THE HIGH WALLS
OF JERUSALEM

Also by Ronald Sanders

Socialist Thought: A Documentary History *(coeditor)*
Israel: The View from Masada
The Downtown Jews
Reflections on a Teapot
Lost Tribes and Promised Lands
The Days Grow Short: The Life and Music of Kurt Weill

THE HIGH WALLS OF JERUSALEM

A History of the Balfour Declaration
and the Birth of the
British Mandate for Palestine

RONALD SANDERS

Holt, Rinehart and Winston | New York

Copyright © 1983 by Ronald Sanders
All rights reserved, including the right to reproduce this
book or portions thereof in any form.
First published in January 1984 by Holt, Rinehart
and Winston, 383 Madison Avenue, New York,
New York 10017.
Published simultaneously in Canada by Holt, Rinehart
and Winston of Canada, Limited.

Library of Congress Cataloging in Publication Data
Sanders, Ronald.
The high walls of Jerusalem.
Includes bibliographical references and index.
1. Balfour Declaration.   2. Zionism—Great Britain.
3. Great Britain—Foreign relations—Near East. 4. Near
East—Foreign relations—Great Britain.   I. Title.
DS125.5.S26   1983   956.94′001   82-23265
ISBN: 0-03-053971-4

First Edition

Design by Victoria Hartman
Maps by David Lindroth
Printed in the United States of America
1 3 5 7 9 10 8 6 4 2

ISBN 0-03-053971-4

For George and Esther Gingold
With Love and Gratitude

Behold the high walls of Jerusalem,
Which Titus and Vespasian once brake down:
From off these turrets have the ancient Jews
Seen worlds of people mustering on these plains.
Oh Princes, which of all your eyes are dry,
To look upon this Temple, now destroy'd?
Yonder did stand the great Jehovah's House,
In midst of all his people, there he dwelt . . .
There was the Ark, the shewbread, Aaron's rod,
Sanctum Sanctorum and the Cherubines.
Now in that holy place, where God himself
Was personally present, pagans dwell.

Thomas Heywood, *The Four Prentices
of London* (ca. 1600)

Contents

EPILOGUE | 1918–1948

List of Maps

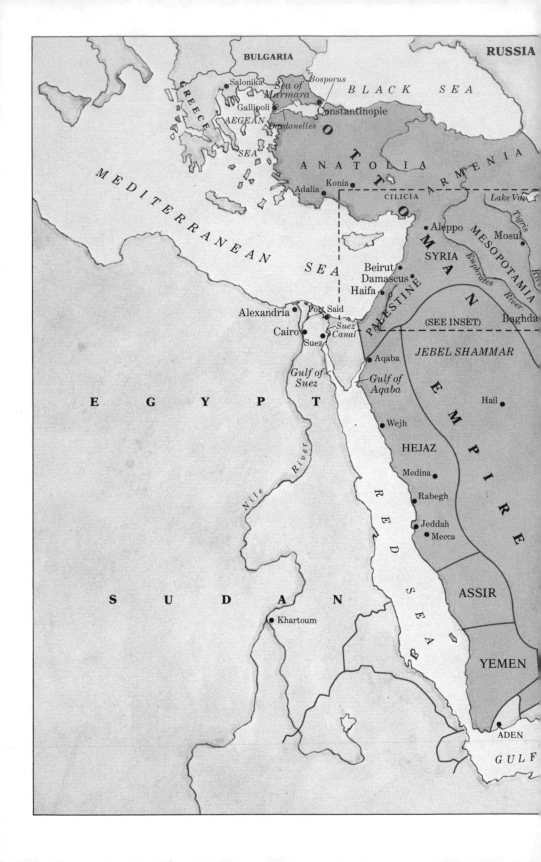

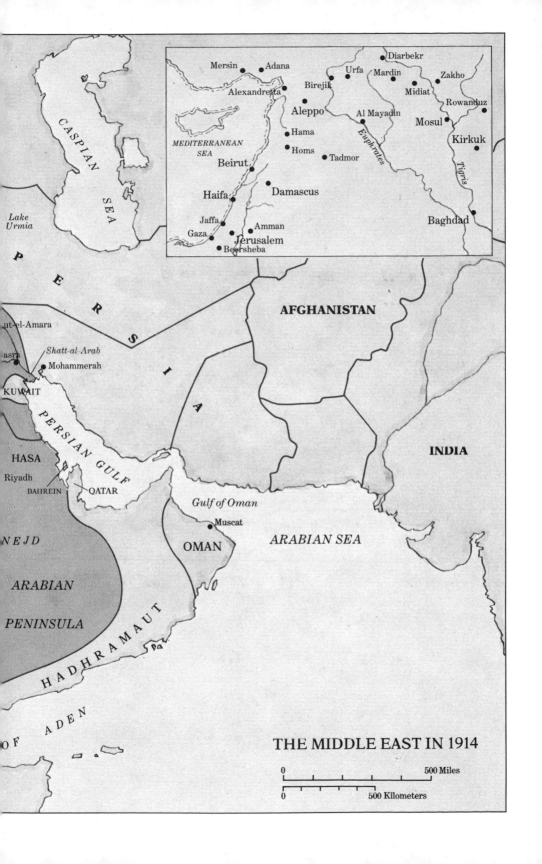

THE MIDDLE EAST IN 1914

MEDITERRANEAN SEA

CASPIAN SEA

Lake Urmia

Mersin Adana

Alexandretta

Diarbekr

Urfa Mardin

Birejik

Zakho

Midiat

Aleppo

Al Mayadin

Rowanduz

Mosul

Kirkuk

Hama

Homs

Euphrates

Tigris

Beirut

Tadmor

Haifa

Damascus

Jaffa

Amman

Gaza

Jerusalem

Beersheba

Baghdad

PERSIA

AFGHANISTAN

nt-el-Amara

Shatt-al Arab

asra Mohammerah

KUWAIT

PERSIAN GULF

HASA

Riyadh

BAHREIN QATAR

NEJD

ARABIAN

PENINSULA

HADHRAMAUT

OF ADEN

INDIA

Gulf of Oman

Muscat

OMAN

ARABIAN SEA

0   500 Miles

0   500 Kilometers

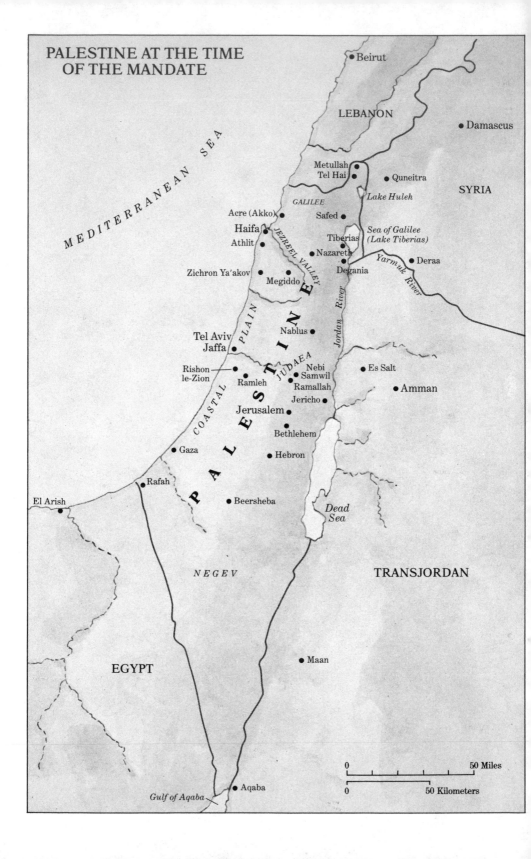

PALESTINE AT THE TIME OF THE MANDATE

MEDITERRANEAN SEA

LEBANON

Beirut

Damascus

SYRIA

Metullah
Tel Hai

Quneitra

Lake Huleh

GALILEE

Acre (Akko)

Safed

Haifa

Sea of Galilee
(Lake Tiberias)

JEZREEL VALLEY

Athlit

Tiberias

Nazareth

Deraa

Zichron Ya'akov

Degania

Yarmuk River

Megiddo

Nablus

Jordan River

Tel Aviv
Jaffa

JUDAEA

Es Salt

Rishon
le-Zion

Nebi
Samwil

Ramleh

Ramallah

Amman

Jericho

Jerusalem

Bethlehem

Gaza

Hebron

Rafah

El Arish

Beersheba

Dead
Sea

NEGEV

TRANSJORDAN

EGYPT

Maan

COASTAL PLAIN

P A L E S T I N E

0   50 Miles

0   50 Kilometers

Aqaba

Gulf of Aqaba

Acknowledgments

I want to thank a few people who were especially helpful to me personally in the preparation of this book.

My friends Alice and Frank Prochaska of London, both gifted historians, provided comfort, guidance, and valuable advice at a crucial stage of my work. I also thank Alice Prochaska in particular for initiating me into the mysteries of the Public Record Office.

Two guardians of archives, among the many with whom I dealt, stood out for helpfulness from among the rest: Mrs. Trude Levi of the Mocatta Library in London, and Gillian Grant of the Private Papers Collection at the Middle East Centre, St. Antony's College, Oxford.

Marian Wood, as ever, brought to bear her outstanding skills as an editor and literary adviser. Trent Duffy applied his high editorial standards in the final stages of preparation of the manuscript and during the physical production of the book.

My wife, Beverly Sanders, not only sustained me during these labors, but also provided the aid of her professional editorial skills, and typed the lion's share of the manuscript.

Preface

On November 2, 1917, Arthur James Balfour, the British foreign secretary, sent a letter to the second Lord Rothschild that contained the following official statement of policy:

> His Majesty's Government view with favour the establishment in Palestine of a national home for the Jewish people, and will use their best endeavours to facilitate the achievement of this object, it being clearly understood that nothing shall be done which may prejudice the civil and religious rights of existing non-Jewish communities in Palestine, or the rights and political status enjoyed by Jews in any other country.

The Balfour Declaration, as it came to be known, was issued almost exactly three years after Turkey's entry into the First World War on the side of Germany and Austria. A month later, British troops captured Jerusalem, ending four hundred years of Ottoman rule there.

From these events can be traced the beginning, not only of the three decades of British government in Palestine—first under a military administration, then under a League of Nations mandate—out of which the State of Israel was born, but also of the political map of the Middle East as we know it today. Palestine had not existed as a distinct entity for centuries prior to the First World War—there was no such subdivision of the Ottoman Empire—those represented today by Lebanon and Syria were vague, and Jordan had never really existed at all. They were the work of the postwar conference tables and, as such, the outcome of aims evolved during the war by the powers that had finally emerged victorious. These aims combined self-interest with some genuine ideals, and among the ideals—particularly on the part of the British Government—was a determination to sponsor the political fulfillment of those nationalities that had hitherto been frustrated under Turkish rule.

In the Middle East, they were considered to be threefold: Arab, Jewish, and Armenian. The British policy makers recognized that there was potential for conflict between the aspirations of these groups—especially between those of Arabs and Jews—but tended during the war to regard them as ultimately compatible. Wise government, it was believed, would reconcile them. The supporters of the Balfour Declaration in England—and these included some of the most enthusiastic supporters of Arab nationalism as well—thought of it less as a source of future difficulties in the Middle East than as a keystone of the entire system on which the region's better future was to be built. Palestine, with the Balfour Declaration as its underlying principle, was the quintessential mandate.

It is the purpose of this book to tell the story of how that declaration came about. The narrative on the following pages, which is preceded by a two-chapter prologue giving the nineteenth and early twentieth century background and succeeded by a two-chapter epilogue sketching the thirty years that ensued until the end of the mandate and the emergence of the Jewish state, focuses upon the entire context of relevant events between November 1914 and December 1917. It describes the efforts of Zionists in Britain, as well as of the statesmen who became their ardent sympathizers, to bring about the achievement of their hopes; equally, it shows the struggles of Arab nationalism and the entire evolution of British policy on its behalf. Overarching all is the framework of the war itself—of the most destructive conflict mankind had ever seen and the peculiarly exhilarating quality that the war in the Middle East had alongside the murderous frustrations of the western front. And, on the other hand, there is a picaresque human side to the story as well, for its most characteristic and yet most unusual aspect is the seemingly unlikely rise of a humble provincial chemist, Chaim Weizmann, to the highest levels of decision making.

It has been possible to tell all the aspects of this story in greater detail than ever before for two reasons above all. One is the opening, in the 1960s, of the British Foreign Office archives for the period concerned. The other is the still continuing appearance in print of the complete letters and papers of Chaim Weizmann. This monumental publication of many volumes, richly edited, is a great work of scholarship, a tribute to the care and dedication of those who have created it.

—R.S.

A Note to the Reader

On spelling. In the spelling of the numerous terms and personal and place names from Hebrew and from Arabic that occur in this book, I have used no established system, but have been guided by my own sense of what forms seem either the most familiar or the most accessible to the reader. In my own text, I remain consistent throughout to each form I have chosen; but in the quotations, I have found it most suitable to adhere to the forms used in the originals. This means that certain personal and place names are spelled in a variety of ways throughout the different quotations, but the reader will always find the names recognizable.

In the spelling of ordinary English words, however, I have uniformly put the quotations into standard American forms. Most of the texts quoted are British in origin, yet I find that even many of these were not perfectly consistent with the established British forms of today. Other texts—such as many of the letters of Chaim Weizmann to his foreign-born colleagues—were translated from non-English originals anyway. Still others were quoted from sources published in the United States, in which the spelling was Americanized. To avoid unnecessary chaos, then, I have taken this small liberty in spelling, except with sources of established literary value; also, the final, historic text of the Balfour Declaration itself is presented in its original spelling.

On the terms "Middle East" and "Near East." During the period dealt with in this book, "Near East" was the established term for the area under consideration. It had a particular nuance before 1914, however, when it tended to refer to the whole Ottoman Empire, including the parts that were in Europe. It is therefore a term that can be misleading as well as seem exotic to the reader of today.

For the purposes of this book, it has seemed more useful in most contexts to use the term that is now better established—"Middle

East"—even though its use in this sense is slightly anachronistic in the period covered. It, too, has had various meanings; but I am fairly well within established conventions by using it in these pages to refer to the region bounded in the north and east today by Turkey, Iran, and the Persian Gulf, and culminating in the southeast and the southwest, respectively, in the coasts of the Arabian peninsula and the inland boundaries of Egypt and the Sudan.

PROLOGUE

Antecedents
·1838—1905·

·1·

LONDON AND JERUSALEM:
A VICTORIAN ROMANCE

Among the persisting undercurrents of English political and intellectual life in the nineteenth century was an aspiration to help bring about a Jewish revival in Palestine. Its ripples could be discerned from time to time, and on at least four occasions it rose to the surface with sudden force. Two of these occasions were political and were dissipated in almost the very moment they occurred; the others were literary and took the form of two novels that have since become classics in their respective ways.

The first political occasion came at the conclusion of a decade that had begun in 1831 with the invasion of Palestine by the troops of Mehemet Ali, ruler of Egypt. After a succession of victories over Palestine's Turkish overlords—who were nominally Egypt's suzerains as well—the Egyptian army had soon taken possession of all of Syria.* France and England took different views of this event. For the French, whose ancient appetite for Syria—dating back to the Crusades—had been whetted by Napoleon's abortive attempt to conquer it in 1799, Mehemet Ali had provided an opportunity to gain a sphere of influence, and they proceeded to cultivate friendly relations with him. The English, on the other hand, saw him as a disposable threat to the integrity of the Ottoman Empire, which they were determined to maintain, preferring its waning power in the area to that of any stronger rival.

Lord Palmerston, the British foreign secretary, made his decisive move in July 1840, when he gathered representatives of the

---

* Until the twentieth century the term "Syria" usually referred to the entire region today comprising Israel, Lebanon, and most of Syria and Jordan.

Austrian, Prussian, and Russian governments to agree on terms whereby Mehemet Ali was to be induced to withdraw from at least the north of Syria. The resulting Treaty of London was rejected by the Egyptian ruler, and in September the British bombarded and occupied Beirut. France did not come to the aid of Mehemet Ali, who was forced to evacuate all of Syria.

Was Palmerston's triumph in this instance an early display of British ambition for empire in Egypt and southern Syria? If it was, then the ambition manifested itself in what were to go on being peculiarly British terms. "There exists at present among the Jews dispersed over Europe," Palmerston wrote that August to Lord Ponsonby, his ambassador at Constantinople, "a strong notion that the time is approaching when their Nation is to return to Palestine; and consequently their wish to go thither has become more keen, and their thoughts have been bent more intently than before upon the means of realizing that wish." He therefore instructed Ponsonby "to bring these considerations confidentially under the notice of the Turkish Government, and strongly recommend them to hold out every just encouragement to the Jews of Europe to return to Palestine."

Palmerston thought that a combination of Jewish industriousness in Palestine and investment there by wealthy Jews abroad—the name Rothschild doubtless came to mind—"would tend greatly to increase the resources of the Turkish Empire, and to promote the progress of civilization therein." In other words, it would strengthen that soft Syrian underbelly that had been so susceptible to Mehemet Ali's assaults. Palmerston must also have realized that Britain was the only one of the three Christian powers particularly concerned with the Levant to have lacked, until now, a specific religious group there to receive its protection and gratefully stand up for its interests. France had the Roman Catholics and Maronites, Russia had the Greek Orthodox; now England, lacking any substantial Protestant community there, would stand on its Old Testament solidarity with the Jews. Indeed, Palmerston had already taken an important step in this direction two years before, when he established a vice-consulate at Jerusalem—no other European country yet had diplomatic representation there—and instructed W.T. Young, who was assigned to the post, "to afford protection to the Jews generally" and report on their condition.

Palmerston had solidly practical grounds, then, for his incipient policy regarding Palestine and its Jews; but he also had spiritual grounds, and one need not have looked far among the people closest to him to find their source. In December 1839, Palmerston, a true son of the Regency, had at the age of fifty-five concluded a lifelong bachelorhood and a liaison nearly as long with Lady Emily Lamb Cowper—sister of Lord Melbourne, the prime minister—by marrying her, two years after her husband's death. Of Lady Cowper's children, Palmerston's favorite was Minnie, who may even have been his illegitimate daughter, and who had been married since 1831 to Lord Ashley, the future seventh earl of Shaftesbury—the highest born and one of the most eminent of England's social reformers and evangelicals.

An officer in the London Society for Promoting Christianity Among the Jews, which had been founded in 1808 as a means of doing charitable works and hastening the Second Coming at the same time, Ashley urgently believed in the return of the Jews to Palestine. It was he who had inspired the foreign secretary to extend consular protection to the Jews of Palestine, at which time he wrote in his diary: "Palmerston had already been chosen by God to be an instrument of good to His ancient people." And in January 1839, he had published an article in the *Quarterly Review* that spoke of "the growing interest manifested in behalf of the Holy Land" on the part of both Christians and Jews. A Christian who had recently traveled in Poland, he said, "informs us that several thousand Jews in that country and of Russia have recently bound themselves by an oath, that, as soon as the way is open for them to go up to Jerusalem, they will immediately go thither." When Ashley heard about Palmerston's letter to Ponsonby, he described it in his diary as "a prelude to the Antitype of the decree of Cyrus."*

There was even a potential British Nehemiah to carry out the task of rebuilding in Zion, for these were the very days in which Sir Moses Montefiore began a succession of journeys to Palestine and undertook charitable works there that were to become legendary. Born in 1784, Montefiore was the grandson of a Sephardic Jewish emigré from Italy. Rising from moderately prosperous origins to great wealth—his marriage in 1812 to Judith Cohen, whose sister

---

* "Thus saith Cyrus king of Persia, All the kingdoms of the earth hath the Lord God of heaven given me; and he hath charged me to build him an house in Jerusalem, which is in Judah. Who is there among you of all his people? The Lord his God be with him, and let him go up." 2 Chronicles 36:23. This brought about the return of the Jews from Babylonian exile in 537 B.C.E. and the rebuilding of the Temple of Jerusalem.

Hannah was the wife of Nathan Mayer Rothschild, gave a substantial boost to his advancement as a financier—he retired from the London stock exchange in his early forties to devote himself to philanthropy. He made his first journey to Palestine in 1827, accompanied by his wife, and came away determined to make the largely impecunious Jews of that country prominent among the objects of his benevolence.

By the time he visited Palestine again in 1839—two years after he had been knighted by the new young queen—Montefiore had become imbued with a larger and more significant ideal. Doubtless he had been partly inspired by Ashley's article in the *Quarterly Review*. He must also have been stirred by the fact that the British Government was now providing consular protection to Palestine's Jewish community, which, under Mehemet Ali's relatively enlightened rule, had grown rapidly in size. The Jewish population of Jerusalem was now 5,500, ten times what it had been in 1827, and the number of Jews in the country as a whole was nearly 10,000. Many of these were pious immigrants, come to the Holy Land to live out their lives in study and prayer and be supported by the *Halukkah*—charitable donations from Jewish communities abroad. But there was also a vigorous mercantile element of growing size, largely Sephardic Jews from the neighboring regions, and living mainly outside of Jerusalem.

It was because of the plan taking shape in his mind that Sir Moses made Safed his first stop when he arrived in Palestine at the end of May. The Galilee had been the principal center of Jewish population in the country since the Roman destruction of Jerusalem, and Safed's Jewish community—now about 1,500 souls—had been the largest in the country until it was overtaken by that of Jerusalem during the 1830s. But what particularly interested Montefiore in Safed was the fertile soil that surrounded it. "From all information I have been able to gather," he wrote in his diary,

> the land in this neighborhood appears to be particularly favorable for agricultural speculation. There are groves of olive trees, I should think, more than five hundred years old, vineyards, much pasture, plenty of wells and abundance of excellent water; also fig-trees, walnuts, almonds, mulberries, etc., and rich fields of wheat, barley, and lentils: in fact it is a land that would produce almost everything in abundance, with very little skill and labor.

This led to reflections upon the idea that had brought him there. "I am sure if the plan I have in contemplation should succeed," he went on,

> it will be the means of introducing happiness and plenty into the Holy Land. In the first instance, I shall apply to Mehemet Ali for a grant of land for fifty years; some one or two hundred villages; giving him an increased rent of from ten to twenty per cent, and paying the whole in money annually in Alexandria, but the land and villages to be free, during the whole term, from every tax or rate either of Pasha or Governor of the several districts; and liberty being accorded to dispose of the produce in any quarter of the globe. The grant obtained, I shall, please Heaven, on my return to England, form a company for the cultivation of the land and the encouragement of our brethren in Europe to return to Palestine.

After going on to visit Tiberias, Hebron, and Jerusalem—where he considered a possible purchase of agricultural land right outside the city walls—Sir Moses proceeded to Egypt and discussed his plan with Mehemet Ali.

The following year, Montefiore found reason to make a third journey to the Near East—this time to exert his influence in opposition to a ritual murder charge that had been leveled against the Jews of Damascus. Just before departing, he and a group of other Anglo-Jewish leaders went to see Palmerston to discuss the problem, and the foreign secretary promised to use his own influence with both Mehemet Ali and the Turkish government "to put a stop to such atrocities." Sir Moses took this opportunity to praise Vice-Consul Young's "humanity at Jerusalem," and to mention that the Jews of Palestine "were desirous of being employed in agricultural pursuits."

A few months later, Palmerston wrote his letter to Ponsonby about the return of the Jewish nation to Palestine.

But nothing was to come of any of this. By the end of the following year, Mehemet Ali was no longer a threat to the stability of the Near East, and Lord Melbourne's cabinet had fallen. Palmerston was not to return to the Foreign Office for five years, during which time his concerns became focused elsewhere. The idea, which had reached the level of cabinet discussion and the pages of *The Times*, continued to be discussed in governing circles for a while, but with diminishing commitment. Nor was there, in spite of what Ashley had written in the *Quarterly Review*, any clear and organized commitment from the only source that would have made such an enterprise possible—the Jewish masses of Eastern Europe. Such manifestations on their part were still two or more generations away. As for Ashley's hopes, these had perhaps achieved a certain satisfaction with the appointment, in the fall of 1841, of the Reverend Michael Solomon Alexander—a converted Jew and professor of Hebrew and Arabic at King's College—as the first Anglican bishop of Jerusalem. Unofficially, his task was to convert Jews, but he was to succeed in winning over only a handful by the time of his death in 1845.

Benjamin Disraeli must have watched all this with considerable interest; in his novel *Tancred*, he even refers to "the good bishop" of Jerusalem, "who is himself a Hebrew." In 1844, having reached a lull in what was proving to be a brilliant but unorthodox political career, Disraeli made a temporary return to his earlier calling as a writer of fiction, and in the ensuing three years produced a trilogy of outstanding political novels: *Coningsby*, *Sybil*, and *Tancred*. The third, based in large part on a journey to Palestine that the author himself had made in 1831, presents yet another vision of Jewish—or, in this case, pan-Semitic—revival there. As for the "Hebrew" bishop of Jerusalem, Disraeli's interest in him was not of merely passing significance. Himself born a Jew of Sephardic descent, Disraeli had been converted to Christianity by his father at the age of thirteen, but had subsequently become preoccupied with an idea of Jewish peoplehood—of Jewish *race*, as he liked to put it—that was not strictly a matter of religious affiliation. "All is race," Disraeli's fictitious Jewish philosopher and financier Sidonia tells the Christian Englishman Tancred: "there is no other truth."

Among the many themes in the trilogy is a persistent, at times obsessive, concern with the Jewish "race" and its contributions to Christian civilization. "Christianity is completed Judaism," says one character in *Sybil*. In *Tancred: or, The New Crusade*, Disraeli goes a step further and suggests that Judaism is a major source of English civilization as well. Oppressed with the emptiness of his privileged existence, young Lord Montacute—whose Christian name, Tancred, is significantly that of a great Crusader—decides to go on a pilgrimage to the Holy Sepulcher. But when he approaches Sidonia for advice before departing, the latter makes him realize he is after something more—that what he really wants to do is "penetrate the great Asian mystery." Disraeli never says precisely what this is; but it is at least partly implied in such moments as when, after Tancred has reached the Judean hills, the author reflects upon how,

> for this English youth, words had been uttered and things done, more than thirty centuries ago, in this stony wilderness, which influenced his opinions and regulated his conduct every day of his life, in that distant and seagirt home, which, at the time of their occurrence, was not as advanced in civilization as the Polynesian groups or the islands of New Zealand. The life and property of England are protected by the laws of Sinai. The hard-working people of England are secured in every seven days a day of rest by the laws of Sinai.

Tancred seems to discover himself to be a Hebrew in every respect but "race." He falls in love with a beautiful Jewess of Bethany and becomes involved in the political intrigues of the Levant of Mehemet Ali, exhorting his friends there to an ideal of Semitic revival. The task, he tells them, is "to free your country, and make the Syrians a nation"—by which he means a nation of Muslim and Christian Arabs as well as of Jews, for to Disraeli these are a single race. As one character puts it, "the Arabs are only Jews upon horseback." Jerusalem, the author says, "will ever remain the appanage either of Israel or of Ishmael"; either one has the right to sit "upon the throne of David"—but not anyone else.

The book abounds in criticism of the attempts of Frenchmen through the ages, starting with the Crusades, to force themselves upon this throne that was not theirs either by racial or by moral right. So far out of sympathy is the French nation with everything Semitic, Disraeli observes, that in its revolution it even had made a violent effort "to disembarrass itself of its Asian [i.e., Judeo-Christian] faith." The English are quite different: "I am not, alas, a true Arab, though I love Arabia and Arabian thoughts," Tancred says; and he is believed. The book implies that, whereas French rule would suppress the Syrian nation, a benign English suzerainty would enable it to flourish. "If the English would only understand their own interests," an Arab tells Tancred, "with my co-operation, Syria might be theirs."

"The English," said Tancred, "why should the English take Syria?"

"France will take it if they do not."
"I hope not," said Tancred.

But if he hesitates to draw the inevitable conclusion, his rambunctious Arab friend Fakredeen is quite ready to leap beyond it. "Let the Queen of the English collect a great fleet," he says,

> let her stow away all her treasure, bullion, gold plate, and precious stones: be accompanied by all her court and chief people, and transfer the seat of her Empire from London to Delhi. There she will find an immense empire ready made, a first-rate army, and a large revenue. In the mean time I will arrange with Mehemet Ali. He shall have Bagdad and Mesopotamia, and pour the Bedoueen cavalry into Persia. I will take care of Syria and Asia Minor. . . . We will acknowledge the Empress of India as our suzerain, and secure for her the Levantine coast.

Disraeli's "great Asian mystery" thus culminates in a fantastic vision of Eastern empire that, in years to come, he would not entirely forget.

The next notable manifestations, literary and political, of British interest in a Jewish revival in Palestine occurred while Disraeli was prime minister. This hardly seems accidental; Disraeli was now setting the tone for an era in which the old romance of the Orient that he had exemplified was reviving in a more pointed fashion. After holding office for most of 1868, he had returned to power in 1874 and soon begun to demonstrate an undying, and now rather practical, preoccupation with "the great Asian mystery." It was in November 1875, six years to the month after the opening of the Suez Canal—that alarming display of French genius and ambition on the route to India—that Disraeli suddenly purchased for Great Britain the 44 percent of the shares in the Canal Company hitherto owned by Mehemet Ali's grandson, the insolvent Khedive Ismail of Egypt. This imperial *coup de théâtre* was made possible by a loan of £4 million from Lionel de Rothschild, who, in 1858, had become the first professing Jew to sit in Parliament, and whose right to be so had been championed above all by Disraeli during a struggle of more than ten years to seat him. The spirit that had created *Tancred* became even more evident the following April, when Disraeli succeeded in ushering through Parliament the Royal Titles Bill declaring the Queen to be Empress of India.

The reviving British interest in the Orient was further stimulated by the fact that, during the spring of 1876, the Ottoman Empire became once again the main theater of world events—this time with Bulgaria at the center of the stage. Insurrection against Ottoman rule, which had begun the previous year in Bosnia and Herzegovina, was spreading through the Balkans; but its manifestation in Bulgaria that May was put down with particular cruelty by troops of irregulars, and reports of atrocities and of deaths in the tens of thousands reached the British press. A public outcry arose, particularly among Liberals, who had, since the days of Palmerston and of the Crimean War (when Britain and France had gone to war against Russia to defend the Ottoman Empire), come to dislike the Turks and to look with strong sympathy upon the cause of small nationalities in Europe. The Tory Disraeli, on the other hand, whose oriental passion had always embraced the Turks as well, sought at first to minimize the reports. Although they did prove to be a bit exaggerated, no quibbling about exact mortality figures was going to matter after September 6, however, when the prime minister's defeated rival, William Ewart Gladstone, emerged from retirement with a pamphlet called *The Bulgarian Horrors and the Question of the East*. In it, he characterized the Turks as "the one great anti-human species of humanity" and called upon them to clear out of Bulgaria, "bag and baggage." Later that year, Gladstone, suspecting that what one of his friends called Disraeli's "Judaic feeling" was a factor in British foreign policy, found new focus for his fury when he read *Tancred* for the first time. Certainly Disraeli's prejudices were oriental enough that, when war broke out between Russia and Turkey the following year, it was widely assumed he would once again bring in England to fight on the Turkish side. But though he came close to doing so, he prudently avoided it in the end.

In the meantime, another symptom of the eastward-leaning interests of the day was the considerable scientific literature that was coming into being on Palestine and its possibilities for revival. In this era of Austen Henry Layard of Nineveh and Sir Richard Burton of Arabia, the British were showing a special gift for Near Eastern archaeology and exploration and the Palestine Exploration Fund had been established in 1865 to apply that gift to scientific research into the background of the Bible. In 1867, it had sent Charles Warren, a lieutenant in the Royal Engineers, to make archaeological soundings at Jerusalem in an effort to determine the exact locations of the Temple and of the Holy Sepulcher. By the mid-1870s, the fund was conducting a definitive topographical, geological, archaeological, and anthropological survey of the Holy Land under the direction of a gifted young orientalist, Lieutenant Claude Reignier Conder. The results were being published in articles and were soon to appear in many volumes.

Some of the fund's explorers were producing a less formal literature as well. Charles Warren's treatise, *The Land of Promise: or, Turkey's Guarantee*, appeared in 1875. In it, he proposed the colonization of Palestine under the auspices of a British chartered company that would, in compensation, take over a portion of the Turkish national debt. "Let this be done," he added, "with the avowed intention of gradually introducing the Jew, pure and simple, who is eventually to occupy and govern this country." On the basis of his experience, Warren was able to provide abundant technical arguments for his position, dealing mainly with the soil of Palestine and its prospects for rehabilitation. But he was also ready to argue in a less scientific vein. "It is written over and over again in the word of God," he said, that "Israel are to return to their own land." And then he concluded in the tones of a political prophet: "That which is yet to be looked for is the public recognition of the fact, together with the restoration, in whole or in part, of Jewish national life, under the protection of some one or more of the Great Powers."

It was in this atmosphere that George Eliot wrote and published her novel *Daniel Deronda*, the second of the notable literary manifestations of the century concerning a Jewish revival in Palestine. Her own fascination with the history of Israel went back to her young womanhood, when she had been fully in the grip of the evangelical passion epitomized in that era by the young Lord Ashley. In 1839, when she was nineteen, she had begun compiling a "Chart of Ecclesiastical History," which was meant to show in parallel columns the principal dates in the histories of Rome, Christianity, and the Jews, from the birth of Christ to the Reformation. In 1846, as a professional translator of German, she had produced the first English version of that pioneering exercise in historical criticism of the Bible, David Strauss's *The Life of Jesus*. By 1854 her personal library had come to include a Hebrew grammar; and signs of a Hebrew vocabulary show up in her writings from her very first published works of fiction some three years later. By the end of 1867, she had embarked upon a serious study of that language, under the tutelage of Emanuel Deutsch, a Berlin-educated Jewish scholar who had just published a widely read article on the Talmud in the *Quarterly Review.*

Deutsch made a journey to Palestine in 1869 that greatly moved him, and he was traveling in the Near East again four years later when he died at the age of forty-three. By then, George Eliot was already planning the novel that would commemorate him. She read widely in Jewish history, made herself familiar with the work of the Palestine Exploration Fund, and found out what she could about Jewish agricultural settlement in Palestine. She learned of the Mikveh Israel ("Hope of Israel") school, founded near Jaffa in 1870 by the Alliance Israélite Universelle of Paris to train young Palestinian Jews as farmers. No doubt she also learned about the ongoing British involvement in such enterprises: modern Jewish agricultural settlement in Palestine had begun in 1852 when James Finn, W.T. Young's successor at the Jerusalem consulate, raised money and purchased some eight to twelve acres outside the city walls to be set aside as "the Industrial Plantation for employment of Jews of Jerusalem." Three years later, during his fourth journey to Palestine, Sir Moses Montefiore had acquired pieces of land near Jerusalem, Jaffa, and Safed, for agriculture and other useful purposes. By the time George Eliot finished her novel on Jewish themes, Montefiore had made, in 1875, his seventh journey to Palestine—at the age of ninety.

Daniel Deronda, which first appeared in installments during the spring and summer of 1876, is touched with the spirit of *Tancred,* even though George Eliot had not liked that novel when she read it thirty years before. Young Deronda seems in the end like a Tancred who, even before sailing to Palestine, has discovered himself to be Jewish after all. Growing up in the home of Sir Hugo Mallinger, whom he calls uncle, he knows nothing of his parentage at first, but a destiny then unfolds for him that seems as inexorable as the gradual revelation of his identity that accompanies it. In love with Mirah and deeply moved by the Jewish learning and idealism of her brother Mordecai—the character who is based on Emanuel Deutsch—Deronda has already become absorbed in the study of Jewish life and literature by the time he learns the truth of his origins. It is as if he had, from the beginning, fallen under the control of a hidden but powerful magnetism of "race"—to apply Sidonia's term to a situation he would have understood completely.

The mystery of this force is embodied in the novel by its own Sidonia—by Mordecai, who has the qualities of a prophet. Imbued with an ideal of Jewish national regeneration, the sickly Mordecai sees himself from the outset as an intermediary between that ideal and some person better equipped physically than he to carry it out. This person

> must be a Jew, intellectually cultured, morally fervid—in all this a nature ready to be plenished from Mordecai's; but his face and frame must be beautiful and strong, he must have been used to all the refinements of social life, his voice must flow with a full and easy current, his circumstances be free from sordid need: he must glorify the possibilities of the Jew, not sit and wander [sic] as Mordecai did, bearing the stamp of his people amid the signs of poverty and waning breath.

From their first meeting Mordecai sees in Deronda the man he has sought, and he alone in the novel is fully convinced that the latter is a Jew long before the fact is revealed.

As for the mission Mordecai has in mind, its focal point is the eventual return of his people to the Land of Israel. "Revive the organic centre," he says:

> let the unity of Israel which has made the growth and form of its religion be an outward reality. Looking towards a land and a polity, our dispersed people in all the ends of the earth may share the dignity of a national life which has a voice among the peoples of the East and the West—which will plant the wisdom and skill of our race so that it may be, as of old, a medium of transmission and understanding.

Mordecai also understands practical politics and envisions the ways in which

> the world will gain as Israel gains. For there will be a community in the van of the East which carries the culture and the sympathies of every great nation in its bosom; there will be a land set for a halting-place of enmities, a neutral ground for the East as Belgium is for the West.

Deronda perceives that this secular mission is the most suitable of modes whereby he can take up the traditions of his ancestors. He knows he cannot be like his orthodox grandfather. "That is impossible. The effect of my education can never be done away with. The

Christian sympathies in which my mind was reared can never die out of me." Rather, he can only be some kind of nonreligious Jew, who will "identify myself, as far as possible, with my hereditary people, and if I can see any work to be done for them that I can give my soul and hand to, I shall choose to do it." What he has discovered is a fulfillment of that ideal of the religion of humanity—a reworking for the liberal, scientific age of the pious values of one's forefathers—that was always among the central concerns of George Eliot's life and work. The fact of being a Jew has enabled him "to make his life a sequence which would take the form of duty." In the end he marries Mirah and resolves to go to the East, "to become better acquainted with the condition of my race in various countries there" and then seek to restore "a political existence to my people, making them a nation again, giving them a national centre, such as the English have, though they too are scattered over the face of the globe." At the novel's end, Mordecai dies as Deronda and Mirah prepare to make their journey.

"Doubtless," George Eliot had told her publisher while still writing the book, "the wider public of novel-readers must feel more interest in Sidonia than in Moredecai. But then, I was not born to paint Sidonia." As for the man who was, it would have been interesting to know what he thought of *Daniel Deronda*. But Lord Beaconsfield—as Disraeli now had become—is said to have replied when asked if he had read it, "When I want to read a novel, I write one."

This time, however, Beaconsfield nearly had a chance to pursue the aims of Tancred and Daniel Deronda as a political act rather than a novel. The occasion arose shortly after the Congress of Berlin in the summer of 1878, which decided upon the new map of the Near East at the end of the Russo-Turkish War. That November, Beaconsfield's foreign secretary, Lord Salisbury, received a letter from one Laurence Oliphant submitting "a project which I have already communicated to the Prime Minister; and which he has directed me to formulate in writing and address to the Foreign Office." What Oliphant proposed was the formation of a Palestine development company, which would seek to obtain a land concession from the Turkish government for a period of twenty-five years or more. Most of the immigrants into this territory, he wrote, "will probably consist of oppressed Jews from Rumania and the South of Russia." As for the financing of the project, he wrote elsewhere that "any amount of money can be raised upon it, owing to the belief which people have that they would be fulfilling prophecy and bringing on the end of the world. I don't know why they are so anxious for this latter event," he hastened to add,

> but it makes the commercial speculation easy, as it is a combination of the financial and sentimental elements which will, I think, ensure success. And it will be a good political move for the Government, as it will enable them to carry out reforms in Asiatic Turkey, provide money for the Porte,* and by uniting the French in it, and possibly the Italians, be a powerful religious move against the Russians, who are trying to obtain a hold of the country by their pilgrims.

The author of this proposal was a forty-nine-year-old journalist, writer of novels and travel books (he had seen Russia and its Jews with his own eyes), sometime diplomat and member of Parliament, disillusioned Christian, and, in recent years, adherent of an American-based mystical order called the Brotherhood of the New Life. From 1867 to 1870, Oliphant and his mother had lived and worked in the brotherhood's two agricultural settlements in New York state, at Amenia and at Brocton. By the time of his letter, his ties with it had loosened; but showed some continuing attachment to its ideals, not only in his occasional mystical writings but in the character of his marriage, which had been contracted in 1872 and had remained deliberately chaste. It would seem likely that his sudden desire to return the Jews to Palestine had sprung from this mystical background; but Oliphant himself—perhaps protesting too much—always disparaged religious motives and claimed that his own were purely practical. Doubtless he had been struck by *Daniel Deronda*, which first appeared in *Blackwood's* magazine, a regular outlet for his own writings. But what had immediately inspired him, he made it clear, was the literature of the Palestine Exploration Fund, which had just completed the western part of its survey under another young officer of the Royal Engineers, Lieutenant Horatio Herbert Kitchener.

"The investigations and reports of the engineer officers who have surveyed the land under the auspices of the exploration fund," Oliphant said in his letter to Salisbury,

> testify to the vast undeveloped natural resources of Palestine, which it is estimated by Captain Warren, Lieutenant Conder, Lieutenant Kitchener and other competent judges could maintain at least ten times its present population, and I should be

* The Sublime Porte, as the government at Constantinople was known.

prepared to satisfy your Lordship, without entering upon the details here, that it would be well worth the attention of the capitalist.

By this time Oliphant was in touch with Conder, who had just begun publishing his own ideas about a Jewish return to Palestine.

Oliphant received from both Beaconsfield and Salisbury, he later wrote, "the kindest encouragements and assurances of support, so far as it was possible to afford it without officially committing the government." He claimed also to have won "the warm interest and cordial sympathy" of the Prince of Wales. The next thing was to choose a site, and, early in 1879, armed with letters of recommendation from the Foreign Office and the French Foreign Ministry, Oliphant departed for the East. Sailing to Beirut, he made his way overland from there with a small party and searched northern Palestine until he at last came to a place that suited his specifications. Just east of the Jordan and north of the Dead Sea, it was—in striking contrast with the arid regions that immediately surrounded it—abundantly fertile, even tropical in character: Oliphant called it "the Land of Gilead." He was also struck by the realization that, if this region were settled, "the western section of the colony would be within an easy day's journey from Jerusalem, from which city in the early stages of its development supplies and necessaries could be drawn." A railway line running through Jericho, he envisioned, "would put the colony in close and direct communication with Jerusalem," which now had a Jewish population of about 15,000. He also dreamed of a railway connection between this region and the port of Haifa, "the true outlet for its produce."

Oliphant began a series of articles for *Blackwood's* after moving on to Constantinople, where he tried to persuade members of the sultan's government of the value of his scheme. No doubt he told them, just as he wrote in his articles, that a colony founded by Jewish enterprise "under the auspices of the Sultan, would enjoy a protection of a very special character, and that the influence of the race upon the several governments under which they possess civil rights would be exercised in its favor." These are the tones of Palmerston, now also resonant with the era of Disraeli; and like those two statesmen, Oliphant assumed that, whatever advantages the plan might offer the Turks, its chief beneficiaries would be the English. "The nation," he wrote,

> that espoused the cause of the Jews and their restoration to Palestine, would be able to rely upon their support in financial

operations on the largest scale, upon the powerful influence which they wield in the press of many countries, and on their political cooperation in those countries—which would of necessity tend to paralyze the diplomatic and even hostile action of Powers antagonistic to the one with which they were allied. Owing to the financial, political, and commercial importance to which the Jews have now attained, there is probably no one Power in Europe that would prove so valuable an ally to a nation likely to be engaged in a European war, as this wealthy, powerful, and cosmopolitan race.

It is clear what nation is meant,

for as we have special interests, so we have come under special obligations in regard to this quarter of the globe. The population of Palestine in particular, of which 25,000 belong to the Hebrew race, is looking to England for protection and the redress of grievances; and those who see in the relations which our own country now occupies towards the Holy Land, the hand of Providence, may fairly consider whether they do not involve responsibilities which cannot lightly be ignored.

These words must have been gratifying to Lord Beaconsfield. But there was no longer anything he could do about them, since his government had fallen almost as soon as they were published. After six years in Opposition, Gladstone and the Liberals were back in power, leaving Oliphant only to hope, as did the London *Jewish Chronicle* in its issue of April 9, 1880, "that the Liberal leaders may see fit to give, if it be only unofficially, some kind of countenance, as did the Conservative authorities, to Mr. Laurence Oliphant's scheme for the peaceful and non-political colonization of a portion of Palestine by our people."

This was not to be. Schemes that smacked of imperial aggrandizement were not for Mr. Gladstone and his colleagues—albeit, before long, they were to make a major stroke for empire in the Near East in spite of themselves. In the summer of 1882, Gladstone resolved a state of revolution and political crisis in Egypt by sending in the British army, which, in the sequel, was not to leave the country for seventy-four years. But by then Oliphant's main political hope was gone: on April 19, 1881—four months after the death of George Eliot—Lord Beaconsfield had died, obscuring forever that particular vision of the great Asian mystery.

·2·

HERZL IN ENGLAND

"I am Daniel Deronda," Colonel Goldsmid told his Viennese guest one November evening in Cardiff in 1895. "I was born a Christian. My father and mother were baptized Jews. When I found out about this, as a young man in India, I decided to return to the ancestral fold. While I was serving as a lieutenant, I went over to Judaism."

Like Deronda, Albert Goldsmid had signaled his return by looking to Eastern Europe and Palestine, seeking the betterment of his people and their revival as a nation. In the spring and summer of 1881, following the assassination of Tsar Alexander II, a wave of pogroms had spread devastation through the Jewish communities of southern Russia, causing an upheaval throughout Eastern Europe that was to manifest itself in years to come as the largest Jewish exodus of all time. From the beginning, this vast population movement was aimed primarily at the shores of the United States and Canada; but other countries in the west, including Great Britain, felt its impact as well. And Palestine also felt it: for another result of this upheaval was the first concerted effort by significant numbers of Jews to found agricultural colonies there.

Among the sources of inspiration for this effort had been the writings and activities of Laurence Oliphant, with whom Goldsmid, then a thirty-five-year-old major, became closely associated early in 1882. Together they participated, at London's Mansion House, in the organization of a relief fund for the persecuted Jews. Oliphant promptly left for Eastern Europe to help administer the fund; Goldsmid was to have joined him, but could not, and instead became a recipient of his enthusiastic letters. "There is an immense movement going on in Roumania," Oliphant wrote, "and subscriptions amongst Jews alone there for Palestine colonization purposes, it is hoped, will amount to fifty thousand francs a month." This was what really interested both men, and Oliphant quit his fund assignment. At Jassy he "attended a meeting of delegates from twenty-eight Palestine colonization committees. . . . It was very interesting and encouraging. My correspondence from all parts of Russia tells me that the movement is universal; but for the moment everything is at a standstill, until I have been to Constantinople to find out the dispositions of the Turkish Government." In Constantinople, he found the government of Sultan Abdul Hamid firmly opposed to Jewish colonization.

A few determined settlers got through anyway, and by the end of 1882, four Jewish agricultural colonies were functioning in Palestine. Oliphant, still seeking his own place in the scheme of things, retired with his wife and a small entourage to Haifa, from which he observed the life of the new settlements and wrote articles about them. It was partly owing to his influence that Baron Edmond de Rothschild, head of the Paris branch of the family, decided at this time to start providing financial support to the colonies and help in the founding of new ones. Meanwhile, the new movement's popular roots were growing stronger: in 1884, representatives of the various colonization societies that called themselves Hovevei Zion ("Lovers of Zion" in Hebrew) gathered in Kattowitz, in Upper Silesia, to lay the groundwork for an international organization—and also, incidentally, to celebrate the one hundredth birthday of Sir Moses Montefiore. By 1890, when Major Goldsmid and his kinsman Elim d'Avigdor cofounded an English Hovevei Zion society, both Montefiore and Oliphant were dead, but a new generation was carrying on their work. Goldsmid became "chief" of the society in 1893 and organized it in quasi-military fashion, with branches called "tents."

Now commanding colonel of the Welsh regimental district at Cardiff, Goldsmid had reason to see some resemblance between himself and Daniel Deronda. But his claim, whatever he may have believed, could hardly have been an exclusive one: George Eliot had drawn a portrait for an entire generation, and indeed, Colonel Goldsmid's guest that evening could have laid as strong a claim to it as anybody. Not that Dr. Theodor Herzl had not known he was a Jew all the thirty-five years of his life; on the contrary, he had attended a Hebrew school during his childhood in Budapest. Even in Vienna, where he had studied at the university and then gone on to achieve some eminence as a journalist and a playwright, his personal milieu had been largely Jewish: the woman he married, his closest friends, the publishers of the *Neue Freie Presse*—the highly esteemed Liberal newspaper for which he worked—all were of that lineage. But in those first decades following the Jewish emancipation in Austria and Germany, the predominant attitude of Theodor Herzl and his circle had been the one typical among European intellectuals of the day: indifference to *religion* in any form.

A new sense of Jewish peoplehood had begun to dawn upon Herzl at the end of 1891, when his paper assigned him as its correspondent in Paris. In the ensuing years, the public agitation over the Panama scandal and the trial of Captain Dreyfus demonstrated to a young man already troubled by the persistence of anti-Semitism in Austria and Germany that there were no limits upon this disease if it could so virulently infect even the land of the great revolution. His imagination began seeking dramatic cures—first in the form of a play, then in thoughts of a novel, and finally in a succession of plans for some grand *coup de théâtre* on the stage of life itself. Soon he had vaguely formulated a scheme for the mass regeneration of European Jews and their emigration to some distant land where they could form a political entity.

Palestine naturally came to his mind, but he also thought of— and was inclined to favor—unsettled places in the New World. One of his dearest friends had died in Brazil a few years before on an expedition investigating the possibility of resettling Russian Jews there. And recently Baron Maurice de Hirsch of Vienna and Paris, one of the most eminent Jewish philanthropists of the day, had founded the Jewish Colonization Association and begun establishing agrarian communities in Argentina. Herzl's activity on behalf of his own germinating idea had actually begun in the spring of 1895 with a visit to Baron de Hirsch. The arrogance of brilliant youth clashed with that of great wealth, and the two men did not hit it off; but Herzl, hotly pursuing a momentary vision of Jewish philanthropic support, sat right down and composed an "Address to the Rothschilds." He did not send it, but he did show it to friends and associates in Paris and Vienna, talking obsessively about his idea and discovering that he had "the power to stir people." This tall man with dark eyes and hair, a princely Assyrian beard, and a magnetic personality, was a living version of that emissary—"beautiful and strong . . . used to all the refinements of social life"—of whom George Eliot's Mordecai had dreamed.

Among the people Herzl had stirred was his fellow Paris correspondent Max Nordau, a man even more detached from his Jewish origins than Herzl, and, as the author of such works of social criticism as *Degeneration* and *The Conventional Lies of Civilization*, one of the literary eminences of the day. Nordau knew writers in England, and it was at his suggestion that Herzl had gone there. On Thursday, November 21, freshly arrived in London, Herzl had paid a visit to Israel Zangwill, whose book of sketches of Jewish life in the East End, *Children of the Ghetto*, had been very well received when it was published three years before. Zangwill, who bore some physical resemblance to Disraeli despite his own East European parentage, proved to have the latter's penchant for viewing the Jews as a biological race—to the chagrin of his visitor, who had seen too much of the racial anti-Semitism of the Continent. Speaking French, Herzl argued that "we are an historical unit, a nation with anthropological diversities. This also suffices for the Jewish state." Despite this difference in their outlooks, Zangwill was deeply impressed with Herzl and made arrangements for him to see other prominent English Jews.

Herzl soon found himself with a succession of invitations. One was from the chief Ashkenazi rabbi of the British Empire, Dr. Hermann Adler, with whom conversation was easy since he was a native of Germany. On Saturday evening, after the close of the Sabbath, Herzl was among a handful of guests invited to dinner at Rabbi Adler's home. Over glasses of red wine from Rishon le-Zion, one of the Palestine colonies, he expounded his ideas. When Herzl had finished, Rabbi Adler remarked that "this was the idea of *Daniel Deronda*"—a book the young Viennese author had not yet read.

On Sunday, Herzl had lunch with Sir Samuel Montagu, banker and Liberal member of Parliament for Whitechapel. Montagu—who had been born Montagu Samuel, but switched the names around to distinguish himself within a prolific clan that had come to England from Germany in the eighteenth century—was a cofounder of the Mansion House Relief Fund and a member of the English Hovevei Zion. It was in the name of the latter organization that he had, in 1892, made an offer to the Turkish government to purchase land for Jewish settlement in the Hauran district, east of the Jordan. It had been refused.

At lunch in Montagu's home, Herzl had a glimpse of the synthesis of traditions that had been uniquely achieved by the aristocrats of English Jewry. "A house of English elegance, in grand style," he later wrote in his diary. "Kosher food, served by three liveried footmen." In the smoking room afterward, Herzl unfolded his scheme. Sir Samuel, "a splendid old chap," was roused to enthusiasm and envisioned settling in Palestine with his whole family; he would not even consider Argentina, which Herzl still regarded as a possibility. He was ready, he said, to join in "as soon as one of the Great Powers takes the matter seriously."

That evening, Herzl spoke before the Maccabaeans, an organization of intellectuals dedicated to the spread of Jewish culture. Zangwill was prominently involved in it, and Colonel Goldsmid was a former president. Herzl was unanimously elected an honorary member.

The next day, Herzl left for Colonel Goldsmid's home in Cardiff. Zangwill had made the arrangements by telegram for this visit, and Herzl looked forward to it as the most important one of his stay. Goldsmid knew only a little German and—though Herzl's rudimentary English was rapidly improving—communication was difficult between them; nevertheless, their relations soon were more than cordial. On the afternoon of his arrival, Herzl explicated his plan to the colonel; it was painful going, but when he was through, his host declared in English, "That is the idea of my life."

From that point on, the forms and technicalities of communication were unimportant. "We understood, we understand, each other," Herzl wrote. "He is a wonderful person." It was after dinner that night, Herzl and Goldsmid having retired alone to the smoking room, that the latter made the comparison between himself and Daniel Deronda. "My family was indignant at this," he went on after having described his conversion. "My present wife was also a Christian of Jewish descent. I eloped with her, and we had a civil marriage in Scotland, to begin with. Then she had to become a Jewess, and we were married in a synagogue." Goldsmid pointed out that he now was an orthodox Jew, which "has not done me any harm in England," and that his daughters, Rahel and Carmel, were being taught Hebrew and given a religious upbringing.

Herzl thought it all was indeed like a novel—"that, and his tales of South America," for Goldsmid had recently spent a year in Argentina, administering Baron de Hirsch's colonies. This was a most important point: like Sir Samuel Montagu, but this time on the basis of real experience, Goldsmid rejected Argentina out of hand and insisted "that only Palestine can be considered." He argued that "the pious Christians of England would help us if we went to Palestine. For they expect the coming of the Messiah after the Jews have returned home." These were echoes of Oliphant, and they clearly were having their effect upon Herzl, who wrote: "With Goldsmid, I suddenly find myself in another world." And the next day he wrote: "Goodbye to Colonel Goldsmid. I have already taken him to my heart, like a brother."

Herzl concluded his English stay with a visit to the London home of Rabbi Simeon Singer, spiritual leader of the New West End Synagogue in the Bayswater section. Singer, who had helped Sir Samuel Montagu draft his petition to the sultan in 1892, was enthusiastic about Herzl and invited several distinguished Jewish guests to meet him. Among these was Asher Myers, editor of the *Jewish Chronicle* of London, the august weekly that had been the journalistic spokesman for English Jewry since 1841. Myers had his doubts about Herzl and disliked his lack of religious commitment; nevertheless, he asked Herzl to send him a summary of the pamphlet he then was preparing, a revised and expanded version of the "Address to the Rothschilds." Herzl did so after he got back to Paris, with the result that, in January 1896, Herzl's plan made its first appearance in print in the pages of the *Jewish Chronicle*. His full-length bid to change history, *Der Judenstaat (The Jewish State)*, was published in Vienna the following month.

By the time he made his next trip to London, in July 1896, Herzl had taken considerable strides. Although the public response to his pamphlet had been mixed—indeed, Hovevei Zion throughout Europe were incensed at the clamorings of this outsider who knew nothing of their work—he had won significant adherents all the same. The Jewish nationalist student circles of his own Vienna—within which the term "Zionism" had recently been coined by Nathan Birnbaum, one of their leaders—took warmly to his ideas and personality and through their network of contacts began promoting their goal of a general Zionist congress. Ordinary Jewish folk wrote him letters of thanks, even as assimilationist rabbis and community leaders denounced his stress on Jewish nationality over religion.

Important political contacts also had come about. The Reverend William Hechler, chaplain to the British embassy in Vienna and author of a pamplet called *The Restoration of the Jews to Palestine According to the Prophets*, had presented himself to Herzl in March: having once tutored the son of the grand duke of Baden, he knew both the grand duke and the latter's nephew, who had since become Kaiser Wilhelm II. And within six weeks he had not only discussed Herzl with those two eminences, but brought about a meeting between him and the grand duke, who was favorably impressed. In June, Herzl had been brought to Constantinople by Philip Michael de

Newlinski, a Viennese journalist of Polish aristocratic extraction and former political attaché to the Austrian embassy in Turkey. As attaché, he had formed a friendship with Sultan Abdul Hamid II. Through Newlinski, Herzl was able to discuss his scheme with various Turkish statesmen. Though he did not get to talk with the sultan himself, Newlinski did; the upshot was a strong impression that the Ottoman government might entertain some proposal that had strong political and financial backing. The Argentine alternative, which had survived into the pages of *Der Judenstaat*, was now scarcely more than a memory.

The previous month, Sir Samuel Montagu (whose name Herzl was to find helpful in Constantinople) had presented a copy of Sylvie d'Avigdor's translation of *The Jewish State* to William E. Gladstone. The eighty-six-year-old statesman had found its subject "highly interesting." Yet, when Herzl arrived in London on July 5, Sir Samuel was among the people he found strangely cooled toward him. Though Herzl had written Sir Samuel that he was bringing "from Constantinople the *presque-certitude* that we would regain Palestine," he found it hard to gain a suitable appointment with him right away. Goldsmid also was unavailable at first, claiming to be kept in Cardiff by a battalion inspection. Rabbi Simeon Singer was the only one of the old enthusiasts available that first day, and even he had to be "stirred . . . up a bit," as Herzl put it in his diary: "In fact, I shall first have to light a fire under everybody here."

What had happened? In the ensuing days, Herzl was to get together with both Goldsmid and Montagu more than once and have other vital encounters as well: an interview for the *Daily Graphic* with Lucien Wolf, its foreign editor, himself a well-known author of works on Jewish history; a conversation with Claude Montefiore—grandnephew of Sir Moses, distinguished Liberal-Jewish theologian, and recently elected president of the Anglo-Jewish Association—in which Montefiore demonstrated opposition to all ideas of Jewish nationality or statehood; and another pleasant appearance before the Maccabaeans, this time with a speech written by Herzl in German, translated by Sylvie d'Avigdor, and carefully rehearsed by Herzl in English an hour earlier. But despite all this activity—and the appearance, during his stay, of a *Sunday Times* interview with Zangwill that focused mainly on Herzl—England was clearly not as receptive to him as it had been on his first visit, and Goldsmid and Montagu had indeed grown cooler.

The fact was that the young man from Vienna had become a major presence on the Palestine colonization scene, and the full implications of his position now had to be soberly considered. What he stood for above all was a grand political stroke: a purchase, a concession, a charter—some decisive arrangement with the Turks for an autonomous entity in which masses of Jews could be immediately resettled. What he did not stand for was the kind of slow, gradual colonization under existing political conditions—he scornfully referred to this as "infiltration"—that had been Hovevei Zion policy from the beginning. Herzl seemed, then, to be on a collision course, not only with that organization, but also with the great benefactor in Paris who had been making it all possible. "Edmond Rothschild's sport must cease at all costs," he told his glum listeners in the "headquarters tent" at the Bevis Marks synagogue on the evening of July 14, his last in London for this trip; whereupon one member piously expressed the hope "that Jewish history would not have to record any strife between Edmond Rothschild" and Herzl. But Colonel Goldsmid, who had promised to write Herzl a letter of recommendation to the baron, sat there and no doubt wondered.

The fact is, Herzl—who had begun his Zionist work with a visit to Baron de Hirsch that ended in a quarrel and an "Address to the Rothschilds" that never was sent, and who now pondered the "complete elimination" of Sir Samuel Montagu from his plan—had a vehement dislike of the rich and of the tradition of Jewish philanthropy, even while he continued believing they were indispensable. He was no Socialist, but he might very well have become one had he not discovered the Jews to suffice as his proletariat. And this, too, had begun to happen in London, on the evening before, when he addressed a mass meeting of Jewish workingmen—immigrants from Russia and Rumania—in the East End. Significantly, this appearance had been advised against by Sir Samuel Montagu, MP for the district.

The Workingmen's Club had been filled to capacity for the occasion. "People crowded into every corner," Herzl wrote. "A stage served as the platform from which I spoke extemporaneously. I had merely jotted down a few catchwords on a piece of paper. I talked for an hour in the frightful heat. Great success." Among the succession of speakers who then stood up to eulogize him were individuals from the Hovevei Zion, including Dr. Moses Gaster, one of the founders of that organization's branches in his native Rumania, and now the *haham* (chief rabbi) of England's Sephardic congregations. "As I sat on the platform," Herzl meditated, ". . . I experienced strange sensations. I saw and heard my legend being born." He was being recognized as "the man of the little people," and the issues had thus become clear: "Now it really depends only on myself whether I shall become the leader of the masses; but I don't want to be, if in some way I can buy the Rothschilds at the price of my resignation from the movement." Less than a week later, in Paris, Herzl swallowed his resentment and went to see Baron Edmond de Rothschild; but the baron had just received a letter from Colonel Goldsmid describing Herzl's scheme as "downright dangerous," and the meeting was a failure.

In the ensuing year, Herzl—indefatigably speaking, writing, traveling, organizing—succeeded in creating a mass movement. And on August 29, 1897, a dream was realized: the First Zionist Congress assembled in Basel for three days of deliberations. Its 197 delegates, plus representatives of the press, had come from all over Europe, from America, and from Algeria; English friends—Zangwill, Gaster, and Hechler among them—were there, although the Hovevei Zion of England, like that of France, had boycotted the congress, and some of the Russian branches had been resistant. But the Hovevei Zion was now nearing the end of its days, withering before the overwhelming personality of the "marvelous and exalted figure"—in the words of one witness—who stood before the congress in frock coat and white tie: "It is no longer the elegant Dr. Herzl of Vienna; it is a royal scion of the House of David, risen from among the dead, clothed in legend and fantasy and beauty." As for Herzl himself, he went home at the end of the congress and wrote in his diary: "At Basel I founded the Jewish State. . . . Perhaps in five years, and certainly in fifty, everyone will know it."

Fifty years was sound prophecy, but Herzl hoped for five with all the breath of his life. A basic program—henceforth to be known as the Basel Program—had been drawn up at the congress in such a way as to alarm neither the Hovevei Zion nor the Turks unnecessarily: "The aim of Zionism," its opening sentence read, "is to create for the Jewish people a home in Palestine secured by public law." In particular, Max Nordau's idea of using *Heimstätte* ("home" or, literally, "homestead" in German, the official language of the congress) rather than "state" was a way of avoiding provocation. Yet for all this prudence, and despite its occasional signs of friendliness, the Ottoman government remained unyielding to Zionist blandishments.

So also did the German government, despite three euphoric meetings between Herzl and the kaiser during the course of their respective journeys to Constantinople and Palestine in the fall of

1898. Germany had, in recent years, become the foremost European investor in Turkish railways and other enterprises and was now seeking to consolidate its influence in Constantinople; but this fact, encouraging at first to Herzl's hopes for the kaiser's help, finally led the Germans to rebuff the Zionists as an embarrassment. Herzl never quite recovered from this, though he went on zealously working, hoping, presiding over Zionist congresses and the worldwide organization he had created; finally, in 1902, he vented his frustration by writing a utopian novel, *Altneuland (Old-New Land)*, about the Palestine commonwealth he had not yet been able to create.

Through all this, Herzl continued as always to look upon England as the "Archimedean point" on which to rest his lever. The Zionist organization's bank had been charted there under the name Anglo-Palestine Company, and in 1901 Herzl had seriously considered the possibility of transferring his headquarters from Vienna to London, where the previous year's congress had been held. He knew of the continuing ambitions of some Englishmen concerning the Levant and, in *Altneuland*, had stressed the importance of Palestine on the overland route to India. And England was still, in spite of everything, the home of some of his best friends—including some valuable new ones, such as Joseph Cowen and Leopold Greenberg, two slightly younger men who had been drawn into the Zionist movement by Herzl's personality. Cowen, a cousin of Israel Zangwill's and a successful businessman, had been lovingly depicted in *Altneuland* as Joe Levy, the energetic leader who presided over the technological tasks of rebuilding a modern Palestine. Greenberg was a journalist with high political connections: a native of Birmingham, he was a friend of its most celebrated citizen, Joseph Chamberlain, the colonial secretary and the dominant figure in English politics.

Herzl had once tried on his own to see the prime minister, Lord Salisbury—who, as Disraeli's foreign secretary in 1879, had looked favorably upon Oliphant's Gilead project and had also, in an earlier tenure as prime minister, supported Sir Samuel Montagu's similar plan for the Hauran. But Lord Salisbury had then been preoccupied with a major colonial embarrassment, the Boer War, and he had not seen Herzl. That war was now coming to an end, however; and in the spring of 1902, Leopold Greenberg was at work establishing contact between Herzl and British governing circles at last.

The occasion for this was provided by what was, in part at least, a rare intimation of political anti-Semitism in the one country Herzl had thought to be completely free of it. The vast East European

Jewish emigration that had begun in 1882 was reaching its height; it had accounted for some 95,000 of the new arrivals in Great Britain over the intervening twenty years. Of these, 54,000 had settled in London, mainly in the East End, where they formed a world of their own. They aroused a variety of resentments, but one in particular dominated the rest. As a great historian of England has pointed out: "It was their insatiable appetite for work which made them formidable. For the Jew no amount of wealth was so great that he would not seek to earn more, no wage so small that he was ashamed to work for it. This trait produced the vast fortunes whose display in Park Lane outraged British traditions, also the mass of sweated labor employed by the tailors, shoemakers and cabinet makers of Whitechapel." The agitation now arising among English workers, and being exploited by that type of parliamentary Conservative who saw in this issue a chance to be their friend, was nominally against the competition of all "aliens"; but when the Royal Commission on Alien Immigration was appointed to investigate the problem in the spring of 1902, the term was mainly a euphemism for Jews.

Owing to Greenberg's influence, one of the witnesses called by the commission was Theodor Herzl. The Zionist leader had to steer a difficult course. Certainly some of the more anti-Semitic members of the commission hoped he would say that Jews should go to Palestine and not England, and the prospect of his doing so had been worrisome to its one Jewish member, Lord Nathaniel Mayer Rothschild. Lay leader of English Jewry, a peer since 1885, eldest son of that Lionel de Rothschild who had fought for years to be the first member of his faith to sit in Parliament, Lord Rothschild looked upon Zionism's claim that Jews were not just a religious group, but a nation, as the antithesis of everything he and his family stood for. He had always refused to see Herzl; but three days before the latter's scheduled appearance, he got together with him at last, hoping to dissuade him from saying anything that might make him a pawn in the hands of British anti-Semites. Their vehement confrontation ended in a standoff. Herzl refused to be dictated to, but in the end he placated Lord Rothschild by describing a plan he was going to offer the commission.

Herzl presented his testimony, carefully written out in English by Greenberg and himself, on July 7. Stressing the desperate condition of the Jews of Eastern Europe, he made clear his view that Jewish immigration to England was likely to increase in the near future—Lord Rothschild had not wanted him to make a point of this—but he carefully avoided any explicit statement that would tend to favor restrictive legislation. On the contrary, he argued that restriction would be contrary to British traditions. Then, setting aside that particular question, he moved on to the one about which he felt qualified to speak.

Ultimately, he said, the only solution was the one he had been advocating since 1895: "the recognition of Jews as a people, and the finding by them of a legally recognized home, to which Jews in those parts of the world in which they are oppressed would naturally migrate, for they would arrive there as citizens just because they are Jews, and not as aliens." This was more in the spirit of *Der Judenstaat*, with its aspiration for a Jewish refuge in virtually any available place, than in that of the Palestine-oriented Zionist movement, and it is significant that Herzl did not mention Palestine in this context. He advised the commission that "a diverting of the stream of migration" was needed. "The Jews of Eastern Europe cannot stay where they are—where are they to go? If you find they are not wanted here, then some place must be found to which they can migrate without . . . raising the problems that confront them here."

Sensing the direction in which he was going, one member of the commission asked about Argentina. Herzl replied that the project of Baron de Hirsch—who had died in 1896—was a failure because "when you want a great settlement, you must have a flag and an idea. You cannot make these things only with money." Lord Rothschild now took up the baton and asked the witness for an elucidation of the word "Zionism"—"whether you mean that there should be a combined movement to re-establish a Jewish State in Palestine, or whether, by the word 'Zionism,' you simply mean that some great endeavor should be made to colonize some part of the world entirely with Jews." Herzl repeated the formula of the Basel Program stressing a home in *Palestine*, but added: "Now, it is certainly the goal, but there may be moments where immediate help or a step forward is indispensable, and so Zionists believe that, maintaining always their principle and program, they should, in the meantime, try to alleviate the hard conditions of oppressed Jews by adequate means." Rothschild pressed for the point by asserting it himself in the form of a question: "I will not say the dream, but the object that a Zionist has in view is to find a fresh opening for oppressed Jews, apart from the present openings they have got—a fresh home for them, whether it be in Palestine itself or whether it be on the road to Palestine or elsewhere?" They understood one another perfectly; Herzl replied that he had a plan to offer, but that he preferred to present it to the chairman privately, who could then convey it to his colleagues as he saw fit.

Herzl called upon the commission chairman, Lord James of Hereford, the very next day. His plan was to colonize some portion of British-held territory that was as close as possible to Palestine—he suggested either Cyprus or the region of the Sinai around El Arish, which was then often called "Egyptian Palestine." Lord Rothschild obviously had approved of this plan because it meant both an honorable solution to the overcrowding of ghettoes at home and a "Jewish state" whose subjects would be British after all. Lord James "thought that I could carry out the Sinai-El Arish-Cyprus plan only with the aid of Lord Rothschild. The Rothschilds would have to become my agents in this country. They were highly respected here, where there was no anti-Semitism." James emphasized that no money should be expected from His Majesty's Government. But Herzl's view of the conversation afterward was: "I believe Lord James liked the matter better than he cared to show me."

Certainly the idea was to appeal to Joseph Chamberlain, who had suffered a driving accident at the time of Herzl's testimony, but was ready to see him in the fall. By then Lord Salisbury had retired, but Chamberlain—still recuperating, too controversial a figure and, after all, a Liberal Unionist rather than a Conservative*—had been passed over for prime minister in favor of Salisbury's nephew, Arthur James Balfour; Chamberlain nevertheless continued to wield his power at the Colonial Office. At first, upon entering Chamberlain's rooms on the afternoon of October 22, Herzl found the well-known, monocled, clean-shaven face to be a "motionless mask." The colonial secretary listened to his visitor for a while, then explained that he was not qualified to discuss El Arish and the Sinai, since Egypt was technically not a colony and was therefore under the jurisdiction of the Foreign Office; and as for Cyprus, he could not approve, since Greeks and Muslims lived there in considerable numbers and would certainly resist large-scale Jewish immigration. But Chamberlain listened with growing fascination as Herzl developed his arguments in favor of El Arish and began to understand the "desire to obtain a rallying point for the Jewish people in the vicin-

---

* The Conservatives in this epoch in fact styled themselves Unionists, to characterize their position regarding Ireland, but this term was not exclusively used and has been neglected for the purposes of this narrative.

ity of Palestine," in return for which Britain would "reap an increase in power and the gratitude of ten million Jews." In the end, Chamberlain expressed agreement with the idea, provided it had the approval of Lord Cromer—technically only the British agent and consul general in Cairo, but since 1883 the virtual ruler of Egypt. He also arranged an appointment for Herzl with Lord Lansdowne, the foreign secretary.

Two days later, at 4:30 P.M.—after a friendly lunch at New Court, during which Lord Rothschild had told him he was "a great man"—the Zionist leader found himself back on Downing Street, this time making his way to Lord Lansdowne's "exquisite salon." After being greeted "charmingly" by the foreign secretary—"a nice English gentleman, most modest in manner and not of conspicuous intelligence"—Herzl began his exposition, first in English, then in French. Lansdowne "listened most amiably, raised few objections, and finally asked me to let him have a written memorandum of the matter—evidently for the Cabinet." Lansdowne said he would write to Lord Cromer for his opinion, and when Herzl pointed out that he was planning to send Leopold Greenberg to Cromer as the Zionist representative, the foreign secretary offered to provide a letter of introduction. As a final flourish, Herzl offered to be of whatever service he could at Constantinople, where he claimed "a good personal relationship with the Sultan," and where, he believed, "English influence has suffered a bit."

Herzl returned to this matter of useful influence in the memorandum he wrote for Lansdowne on his way back to Paris the following day. "At one stroke," he suggested, if the plan is approved, "England will get ten million secret but loyal subjects active in all walks of life all over the world. They sell needles and thread in many small villages in the East; but they are also wholesale merchants, industrialists, stock brokers, scholars and artists and newspapermen and other things." Urging the British government to "recognize what value there is in gaining the Jewish people," Herzl's memorandum hinted at a moral bargain. It was the immigration to the East End of London that had caused Englishmen to concern themselves with the Jewish Question of Eastern Europe. Now, this immigration

is still no calamity worth mentioning, and I hope it will never become one to the extent that England would have to break with the glorious principle of free asylum. But the fact that a Royal Commission was appointed for the matter will make it sufficiently plausible in the eyes of the world if the British government considers itself impelled to open up a special territory for the Jews who are oppressed everywhere and thus gravitate to England.

Herzl thus closed the circle of argumentation that had begun with his own appearance before the royal commission in July.

Things now seemed to be moving rapidly. While Herzl, physically exhausted and feeling symptoms of the deadly heart disease that had been troubling him for years, retired for a brief rest cure to the Alpine village of Edlach, Greenberg went to Cairo. There he found not only Lord Cromer, but also the Egyptian prime minister, Boutros Ghali Pasha, to be friendly to the plan. He wired a favorable report to Herzl, and the latter wrote breathlessly in his diary: "Is it possible that we stand on the threshold of obtaining a—British—Charter and founding the Jewish State?" On December 18, after Chamberlain had begun a personal tour of Britain's African colonies and had consulted with Cromer in Cairo, the Foreign Office sent Herzl a letter saying that Lord Cromer, while warning "that no sanguine hopes of success ought to be entertained," had suggested that a commission be sent to survey the El Arish region with reference to the plan. The letter went on to assure Herzl that if the commission's report proved favorable, the Zionists would be offered good terms for colonization. Herzl regarded this as a "historic document"—the first recognition by a Great Power of the Zionist movement as a political entity with which to negotiate.

A six man commission was appointed, with Colonel Albert Goldsmid as one of its members. In spite of everything, Goldsmid and Herzl had remained in touch over the years, and the bitterness of earlier exchanges was long gone. Herzl's real achievements had finally overcome Goldsmid's misgivings at his ambitiousness, and the colonel had even become affiliated with the Zionist movement; indeed, he was about to replace Greenberg in Herzl's esteem. Goldsmid and the other commission members left at the end of January 1903 for Egypt, where it was their task to take the field and regularly report to Greenberg in Cairo. Greenberg, in turn, was to send comprehensive reports to Herzl in Vienna; but before February was over something had gone wrong. Cromer, after encountering disapproval of the plan among Egyptian leaders, had begun showing resistance, and one day Herzl received a wire from Greenberg saying he had presented Cromer with an "alternative proposal." Herzl had no idea what this was, but his suspicion that Greenberg was taking things into his own hands was not allayed when the latter made a trip back to London without stopping in Vienna. Greenberg finally did get to Vienna in mid-March, but by this time Herzl was utterly aroused and went to Egypt himself.

The commission's report was in, and the central problem it posed was that of water supply. Herzl suggested that the Nile be tapped—"only surplus Nile water," he told Cromer, "what comes from the winter; the water that would otherwise flow into the sea, unused. We will build reservoirs for it." But Cromer, whom Herzl described as "the most disagreeable Englishman I have ever faced," would not discuss the matter until his own expert had examined the terrain at El Arish. Cromer did put Herzl in touch with a lawyer to work out the lines for a territorial concession, but the initial momentum clearly had passed by the time the Zionist leader left Cairo, on April 4. He appointed Colonel Goldsmid to stay there as his representative—the position Greenberg had held—and it was Goldsmid who was left with the disagreeable task of sending Herzl a telegram on May 12 informing him that the negotiations had fallen through. Goldsmid relayed the official reason in a follow-up letter: Cromer's expert concluded that five times as much water would be needed as had been claimed in the commission's report and maintained that the laying of irrigation pipes would tie up Suez Canal traffic for weeks. Herzl tried to refute the arguments, but they clearly stood for a deeper-lying opposition.

It was all over; and to compound the failure, during Easter week a pogrom had broken out in the south Russian town of Kishinev that proved to be the worst in that country since 1881. Some forty-five Jews were killed and more than a thousand injured. Amid worldwide protests at this outrage, Herzl responded to it by writing a letter to the Russian minister of the interior, Vyacheslav von Plehve, asking to see him. Indeed, he was to do so that summer, to the anger of the many Jews the world over who considered von Plehve to be the man chiefly responsible for the pogroms. But for Herzl, resentment was not good enough; Kishinev had revived his passion for action, the desire to achieve the kind of sudden and dramatic solution that had once again been denied him.

Miraculously, another chance for such a solution had presented itself even before the El Arish project died, and it had come from the same source. In London shortly after returning from Egypt, Herzl had gone to see Joseph Chamberlain, who was just back from his African journey. "I have seen a land for you on my travels," he said on that occasion, according to Herzl, "and that's Uganda." Chamberlain may not have put it precisely this way, though the name "Uganda" was to stick in Zionist circles; what he meant was British East Africa, in any one of several places along the recently completed Uganda railway. "It's hot on the coast, but farther inland the climate becomes excellent, even for Europeans. You can raise sugar and cotton there. And I thought to myself, that would be a land for Dr. Herzl. But of course he wants only to go to Palestine or its vicinity." To which Herzl had replied: "Yes, I have to"—for the El Arish negotiations were then still going on.

How had the idea occurred to Chamberlain? As far back as January 2, while still on his trip, he had made some notes on the East African protectorate and sent them to the Foreign Office. Among other things he wrote: "If Dr. Herzl were at all inclined to transfer his efforts to East Africa there would be no difficulty in finding land suitable for Jewish settlers, but I assume that this country is too far removed from Palestine to have any attractions for him." It had attracted few settlers so far and seemed to cry out for more; meanwhile, the things Herzl had said to him in October evidently were still resonating in Chamberlain's mind. But this was not the first time East Africa had been discussed as a place for possible Jewish settlement: Lord Rothschild, in his very first conversation with Herzl back in June, had also suggested that he consider "Uganda." Was there an earlier source for this idea?

There was one precedent that seems to have been on many minds, though it was not an entirely fortunate one: the Freeland colony, inspired by the writings of the Viennese economist and journalist Dr. Theodor Hertzka. In 1890, this man with a name so startlingly similar to Herzl's had published *Freiland*, a utopian novel that envisioned an ideal communitarian colony at the foot of Mount Kenya. Herzl, in his preface to *Der Judenstaat*, had referred to this book as "an ingenious bit of fantasy, devised by a thoroughly modern mind schooled in the principles of political economy, and as remote from life as the equatorial mountain on which this dream state is located." But a group of Hertzka's followers had in fact formed an International Freeland Society and petitioned the British Foreign Office for the right to establish a colony in 1893. The following year they established themselves at Lamu at the foot of Mount Kenya; but the colony soon fell apart in internal dissension. Was there, then, some connection in men's minds—as there was in Herzl's own—between these two utopian novelists from Vienna?

Be that as it may, a crucial conversation took place between Leopold Greenberg and Joseph Chamberlain, in the latter's office, on

May 20, 1903, a little more than a week after the collapse of the El Arish negotiations. Stressing that Palestine was still the ultimate goal of the Zionists, Greenberg asked if Jewish settlement on Cyprus could not in the meantime be reconsidered. Chamberlain said it could not, and then brought up East Africa. "I hope that Dr. Herzl will take my suggestion seriously," he said, and Greenberg promptly sent a report on the conversation to Herzl in Vienna. Herzl wired back urging him to ask Chamberlain for details right away. The Sixth Zionist Congress was due to meet at Basel in August, and Herzl was eager to present something that would mean possible relief for the persecuted Jews of Eastern Europe.

Greenberg went back to Chamberlain and tried to arrive at an exact location for possible Jewish settlement within the East African protectorate, but the colonial secretary had nothing definite yet in mind. This drawback was then set aside, and Herzl and Chamberlain, with Greenberg as intermediary, agreed that an investigating commission would be sent to whatever territory was chosen. Meanwhile, they decided to draft a provisional charter. The task of drawing this up was placed in the hands of the law firm of Lloyd George, Roberts and Company: Greenberg thought this was a good idea because David Lloyd George was a member of Parliament and, having recently become famous as Britain's most fiery denouncer of the Boer War, a man well versed in African affairs.

The draft charter for "New Palestine" was forwarded by Lloyd George's office to Chamberlain on July 13, and copies were sent on to the Foreign Office for perusal. While Greenberg waited impatiently in London for the outcome, Herzl departed for Russia, where he obtained assurances of support for Zionism from the hated von Plehve and from the foreign minister, Count Witte—they being as eager as Herzl to get Jews out of Russia. During the journey, Herzl also witnessed some moving demonstrations in his favor by Jewish crowds and was all the more eager for a triumph. As for the British Government, the potential face-saving value of a territorial offer to the Jews took on a certain urgency at the beginning of August, when the aliens commission report was finally published, urging some degree of restriction upon immigration.

It was on August 14 that Sir Clement Hill of the Foreign Office finally wrote, on behalf of Lord Lansdowne, the letter that constituted the first official diplomatic recognition of a Jewish political entity since the extinction of the Judean state more than eighteen hundred years before. "I am now directed by his Lordship," the letter read, "to say that he has studied the question with the interest which His Majesty's Government must always take in any well considered scheme for the amelioration of the position of the Jewish Race." Protesting that the time had been too short for any *detailed* plan concerning the proposed Jewish settlement in East Africa, the letter went on to say that Lord Lansdowne would be happy to give members of any investigating commission sent there "every facility to enable them to discuss with His Majesty's Commissioner the possibility of meeting the view which may be expressed at the forthcoming Zionist Congress in regard to the conditions upon which a settlement might be possible." And then followed the crucial statement: "If a site can be found which the [Jewish Colonial] Trust and His Majesty's Commissioner consider suitable and which commends itself to His Majesty's Government, Lord Lansdowne will be prepared to entertain favorably proposals for the establishment of a Jewish colony of settlement, on conditions which will enable the members to observe their national customs."

Herzl read the Foreign Office letter to the Sixth Zionist Congress at its opening session on August 22. The effect was stunning; there was an outburst of applause, and one of the secretaries of the congress saw on the faces throughout the hall universal expressions of "amazement, admiration . . . [at] the magnanimity of the British offer." The impact of this historic gesture and Herzl's profound sense of the dramatic had won the moment; but the euphoria was quickly to pass. What about Palestine? It was as if Herzl, in his overwhelming eagerness for a political triumph, had gone back to his beginnings as the writer of the "Address to the Rothschilds": Argentina would do, or "Uganda."

By the time the separate federations had retired to their caucuses, the full implications of the letter were being considered, and there were widespread changes of heart—particularly among the Russian delegations, for whom the love of Zion was fierce and undying. The opposition mounted and a highly emotional debate ensued during the remaining sessions of the congress. Herzl stayed aloof during the debate. Max Nordau—who himself had doubts about the idea—took the role of Herzl's principal spokesman, at one point characterizing "Uganda" as a much-needed *Nachtasyl* ("refuge in the night") for persecuted Jews on the road to Zion; he was often to be reproached for this term in years to come.

When, amid breathless tension, the roll-call vote was finally held on the afternoon of August 29, Herzl actually won: 295 votes to 177. But it was a Pyrrhic victory. About a hundred delegates abstained—

some of them leading figures in the movement—and the majority had given their support because the resolution they voted on was for nothing more than appointing a committee of inquiry to look more closely into the offer. They had not made a final decision in favor of establishing a colony. Furthermore, when the vote was announced, the entire minority of 177 delegates who had opposed the resolution—most of them from Russia—rose from their seats and strode out of the hall. They assembled in a caucus room, where many of them wept and assumed attitudes of mourning. Herzl later went to see them in person and, though one voice shouted "traitor," he was listened to cordially as he pleaded his case and insisted that his ultimate loyalty always was to Palestine. This calmed them, and they reappeared at the next day's session and issued an explanation of their behavior. The congress closed peaceably, but it was clear that the Zionist movement was seriously threatened with dissolution.

In the evening after the final session, the weary Herzl went with Joseph Cowen to the latter's hotel room, where they were joined by Nordau and Israel Zangwill, his closest friends at the congress. Herzl outlined for them the position he would take two years hence at the seventh congress—"that is, if I live to see it." By then, he would "either have obtained Palestine or realized the complete futility of any further efforts." In the latter case, he would give a speech of resignation, again defending his acceptance of the East African offer, and would add: "Although I was originally only a Jewish State man—*n'importe où*—later I did lift up the flag of Zion and became myself a Lover of Zion. Palestine is the only land where our people can come to rest. But hundreds of thousands need immediate help."

This was virtually his dying plea. Less than a year later, on July 3, 1904, in Edlach, where he had gone for another rest, Theodor Herzl's troubled heart stopped beating altogether. He was forty-four. Colonel Goldsmid, the other Deronda of his generation, died the same year at the age of fifty-eight. At the seventh congress in 1905, after indifferent reports both from the committee of inquiry and the investigating commission, and after a clamor of protest against the whole idea from the white settlers of East Africa, the "Uganda" offer was rejected once and for all.

PART ONE

·1914·

·3·

TURKEY ENTERS THE WAR

On July 29, 1914, the day after Austria declared war on Serbia and Europe quickened its preparations for a looming general conflict, Winston Churchill, Britain's first lord of the Admiralty, took some moments to ponder a Turkish matter within his jurisdiction. Two dreadnought battleships, the *Sultan Osman* and the *Reshadieh*, were being completed for Turkey in British shipyards; indeed, the *Sultan Osman* was ready for delivery, but had been held up by a series of minor complications. Growing impatient and even suspicious, Djemal Pasha, the Turkish minister of marine, had dispatched a crew of five hundred men to board the vessel, and they had been waiting in a steamer near the Armstrong shipyard on the Tyne. Churchill had just received a note from the Foreign Office—which was worried about Turkey's intentions on the international scene—informing him that the *Sultan Osman* was being equipped with coal that very day and that its crew were under orders to proceed immediately to Constantinople.

"There seemed to be a great danger," Churchill later wrote, "of their coming on board, brushing aside Messrs. Armstrongs' workmen and hoisting the Turkish flag, in which case a very difficult diplomatic situation would have been created." He immediately gave orders that this should be prevented by every means and readied himself for even more decisive action. Two days later, he persuaded the cabinet that both ships should be taken over by the Royal Navy, and on August 1, the *Sultan Osman* was boarded by British sailors.

"Never, never," Djemal Pasha was to write, "shall I forget my mental anguish when I heard this frightful news." The ships, which had cost Turkey more than £3.5 million, had been paid for by popular subscription. Contributions had been solicited amid a patriotic clamor. "Agents had gone from house to house," according to the

American ambassador at Constantinople, Henry Morgenthau, "painfully collecting these small sums of money; there had been entertainments and fairs, and, in their eagerness for the cause, Turkish women had sold their hair for the benefit of the common fund." As far as Djemal was concerned, "this incident justified the mobilization of our army, and thus gave us good reason for returning a *tu quoque* answer to the Entente ambassadors who found this general mobilization unnecessary." But the Turks were to enjoy a more pointed revenge within the next few days.

On the afternoon of August 3, when Germany declared war on France, the German battle cruiser *Goeben* and light cruiser *Breslau* were making their way southwestward over Mediterranean waters toward the Algerian coast. They were the only German ships in the Mediterranean, but the *Goeben* was as large as a British dreadnought and, according to Winston Churchill, "far outstripped in speed every vessel in the French navy." Three squadrons of the French fleet were speeding to head off any move the German vessels might make toward France itself; but the only ships in the area fully equipped to deal with the *Goeben* were three British battle cruisers, two of which were ordered out from the Adriatic to shadow it. Early in the morning of August 4, they spotted the *Goeben* and the *Breslau* returning northeastward after having shelled Philippeville and Bône, and proceeded to follow; they could do nothing more, as England and Germany were not yet at war. "Very good," the Admiralty wired back after receiving the news. "Hold her. War imminent."

The two German ships headed for the Strait of Messina and entered it before the midnight deadline after which Britain and Germany were officially at war. Within the strait they met German colliers and recoaled; but the British ships—there now were three—which had gathered at the northern entrance did not go in after them, for to do so would have been to violate the neutrality the Italian government had just declared. The British simply waited, assuming that the *Goeben* and the *Breslau* would come out again at the north, since this was the way to the western Mediterranean and the Strait of Gibraltar. If the German ships went out the other way, there seemed no place for them to go; for the only friendly port in that direction was the Austrian one of Pola at the northern end of the Adriatic—and the Adriatic was covered by a British fleet.

What the British did not know was that Admiral Wilhelm Souchon of the *Goeben* had received orders by wireless to proceed to Constantinople. It was at 5:00 P.M. on August 6 that he finally sailed his two ships out of Messina harbor, bands playing and flags flying as if about to go into battle; then he vanished. Early the following morning Rear Admiral Ernest Troubridge realized that the *Goeben* and the *Breslau* were passing to the south of his Adriatic fleet, and he began to lead a squadron in pursuit; but when dawn came he remembered the superiority of the *Goeben*'s guns and an Admiralty warning, issued before hostilities began, not to take action "against superior forces," and he backed off.

The chase was not yet over, however. The *Gloucester*, a British light cruiser, which alone had patrolled the southern entrance of the Strait of Messina, remained in pursuit and even engaged the *Breslau* in fire off the coast of Greece that afternoon; but it was chased off by the *Goeben*, and the Admiralty ordered its captain to desist. By now the three British Mediterranean-based cruisers were in hot pursuit, and their chances of reaching the *Goeben* and the *Breslau* were good, for the two German ships found themselves having to wait at the entrance to the Dardanelles while the Turkish government decided whether to let them in after all.

Then a "sinister fatality" intervened, in Winston Churchill's words, and a "blameless and punctilious Admiralty clerk" mistakenly sent out word that England had declared war on Austria— four days before the fact, as it was to turn out. When Admiral Sir Berkeley Milne, leading the squadron that pursued the German ships, received this message, he promptly reverted to his general instructions covering the event of war with Austria, turned about, and headed for Malta to concentrate his fleet there. By the time he received a correction, it was too late: on the evening of Tuesday, August 11, the *Goeben* and the *Breslau* sailed into the Dardanelles.

Since Turkey had proclaimed neutrality a week before, the two German ships were now presumably out of the war. No one knew that Turkey had signed a secret treaty of defensive alliance with Germany on August 2—a fact that naturally did not bode well for the Entente formed by Great Britain, France, and Russia. The Turks themselves do not seem to have known precisely what they had committed themselves to do—counsels were divided among them. They were determined, however, not to go to war for the time being.

The result was that, on the morning of August 12, there were some Turkish ministers ready to propose to Baron von Wangenheim, the German ambassador, that his government "consent to the two ships being disarmed—temporarily and superficially only." Wangenheim refused, and someone then suggested that Germany "sell" the

Goeben and the *Breslau* to the Turkish government. This idea was found acceptable, and Djemal sent an official communiqué to the press announcing the purchase. "I asked the press," he later wrote, "to speak enthusiastically of the circumstance that we had obtained possession of the ships as compensation for the *Sultan Osman* and the *Reshadieh*, of which the English had robbed us."

This was ominous, but it still did not produce great consternation. "As we shall insist," Prime Minister Herbert Henry Asquith wrote on August 12, "that the *Goeben* shall be manned by a Turkish instead of a German crew it does not much matter, as the Turkish sailors cannot navigate her except on to rocks or mines." The next day *The Times* could confidently state that negotiations were "now pending with the Ottoman Government for the removal of the German officers and crews from these vessels"; and on August 15, it announced that the two ships, duly renamed the *Jawuz Sultan Selim* and the *Midilli*, were going to be placed under the command of Rear Admiral Arthur Henry Limpus, the head of a British naval training mission that had been in Turkey for two years.

In another few days, however, Admiral Limpus was sent home, and the German crews of the two ships had been solemnly proclaimed members of the Turkish navy. Admiral Souchon and his men even took to wearing Turkish fezzes; but the pretense was not always perfectly maintained. "One day," Ambassador Morgenthau writes, "the *Goeben* sailed up the Bosphorus, halted in front of the Russian Embassy, and dropped anchor. Then the officers and men lined the deck in full view of the enemy embassy. All solemnly removed their Turkish fezzes and put on German caps. The band played '*Deutschland über Alles*,' the 'Watch on the Rhine,' and other German songs, the German sailors singing loudly to the accompaniment. When they had spent an hour or more serenading the Russian Ambassador, the officers and crews [*sic*] removed their German caps and again put on their Turkish fezzes. The *Goeben* then picked up her anchor and started southward for her station, leaving in the ears of the Russian diplomat the gradually dying strains of German war songs as the cruiser disappeared down stream."

Morgenthau also describes an encounter on the street, later that month, between one Turkish minister and a prominent Belgian jurist.

"I have terrible news for you," the Turkish statesman said. "The Germans have captured Brussels."

"I have even more terrible news for you," the Belgian replied, pointing to the *Goeben* and the *Breslau* in the harbor. "The Germans have captured Turkey."

Germany's capture of Turkey had begun as far back as the first days of her large-scale investment there, which were highlighted by the kaiser's two visits in 1889 and in 1898. Since then, major political upheavals had intervened in Turkish history to make that capture even more effective. It was in 1908 that Sultan Abdul Hamid II, in power since 1876, faced the explosive results of his peculiar combination of policies—progressive in education and technology, retrograde in constitutional reform. In July of that year, a group of young army officers—representing a newly educated generation of the emerging middle classes and imbued with the ideals of a politically progressive movement that called itself Young Turkey—raised the standard of revolt in the Resna hills near Salonika. One of the two leaders, Enver Bey, was a twenty-six-year-old major of outstanding military record; the other, Ahmed Niyazi, had close connections with the Young Turk organization based in Salonika that called itself the Committee of Union and Progress.

With the backing of the committee, Niyazi and Enver sent a telegram to the sultan demanding the restoration of the lapsed Constitution of 1876. Abdul Hamid's first reaction was to send troops, but upon arrival they defected to the movement. He had no choice but to acquiesce, and in December a parliament was convened for the first time in thirty-one years. Abdul Hamid did not take readily to the role of constitutional monarch, however, and in April 1909, after having tried to foment a counterrevolutionary movement in the army, he was deposed in favor of his brother, Mehmed V.

The sultanate had been preserved, but the Ottoman Empire was now effectively in the hands of the Committee of Union and Progress. These were shaky hands, however. Even in its first moment of triumph in the summer and fall of 1908, the revolution had provoked a series of international crises that were detrimental to Turkish interests. On October 5, Bulgaria, which, since the Congress of Berlin, had been a semiautonomous chimera still largely subject to Turkish domination, proclaimed itself a united and independent state at last. The very next day, Austria announced her annexation of Bosnia and Herzegovina, which she had been allowed to occupy since the Congress of Berlin, theoretically on a temporary basis. Serbia, which regarded these two provinces as potentially part of a future south Slav state, was offended, and so therefore was her protector Russia—

in an ominous beginning to the crisis that was to precipitate war in 1914—but Turkish spirits also fell at yet one more permanent loss of what once had been Ottoman territory. Nor was this the end: on October 7, still another day in rapid succession, the island of Crete, also till then in an ambiguous relationship of dependence with the Ottoman Empire, declared its union with Greece.

These events raised a fundamental question about what the Committee of Union and Progress stood for. Throughout the nineteenth century, European liberalism had fought not only for constitutional and social reform, but also for the rights of politically unfulfilled nationalities. This tradition placed the Young Turks in an untenable situation. On the one hand, they were indeed Turkish nationalists, representing that ideal in Constantinople for virtually the first time in history; but on the other hand, they were Ottoman reformers, seeking to consolidate an ailing multinational empire. The contradictions of their position emerged from the moment the new parliament was convened, when the various nationalities of the empire took the opportunity to demand political and cultural autonomy and to call for the decentralization of Ottoman rule. These were principles that the Committee of Union and Progress could not accept, and its reaction against them signaled the oncoming transformation of a European-inspired revolutionary movement into an oligarchical dictatorship based on the old-fashioned Turkish bureaucratic corruption. Sympathetic outside observers of the new *hurriyeh* ("freedom") in Turkey began to wonder if it was able to live up to its name.

"It is a wonderful brew, this advanced thinking," reflected a veteran English traveler in the Asiatic parts of the Ottoman Empire, Mark Sykes, after a journey there in the spring of 1909:

> The ingredients are Gallic and Teutonic: Gallic in negation of religion, in insane attachment to phrases, in superficial logic, in purposeless irreverence; Teutonic in obstinate rigidity, uncompromising woodenness, in brutal assertiveness. . . . The great thinkers had been thinking and talking for nearly five months. They had written leading articles for even longer, and since their phrases were growing stale they were beginning to fight among themselves, to accuse each other of tyranny, reaction, espionage, and chicane. They violated the addle-pated Constitution they professed to adore, but did not remodel it. . . . The navy, with its 6,000 officers and 4,000 men remained; the civil service, with its countless hordes of greedy incompetents remained; the corrupt police, with its useless divisions, remained;

the tax-wrung peasantry remained; the hopelessly congested finances remained; the war in the Yemen remained. After five months of speechifying these things remained because they were facts and the speechifying had all been about other men's ideas.

In the next five years, the regime in Constantinople faced a series of crises within the country and outside it. A Liberal opposition came into being and sought both to represent the claims of the national minorities and to combat the dictatorial tendencies of the Committee of Union and Progress. For a while the committee was able to withstand this challenge; then Italy, laying claim to Tripoli, went to war with Turkey in October 1911 and, in the ensuing year, not only annexed Tripolitania but occupied the Dodecanese Islands near the Anatolian coast. This produced a succession of political upheavals in Constantinople, which first put the committee into a renewed position of power, then brought an opposition regime in its stead.

The war with Italy ended in October 1912, but no sooner had a peace treaty been signed than the three states of the Balkan League—Bulgaria, Serbia, and Greece—combined with Montenegro in a declaration of war upon Turkey. The result was a disastrous defeat for the Turks and the loss of almost all the territory that had remained to them in Europe. Enver Bey, freshly returned from the front in Tripoli, responded to events by organizing a group of conspirators who forced their way into the cabinet chamber on January 23, 1913, shot dead the war minister, and forced the Liberal government's resignation at gunpoint. A few months later, Mahmud Shevket Pasha, the man whom Enver's coup had restored to power as grand vizir, was himself assassinated in reprisal. But by the end of the summer, the committee had stabilized its position, above all on the strength of a major triumph: a second Balkan war had broken out, this time between Bulgaria and her former allies over their conflicting victorious claims, and Turkey had been able to take advantage of the situation by reclaiming some lost territory in Thrace, including Adrianople.

Starting in the summer of 1913, Turkey, though still nominally a constitutional sultanate, was under the rule of a triumvirate led by Enver Bey, who was soon to become minister of war. The other two members were Djemal Pasha, later to be minister of marine but then still military governor of Constantinople, and Talaat Pasha, the minister of the interior. Of the three, Enver not only tended to have the most authority, but also was—fatefully for the Ottoman Empire—the most pro-German. He had first gone to Berlin shortly after the revolution on a military mission, then had returned there for some time as a military attaché. During this stay he had developed a fondness for Germany that was flatteringly reciprocated in the highest circles; for the kaiser recognized in this ambitious son of a minor railway official a man who could be a useful instrument for German ambitions in the Ottoman Empire. Enver had come home from this assignment "almost more German than Turkish," in the words of Ambassador Morgenthau. Slim and dashing in his uniform, "he had learned to speak German fluently, he was even wearing a moustache slightly curled up at the ends; indeed, he had been completely captivated by Prussianism."

Enver's leanings were made manifest when, in June 1913, Baron von Wangenheim sent a telegram to his government in Berlin saying that Constantinople, "convinced that German policy is sincere and friendly toward the consolidation of Asiatic Turkey," was submitting "a request for a leading German general for the Turkish Army," to be responsible for its "uniform and purposeful reformation." Wangenheim added that in his judgment "the selection of a German general would silence all those who would make the German reformers responsible for the Turkish defeats. It would also check British influence seeking to have British administration reformers called to Turkey." Admiral Limpus's mission had in fact already been there a year; but British influence at Constantinople, which had been steadily declining since the Egyptian takeover in 1882, was at a new low since the Balkan Wars, when Asquith's Government had shown the traditional small sympathy of the Liberals for Turkish claims. There also was a French mission in Turkey to reform the police, but this seems to have had little political significance.

Berlin responded by sending General Otto Liman von Sanders, one of the senior division commanders in the German army. This appointment aroused concern in foreign embassies, especially the Russian; and matters were made worse when Liman, upon his arrival in December, was made Djemal's successor as commander of the First Army Corps in Constantinople. A diplomatic crisis ensued, during which Russia was strongly supported by her ally, France, and Britain remained somewhat at a distance. Germany and Turkey would not back down, but the crisis was resolved in January when Liman was promoted to full general's rank in the German army, which entitled him to the Turkish rank of field marshal. Having thus been kicked upstairs, he was no longer eligible for the Turkish First Army command, and was given the post of inspector general instead. This was found acceptable by all governments, though basic Russian suspicions were unallayed.

Mark Sykes, revisiting Turkey in 1913, noted with disapproval that the Teutonic influence was winning out over the others:

> German training was never meant for such men as the Asiatic provinces put forth. With them, a rough and ready disciplinarian with energy, a common-sense disregard of unimportant details, a readiness to share privations or hardships, a sense of humor, and a quick gusty passion, might carry Turkish soldiers anywhere; but modern Germany cannot teach these things. Her machine-made officers and her military system are inhuman, precise, bookish and rigid—though excellent, of course, in Germany. Because they are so, they naturally appeal to the schoolboy officers of Turkey. There is so much that can be learned by mere rote and mimicry, and a little German varnish can be made to go so far. A moustache improver, a ridiculous stiff swagger, a brusque, overbearing, staccato voice, can be mastered in a week, and once mastered can be assumed when required, leaving twenty-three hours out of twenty-four to idling, intriguing, secret drinking and any other illicit means of wasting time that Constantinople affords.

Of all the signs of Germany's incursions into Turkey, the most renowned was the railway that had been begun in 1903 under the auspices of an international syndicate headed by the Deutsche Bank, which planned to extend tracks ultimately to link Berlin with Baghdad. The new extension of track, begun at Konia, had subsequently been laid through Aleppo, and by 1913 was in the process of crossing the upper Euphrates to the northeast of that city. A branch line also was being built to Alexandretta, the port that meets the Mediterranean at its northeasternmost corner. Another part of the system—Ottoman-owned, but adding strength to the German part—was the Hejaz railway, covering the old pilgrimage route from Damascus to Medina.

To Mark Sykes, all these were the achievements of a "disgraceful career," which he summed up this way:

> Begun by the German Emperor's visit which condoned the Armenian massacres, after years of intrigue with the vilest scour-

ings of the palace, and further years of intrigue with the viler scourings of the Committee, the great venture is now fairly started; but, though the idea is sound, its parentage and antecedents militate against its being anything but what it is—a pretentious piece of petty chicanery.

Sykes conceded that it brought advantages, but insisted that it also brought much evil:

It enabled the Turkish War Office to collect more men than it could deal with; it helped drain Anatolia of inhabitants; it helps to increase the cost of living by drawing off the cereals and sending up the price of bread. Of course, this means more money; but it also means more poverty. The railway brings alcohol, dirty pictures, phonographs, and drinking saloons. Moreover, it produces a most horrible kind of greasy, grimy-faced, ragged, and unwholesome people, now well-paid employees, but formerly happy, wholesome peasants.

Meanwhile, even as Sykes made these observations, a yet closer scrutiny of the railway under construction was being made by English eyes. It was just north of the dusty little village of Jerablus that German engineers, working with Arab and Kurdish laborers, were then building the steel bridge that would take the tracks across the Euphrates. But this also was a place for the testing of British scientific skill; for a short distance north of the bridge was the great mound under which lay Carchemish, a major site of the Hittite civilization among the many ancient layers of its history. In 1910, the British Museum had obtained permission from the Ottoman government to reopen excavations it had begun there more than thirty years before, and the dig had commenced in the spring of 1911 under the direction of the prominent Oxford archaeologist, David G. Hogarth. The following year, Hogarth stayed home, and the new supervisor was C. Leonard Woolley, then thirty-two years old and one of the promising younger scholars in the field.

But a yet younger and equally promising man had been with the expedition from the beginning: Thomas Edward Lawrence, who was Hogarth's latest disciple. Having come down from Jesus College in 1910 with a first in modern history—writing a thesis on Crusader castles, he had made a lone journey through Syria in 1909—Lawrence was at Carchemish on a Magdalen demyship (a four-year traveling scholarship) that Hogarth had obtained for him. He and Woolley, both of whom looked several years younger than their respective ages, cut rather dashing figures at Carchemish: in their personal styles, they combined the wry diffidence and boyish eccentricity of Oxford scholars with a gift for playing rough-and-ready soldiers of empire whenever they felt called upon to do so. Woolley, in pith helmet and boots, more than once settled disputes that arose by brandishing his revolver. Lawrence also was courageous and a good shot: once he wounded in the hand a man who had begun shooting at him some distance away.

According to Woolley, the younger man "always wore a blazer of French grey trimmed with pink, white shorts held up by a gaudy Arab belt with swinging tassels (it was a belt worn only by bachelors, and Lawrence had his tassels made bigger than anyone else's), grey stockings, red Arab slippers and no hat." Gradually acquiring fluency in Arabic, he soon achieved "a marked ascendancy over the Arab workmen, partly by his genuine interest in and sympathy with them, partly because his impish humor was of a sort that they could relish." Lawrence formed a particularly close relationship with a teenage Arab water boy called Dahoum, whom he took home to his family on one of the summer vacations during the dig.

Since the southern end of the Carchemish mound was less than a quarter of a mile from the German camp, the latter was quite visible to the English archaeologists. Indeed, the German engineers suspected them of spying for the British Government, and it is entirely possible, though by no means certain, that they were doing so. Certainly Lawrence showed an intense involvement in the Germans' activities when he wrote home to Hogarth on December 12, 1911: "Tonight one of these engineers told me that the plans are being changed for the third time. They now propose a temporary bridge to the N. of the [archaeological] site, for materials etc., and the permanent one to the South. . . . The building of the approaches and temporary bridge will be begun as soon as the final plans are published: in any case by the spring." This concern at the threat of being surrounded by German bridges and camps was a natural one; particularly since the Germans, in need of extra earth to build up the supports of the bridge, had developed a vexatious habit of taking rubble from the mound. Woolley had been willing to let them take material that was of no archaeological value, but they had not always shown discrimination.

The idea of building a temporary bridge to the north was soon abandoned, but tension mounted between the two camps over the rubble question. In the spring of 1912, Herr Contzen, the German chief engineer, asked Woolley if he could take away certain earth mounds that were quite close to the new railway tracks, though within the archaeological concession. "Now these earth mounds so lightly spoken of," Woolley later wrote, "were nothing less than the city walls of Carchemish, so I told him that I was sorry but could not allow anything of the sort. He started to argue the point, and when I remained firm tried to bluster; but I told him that, while I sympathized with his feelings, I was there for archaeological purposes, and could not permit such an act of vandalism as he proposed; if he liked to take the earth from my rubbish-mounds he might do so, but the walls of Carchemish could not be touched."

There matters stood until the summer, which found Woolley back in England and Lawrence traveling in the Lebanon. One morning, Contzen gathered about a hundred workmen and started to build a light service railway to the foot of the Carchemish site. Nothing stood now between him and the desired rubble—except Haj Wahid, a brawny Arab from Aleppo and the expedition's factotum, who suddenly appeared carrying a rifle and two heavy revolvers and threatening to shoot the first man who drove a pick into the walls. Haj Wahid then maintained a vigil for three days, during which the Germans and their workers did not make a move. Meanwhile, he had dispatched someone to wire Lawrence. Upon receiving the message, Lawrence rushed to Aleppo, contacted the local minister of public instruction and the representative of the Baghdad railway, and sent word to Constantinople of what was happening. On the morning of the fourth day Haj Wahid had been called off by the Baghdad railway representative and Contzen's workers had begun removing precious dirt. Then Lawrence suddenly appeared with the minister of public instruction, who ordered the Germans to desist and pull up the rails. Contzen complied, keenly aware of the humiliation he had been made to suffer at English hands.

"The natives, of course," Woolley wrote, "looked upon the whole thing as a contest for supremacy between Germans and English; the former had made themselves generally unpopular, and the Arabs, including those in railway employ, lost no opportunity of having a dig at the Germans." It was like a mildly comic rehearsal for the more serious conflict that threatened to come. As for Lawrence, his attitude toward the Germans at Jerablus was one of utter contempt "because they did not know how to treat Arabs." Lawrence thought the Germans "idle and incompetent and corrupt, and loved to score off them and hold them up to ridicule, but it was their behavior to the men that made him despise them."

These better English relations with the local peoples extended also to the Kurds, who formed an increasingly dominant portion of the Germans' work force during the years at Jerablus. Lawrence kept in close touch with the local Kurds during the first Balkan war, when they had hopes of sacking Aleppo. He formed a solid friendship with Basrawi, the most prominent Kurdish chief in the area. "Whenever Basrawi went in to Aleppo by train," according to Hubert Young, a British army lieutenant who passed through Carchemish in the summer of 1913, "Lawrence used to make him a present of his ticket, telling him that he was a guest on the line. One day Basrawi turned up at Jerablus station without having seen Lawrence on the way. He found [Contzen] the German engineer going to Aleppo, and got into the same carriage, and when the ticket collector appeared, he referred him to the German with a courteous wave of the hand, as if to say, 'There sits my host.' The German knew nothing of Basrawi, and rather rudely declined to pay. The consequence was that as soon as Basrawi got back all the Kurdish workmen disappeared from the bridge works, and did not come back until the German had apologized and promised him a free trip to Aleppo whenever he liked."

This proved the foreshadowing of a graver confrontation between Germans and Kurds, which took place in the spring of 1914. By this time, Contzen had returned home and been replaced by a Herr Hoffman, "a well-meaning man, a great improvement on his forerunner," in Woolley's opinion, but far from capable of handling the kind of forces about to be unleashed upon him. Hoffman had adopted a policy of paying the workers directly rather than through a contractor as before; but he had not yet sufficiently checked his books, nor entirely reformed a system that was still protected on payday by a cordon of armed Circassian guards. It was during a payment lineup in March that one Ali, a Kurd from Mesopotamia, found himself picking up a smaller sum of money than he had expected.

"He protested," Lawrence wrote soon after the incident, "but the paymaster refused to listen to him. This paymaster was a German clerk, an awful rotter who used to treat his men as beasts, and to swindle them in wages right and left. . . . However, when Ali found his complaints unheeded, he threw his money back on the table. The German said to his Circassian 'Hit him,' and the Circassian knocked the Kurd down. Getting up, he grabbed a stone and slung it at the Circassian who pulled out a revolver and shot at him. Then the other hundred or hundred and fifty Kurds waiting their pay also picked up stones, and flung a volley, which broke the windows of the office in which three or four Germans were. They all grabbed rifles and revolvers, and through the windows blazed out at everyone they saw."

Lawrence and Woolley were at that moment in their house, about two hundred yards away; they had just returned from a mission of two months' duration in the Sinai and eastern Palestine, where they did a survey for the Palestine Exploration Fund and some real spying besides, mapping the region for military use. When they heard the commotion, they rushed to the scene, getting shot at on the way. Upon arriving, they saw two lines of battle drawn up: the Germans and Circassians on one side, fully armed; the Kurdish workmen on the other, some with rifles but most with iron bars and stones. The two Englishmen, along with Haj Wahid and some other Arab friends who had arrived, placed themselves between the two lines and sought to calm the workers. "So we talked to them," Lawrence recalled, "and pushed them back, and took away their guns: even knocked down one or two, quite good-humoredly, and kept them on the wall-top." In the end, and despite occasional nervous outbursts of fire from the German side, a standoff was achieved.

One Kurd had been killed and twenty more wounded, so the workers still required satisfaction before they would return to their jobs. During the next few days the German consul from Aleppo sought a solution, but the only man with the authority to speak for all the Kurds was Basrawi, and the Germans literally could not get near him now, for fear of their lives. Lawrence and Woolley therefore had to act as go-betweens, and it was they who dictated to the German consul the terms they would take to Basrawi in his name: the payment of £120 in blood money, along with the dismissal of the Circassians, the paymaster, and one of the more objectionable engineers. Basrawi accepted and went to the consulate in Aleppo to sign a treaty of peace, "with a very fat present to himself," Lawrence added. It was further arranged that some of Basrawi's men be hired, in the railway company's pay, to patrol the camp for abuses. "It's really very comic now," Lawrence concluded, "every engineer walks about with a huge frowning Kurd behind him, armed to the teeth, and very ready to shoot him down if he misbehaves. The improvement in German manners is incredible: only they don't seem to love us more than before."

The impact of German ambitions in the Ottoman Empire was also being felt in Palestine. By this time, there were 85,000 to 100,000 Jews there among a total population of 600,000 or so; of these, 65,000 lived in Jerusalem—mainly in the new residential areas outside the Old City walls—where they formed some two-thirds of the population, while the rest were scattered through the other towns and the more than forty rural settlements that had been established since 1881. Yet this thriving element was not yet perfectly clear about its cultural identity—least of all about its language. The new type of settler was predominantly committed to the revival of Hebrew, and a major achievement of recent years was the founding of a Hebrew high school in Tel Aviv, the new garden suburb of Jaffa. But among the more traditional Jewish communities, Arabic and Ladino were the preferred languages of the Sephardim, and Ashkenazim of strict piety spoke only Yiddish, refusing to profane the holy tongue with everyday matters. Most of the schools teaching secular subjects used the language of the country from which their charitable endowment had come: at the Evelina de Rothschild School for Girls in Jerusalem, it was English; at the Mikveh Israel agricultural school and other Alliance Israélite institutions, it was French; and at the schools run by the formidable Hilfsverein der Deutschen Juden, it tended more and more to be German.

The claims of German had some strength. Everyone who speaks Yiddish—and that meant the vast majority of both the old and the new type of Jewish settlers in Palestine—can understand some German and can learn more without much difficulty. German seemed in this era to be the magnet to which Jewish culture was inexorably drawn, and even outside Germany and Austria a substantial number of educated Jews could speak it. When Theodor Herzl presided over Zionist congresses at which German was the official language, this seemed to him and his colleagues perfectly natural for such an assemblage; and in *Altneuland*, he depicted the citizens of his ideal Jewish state speaking the whole range of a single tongue from Yiddish to *Hochdeutsch*. Indeed, the Zionist organization, which had located its headquarters successively in Vienna, Cologne, and now Berlin, was in danger of presenting a preponderantly German image before the eyes of the world—a danger that hardly seemed one at all to many German Zionists.

The Hilfsverein der Deutschen Juden was not Zionist, but the scope of its Jewish charity was as grand as Germany's imperial aspirations. By 1914, it ran some thirty schools all over Palestine, ranging from kindergartens to two seminaries, one for teachers and one for rabbis. Hebrew had always been a prominent element in these schools, but since 1911 German had been displacing it as the principal language of instruction, to such an extent that the Teachers'

Union of Palestine, which staffed the Hilfsverein schools but was strongly Hebraist in orientation, raised an organized protest in the summer of 1913.

But this proved to be only the overture to a more vehement controversy. That same year, construction had begun of a technical college in Haifa which was to be the first secular Jewish institution of higher education in Palestine and the institutional crown of the colonization movement thus far. Funds had been raised for it through independent contributions all over the world, and it was neither exclusively Zionist nor exclusively Hilfsverein in its sponsorship; but control of it was in the hands of the latter, while three Zionists were among its board of governors. In the fall of 1913, the three Zionist members brought in a proposal from their organization that Hebrew be the language of instruction in at least one science department of the college and in all courses at the secondary school that was to be attached to it. This was rigorously opposed by the Hilfsverein, which stood on German alone, and the Zionist members resigned from the board of governors.

The Teachers' Union responded with a wave of strikes and resignations at all the Hilfsverein schools and with a movement to pull out of them altogether and set up another system in their place. The controversy reached the German newspapers, and on February 5, 1914, the *Berliner Tageblatt* carried a statement signed by some prominent German-Jewish philanthropists to the effect that the Zionists were undermining humanitarian institutions. One Zionist leader in England, Dr. Chaim Weizmann, saw the question at stake as "the Hebraization or Germanization of our schools in Palestine," and wrote to a colleague that the Hilfsverein policy was going to make the college "a *Stützpunkt* [point of support] of Germany in Palestine." There was widespread suspicion that the Hilfsverein was receiving encouragement in this affair from the German government; and indeed it was.

But all such controversies were superseded by the immense conflict that began that summer. Indeed, for several weeks in late August and early September, the Middle East was all but entirely forgotten while the fate of the European continent hung in the balance; but the smoke of the Marne had hardly begun to clear, and the immense line of trenches from the North Sea to the Alps was only starting to be dug, when Turkey regained the attention of the West. On September 9, while the Battle of the Marne was still raging, the Ottoman government gave a new signal of possible bellicosity by announcing the abolition of the Capitulations—the centuries-old system of agreements and concessions under which the nations of the West had carried on commerce in the Turkish empire. This provoked alarm in Britain concerning Turkey, but the Liberal *Manchester Guardian* was still ready to write cautiously on September 12: "There is only a feeling of sympathetic goodwill towards her in the difficulties which we believe to surround her Government's efforts to save the country from being dragged into the European war against its own sense of right and prudence." By October 2, however, the same newspaper had to acknowledge "alarming rumors" about Germanophile tendencies in Constantinople and to protest firmly that the "net effect of a Turkish declaration of war would be a great increase in carnage without any change in its results."

Such warnings were to no avail. On the morning of October 29 the *Goeben* and the *Breslau*, still flying the flag of Turkey and accompanied by other ships of her fleet, bombarded the Russian Black Sea ports of Odessa, Nikolayev, and Sevastopol: they had thus completed the fateful trajectory begun in the western Mediterranean nearly three months before. Russia declared war on Turkey on November 2, and England and France followed suit three days later.

·4·

HERBERT SAMUEL RAISES
THE PALESTINE QUESTION

"It is not the Turkish people," Prime Minister Asquith told his cheering audience at London's ancient Guildhall on the evening of November 9, "it is the Ottoman Government, that has drawn the sword, and which, I venture to predict, will perish by the sword. It is they and not we who have rung the death-knell of Ottoman dominion, not only in Europe, but in Asia."

This careful declaration of war against a regime and not a people, made among a succession of speeches at the annual Lord Mayor's banquet, was an effort at reassuring the vast Muslim populations of the British Empire—some 70 million in India and 16 million in Egypt and the Sudan—that His Majesty's Government had "no quarrel with Musulman subjects of the Sultan." It was a point that had to be stressed after the proclamation two days before by the sheikh al-Islam in Constantinople, the highest theological authority in the Ottoman Empire, that it was now a duty of good Muslims to take up arms against Britain, France, and Russia. Clearly, it was not to be long before the sultan, who also was the caliph of Islam, would declare a *jihad*—a holy war—against the Entente Powers. What then would be the response of the millions of Muslims that all three of them governed?

"Nothing is further from our thoughts or intuitions," Asquith protested, "than to initiate or encourage a crusade against their belief. Their holy places we are prepared, if any such need should arise, to defend against all enemies and to maintain inviolate." Once again, it was a regime, not a people, that had been a "blight which for generations past has withered some of the fairest regions of the earth"; and it was only a regime to which he was referring when he concluded with these ominous words: "The Turkish Empire has committed suicide."

On November 11, the sultan announced a *jihad* to his own army and fleet, though he did not yet proclaim it to the entire Muslim world. But in the meantime, Asquith's words had aroused responses in quarters he had not necessarily intended to reach. "I don't know whether you have read the speech of the British Prime Minister," Chaim Weizmann wrote from Manchester that same day to some Zionist colleagues in New York. "He publicly announced yesterday* that he was convinced the end had come, not only of European Turkey but also of Asiatic Turkey. I think the time has now come to speak openly—to point out to the world the attitude of the Jews to Palestine." And the edition of the weekly *Jewish Chronicle* that appeared on Friday, November 13, did indeed speak openly, if cautiously, in a leader buried among several other items and entitled "What About Palestine?" It began:

> The Prime Minister, in his speech at the Lord Mayor's banquet at the Guildhall on Monday last, referred to the action of Turkey in taking the part she has chosen in the War, and he predicted that the Ottoman Government as it had drawn the sword so it will perish by the sword. Mr. Asquith added words which must be of the utmost significance to the Jews. "It is the Ottoman Government," he said, "and not we, who have rung the death-knell of Ottoman dominion, *not only in Europe but in Asia.*" We have italicized the last words because, so far as we recollect, this is the first time that any responsible Minister has extended the "bag and baggage" policy as applied to the Turkish Empire, further than to European Turkey. If, as a result of the War, the dominion of Turkey in Asia is to be ended, then what is to be the fate of Palestine?

The writer—who undoubtedly was Leopold Greenberg, Herzl's old associate and, since 1907, co-owner and editor of the *Jewish Chronicle*—went on to formulate a Jewish case concerning Palestine. It was bound to seem tepid to other Zionists, but it would have appealed strongly to such Englishmen as those who had made up the Aliens Commission a dozen years before. At this point in the war, Jewish concern centered on the fate of coreligionists in Poland and Austrian Galicia, on the eastern front between Russia and the Cen-

* That is, the speech had appeared in the newspapers the previous day, November 10.

tral Powers. The fact that the Jews of these areas were welcoming the German troops was both an appalling reminder to Englishmen that their Russian ally had not mended its ways regarding Jews and a point eagerly exploited by German propaganda. This was the situation to which the *Jewish Chronicle* writer was referring as he continued:

> This war will inevitably de-house and de-home many thousands of our people, who must seek some place for emigration. Is Palestine, with its traditional and historic associations, altogether a *place négligeable* in this connection? After all, it might be found that a large number of our people could, with advantage to themselves and to Jewry as a whole, emigrate to settle in Palestine when means are taken for assuring to that land good and righteous government and security of person and property. A considerable number of our people have managed to do remarkably well there, without these advantages, and largely because of the love of the land which is in them—no small element in successful colonization.

The Zionist aspect of the argument comes almost as an afterthought: the main thing is the old goal of a *Nachtasyl*, of a suitable place of refuge for persecuted Jews. In this case, the available "Uganda" happens to have Jewish traditions already. As for "good and righteous government," such words on the pages of the *Jewish Chronicle* had usually been synonyms for "British rule." But caution is the watchword throughout this article.

Significantly, the only bold statement in print on this subject during these first days after Turkey's entry into the war came from a prominent Gentile: H.G. Wells. In an open letter addressed to Israel Zangwill and published in the *Daily Chronicle* on November 4, several days before the Asquith speech and even before England's actual declaration of war on Turkey he wrote: "And now, what is to prevent the Jews having Palestine and restoring a real Judaea?" Zangwill was hardly the ideal person to whom to address this question. An ardent supporter of the East African offer, he had refused to acquiesce in the final rejection of it at the Seventh Zionist Congress in 1905, seceding instead from the organization to form one of his own. For nine years, his Jewish Territorial Organization (ITO) had been searching the world for an asylum, carrying on negotiations with governments, exploring Angola and Cyrenaica among other places, all to no avail. Recently, Zangwill had also become irritated, along with other Anglo-Jewish spokesmen, at remarks in the press by Stephen Graham, a writer and journalist specializing in East European affairs, to the effect that the Jewish problem in Poland might best be solved if all that country's Jews emigrated.

Zangwill's reply appeared on November 9. "Dear Mr. Wells," he wrote,

> Your "War in the Air," published in 1908, has become a reality so soon that I dare not reply too skeptically to your suggestion that the time is ripe to recreate the old Judaea in Palestine. That idea is certainly in the air. And, enormous as are the obstacles and difficulties—difficulties which have led me to suggest a new Judaea in Canada or elsewhere—they would assuredly lessen if Englishmen of your stamp would work to ensure British suzerainty for the new State. But grateful as all true Jews would be for such help from Englishmen, they could only accept it if its motive was pro-Jewish, not anti-Jewish, justice and not Jew-hate. Palestine could only receive and support the Jews in small installments, and as the majority of the thirteen millions must long inhabit their present homes, an offer of Palestine, coupled with an aspiration, or worse, a policy for the clearance of other countries of Jews—such as Stephen Graham has so naively suggested for Poland—would be a trap from which I should do my best to dissuade my fellow Jews. Nay more! No bait of Palestine will lessen the insistence of our demand for equal rights in Russia, Rumania, or wherever anti-Semitism drags down civilization.

Zangwill really had heard enough about the question for the time being.

The boldest statement of any importance to be made about the Jews and Palestine at this time did not appear in print at all, but its implications and ultimate consequences were to be historic. It was made in high Government circles by a man keenly aware of himself as "the first member of the Jewish community ever to sit in a British cabinet," a man regarded by almost anyone who knew him as the least likely of spokesmen for what was, in effect, the most Zionist of ideas.

There is a mystery surrounding the personality of Herbert Samuel. An offspring of a distinguished old Anglo-Jewish family, of the type that had become increasingly opposed to Zionism over the years, he was a nephew of Sir Samuel Montagu—who had become Lord Swaythling shortly before his death in 1911—one of Herzl's most ardent opponents after their early halcyon days had passed.

Indeed, although Herbert Samuel was independently wealthy, he really owed his fortune to Lord Swaythling, who had taken his brother Edwin (Herbert's father) into his banking enterprise many years before. Nor does this seem to have been the only way in which the eminent uncle had an impact upon the life of Herbert Samuel, who had lost his father when he was only seven. For fifteen years Samuel Montagu had sat as the Liberal MP for Whitechapel, where he had championed the cause of the poor—Jews and non-Jews alike— and had supported the workers during the great dockers' strike of the summer of 1889. This strike had been a major formative event in the outlook of eighteen-year-old Herbert, who was about to go up to Balliol College, Oxford. At the time, his elder brother Stuart was campaigning in Whitechapel for election to the newly formed London County Council. Herbert, in helping him, learned to share the concern with the East End poor that absorbed both his brother and his uncle. Stuart won the election (he was eventually to succeed his uncle as Liberal MP from Whitechapel, a position he still held in the fall of 1914), and Herbert emerged from the experience ready to become, in his own subsequent parliamentary career, a confirmed social reformer and Liberal of the new progressive stamp.

There was at least one way, however, in which Herbert Samuel had quite plainly departed from his uncle's influence over the years. Whereas Lord Swaythling's religious orthodoxy had been legendary for its zeal, Herbert, under the influence of his philosophical studies, repudiated his ancestral faith while at Balliol. This had been done, however, in the spirit of worldly prudence and careful compromise that was ever to seem central to Samuel's personality in the eyes of his colleagues and friends. Even when writing the disappointing news of his loss of faith to his mother, he had stressed that he would never renounce his affiliation with the Jewish community; and this was a promise he kept. He remained a member of the New West End Synagogue in Bayswater, which he and his family had always attended, and it was there that he was married in 1897 to Beatrice Franklin, daughter of another old Anglo-Jewish family of German origin and, in fact, a distant relative. At home, in the midst of his growing family, he maintained a moderate observance of some of the basic Jewish rituals and traditions. Occasionally he would attend Jewish community functions outside the synagogue as well.

Somewhere in the course of all this, Herbert Samuel had quietly developed Zionist sympathies. Where had they come from? Evidently there was a touch of Deronda in this man: after refuting theology in the late nineteenth century Oxford manner, he still shared the bent of George Eliot's hero to "identify myself, as far as possible, with my hereditary people," and his philosophical mind may well have gone on craving a secularized humanist religion. Certainly he had an example of Deronda's work close at hand during Sir Samuel Montagu's Hovevei Zion days, which culminated in his uncle's attempt to buy land in the Hauran for Jewish settlement in 1892. And also close at hand was the influence of Rabbi Simeon Singer, Sir Samuel's collaborator in that attempt and one of Herzl's early ardent supporters. Singer had presided over services at the New West End Synagogue from 1879 to his death in 1906—years during which his congregant Herbert Samuel grew from childhood to early middle age.

Also among Samuel's acquaintances was a rabbi more eminent and a Zionist more ardent than anyone else he could possibly have known: Dr. Moses Gaster, still *haham* of England's Sephardic community in 1914 and even more prominent in English Zionism than he had been on that day in July 1896 when he introduced Theodor Herzl to a cheering audience of East End workingmen. Gaster's wife, Leah, had been a good friend of Samuel's wife, Beatrice, since childhood; and though the two men never became close friends, they certainly saw a good deal of one another.

But however Samuel may have arrived at his ideas concerning Zionism, he characteristically harbored them with such prudence and reserve that not even his closest friends seem to have known about them. Typically, little is known of his ideas on another likely influence, the East African offer to the Zionists. In the spring of 1902, just before the beginning of his career as a member of Parliament, he had traveled to Uganda and then written a series of articles about it; yet, outside of a passing remark in the *Jewish Chronicle* of January 12, 1906, that he "has traveled in East Africa and given his views on the proposed Jewish settlement in that region," the record shows little or nothing of his responses to that episode. Clearly he liked to avoid labels that could be politically embarrassing: he had, for example, maintained close relations with the Fabian Society all his life, but he never called himself a Socialist. As for Zionism, he was later to write of these years: "With plenty to do elsewhere, I had left to others the pursuit of this apparently distant ideal."

Distant it was bound to seem when he held a succession of cabinet and government posts from 1909 onward—first as chancellor of the Duchy of Lancaster; then, from February 1910 until February 1914, as postmaster general; and, by the autumn of 1914, as president of the Local Government Board. Indeed, nothing was likely to have been further from his mind during the troubled months of 1912 and 1913 when, along with other Liberal leaders, he had to defend himself against charges of corruption—successfully, as it turned out—for his manner of dealing in shares in the Marconi Company.

Samuel later wrote of his long-dormant concern with Palestine that "the moment Turkey entered the war the position was entirely changed." Long a committed Liberal imperialist who saw British influence as beneficial to the less-developed parts of the world, he now regarded as crucial the question of "who was to succeed the Turk in controlling the country that bordered on the Suez Canal." It is even likely that he had begun thinking this way before the war, when the Balkan Wars had begun dramatizing Turkey's decline.*

It was on November 9, 1914, only hours before Asquith was to make his remarks at the Guildhall about the Ottoman Empire, that Samuel went to see Sir Edward Grey at the Foreign Office to talk about Palestine. We may pause a moment to consider the scene in the palatial corner room occupied by the foreign secretary, one flight above Downing Street and with tall windows overlooking the Horse Guards Parade to the north and the pelicans and waterbirds of Saint James's Park to the west. The two men who sat facing one another had in common not only their membership in the Liberal party and in Asquith's cabinet, but also a privileged background that made it unnecessary for them to earn their livings.

Otherwise, they were very different from one another. Samuel, whose home was a large town house on Porchester Terrace, just a short walk to the north of Kensington Gardens, had lived in London all his life and had his homes entirely in the Paddington and Bayswater districts; he was a man of the city. Of middle height and compact build, wearing the black moustache he had grown in his first days as a parliamentary candidate—doubtless to mask an extremely youthful appearance—he still had a boyish handsomeness three days after his forty-fourth birthday. The great dignity with which he held himself was perhaps more self-conscious than that of an English Christian gentleman would have been, and his small gray eyes had an intense alertness about them that still bespoke his origins in a people for whom alertness meant survival.

Grey's tired eyes, on the other hand, when they were not strain-

---

* Moses Gaster records in his diary for Saturday, January 10, 1914, that he and his wife were at the Samuels' for dinner and that they had a "long conversation" on politics, on Britain's Near Eastern policies, and on Zionism. He adds cryptically, referring either to the whole company or to Herbert Samuel in particular: "Seemed rather impressed—altogether tendency leaning more favorably to Palestine."

ing over the wartime piles of Foreign Office memoranda that were
rapidly costing him his vision and general physical health, were
likely to have turned in the direction of Fallodon, the splendid
Northumberland estate in whose streams he had through the years
developed himself into one of England's outstanding fishermen, the
author of a well-known book on angling. A tall Englishman of the
hawkish physical type, with the lean strength of one who had spent
much of his life outdoors, he was the scion of a family that included
in its genealogy the second Earl Grey, who had been prime minister
in 1832 and presided over the passage of the great Reform Bill. "Sir
Edward Grey," his colleague David Lloyd George, a self-made man,
was to write disdainfully, "belongs to the class which, through hered-
ity and tradition, expects to find a place on the magisterial bench to
sit in judgment upon and above their fellow-men, before they ever
have any opportunity to make themselves acquainted with the tasks
and trials of mankind—and some of them preserve those magisterial
airs through life. They are remote from the hard work of the community." Lloyd George acknowledged some exceptions—Palmerston,
Salisbury, Balfour—but Grey, who had traveled abroad very little for
a foreign secretary but always returned to Fallodon when he could,
was far from being one in his eyes.

Yet there were those who regarded Grey, Britain's foreign secretary for nine years by this time, as one of the great holders of that
office, and who thought he had done as much as any man could to
keep England out of the war that others, such as Lloyd George,
blamed him for having blundered into. There was at any rate a
grandly tragic quality about this man, so alone since his beloved wife
had died in 1906 and left him childless as well, who had stood at the
window of his room at the Foreign Office the previous August 3 at
dusk, watching the lamps being lit, and said: "The lamps are going
out all over Europe; we shall not see them lit again in our life-time."

At the moment when Samuel came to see him, the war in Turkey of only four days' standing may still have seemed a bit remote to
Grey. On the western front—still the main theater of war for England as well as for France—British troops were engaged in a fierce
fight, defending the salient they had helped establish around Ypres
against a new German offensive. Not that there was no British action in the Turkish theater: just three days before, a landing had
taken place at the Shatt-al-Arab on the Persian Gulf, with Basra as
its objective. But this was made up entirely of troops from India and
was under the jurisdiction of the India Office, a virtual suzerainty in
its own right with which the Foreign Office did not try hard to inter-

fere. The Foreign Office had, however, established the fundamental outlines of a policy in the Middle East, in the event of Turkey's entry into the war, a good many weeks before that event actually occurred. On August 29, Grey had written to Sir Louis Mallet, the British ambassador at Constantinople, urging him to warn the Turkish leaders that if they entered the war Britain would feel free, not only to annex Egypt at long last, but also "to support Arabs against Turkey and another Moslem authority for Arabia and control of holy places" of Islam.

Samuel began the conversation, telling Grey that "now that Turkey had thrown herself into the European War and that it was probable that her empire would be broken up, the question of the future control of Palestine was likely to arise." Indeed, the question may well have occurred to Grey already; but if it had, he assuredly had concluded that the future of Palestine—like that of all Syria—was entirely a French matter. Samuel was prepared for this: "The jealousies of the great European Powers would make it difficult to allot the country to any one of them." As a solution to that problem, he concluded, "perhaps the opportunity might arise for the fulfillment of the ancient aspiration of the Jewish people and the restoration there of a Jewish State."

In his record of the conversation, Samuel says he went on to protest "that I myself had never been a Zionist, because the prospects of any practical outcome had seemed so remote that I had not been willing to take part in the movement. But now the conditions are profoundly altered. If a Jewish State were established in Palestine it might become the center of a new culture. The Jewish brain is rather a remarkable thing, and under national auspices, the state might become a fountain of enlightenment and a source of a great literature and art and development of science." Samuel notes that he also spoke of the regenerating effect such a state would have upon Jews wherever they lived.

But, for all this stress on large historic ideals, Samuel was careful to couch most of his presentation in immediate practical terms. He said he "thought that British influence ought to play a considerable part in the formation of such a state, because the geographical situation of Palestine, and especially its proximity to Egypt, would render its goodwill to England a matter of importance to the British Empire." This was very much to the point, and Samuel did not hesitate to expand upon it, suggesting that "English and American Jews ought to take the leadership in such an enterprise, if it were undertaken. The Germans could do nothing in present circumstances; the

French were not sufficiently influential, nor the Italians; it was important that the new state should be founded under the auspices of the most progressive of the countries in which the Jews found themselves."

On the other hand, no such plan could be undertaken without reference to one of the least progressive of such countries. Russia and her vexing Jewish question were inevitably a prominent part of the picture Samuel was drawing. "She already had a great Jewish population, and the conquest of German and Austrian Poland and of Galicia would bring with it a great accretion. Her armies had been welcomed in Poland by the whole of the people except the Jews. She would, if she were wise, wish to gain the loyalty of her Jewish subjects, new and old, but for my own part I doubted whether her own public opinion would allow her Government to grant them equal rights."

These last words would have been regarded as heresy in those Anglo-Jewish establishment circles from which Samuel's own family came and which had created such an institution as the Anglo-Jewish Association to fight for the rights of coreligionists wherever they lived. It had been doubts such as this one, imputed to Zionists in general and unfortunately echoed in the press in recent weeks by Stephen Graham, that had roused the Anglo-Jewish Association's hostility toward Zionism to even greater heights than before the war. But Samuel, whether or not he had discussed this delicate point with any Zionists, was lighting upon a practical argument of great importance to their case when he went on to explain to Grey: "If Russia took a leading part in the re-establishment of the Jewish State, the sentimental appeal to the Jews within her own territories would be so strong that it could not fail to have an immediate and a powerful influence on their attitude."

As Grey listened to Samuel's presentation, his thoughts must surely have gone back to the days of the East African offer to the Zionists. Though he sat on the Opposition benches, he was even then being groomed for leadership of the Foreign Office in a Liberal government. He had been doubtful about East Africa as the right choice, but had warmly expressed his support, during a House of Commons debate, for the idea of finding a refuge and a home for the Jews somewhere within the British Empire. Indeed, early in 1906, shortly after assuming his present office, he had been contacted by Leopold Greenberg, who then still hoped to reopen the El Arish plan. Nothing seems to have come of this, however, no doubt owing to continuing resistance in Cairo.

Samuel was now hardly talking about the British Empire as far as Grey was concerned, but when he was done, the foreign secretary had to admit that "the idea had always had a strong sentimental attraction for him. The historical appeal was very strong." He said that he "was quite favorable to the proposal and would be prepared to work for it if the opportunity arose."

Opportunity was the problem, of course, since Britain wanted to do nothing to offend her French ally, whose cultural and financial hegemony in at least the northern part of Syria was of long standing. Grey therefore hedged a little as he went on to assure Samuel that if "any proposals were put forward by France or any other Power with regard to Syria, it would be important not to acquiesce in any plan which would be inconsistent with the creation of a Jewish state in Palestine."

Grey then asked a rather odd question; he wanted to know if, in Samuel's scheme, all of Syria "must necessarily go with Palestine." Samuel hastened to say no, pointing out that "on the contrary it would be inadvisable to include such places as Beyrout and Damascus, since they contained a large non-Jewish population which could not be assimilated." While it is true that a few knowledgeable advocates of a Jewish state at this time were ready to project outlandish boundaries for it, one may safely assume that Grey's question had been at least partly founded in a certain vagueness about Levantine geography; for this was not to be the last time that such a vagueness on his part would display itself. But we may also see in this question the first dawning of a significant realization: that the palpable French influence in Syria did not really extend as far south of Beirut and Damascus as Frenchmen liked to imagine. Could a distinct line perhaps be drawn between Palestine and a French Syria to the north of it? Samuel seemed to have been pondering just such a question when he assured Grey that "it would be a great advantage if the remainder of Syria were annexed by France, as it would be far better for the state to have a European power as neighbor than the Turk." A separate Palestine did not have to mean the death knell of French ambitions in Syria; just a modification of them.

Samuel further satisfied Grey by stressing that the Jewish state "should be neutralized, since it could not be large enough to defend itself"—an echo of Mordecai's conception, in *Daniel Deronda*, of Palestine as "a neutral ground for the East as Belgium is for the West." He also said it was essential "that the free access of Christian pilgrims should be guaranteed." All of this sufficiently impressed Grey that he concluded the conversation by asking Samuel to prepare a memorandum on the subject for presentation to the cabinet in the near future.

As Samuel walked out of the Foreign Office, he could only have felt great satisfaction at what had just transpired. Two members of a British cabinet had just thoroughly and concretely discussed a plan for a Jewish state in Palestine! What more could he have asked for his idea's first day of trial?

But it was not over. "I had an opportunity today," he later noted for that same Monday, November 9, "of a brief talk with Lloyd George on the subject. He had referred in the Cabinet to the ultimate destiny of Palestine, and said to me that he was very keen to see a Jewish state established there." It was not long after this that Samuel was regularly to make a point of describing Palestine as "a country the size of Wales." Had the comparison come up in this brief talk?

·5·

LLOYD GEORGE TAKES NOTE

W hen David Lloyd George, chancellor of the Exchequer, opened his November 21 issue of the *New Statesman*, he found in it an article on "The Future of Palestine" that aroused his interest. Signed simply "A.M.H.," it was written by Albert Montefiore Hyamson, an official in the Post Office Department and a known writer and lecturer on Jewish history.

"Mr. Asquith," the article began,

> has announced that the end of the Turkish Empire is at hand; that the death knell of Ottoman dominion, not only in Europe but in Asia, has been sounded. More than once in the past Turkey has received notice to quit Europe, but this is the first time that the liquidation of Turkey in Asia has become a definite prospect, and with Mr. Asquith's words at the Guildhall the hopes of the Zionists have suddenly passed from an ideal into a matter of practical politics.

This alone was as forthright a statement of the point as had yet appeared outside the correspondence columns of a responsible non-Jewish journal; and it was especially striking in this politically progressive, highly intellectual organ founded by the Fabian Society only the year before, which in the previous week's issue had carried George Bernard Shaw's long, scathing, and instantly controversial critique of militarism's latest mad outburst, called "Common Sense and the War." But the article contained much more.

Hyamson, after a brief reference to the destructions of the Jewish state in antiquity, went on to summarize the history of the aspirations to revive it in modern times. Herzl's career, his negotiations with the sultan over Palestine, his subsequent dealings with the British Government over El Arish and East Africa, all were touched upon, along with the violent reaction against the latter at the Sixth

Zionist Congress in 1903. "The remarkable friendliness displayed by the British Government to the Jews was recognized and appreciated by every speaker," Hyamson stressed, "but it was felt that much of the forces which were behind a settlement in Palestine would be lacking if the scene were changed to another quarter of the globe."

Lloyd George, whose law firm had drawn up the tentative charter for a Zionist colony in East Africa, must have pondered these words with special interest—as well as the passage that followed, which described the secession "of Mr. Zangwill and his friends," and the subsequent efforts of their Jewish Territorial Organization to find a place for Jewish settlement somewhere in the world. The chancellor of the Exchequer knew Zangwill personally and in recent years had made him the guest at one if not more of his celebrated political breakfasts.

"If the Government of Turkey," Hyamson's article went on, "had remained in the hands of Abdul Hamid it is impossible to say whether Herzl's idea would have been realized or not. With the advent of Young Turkey, however, all possibility of such an event disappeared; with it passed away Zionism as a political movement." Herzl's vision of a charter and an overnight mass exodus, mainly from Eastern Europe, was temporarily put aside by the Zionist movement in favor of what he had scornfully called "infiltration." Zionism "became entirely a movement for the recreation, after the lapse of two thousand years, of a Jewish center in Palestine. Jerusalem was to be, not the capital of a Jewish State, but the center of Jewish culture." Political aspirations were put aside for some distant future, while the Jewish community in Palestine quietly grew and consolidated itself.

"Left alone the future of the Jews in Palestine would have been secure," Hyamson assured his readers. "But the country is now in the melting-pot and the crisis has come too soon for the Jews to be able to cope with it unaided. The crisis, however, is not one for the Jews of Palestine alone, but for the Jews of many other lands." Hyamson then ventured into the delicate territory, also touched upon by Herbert Samuel in his conversation with Sir Edward Grey, of anti-Semitism in Eastern Europe and the future of the Jews now living there. Alluding to the recent remarks by Stephen Graham about the Jews of Poland, Hyamson argued that they had a valid claim to a historic role in that country's national aspirations, and that in any case Poland's 2.6 million Jews could not be absorbed by Palestine or any other country. Nevertheless, he acknowledged "the necessity for some land in which Jews would be able to find a home, where they would not be considered intruders." This, he asserted, could only be Palestine.

The discussion had thus returned to the context of the largest current political questions. "Today we are told is the day of small nationalities," Hyamson went on, thus putting his theme in terms that doubtless were gratifying to the chancellor of the Exchequer, who had begun his political career as a Welsh nationalist. "Their interests are to be considered when peace is concluded. It should not be overlooked that the Jews of Palestine—let us call them the Hebrews after their language—are also a small nationality." But this led inevitably to another point: for the events of the past hundred years had shown that small nationalities do not achieve and maintain independence without Great Power protection. And the Jews of Palestine, Hyamson pointed out, "are the weakest of the nationalities and they cannot stand alone. For many years, perhaps for centuries, they will need a protecting power while they grow into a nation. To give Palestine self-government today would be a blunder and a crime."

Who, then, was to be the protecting power? Hyamson granted that there were several who "profess to have 'interests' in Palestine and Syria, but in no case is the claim overwhelming." His own choice, however, was England, which "has sentimental, educational, and archaeological interests in Palestine. It has besides in point of fact commercial interests which dwarf those of all other powers into insignificance," and he proceeded to spell them out. In the preceding year, Britain had imported all the oranges produced for export by the Palestine Jewish colonies and, along with Egypt, consumed a large part of their wine. The total of British imports from and exports to Palestine was now six times that of either France or Russia, and twice as large as even that of the rest of the Ottoman Empire. Yet none of this was the main point. "Still more weighty is the consideration that if the inhabitants of Palestine were consulted as to the State in which they would prefer to give their allegiance in the future, it is almost certain that the overwhelming majority of the non-Jewish population would choose Great Britain." It was in particular the relative prosperity and good government that Egypt had come to enjoy since 1882 that was inspiring a predilection, by now quite evident, for the British among Arabs all over the Middle East.

"As for the Jewish inhabitants," Hyamson continued, "with exceptions that one could almost count on the fingers of one's hands, they would certainly vote for Britain." This was intended for all readers who might still have feared that Zionists were by nature pro-German. "Britain is in fact the only power that has ever shown sympathy with the Jewish people," Hyamson added, and entered into a final bit of historical summary to make the point:

> English political writers have repeatedly advocated a British protectorate of Palestine for the benefit of the Jews. Palmerston brought all the influence of British diplomacy to bear at Cairo and at Damascus on the occasion of the persecutions that followed the Blood Accusation of 1840, instructed the British Consul at Jerusalem to extend his protection to the Jews, and himself made representations on their behalf to the Porte. At a later date both Beaconsfield and Salisbury supported Laurence Oliphant in his negotiations with the Porte for a concession which was to pave the way to an autonomous Jewish State in the Holy Land.

Thus, he concluded, the Jews of Palestine had "every reason to be grateful to Britain and they are not unmindful of their obligation." As for the other side of the picture, "Christendom owes a debt to Jewry for the persecutions of the past nineteen hundred years. It would seem that she now has the opportunity of commencing to pay it." But there was only one agent suitable to handle the payment as far as Hyamson was concerned: "Let Britain remember her past and think of her future, and secure to the Jews under her protection the possibility of building up a new Palestine on the ruins of her ancient home."

"I was brought up in a school," Lloyd George was to say some years later about his childhood, "where I was taught far more about the history of the Jews than about the history of my own land. I could tell you all the kings of Israel. But I doubt whether I could have named half a dozen of the kings of England, and not more of the kings of Wales."

There may be some exaggeration here, but there can be no doubt that in the years when young David Lloyd George, after losing his father in infancy, grew up in the Welsh village home of his uncle Richard Lloyd—shoemaker, part-time preacher, and zealous Nonconformist—the Bible was prominent in forming the landscape of his imagination. The psalms of Israel and the hymns of Welsh choirs mingled in his ears to sound the common chord of small, pious, stiff-necked nations struggling against the forces that sought to overwhelm them from without. "The spiritual wants of the Welsh people," he told an audience in London shortly after he had first come there as a member of Parliament in 1890 at the age of twenty-seven, "are attended to by Nonconformity. The Nonconformist chapels are crowded, but the churches of the Establishment are forsaken in every rural district in Wales." And then came the inevitable biblical example: "If you recollect, it was Elisha who cleansed Naaman's leprosy but it was Gehazi who secured the emoluments. It is Nonconformity that cleansed the moral leprosy which had afflicted Wales under the quack doctoring of the Established Church, but it is the Gehazi of the Establishment that is enjoying the emoluments." Those among his listeners who recalled that Elisha had then punished Gehazi by afflicting *him* with leprosy would above all have recognized the Hebraic fury underlying the lilts of Welsh nationalism.

Not that a passion for the Old Testament had made Lloyd George a lover of Jews all his life. During and just after the war against the Boers, when he rallied to the cause of that small nationality with a fury that made him the most celebrated—and the most widely detested—critic in the land of his Government's South African policy, he occasionally gave vent in indecorous ways to his anger at the considerable Jewish presence in the Transvaal. More than once, with reference to the home constituency of Joseph Chamberlain—the minister most responsible for the war—as well as to the Jewish immigrants of South Africa, did he assert that the British Empire was "being run by Brummagem [Birmingham] and Jerusalem." Once in a 1905 by-election, while campaigning for a Liberal named Baker against a Tory named Cohen, he responded to the latter's criticism of his colleague for being a Canadian by proclaiming that "a British subject born in Ontario is no worse than a British subject who traces his ancestry from Jerusalem. As for me, in a case like that I am for Colonial Preference." This was only the beginning: "Would you like to know how to make a fortune?" he asked his audience, warming to his subject. "I will tell you. First get up a war, like Mr. Chamberlain's. Choose a country with gold in it. Get the *Daily Mail* to back you up. . . . Having got your war, go down there and start business. If you have a British name, like Jones or Smith, or Baker, change it at once. Make it Beit, Dunkelsbuhler, or, say, Cohen!"

But perhaps such outbursts were the unavoidable excesses of a platform bard who all his life, in Asquith's view, could "only think talking," and who, in his still angry early forties, had not yet smoothed all his rough edges. It was in the next few years that he underwent a noticeable ripening of personality, particularly after his appointment to Asquith's cabinet in April 1908. "The present Chancellor of the Exchequer," noted the German ambassador to London just three months later, "has in a short time educated himself from an ultra-radical Welsh lawyer into a leading and esteemed personality in his Party and in the Cabinet." His Celtic charm soon mellowed into an instrument for dealing diplomatically with men of different backgrounds and persuasions, even for manipulating them. He acquired Jewish friends, notably Sir Rufus Isaacs, who subsequently became Lord Reading and England's first Jewish lord chief justice, and alongside whom, during the Marconi scandal, he had to defend himself against allegations by critics who often—when dealing with Isaacs and Herbert Samuel—did not stop short of displays of anti-Semitism.

When, at the outbreak of war in August 1914, Lloyd George had to take special measures to avert a financial crisis, one of the men he invited in to advise him was Lord Rothschild, whom he had once publicly placed "among Philistines, not all of whom are uncircumcised." He began apologetically: "Lord Rothschild, we have had some political unpleasantness." But he was waved aside in the celebrated brusque manner and told: "Mr. Lloyd George, this is no time to recall those things. What can I do to help?"

As it happened, the financial moratorium that Lloyd George had declared at the beginning of the war came to an end on November 4, the day before England declared war on Turkey. From the outset, he found that the war in the East was the one that made the greater appeal to his emotions. He regarded the war in the West as a great mistake and had remained doubtful about whether Britain should take part in it as late as August 2; since the night of August 4, no statesman had devoted more energy than he to the war effort, but for him the task in Europe remained simply that of bringing a historic disaster to an end as soon as possible. In the Middle East, on the other hand, he felt that a chance had come to make the world better than it had been before. He certainly agreed with the prime minister that Ottoman rule there was a blight and that its death knell had now been rung. "The Turk," he told a cheering London audience with Elisha-like fury on the evening of November 10,

is the greatest enemy of his own faith because he has discredited it by misgovernment. What have the Turks contributed either to culture, to art, or to any aspect of human progress that you can think of? They are a human cancer (cheers), a creeping agony in the flesh of the lands which they misgoverned, and rotting every fiber of life. And now that the great day of reckoning has come upon the nation I am glad. (Cheers) I am glad the Turk is to be called to a final account for his long record of infamy against humanity in this gigantic battle between right and wrong.

But Lloyd George's thinking on the subject tended to go beyond Asquith's in two essential ways. For one thing, this erstwhile pro-Boer, who had been far more radical on that subject than his colleagues Asquith and Grey, was now rather more imperialistically inclined than they: even as far back as the summer of 1908, the German ambassador had noted of the new chancellor of the Exchequer that he "thinks imperially." As with Herbert Samuel, a vision of beneficent British empire had captured Lloyd George's imagination over the years, and there now seemed no better place to realize it than in the Ottoman dominions. Moreover, Lloyd George—unlike Asquith and somewhat more ardently than Grey—had a particular focus for Middle Eastern reform in the ideal of a Jewish Palestine. This aim of a revival of the ancient Israel whose history he had so thoroughly absorbed as a boy had doubtless become vivid to him at the time of his involvement in the East African offer to the Zionists in 1903, and again in 1906, when Leopold Greenberg had sought the services of his law firm in an effort to reopen the El Arish plan with Sir Edward Grey. Later that same year he had sent, through Greenberg, a friendly message to a Zionist meeting in Cardiff. If Lloyd George was not always sure how he felt about Jews in Park Lane or Johannesburg, but loved the thought of them as regenerated Hebrews in the Land of Israel, he was far from the only Englishman to have been this way. But his position in affairs was a special one and, as we know from Herbert Samuel, he had already brought up the matter of Palestine in cabinet by the time of Asquith's Guildhall speech. Since then, his conversation with Samuel and the *New Statesman* article by Hyamson had provided him with ample sources of sustenance for the position on Palestine that was shaping in his mind.

On Friday, November 27, at 9:15 A.M., Lloyd George had another one of his political breakfasts at 11 Downing Street, this time with C.P. Scott, editor of the *Manchester Guardian*. Scott and Lloyd George had been close political allies since their common pro-Boer days, when the editor of England's foremost Liberal newspaper had put in a few years as a member of Parliament. Starting around 1911, their relationship had developed into a kind of political intimacy that eventually made Scott, who would take the train down from Manchester as often as once a week, by far the favorite guest at these breakfasts.

The two men were a striking contrast in some ways: Scott, the elder by seventeen years, a tall, slim, austere widower, with a great white beard and piercing blue eyes that made him resemble a Hebrew prophet; Lloyd George, short, talkative, his wispy moustache and great mane of dark hair just beginning to turn to silver, who briskly strode the corridors of power with an overwhelming vitality. Indeed, there were those who thought that the crafty Welshman had overwhelmed the influential editor for his own demagogic purposes, flattering him with confidences that were just so many moves in a game of political manipulation. But Scott was no mere innocent and surely perceived that his friendship with Lloyd George was worth the risks it entailed.

Lloyd George began the conversation with a diatribe against the navy and the first lord of the Admiralty. Over the years, Lloyd George and Winston Churchill—two men of differing outlooks and diametrically opposite backgrounds, yet oddly similar in their powerful and unorthodox political presences—had alternated between friendship and intense rivalry, the latter having been the case in the months preceding the war, when Churchill had advocated a naval buildup that Lloyd George bitterly opposed. As he looked over the events of the past four months with his guest, the chancellor of the Exchequer could express a glum satisfaction at Churchill's expense. There had been a "reversal of expectations. The Army which we regarded as capable of little had done wonders. On the other hand in the conduct of the Navy on which we thought we could implicitly rely there had been some very uncomfortable incidents."

Among these was the sinking of three cruisers by a German submarine in September, for which Lloyd George blamed the Admiralty, and the "escape of the *Goeben* from Messina—a dreadful business, which was directly responsible for the entry of Turkey into the War." He spoke scathingly of the admirals involved—of Troubridge, the commander in the Adriatic, who had backed off from the chase on August 7 and who had subsequently been court-martialed for this and acquitted; and of Sir Berkeley Milne, the commander in the Mediterranean, who had been negligent and yet had not been court-martialed at all. Indeed, Milne still had his command: "He has powerful social connections," Lloyd George offered as an explanation to Scott.

After reviewing some other setbacks that he blamed on the Admiralty—including the abortive British landing and defeat at Antwerp at the beginning of October—Lloyd George moved on to the war with Turkey. Perhaps a bit disingenuously, he spoke against it and "partly blamed Churchill also for that. The situation was not desperate even after the attacks by the *Goeben* on Russian Black Sea ports." But in the few days following these attacks, British ships had responded with provocative actions, including bombardments of Aqaba and a Dardanelles fort; these had "brought us at once into war. Our whole endeavor should of course have been for postponement. The effect of bringing Turkey in has been to lock up 50,000 of our troops . . . besides our territorials (including a Lancashire regiment) and 300,000 Russian troops, both of which forces would have been invaluable elsewhere." Nevertheless, Lloyd George showed the true bent of his feelings when he and Scott went on to discuss aspects of the settlement they envisioned at the war's end. "In feeling," Scott goes on in his notes, "George is not strongly anti-German. He said he should have much greater pleasure in smashing Turkey than in smashing Germany."

Scott went on to speak of what he had considered "the hardly noticed statement by Asquith at the Guildhall that the Turkish dominion in Asia must now come to an end as well as that in Europe, and of the enormous questions which that raised." Lloyd George admitted their difficulty, but—even as it occurred to Scott that the cabinet, including the chancellor of the Exchequer, had probably given only cursory consideration to the matter so far—he said he "thought the time had come to deal" with this. Then he gave some of his own views about the future disposition of the doomed Ottoman Empire. "Russia he assumed would take Constantinople and Armenia and Great Britain Mesopotamia.* When I asked what was to become of the rest of Asia Minor and the 10 million Turks in it he thought it would be a good plan to give it to Germany as a solatium. When I remarked that it might not suit Russia to have Germany on the other side of the Bosphorus, he said he meant that she [i.e., Russia] should have control of the whole of the straits with enough territory to secure that."

* The region between the Tigris and Euphrates, Mesopotamia is now largely comprised within modern Iraq.

As a final point, Scott "raised the question of Palestine, and the Zionists." In Manchester, Scott had recently made the acquaintance of Dr. Chaim Weizmann, reader in biochemistry at the university there and by this time, ten years after he had settled in the country, one of the prominent leaders of the Zionist movement in England. Weizmann had made a deep impression upon the *Guardian* editor, who had promised he would bring up the Palestine matter with Lloyd George. "It was not quite new to him," Scott observed, no doubt with some surprise, "as he had seen the article in the 'New Statesman' and mentioned also that he had had a 'whole hearted' i.e. 'heart to heart' conversation with Samuel and had been astonished to find how that cold and dry person suddenly kindled and they had sympathized on the common ground of the small nationality. He was interested therefore at the suggestion of a partly Jewish buffer state, but thought France would have strong objections. As to Russia she might prefer Jews to Catholics in the Holy Places. But he was interested and when I mentioned Weizmann said he would like to see him and he would ask Samuel too and perhaps I would come."

Scott returned to Manchester on Saturday and wrote to Weizmann the next day. He thought he could arrange for a breakfast at 11 Downing Street the following Friday, and Dr. Weizmann prepared himself for a meeting with the chancellor of the Exchequer.

·6·

THE GENTLEMAN FROM PINSK

"Starting with nothing I, Chaim Weizmann, a *yied* from Pinsk and only *almost* a Professor at a provincial University, have organized the *flower* of Jewry in favor of a project which probably by Rothschild (Lord) and his satellites is considered as mad."

Writing on Saturday, November 28, the day after his fortieth birthday, Weizmann was reminding two young friends in London, Harry Sacher and Leon Simon, of his long struggle to organize a Hebrew university in Jerusalem, which had seemed well on its way to fruition when the war broke out. But he also was thinking of more than that one project. Sacher, a newspaperman and former staff member of the *Manchester Guardian,* had been trying, on behalf of the English Zionist Federation, to make contact with Lucien Wolf, the journalist and historian who had interviewed Theodor Herzl in 1896 and who had since become the foremost political spokesman for the Anglo-Jewish establishment. The Zionists were hoping to achieve through Wolf a rapprochement with that establishment and a common political front representing worldwide Jewish interests in the war. But Wolf, who had left his Zionist sympathies behind in 1905, when he joined Zangwill in the formation of the Jewish Territorial Organization, had replied by asking haughtily, "Who are the persons representing your organization and in what measure do they represent the great body of Zionists?" And Chaim Weizmann was giving Sacher and Simon his reply.

"My success," he continued, "was due to one fact and you must impress it upon the porter of Mr. Rothschild—I represented the opinion of all thinking Jews and that opened all doors for me.

"Further! If people speak at present of Palestine, if *goysche* statesmen take us seriously it is because we have worked there for the last thirty years and we have been preaching Palestine to Jewry for a ¼ of a century. We did the work in the teeth of all those magnates, we were sneered at by individuals like L.W., who after having sneered at us for 10 years finds at last, that he knows nothing about Zionism, nothing about our work and had to ask you for literature on the subject."

Then he repeated, "I, Chaim Weizmann and you Harry and you Leon—to say nothing of A.H. [Ahad Ha'am]—are the accredited representatives of the Jewish people." Weizmann was at the time one of two vice-presidents of the English Zionist Federation—its president was Joseph Cowen, the Joe Levy of Herzl's *Altneuland*—and he held a minor executive post in the World Zionist Organization. As for Ahad Ha'am ("One of the People," the Hebrew pen name of Asher Ginzberg), who was now living in London, he was perhaps Zionism's foremost philosopher, but few would have accorded him any political importance. Weizmann alone was electing himself and his circle to a position of preeminence in Jewish history—and some were even beginning to notice his claim.

The writer of this letter had grown up in the heartland of Russian Jewry. "The townlet of my birth, Motol," he was to explain in his autobiography, "stood—and perhaps still stands—on the banks of a little river in the great marsh area which occupies much of the province of Minsk and adjacent provinces in White Russia; flat, open country, mournful and monotonous but, with its rivers, forests and lakes, not wholly unpicturesque." Some twenty-five miles north of Pinsk, Motol was well within the Pale of Settlement, the vast but unpropitious area along the western and southwestern edges of the Russian Empire within which the tsars had confined virtually all their Jewish subjects since the end of the eighteenth century.

Jews were far from being the only residents of the pale—in Motol, for example, there were 400 or 500 Christian families and less than 200 Jewish ones—but in most parts of it, except for the daily intercourse of commerce and work, their life as a community was self-contained. "In those days," the Yiddish author Mendele Moicher S'forim wrote with sad irony of a fictitious village in the pale, "all of Tuneyadevka found itself in the Land of Israel—at least in the visions they conjured up." In Motol the streets were of dirt, and there was neither a post office nor a railroad; but for its Jews, speaking in Yiddish and praying in Hebrew, the harshness outside their wooden synagogues and homes was made up for within by the rituals, flavors, and glories of a distinct and ancient peoplehood. "At table grandpa used to tell me stories of the deeds of great Rabbis and of other mighty figures in Israel," Weizmann recalled.

In the fall of 1885, when he was not yet eleven years old, Chaim was sent by his father, Ozer Weizmann—a timber merchant, mildly prosperous by Motol standards and forward looking in his views—to a secular Russian gymnasium in Pinsk. Well over half of the 30,000 inhabitants of that provincial metropolis were Jews, but they tended to be more modern in their ways than most of their coreligionists in Motol. One Pinsk resident was to write of these very days:

> A remarkable change had taken place in the minds of my parents since I had overcome all difficulties and become a student of a royal college. Not only were they reconciled to me, but they were distinctly proud of me. Old Rabbi Abraham now delighted in conversation and discussion with his grandson, who seemed to him almost like an inhabitant of another world, of the *terra incognita* of modern knowledge and science.

Rabbis and grandfathers like Abraham were rare in the smaller Jewish communities of the pale. "And please, my dear teacher," the boy Chaim Weizmann wrote in Hebrew to a man in Motol who had taught him that language, "do not imagine that when I attend the Gymnasium I shall throw off the garb of Judaism. No! On no account."

In his case, only the most ironbound religious traditionalist would have found anything to worry about. Long a center of the nineteenth-century Hebrew literary revival known as the *Haskalah* ("Enlightenment"), Pinsk had become a prominent gathering place of Hovevei Zion—a movement young Weizmann had heard about and admired even while still in Motol. In his seven years at the gymnasium, Weizmann, who discovered there a passion for chemistry, no doubt already began loosening his grip on traditional religious practices, but at the same time he became strengthened in a Jewish national ideal that was as powerful as the vision of a Hebrew prophet. As a budding scientist, he was on his way to becoming a man of the modern world; and as a Zionist, he bore within himself a voice which, when mellowed to maturity, was to sound like that of the Jewish people itself as it moved men and women of backgrounds vastly different from his own.

Weizmann completed his education in Germany and Switzerland, attending the Darmstadt Polytechnic from 1892 to 1893, the Charlottenburg Polytechnic in Berlin from 1893 to 1897—taking off for the year 1895-96 to help his father in Pinsk, where the entire family of fourteen had settled by then—and Fribourg University, where he obtained his Ph.D. in chemistry, magna cum laude, in 1899. That summer he began lecturing at the University of Geneva, and soon afterward also obtained a contract to do research for the Bayer Chemical Works at Elberfeld in Germany. This might have been career enough for most men; but with indefatigable will and at some peril to his occasionally delicate health, Weizmann also led a life of full commitment to Zionism during these years, arguing and discussing into the night in the cafés of Berlin, Bern, and Geneva, propagandizing under the noses of the hostile authorities whenever he was back in Russia, and attending every Zionist congress from 1898 onward as a delegate from Pinsk.

Geneva in particular was an important training ground for his growing ability to persuade, for not only was its university filled with Jewish students escaping the *numerus clausus* back in Russia, it also had become a principal exile of Russian radicals, Jews and non-Jews alike. At this time Georgii Plekhanov was there; the foremost mentor of Russian social democracy, Plekhanov was enjoying—though he was not a Jew himself—particular influence among the young adherents of the Jewish Workers' Federation, or Bund. Founded in 1897, the year of the First Zionist Congress, the Bund represented an attempt to combine Marxist ideology with a Jewish nationalism based on Yiddish language and culture and with a commitment to the Russian homeland; Plekhanov joked that a Bundist was a Zionist who was afraid of seasickness, but anti-Zionism was an important part of the Bundist outlook, and this was what Weizmann and his friends took on in numerous debates, on the platform and at the café tables. At one public meeting, Weizmann even took on Plekhanov himself, who, he claimed "was debunked and routed, and retreated in the most ignominious manner." Weizmann won many converts. His powers of persuasion also extended to Vera Khatzman, a medical student from Rostov, seven years his junior, who agreed to become his fiancée.

Weizmann began making his mark in the Zionist organization in 1901, when he was one of the organizers of a group of younger delegates that called itself the Democratic Fraction and sought to promote cultural activities. In a short time he became the principal spokesman within this group for the idea of a Jewish university, and an office devoted to the project was set up in Geneva under Weizmann's direction. But this activity was eclipsed, at least for the time being, by the major crisis that erupted in the Zionist movement when Herzl announced the East African offer in the summer of 1903.

Decades later, Weizmann was to recall vividly the scene in Basel, when some of the delegates who gathered in the hall on the first day of the congress noticed that the usual map of Palestine behind the dais had been replaced by one of East Africa. He describes how, at the end of the first session with its dramatic announcement, one woman ran up to the platform and tore down this map "with a vehement gesture"; and how this same young woman, Rosa Grinblatt, later exclaimed to Herzl, "Monsieur le Président, vous êtes un traitre!" But though Weizmann, in later years, liked to depict himself as an anti-"Ugandist" of similar ardor from the outset, the fact is that his initial response to the historic offer from the British Government was rather more circumspect. "Congress does not conceive the action in Africa as the ultimate aim of the Zionists," he wrote in a draft resolution that he proposed to the Russian caucus at Basel, "but deems it necessary to regulate emigration, and consequently finds that the Zionists must unify all colonization societies or convene a congress in order to decide on East Africa." The caucus voted against this proposal, but Weizmann continued to take "a positive attitude" to the British offer for another day or so; by the final roll call, however, he had become convinced that the Western European delegates were losing sight of Palestine, and he joined the other Russian delegates in voting against East Africa.

Even then, he was not ready to reject East Africa out of hand, and he became a member of the committee of inquiry set up by the Zionist congress to look into the matter further and eventually appoint an expedition to explore the site. It was his work on this committee that provided him with his first experiences in diplomacy. It provided as well—from the standpoint of his personal life—a most important opportunity to take a good look at England in the fall of 1903, his second time in the country (the first had been at the Fourth Zionist Congress, held in London in 1900). During this visit he saw Major William Evans-Gordon, the moving spirit behind the Aliens Commission, whom he had shown around Pinsk the previous fall when the latter had been touring Russia on a mission to investigate the condition of the Jews there. Evans-Gordon spoke good German, and like Herzl, Weizmann got on well with this man whom Lord Rothschild considered an incorrigible anti-Semite, but who was in fact eager to help settle destitute Jews almost anywhere in the world that was reasonably distant from Manchester, Leeds, or Whitechapel. Evans-Gordon had originally been a supporter of the East Africa scheme, but he had changed his mind by the time Weizmann saw him in October, apparently because of the opposition to it of Sir Harry Johnston, the former British commissioner in Uganda, whom Weizmann also saw on this trip. Both Johnston and Evans-Gordon assured Weizmann of their ardent support for Zionist aspirations in Palestine. "I have reached the inescapable conclusion that Africa has already collapsed," Weizmann wrote to his fiancée from London on October 12, 1903, adding that "if we are to get help from any quarter it will be in England which, I don't doubt, will assist us in Palestine."

There had been a touch of the Anglophile in Chaim Weizmann from his earliest days, when his grandfather's stories of some of the mighty figures of Israel had included Sir Moses Montefiore prominently among them. One tale was about a visit to Vilna, when members of that ancient and distinguished Jewish community "unharnessed the horses and dragged the carriage of Sir Moses Montefiore in solemn procession through the streets. It was a wonderful story," Weizmann recalled, "which I heard over and over again." In the letter he had written to his Hebrew teacher just before leaving for the gymnasium in Pinsk, there was a passage in which he praised the Hovevei Zion—consolidated just the year before in the conference at Kattowitz that had honored Sir Moses—and then added: "We must also thank the two patriots who are Moses Montefiore and [Baron Edmond de] Rothschild." But equal mention for the baron did not mean equal affection for France; for in a passionate peroration at the end of the letter, the ten-year-old Chaim Weizmann wrote, "All have decided: The Jew must die, but England will nevertheless have mercy upon us."

At first, Weizmann was not at all taken with "this monstrous London" when he arrived there on October 8, 1903, for his visit—least of all with Whitechapel, where he stayed with a friend: "Lord, what horror!" he wrote to Vera Khatzman of the London ghetto. "Stench, foul smells, emaciated Jewish faces. A mixture of a London avenue and Jewish poverty in the suburbs of Vilna." But his impressions of the city in general grew more favorable as his mission approached accomplishment, and on October 12 he wrote to Vera: "This is the hub of the world and, really, you sense the breathing of a giant, the city of cities." By this time he had already spoken to both Evans-

Gordon and Rabbi Moses Gaster "about my wish to move to London. They promised to be on the look-out for something for me." As for Vera, he wrote her the next day that "I have also enquired about women doctors. One has to pass a simple examination, and then one may set up in practice, and do well. What a marvelous city London is!"

Dissatisfied with life in Geneva, impressed that the Zionist movement was reaching a historic turning point, Weizmann at nearly twenty-nine wanted to make a new beginning before settling down to marriage. Like most emigrating Jews of his generation, he even thought of America; at any rate, he was drawn to the Anglo-Saxon cultures westward of the European continent. Perhaps if he had been a chemist alone he would have gone to the United States; but as a young Zionist of ambition, he surely sensed the value to himself of staying closer to the movement's centers of activity.

It was on July 10, 1904, that Weizmann arrived in England to stay. Theodor Herzl had died a week earlier: "He is no longer with us," Weizmann had written on July 6 to Vera, home in Rostov for the summer vacation. "At this moment all the differences between us have disappeared, and I only have the image of a great creative worker in front of my eyes. I feel a great weight on my heart." And then he added, as if sensing his destiny: "I feel that a heavy burden has fallen on my shoulders, and the shoulders are weak and tired."

Indeed, in the two or three weeks that followed his arrival in London, Weizmann's principal energies were once again devoted to Zionist work, even before he had secured a professional situation for himself. In addition to Gaster, Cowen, Greenberg, and other British Zionist leaders, he saw Evans-Gordon once again, and, through him, two prominent Government officials: Earl Percy, the parliamentary under-secretary of state for foreign affairs; and Sir Clement Hill, superintendent of the African protectorates, who had written the letter making the East African offer to the Zionists on Lord Lansdowne's behalf. Both of them had become quite negative about the East African idea, and Weizmann felt confirmed in his own by now vehement opposition to it.

But there also were the necessities of a livelihood, and these brought about a retreat to the provinces. Out of a network of connections came a dual opportunity to make a professional start in Manchester—as a laboratory assistant at the university and as a researcher for the Clayton Aniline Company—and Weizmann had settled in that city by autumn. Both professionally and politically it was a modest beginning; but Manchester was not without its advantages for him. England's second city in size with a population of more than 600,000, it also had the second largest Jewish population; and though the vast majority of Manchester's nearly 30,000 Jews were recent arrivals from Eastern Europe—Cheetham Hill, north of the city, was its Whitechapel in this respect—the new and the old Jewish settlers formed a more integrated community than did those of London. "There was a certain freedom of association and tolerance" between them, according to Israel M. Sieff, one of the friends Weizmann was to make in Manchester. And as for the older Jewish community there, mainly German in origin, its contribution to the economic, social, and cultural life of this flourishing provincial city had been crucial. James Agate, the *Guardian*'s drama critic, was to write of this era that "in my time Manchester was a city of liberal culture, awareness and gaiety, which it owed almost entirely to the large infusion of German-Jewish brains and taste." The impact of these virtues was felt all over town, from the important chemical industry and the Hallé, the finest of British orchestras, to the Victoria Memorial Jewish Hospital and the Jews' School on Derby Street, where the children of poor coreligionists from Eastern Europe were receiving their free elementary educations.

Such a milieu was to prove itself particularly suitable to a young Jewish activist who was really an outsider to any of the Jewish establishments in London—including the Zionist one, dominated by Joseph Cowen and Leopold Greenberg, who were not giving up easily on either the East Africa or the El Arish plan, and with whom Weizmann had come to exchange a mutual and hearty disrespect. Manchester was to be Weizmann's political fulcrum, and it was not long after his arrival that he was given a glimpse of how this might work. Another of the city's virtues was that it included the constituency of the present prime minister, and in January 1905, the young immigrant was given an opportunity that would never have arisen in London: he was to meet Arthur James Balfour himself.

This first meeting between Weizmann and Balfour was brief and perfunctory, but since it was the prelude to a far more significant one that was to take place a year later, we should dwell a moment upon its background. Weizmann was at the time enjoying a certain patronage from one of the leaders of Manchester Jewry, Charles Dreyfus. Born in Alsace in 1848, Dreyfus had earned his doctorate in chemistry at Strasbourg, then moved to England and become a founder of Clayton Aniline. After an initial contact between them that Moses Gaster had helped to arrange, Dreyfus was now not only providing Weizmann with a good job, but consoling him in his loneliness—Vera still had to finish her medical studies in Geneva—with frequent invitations to dinner. Indeed, Dreyfus and his wife, Hedwig, the chief benefactors of the Victoria Memorial Jewish Hospital, also were ready to help the future Mrs. Weizmann obtain employment when the time came.

Furthermore, Dreyfus, who was president of the Manchester Zionist Association, was a man of some political importance. He was a member of the municipal council and—rather unusually among Manchester Jews, who were predominantly Liberal in their politics—a figure in the local Conservative party, of which he became the East Manchester chairman at around this time. It was in this capacity that he had come to know Balfour, for East Manchester was the prime minister's parliamentary constituency. Now, there are clear signs that Balfour was perturbed by the related problems of the Aliens Commission recommendations and the East African offer, even if they were far from the major issues confronting him at this time. They were major enough in Manchester at any rate, where the Jewish community had reacted in pointedly political terms the previous spring at the first reading of a proposed Aliens Bill, restrictive in intent. Balfour had undoubtedly already asked Dreyfus why so many Jews, desperate for a refuge, were opposed to East Africa; and Dreyfus, who had abstained in the vote on the proposal at the Sixth Zionist Congress, had probably given an answer as ambiguous as his own position continued to be.

But Dreyfus was now in the grip of a decisive young man. On Sunday, January 22, 1905, he and Weizmann went to Leeds to take part in the annual conference of the English Zionist Federation, and the latter was unanimously elected to the organization's executive. "Greenberg and Cowen are wooing me," Weizmann later offered as an explanation to Vera, but this did not stop him from attacking their positions in a mass meeting that evening, before an audience of some twenty-five hundred, most of them immigrants from Eastern Europe. Speaking in Yiddish to the delight of his listeners—and thereby demonstrating one of his powerful weapons in opposition to the Anglo-Zionist leadership—he delivered a point-by-point criticism of the program they had drawn up that day, which included remarks about both the East African offer and the Aliens Bill. He objected to the inclusion of the latter, he said, because "the introduction of politics into Zionism was dangerous."

After Weizmann had finished, Greenberg stood up and said he "considered it one of the duties of Zionists to oppose such legislation as the Aliens Bill." As for East Africa, which Weizmann had roundly denounced, Greenberg "repeated, now for the fifth time, what he had indeed written to Dr. Herzl when transmitting him the offer of the British Government, namely, that in his view it was not a matter in which the colonization in East Africa ought to be undertaken by Zionists, but must be done by another body in which Zionists should assist." This had been the gist of Weizmann's own position in his first reaction to the offer at the sixth congress, but that moment was long past. Otherwise, Greenberg and Cowen had delivered speeches that evening which Weizmann described to Vera as "ultra-*Palestinian*," adding that "all the delegates attributed this to my presence."

This authentic voice of the Russian-Jewish passion for Zion alone was certainly something for a Manchester political leader to hear in person, and Prime Minister Balfour had his opportunity to do so the following Friday night, when he delivered a public address in his own constituency. Dreyfus had had Weizmann to dinner that evening, and they had arrived together afterward to hear Balfour's speech. The introductions evidently were made right on the platform after the speeches were over. "Yesterday I went to Balfour's meeting," Weizmann wrote to Vera on Saturday, "had a talk with him about Zionism (a brief one, about five minutes), and he promised that when I come to London I shall have the opportunity of talking with him at greater length and in greater detail on the same subject."

This is all we have on that first encounter between them; Weizmann's description of it is even more abbreviated in a letter he wrote Sunday to his colleague in Russia, Menahem Ussishkin, who was the leader of an anti-"Ugandist" movement so strong that it threatened to break up the Zionist organization. But to Ussishkin, Weizmann had much to say about the political schemes that the event had inspired within him. "The local Zionist leader, Dr. Dreyfus, is a very good friend of Balfour and other powerful eminences," he wrote. "I therefore suggest the following: contact Dreyfus and use him to establish relations with the English government." Dreyfus may not have thought of himself as being manipulated by this young man more than a quarter of a century his junior, but certainly his hitherto indecisive position against East Africa had been firmed by the relationship. "Dreyfus is in favor of Palestine," Weizmann went on with almost audible self-satisfaction, "and we could present a report on our true aspirations to Balfour and others. Dreyfus must be promoted. He wields enormous influence (he is due to become the next mayor), and is a future Member of Parliament and a good Zionist. By this, *eo ipso*, Greenberg and Co. are rendered completely paralyzed."

As for Balfour, he certainly had other things to worry about: above all, his Government was now deep into the debate about free trade versus imperial preference, raised by Joseph Chamberlain's proposals for tariff reform in 1903, that threatened to bring it down. But the Aliens Bill remained a vexation and an embarrassment that could not be ignored, for it was popular with organized labor, which was being wooed by the Conservatives in these pre-Labour party days. An earlier version of the bill had been blocked in 1904, but it came up again in the spring and summer of 1905, and Balfour again had to face the criticism of the Jewish community. During the House of Commons debate on it in July, the Liberal member from Whitechapel, Stuart Samuel—who, along with his brother Herbert, was among the bill's most ardent opponents in Parliament—charged the prime minister with inhumanity and indifference to the sufferings of Jews in Russia. "So far as he knew," Balfour replied in the name of himself and his colleagues, "alone among the nations of the world, and certainly alone among the Governments of this country, they had offered to the Jewish race a great tract of fertile land in a British possession in order that they might, if they so desired it, find an asylum from their persecutors at home." But such a defense was only grist for the mill of critics like Rabbi Moses Gaster, who had said on a public platform in April that the East African offer "may be classed as 'blood money' paid in advance for the Aliens Bill."

That summer the bill was passed, and nearly three hundred years of virtually unrestricted "right of asylum" in Britain was put to an end. Immigration was restricted to eight ports, at which officials would examine the new arrivals and weed out the "undesirables"—those who were completely impecunious and without any prospect of employment, as well as the seriously diseased, the mentally ill, and bearers of criminal records.

Enforcement of the Aliens Act was scheduled to begin on January 1, 1906; this, in the event, coincided with a general election, for Balfour's long-tottering Government had finally resigned on December 4. The issue of the day was free trade versus protection, but with *The Times* and the *Guardian*, as well as the *Jewish Chronicle*, sending out reporters to cover scenes of individual refugees and families being turned away at the ports of entry, a not inconsiderable election issue had also arisen among the ranks of that new phenomenon in British politics, "the Jewish vote." The *Jewish Chronicle* denied indignantly that such a thing existed, but at the same time cultivated it, even devoting several pages in one of its numbers to a list of all the Jewish candidates, whatever their party, with a brief biography of each. On January 1, a prominent member of the Jewish Board of Deputies—one of the two central organizations, along with the Anglo-Jewish Association, of the country's Jewish establishment—had an open letter in *The Times* to Joseph Chamberlain asking him for his views on the new outbreak of pogroms that occurred in Russia in the fall. "I should have thought it hardly necessary," the colonial secretary promptly replied, "that I should again express my deepest sympathy with the Jewish people in their present trials and my horror at the outrages which have been perpetrated upon them in connection with the disturbances in Russia." A great meeting protesting these disturbances was organized for Sunday, January 7, in Queen's Hall, and Israel Zangwill had sent a letter about it to the new Liberal prime minister, Sir Henry Campbell-Bannerman, who replied in *The Times* approving this expression of "sympathy with Jews in Russia, and horror at the cruelties that have been inflicted on so many of them."

Such ritual expressions of goodwill may have been no more than that in London, but in Manchester they had an impact; and it was there that Winston Churchill, who had deserted the Tories over the tariff reform issue in 1904 and was now the Liberal candidate in Northwest Manchester—which included Cheetham Hill—was running an American-style campaign that unabashedly courted the Jewish voter. Churchill had vigorously opposed the Aliens Bill from the beginning, and in October had given a speech in Manchester in which he described the new legislation as a "sham [that] contained absurdities . . . which would make a deaf and blind mute roar with laughter." Now, during the campaign, a typical scene was this one described in the *Manchester Guardian* of Tuesday, January 9:

> Mr. Churchill, in addressing a Jewish audience at the rooms of the *Achei Brith* Society on Sunday evening, appealed for their support on account of the work he had done for Jews in connection with the Aliens Bill. With regard to the first measure on the subject [in 1904], men like Sir Charles Dilke, Mr. Herbert Samuel, and himself had striven their utmost to wreck that bill,

and he (Mr. Churchill) it was who got the credit, together with the odium, of defeating it. He had been subject to the foulest abuse and grossest insults on account of his antagonistic attitude to that bill, and charges of corruption and all kinds of taunts had been hurled at his head.

This sort of thing was enormously popular in Cheetham Hill, though Churchill—who, like his party, made the free trade issue the main burden of his campaign—was careful to stand on his record where the Aliens Act was concerned and not make promises for the future. Indeed, he had already begun to hint that the Liberal policy would be to mollify the administration of the act rather than to seek its repeal. But there also was another Jewish issue burning in Manchester that he could not handle so deftly: that of Zionism versus territorialism.

The Seventh Zionist Congress had taken place the previous August, and it had definitively rejected the East African offer. The great division over that question was now, strictly speaking, no longer one between two factions of the Zionist organization, but between that organization and the one that had since been founded by Israel Zangwill and his associates. An inveterate writer of letters to the editor, Zangwill had already placed a statement of his views on the matter in *The Times*, and on December 26 Churchill was asked for his own feelings on the subject by Dr. Joseph Dulberg, the secretary of the Manchester branch of the Jewish Territorial Organization. This was quite close to home, since Churchill had been appointed under-secretary for the colonies in the new Liberal Government. Indeed, he could not reply without first consulting with his chief, Lord Elgin, the new colonial secretary.

Churchill's reply, written on January 1, appeared in *The Times* the next day. "My Dear Sir," it began,

> I have delayed to answer your letter of the 26th of December until I have had an opportunity of studying the documents in this office which relate to the subject. You are no doubt aware of the numerous and various difficulties which present themselves to a scheme of establishing a self-governing Jewish Colony in British East Africa, of the differences of opinion among the Jews themselves, of the doubtful suitability of the territory in question, of the rapidly extending settlements by British colonists in and about the area and of the large issues of general state policy which the scheme affects.

Churchill added that these difficulties, which had beset the previous occupants of the Colonial Office, could hardly be absent from Lord Elgin's mind, though the present colonial secretary would approach them with a profound sense of sympathy for the Jewish people. "But I will own," he went on,

> that I hope that they may be surmounted. I agree most heartily with the spirit of Mr. Zangwill's letter to the *Times* of December 12, 1905. I recognize the supreme attraction to a scattered and persecuted people of a safe and settled home under the flag of tolerance and freedom. Such a plan contains a soul, and enlists in its support energies, enthusiasm, and a driving power which no scheme of individual colonization can ever command. . . . There should be room within the worldwide limits of the British Empire, and within the generous scope of Liberal institutions, for the self-development and peculiar growth of many races, and of many traditions, and of many creeds. And from an imperial point of view it is on the varied excellence of its parts, that there is most surely to be founded the wealth, the happiness and the higher unity of the whole.

This skillful performance, in which Churchill demonstrated himself a friend of the Jewish people once again without taking a perfectly clear position on the issue at hand, was necessitated not only by the difficulties of the problem from the Government standpoint, but by the palpable presence of the Zionists. Churchill had already met Chaim Weizmann on December 10, when they found themselves on the same speakers' platform protesting the new outburst of Russian pogroms the previous month; and on December 27—the day after Dulberg's letter was written—Weizmann had received a letter from Churchill's election agent asking him to exert his influence among the Jews of Cheetham Hill in favor of the Liberal candidate. Weizmann wrote to Zionist headquarters in Cologne asking for instructions on this point, but before he got any he was being courted by Liberals and Conservatives alike. On Friday, January 12, the day before the election, Churchill saw Weizmann in person and informed him that Lord Elgin was "prepared to receive a Zionist delegation and give a hearing to Zionist *desiderata*." By then, however, two important developments had taken place: Zionism had made itself a factor in the national elections and Weizmann had had a long meeting with Arthur James Balfour.

Both events occurred on January 9. That day, a letter was composed by the president of the English Zionist Federation, Sir Francis Montefiore—a nephew of Sir Moses, and a man whose abilities Weizmann considered to be far less distinguished than his name—which was sent to all candidates and to *The Times*, where it was published on January 12. It began with references to both the Aliens Act and the recent pogroms in Russia and summed them up in a way to prod liberal consciences: "These—the orderly, careful legislation of the British Parliament and the villainous outrages inflicted by mobs of hooligans—are equally parts of the Jewish question." But Montefiore readily acknowledged the difficulties of recent solutions sought:

> Emigration under direction, and colonization on a large scale in any place that can be made available, are suggestions put forth to meet present Jewish difficulties. But, however carefully emigration may be undertaken, the result must in the long run be the mere shifting from place to place of the trouble. Colonization on a large scale in any territory that can be found for the purpose takes no account of the true national sentiment of the Jewish people, and lacks the local magnetism and attraction necessary for rendering such colonization other than a philanthropic effort. And philanthropy will not solve the Jewish question.

After a reference to the unsuccess of the Hirsch colonies in Argentina, Montefiore went on to offer "Zionism, the Jewish national movement," as the only solution. "It proposes to establish for the Jewish people a legally-secured and publicly-recognized home in Palestine, the land to which the Jew during 2,000 years of exile has never relinquished his moral claim and never ceased to direct his fondest hopes." Then followed a reference to the El Arish plan, which many Zionists, along with Leopold Greenberg, still hoped could be revived: "Such urgent needs of our people as can be alleviated by colonization Zionism believes can best be met by colonization in the neighboring lands of Palestine, with the granting of autonomous rights; colonization which could be compatible with and subservient to the national movement." And finally came the exertion of political pressure upon each candidate receiving the letter in the mail: "I shall be glad to know whether you are in agreement with our objects and upon hearing from you to that effect I will take care that such intimation shall be conveyed to the Jewish voters and others who sympathize with our aims in your district, so that they may render you what support they are able in your candidature."

This letter evoked upward of 250 favorable replies from candidates of all the parties, and it was undoubtedly what Winston Churchill was responding to when he spoke to Weizmann on January 12. As for Balfour, he probably had not seen the Montefiore letter by the time of his own meeting with Weizmann on the afternoon of the very day the letter was dated; but he may have heard that it was forthcoming, and in any case, he had had plenty of opportunity to notice that there was a distinct Jewish element in the campaign. Not that there was much of it in his own East Manchester constituency; but he had concerned himself with the difficulties his colleague W. Joynsen-Blake was having against Churchill in Northwest Manchester. Furthermore, the prime minister's brother Gerald was having a very difficult time in his campaign in Leeds, where anger at the Aliens Act among its large Jewish community was a distinct political factor. Arthur James Balfour had discussed Zionism before with Charles Dreyfus, who was his campaign chairman in this election; and now Dreyfus arranged another meeting between his candidate and Weizmann, a year after their last one.

Unlike that first, brief encounter, however, this one lasted more than an hour; and, considering what was said in it from the standpoint of future events, it must be deemed of historic import. Certainly its two participants came to consider it such many years later, after so much had happened, and their subsequent tellings of the story were to take on the aura of legend and romance. We must try to penetrate the aura and perceive what happened as best we can.

"I had a meeting with Balfour today," Weizmann wrote to Vera on the evening of January 9, "and had a long and interesting talk with him about Zionism. He explained that he sees no political difficulties in the attainment of Palestine—only economic difficulties. We talked about territorialism. I explained to him why this was not possible."

Adding only that he promised to send Balfour a memorandum, Weizmann thus concluded the only known contemporaneous account of the conversation. Ten months later he wrote to David Wolffsohn—Herzl's successor as president of the World Zionist Organization—in Cologne, reporting a conversation with Balfour that may have been a subsequent one; but there is no reference in Weizmann's autobiography to a second conversation that year, or any positive evidence to support the existence of one, so the report in the letter to Wolffsohn is generally held to refer back to the January meeting. "I saw Balfour," Weizmann told the Zionist president. "He seems unable to understand why Rothschild, etc., are so hostile to Zionism." After the death of Herzl and the failure of the East Africa project, Lord Rothschild had gone back to his old anti-Zionist position. "This has done much harm to Zionist policies in England," Weizmann went on, paraphrasing Balfour, "because public opinion among prominent Christians is influenced by Jews like Rothschild, etc. I tried to explain things to him as best I could. He wants another *rendezvous* with me in London. Shall I go?" But there was not to be another *rendezvous* between them until 1914.

We must now revert to descriptions of the scene made decades later. "He delivered the best platform speeches of his life," Blanche Dugdale has written of the campaign conducted by her uncle, Arthur James Balfour, in 1906, "during the ten grim January days in which Manchester rain pelted unceasingly upon Manchester cobblestones. His headquarters were, as usual, in the Queen's Hotel. Through the green-painted pillars of that Victorian portico the stream of pressmen, Party organizers, supporters, and busybodies passed continually in and out. Upstairs, in the suite of first-floor rooms, Balfour's sister and his secretaries guarded his moments of quiet." It was to these rooms that Chaim Weizmann was brought. "I surmised," he writes in his autobiography, "that Mr. Balfour had consented to see me for a few minutes—'a quarter of an hour,' Dreyfus warned me— simply to break the monotony of his routine. He kept me for well over an hour."

The image floats vividly before the mind: on the one side, the dark, intense young Jewish immigrant, already looking older than his thirty-one years with his bald head and goatee of the Russian *intelligyent*; on the other, tall languorous Balfour, beloved by political cartoonists for presenting in his person one of the quintessential images of English aristocratic diffidence, moustache drooping like his back. They were two utterly contrasting images of leanness, a wire and a willow, but if Weizmann was someone who could discuss a point as readily as he could breathe and Balfour had a reputation for not even reading the newspapers, they had in common a keenness of mind that missed nothing. "I had been less than two years in the country," Weizmann was to recall, "and my English was still not easy to listen to. I remember how Balfour sat in his usual pose, his legs stretched out in front of him, an imperturbable expression on his face. We plunged at once into the subject of our interview."

Weizmann's ensuing account of the conversation in his autobiography adds nothing of substance to what we know from his 1906 letters; what it does add is aura, and some distortions of memory. The Balfour of the letters seems rather more sophisticated about Zionist matters than the Balfour of Weizmann's *Trial and Error*; and everything we know about him and what happened with regard to Zionism while he was prime minister suggests that the earlier image is the truer one.* But we may nevertheless be sure that Weizmann went on at length that day, greatly deepening Balfour's knowledge and understanding of the subject, making it dazzlingly clear to him why only Palestine and not East Africa or anywhere else would do. And Weizmann's autobiographical account ends with an exchange that is far too good to deserve critical handling by some prosaic historian:

"Mr. Balfour," he suddenly said, "supposing I were to offer you Paris instead of London, would you take it?"

"But, Dr. Weizmann," Balfour replied, "we have London."

"That is true," came the rejoinder. "But we had Jerusalem when London was a marsh."

One suspects that for Balfour, a philosopher by avocation, this encounter was one of the few pleasant moments in those ten grim days. Certainly there was nothing pleasant for him in their conclusion. On Saturday, January 13, Britain went to the polls, and the result was a landside victory for the Liberals that gave them 377 seats in the House of Commons, a majority of 84 over the other parties combined. Indeed, the Conservative defeat was even worse than this, as another 53 seats were won by the new Labour candidates, the wave of the future. In Manchester, the Liberals were returned for every constituency: Balfour lost and Churchill won. The *Jewish Chronicle* willingly celebrated the latter victory in ethnic terms. "Much excitement and enthusiasm," it wrote in its January 19 issue,

> reigned in Cheetham on Saturday last, during the polling. Several Jews, who had volunteered to act as canvassers, had during the week called upon all the Jewish voters with the satisfactory result of obtaining promises from five-sixths of them that they would give their vote to Mr. Winston Churchill on account of his splendid and energetic efforts to throw out the Aliens Bill. A large number of merchants and businessmen professed their adherence to the principles of Free Trade, and voted accordingly

---

* It should be pointed out that the instances are many in which Weizmann's letters, as well as other sources, prove various recollections in *Trial and Error* to be incorrect and that frequently the distortions are more serious than the one dealt with here.

for the Liberal candidates. After Sabbath some of these can-
vassers were busy giving their help at the various committee-
rooms, and others were bringing voters to the poll in motor-cars
and carriages. When the result became known about ten-o'clock
at night that Mr. Winston Churchill had been elected by the
large majority of 1,241, the delight among the community knew
no bounds, and men excitedly congratulated one another.

Churchill made a special point of thanking his Jewish supporters, among others, and of telling them he would continue to assist
them and study their interests; but in the last analysis, no one could
claim he had received a mandate to act upon any specifically Jewish
issues. He promised that the Aliens Act would be very mildly administered under the Liberals; and so it was. As for Zionism and territorialism, there was little he or anyone else could do about these
two movements at this moment of crisis and indecision in their own
history. Other issues had determined the national outcome; in the
end, perhaps Gerald Balfour's defeat in Leeds was the only one that
could be directly attributed to Jewish anger over the Aliens Act—and
even this conclusion was debated for weeks in the pages of the *Jewish Chronicle*.

As for Arthur James Balfour, there were large questions to concern him now, such as how to regain a seat for himself in Parliament
and how to maintain his leadership of the party and rebuild it.
Young Dr. Weizmann could hardly have been in his thoughts very
much in the weeks following the election—but he was not entirely
absent from them, either. According to Weizmann's autobiography,
Balfour wrote a letter shortly after their meeting to one of his Jewish friends, Mrs. Leopold Rothschild—her husband was Lord Rothschild's brother—in which he said: "I had a most interesting
conversation with a young Russian Jew, a lecturer at the university." On March 23, Weizmann wrote to Vera that "Balfour has written to Dreyfus that he would very much like to know me better. I
shall probably be seeing him in London." Dreyfus replied to Balfour
on the twenty-fourth, enclosing information about "the Russian
gentleman who had the honor of an interview with you in Manchester." Balfour sent this information on to "a Jewish friend—an anti-
Zionist," perhaps Mrs. Rothschild, with the remarks: "I enclose a
letter from Dr. Dreyfus, to whom I wrote to find out the name of the
Russo-Jewish gentleman of whom I spoke to you. I did not, as you
will see by Dr. Dreyfus's account of him, in any way overstate
his intellectual qualifications." And there the story rests until another era.

·7·

DR. WEIZMANN MISSES LLOYD GEORGE AND SEES HERBERT SAMUEL INSTEAD

By the outbreak of war in 1914, Chaim Weizmann and his friends had gone through a struggle for power within the English Zionist Federation (EZF) that had nearly caused it to fall apart. For a time, the insurgency had been led by Rabbi Moses Gaster, who had been among the most rabid opponents of the East African scheme from its inception: so much so that his early admiration for Herzl had given way to a determination, while the latter was still alive, to overthrow and succeed him as president of the World Zionist Organization. Failing to achieve this even after Herzl's death, Gaster found an outlet for his ambitions by winning the presidency of the EZF in 1907. The Greenberg-Cowen faction seemed thus to have been superseded, but Gaster proved so lordly and inflexible that the organization soon began losing membership and influence. In 1909, he was made to step down and was succeeded in the presidency by Charles Dreyfus, who—since the demise of his political career with the Tory disaster of 1906—had become known in the EZF as a man who would offend no one. Certainly Weizmann no longer pinned any hopes on him; but in the ensuing months, Weizmann also began loosening his hitherto strong ties with Gaster and found his way to a businesslike understanding with Joseph Cowen. In February 1911, Cowen was elected to the presidency of the EZF, and Weizmann, now a naturalized British subject,* became one of its two vice-presidents.

---

* On official documents, Weizmann used the Anglicized forename Charles. For some years thereafter, his letters, when addressed outside his circle of family, friends, and Zionist colleagues, usually were signed "Ch. Weizmann."

The fact was that Weizmann—living quietly in Manchester with his wife Vera and their small son, Benjamin—had begun creating a power base all his own, both inside and outside the organization. In his home city he had formed a friendship with a gifted journalist seven years his junior, Harry Sacher, that was leading to connections with an emerging and influential younger generation of Zionists there and in London. As for London, he and Gaster both had strong support from the Maccabaeans, who had vied briefly with the demoralized EZF for leadership of British Zionism. Furthermore, Ahad Ha'am had been living in London since 1908, and this distinguished spokesman and critic of old Russian Hovevei Zion ideals was adding to Weizmann's reputation by treating him virtually as his foremost disciple.

But it was above all on account of his renewed efforts to create a Jewish university—now definitely to be Hebrew speaking and in Jerusalem—that Weizmann was developing a personal following. From the beginning of 1913, this had been his main preoccupation, and in the course of his travels on its behalf he had formed contacts with such non-Zionist Jewish eminences as Dr. Paul Ehrlich, the illustrious Berlin immunologist, and Baron Edmond de Rothschild. Indeed, he got on far better with the baron than Herzl had, and this still-undaunted supporter of Palestine agrarian colonies had confided to him in March 1914: "Without me the Zionists could not have accomplished anything, without the Zionists my project would have died."

It was no doubt partly in recognition of his political skills, as well as of the fact that he was now the foremost of the old anti-"Ugandists" in the ranks of the EZF, that Cowen and Greenberg charged Weizmann with a delicate mission in September 1914. Zionism was without leadership of worldwide stature—indeed, in Berlin, where the movement's headquarters had been located since 1911, an already divided and lackluster leadership was now in total disarray as a result of the war—and Cowen and Greenberg thought the time had come to try to recover Israel Zangwill for the cause. Originally their plan had been to have Weizmann join them for a meeting with Zangwill in London, but the somewhat disdainful author had been unwilling to come up from his summer home in East Preston, near Brighton. The upshot was that Cowen wrote to Weizmann at the end of September asking him to go down to Brighton by himself. A meeting was arranged for Saturday, October 3; but Weizmann, though he was in London on Tuesday, September 29, did not show up for the appointment.

"I regret deeply that it was impossible for me to go over to East

Preston from London," he wrote to Zangwill on Sunday, "as I was suddenly called away to Manchester." It may be that his wife had been ill, but Weizmann did not offer any further explanation; instead, he got right to the business at hand:

> Cowen and Greenberg, no doubt, have mentioned to you the object of our meeting. Whatever differences of opinion have separated you from the general Zionist body, differences which, I am afraid, are still in existence, I am nevertheless convinced that at the present critical moment, we must try and find the possibility for working together and save what can be saved from this debacle which befell our people.

After referring to the dangerous situation of the Jews in Russia, with which Zangwill was especially concerned, and of those in Palestine, he went on:

> I am inclined to think with you that at the present historical moment, through which the civilized world is passing, we may hope that the powers, which are going to alter the map of Europe, will find time to consider the fate of 13 millions of Jews, who, no doubt, represent a small nation, which has given to the world as much as any other nation, and which, in the present struggle, is taking a very prominent part.

"Needless to say," he added, "that we look to you as one who would be able to take the lead in this matter," and then concluded pointedly:

> You know, Mr. Zangwill, that I have been one of your most convinced adversaries, and I never hesitated to tell you so when the opportunity arose. In the same time I would like you to know that this was a *mahaloket l'shem shamayim** [a controversy for the sake of Heaven], and certainly there was no personal feeling of any sort in the controversy. This is what emboldened me to come to you now in a time of stress like this and ask you to accept our cooperation for the good of Jewry.

Zangwill replied two days later, telling Weizmann he had gone to Brighton Saturday and was disappointed not to find him at their prearranged meeting place; particularly because, as he wrote, "your letter leaves me quite in the dark as to what you propose to do." As

---

* In Hebrew letters in the original.

for their old rivalry, he graciously observed: "I have always under-stood that we were divided by a question of principle, and those divided by principle are always nearer than friends without princi-ple." It was again Weizmann's move.

He took some time to formulate his reply, then wrote it on Octo-ber 19. "My plans," he said,

> are based naturally on one cardinal assumption, viz., that the Allies will win and, as I sincerely wish and hope, win well. No doubt fundamental changes will take place after this war, changes which probably in their character will be determined by the principle of nationality. England, which champions the cause of small nationalities will—I believe—guarantee the maxi-mum amount of justice to a world tired out by this terrible war.

What did this mean for the Jews? "The one nation whose position may remain unaltered are we, who fight everywhere and will win nowhere." Weizmann then entered into an analysis of the Russian-Jewish situation, telling Zangwill frankly that he did not share his "optimism that a change for the better in Russia may take place after the war." Only a revolution could do that, he said—but even then, improvement would be slow; and in the meantime, "we must at least *claim* more, much more, and not reduce the Jewish problem to a Russian problem. . . . The Jewish question now ought to be raised on a higher plane and the Russian position must follow as a matter of course." Then he came to his point:

> Now, when the general reckoning comes, is a time to put forward our claim for the establishment of an organized autono-mous Jewish community in Palestine. Nobody doubts our in-tellectual achievements, nobody can doubt now, that we are capable of great physical efforts, that would all the mental, moral and physical forces of Jewry be concentrated on one aim— the building up of a Jewish community—this community would certainly not lag behind and [could] stand comparison with any modern highly civilized state.

Weizmann furthermore had no doubt "that Palestine will fall within the influence of England"—a point on which he evidently had greater confidence than the British foreign secretary. "Palestine," he went on, "is a natural continuation of Egypt and the barrier separating the Suez Canal from Constantinople, the Black Sea and any hostility which may come from this side." It would be, he added—taking a cue from Mordecai in *Daniel Deronda*—"the Asiatic Belgium." And he concluded with a vision of Anglo-Hebraic unity against pagan militarism that could have been conceived by Disraeli himself, had he witnessed this war: "I conceive this war," Weizmann said, "as the struggle between Siegfried and Moses, and I believe in the indestructibility of Moses who withstood worse things than 17 inch guns."

Zangwill wrote his answer on October 28. He was unable to see how the fate of Russia's "six or seven million Jews can be ameliorated by anything that happens in Palestine." As for Palestine, "I should find it difficult," he wrote, "to demand that the Jewish minority should rule over the Arab majority." He protested that "I could only lead if I could see the way to go," and that otherwise "it would be a case of the blind leading the blind." He suggested that he might nevertheless be of some assistance in bringing Weizmann's views to people of influence, though he warned that in view of all his own efforts on behalf of the Jews of Eastern Europe, "I have to be on my guard against abusing the patience of the authorities." This certainly was refusal enough, although there was to be one more attempt to win Zangwill over, on November 7, when Weizmann, Cowen, and Greenberg all finally went down to Brighton to meet with him and one of his associates in the Jewish Territorial Organization. In person, he dropped his circumspection and frankly stated his antagonism to "any national view of the Jewish problem." There was to be no Zangwill on the Zionist scene, no doubt to Weizmann's relief.

Weizmann was, in the meantime, making contact with people of influence on his own. It was in the middle of September, when plans were being laid by Cowen and Greenberg for a reconciliation with Zangwill, that Weizmann met C.P. Scott for the first time. He had wanted to meet the distinguished editor for years and had even collaborated with Harry Sacher in 1907 in covering the Eighth Zionist Congress for the *Guardian*, but the long-sought-after encounter did not take place until 1914—and then apparently by accident.

The occasion was a tea party in Withington—the comfortable Manchester suburb in which the Weizmanns were living—given by one Mrs. Eckhard; along with her husband, she was among the pillars of the city's old German-Jewish community. The Eckhards were friends of the Dreyfuses and, like them, benefactors of the Victoria Memorial Jewish Hospital, where Vera Weizmann was employed; in fact, this party was in particular for the supporters and staff of the department in which Vera worked, the postnatal clinic for mothers, which was the special charity of Mrs. Eckhard and Mrs. Dreyfus. The Weizmanns were beginning to look upon this sort of thing, around which their social and professional lives had largely been built for the past eight years, with all the disdain of Russian *intelligentsiya* for the provincial bourgeoisie—perhaps Vera even more so than Chaim, for she was far more Russian than he, having been one of the small number of Jews who had grown up outside the Pale of Settlement, in Rostov-on-Don, and she was capable of a hauteur not untypical of her background and education. But this party was now to provide a crucial link in a chain of events that would soon lead the Weizmanns out of the provinces forever.

It is not clear who made the introductions between Chaim Weizmann and the tall, distinguished-looking gentleman with the white beard whose name he did not catch. One does not even know if Scott, whose conscience was troubled by Britain's alliance with reactionary, anti-Semitic Russia, had asked to meet this fairly well known spokesman for Russian Jews in Manchester or was introduced to him by chance. In any case, once their conversation had begun, Scott was most interested in hearing Weizmann's views on Russia and its anti-Semitism, which were expounded to him vehemently and at length. He then asked if Weizmann would like to call the next day at his office to continue the discussion.

"And what is your office?" the chemist asked.

"The *Manchester Guardian*," Scott replied.

When he realized at last to whom he had been talking, Weizmann feared for a moment that he had offended with his diatribe against England's Russian ally. But Scott was far from offended, and they had their meeting the following day, Wednesday, September 16. "I had a long talk with C.P. Scott (the editor of the *Guardian)* today," Weizmann wrote gleefully that evening to Leopold Greenberg, "and he will be quite prepared to help us in any endeavor in favor of the Jews. He expressed his willingness to see Grey, when we have a practical proposal to submit. Scott carries great weight and he may be useful."

The bluster of that last sentence in particular suggests that Weizmann was leaping too eagerly, for Greenberg's benefit, to conclusions about Scott's potential as a Zionist sympathizer. Turkey had not yet entered the war, and the *Guardian*'s leader pages were fervently expressing the wish that she would not do so. Scott was far more reluctant than Lloyd George had become to ponder an extension of British imperial commitments. It is most likely that Scott had preferred to confine the discussion as much as possible to Russian and Russian-Jewish questions, and it was surely with reference to those questions that he spoke to Weizmann of contacting Sir Edward Grey. But ironically, Weizmann turns out in the end to have known his man; for Scott was soon to become one of his warmest supporters.

Weizmann did not wait long after Asquith's Guildhall speech to renew the contact with Scott. "Things have moved quicker than we all perhaps expected," he wrote to the *Guardian* editor on November 12.

> Turkey has come in and no doubt this will have fatal consequences for her. The remark in Asquith's speech, that the end has come not only for Turkey in Europe, but also for her Asiatic dominions is certainly significant. Don't you think that the chance for the Jewish people is now within the limits of a discussion at least. I realize of course, that we cannot "claim" anything, we are much too atomized for it, but we can reasonably say, that should Palestine fall within the sphere of British influence and should Britain encourage a Jewish settlement there, as a British dependency, we could have in 25-30 years about a million of Jews out there, perhaps more.

Weizmann then developed his position with some of the points he had previously wasted on Zangwill, whose final demurral had occurred five days earlier: a Jewish settlement in Palestine would develop the country and raise the level of civilization there, would form a barrier between the Suez Canal and any possible aggression from Constantinople, would be "an Asiatic Belgium." This, he said, would be for the sake of a Jewish people now fighting on all the battlefields of Europe without much hope for the future. "I hope for nothing from Russia," he went on, aiming for Scott's most vulnerable point where these matters were concerned. "In fact things there are getting worse than ever." He concluded by saying that "if you think the matter sufficiently interesting and ripe I would be exceedingly glad to hear from you."

Scott replied by inviting Weizmann to come to his office again, and their meeting took place on November 15. Eastern Europe again formed part of the discussion—Scott even asked Weizmann to do an article on Poland—but this time they freely discussed Zionism as well, and Weizmann found the sixty-eight-year-old editor "so unaffected, so open, so charming that I simply could not help pouring out my heart to him. I told him of my hatred for Russia, of the internal conflicts of the Jews, of our universal tragedy, of our hopes and aspirations for Palestine, of the little we had already done there, and of our almost Messianic dreams . . . for the future. He listened with the utmost attention."

The next day Weizmann wrote to Scott thanking him heartily

> for the kindness you have shown to me and for the patience with which you have listened to my perhaps somewhat voluminous talk. It is the first time in my life I have "spoken out" to a non-Jew all the intimate thoughts and desiderata, you scarcely realize what a world of good you did to me in allowing me to talk out freely. In this cold world we "the fantatics" are solitary onlookers, more especially now. I shall never see the realization of my dream—"the 100% Jew"—but perhaps my son will see it. You gave me courage and please forgive my brutal frankness. If I would have spoken to a man I value less, I would have been very diplomatic.

Scott, who had asked Weizmann to prepare a memorandum on Zionist aims and achievements, was beginning to feel the younger man's spell. "I was immensely interested in all you told me of your hopes and plans," he wrote back on November 22. "There are so few people who have the courage of an ideal and at the same time the insight and energy which make it possible." He told Weizmann not to bother about the article on Poland. Meanwhile, he remembered a promise he had made during the conversation to put Weizmann in touch with Lloyd George, and it was on the following Friday that he raised the matter with the chancellor of the Exchequer.

> "I have just had a letter from Mr. Scott (editor of the *Manchester Guardian*)," Weizmann wrote excitedly to Ahad Ha'am on Monday, November 30, "telling me that he saw Lloyd George on Friday, talked to him about Palestine and found him 'interested.' Lloyd George said that he had read the article in the *New Statesman*, and also (alas!) had spoken to Herbert Samuel." Weizmann, who must have thought Samuel had been brought into the picture simply because he was the only Jew in the present Government, still assumed—along with almost everyone else—that he shared the anti-Zionist outlook of the Anglo-Jewish establishment. "L.G.," Weizmann went on, "expressed his wish to see me in the presence of Samuel."

The meeting was to be a Lloyd George breakfast at 9:15 the following Friday, and on Thursday Weizmann prepared to go to London, planning to spend the night at Ahad Ha'am's home in Hampstead. Then at the last minute a telegram came from Scott in London: "Unable arrange George away." Scott followed this up with a letter asking if Weizmann could be in London the next Wednesday or Thursday, December 9 or 10; he would try to arrange a meeting on one of those days. This time Weizmann made plans to be in London whether Lloyd George was available or not; and as he prepared to board the 4:15 on Wednesday afternoon, he received another telegram from Scott informing him that Lloyd George, who was otherwise occupied, wanted him to call upon Herbert Samuel the next day.

And so it was that, at 4:15 on the afternoon of Thursday, December 10, Weizmann found himself sitting down with the president of the Local Government Board in the latter's room in Whitehall. Samuel was only four years his senior, but the two men were very nearly as different in their backgrounds as two Ashkenazic Jews could be; and Weizmann was no doubt doubly apprehensive as the conversation began, since he had already met that day with two prominent Anglo-Jewish critics of Zionism: Sir Philip Magnus, a well-known Jewish educator, and Lucien Wolf.

Weizmann started with an exposition of the Zionist outlook, which, he said, considered the Jewish problem "from one definite point of view. For us the position of the Jews in Eastern Europe, terrible as it is, is only one aspect of the problem, the economic one." What he meant was the material situation of East European Jewry in the broadest sense, which was now being most vividly illustrated "by the 300,000 Jews fighting in the trenches in Poland, who have no hope before them, and who know that the oppression and ill-treatment of the Jews in Russia are being pursued with still more rigor than before the war." The *moral* aspect of the problem, on the other hand, was represented by the Jews of the West—of England, for example, where they "must prove that they are English, and instead of proving that they are 100% English, they behave as though they were 105% English, and this alone provokes suspicion." Whether Samuel looked uncomfortable at this or not, Weizmann was at any rate determined not to spare his feelings unnecessarily.

Urging that "the genuine patriotism of the Russian Jews under such circumstances calls for some more than superficial explanation," Weizmann went on to suggest "that this abnormal position of our people in East and West is due to one fundamental cause." This was "that we are a nation in as much as we resist all influences making for the destruction of our race, and not a nation because we assimilate ourselves superficially, and are always ready to attach ourselves quickly to surroundings. That is the reason why we are so widely misunderstood. We are a people without a status, and if in normal times such a position is tolerated, in times of crisis it becomes dangerous." Coming to his main point, Weizmann drew upon a capacity for witty analogy that he had begun showing of late—he nowadays referred, for example, to his projected Hebrew university as "the Jewish Dreadnought"—and said: "If the Jews had at present a place where they formed the important part of the population, and led a life of their own, however small this place might be, for example, something like Monaco, with a University instead of a gambling hall, nobody would doubt the existence of the Jewish nation, all the fatal misunderstandings would disappear, we should have a definite passport, and we should therefore not be suspected."

He ended with a final look at the Russian-Jewish question, which he knew was still the main Jewish question in the eyes of British leaders, whatever their religious background. "It is possible," he went on, "that Russia, who finds herself for the first time in her history in decent company may learn something from this company, but unfortunately there is also a possibility of the reverse taking place. Anyhow," he added, experiencing another of his occasional moments of prophetic insight, "there is little hope that the Russo-Jewish problem will be ameliorated by pressure from without; I think that the emancipation of the Russian Jews will come along with the emancipation of the Russian people, and certainly we shall pay dearly for it, perhaps as dearly as the Jews pay now for the war."

With this, Weizmann ended his discussion and waited for a response from Samuel, who had been listening attentively throughout. The president of the Local Government Board began by remarking drily that he "saw at once" that Weizmann "was a Zionist." The humor of this escaped his listener, who was still not accustomed to Oxonian understatement; but Samuel could not miss making an impression with his very next words. He was "not a stranger to Zionist ideas," he said; "he had been following them up a little of late years, and although he had never publicly mentioned it, he took a considerable interest in the question. Since Turkey had entered into the war, he had given the problem much thought and consideration, and he thought that a realization of the Zionist dream was possible."

Weizmann must have been utterly astonished. But as if this were not enough, Samuel went on to say he believed Weizmann's "demands were too modest, that big things would have to be done in Palestine; he himself would move and would expect Jewry to move immediately the military situation was cleared up. He was convinced that it would be cleared up favorably. The Jews would have to bring sacrifices and he was prepared to do so."

At this point the incredulous Weizmann "ventured to ask in which way the plans of Mr. Samuel were more ambitious" than his own. Samuel, however, "preferred not to enter into a discussion of his plans," saying that "he would like to keep them 'liquid,' but he suggested that the Jews would have to build railways, harbors, a University, a network of schools, etc." The university idea made "a special appeal to him." He hoped that "great things" would be "forthcoming from a seat of learning, where the Jews can work freely on a free soil of their own." The normally reserved Samuel, carried away with the enthusiasm of his vision, even added something that Weizmann had certainly never included in his ambitions: perhaps, he ruminated, "the Temple may be rebuilt, as a symbol of Jewish unity, of course, in a modernized form."

This could only have taken Weizmann's breath away; but it was hardly the moment for the appreciative chemist from Manchester to tell the unexpectedly Zionist cabinet minister what were the obstacles in the way of *that* particular messianic vision. It was a moment, rather, to ponder an amazing phenomenon of the world upheaval they were living through. "After listening to him," Weizmann recalled soon thereafter, "I remarked that I was pleasantly surprised to hear such words from him; that if I were a religious Jew, I should have thought the Messianic times were near; that as I came up to him I had debated in my mind whether I should speak to the Jew or the British Cabinet Minister; that I am happy to have spoken just as I did, and still happier to have heard his reply."

Samuel then assured Weizmann that these ideas were "in the mind of his colleagues in the Cabinet," and advised him "to work quietly, continue the investigation step by step and prepare for the hour to come." He asked Weizmann to keep him informed of his activities and to let him know of the arrival, expected any day, of two members of the executive of the World Zionist Organization, which was transferring a part of its main headquarters from Berlin to neutral Copenhagen.

Weizmann, for his part, concluded by saying that many of the projects Mr. Samuel envisioned had already been under way when the war broke out—"for instance, the University project"—and "that certainly all these things would flourish as soon as civilized conditions were established in Palestine." What he and other Zionists asked for, Weizmann said, "was simply encouragement from the

British Government, which we hoped would be the master of Palestine, in our work there, and further a wide measure of local Government, and freedom for the development of our own culture."

As Weizmann prepared to take his leave, Samuel asked him if he knew his friend Rabbi Moses Gaster. Gaster! Weizmann not only knew him, he was having dinner at his home the following evening. Responding in the affirmative to Samuel's question, Weizmann knew that he had no choice but to tell Gaster about this meeting, which he had not intended to mention outside a very restricted circle of family, friends, and colleagues. Gaster had once been part of that circle; indeed, the chief Sephardic rabbi, who was eighteen years Weizmann's senior, had for a time been his foremost mentor in England until Ahad Ha'am arrived in 1908 and superseded Gaster in that role. Since then, temperamental differences and tensions over their respective power struggles within the Zionist movement had caused Weizmann and Gaster to drift apart. Yet they had never lost touch, and Weizmann found it a bit irksome that Gaster, who clearly knew something of Samuel's feelings about Zionism, had never even mentioned that he knew the man. But it was Gaster's turn to be irritated once he found out what had happened with Samuel.

This was a relatively small matter, however; Weizmann had other important visits to think about as he stepped out of the Local Government Board onto the London streets. The next morning there was Dorothy de Rothschild, Baron Edmond's English daughter-in-law: just the previous month he had made contact with her, and on November 25 had had a fruitful meeting with her husband, James, when he was in on leave from the front. Not only were they sympathetic to Zionism, they were well connected with the British Rothschild circles that Weizmann had never yet been able to penetrate. They also were friends of Lloyd George.

But an even more important meeting had become a likelihood for the next day or two, though he had yet to confirm it. There was a good chance that Weizmann was going to see Arthur James Balfour again at last, for the first time in more than eight years.

·8·

MR. BALFOUR

Weizmann had never lost the feeling that a special relationship between himself and Balfour had come into being in 1906. Early the following year, he had written to Cowen and Gaster suggesting that they try to organize "a special Palestine Association" among English non-Zionist and Christian eminences, which would include men like Balfour and Winston Churchill. Nothing came of this, and it was not until December 1911, when the leaders of the Zionist organization in Berlin pondered what political moves they ought to make in the wake of Italy's victories over Turkey, that Weizmann again thought of this old contact. "I know Balfour, to whom I talked about Zionism some years ago," he wrote to his colleagues, mentioning a few lesser eminences as well and formulating the line he would take if he saw them. "The only way for us to approach the English is to show them how vital it can be for England to have a friendly and 'strong' element in Palestine, in the Asian Near East in general, that we can be the link between England and the Muslim world." And he concluded: "Would you like me to speak to Balfour, etc., on the lines indicated above?"

Weizmann's Berlin colleagues were interested; Balfour had lost the leadership of the Conservative party the previous month, but no one doubted that he was still a political presence to contend with, and it probably was also felt that he would now be more accessible than before. After receiving their go-ahead, Weizmann endeavored to make his contact. He was able to write to them on January 14, 1912: "I am at present engaged in correspondence with Balfour, and it looks as if I shall be calling on him on 3rd February, either in London or at his castle at Whittingehame for a long talk." Actually, Weizmann had not heard from Balfour himself, but from his secretary, Wilfrid M. Short, who then suddenly wrote saying that Balfour had gone to France but would make an appointment upon returning.

"It has not now been possible," Weizmann had to report on January 21, "for me to see anyone from the government in London. Most of the gentlemen are on the Riviera. Mr. Balfour has gone away and will be back towards the middle of February, as the enclosed letter will show you. I shall see him, of course, just as soon as possible."

This proved not to be easy, however, and by the time Weizmann arrived in Berlin for a committee meeting in the middle of March, he still had not seen Balfour. He began trying again after his return home in April, but now a new factor entered the picture. The Zionist organization, having come to the conclusion that it was crucial to make political contacts in London, decided to send over one of its most seasoned diplomatists, Nahum Sokolow. A man of many talents and languages, the Polish-born Sokolow had made his reputation in the Jewish world mainly as a Hebrew writer and journalist; but as a leading functionary of the Zionist organization since 1906, he had held sensitive conversations through the years with members of various European governments. Fifteen years older than Weizmann, he was still treated by the latter at this time with a respect that only occasionally veered over into irritability. But on this occasion there were intimations of rivalries to come.

Sokolow arrived in the middle of June and wanted to see Balfour among other Englishmen of influence. It was still considered up to Weizmann to arrange this, and on June 20, when they got together in London, he promised Sokolow that he would bring about a meeting between him and Balfour by using the good offices of Charles Dreyfus. No doubt the idea of calling upon Dreyfus had been Sokolow's, since Weizmann, who had left the employ of Clayton Aniline with great relief a few years before, was no longer eager to ask Dreyfus for anything, least of all a favor that implied a surrendering of his own status. As a matter of fact, he did not approach Dreyfus until July 2; in a letter written to Sokolow the next day, Weizmann claimed that Dreyfus had been away during the interval, but said that he now had seen Dreyfus and that the latter "promised to write to you and Balfour." After a few more lines he even added, "I shall write at once to Dr. Dreyfus to remind him again of his promise"—but Sokolow may well have felt that this was a case of protesting too much. He did not think much of Weizmann's skill in this sort of thing anyway, and so he now contacted Dreyfus himself. Dreyfus replied that Balfour was away on holiday and would not be available until Parliament was reconvened.

It is not likely that Sokolow got to see Balfour either that summer or during a subsequent sojourn in London at the end of the year.

As for Weizmann, he gave up for the time being, but not without a wry sense of some continuing claim upon the former prime minister. "By the way," he wrote in January 1913 to Vera in Cannes, where she had gone with their son, Benjamin, for a short vacation, "my friend Balfour is now in Cannes, playing *golf* there. Tell him that I am displeased with him." His letters then were silent on the subject until after the outbreak of war.

By November 1914, the influence Balfour had never completely lost in governing circles was becoming visible again. Just the previous month he had been appointed by Asquith to full membership on the Committee of Imperial Defence, which had first been founded under his Government and for which he had done advisory work in recent years. This gave way to a newly organized War Council on November 25, of which Balfour also was a member. There could no longer be any doubt that the former prime minister, who had interested himself deeply in defense questions since he had presided over the creation of the Anglo-French Entente in 1904, was now one of the makers of Britain's wartime policies.

Under the circumstances, it was quite natural for Chaim Weizmann, among the flurry of letters he wrote after the Turkish entry into the war and Asquith's Guildhall speech, to send one off to Balfour. But this time he thought again and decided to be more prudent than he had been in 1912. "I have written to Balfour and now await his reply," he told Ahad Ha'am in a letter of November 12; but he amended this a week later: "After I had written to Balfour and told you about it, I decided that it might be better if Prof. Alexander, who knows B. well, wrote to him." There was no need for Dreyfus now; Samuel Alexander, a member of an old Anglo-Jewish family and a professor of philosophy at Manchester University, who had befriended his younger colleague Weizmann in recent years, was well known to his fellow philosopher Balfour. The man who was working on the series of lectures that would be published as *Space, Time, and Deity* had no trouble reaching the author of *A Defence of Philosophic Doubt* and *The Foundations of Belief* without the intervention of a secretary.

"I have the liveliest and also the most pleasant recollections of my conversation with Dr. Weizmann in 1906," Balfour replied to Alexander, "and should be very glad to hear from him. If I am in London later in the year, and he happens to be up in Town, I shall be happy to see him; but my plans are uncertain, and it is safer for him to write. This would not prevent our talking matters over if opportunity served."

Weizmann sought to make opportunity serve on the occasion of his very next visit to London, the one that began on Wednesday, December 9; and by Saturday morning, an appointment had been arranged. At noon that day he was to call at 4 Carlton Gardens, Balfour's London home.

Arthur James Balfour was one of the most complex men ever to have held the office of prime minister. For many, however, the explanation of him was simple: he was a decadent who had wandered into politics, a rather listless member of the privileged classes who could make a career in government because his mother's brother was Lord Salisbury, Disraeli's distinguished successor to the leadership of the Conservative party. It was Salisbury who had catapulted his nephew and one-time personal secretary into national prominence by appointing him chief secretary for Ireland in 1887, just in time to enforce the Coercion Act against the angry and rebellious Irish Land League. The result was that this delicate thirty-nine-year-old bachelor of the salons, hitherto known among his colleagues as "pretty Fanny," soon achieved notoriety under the nickname "Bloody Balfour" in honor of his readiness to endorse police actions against demonstrators even when people had been killed. Balfour's parliamentary critic William O'Brien saw him as a man who harbored "a lust for slaughter with a eunuchized imagination" and took "a strange pleasure in mere purposeless human suffering, which imparted a delicious excitement to his languid life."

The elegantly detached appearance presented by Balfour during debates greatly stimulated such outbursts of anger against him. "Presently," runs one description of him in the 1890s, when he served as leader of the House of Commons under his uncle's Governments,

> from behind the Speaker's chair emerges a tall, gaunt figure, limp and lackadaisical, angular and artless is its owner. It is Arthur, sweet Arthur, who had dropped in to see that all is well within the Chamber. He makes his way to his seat into which he flops weary. . . . The elongated body slides down until the neck, thin and delicate as a woman's, reaches the ridge of the Treasury Bench behind. Up go two square-toed, thick soled, spatted feet on the table opposite. The legs are arched and suggest a switch-back railway. The soft brown meditative eyes, denoting the man of thought rather than the man of action, are now peering upwards through glasses into the amber glow of the fanlight on the ceiling. As he gazes, he yawns.

Even his young supporters in the party often were, in the words of one of them,

> aghast at the halting nature of his official statements in the House; they seemed so ill-prepared, so tiresome to the speaker himself. And when he approached statistics his lapses were positively alarming at times: "Did I say *thousands*? Oh, I meant *millions*"; and then calmly, to our consternation, "But that makes no difference to my argument."

This may well seem to sum up the man who, after succeeding his uncle as prime minister in 1902, allowed his Government to fall apart over an issue—free trade versus protection—that evidently bored him, and then went on to preside over one of the worst defeats in his party's history.

But there were quiet contradictions to this popular image. If it was true that Balfour rarely emerged from his bedroom before noon, it also usually turned out that he had been doing his parliamentary homework all morning in bed—and doing it well. "No Minister in charge of a Bill ever worked harder," Winston Churchill said of him, "or was more thoroughly conversant with all the essentials of the legislation he was proposing." When he was proposing legislation that truly aroused him, such as the Education Act of 1902—a milestone, albeit a highly controversial one, in the democratization of the British educational system, which strongly appealed to the spirit of Tory radicalism he had inherited from Disraeli—his efforts on its behalf were inexhaustible. His absolute parliamentary mastery was the reason why his ad libitum and seemingly careless speeches on the floor of the House—"I say what occurs to me," he told Churchill once, "and sit down at the end of the first grammatical sentence"—would hold his listeners, opponents and supporters alike, fascinated for as much as an hour at a stretch. If he occasionally confused thousands with millions, "the curious thing," Balfour's one-time private secretary Ian Malcolm added to his description of such an instance, "was that it did make no difference to the foundation of his conviction; for he was always speaking (as we were to live to find out) for or against some principle of theory or action to which the accuracy of figures was only of secondary importance." His approach to all things was diffidently—and hence maddeningly—Olympian: "He saw a great deal of life from afar," Ramsay MacDonald was to say of him, not without resentment.

Balfour was always in part the philosopher he had briefly thought of becoming after his student years at Eton and Trinity

College, Cambridge. "Do it if you like," his mother had told him, "but remember that if you do, you will find you have nothing to write about by the time you are forty." And so he followed his uncle into politics instead, but was barely past thirty when he produced a full-length epistemological treatise, *A Defence of Philosophic Doubt.* In it he took on the great metaphysical controversy of the day: science versus religion.

Balfour was no stranger to either persuasion. One of his younger brothers, Francis, was already an embryologist of great distinction. On the other hand, he had never stopped cherishing the devout upbringing that he, along with his four brothers and three sisters, had been given by their widowed mother on the great Balfour family estate of Whittingehame in Scotland. Fully conscious of their double heritage, the strong-willed Lady Blanche Gascoigne Cecil Balfour had even had them all baptized in both the Church of England and the Scottish Presbyterian Church. Convinced by his own life's experience that variant conceptions of ultimate truth could coexist in the world, Arthur Balfour endeavored in his treatise to defend religion against science without repudiating the latter— although the philosophic doubt of the title was by all means aimed against science's basic assumptions. What he wanted to demonstrate was that these assumptions were as much a matter of faith as were religious beliefs. Causality, for example, could hardly be posited as a uniform principle everywhere in the universe without—he argued— implying the existence of divinity.

This closely reasoned work was entirely up to the academic standards represented by such men as the Cambridge philosopher Henry Sidgwick, Balfour's own brother-in-law, who at least for a time shared his skepticism about science, and it brought its author a solid reputation in this field. His next book, *The Foundations of Belief,* which was mainly a polemic against agnosticism, was not so well received in academic circles when it appeared in 1895. There was a widespread feeling that the parliamentary debater had overcome the philosopher and that reasoning had given way to rhetoric. "Morality is more than a bare code of laws," Balfour intoned in this book against the ethics of what he called "naturalism"; and to change the moral tradition, he went on, would necessitate changing

something more important than the mere customary language of exhortation. The old ideals of the world would have to be uprooted, and no new ones could spring up and flourish in their stead; the very soil on which they grew would be sterilized, and the phrases in which all that has hitherto been regarded as best and noblest in human life has been expressed, nay, the words "best" and "noblest" themselves, would become as foolish and unmeaning as the incantation of a forgotten superstition.

Such literary speechmaking made the book popular in spite of the professors, and Thomas Henry Huxley was sufficiently aroused by it to try composing a rebuttal with his last dying breath.

Far from being a religious fundamentalist or even a pietist in the conventional sense, Balfour was really a philosophical seeker after some humanistic reconstruction for his own times of the Christian ideals of old. In this sense, he was not unlike George Eliot, whose novels he appreciated and whom he and his brother Gerald had met in person on occasion. Perhaps one of the more significant expressions of his own ideal of a modern "religion of humanity" was an essay he published in 1887 dealing with the art he loved the most, music, and focusing upon his favorite practitioner of that art, George Frideric Handel. Balfour saw in Handel's career some of the tension of his own, between the ideal and the worldly, and wrote of the composer prior to his great oratorios that

on the whole it would, I suppose, be true to say that after expending for more than thirty years his time, his money, his health, and his unequaled genius, on the cultivation of the Italian opera, he left it richer, indeed, by innumerable masterpieces, but in other respects very much where he found it—fettered, that is, by endless conditions, imposed not so much to satisfy the requirements of dramatic propriety as to moderate the rivalries of competing singers.

"It seems at first sight strange," he added significantly, "that any man of genius should have patiently submitted to rules which, from the point of view of art, were perfectly arbitrary."

And yet, in the end, it was a confluence of worldly circumstances—"the rivalries and quarrels already adverted to, which made it impossible profitably to perform operas,—and the observance of Lent, which made it possible profitably to perform oratorios"—that caused Handel's transformation into a composer who, "in the age of Voltaire and of Hume," could produce "the most profoundly religious music which the world has yet known." How like a statesman's career, at that! And the implications did go beyond music, for even among the greatest poets and scholars, few "have succeeded in touching the words of our English Bible without rushing on disaster." It was only of Handel that it could be said that

> the most splendid inspirations of Hebrew poetry gain an added glory from his music, and that thousands exist for whom passages of Scripture which have for eighteen centuries been very near the heart of Christendom acquire a yet deeper meaning, a yet more spiritual power through the strains with which his genius has inseparably associated them.

Balfour found this Hebraic power to be at its height in the *Messiah* and *Israel in Egypt*; of the latter in particular he wrote that "it stands out amid all creations of the last century, whether of poets, painters, or musicians, unique in its unborrowed majesty."

How often, then, did the glorious strains of "But as for His people, He led them forth like sheep" run through Balfour's head in those moments when he pondered the Jewish question? For there can be no doubt that, if he sympathized with the plight of Jews in the Russian Egypt, he was not at all eager to see England become their Canaan. "A state of things could easily be imagined," he told the House of Commons on July 10, 1905, during the debate on the Aliens Bill, "in which it would not be to the advantage of the civilization of this country that there should be an immense body of persons who, however patriotic, able and industrious, however much they threw themselves into the national life, remained a people apart, and not merely held a religion differing from the vast majority of their fellow-countrymen, but only intermarried among themselves." Balfour found himself having to explain these remarks within a few days to a colleague who had received a letter of complaint and sent it on to him. "The letter you send me," he wrote,

> exhibits a very curious misapprehension of my attitude on the part of its writer.
>
> He states, in the first place, what I think he would have avoided stating had he read all the speeches which I have made upon the subject. My opinions briefly are these: (1) Antisemitism is in itself a great evil, and has been the cause of most abominable crimes wherever it has prevailed. It is all-important to prevent its growth in this country by all legitimate means; (2) The Jews are not only a most gifted race, but have proved themselves ready and anxious to take part in the national and civic life of the countries where they are settled. But, from my point of view, it is an undoubted disadvantage that they do not inter-

marry with the rest of the population; and I think so, not because I dislike the Jews, but because I admire them; and I think that their rigid separation in this respect from their fellow-countrymen is a misfortune for us. If they think it wrong, I do not, of course, complain of their obeying what they hold to be a binding law; but I must be permitted, from my own point of view, to regret their decision.

These regrets, though exacerbated mainly by Whitechapel, seem even to have applied on occasion to Balfour's wealthy Jewish friends. After one visit to the Sassoons a few years earlier, Balfour had written to his friend and possible mistress Lady Elcho that the house was "peopled with endless Sassoon girls. . . . I believe the Hebrews were in an actual majority—and though I have no prejudice against the race (quite the contrary) I began to understand the point of view of those who object to alien immigration." Lady Battersea, a member of the Rothschild family, was to remember a visit to Whittingehame in 1895 during which Balfour plied her with questions about Jews, synagogues, alien immigration—and about Claude Montefiore, president of the Anglo-Jewish Association and England's foremost spokesman of Liberal Judaism. Balfour clearly was as perturbed by "105%" Englishness as Chaim Weizmann was.

"I spoke to him practically in the same strain as I did to Mr. Samuel," Weizmann later wrote of his visit to Balfour that Saturday, December 12, 1914, "but the whole turn of our conversation was more academic than practical." Weizmann was at first ready to expound the basic Zionist position, but found he did not have to do so, for Balfour remembered everything they had discussed in 1906. Instead, Weizmann—who had himself visited Palestine in 1907—summarized what had been done in the intervening years, telling Balfour about the colonization work, about the Haifa Technical College and the language dispute involving it, about other cultural projects such as the Bezalel School of Arts and Crafts in Jerusalem, about his own university project. He expressed regret that all this had to be interrupted, but Balfour stopped him.

"You may get your things done much quicker after the war," he said.

Balfour then expounded for Weizmann his own view of the Jewish question, saying that in his opinion it "would remain insoluble until either the Jews here became entirely assimilated, or there was a normal Jewish community in Palestine—and he had in mind Western Jews rather than Eastern." No doubt expecting his listener to be shocked, Balfour said he had discussed the Jewish question with Co-sima Wagner during a visit to Bayreuth in 1912—he was quite inter-ested in Wagner's music, though he did not like the later works and found Wotan a "tiresome old gossip"—and he and that notoriously anti-Semitic lady had agreed on some points at least.

Weizmann, undaunted by this, broke in "and offered to tell him what Mrs. Wagner said." Balfour agreed, and Weizmann "told him that Mrs. Wagner is of opinion that the Jews in Germany have cap-tured the German stage, Press, Commerce, Universities, etc., that they are putting into their pockets, after only a hundred years of emancipation, everything for which Germans have worked for cen-turies, and that she, Mrs. Wagner, and people who think like her, resent very much having to receive all the moral and material cul-ture at the hands of the Jews." Weizmann then went on to say he even agreed with her as to the facts, and in the belief "that Germans of the Mosaic faith are an undesirable, demoralizing phenomenon," but he disagreed entirely about the conclusions to be drawn.

"The essential point which most non-Jews overlook," he ex-plained, "and which forms the very crux of the Jewish tragedy, is that those Jews who are giving their energies and their brains to the Germans are doing it in their capacity as Germans, and are en-riching Germany and not Jewry, which they are abandoning." In-stead, they have let themselves become absorbed there—and in England and France as well—into the surrounding communities, which then reproach the Jews for this "absorption" and react with anti-Semitism. In Germany these Jewish "Grandees," as Weizmann called them, were losing all contact with the Jewish people: "they must hide their Judaism in order to be allowed to place their brains and abilities at the disposal of the Germans. They are to no little extent responsible for German greatness. The tragedy of it all is that whereas we do not recognize them as Jews, Madame Wagner does not recognize them as Germans, and so we stand there as the most exploited and misunderstood of peoples."

With that Weizmann ended his confrontation between Moses and Siegfried. Balfour, deeply moved—Weizmann thought he saw tears in his eyes—took his visitor by the hand and said that the road followed by a great and suffering nation had now been illuminated for him. When he asked what could be done about the problem, Weizmann once again gave his view that "Palestine and the building up of a Jewish nation from within, with its own forces and its own traditions, would establish the status of the Jews, would create a type of 100% Jew."

Then they began talking about Russian Jewry, whereupon Balfour was suddenly reminded of Claude Montefiore, who had come to him three months before, asking him to intercede on behalf of the Jews of Rumania.

"What a great difference there is between you and him," he told Weizmann. "For you are not asking for anything—you demand, and people have to listen to you because you are a statesman of a morally strong state."

Reflecting on men like Claude Montefiore and Lord Rothschild, Balfour added that he "regretted that he had known only Jews of one type." Weizmann, ever impatient with the predominantly philanthropic approach of such men to the Jewish question, replied by drawing Balfour's attention to "that fatal error into which West European statesmen have fallen, looking at East European Jewry as at a Pack of *Schnorrers* [Beggars], Western Jews contributing to the propagation of this view. Our bodies are in chains," he went on, "but we are trying to throw off our chains and save our soul." Balfour asked him whether he wanted anything practical at present, and Weizmann said that, as long as the guns were roaring, all he wanted was "to explain to him how great and deep is the bloodstained tragedy of the Jews." But he hoped to call again when "the military situation became clearer."

They had been together an hour and a half. Balfour saw Weizmann out into the street, and as they stood in the elegant splendor of Carlton Gardens, with the Mall stretching out beneath them only a few feet away, he held Weizmann's hand and said:

"Mind you come again to see me. I am deeply moved and interested, it is not a dream, it is a great cause and I understand it."

As Weizmann walked off, could Balfour possibly have felt he had just heard a voice that could rebuke the Red Sea? After all even Handel, that most English as well as Hebraic of composers, had spoken with a foreign accent.

That evening Balfour went to Bristol and gave a speech denouncing the arrogance of the German "superman" ideal.

PART TWO

·1915·

·9·

LLOYD GEORGE SEES DR. WEIZMANN, AND HERBERT SAMUEL PRESENTS HIS MEMORANDUM

"I received today two long memoranda," Prime Minister Asquith wrote on January 1, 1915, "one from Winston, the other from Lloyd George—the latter is quite good—as to the future conduct of the War. They are both keen on a new objective and theater as soon as our new troops are ready, Winston of course for Borkum and the Baltic, Lloyd George for Salonika, to join in with the Serbians, and for Syria."

Churchill and Lloyd George were both seeking alternatives to the extraordinary situation that had developed in France. "All the wars of the world," Churchill wrote years later, "could show nothing to compare with the continuous front which had now been established. Ramparts more than 350 miles long, ceaselessly guarded by millions of men, sustained by thousands of cannon, stretched from the Swiss frontier to the North Sea." An anticipated war of movement had fast deteriorated into a series of slogging matches, their deadliness all the more horrifying for the atmosphere of futility that was beginning to arise around them: fifty thousand Englishmen had been killed or wounded at Ypres alone, defending a salient.

"I cannot pretend to have any military knowledge," Lloyd George wrote in his January 1 memorandum, recalling a visit to the front he had made in October and early November, "but the little I saw and gathered in France as to the military position, coupled with such reading on the subjects as I have been able to indulge in, convinced me that any attempt to force the carefully prepared German lines in the west would end in failure and in appalling loss of life, and I then expressed this view to my colleagues." Half a million new British troops were now in training, but would it really be of use to send them to the western front? Couldn't they be more effectively employed in some new area entirely?

Lloyd George had two operations in mind. One would be on the Balkan front. The Serbs were fighting the Austrians virtually alone, unaided by their old Greek and Rumanian allies—who were maintaining a precarious neutrality—and potentially threatened by the Bulgarians, who also were neutral but were still spoiling for revenge after the Second Balkan War. He proposed a British landing there, preferably at Salonika, which was in Greek hands. This, he reasoned, in addition to its direct military advantages, would bring in not only Greece and Rumania on the side of the Allies, but Italy as well.

The second operation he proposed—and he thought the two could be carried out simultaneously—involved "an attack upon Turkey." For a number of weeks there had been talk of a large Turkish force assembling in Syria and Palestine under the command of Djemal Pasha, the former minister of marine. There had been skirmishes on the Sinai frontier from the very beginning of the war with Turkey, but now a full-scale attack upon the Suez Canal was imminent. "I would let them entangle themselves in this venture," Lloyd George suggested, "and whilst they were engaged in attacking our forces on the Suez Canal, I would suggest that a force of 100,000 should be landed in Syria to cut them off." This, he argued, was not such a large force that the western front would be weakened by being deprived of it; furthermore, it would never have to be far from the sea, so that it would always be near its supplies, while Turkish supply lines would be attenuated. Such an operation would "give us the chance of winning a dramatic victory," he said, "which would encourage our people at home, whilst it would be a corresponding discouragement to our enemies." And he added that "it would be a great advantage from this point of view if it were in territory which appeals to the imagination of the people as a whole." Lloyd George did not explicitly mention Palestine, but it certainly was what he had in mind with these words.

No discussion of new theaters of operation or the redistribution of troops was possible, however, without the interested participation of Lord Kitchener, the all-powerful secretary for war. Kitchener, whom we last saw as a young subaltern surveying Palestine in the 1870s, had risen to the top of the military profession and to a peerage while serving almost exclusively in Asia and Africa. Having comported himself with valor on the unsuccessful mission to rescue General Charles Gordon from the Mahdi at Khartoum in 1885, he himself led the capture of that city in 1898, thereby achieving a reputation as a national hero that remained unsullied even through the Boer War, in which he served as commander in chief. From 1902 to 1909 he was commander in chief in India, and in 1911 had moved on to the post long coveted by him, that of British agent and consul general in Egypt, which Lord Cromer had run as a virtual autocracy. Kitchener, who, unlike Cromer, had some command of Arabic, had run it that way too, and had fully intended to go on doing so when the outbreak of war found him vacationing in England. Asquith had virtually snatched him off the boat that would have started him back to Egypt, and appointed him secretary for war with the promise that the Cairo post would again be his at the war's end. It seemed likely, then, that Kitchener would be sympathetic to the idea of a campaign in the Middle East.

The crucial prod in this direction came on January 2 from Russia. On that day Kitchener received from the Foreign Office a copy of a telegram sent by Sir George Buchanan, the British ambassador in Petrograd, which relayed an urgent appeal from the Russians. They wanted a British naval or military demonstration against Turkey to help alleviate the pressure on their troops in the Caucasus, where they were engaged in heavy fighting against the Turks. There was widespread fear that Russia would not be able to remain in the war, and Kitchener immediately acted upon this message in two ways. That same day, he wrote a letter to Sir John French, the commander in chief of the British Expeditionary Force in France, in which he said: "The feeling here is gaining ground that although it is essential to defend the line, troops over and above what is necessary for that service could be better employed elsewhere." Referring to the apparent stalemate in the West, he suggested that "the German lines in France may be looked upon as a fortress that cannot be carried by assault," so that it might be sufficient just to hold the line there while sending fresh troops somewhere that would be helpful to the Russians. Not surprisingly, French—who had already had his quarrels with Kitchener—reacted violently against the suggestion.

Kitchener's other move upon hearing of the Russians' distress was to contact Winston Churchill at the Admiralty, asking if a naval demonstration could not be held against the Turks at the Dardanelles. Churchill had been an advocate of some action directly aimed at Turkey from the moment that country took up hostilities. One of his ships had bombarded the Dardanelles even before Britain's declaration of war, and it was he who had proposed the attack on Haifa that had been discussed at the first meeting of the newly organized War Council on November 25. He had also proposed a Dardanelles attack at that meeting. More recently, under the influence of his colleagues at the Admiralty, his vision of some major operation to the East had focused itself on the North and Baltic seas, and in these first days of 1915 he was preoccupied with the possibilities of landings at the German island of Borkum and at Zeebrugge on the Belgian coast. But the idea of a Dardanelles campaign had never faded for him; only two days before, on December 31, when he read another proposal for a campaign against Turkey that had been written by Colonel Sir Maurice Hankey, secretary to the War Council, Churchill had told Asquith: "I wanted Gallipoli attacked on the Turkish declaration of war."

Nevertheless, when Kitchener came to him with the idea, Churchill hesitated. A "mere demonstration" was hardly what he had always had in mind. There was a real possibility of being able to force the Dardanelles one day, of bringing British ships right up to Constantinople, and the effect of a limited demonstration would only be to stir up defenses there to the detriment of any such future attempt. But Churchill doubted whether the straits could be forced by a naval assault alone, and he asked Kitchener if troops could not be found to help in the operation. Kitchener did not think so, but he went back to the War Office to discuss the matter with his aides. Later that same day he wrote to Churchill saying, "I do not see that we can do anything that will very seriously help the Russians in the Caucasus," and adding emphatically: "We have no troops to land anywhere." He also gave his view that Lloyd George's proposed landing on the "coast of Syria would have no effect," and ended by reiterating: "The only place that a demonstration might have some effect in stopping reinforcements going East would be the Dardanelles. Particularly if . . . reports could be spread at the same time that Constantinople was threatened."

This was inevitably not to be the end of it, however: the idea of a new opening in the East was now in the air, and it carried the exhilarating whiff of some fresh start in a war that was otherwise stagnating. On January 3, Churchill's rambunctious septuagenarian colleague, Lord Fisher—only second in command at the Admiralty, but always mindful of the fact that he had been first sea lord before Churchill ever got there—came in with an elaborate, eight-point plan of attack upon Turkey. It was too vast to be practical, but Churchill, now roused by the Dardanelles idea, wired Vice-Admiral Sackville

Carden, the commander in the eastern Mediterranean, asking for his views on the matter. Carden replied on January 5, saying he thought the Dardanelles "might be forced by extended operations with large number of ships"—in other words, by a purely naval assault. The astonished Churchill presented Carden's telegram at the War Council meeting that afternoon, while also expressing his continuing advocacy of an operation in the North Sea. Kitchener continued to press for action in the Dardanelles, and Churchill, spurred by the growing interest in the idea among his Admiralty colleagues, wired Carden asking for a detailed exposition of his views.

Carden's reply came on January 12; it was a fully wrought plan of attack that envisioned penetration by the fleet into the Sea of Marmara within a month after the operation had begun. It "produced a great impression upon every one who saw it," according to Churchill, who sent copies to Asquith and Kitchener. He presented it to the War Council the following afternoon, declaring that once the forts in the Dardanelles had been reduced and the mine fields cleared, "the Fleet would proceed up to Constantinople and destroy the *Goeben*." The idea was greeted, according to Hankey, with "tremendous enthusiasm." Lloyd George, who until now had been advocating his own plan against Kitchener's opposition, said he liked this one. Balfour undoubtedly shared in the enthusiasm of this moment, for he was to become one of the most outspoken supporters in the War Council of a purely naval assault. As for Kitchener, with striking understatement he said he "thought it was worth trying," and added that if the bombardment did not work the whole thing could be called off.

Churchill accordingly sent Carden a telegram early in the morning of January 15, instructing him to make preparations for an attack upon the Dardanelles.

It was on the fifteenth that Chaim Weizmann was to have his long-awaited meeting with Lloyd George, but he had remained busy in the meantime. On Christmas Day he had paid another visit to Herbert Samuel, this time at the latter's home and in the company of Dr. Moses Gaster—who, upon hearing of Weizmann's first meeting with Samuel, had been most eager to arrange this one for all three of them. Weizmann and Gaster gave Samuel "a brief *aperçu* of the Zionist movement," and assured him that although, "in view of the atomized state of Jewry," there was "a grave danger that all sorts of local and self-appointed bodies may flood him or the Foreign Office with projects and memoranda," they themselves spoke "on behalf of an international Zionist organization and of a great hinterland of sympathizers, who might not be formally Zionists." They said they would try to present him with their credentials when the time came.

Samuel made it quite clear "that the British Government would not look at any proposal which did not emanate from and was not backed by international Jewry." When Weizmann mentioned that he was leaving for Paris the next day to see Baron Edmond de Rothschild—he explained the baron's activities on behalf of the Palestine settlements—Samuel asked to have a report of the interview and urged that they "should try and create a representative instrument which would be sufficiently strong to negotiate when the time came." Samuel had doubtless become fully aware of the disrupted state of world Zionism, and he also clearly had little faith in the authority of the English Zionist Federation as it was then constituted. The fact that it had thrown over his friend Gaster a few years before also probably did not help to redeem it in his eyes. He was in effect appointing Gaster and Weizmann to start anew in organizing an authoritative consensus among world Jewry for the purpose at hand—a Zionist body politic, as it were, with which the British Government could treat when the time came. There was more of one still in existence than he realized, as a matter of fact; but he was right in perceiving that for the moment it was without valid leadership.

Samuel went on to assure them that Sir Edward Grey was "interested in the project, especially from the point of view of creating a Jewish cultural center, a 'Nidus' as Sir Edward called it, which would reflect glory not only on the Jews, but on the whole world; a sort of a generating station which would set into motion all that is best in Israel." The three men then discussed the various political possibilities for Palestine in a postwar settlement, and Gaster and Weizmann expressed their opinion that a British protectorate—such as had at last been officially established in Egypt a week before—was the most desirable; in this way, the Jewish community there could develop and grow at a reasonable pace. The two Zionists knew perfectly well what Samuel was only beginning to realize: that 85,000 or so Jews (a number that had furthermore been depleted since the start of the war) were far from ready to establish a state of their own in a country also populated by more than 500,000 Arabs. What they wanted was a protecting power that would preside over the immigration and consolidation required to make such a state a possibility in the future.

Baron Edmond de Rothschild expressed concern over precisely this point when Weizmann saw him in the rue Laffitte on Monday,

December 28. "The whole thing has come to us 5 or 10 years too soon," the tall, slim, white-bearded baron said. "When I created my colonies in Palestine I had in view that a time might come when the fate of Palestine could be in the balance, and I desired that the world should have to reckon with the Jews there at such a time. We did a good deal in the last 10/15 years; we meant to do still more in the years to come; the present crisis caught us in the middle of our activities; still one has to reckon with the facts and now we have to use the opportunity which will probably never return again."

The baron, who had acknowledged the value of the Zionists' achievement to Weizmann when they last had met, was now clearly ready to lend them his discreet support without joining them—as his son James and daughter-in-law Dorothy already were doing. He advised discretion to Weizmann and his colleagues as well, suggesting that they "work at present through a very small committee" without broadcasting their plans; they should try to find out exactly what the British Government wanted them to do, and not enter the public arena until their plans were "fully matured." He also urged them to leave Claude Montefiore and other prominent English Jews "entirely out of calculation, as they are of no value, being themselves shaken in their position." He maintained that the Zionists were the only body capable of dealing with the present situation and that the work of the moment should be carried out by the Zionist executive. "When the time comes to act publicly," he said, "the Zionists could without difficulty find valuable support amongst Jews, who, although not identified with Zionism at present, are fully sympathetic of this cause, like his own son, his daughter-in-law, [Henry] Morgenthau, etc. They would form a valuable committee and the Zionist Executive would be embraced in this Committee." He also thought that "American Jewry would certainly lend its support" and said he would take open action himself "when the diplomatic situation and relation between France and England concerning Palestine is cleared up. He thought that Herzl's idea of a Charter might be taken up now."

Weizmann returned to London the next day exuberant over this interview, which had taken up five hours during two sessions that morning and afternoon. In London he stayed on to receive the two members of the Zionist executive, Nahum Sokolow and Yehiel Tschlenow, who arrived from Copenhagen at last on December 31. They planned to travel on as soon as possible to the United States, where they were to take part in a campaign to mobilize American Jewry for the Zionist cause; Weizmann even thought of going over, too, though the baron and others were advising him against it. But in the meantime, Sokolow was familiar enough with London to resume some of the diplomatic work he had left off doing nearly two years before. As for Tschlenow, a fifty-one-year-old physician, he had been one of the foremost leaders of the Zionist movement in Russia; indeed, the question remained whether he would not be of more value if he returned there.

The two new arrivals established themselves in the boarding-house in which Sokolow had stayed during his previous visits, on Sutherland Avenue in Maida Vale, and Weizmann left them and returned to Manchester on Monday, January 4. There he composed for their benefit a long report on his activities since the beginning of the war, which he sent them on the seventh.

The three of them had arranged to meet with Herbert Samuel, but before this meeting occurred Weizmann got to meet Lloyd George. On Monday, January 11, Samuel wrote Weizmann a letter saying: "Mr. Lloyd George, whom I have seen today, would be very glad if you could breakfast with him next Friday. I should be there also, and we should have a good opportunity of discussing the matter in which we are both interested." Weizmann wasted no time in notifying Samuel of his acceptance, and he also sought the advice of C.P. Scott, whom he had just seen on Sunday. "You will probably find," Scott wrote to him on Thursday about Lloyd George,

that he will take the lead in the conversation and put questions to you which will give you plenty of openings. . . . He will, I am sure, be much interested in your view of the Jews of Judaea as a possible link between East and West . . . and as a channel of ideas and of enterprise in the Arabian Peninsula. But no doubt he will want to discuss with you much more concrete matters than those—the present strength of the Jewish element in Palestine and the possibility of its rapid expansion; its relation to the local Arab population which so greatly outnumbers it; the potential value of Palestine as a "buffer-State" and the means of evading for ourselves an undesirable extension of military responsibility; the best way of allaying Catholic and Orthodox jealousy in regard to the custody of the Holy Places—and the like.

We may assume, then, that these matters and more were discussed during the breakfast meeting between Lloyd George, Weizmann, and Samuel that began at 9:15 in the morning that Friday,

January 15, at 11 Downing Street. Unfortunately, the only description we have of it is the hazy recollection Weizmann set down decades later in his autobiography. Though the facts are garbled, one may still feel quite confident about the impressions.

"I was terribly shy and suffered from suppressed excitement," Weizmann writes, "knowing how much depended on this meeting. At first I remained a passive listener. They talked about the war in a way that seemed to me extraordinarily flippant. I was very, very serious minded, did not quite appreciate English humor, and did not understand at first that behind this seeming flippancy there was a deadly seriousness. Lloyd George began to fire questions at me, about Palestine, about our colonies there, about the number of Jews in the country and the number who could go there. I answered as best I could." Weizmann adds that Dorothy de Rothschild later reported that Lloyd George had said to her of this meeting: "When Dr. Weizmann was talking of Palestine he kept bringing up place names which were more familiar to me than those on the Western Front."

We may also assume that, at this breakfast meeting of January 15, Herbert Samuel at least summarized the draft memorandum on Palestine that he had been working on since his discussion of the subject with Sir Edward Grey on November 9. He may not have finished it yet, but he was to submit a completed draft only a week later for Grey's approval before circulating it among the cabinet. If we read this draft of a week later, we may have a reasonable sense of the spirit of Samuel's remarks to Lloyd George and Weizmann that morning.

"The course of events," it began somewhat dithyrambically (to borrow Asquith's term for it),

> opens a prospect of a change, at the end of the war, in the status of Palestine. Already there is a stirring among the twelve million Jews scattered throughout the countries of the world. A feeling is spreading with great rapidity that now, at last, some advance may be made, in some way, towards the fulfillment of the hope and desire, held with unshakable tenacity for eighteen hundred years, for the restoration of the Jews to the land to which they are attached by ties almost as ancient as history itself.

This, so far, was still the Samuel of November and December speaking; but in the meantime he had also learned some prudence—from Weizmann, among other people. "Yet it is felt," he went on,

that the time is not ripe for the establishment there of an independent, autonomous Jewish State. Such increase of population
as there has been in Palestine in recent years has been composed, indeed, mostly of Jewish immigrants; the new Jewish
agricultural colonies already number about 15,000 souls; in Jerusalem itself two-thirds of the inhabitants are Jews; but in the
country, as a whole, they still probably do not number more than
about one-sixth of the population.

Under these circumstances, it was not likely that a Jewish government in Palestine, "even if established by the authority of the
Powers, would be able to command obedience. The dream of a Jewish State, prosperous, progressive, and the home of a brilliant civilization, might vanish in a series of squalid conflicts with the Arab
population." The country would thereby also find itself defenseless
against external aggression. "To attempt to realize the aspiration of
a Jewish State one century too soon," Samuel concluded, "might
throw back its actual realization for many centuries more."
    What was to be done, then? For his answer, Samuel now had
men like Weizmann and Gaster enlisted in support of his own inclinations. "I am assured," he went on, "that the solution of the
problem of Palestine which would be much the most welcome to the
leaders and supporters of the Zionist movement throughout the
world would be the annexation of the country to the British Empire." He believed that this solution would also be welcome to non-
Zionist Jews. Under British rule, he hoped, "facilities would be given
to Jewish organizations to purchase land, to found colonies, to establish educational and religious institutions, and to spend usefully the
funds that would be freely contributed for promoting the economic
development of the country." He also hoped that Jewish immigration, "carefully regulated, would be given preference so that in the
course of time the Jewish people, grown into a majority and settled
in the land, may be conceded such degree of self-government as the
conditions of that day may justify." Samuel made special provision,
however, for the Christian and Muslim Holy Places; for the former
he proposed an extraterritorial regime controlled by an international commission, and for the latter, Muslim representation on the
British governor's council.
    Samuel then spelled out five specific arguments in favor of his
policy from the standpoint of British interests. First, it would "enable England to fulfill in yet another sphere her historic part of
civilizer of the backward countries. Under the Turk, Palestine has

been blighted. For hundreds of years she has produced neither men nor things useful to the world. Her native population is sunk in squalor. Roads, harbors, irrigation, sanitation, are neglected." Almost the only signs of vitality were in the Jewish colonies, as well as in the small number of German Protestant colonies that had been founded in the middle of the nineteenth century. Corruption and extortion were rife among the Turkish administrators. But under British administration,

> all this will be quickly changed. The country will be redeemed. What has been done in Egypt will be repeated here, and the knowledge of this would make many of the present inhabitants not merely acquiesce, but rejoice, in the change. The British Agent in Egypt recently reported (on the 7th January) that the information of the Intelligence Department there indicated that a large proportion of the population would welcome a British occupation. There have been many previous indications of the same feeling.

A second argument was that, though the British Empire had "little addition to its greatness left to win," the inclusion in it of Palestine, which "bulks so large in the world's imagination," would "add a luster even to the British Crown." Mentioning the widespread and deep-rooted sympathy in the Protestant world "with the idea of restoring the Hebrew people to the land which was to be their inheritance," Samuel concluded that there was "probably no outcome of the war which would give greater satisfaction to powerful sections of British opinion." Furthermore—and this was the third argument—in a war in which France sought to regain Alsace-Lorraine and had designs upon Syria as well, and in which Russia had ambitions involving not only the Caucasus but Constantinople itself, was not England entitled to something too? "Although Great Britain did not enter the conflict with any purpose of territorial expansion," Samuel wrote, "being in it and having made immense sacrifices, there would be profound disappointment in the country if the outcome were to be the securing of great advantages by our allies, and none by ourselves." The German colonies in Africa were possible territories for acquisition by the British, but Samuel was insistent that, for the sake of good feeling after the war, the Germans should be allowed to keep these. A more lasting peace would be achieved if Britain confined her claims to Mesopotamia and Palestine.

Samuel's fourth argument was on strategic grounds. "The belt of desert to the east of the Suez Canal is an admirable strategic frontier for Egypt," he conceded, but only so long as the enemy were a relatively weak power such as Turkey; "it would be an inadequate defense if a great European Power were established on the further side." He did not name the power, but he of course meant France, which was already making claims on all of Syria, and which usually had been considered England's traditional enemy prior to 1914. To be sure, the French would be in the Lebanon in any case, but the mountainous terrain of northern Palestine would form a more defensible frontier against them than the Sinai would. "A common frontier with a European neighbor in the Lebanon is a far smaller risk to the vital interests of the British Empire than a common frontier at El Arish."

Finally, Samuel argued as he had to Sir Edward Grey that this policy "would win for England the lasting gratitude of the Jews throughout the world." Mentioning the 2 million Jews of the United States in particular—who were a matter of growing concern in England, where it was thought that the pro-German and anti-Russian sentiments among them were significantly influencing the attitudes of neutral America toward the war—he stressed that "they would form a body of opinion whose bias, where the interest of the country of which they were citizens was not involved, would be favorable to the British Empire." This "devoted gratitude of a whole race," he pointed out, "in time to come, may not be without its value."

Samuel concluded his paper by reviewing some of the alternatives to British control for Palestine. First was the one that Sir Edward Grey and other colleagues in the Government still thought to be almost unavoidable: annexation by France. Samuel criticized this alternative by pointing out that, though French interests were considerable in northern Syria, in Palestine they were small. Indeed, France hardly had any commercial interests there outside of the railway line from Jaffa to Jerusalem—and that, Samuel hastened to remark, "could doubtless be bought out for no large sum." There were a few French monastic establishments in Palestine, but not many French residents outside of them. Samuel again cited the January 7 report of the British agent in Egypt, this time to the effect that the French would be unwelcome to the Palestine population; they "would certainly be unwelcome to the Jews"—as he knew from the vehemently anti-French arguments of Weizmann and others. "If, as the outcome of the war," he argued, "France recovers Alsace and Lorraine, and obtains the greater part of Syria, including

Beirout and Damascus, she ought not to grudge to Great Britain Mesopotamia and Palestine." As for her ancient protection of Catholics in the country, France could maintain this through leadership of the international commission proposed for the Holy Places.

Another alternative was international control, but Samuel feared that this would not only be chaotic, it would also "prove to be a stepping-stone to a German protectorate." Germany already "has been very active in Palestine," he pointed out. "She has spent considerable sums of money there with a view to increasing her influence. She has founded a bank, agricultural colonies, schools, hospitals." Samuel doubtless knew by now about the language controversy of only a year before. "In twenty years' time Egypt's neighbor," he put it pointedly, "ostensibly internationalized, may have become so permeated by German influence as to furnish a strong case for German control."

After quickly disposing of two other possible alternatives— annexation to Egypt and continuing control by a reformed and pro-Zionist Turkish administration—as more difficult than they were worth, Samuel moved on to his summing up. His proposal, he stressed, would not solve the Jewish question in Europe. "A country the size of Wales, much of it barren mountain and part of it waterless, cannot hold 9,000,000 people. But it could probably hold in time 3,000,000 or 4,000,000, and some relief would be given to the pressure in Russia and elsewhere." Rather, the main advantage was

> the effect upon the character of the larger part of the Jewish race who must still remain intermingled with other peoples, to be a strength or to be a weakness to the countries in which they live. Let a Jewish center be established in Palestine; let it achieve as I believe it would achieve, a spiritual and intellectual greatness; and insensibly, but inevitably, the character of the individual Jew, wherever he might be, would be ennobled. The sordid associations which have attached to the Jewish name would be sloughed off, and the value of the Jews as an element in the civilization of the European peoples would be enhanced.

And Samuel concluded this lyrical peroration with the words Thomas Babington Macaulay had uttered in the House of Commons during the long struggle to enable Lionel de Rothschild to take the seat to which he had been duly elected: "Let us not presume to say that there is no genius among the countrymen of Isaiah, no heroism among the descendants of the Maccabees." It was a remark from the era of Disraeli being reechoed by a man who had once, upon becoming a Liberal in his youth, pointedly removed a portrait of the great Tory prime minister from the place where it had hung over his bed during his childhood years: had something of it engraved itself upon his soul after all?

The present Liberal prime minister would have thought so at any rate. "I have just received from Herbert Samuel a memorandum headed 'The Future of Palestine,'" Herbert Henry Asquith wrote on January 28.

> He goes on to argue, at considerable length and with some vehemence, in favor of the British annexation of Palestine, a country the size of Wales, much of it barren mountain and part of it waterless. He thinks we might plant in this not very promising territory about three or four million European Jews, and that this would have a good effect upon those who are left behind. It reads almost like a new edition of "Tancred" brought up to date. I confess I am not attracted by this proposed addition to our responsibilities, but it is a curious illustration of Dizzy's favorite maxim that "race is everything" to find this almost lyrical outburst proceeding from the well-ordered and methodical brain of H.S.

Samuel must have received some criticism to this effect, for he then proceeded to compose a second draft that would be less lyrical, more well-ordered and methodical.

·10·

ISRAEL IN EGYPT

The Palestine Jewish community whose future was being planned by Herbert Samuel had suffered considerable distress since the outbreak of the war. Its troubles had begun as far back as August, for the Jews of Palestine were particularly dependent upon the financial and commercial lines with Europe that were then suddenly cut off. This dependency was shared equally by the old type of settler—mostly the pious communicants in Jerusalem and the other cities holy to Judaism who lived on the *Halukkah*, the charitable donations from abroad—and the new, mainly those in the agricultural colonies, which derived much of their income from export.

"The months of August and September are the normal period for the ingathering of the staple products of Palestine," David Levontin, managing director of the Anglo-Palestine Company in Jaffa, told an interviewer at the beginning of October. "Last year the almond crop was valued at 600,000 francs [$120,000, at the prewar exchange rate of 5 francs to the dollar]. The value of the wine crop fluctuates from 800,000 to a million francs. Half a million boxes of oranges valued at 1½ million francs are normally prepared for export. The outbreak of war paralyzed everything. The price offered for almonds fell from 3 francs per kilo to 1 franc 15 centimes. This would have meant a loss of 400,000 francs. Freight for oranges became practically unobtainable. Checks drawn in advance for wine export were unpresentable, and the negotiation of bills became practically an impossibility." The Anglo-Palestine Company resorted to emergency financial measures, but an urgent appeal for help was issued to the Jews of neutral countries—that is to say, mainly of the United States of America.

Henry Morgenthau received the appeal in Constantinople and

responded with characteristic energy. A Jew himself, Morgenthau had been so enthusiastic about the Palestine settlements when he visited them in the spring of 1914 that many people mistakenly thought he was a Zionist. He now gave reinforcement to that belief by making contact with two other eminent non-Zionist Jews back in New York, the philanthropists Nathan Straus and Jacob Schiff, and through them, with the American-Jewish relief organizations that had been established at the onset of war in Europe. They, too, acted with speed, and by the middle of September the cruiser *North Carolina*—President Wilson heartily endorsed such philanthropies—was on its way to Palestine with $50,000 in gold on board. Ambassador Morgenthau sent his son-in-law, Maurice Wertheim, who had been visiting him in Constantinople, to meet the ship en route.

"On the morning of the 24th September," a correspondent wrote to London, "a large American cruiser anchored off Jaffa. The political troubles—rumors of war between Turkey and England—brought thousands of spectators to the shore. All were eager to know whether the warship had come to take away American citizens from Jaffa. A boat was lowered and made for the shore. And what a surprise! Mr. Wertheim, the Ambassador's son-in-law, accompanied by the sailors, brought ashore four bags of gold containing £10,000. This large sum was conveyed by the sailors to the Jewish bank."

The relief thus provided turned out to be short-lived, however, particularly under the even graver conditions that arose after Turkey's entry into the war. Some fifty thousand of the Jews in Palestine were still technically Russian subjects and, therefore, enemy aliens. Djemal Pasha, upon becoming military commander in chief in Syria and Palestine—and hence virtual dictator in the area—announced that all enemy aliens would have to become Ottoman subjects or leave the country. The tiny number who still had British certificates of protection—that Palmerstonian policy had lasted until 1890—made preparations to depart for Egypt, but the vast majority faced repatriation to Russia, a prospect few of them could consider. The Zionist leadership in the country decided that "Ottomanization" was the only viable course, even though that too had its dangers, and proceeded both to negotiate with the Turks for facilitating it and to propagandize for it among their coreligionists. Then disaster struck in another form.

On Tuesday, December 15, the American cruiser *Tennessee* entered Turkish waters off Jaffa, and the authorities on shore thought it was Russian. All non-Muslim residents of the city were promptly ordered to remain in their homes under pain of death, and a large force of Bedouin policemen was supplied with guns to enforce the ruling. Then, when the ship departed on Thursday, a roundup was held among the Jews of Jaffa.

Men, women, and children were broken in upon, often roused from their beds, allowed to pack only a few of their belongings, and herded at gunpoint to the harbor. There they were awaited by an Italian ship that had been engaged to take them to Alexandria. The cost of it was defrayed by the women's jewelry, which was brusquely confiscated by the Turkish officials; but the now homeless Jews also had to reach into their pockets to pay for the Arab boatmen to take them to the ship—for Jaffa was an anchorage rather than a true harbor, and large vessels always remained some distance from the shore. "At the harbor that evening," according to the stunned Zionist leader Arthur Ruppin, who was spared this particular misfortune by dint of being a German citizen, "I had to watch whole families with their hurriedly collected belongings—old people, mothers with babies—being driven on to the boats in infinite disorder." In some cases, parents and children were separated, and there were also incidents aboard the boats when a few of their proprietors used threats and violence to extort still more money and goods from the hapless passengers.

By the end of the month, some eight hundred Jewish refugees had reached Alexandria from Palestine, and still more were on the way. "Although these expulsions are no worse than the things being done by all the European nations now at war," wrote the fair-minded Ruppin in his diary, "and they may even be carried out with greater moderation and more decency, the authorities here are particularly incompetent, and this causes much hardship and anger. Moreover, we are now losing within a few days more people than we gained during years of immigration, and who knows what else the immediate future may hold?" On January 18, he had to record that "nearly 4,000 Russian, French and English Jews who did not want to become naturalized have been forced to leave Palestine," and the expulsions were still not at an end.

By then it had become clear that what was afoot was a systematic campaign against Zionism, instigated mainly by Djemal Pasha's cousin, Beha ad-Din, a former specialist in Palestine Jewish affairs for the Ministry of the Interior and governor of Jaffa at the time of the first expulsions in December. In mid-January, Beha ad-Din was dismissed from the governorship after an inquiry held upon the urging of Ambassador Morgenthau, but he was then simply kicked upstairs and appointed an adjutant and political adviser on his powerful cousin's staff. The result was an application of Beha ad-Din's anti-Zionist policies to all of Palestine and not just the Jaffa district. This was reflected in mid-January by an announcement forcibly published in the Hebrew newspaper *Herut* (*Freedom*) of Jerusalem:

> The Government—in opposing the acts of those elements which, through intrigues, are trying to create in the Palestinian region of the Ottoman Empire a Jewish state under the name of Zionism and who are thus harming the sons of their own race—has ordered the confiscation of the postage stamps, Zionist flags, paper money, bank notes of the Anglo-Palestine Company, Ltd. in the form of checks which are spread among these elements and has decreed the dissolution of all the clandestine Zionist societies and organizations.

This meant the removal from circulation of the emergency bank notes that had been issued to save the Jews of Palestine from destitution.

Although the number of refugees in Alexandria had reached nine thousand by the end of January, little was known outside Palestine itself of the specifically anti-Zionist turn that Turkish policy had taken there. Even Morgenthau's information was hazy for a time, for the American consul in Jerusalem, Otis A. Glazebrook, did not want to antagonize the Turks by giving detailed reports. The only solid information was being obtained at that moment by Captain Decker of the *Tennessee*—the ship that had unwittingly touched off the whole situation and that was now shuttling back and forth between Jaffa and Alexandria, providing free transportation for the refugees. Decker was interviewing Zionist spokesmen such as Arthur Ruppin in Jaffa as well as the refugees themselves and was compiling a report on the situation for official American use.

As for the British press, its poor state of knowledge on the internal Jewish situation in Palestine was dramatized in the February 5 number of the *Jewish Chronicle*, which had been covering the refugee situation in considerable detail. Quoting a *Daily News* correspondent to the effect that "the refugees think that recent articles in the London Press on Jewish nationalist aspirations are the main cause of Turkish persecution," the *Jewish Chronicle* writer went on to say:

> Further statements from the same correspondent appeared in the *Daily News* of Tuesday last, giving, on the authority of M.

Vladimir Jabotinsky, a well-known Russian Zionist, an alarming account of the state of affairs in Palestine. M. Jabotinsky, who is in Alexandria, appears to have derived his information from refugees there and to have made disquieting statements concerning Zionist institutions in Palestine. But on enquiry in authoritative quarters we are informed that the report is unfounded.

It was late in December 1914 that Vladimir Jabotinsky, a roving correspondent for the Moscow liberal daily *Russkiye Vyedomosti* (*Russian Journal*), had arrived in Alexandria from Italy after having made his way through Sweden, England, France, Spain, Italy, and much of North Africa since the beginning of the war. He was to recall years afterward how the British customs official, fumbling with his Russian passport, trying to ferret out from the jumble of thirty-odd visas his permit to land in Egypt, had turned to an officer and said: "A few days ago a boatful of Zionists, almost a thousand of them, arrived from Jaffa—the Turks kicked them out of Palestine."

This was an appropriate confluence of destinies for a man who had been both a journalist and a Zionist for most of his adult life, and who had, after an initial feeling of indifference about the outcome of the war that broke out in Europe that summer, begun to feel the proddings of a personal mission once Turkey entered it. But then, Vladimir Jabotinsky had an appetite for destiny and a gift for going out and discovering its confluences when they did not come to him. Born in Odessa in 1880, he had in full measure the particular quality of romantic daring that heaven seems to have reserved for Jews of his generation who were nurtured in and around that city.*
At the age of eighteen, he had gone to Switzerland and then Italy to study law, and in Rome he earned his living as correspondent for two Odessa dailies, writing under the whimsical pen name "*Altalena*" ("Seesaw," in Italian). In 1901, he returned home and joined the staff of the *Odesskiye Novosti* (*Odessa News*), for which he wrote daily feuilletons that became quite popular, and it was there that he became a Zionist two years later. Aroused by the threat of a pogrom in Odessa, he had joined a Jewish defense organization in the spring of 1903, and then when the disaster struck not in Odessa but in Kishinev, he had responded by discovering a fierce ardor of Jewish nationalism within himself.

Jabotinsky, who had learned a little Hebrew in childhood and hardly any Yiddish at all, was thus a rare phenomenon among

---

* Others who come to mind are Trotsky and Isaac Babel.

Russian-Jewish Zionists: an utterly *Russian* intellectual, a cosmopolitan—for the Jewish life of Odessa was more like that of Vienna than of Pinsk—who had come upon his sense of peoplehood mainly in reaction to anti-Semitism. In this respect—and in others as well—he resembled Herzl, whom he passionately admired, and Nordau, with whom he formed a lasting friendship. As far as Chaim Weizmann was concerned, "Jabotinsky, the passionate Zionist, was utterly un-Jewish in manner, approach and deportment. He came from Odessa, Ahad Ha'am's home town, but the inner life of Jewry had left no trace on him. When I became intimate with him in later years, I observed at closer hand what seemed to be a confirmation of this dual streak; he was rather ugly, immensely attractive, well spoken, warmhearted, generous, always ready to help a comrade in distress; all of these qualities were, however, overlaid with a certain touch of the rather theatrically chivalresque, a certain queer and irrelevant knightliness, which was not at all Jewish."

This judgment, though written in an era when Weizmann could no longer talk about Jabotinsky without becoming testy, was essentially correct. There was, in fact, something Mediterranean in the personality of this man who had grown up in Russia's epitome of a sunny southern port and spent part of his young manhood in Italy: this was perhaps why, when he went to Constantinople in 1909 to be the editor there of four Zionist periodicals—two in French, one in Hebrew, and one in Ladino—he experienced what was to be a lifelong admiration for the Sephardic Jews, whose natural, seemingly aristocratic grace struck him as a quality that had been bestowed upon very few of his fellow Ashkenazim. There was something of the spirit of Disraeli in him.

His experience of Constantinople in the first flush of *hurriyeh* ("freedom") had not caused him to share Disraeli's fondness for Turks, however. "The Young Turks then ruled the Sublime Porte," he was to write, "and there and then I reached the steadfast conviction that where the Turk rules neither sun may shine nor grass may grow, and that the only hope for the restoration of Palestine lay in the dismemberment of the Ottoman Empire." This was why Turkey's entry into the war had awoken new feelings within him. It was on a wet November morning in Bordeaux, he later recalled, that "I read in a poster pasted on a wall that Turkey had joined the Central Powers and begun military operations." Until that moment, he realized, he "had been a mere observer, without any particular reasons for wishing full triumph to one side and crushing disaster to the other. My desire at that time was: stalemate, and peace as soon as possible. Turkey's move transformed me in one short morning into a fanatical believer in war until victory; Turkey's move made this war 'my war.' "

After a brief visit with Max Nordau in Madrid—Hungarian-born correspondent for a Berlin newspaper, Nordau had been expelled from France as an enemy alien—Jabotinsky visited Morocco, Algiers, and Tunis in the course of a new journalistic inquiry occasioned by the Turkish presence in the war. On November 23, the sultan had finally issued the call for *jihad* to the entire Muslim world, and Jabotinsky wanted to investigate the response in the countries of the Maghreb. In fact, there had been scarcely a response to the call anywhere; and Jabotinsky, seeking the reason for this, found that Muslims would not tell him but Sephardic Jewish merchants would.

"The appeal to a Holy War? Nonsense," they told him. "Ridiculous even to ask. Only you naïve Europeans still believe that it is possible to raise masses in the Orient in the name of Islamic solidarity and make them accept any serious risks. The Turks themselves don't believe it: for the last hundred years Europe has been inflicting on them defeat after defeat, stripping them of their best provinces one after another, yet not one single Muslim people has budged an inch during all this time to help the Sultan—even though they call him 'Caliph of all the Muslims.' The Germans, who are just as naïve as all other Europeans, have persuaded the Turks to try once more. It is hopeless: not a soul here will lift a finger to help the Turks."

Now convinced that the days of the Ottoman Empire were numbered, Jabotinsky arrived with heightened expectations in Alexandria, where he was all the more aroused by the "lively Zionist atmosphere" that had grown there. The refugees, who had at first been herded into the Hotel Metropole, commandeered for the purpose, were gradually being transferred from that "stuffy unattractive building which sounded finer than it really was" to more ample quarters. Emile Cattaui, a member of one of Egypt's most ancient and eminent Jewish families, donated a cinema that he owned, and four hundred refugees made it their home. With the help of members of the large contingent of Australian Expeditionary Force soldiers that had recently arrived in Egypt, twelve hundred more were eventually resettled in the Gabbari military barracks outside of town. Sheds to accommodate still more were built on the outskirts of town. All this was done under the direct auspices of the British authorities, aided by local volunteers. "A special department was created for the affairs of the refugees," Jabotinsky observed, "with a fine, friendly Englishman, Mr. Hornblower, in charge."

Jabotinsky worked as a volunteer for several weeks at the Gabbari barracks. Three hundred of the refugees there were Sephardim, he later recalled, and there consequently were "two kitchens, an Ashkenazic and a Sephardic (at first there had been only one, but the Sephardim rebelled because they could not tolerate Ashkenazic food, especially the soup). We also had a Hebrew school and a chemist, and were altogether a completely independent community, having even a regiment of watchmen." He was particularly impressed by a group of students from the Herzliya School in Tel Aviv, who would refuse even to take medicine if the chemist did not speak to them in Hebrew. After a few weeks, they "organized a football club and won a match against the scouts of Alexandria."

Young men like these helped arouse anew in him an idea that he had been harboring almost from that moment in Bordeaux when he learned of Turkey's entry into the war. On November 5 he had written a letter to a Zionist colleague in Russia in which he suggested that a Jewish unit ought to be formed under the auspices of the British army—or even of the British and French armies together—for the purpose of fighting the Turks and taking part in the conquest of Palestine. He had discussed the idea with Nordau, who was disappointingly skeptical: where would you get the soldiers? he had asked. "English, French, Russian Jews were serving in their respective armies; in the neutral countries in Europe there were few Jews; America was far away; and besides, Jews nourished some foolish sentimental predilection for the Turk, 'our cousin Ishmael.'"

This had no doubt discouraged Jabotinsky—but now, the answer to all those objections was before his eyes, here in the Gabbari barracks. What army would these people be both willing and eligible to serve in but a Jewish one? They would certainly not serve in the Russian army, and the British army did not accept foreigners. But who in the world would be more determined fighters against the Turks than these particular Jews? Jabotinsky saw in them the material to bring his idea to life; and the occasion for doing so was about to present itself as well.

The British had known since November that Djemal Pasha was preparing a part of his Fourth Army for an attack on the Suez Canal and that his Arab troops were being trained by German officers under the supervision of the Bavarian colonel Kress von Kressenstein. The Reverend Canon Carnegie Brown, among others, had returned to England that month from missionary work in Jerusalem and reported that the city was "an armed camp, dominated by the Kaiser's officers." This initial surge of mobilization had then slowed down, but the pace was renewed in late December—every step of the way being watched by British reconnaissance planes and intelligence observers and reported not only along official channels but in bold headlines in the daily press. "Up to December 18," *The Times* reported on New Year's Day, "there were no more than 10,000 troops in Southern Palestine. The arrival of a German General [Kress had thus been promoted by the Cairo correspondent] with 30,000 soldiers was expected that day, but not more than 3,000 troops actually arrived. These were to be followed by General Kress von Kressenstein with a large German staff and automobiles."

There was at this time a tendency in British public opinion to regard the Turks not only as poor soldiers but even as something of a joke as military opponents. They had done poorly in their recent wars against Italy and the Balkan countries, and Britain's Indian troops had just handled them with seeming ease in the Shatt-al-Arab, taking Basra on November 22 and Kurna on December 9. Their inefficiency as administrators was notorious, and for the Anglo-Saxon sensibility this enhanced a popular image of feckless desert pietists wandering lost in the sandstorms of the twentieth century. "On December 19," *The Times* reported of the scene in Jerusalem with ill-suppressed irony,

> the Holy Banner arrived from Medina, escorted by a camel corps. The banner proved to be not the Prophet's standard, but a new banner, presumably mounted on an ancient staff. The aged Mufti of the Great Mosque of Medina accompanied it. A procession escorted the banner to the Court of the Mosque of Omar, where a thunderstorm broke upon the *cortège*, drenching the banner. The Mufti, who took to his bed, died three days later. This was interpreted as an evil omen by the majority of the Arab population, who were never enthusiastic about the war.

The indifference, or possibly worse, of "the luckless population of Syria"—who provided supplies without recompense as well as troops—was a theme often stressed. "The Arab and Syrian troops, who form so large a proportion of their army," *The Times* wrote of the invasion forces on January 14, "have no hearts in the business, and are more anxious to expel the Turks from Syria than install them in Egypt."

Nevertheless, the force of twenty thousand men and eleven

thousand camels that Djemal had collected at Beersheba since late December willingly began its desert march toward the canal on January 14 and 15. Kress and his engineers had dug wells in advance along the way—even in areas which, like El Arish, were on the Egyptian side of the Sinai border but had been evacuated by British troops as unnecessary and overly distant outposts—but the soldier in Djemal's force was not permitted to carry more than one gourd of water at a stretch. This was part of his "desert ration," which also consisted of one kilogram altogether of biscuits, dates, and olives for the entire expedition. "I can have no greater duty," Djemal was to write, "than to offer a respectful tribute to these heroes who accomplished their march, though subject to privations innumerable, and dragged their guns and, above all, their pontoons (all that was available for crossing the canal) through a sea of sand." Persuaded by this display of courage among other things that "the majority of the Arabs stood by the Caliphate with heart and soul," Djemal looked forward to being greeted in Egypt by a Muslim population that, flocking to the call of *jihad* and the presence of his troops, would enable him to raise the Ottoman standard over their land once again.

After two diversionary maneuvers along the canal on January 26 and 27, the Ottoman forces made their main attack at 3:00 A.M. on Wednesday, February 3. The feints had been carried out at less well defended positions to the north and to the south, but the Turkish bid for victory was now aimed at Tussum, just below Ismailia, the thoroughly fortified midpoint of the canal route. Ismailia was the Suez lifeline, where both the railroad from Cairo and the Sweet Water Canal from the Nile—the sole source of drinking water for the area— arrived and branched to the north and south. Significant damage could have been caused by an attack anywhere along the route, but it was at Ismailia alone that victory would have meant the conquest of the entire canal—a fact of which the British were as aware as were the Turks and Germans. In front of that town and just east of the canal, Indian troops even occupied five posts on the side from which the invaders were coming, though the main British forces—and all of their artillery—were on the west bank, quaintly treating as a moat the very body of water they were defending. The British and French warships on the canal also were clustered mainly in this vicinity.

"Unfortunately," Djemal has recorded, "there was some slight delay in the approach of the attacking force to the Canal." Darkness was the Turks' best ally, and they had originally planned to make their attack right after nightfall on Tuesday, February 2; a thick sandstorm had intervened, however, and held them up until an hour perilously close to dawn. "Morning broke as the pontoons were being put into the water and the crossing began," Djemal goes on, "so that the operation took place under the eyes of the English. The defensive measures they immediately adopted at the crossing points destroyed all our pontoons except three. As it was impossible to send reinforcements to the six hundred heroes we had succeeded in getting on to the opposite bank at the very outset, they were all captured by the English." Djemal says that a duel then ensued between the Turkish artillery and the guns of British ships on the canal, and that an auxiliary cruiser was destroyed, though British sources make no mention of this.

Kress von Kressenstein, who thought that one cause of the failure was the indiscipline of the Arab troops he had tirelessly attempted to train for two and a half months, wanted to make another major assault the following night. Djemal thought this would be hopeless.

"Your Excellency!" Kress replied, according to Djemal's account, "in my view it is now the duty of the Expeditionary Force to die to a man on the Canal!"

Djemal, though not noted for kindness to those under his jurisdiction, did not agree. After one more abortive attempt to cross the canal was made that day in another sector, he ordered a retreat to Beersheba. On the afternoon of Friday, February 5, normal traffic was resumed on the canal. Turkish losses had been more than two hundred killed, about four hundred wounded, and over seven hundred taken prisoner; British casualties totaled about one hundred and fifty. Though there were some raised eyebrows at home over the British line of defense—"Is the garrison of Egypt defending the Canal, or is the Canal defending the garrison of Egypt?" was the question widely asked—the public had been given little reason by the outcome of the Suez attack to improve its estimate of Turkish military prowess.

It was shortly after Djemal's attack that Jabotinsky was given an urgent reason to promote his idea. If the Ottoman government had regarded Jews from Russia as enemy aliens, so now did the Russian consul in Alexandria regard the young men among them as eligible for conscription into the tsar's army. "The position was an unpleasant one," Jabotinsky was to recall. "The British Administration in Egypt was fully expected to accede to such a demand and was even obliged to employ every means at its disposal to carry it out." A deputation to see the British governor of Alexandria about this problem was organized by Edgar Suarès, a wealthy banker and president of that city's Jewish community, and Jabotinsky joined it as a member. "And at that interview I, an old admirer of Sephardi Jews (they are the finest Jews in the world), discovered another quality, which I had not known them to possess—the courage with which a Sephardi addresses the governor of a country at war." It did courage no harm, however, that Suarès and the governor were friends.

"Hush," the governor said, laughing after a firm but jovial exchange about the matter, "your young fellows will not be given away either. Still, the position is complicated—a treaty—time of war—but there's no question of giving up your men."

It seemed to Jabotinsky, however, that the situation could not hang in the balance much longer. He also thought the British were bound to invade Palestine soon and that a Jewish corps should be ready to go with them when they did. Right after the interview, then, he took what he considered to be the next crucial step: he went to see Joseph Trumpeldor.

If there was any man in Egypt—indeed, in the world—around whom the first Jewish army since antiquity could be built, it was Trumpeldor. Born in 1880 in Pyatigorsk, near Rostov-on-Don, he was the child of a Jew who had been conscripted into the Russian army for twenty-five years and who had consequently been allowed upon retirement to live outside the Pale of Settlement. Joseph himself had been drafted into the army in 1902 and had volunteered to serve at Port Arthur during the Russo-Japanese War. There, during the long siege, he distinguished himself by a courage he had become grimly determined to show as proof against the old belief that Jews were cowards. Though his left arm was severely wounded and had to be amputated, he asked upon recovery to be returned to the front. This request was honored, and, upon the surrender of Port Arthur in January 1905, he was removed to a prisoner of war camp in Japan. There he is said to have devoted himself to the welfare of his fellow prisoners in general, and to that of the Jews among them in particular. With the latter, he formed a Zionist circle. Trumpeldor seems to have been attracted by Zionism even before entering the army: proud and chivalrous like Jabotinsky, he perhaps had experienced a similar upsurgence of Jewish national pride when he had been unable to attend a Russian gymnasium on account of the *numerus clausus*.

Upon his return home in 1906, Trumpeldor not only was rewarded with military honors and officer's rank—Jewish officers were almost completely unheard of in the Russian army—but also was able to study law at the University of Saint Petersburg. This dimmed neither his Zionism nor his ideal of living communally on the soil (aroused in him by his reading of Tolstoy), and in 1912 he went with a group of comrades to live and work in Palestine. By then, the first *kvutzah** or collective farm, Degania, had been founded near the southern shore of Lake Tiberias, just east of the Jordan, and it was a natural magnet for Trumpeldor. Not only was its organization communal, but it was relatively remote from other Jewish settlements, and this called upon an old ambition within him to organize Jews for self-defense.

One of Trumpeldor's young comrades at Degania, Joseph Baratz, who observed along with the others that "with his one arm he did more work than other people did with two," later remembered serving with him as a watchman one night when marauders came. "We ran after them, exchanged a few shots and drove them out. One-armed Trumpeldor handled his rifle better than I did and had a surer aim." When the war came and was followed by the oppressions of Djemal Pasha, Baratz accepted Ottomanization along with much of the Zionist leadership, but Trumpeldor refused it and left for Alexandria. Baratz recalled his having said that he was going to join the British army.

In Alexandria, Trumpeldor enjoyed the relative luxury of private quarters, for the same Consul Petrov who wanted to conscript his fellow "Russians" from Palestine honored Trumpeldor's record on a similar principle, even seeing to it that he received his pension. "I found him at home," Jabotinsky recalls. "He looked very much like an Englishman or a Swede. Rather tall and very slim, with close-cropped hair, he was clean-shaven, with thin lips and a quiet smile. He spoke Russian excellently, though under the influence of Palestine he had developed a slight singsong intonation. His Hebrew was slow, and poor in words—but it sufficed. His Yiddish was atrocious. He was well educated, well read in Russian literature, and apparently gave much thought to every line he read."

Jabotinsky relates that they did not have to talk very long at that first encounter; Trumpeldor quickly got the point and after a quarter of an hour simply said yes to his scheme. That evening, the two of them gathered with several members of a Jewish steering committee that had been formed mainly from among the refugees themselves, and Jabotinsky's idea was discussed; a vote was held and a majority approved it.

* This, rather than *kibbutz*, was the term then in use.

That was on Tuesday, March 2; about a week later, a public meeting for refugees of military age was held at the Mafruza barracks. An audience of about two hundred gathered to listen to Jabotinsky, Trumpeldor, some members of the steering committee, and the chief rabbi of Alexandria, Raphael della Pergola. The speakers gave a review of the situation, explaining that "the English would not do what Consul Petrov had demanded, but it was not desirable to remain in the barracks indefinitely." They spoke of the situation in Palestine, which had worsened in January and February—actually, Djemal Pasha had begun to ease his anti-Jewish policies since the beginning of March, but they did not know this yet. In any case, it seemed most unlikely that the Turks, if victorious, would permit Jewish colonization after the war. The upshot of the meeting was that a petition was drafted in Hebrew "to form a Jewish Legion and to propose to England to make use of it in Palestine." One hundred signatures were affixed to it.

Petition in hand, a delegation that included Trumpeldor and Jabotinsky went to Cairo to present the case to the British authorities. The first person they saw was Ronald Graham. As the British adviser to the Egyptian minister of the interior, Graham was, in effect, minister of the interior. A career diplomat and Arabist in his mid-forties, he seemed cool and taciturn to the point of curtness, though this appearance may have belied his true attitude. "How many men do you expect?" he asked. Then, after writing the answer in a notebook, he said: "It does not rest with me, but I shall try."

The next person they went to see was Lieutenant General Sir John Maxwell, commander in chief of the British armed forces in Egypt. In preparation for this interview, Trumpeldor had been persuaded by his colleagues to put on the four Saint George crosses—two bronze and two gold—that he had won for service in the Russo-Japanese War. When he entered, Maxwell looked at him sharply and said in French, "Port Arthur, I understand?"

In spite of this good start, however, Maxwell's reply to their proposal was disappointing.

"I have heard nothing about an offensive in Palestine," he said, "and I doubt whether such an offensive will be launched at all. I am prohibited by regulations from admitting foreign soldiers into the British army. I can make only one suggestion—that your young men form themselves into a detachment for mule transport, to be made use of on some other sector of the Turkish front. I cannot do more than that."

A mule detachment! Maxwell had spoken to them in French, and it was the term *corps de muletiers* that had had, according to Jabotinsky, "a most unflattering sound in our civilian ears: what a shocking combination—Zion, the rebirth of a nation, the first really Jewish troop in the whole history of the Exile, and 'mules.' " That night, in a hotel room, the delegates debated the matter with a Talmudic intensity.

"Talking as a soldier," Trumpeldor said, "I think you overrate the difference. Trenches or transport is practically the same—all so essential that you can't do without it; and even the danger is often the same. You are just afraid of the word 'mules,' and that is childish."

"But a mule," one of them objected, "is almost a donkey. Sounds like calling names, especially in Yiddish."

"In Yiddish," Trumpeldor replied, " 'horse' is also not a compliment: *'sei nit keyn ferd.'* Yet if it were to be a cavalry detachment you would all feel terribly proud. In French, to call a person *chameau* is grossly offensive, but they have a Camel Corps in the French Army, and in the English Army, too; and to serve in them is considered a particular honor. It's all nonsense."

"But that 'other front' which is not Palestine—"

"Also not at all essential, speaking as a soldier. To get the Turk out of Palestine we've got to smash the Turk. Which side you begin the smashing, north or south, is just technique. Any front leads to Zion."

The debate lasted until dawn, with nothing resolved. On the way back to their own hotel, Jabotinsky said to Trumpeldor, "You may be right; but I, personally, would not join a unit of that sort."

"I probably will," Trumpeldor replied.

A few days later, Jabotinsky resumed his travels and sailed to Athens. Before the end of the month he was in Brindisi, and it was there that he received a telegram from Trumpeldor saying: "Maxwell's offer accepted."

·11·

ENGLAND PREPARES TO
SMASH THE TURKS

Vice-Admiral Carden had begun his assault at 9:51 A.M. on February 19. Twelve warships—three of them French—were deployed at the mouth of the Dardanelles in three divisions led by the newly built battleship *Queen Elizabeth* under Carden's command. They began a slow bombardment of the Turkish outer forts, which was sustained all morning and into the early afternoon with no reply from the enemy guns. At 2:00 P.M. Carden decided to move to a six-thousand-yard range, but there was still no Turkish fire. Then, at 4:45 P.M., the *Suffern*, the *Cornwallis*, and the *Vengeance* moved closer still, and a real exchange began at last. But by this time the sun was setting and Carden ordered a withdrawal. Vice-Admiral John de Robeck of the *Vengeance*, Carden's second in command, asked for permission to continue but was refused. That night Carden reported to the Admiralty that, though there had not been any direct hits on Turkish gun emplacements, the magazines at two of the forts had been destroyed, along with their communications to control positions. Then a storm blew up and Carden wired London again, saying he would not resume until it was over.

It was more modest a beginning than had been anticipated. Nevertheless, hopes remained high when Carden made his second attack on February 25. Vice-Admiral de Robeck now led the way in the *Vengeance*, and this time the onslaught forced the Turkish gunners to abandon their positions and retire to the north. The four outer forts were silenced, and in the ensuing days English and French sailors were able to land on both shores and roam about freely, destroying abandoned guns, searchlights, and emplacements. The Allied minesweepers now proceeded up the strait, making their way slowly against the current and occasional skirmishes with the mobile Turkish rear guard. Now and then an Allied warship was hit, but there was no serious damage and casualties were minor. On March 2, having penetrated for a distance of about six miles, Carden wired the Admiralty that, weather permitting, he hoped to reach the Sea of Marmara in about fourteen days.

The news was received with elation at the Admiralty. At the War Council held at 10 Downing Street the next day, Churchill read two telegrams from Carden, one saying that the forts at the entrance to the Dardanelles had been "practically demolished," the other that the Allied ships were now in the process of destroying forts number eight and nine. The members then proceeded to discuss what should be done once the fleet had forced the Dardanelles and what should be the future disposition of Constantinople once it had fallen. By this time Kitchener had come around to the view that it would be desirable to use troops at some point in the campaign after all, and he had promised they would be forthcoming—though he had yet to make it clear when, from where, or under what circumstances. Churchill tried to press him for a commitment, hinting about the considerable forces that were now gathered in Egypt and also mentioning that troops had been promised by Russia and even Greece once the ships had penetrated the straits.

But Kitchener requested another week for making his decision. The war secretary's colleagues were beginning to suspect that the highly personal and murky methods by which he had conducted colonial campaigns—Kitchener often consigned vital pieces of information to scribblings on scraps of paper or even to memory alone—had not really qualified him for the enormously complex task that had been his since last August. But he remained unassailable, chiefly on account of his great prestige with the British public. His Majesty's Government had so far maintained intact its tradition of not resorting to conscription, and if the nation's growing military needs were still being met by masses of volunteers, this was largely because of the strong man with military hat and gigantic handlebar moustache who pointed out from posters everywhere saying, "Your Country Needs YOU." The prime minister's wife, Margot Asquith, celebrated for her mordant wit, had even quipped that if Kitchener was not a great man he was at any rate a great poster—an estimate in which several members of her husband's cabinet were ready to concur.

Kitchener, however, was not the only source of Churchill's difficulties among the cabinet at this moment. Two other matters were brought up at the March 3 War Council concerning which Sir Edward Grey, unbeknownst to his colleagues there as yet, had ideas that were bound to clash with those of the first lord of the Admiralty. As we have seen, Churchill looked forward to the cooperation of Greece—for the moment still neutral—once the Dardanelles had been forced: Prime Minister Eleutherios Venizelos, always friendly to the Allies, was considered most likely to have his way in this matter over the pro-German King Constantine once it became clear that Turkey was about to be dismembered. But Grey knew that Greek participation in the campaign was not compatible with Russian ambitions concerning Constantinople and the straits, to which he was firmly committed. At the War Council he brought up these ambitions, saying it was absurd "that a huge empire such as Russia should have only ports that were icebound part of the year" or were subject to the whims of the Turks. Balfour was among those who agreed with Grey that Russia should get special consideration in the Dardanelles, but Churchill firmly dissented from this view. "We should stick to our general principle," he said, "that the settlement of all territorial questions should be left until the end of the war."

This was decidedly not Grey's principle; and it was the very next day that the foreign secretary found himself embarking on what was to be a course of territorial commitments, by means of hidden covenants secretly arrived at, for which he was to become notorious. On Thursday, March 4, Sergey Dmitrievich Sazonov, the Russian foreign minister, sent this message to the British and French ambassadors in Petrograd:

> The course of recent events leads His Majesty Emperor Nicholas to think that the question of Constantinople and of the Straits must be definitively solved, according to the time-honored aspirations of Russia.
>
> Every solution will be inadequate and precarious if the city of Constantinople, the western bank of the Bosphorus, of the Sea of Marmara and of the Dardanelles, as well as southern Thrace to the Enez-Midye line, should henceforth not be incorporated in the Russian Empire.
>
> Similarly, and by strategic necessity, that part of the Asiatic Shore that lies between the Bosphorus, the Sakarya River and a point to be determined on the Gulf of Izmit, and the islands of the Sea of Marmara, the Imbros Islands and the Tenedos Islands must be incorporated into the Empire.
>
> The special interests of France and of Great Britain in the above region will be scrupulously respected.

The Imperial Government entertains the hope that the above considerations will be sympathetically received by the two Allied Governments. The said Allied Governments are assured similar understanding on the part of the Imperial Government for the realization of plans which they may frame with reference to other regions of the Ottoman Empire or elsewhere.

At the same time, the Russian government made it clear in separate communications that it would not allow Greek participation in an assault on Constantinople.

Grey had no doubts where he stood on this matter, even when, in the next few days, Churchill hinted that the Greeks could be immensely helpful at this very moment. "Admiral Carden is asking for more destroyers to protect the Fleet from submarine dangers," Churchill wrote to Grey on March 10. "We have none to send him. The Greek flotillas would have been of inestimable value now. The Russian discouragements have very likely been a determining factor against fresh aid. If you see an opportunity you should bring this point home to the Russians." Grey did not seem ready to do so. At the War Council that day, he had pressed the Russian case that had been presented to him in Sazonov's letter.

As it turned out, most of his colleagues at the War Council had acknowledged the validity of the Russian claim—provided, as Asquith put it, "that both we and France should get a substantial share of the carcase of the Turk." Lloyd George, whose enthusiasms concerning the area were once again aroused, observed that "the Russians were so keen to obtain Constantinople that they would be generous in regard to concessions elsewhere." Churchill seems to have remained silent on the matter during the session. It was agreed that Russia should be informed of Britain's acceptance of her demands, on condition that she be prepared to accept Britain's own desiderata "as soon as there has been time to consider them." Grey also was instructed to warn Russia that there would be opposition to this decision among "a large section of public opinion in this country."

Accordingly, the following note was sent to the Russian government on March 12:

Subject to the war being carried on and brought to a successful conclusion and to the desiderata of Great Brtain and France in the Ottoman Empire and elsewhere being realized, as indicated in the Russian communication herein referred to, His Majesty's Government will agree to the Russian Government's *aide-mémoire* relative to Constantinople and the Straits, the text of which was communicated to His Britannic Majesty's Ambassador by his Excellency M. Sazonov on February 19/* March 4 instant.

Grey attached a memorandum to this, making some observations preliminary to a detailed statement of British desiderata, which was to be given sometime in the near future. Spelling out the most basic desiderata in advance—these regarded Arabia and Persia—the memorandum also stressed the import of the concession being made to Russia, this "definite promise that her wishes shall be satisfied with regard to what is in fact the richest prize of the entire war." It was pointed out, in accordance with the War Council's instructions, that this promise "involves a complete reversal of the traditional policy of His Majesty's Government, and is in direct opposition to the opinions and sentiments at one time universally held in England and which have still by no means died out." The principles of Palmerston and Disraeli were being finally repudiated, in other words. Therefore, the memorandum goes on, Russia should, "in the opinion of His Majesty's Government, not now put difficulties in the way of any Power which may, on reasonable terms, offer to cooperate with the Allies." Greece was then specifically mentioned as such a power.

But this bit of arm twisting was to no avail. On March 14, Churchill cabled Grand Duke Nicholas, supreme commander of the Russian armies, asking whether the Russians would accept Greek participation in the campaign now that Constantinople had been promised to them. The answer was no.

In the course of the exchanges leading to the secret agreement with Russia concerning Constantinople and the straits, the overlapping questions of Palestine and of French interests in Syria were pointedly discussed. Members of the British Government were beginning to believe that the traditional French claim—dating back at least to the sixteenth century, if not to the Crusades—to all of Syria down to the Egyptian border could not reasonably be honored. Even if one set aside the question of a defensible border for Egypt, there remained the growing British involvement in Mesopotamia and what that implied concerning Syria. Strategically and economically, Mesopotamia was tied to the Levant, so that the British involvement

* The same date as March 4 according to the Russian Old-Style calendar.

made little sense without the assurance of an outlet to the Mediterranean. The question of a possible British port on the Levantine coast had arisen almost as soon as the war in the East began. Haifa, the only Mediterranean port linked with the Hejaz railway, was one natural choice, and in fact the War Office files contained a plan for a possible attack on that town that had first been developed as far back as 1906. Another possibility was Alexandretta, but such a claim would be aiming an arrow right at the heart of French interests in Syria.

At the War Council of March 10, during which the Russian claims to Constantinople and the straits were acknowledged, Kitchener again raised the matter of Alexandretta. He had just surprised everyone present by announcing that a whole division would soon be sent to the Dardanelles, and he and Asquith both thought that Britain was now entitled to press this claim for a Syrian port. Others recognized that France would never accept it. Lloyd George, convinced by the arguments of Herbert Samuel and others that northern but not southern Syria was a legitimate area of French interests, argued that Britain should let France have Alexandretta rather than quarrel with her over it. He was for claiming Palestine instead, "owing to the prestige it would give us." Kitchener retorted that "Palestine would be of no value to us whatsoever"—a rather dogmatic assertion, but forceful, coming as it did from the only person present who had ever been there. Only a few weeks before, the *Jewish Chronicle* had written of him that "it is a point of no ordinary importance that the British Cabinet has within its ranks at this moment a member so intimately conversant with the Palestinian realities, political, racial, strategic, and, in all probability, economic too." Kitchener's old comrade in Palestinian exploration, Claude Conder, now dead, had gone on from that experience to become one of England's foremost gentile Zionists, as the *Jewish Chronicle* well knew; it was not very well known, however, that Kitchener had come to different conclusions.

The argument for Haifa instead of Alexandretta was to re-emerge very soon and gain strength in the ensuing weeks; in the meantime, the fact that many Frenchmen considered their claim on Palestine to have the same validity as their claims in the Lebanon was a problem that still had to be confronted. At the very beginning of the year, Foreign Office members had been amused to receive from Sir Francis Bertie, the ambassador in Paris, a copy of an article in *Le Matin* that lyrically described the Syria and Palestine of the future as "La France du Levant." The French Republic, it said, was destined to follow in the wake of the Crusaders, and

> thus Jesuits; Lazarists; Brothers from Christian Schools; Jews of the *Alliance Israélite* who have taught at Beirut, Alexandretta, Jerusalem, Nazareth or Bethlehem; economists and financiers; engineers who have drawn blueprints, laid rails, dug ports; peasants or small merchants who have emptied their wool stockings to pay debts; thinkers who have proclaimed Liberty; all Frenchmen since those who departed to reclaim Christ's tomb from the infidels; all the Frances which have been ignored or are contending with one another, who for so long have imagined themselves to be without an ideal or even honor: see how past and present history confounds and reconciles them. Eight centuries of battles, prayers, works, missions in those places where Europe meets Asia and Africa, are finally going to win their reward.

"Very French" was the wry comment of one Foreign Office member upon reading it—and, as such, it was a vivid demonstration of why there was hardly a Zionist anywhere who would have preferred French to English control of Palestine. To be sure, there were such manifestations as the article by the socialist leader Gustave Hervé in *La Guerre Sociale* on February 12, in which he argued passionately for the restoration of the Jews to Palestine under French auspices; but for the most part, the French overseas struck Zionists as having always, in Weizmann's words, "interfered with the population and tried to impose upon them the *'esprit français.'* "

What banner, then, the *Jewish Chronicle* asked on March 12, was to fly over Palestine now that the downfall of the Ottoman Empire "has begun in deadly earnest. . . . The French flag, the British flag, the Russian flag—the Jewish flag? What is it to be?" Straddling the British alternative with the French and Russian ones was indeed appropriate at that moment, for if the British and the Russians had arrived quickly enough at an understanding with respect to their claims in the Ottoman Empire, the French and the Russians were now running into a snag—and it was over Palestine.

"I should be grateful to Your Excellency," the French ambassador, Maurice Paléologue, wrote to Sazonov on March 14,

> for informing His Imperial Majesty that the Government of the French Republic, having studied the conditions of the peace to be imposed on Turkey, would like to annex Syria together with

the region of the Gulf of Alexandretta and Cilicia up to the Taurus range. I should be happy to inform my government, without delay, of the Imperial Government's consent.

But there was a delay: Sazonov wanted to know how much was meant by "Syria" and he assigned an assistant minister to find out. "The French ambassador," his assistant informed him the next day, "has told me that it is his impression that Syria 'includes Palestine.' I deemed it useful to remind him that there is in Jerusalem an independent governor."

The unwillingness of Russians to acquiesce in complete French control of Palestine and the Holy Places was at least as old as the Crimean War, which had begun in a jurisdictional dispute there between Catholic and Orthodox monks. Having now heard the French ambassador's impression that this unwelcome claim was in effect being made, Sazonov turned directly to Paris for an explanation. Paléologue's telegraphed instructions from there, on the basis of which he had written his March 14 letter, had mentioned Syria but not Palestine. "Paléologue explains," Sazonov wrote on March 16 to his ambassador in Paris,

> that in his opinion the French Government refers also to Palestine when speaking of Syria. However, since in this telegram there is no question of Palestine, it would be desirable to elucidate whether the explanation of the Ambassador really corresponds to the view of the French Government. This question appears important to us; for, if the Imperial Government should be prepared largely to satisfy France's desires concerning Syria and Cilicia proper, it is indispensable to study the question with closer attention, if the Holy Places are involved.

There the matter rested. France went on to give, as Britain had, her agreement in principle to Russian claims in the Ottoman Empire, but nothing more was said about Palestine for the time being.

In preparing to write a new draft of his memorandum on Palestine, Herbert Samuel had plenty of opportunity to perceive the French obstacle in the way of his plan. On January 30 he saw Chaim Weizmann, who had just returned from his second trip to Paris in a month, during which he had spoken not only to Baron de Rothschild again but also to the British ambassador, Sir Francis Bertie. Weizmann undoubtedly told Samuel of Bertie's unfavorable opinion, which the ambassador had recorded in his diary: "Edmond de Roth-schild sent a co-religionist established in Manchester to 'talk' about what I think an absurd scheme, though they say it has the approval of Grey, Lloyd George, Samuel and Crewe: they did not mention Lord Reading." By this time, through the intercession of Dorothy de Rothschild, Weizmann's ideas had also been favorably received by the secretary for India, Lord Crewe, whose wife, daughter of the former prime minister, Lord Rosebery, was a Rothschild on her mother's side. As for the Jewish lord chief justice, Lord Reading, he was no Zionist, but he had begun to express such sympathies. Bertie, who was to send the article from *Le Matin* to the Foreign Office just a few days later, went on to say of Weizmann's plan: "It contem-plates the formation of Palestine into an Israelite State, under the protectorate of England, France or Russia, preferably of Eng-land. . . . What would the Pope, and Italy, and Catholic France with her hatred of Jews, say to the scheme?"

Samuel had occasion to discuss the French aspect of the matter in another conversation with Grey, which was held on February 5. Samuel found Grey "still anxious to promote a settlement of the question in a way favorable to Zionist ideas," but "very doubtful of the possibility or desirability of the establishment of a British Pro-tectorate. He does not know what views the French Government hold, and was rather disposed to sound them." This was Grey's cau-tious response to the recommendations contained in Samuel's Janu-ary 22 memorandum. Samuel took issue with him, pointing out that this proposed approach to the French government "would open up the whole question of territorial dispositions after the war; the dis-posal of Palestine could not be discussed without raising also the questions of Northern Syria and, probably, of African colonies." Grey, as we have seen, was to discover within a few weeks that, with a British offensive going on in the Dardanelles, it would no longer be possible to avoid discussing Syria with Britain's allies; but he still seems to have been far from ready to raise the possibly irritating Palestine question with France.

Indeed, France was not the only problem at that particular mo-ment. "Grey is also very indisposed," Samuel went on in the note he made of this conversation right afterward, "to assume for the Brit-ish Empire the fresh military and diplomatic responsibilities that would be involved by this extension of frontiers." This was still a delicate question among the Liberal leadership, who, until November at any rate, had firmly believed that they were in the war solely to

defend Europe against German aggression and not to annex territory. Turkey's entry had caused a decisive change in this respect in
the views of Lloyd George and Samuel, but other Liberals were slow
to follow their lead.

Even C.P. Scott, after coming to recognize Palestine as a special
and appealing case, had remained ambivalent a while longer: the
Manchester Guardian leader on the December 18 proclamation of a
British protectorate over Egypt, which Scott probably wrote but certainly at least influenced, had expressed his ambivalence this way:

> A long line of statesmen, from Palmerston to Salisbury and
> Gladstone, have expressed the view that a Protectorate of
> Egypt would be a burden to this country without compensating
> advantages. It is true that, as the old status of Egypt was a
> Protectorate in fact though not in name, its mere conversion
> into a formal Protectorate will not in itself be any addition to
> our responsibilities. But no one quite knows what this war will
> bring forth. It may give us other neighbors on the Asiatic fron-
> tiers of Egypt; it may extend our own sphere of influence. In
> any case, it is likely to entail much more serious organization of
> the frontier defenses.

The writer then quickly stepped back from this dizzying glimpse
from the heights of Pisgah and reverted to a traditional Liberal
warning against overweening imperial ambition. If these were
Scott's reservations in December, we must imagine Grey's to be
greater, even in February; and if the height of euphoria during the
Dardanelles campaign was to arouse in him and Asquith mild displays of the common lust for "the carcase of the Turk," the prime
minister was nevertheless still to be able to write of himself and
Grey in late March: "We both think that in the real interests of our
own future the best thing would be if at the end of the War we could
say that we had taken and gained nothing, and this not from a
merely moral and sentimental point of view." From a practical point
of view, however, they knew perfectly well that they could not stand
aside and let France and Russia have everything.

But in his February 5 conversation with Samuel, Grey was still
groping for the most unselfish alternatives, regarding Palestine as
regarding any place else. "When I asked him what his solution was,"
Samuel went on in his note, "he said it might be possible to neutral-
ize the country under international guarantee; to place the control of
the Holy Places in the hands of a Commission in which the European

Powers, and the Pope, and perhaps the United States, would be represented; and to vest the government of the country in some kind of Council to be established by the Jews."

Samuel retorted with what he now knew, along with Weizmann and other Zionist leaders, to be the chief objection to such an arrangement: he expressed "a doubt whether the Arab population, who number five-sixths of the inhabitants, would accept such a government. Grey said that a possible alternative would be, if it were found necessary to continue the suzerainty of Turkey, to establish a regime somewhat like that of Lebanon, but with the governor appointed by the Powers." But this only brought Samuel back to the original point and he pressed upon Grey "the danger of any other Power than England possessing Palestine, and the risk that an international government might end in some European state becoming dominant." He "pointed out that if Germany had possessed Palestine before the outbreak of this war, she could have prepared a most formidable attack on Egypt." Grey agreed that this was so, both of them doubtless reflecting on the dramatic contrast between what then would have happened and Djemal's failure of two days earlier.

Meanwhile, Samuel had been gathering a widening range of influential opinions in favor of his plan both inside and outside the cabinet. On the subject of Lloyd George's continuing enthusiasm for it, he heard from Lord Reading, who wrote: "I had a talk with L. G. about the matter before his departure for Paris. He is certainly inclined to the sympathetic side. Your proposal appeals to the poetic and imaginative as well as to the romantic and religious qualities of his mind." As for Reading, he had just been quoted in yet another Stephen Graham piece about Russia and its Jews. Graham was now an enthusiastic advocate of Jewish emigration to Palestine, and he had reported a conversation between himself and Lord Reading in which the latter had said that, in the eventuality of a Turkish defeat, "it seems to me that something might be done for the establishment of the Jews in Palestine." Samuel also received a note at around this time from Viscount Haldane—the lord chancellor, but even more importantly, the secretary for war from 1905 to 1912, and as such, the man responsible for some of the most sweeping military reforms in British history. "I have read your Memorandum on Palestine with interest and sympathy," Haldane wrote. "There may be possible questions with the French—as you quite foresee. But it is well worth considering as a possibility."

Samuel even made sallies into the non-Zionist bastions at the very top of the Anglo-Jewish establishment, and got encouraging results. On Saturday, February 13, he was a guest at Tring, the great Rothschild mansion in Hertfordshire. Lord Rothschild, now seventy-four, had gone through a varied cycle of feelings in his contacts with Zionist advocates over the years, but in one aspect of the matter he had always been consistent: he never failed to support programs for the settlement of Jews under British auspices, wherever that might be. An ardent patriot, he now showed himself quite willing to endorse Samuel's idea of a British Palestine—he refused to speak of anything other than a protectorate—into which Jewish immigration would be encouraged. Lord Rothschild's brother Leopold also was present, but, though he too expressed favor for the idea of a British protectorate in Palestine, as a vice-president of the Anglo-Jewish Association he showed some of that organization's qualms about Zionist aims there. Nothing done in Palestine, he insisted, should "be allowed to result in the Jews of Russia and elsewhere being regarded as Palestinians settled in those countries, and not as citizens of them."

On the following day, back at his home in London, Samuel got opinions similar to those of Leopold de Rothschild from the president of the Anglo-Jewish Association, Claude Montefiore. At the age of fifty-six this grandnephew of Sir Moses Montefiore, a lay theologian, was Britain's outstanding philosopher of Liberal Judaism, and an advocate of its traditional view that the bearers of the religion of Moses were scattered as a mission among the nations. As for "modern Jewish Nationalism," he had written that "the aspirations of most Nationalist Jews run counter to the aspirations of most Liberal Jews. To our hopes and desires both for Judaism and for the Jews, the ideals of most Nationalist Jews are opposed. On the other hand, to their hopes and desires our ideals are, in their turn, no less definitely hostile." In all matters other than religion, he had gone on, Liberal Jews want to be "one with the nations among whom they dwell. When an English Liberal Jew speaks of 'my people,' he means the English people; when an American Liberal [i.e., Reform] Jew speaks of 'my people' and 'my country,' he means the people and the country of the United States."

Nothing was to be allowed to compromise this position in his eyes; yet he did welcome Samuel's proposal for a British protectorate, "on the ground that the Jews in Palestine could have British nationality and not an independent nationality." In a better world, as Claude Montefiore saw it, Jews would be Russians in Moscow and Petrograd and Englishmen in London and Jerusalem. He added that he thought the Jewish colonization of Palestine "would be of use as bringing relief to whatever number of Russian Jews can be received there." If not for that, he would consider the establishment of a Jewish center there as "retrograde."

That evening, Samuel described all these conversations to Weizmann, who was then in London. "H. S. told me about his visit to R.," Weizmann wrote the next day to Dorothy de Rothschild,

> and about the willingness of the R.'s to support the Palestinian scheme should Palestine become a British Protectorate. H.S. also had Claude Montefiore in his house and got him to agree to the same thing. S. is satisfied with that result. We must however have no illusions about that. Those gentlemen are primarily in favor of the British Protectorate, in other words they consider it their patriotic duty as Englishmen to desire that Great Britain should occupy Palestine. The Jewish side of the question is a secondary consideration. As it happens, their British patriotism coincides with Jewish interests, but should there arise a conflict, the Jew would have to go overboard.

Nevertheless, he added, "for the present it is gratifying to know that everything works well." He then went on to describe Samuel's conversation of February 5 with Sir Edward Grey, as Samuel had just described it to him. "Here is a serious difficulty," he concluded,

> and curiously enough Mr. Scott, who is our sincere friend, raised exactly the same objections in his conversations with me. According to H.S., there is a body of liberal opinion of which Scott and [Lord] Bryce are the most prominent representatives which would view with disfavor a British Protectorate over Palestine for reasons mentioned above [in the Samuel-Grey conversation].

Weizmann told Dorothy Rothschild that the only course was to convince such men "that the other alternative—a Palestine under international control—presents greater disadvantages to Britain, than a Palestine under British control."

The next day, heeding his own counsel, Weizmann composed a long letter to C.P. Scott. Reporting on the conversation between Samuel and Grey, he summed up for Scott his own arguments against any of the alternatives to British control, and dealt with possible Russian or French objections to it. "As far as Russia is concerned," he began, "I am certain that no difficulties will be met with in this quarter. We have indications which point to it." He then recounted a story he had told Samuel on Sunday evening. "One of my colleagues," he said, "has presented sometime ago a memorandum to the head of the Near East Department of the Russian Foreign Office." Yehiel Tschlenow had sent the memorandum, which advocated a Jewish Palestine under the auspices of some Great Power: none was specifically mentioned, but Great Britain was clearly intended. "The Director of the Department," Weizmann went on, "then expressed a favorable opinion, but he said that he would submit this memorandum to M. Sazonov. Apparently this has been done, because on Saturday last we received a telegram from our friends in Petrograd to say that the memorandum has been well received." Weizmann added that his opinion was that Russia, while "not willing to do anything for the Jews in Russia itself, . . . feels that the least she can do is not to oppose the Palestinian scheme, especially as Russia is in need of money, and it may have to go to the American market for it."

As for France, Weizmann did not think that "she should claim more than Syria, as far as Beyrouth included. The so-called French influence, which is merely spiritual and religious, is predominant in Syria. In Palestine itself there is very little of it, except perhaps a few monastic establishments. The only work which may be termed civilizing pioneer work has been carried out by the Jews." The Catholic claims were balanced by the Orthodox ones, and the only way the religious question could be settled, Weizmann wrote, was to internationalize Jerusalem, Bethlehem, and Nazareth. But as for the rest of Palestine, internationalization "would simply mean that Palestine becomes the play ball of international diplomacy, and each country would endeavor to get a predominant influence. We may have therefore again France or Russia, or even Germany, establishing themselves on the Egyptian flank."

Weizmann finally dealt with the worries of Liberals concerning the extension of British imperial responsibilities by projecting a vision of the next twenty-five years—a period during which, "one has to assume," there was not likely to be any wars. "Great Britain would therefore only have to protect the country from incursions of Arabs, and for this purpose a Militia could be organized from the Colonists." The Jewish settlers would develop the beginnings of an army and a fleet under British auspices, and

we would become a well organized community after 25 years, which could hold its own, not only against the Nomadic tribes round Palestine, but even against a European invader; the last

seems to me an exceedingly remote idea. The advantages which
Britain may derive from such a combination are so evident that
they need not be discussed at great length.

Weizmann concluded by saying he had written this letter because he
was "convinced that the opinion of men like yourself, Lord Bryce
and other advanced liberals will probably be the decisive factor in
this question."

In the case of Scott and Bryce, Weizmann never really had a
great deal to worry about. On March 8, the former ambassador to
Washington and author of *The American Commonwealth* wrote to
Samuel: "I very much agree with your memorandum in principle,
though there are some minor points I should like to discuss with you,
and I am extremely glad you have put the matter before the Cabinet." As for Scott, he had already written to Harry Sacher on
January 16:

> I have had several conversations with Dr. Weizmann on the
> Jewish Question, and he has, I think, opened his whole mind to
> me. I found him extraordinarily interesting—a rare combination
> of idealism and the severely practical which are the two essen-
> tials of statesmanship. . . . What struck me in his view was, first,
> his perfectly clear conception of Jewish nationalism—an intense
> and burning sense of the Jew as Jew . . . and, secondly, arising
> out of that and necessary for its satisfaction and development,
> his demand for a country, a homeland, which for him, and for
> anyone sharing his views of Jewish nationality, could be no
> other than the ancient home of his race. . . . It seems to me a big
> idea and is, I fancy, already producing a revolution in Jewish
> thought—a painful one, no doubt, to many. But the fundamental
> conception—to make the Jew a whole Jew . . . to clear him up in
> his own eyes and the eyes of the world—that seems to me sound,
> at least as an ideal. And there may be a chance now of moving a
> long way towards it.

These words clearly did not yet represent acceptance of a British
protectorate, but they showed a readiness to accept the logic that
had brought Weizmann and Samuel to that conclusion. By March 21,
Weizmann could write to Samuel:

> I am very glad to state that Mr. Scott has expressed the
> following opinion: 1) He does not see how Great Britain can not

declare a protectorate over Palestine if it does not desire any other great power to take it. 2) Once G.B. has taken Mesopotamia it must have Palestine. 3) He is going to see Lord Bryce about it . . . and also Mr. Lloyd George. Mr. Scott thinks that the events are shaping in favor of a British Palestine.

Meanwhile, Samuel had presented the revised draft of his memorandum a week or so earlier. In addition to Weizmann, the Rothschilds, and Claude Montefiore, Samuel had spoken over the weeks with P.J.C. McGregor, the former British consul at Jerusalem, as well as with his predecessor; with the American consul at Jerusalem, Otis Glazebrook, when he passed through London; and with Lucien Wolf, spokesman of the Conjoint Foreign Committee, a common organ of the Anglo-Jewish Association and the Board of Deputies of British Jews, through which those two august bodies now formulated their wartime foreign policy. Samuel also probably spoke to Gaster from time to time, for the two men remained in one another's confidence— even though Gaster was becoming even less willing than before to communicate with Weizmann and with the Zionist executive as represented in London by Yehiel Tschlenow and Nahum Sokolow. For Samuel, the result of all this discussion was a terser document than the January one had been, stripped of rhetoric, and organized so as to address itself immediately to the various alternatives for Palestine. Each of these was taken on and dealt with in the terms that we have seen. Only at the end did Samuel turn to the alternative of a British protectorate, marshaling his by now familiar arguments in a section that was longer than the rest of the memorandum combined.

Asquith responded in equally familiar but more expansive terms to this new draft by recalling the earlier one, writing on March 13 to his friend Venetia Stanley that

H. Samuel had written an almost dithyrambic memorandum urging that in the carving up of the Turks' Asiatic dominions, we should take Palestine, into which the scattered Jews could in time swarm back from all the quarters of the globe, and in due course obtain Home Rule. (What an attractive community!) Curiously enough, the only other partisan of this proposal is Lloyd George, who, I need not say, does not care a damn for the Jews or their past or their future, but who thinks it would be an outrage to let the Christian Holy Places—Bethlehem, Mount of Olives, Jerusalem &c—pass into the possession or under the protectorate of "Agnostic Atheistic France"! Isn't it singular that the same conclusions should be capable of being come to by such different roads? Kitchener, who "surveyed" Palestine when he was a young Engineer, has a very poor opinion of the place, which even Samuel admits to be not larger than Wales, much of it barren mountain, and part of it waterless and, what is more to the point, without a single decent harbor. So he (K) is all for Alexandretta, and leaving the Jews and the Holy Places to look after themselves.

·12·

ZION AT GALLIPOLI

"It [is] not a question of 'crushing' Germany but of defeating her," Lloyd George said to C.P. Scott on March 15. "Personally," he added, he "would rather crush Turkey than Germany." In this season of renewal, England and France were preparing to do both. General Joffre had begun a major new offensive in Champagne, and on March 10 British forces had made a large-scale attack at the village of Neuve Chapelle near Lille. Neither thrust had been outstandingly successful—"We acclaimed it as a great victory when we had gained 1200 yards," Lloyd George complained to Scott—but they seemed to represent progress, and hopes were running high. As for the war against Turkey, the heaviest naval offensive to date was being prepared for the Dardanelles.

On Thursday, March 18, at 10:30 A.M., ten battleships—six of them British and four of them French—entered the straits and steamed forward six miles under a barrage from field guns and howitzers on both shores. Shortly after 11:00 A.M., they stopped at a point some eight miles below the Narrows—where the width of the waterway, normally about four miles on the average, becomes reduced to sixteen hundred yards—and began firing. Under their massive barrage, the thirteen Turkish forts scattered along the two shores below the Narrows were soon silenced, and just before noon there was a huge explosion in Chanak at the Narrows themselves, where a powder magazine evidently had been struck. The French ships then drew closer to Chanak, and the bombardment continued until 1:45 P.M., when virtually all enemy fire had ceased.

It was time for the minesweepers to go to work, and the French squadron had begun to retire, when suddenly, just before 2:00 P.M., there was an enormous explosion on one of its ships. Within two minutes, the *Bouvet* heeled and sank in a cloud of smoke, taking more than six hundred men down with her. No one knew whether she had been struck by a shell or by a mine, but the effect of the disaster was to encourage renewed Turkish fire and to frighten off some of the minesweepers.

Nevertheless, the Allied ships rallied, and by 4:00 P.M. they seemed to have the situation under control again. Then, eleven minutes later, the *Inflexible* struck a mine, and less than five minutes after that, the *Irresistible* was hit. The latter was put out of commission altogether, and, after her men were rescued, an attempt was made to salvage her. But one of the battleships engaged in this operation, the *Ocean*, also struck a mine, and that night she and the *Irresistible* both sank to the bottom. Despite these ship losses, however, British casualties by the end of the day had been just a little over seventy killed or wounded.

Was it a victory with severe but not incapacitating losses, or was it a defeat? Admiral de Robeck, who had replaced Carden in the command after the latter had suffered an attack of nervous exhaustion, seems to have fluctuated in his view of the outcome. Greatly discouraged on the night of March 18, he had been heartened the next day by advisers who thought that another such attack would get them through. Back in London, Churchill and others shared this opinion, and more ships were sent.

But while the British fleet at the Dardanelles retired to repair its ships and heal its wounds, other counsels began to gain strength. General Sir Ian Hamilton, the newly appointed commander in chief of the Mediterranean Expeditionary Force now being sent to the area for a Dardanelles landing, had watched the engagement from a nearby ship and was convinced that the job could not be done without troops. On the very next day he cabled his opinion to Kitchener, who, now that he had finally committed himself to sending troops there, was easily persuaded that a landing on the Gallipoli Peninsula was the only solution. On March 22, Hamilton met with de Robeck on Lemnos—the island the Greek government had been persuaded to let the British use as a base, where two thousand marines and four thousand soldiers from Australia and New Zealand already were stationed—and convinced him of this viewpoint. The next day, de Robeck sent Churchill a telegram saying he would make no further move without a troop landing. It was now the army's turn.

"From the days of my youth," Lieutenant Colonel John Henry Patterson was to write, "I have always been a keen student of the Jewish people, their history, laws and customs." A Protestant from Dublin, Patterson had just arrived in Cairo when, on March 19, General Sir John Maxwell appointed him to command the unit that was to be called the Zion Mule Corps. "It certainly was curious that the General's choice should have fallen upon me," he adds, "for, of course, he knew nothing of my knowledge of Jewish history, or of my sympathy for the Jewish race. When, as a boy, I eagerly devoured the records of the glorious deeds of Jewish military captains such as Joshua, Joab, Gideon and Judas Maccabaeus, I little dreamt that one day I, myself, would, in a small way, be a captain of a host of the Children of Israel!"

Coincidentally, the forty-eight-year-old cavalry officer had first achieved a certain fame as an adventurer in the East African protectorate a few years before land there was offered to the Zionists. An engineer by profession, he had gone to Africa in 1896 to build a railway bridge across the Tsavo River, on what was to become the Uganda line. As the sole European with several hundred Swahili laborers, he had to call upon his skill as a rifleman when the camp was menaced by man-eating lions. The book he subsequently wrote about this adventure, *The Man-eaters of Tsavo*, became something of a classic of its genre and earned him the friendship of Theodore Roosevelt. Patterson also served in the Boer War, then spent several years in India, and subsequently traveled a good part of the Old World and the New.

Upon receiving his appointment, Patterson left promptly for Alexandria, where he got in touch with Rabbi della Pergola, Edgar Suarès, and other leaders of the Jewish community. With their help, and that of an encouraging telegram addressed to the Palestine refugees by Israel Zangwill, recruiting was easily accomplished in two or three days. By March 23, Patterson had under his command about 500 Jewish volunteers, including 8 officers led by Captain Joseph Trumpeldor. He also had 5 British army officers, as well as 20 horses and 750 mules. "I divided the Corps," he writes, "for purposes of interior economy, into four troops, each with a British and a Jewish officer in command; each troop was again divided into four sections with a sergeant in charge, and each section was again divided into subsections with a corporal in charge; and so the chain of responsibility went down to the lively mule himself—and, by the shades of Jehoshaphat, couldn't some of those mules kick!! Sons of Belial would be a very mild name for them."

On Tuesday, March 23, the volunteers were paraded in front of the Gabbari barracks and were sworn in. "It was a most imposing ceremony; the Grand Rabbi, who officiated, stood in a commanding position overlooking the long rows of serious and intelligent-looking lads. He explained to them the meaning of an oath, and the importance of keeping it, and impressed upon them that the honor of Israel rested in their hands." He then asked them to repeat after him the oath of "obedience to the officer commanding the Corps and to such officers as should be placed over them," and they did so with uplifted hands. Rabbi della Pergola then delivered "a stirring address to the new soldiers, in which he compared them to their forefathers who had been led out of Egypt by Moses," and at the end of which he turned to Colonel Patterson and presented him as "their modern leader."

Patterson obtained a campsite at the Alexandria suburb of Wardian; tents were pitched and training began there on April 2. Soon the men were equipped with uniforms bearing the Star of David, and with rifles and ammunition taken from the soldiers killed or captured in the Turkish assault on the Suez Canal in early February. Drilling was conducted in both English and Hebrew. "Never since the days of Judas Maccabaeus," Patterson felt, "had such sights and sounds been seen and heard in a military camp; indeed, had that redoubtable General paid us a surprise visit, he might have imagined himself with his own legions, because here he would have found a great camp with the tents of the Children of Israel pitched round about; he would have heard the Hebrew tongue spoken on all sides, and seen a little host of the Sons of Judah drilling to the same words of command that he himself used to those gallant soldiers who so nobly fought against Rome under his banner; he would even have heard the plaintive soul-stirring music of the Maccabaean hymn chanted by the men as they marched through the camp."

Within two weeks these new Maccabaeans had been inspected by General Sir Ian Hamilton—who "was most complimentary on the workmanlike appearance which the Corps presented"—and had received orders to proceed to Lemnos in order to participate in the imminent military campaign on the Gallipoli Peninsula. "We had a last big parade," Patterson recalls, "and marched from Wardian Camp for some three miles through the streets of Alexandria to the Synagogue, to receive the final blessings of the Grand Rabbi. The spacious Temple, in the Street of the Prophet Daniel, was on this occasion filled to its utmost capacity. The Grand Rabbi exhorted the men to bear themselves like good soldiers and in times of difficulty and danger to call upon the Name of the Lord who would deliver them out of their adversity. His final benediction was most solemn and impressive, and will never be forgotten by those who were privileged to be present." At the last minute, there was a delay of a day and a half while Patterson's unit awaited the delivery of the several hundred wooden frames that, strapped to the mules' backs, would hold kerosene tins filled with water to supply the troops at Gallipoli. These arrived at last, and the Zion Mule Corps sailed out of Alexandria harbor on April 17.

The Gallipoli Peninsula, jutting southwest into the Aegean Sea, forms the western and European side of the Dardanelles. Its fifty-two-mile length begins in the north at the town of Bulair, where it is less than five miles across from the Gulf of Saros to the Sea of Marmara, widens to about twelve miles at the center, then rapidly narrows to its tip at Cape Helles. Its harsh, rocky, scrub-covered terrain is hilly, rising in a relatively gradual slope from the beaches of Cape Helles to the 709-foot height of Achi Baba six miles northeast, but with stark suddenness around most of its perimeter to heights of a thousand feet and more only a few yards from the shore. Along the parts of the coast accessible from the south and the west, there were really only four beaches viable for an Allied landing: those at Bulair, at Suvla Bay midway down, at Gaba Tepe a few miles below it, and at Cape Helles. Another possible landing place was at Kum Kale on the Asiatic side of the Dardanelles, but Kitchener was opposed to a campaign there, and it was decided that the participating French troops would stage a feint instead at this fort near the site of ancient Troy.

An assault across Bulair would have cut off the entire peninsula; but this was just where General Liman von Sanders, who had been put in charge of the Turkish forces at Gallipoli right after the March 18 naval attack, fully expected an Allied landing to take place. Instead, Bulair was set aside as the site of another feinting operation, this one to be performed by the Royal Naval Division. Suvla Bay also was held in reserve for the time being, and the invasion was aimed at the two remaining viable locations. Gaba Tepe, about thirteen miles north of the tip on the western shore, was to be taken by the Anzacs (Australian and New Zealand Army Corps), who were then to move on to the heights beyond, from which Xerxes is said to have reviewed his fleet in the Hellespont. At Cape Helles, the British Twenty-Ninth Division—Kitchener's tardy bequest to the campaign—was to make five landings at once, accompanied by other troops, and proceed from there to the top of Achi Baba. The Turkish forces in the whole southern part of the peninsula were to be crushed between these two assaults, after which Allied ships would be able to pass freely through the Dardanelles.

The invasion began at 4:00 A.M. on Sunday, April 25, with the landing that was aimed at Gaba Tepe. As dawn broke, the Australians leaped from their boats shouting what had become a favorite slogan of theirs while in Egypt, "Imshi Yallah," and rushed for shore against the first outburst of enemy fire. A group of Turkish riflemen was quickly dispersed, and the Anzacs dashed in to take what they had been told would be a beach several hundred yards deep. But suddenly they were at the base of a sharply rising cliff, with Turkish fire raining down from far above them. A mistake in navigation, as it turned out, had brought them not to Gaba Tepe but to a cove near Ari Burnu, several miles to the north. There was great confusion as they scrambled up the rough slopes, many of them falling into gullies along the way. A few even made it to the top, where the Turkish soldiers, never expecting a landing here, were even more confused than they; but it was the Turks' good fortune to have had at hand a gifted though obscure commander named Mustafa Kemal, who rallied his troops and drove the Anzacs off the heights.

At Cape Helles, the attack began at 5:00 A.M. with a tremendous bombardment from the battleship *Albion* upon the village and cove of Sedd-el-Bahr, which was about a mile and a half east of the cape itself and dominated by a medieval castle and a large gun emplacement already in ruins owing to the earlier naval assault. At 6:00 A.M. the bombardment ceased, and in the uncanny silence that ensued the *River Clyde*, a converted collier with two thousand men aboard, began heading for shore, accompanied by about twenty small boats that also were filled with troops. Unlike Gaba Tepe, the natural amphitheater they approached was somewhat familiar terrain, for it was here that British sailors had roamed freely during the February attacks.

But those had been the salad days before the element of surprise was completely dissipated. The Turks now were holding Sedd-el-Bahr so tenaciously that they had returned to their positions under cover after the *Albion* stopped firing and awaited the invaders. At 6:22 A.M. the *River Clyde* ran deliberately aground, and in another moment the silence was broken by an overwhelming outburst from the Turkish rifles and guns. The men in the small boats were mowed down, and in another moment so were those in the *River Clyde* when the gangplanks were lowered and they began streaming down. Only a few lucky ones made it across the dozen or so yards of beach to a sandbank just high enough to shelter them from the Turkish fire above. By midmorning hundreds lay dead on the beach and in the water; but the position somehow was held.

Fortunes varied at the other four landing places around the cape. Just to the west of it, at the place designated W beach (Sedd-el-Bahr was V), heavy casualties were also incurred by troops wading ashore. At the two outermost positions to the east and to the west, however, there were unexpected successes—so unexpected that the advantages gained were quickly lost in this ill-coordinated invasion. The two thousand men who were landed at Y beach, about four miles up the western coast, even reached the heights. But then, instead of encircling the Turkish positions that were wreaking slaughter at V and W, they sat down to make tea, completely unaware of what was happening in the other sectors. There were more British soldiers at Y than there were Turks in the entire Cape Helles area, but such was the atmosphere of confusion that, on the following day, they evacuated the position altogether.

By the afternoon of April 26, the combined beachheads in the Cape Helles area—minus the one at Y—had been established in spite of everything. So also had been the unlikely one at Ari Burnu, in the place that was soon to become known as Anzac Cove. For a while, the Australians had thought that their erroneously established position was to be evacuated, but in the early morning hours General Sir Ian Hamilton had sent a message from his headquarters aboard the *Queen Elizabeth* telling them "You have only to dig, dig, dig, until you are safe." And dig they did, in every spot they could reach on the steep faces of the cliffs, along contours so irregular that it was often impossible to determine where the "front" was: here there were groups of Australians, there groups of Turks, scattered crazily about in the rocks.

It was in particular those trenches at Anzac Cove—which were to earn their makers the permanent name of Diggers—that provided grim reminders of the altogether familiar destiny now overtaking the Gallipoli campaign. That day, the War Office and the Admiralty issued this report to the press:

The general attack on the Dardanelles by the Fleet and the Army was resumed yesterday.

The disembarkation of the Army, covered by the Fleet, began before sunrise at various points on the Gallipoli Peninsula, and, in spite of serious opposition from the enemy in strong entrenchments protected by barbed wire, was completely successful. Before nightfall large forces were established on shore. The landing of the Army and the advance continue.

Thirty thousand troops—about fifteen thousand each at Anzac Cove and the cape—had been landed, and there were more to come; but the advance was not in fact continuing. The heights had not been achieved, and the initial momentum had been lost. As on the western front, a deadly stalemate had begun.

Even this road led to Zion, however, and Colonel Patterson and his men, still aboard their ships on April 26, were eager to get into the fray. The previous day, they had been able only to watch the landing at Cape Helles from over the water. "As we plowed along the calm sea, to the slow beat of the engines," Patterson was to recall of the early morning hours of the twenty-fifth, "each hour seemed a century, but at last we were able to distinguish the misty outline of the Asiatic shore and, a little later on, we saw, coming to meet us like an outstretched arm and hand, a land fringed and half-hidden by the fire and smoke which enveloped it as if some great magician had summoned the powers of darkness to aid in its defense.

"Soon battleships, cruisers and destroyers began to outline themselves, and every few minutes we could see them enveloped in a sheet of flame and smoke, as they poured their broadsides into the Turkish positions. The roar of the *Queen Elizabeth*'s heavy guns dwarfed all other sounds, as this leviathan launched her huge projectiles—surely mightier thunderbolts than Jove ever hurled—against the foe. Every now and again one of her shells would strike and burst on the very crest of Achi Baba, which then, as it belched forth flame, smoke and great chunks of the hill itself, vividly recalled to my mind Vesuvius in a rage."

The Zion Mule Corps was designated to land at Sedd-el-Bahr. "As we approached near to our landing-place, we could see through the haze, smoke and dust, the gleams of bayonets, as men swayed and moved hither and thither in the course of the fight, while the roar of the cannon and the rattle of the machine-guns and rifles were absolutely deafening." Patterson noted that there also was occasional cannon fire from the Turkish positions on the Asiatic shore. As for the British warships, they "were slowly moving up and down the coast blazing away fiercely at the Turkish strongholds, battering such of them as were left into unrecognizable ruins." But in the

transports, which "lay off the shore in four parallel lines, each successive line going forward methodically and disembarking the units on
board as the ground was made good by the landing parties," there
was nothing to do but wait one's turn, and watch.

"We watched the fight from our position in the line for the
whole of that day, and never was excitement so intense and long-
sustained as during those hours; nor was it lessened when night fell
upon us, for the roll of battle still continued—made all the grander by
the vivid flashes from the guns which, every few moments, shot
forth great spurts of flame, brilliantly illuminating the inky darkness. Sedd-el-Bahr Castle and the village nestling behind it were
fiercely ablaze, and cast a ruddy glare on the sky."

They watched the fighting from aboard ship all of the next day,
too, and finally got ashore on the afternoon of April 27. As soon as
they landed, Patterson arranged his men in a long line on the temporary pier that had been set up, and they passed along from the boats
the kerosene tins filled with the drinking water supply. The position
at Sedd-el-Bahr was fully established by now, but there still was fire
from the big Turkish guns on the Asiatic shore, two and a half miles
across the water. As the Jewish volunteers relayed the tins, "the
guns from Asia were making very good shooting, shells striking the
water within a few yards of us, just going over our heads, a little to
the right or a little to the left, but always just missing. I watched my
men very carefully," Patterson says, "to see how they would stand
their baptism of fire, and I am happy to be able to say that, with one
solitary exception, all appeared quite unconcerned and took not the
slightest heed of the dangerous position they were in. The one exception was a youth from the Yemen, who trembled and chattered
with nervousness; but when I went up to him, shook him somewhat
ungently, and asked him what was the matter, he bent to his work
and the cans passed merrily along." There were no casualties during
the disembarkation.

That night, Colonel Patterson and his men received their first
assignment, which was to distribute ammunition along the front.
About two hundred mules were loaded with two thousand cartridges
apiece, and were led into the darkness by men from the Zion detachment, accompanied by Patterson and Major O'Hara, the quartermas-
ter general. It was still the rainy season at Gallipoli, and no sooner
had they set out than a downpour began.

"On we squelched through the mud," Patterson writes, "over
unknown tracks with the water streaming down our bodies and running in rivulets out of our boots. As soon as the rain ceased a biting

cold wind set in, which froze us to the marrow. However, the vigorous walking, helping up a fallen mule, readjusting the loads, getting out of holes into which we had tumbled, etc., kept our circulation going, and when we arrived at a place known as Pink Farm, the furthest point to which we had yet advanced, there was a sudden alarm that the Turks were approaching. Nobody knew then where our front line was, or whether it linked up across the Peninsula." It turned out to be a false alarm. "Gongs could plainly be heard sounding, apparently close by, as though it was some prearranged signal of the enemy, but whatever the reason we saw nothing of the Turks, and no attack was made, so we unloaded our ammunition and were then sent back for more." They ran several such shifts before dawn.

"We have a lot to do," Captain Joseph Trumpeldor wrote to a friend a few days later. "Our Colonel and officers keep thinking that the most strenuous work is only to last another few days; then comes a new transport ship full of men for us to assist. Meanwhile we work day and night without letup; there is scarcely a free moment for eating or drinking. We bring ammunition, machine guns, food and water to the forward positions. Thanks to our work and conscientiousness 'the troops not only have ceased to retreat, but have resumed the offensive and captured new positions,' as it says in one of the Orders of the Day. Our work is quite valuable." Trumpeldor went on to mention the casualties so far—Lieutenant Alexander Gorodisky, wounded in both arms, Sergeant Nissel Rosenberg, grazed in the forehead, both of them recovering, but one man missing in action.

Eventually there were to be other deaths, including that of Gorodisky. "Sometimes while away from Headquarters on these detached duties a man would get killed," Patterson writes. "His comrades always brought the body back to the camp, and then the whole Corps attended the funeral, which was a very solemn ceremony. Over the grave of each hero whom we buried in Gallipoli was erected a little memorial, the Shield of David, with his name and the date of his death engraved underneath. Nothing brought the old days of the Bible back more vividly to my mind than to see, when one of my Zion men was wounded, how his friends would literally fall on his neck, weep, and embrace him most tenderly."

Only Trumpeldor was different. Patterson "never once saw him give way to any of these emotions. On the contrary, he would remark to me over the body of a badly wounded Zionist: 'Ken, ken! (Hebrew for "Yes, yes!") A la guerre comme à la guerre!' And I must say that he himself bore a bullet wound through his shoulder with the greatest fortitude, carrying out his duties as if nothing had happened and absolutely refusing to go into hospital. I am glad to say he made a speedy and good recovery." Sir Ian Hamilton, who thought that Patterson's men did "extremely well," was to remark that they showed "a more difficult type of bravery than the men in the front line who had the excitement of combat to keep them going." One of them, Private M. Grushkovsky, was to win a DSO.

On April 30 the *Jewish Chronicle* wrote:

> The formation in Alexandria of the Zion Mule Transport Corps—a Jewish legion composed almost entirely of Palestinian refugees—marks an era in the history of the Jews as well as in that of England. Never has England been known to depart from its policy of admitting none but British subjects or colonials into its army, and the step which has now been taken, namely the formation of a Jewish battalion under the Union Jack, adds one more rung to the long ladder of kindly acts that have gained for England her superiority over all nations.

Vladimir Jabotinsky, back in London to propagandize for his own Jewish legion idea, had already begun to perceive the value of the Zion Mule Corps as a step toward that goal: "one thing I admit," he was to write, "I had been wrong; Trumpeldor was right."

·13·

DR. WEIZMANN IS ENLISTED
IN THE WAR EFFORT

The first reports of the Gallipoli landings were published on Tuesday, April 27, two days after the event and five days after the second battle of Ypres had begun. "The news," said a *Times* leader,

> that the fierce battle in Flanders which began on Thursday is being continued with unabated fury is coupled this morning with the news that the Allied troops have landed in Gallipoli. But the novel interests of that enterprise cannot be allowed to distract us from what is, and will remain, the decisive theater of operations. Our first thoughts must be for the bent but unbroken line of battle in the West.

But the news from the West was dismaying. The renewed fighting at Ypres brought twice as many casualties as the first battle there and ended in a reduction of the salient. Furthermore, it was there that the Germans introduced a dread new weapon: poison gas. In general, the Germans seemed to have gained an edge not only in ruthlessness but in the technology of war. On May 9, at Aubers Ridge near Neuve Chapelle, a British attack ended as a fiasco, largely—as *The Times* was quick to proclaim—because of an inadequate supply of artillery shells.

The "shell crisis" became the focus of an overall problem of munitions supply that had first begun to be apparent in the fall of 1914. Germany had risen in a single generation to become the second industrial power in the world, and if Britain now made up for being a poor third by having good munitions contracts with the first, the

United States of America, she was still in no way as well organized for a long Continental war as was her enemy. As far back as October, at the instigation of Lloyd George, a cabinet subcommittee had been appointed to investigate the problem of munitions supplies; but by the beginning of January it had fallen into abeyance, largely owing to the unwillingness of Lord Kitchener, its reluctant chairman, to cooperate with it.

If some of the war secretary's colleagues were becoming convinced that his colonial-war mentality was not adequately taking the measure of present events, it was above all in the matter of munitions supply that he was giving them grounds for this feeling. Lloyd George—whose task it was, if anybody's, to worry about excess expenditure—could only ponder with irony the scrupulous regard for economy that had been shown by Kitchener even when he conquered Khartoum. This "one campaign that had brought him renown and rank," Lloyd George was to write, "was waged on the basis of a tender for the total cost of the operation, which he submitted to that most austere of all Chancellors [of the Exchequer], Sir Michael Hicks Beach. The latter refused to give his sanction to operations against the Mahdi without having a most careful estimate of the cost, and the expenses were consequently cut down to the lowest figure. Lord Kitchener undertook to keep within this estimate and succeeded in doing so."

This indeed was the same man who, according to Lloyd George, strode into the cabinet one day in mid-March, just after the news had arrived of the battle at Neuve Chapelle, and said in tones of suppressed emotion: "Oh, it is terrible—terrible!"

"Were the casualties very heavy?" he was asked.

"I'm not thinking for the moment about the casualties," he replied, "but of all the shells that were wasted!"

One must allow for the element of exaggeration in this story told by Lloyd George many years later about the man who was becoming, at this time, his chief bête noire in the cabinet. But even the far more respectful Asquith, who had appointed him, reported of Kitchener on March 18 that he was "really distressed and preoccupied by the reckless way in which ammunition, particularly shells, was expended last week." In Kitchener's eyes the blame fell once again upon the commander of the British Expeditionary Force, Sir John French, his archrival virtually from the moment the war began. French soon defended himself in a report to the War Office. "There is no evidence in my possession," he protested, "to show that the preliminary bombardment of Neuve Chapelle was unnecessarily severe. In fact, at two places it was inadequate, and very heavy losses resulted." He was evidently becoming frustrated, however, at making vain protests through official channels.

By this time, the phenomenal energies of Lloyd George, the former pacifist, had become totally concentrated upon the problems of the war, from those of mobilization and production at home to those of strategy and tactics at the front. Asquith said on March 18 that "it is quite on the cards that I may create a new office for Lloyd George—Director of War Contracts, or something of the kind—and relieve him of his present duties." As far as the chancellor of the Exchequer now was concerned, his major task was to open new channels of munitions production and supply, even if this meant encroaching upon the jurisdiction of the War Office. In early April he succeeded in having a Munitions of War Committee—it was soon popularly known as the Shell Committee—appointed with himself as chairman, and without Kitchener participating in it at all. Significantly, the committee also did not include Churchill, who was rapidly losing political influence after the failure of the purely naval assault at the Dardanelles; but it did include Balfour, whose behind-the-scenes influence everywhere—and especially at the Admiralty—had become considerable, and between whom and Lloyd George a strong tie of mutual respect had come into being despite their old history of antagonisms. The committee also included one of the rising young lights of the Liberal party, Edwin Montagu, who at age thirty-five had just been appointed to the cabinet as chancellor of the Duchy of Lancaster: a close associate of Asquith's, Montagu was the second son of Samuel Montagu, the first Lord Swaythling, and a cousin of Herbert Samuel's.

These men represented forces now lined up against Kitchener, even though friends of his also were on the committee; but the battle was delayed during the rest of April when Lloyd George suddenly, and with characteristic zeal, devoted himself to the problem of drinking. The chancellor of the Exchequer, a light drinker himself, was an old enemy of excessive alcoholic consumption; but now there were statistics to show that drunkenness among munitions workers was a serious curtailment to production. "We are fighting Germany, Austria and Drink," he said at the end of March, "and, as far as I can see, the greatest of these deadly foes is Drink." Within a week, King George V issued a pledge that he and the royal household had renounced alcoholic beverages for the remainder of the war, and he expressed his wish that the nation would follow his example. Lloyd George wanted to go further than mere moral suasion, however; impressed by the fact that the Russians had banned vodka and the French absinthe, he thought for a moment of achieving some equivalent control by nationalizing the liquor trade. But the campaign met strong resistance, from the prime minister down to the humblest workingman; as for the press, there were few editors besides the austere C.P. Scott who could wholeheartedly endorse it. *The Times* went so far as to assert, on April 10, that the munitions shortage was not due to drunkenness among workers, but to "the muddle at the War Office."

Lord Northcliffe of *The Times* and the *Daily Mail*, the foremost press lord in the land, was now prepared to do battle with England's great warlord, Kitchener. He had been issuing warning rumbles for a while, but his great opening salvo was delivered early in May, right after the disaster at Aubers Ridge and the frustrating Battle of Festubert that ensued in that area. Sir John French, no longer able to contain his dissatisfaction over the munitions shortage, had decided to make his correspondence with the War Office available not only to Lloyd George, Balfour, and the Opposition leader Andrew Bonar Law, but also to the *Times* correspondent at the front. The startling headline ran on Friday, May 14:

NEED FOR SHELLS
BRITISH ATTACKS CHECKED
LIMITED SUPPLY THE CAUSE

Doubtless inspired at least in part by the activities of Lloyd George and the Shell Committee, Northcliffe had come forth determined to drive Kitchener out of office.

Certainly he helped contribute to the growing atmosphere of political crisis, which was exacerbated three days later by the resignation of Admiral Fisher as first sea lord in protest over the developments at Gallipoli. Facing a strongly aroused Opposition for the first time since the war began, Asquith asked for the resignation of his Liberal ministers on May 19. He then deftly proceeded to form a Coalition government in which the Liberals retained all the key portfolios. Churchill had to be sacrificed to a Tory resentment that had never really abated since his desertion of that party ten years before—he was appointed Montagu's successor as chancellor of the Duchy of Lancaster—but his replacement at the Admiralty, Balfour, was hardly any longer a Conservative except in name. Herbert Samuel left the cabinet, but remained in the Government by returning to his old position as postmaster general. Bonar Law got the Colonial Office, which meant little in wartime, while Sir Edward Grey retained the powerful Foreign Office post and Asquith stayed on, of course, as prime minister. The Liberal Reginald McKenna, Churchill's predecessor as first lord of the Admiralty and since then home secretary, became chancellor of the Exchequer, while Lloyd George took up the newly created post of minister of munitions, where he could be rival warlord to Kitchener.

As for the secretary for war, that great physical and political mass remained unbudged, and his continuing unassailability was demonstrated on May 21, when Northcliffe dared to renew the attack. "THE SHELLS SCANDAL," the headline ran this time in the popular *Daily Mail*, "LORD KITCHENER'S TRAGIC BLUNDER." That afternoon, an irate mob of jobbers and brokers roamed through offices in the City collecting copies of the *Daily Mail* and made a huge bonfire of them in front of the stock exchange. Subscriptions were canceled. But that was the end of it; Kitchener's ardent supporters soon discovered there was to be no more trouble forthcoming from Northcliffe, who had learned his lesson from the violent reaction he aroused.

Some of the basic problems of munitions production were involved in the manufacture of cordite, the conventional propellant explosive of the day. Consisting of guncotton, nitroglycerin, and mineral jelly mixed, pressed into cords, and dried, the final product resembled brown twine, which was cut to various lengths as required. But the mixture of elements could not have been achieved without a chemical solvent, and the one most widely used in British cordite production was a by-product of alcohol called acetone. Like methyl alcohol, it had usually been distilled from wood pulp, and Britain, not one of the great timber-growing countries, had maintained a supply of acetone by importing it from Austria, Canada, and the United States. But Austrian acetone was, of course, no longer available, and the situation in the American market had become, in Lloyd George's words, "extremely delicate." Prices had gone up and, in any case, it no longer seemed that America and Canada could supply acetone in sufficient quantity for the needs projected over the coming year.

There were two possible routes to a solution of this problem. One was to try to develop types of cordite that could be manufactured with other solvents than acetone; the main problem here, however, was that the other viable solvents also were forms of alcohol or its by-products that were dependent upon wood supply. A second route was to try to produce acetone from sources other than wood. Chemists had, in fact, achieved results along these lines by using bacterial cultures in the fermentation of starches: at a factory in King's Lynn, outside of London, a firm called the Synthetic Products Company had been producing acetone from potatoes since 1912 and was now doing so under a War Office contract. The process used there had been discovered by Auguste Fernbach, a French biochemist who was the director of the Fermentation Laboratory at the Pasteur Institute in Paris.

Fernbach, who had developed this process between 1910 and 1912 while experimenting with ways to produce synthetic rubber by fermentation, had done some of the work of that time in collaboration with a younger disciple from Manchester—Dr. Chaim Weizmann. Indeed, Weizmann, who had shuttled between Paris and Manchester for this work during university vacations, seems to have felt for a time that he was entitled to a share of the royalties earned by Fernbach for the latter's acetone process. But somewhere in the period that intervened between then and the outbreak of war, Weizmann had gone his mentor one better and developed an acetone process based on the fermentation of maize. Weizmann's process was to prove more efficient than Fernbach's as to both quality and quantity of production. But whether it was, in fact, a distinctly different process was a matter that would prove open to question.

Since Weizmann, in his capacity as a Zionist spokesman, had made himself known over the years to some of the British statesmen who had become the most concerned with munitions questions—not only to Lloyd George, but also to Churchill and to his behind-the-scenes associate at the Admiralty, Balfour (the Admiralty having been in charge of the country's main acetone stockpile down to the outbreak of war)—it is not surprising that his acetone work was discovered by them. Rather, what is surprising is that the discovery took so long. Indeed, there is something of a mystery in this and in the story of the devious route Weizmann had to follow before ending up in the Government's employ as a chemist in the spring and summer of 1915.

The story begins on Tuesday, February 9, 1915, when Weizmann had an unexpected visitor to his laboratory at the University of Manchester. It was William Rintoul, head of the research department at Nobel's Explosives Company in Ardeer, Scotland—the largest firm of its kind in Great Britain. Efforts were already being made to clear up some of the complications in the acetone market. Competition for acetone among British firms had been forcing up American prices—legislation enabling the Government to commandeer essential industries was not to be passed until the following month—and Nobel's had agreed to help eliminate such competition by monopolistically purchasing all the acetone it could find. Somewhere in the course of this campaign, Nobel's had discovered Weizmann; since he had not yet taken out a patent on his acetone process, it is not at all clear how this discovery had come about. Years later, Weizmann was to recall having filled out a War Office questionnaire for chemists in August 1914, in which he mentioned his acetone process as something of possible military value and offered it free of charge. But this does not seem to have had any connection with Rintoul's visit, nor does it even seem that Rintoul brought up the matter of acetone right away.

"What the original purpose of his visit was I do not know," Weizmann writes in his autobiography; and one has the impression that Rintoul made a deliberate effort to look as if he had just been passing through. Eventually, however, the conversation made its way to acetone. "You will be interested to hear," Weizmann wrote that evening to Ahad Ha'am, "that I had a visit today from the Chief Chemist of the Nobel factories, who looked over all my experiments and said that he would give a 'favorable report.' "

By the end of the month Weizmann was expecting another visit from Rintoul. What he got, as it turned out, was Rintoul and two or three other people from Nobel's who spent more than a week in Manchester watching him conduct his acetone experiments. Early in March, Weizmann wrote to Dorothy de Rothschild: "The people from Nobel's spent the whole of the week here (it is already the second week) and made all the tests. Everything came off very satisfactorily and they left today. The 'insect' behaved very well; now I hope Nobel's will behave." They did, and in a few weeks Weizmann had received an offer that involved a down payment of £3,000 in cash and further terms that he was eventually to describe as "excellent"— though he wrote to Ahad Ha'am on March 28 that "my solicitor's advice is *not* to budge." In the meantime, he had applied for a patent on the process at last, and it was granted on March 29.

Then there was a short interval, again completely dominated by Zionist work. Weizmann made another trip to Paris, where he again saw Baron Edmond de Rothschild and his son James—Dorothy's husband—who was there recuperating from an injury suffered in an accident at the front. In their discussion of Zionist strategies, they doubtless had much to say about English Rothschild circles, which Weizmann had begun to penetrate and in which an upsetting event had occurred on April 1: Lord Rothschild had died. No one yet knew the political attitudes of his eldest son, Lionel Walter, now the second Lord Rothschild, a retiring man who preferred his collection of natural history specimens at Tring to any of the more worldly activities favored by his father.

Back in Manchester by the middle of April, Weizmann must have begun to wonder what was happening at Nobel's. Suddenly, on Monday, April 19, he got his answer from a different and wholly unexpected quarter. On that day he received a letter from Colonel Sir Frederick Nathan, adviser to the Admiralty on cordite supply, asking him to come to London for an interview the following Wednesday. He did so, and Nathan, explaining that the Admiralty might be interested in Weizmann's acetone process, which had been referred to them by Nobel's, asked for a report outlining past results and possible future procedures. Weizmann mailed it on April 25, and by the end of the month all arrangements had been tentatively made.

"I am handing over the whole process to them," Weizmann wrote to Rintoul on May 2.

> At the present they pay me £500, £250 to be spent on an assistant, and £250 to cover costs of patenting, materials, experiments (preliminary) etc. In view of the fact that the process is going to the Admiralty I did not feel justified in asking for any royalty or remuneration in the case the large scale trial proves successful. I also stated that I lay no claim to any financial remuneration as long as the present crisis is on. Should the Admiralty continue to manufacture acetone by this process after the War I leave it to them to fix my remuneration.

There remained only the drawing up of the official papers and the selection of a plant. Doubtless it was already clear that the plant would be in the London area and that Weizmann would either have to commute from Manchester or resettle himself for the duration of the project.

What had happened in the course of these three months? Why had Nobel's so suddenly appeared, then disappeared with equal suddenness, leaving the whole matter to the Admiralty? There is a significant connection between the two parts of this story in the person of Sir Frederick Nathan, who had been appointed to his Admiralty post around the beginning of the year, but who, just prior to that, had been for five years the works manager at Nobel's. This does not indicate merely that he was the readily available contact between Nobel's and the Admiralty in cordite matters—and indeed, it was to him that Nobel's sent the report it had garnered at Weizmann's laboratory in late February and early March; it also suggests the possibility that Nathan was the man behind Nobel's approach to Weizmann in the first place.

In this connection, it may not be insignificant that Nathan was a member of an old Anglo-Jewish family, an activist in Jewish community affairs, and the brother of Sir Matthew Nathan, a prominent Colonial Service officer who belonged to the Maccabaeans and had known both Herzl and Weizmann personally. "One curious detail," Weizmann wrote about the whole matter to Dorothy de Rothschild on May 3: "the expert who interviewed me is Sir Frederick Nathan, a brother of Sir Matthew. He is very nice indeed and very interesting to talk to. (I kept off Zionism for the time being.)" If they ever did get to talk about Zionism, Weizmann may not have found Sir Frederick among its warmest supporters: his brother, Sir Matthew, at any rate, was to prove hostile in the near future. But in the spring of 1915, the lines between sympathizers with Zionism and opponents of it in the Anglo-Jewish community were not so clear either as they had been before or as they would turn out to be subsequently: commitments were in a phase of readjustment under the overwhelming impact of events. Sir Frederick Nathan, then, may very well have known for some time about Weizmann the Zionist, as his brother did, and possibly did not disapprove. But as an expert in propellant explosives, at any rate, he must also have known about Weizmann's work with acetone if he knew about Weizmann at all.

If at the Admiralty Nathan had been interested in Weizmann's work all along, why then had he let his old colleagues at Nobel's make the initial contacts? One reason is that this was a moment of transition in the wartime relations between Government and industry. In March, a new set of amendments to the Defence of the Realm Act enabled the Government to commandeer factories when it was deemed necessary and in general made the Government a more direct participant than it had been in the processes of war production. But in February, when Weizmann first was approached, Nobel's and other private enterprises were still playing a more prominent and autonomous role in the organization of war production than they were to do by April, when Weizmann was at last contacted directly by the Admiralty. Another reason for Nathan's behavior in February would surely have been mere prudence—a desire to let Nobel's be the cat's-paw for the Admiralty while it was being ascertained whether Weizmann's work merited allowing him access to sensitive sources and outlets. After all, Weizmann, though a naturalized British subject since 1911, was still a foreigner in the eyes of many a native Englishman; and Zionism in particular, with the rump of its executive holding on in Berlin, was still widely thought to have dangerously German associations.

Other possible reasons remain, however, for the Admiralty's discretion. During this period, Weizmann had another meeting with Balfour—who, as we have seen, was already an important influence at the Admiralty and was soon to become first lord. Significantly, it was to turn out to be their last meeting for a long time to come. It took place on the afternoon of March 16, at Weizmann's request, and the only description we have of it is a brief one made by Weizmann in a letter to Herbert Samuel a few days later. "I had an opportunity of talking to Mr. Balfour," he wrote, "who would help us, if the situation with regard to France would be clear." From Weizmann's correspondence just prior to the meeting, however, we may infer that two other matters were brought up at it. For one thing, Weizmann's good friend Harry Sacher, the journalist, had embarked on a literary project—a collection of essays, under his editorship, which would present Zionism to the British public, with himself, Weizmann, Sokolow, and Gaster (but not Joseph Cowen or Leopold Greenberg) among its contributors. Sacher had urged Weizmann to ask Balfour if he would contribute a foreword, and Weizmann had already written to Balfour making this request. There can be little doubt that this came up at the meeting. And if it did, one may surmise Balfour's reply, for the book was to appear the following year with no foreword by him; indeed, all circumstances considered in the middle of March 1915, Balfour could only have regarded the request as somewhat indiscreet.

This may not have been an end to the importunacy, however. Earlier that month, the two members of the Zionist executive who were now in London, Yehiel Tschlenow and Nahum Sokolow—still planning to move on to the United States—had asked Weizmann if he could obtain letters of recommendation for them from both Balfour and Sir Edward Grey. This exasperated Weizmann, who had not even met Grey. "As far as letters from B. and G. are concerned," he replied to his two colleagues on March 7, "I imagine that I'll be able to ask for such letters for myself when I'm ready to go [to America].

After all, I do not know these gentlemen well enough to ask them for letters for my friends." But then he added: "Anyhow, I am writing to Balfour today asking for an appointment and then we shall see"— which suggests he may have brought up this matter, too, in the meeting with Balfour.

Such requests are likely to have helped Balfour conclude that, for the time being at any rate, it was prudent to keep Weizmann and his friends at a distance—not so much in spite of his sympathy for their aims as because of it. And now that the Admiralty was interested in Weizmann for another reason entirely, such prudence was all the more desirable: Balfour was the last man ready to seem to be using Admiralty business as a cover for political purposes. It may even have come to be considered particularly urgent by now to assume such an attitude, since there were other viewpoints at the Admiralty besides Balfour's that were favorable to Zionist aims. The sympathies of the outgoing first lord, Winston Churchill, went back to the 1906 election. Admiral Sir Henry Jackson, former chief of the Admiralty war staff and soon to be Fisher's successor as first sea lord, was about to become an advocate of the British annexation of Haifa, even though he had previously supported the Alexandretta idea. As for Fisher, he wrote to Herbert Samuel on April 29: "I read your excellent paper with conviction as to the inclusion in the English sphere of Palestine, and the excellent committee we have working on the matter* will I feel certain, forward your views. But please say nothing of this, at present, unless you've heard it from elsewhere. I am giving it all my support."

There also was another ministry in which Zionism was to find support and Weizmann to obtain work. In his memoirs Lloyd George tells how, after becoming minister of munitions, he got together with C.P. Scott one day when the question of acetone supply was one of the things weighing on his mind. "I told him of my problem," Lloyd George writes,

> and that I was on the lookout for a resourceful chemist who would help me to solve it. He said: "There is a very remarkable professor of chemistry in the University of Manchester willing to place his services at the disposal of the State. I must tell you, however, that he was born somewhere near the Vistula, and I am not sure on which side. His name is Weizmann." Scott could

* The de Bunsen Committee on British war aims in Ottoman Asia, to be dealt with in Chapter 14.

guarantee that whatever the country of origin, Weizmann was thoroughly devoted to the cause of the Allies, that the one thing he really cared about was Zionism, and that he was convinced that in the victory of the Allies alone was there any hope for his people. I knew Mr. Scott to be one of the shrewdest judges of men I had ever met. . . . I took his word about Professor Weizmann and invited him to London to see me.

These words were written many years after the event, and since it was indeed Scott who first brought up to Lloyd George the subject of Weizmann's acetone work, we can acknowledge the legitimacy of the confusion between that conversation and the earlier one in which Scott had first mentioned Weizmann as a Zionist. The confusion also happens to be convenient, however, in that it makes Lloyd George seem to have been free of any commitment to Zionism until after it was brought to his attention by a brilliant chemist who did war work for him. Indeed, the readiness with which Lloyd George's trick of memory was to make Chaim Weizmann's chemistry an excuse for having adopted a controversial position leads one to suspect that the germ of such a notion was in his mind at the beginning of June 1915, when he took up Scott's latest suggestion regarding the Manchester chemist without a moment's delay.

As for Scott, he no longer needed persuasion about any of the things Weizmann stood for, including his chemistry. Since the fall, there had been a concerted movement afoot to organize a national dyestuffs industry now that the German supply—hitherto the main source for Britain—was no longer available. Manchester was the British center of that industry, so that a good deal of the discussion and activity related to the problem was taking place there, and the *Guardian* was closely covering all of it. Now, dyestuffs chemistry was Weizmann's oldest field of interest as a professional: he had begun his career with a thesis on naphthazarin dyes, had worked at Elberfeld for a plant that subsequently became part of the German I.G. Farbenindustrie, and had come to Manchester in the first place in order to work in dyestuffs, both at the university and at Clayton Aniline. And though his main interests as a chemist had since shifted elsewhere, his work in this field was still well enough recognized that at the end of May 1915 the Board of Trade offered him a post in the forthcoming National Dye Scheme. Scott was surely aware of both this and the Admiralty appointment when, on what must have been his very next trip to London, he reminded the newly appointed minister of munitions of Weizmann's work in acetone.

At Lloyd George's request, Scott arranged for Weizmann to visit the ministry. "I am going up to London again today," Weizmann wrote on Sunday, June 6, "as I was called up by Mr. Lloyd George in connection with my chemical thing." And Scott wrote to Lloyd George that same day:

> If you are seeing Dr. Weizmann tomorrow (he is calling, as directed, on your secretary, Mr. Wolfe), you may like to ask him about the War Office contract with a certain Company for the manufacture of acetone. They are paying a considerable sum . . . for a process originally devised by Weizmann himself and which is now worthless, as Weizmann's new process (which he offered to the War Office for nothing) . . . will work out, he says, very much cheaper.

The stimulus of competition now was in the air; and Lloyd George certainly was ready to try scoring advantages over Kitchener and the War Office at every opportunity. But it could work both ways: if Weizmann was again claiming to be the true creator of the Fernbach process in use at King's Lynn, was not Fernbach likely to make the same claim against him?

The first person Weizmann saw at the ministry on Monday was Lloyd George's secretary, Humbert Wolfe. "He was rather keen on the acetone question," Weizmann was to report to Scott, "but I explained to him that the matter is out of my hands and any arrangement they would like to make they would have to do it directly with the Admiralty, to whom I have handed over the process." When he got in to see Lloyd George, even though it was "only for a very few minutes, he was very busy," Weizmann managed to squeeze in a grand presentation that went far beyond acetone. He subsequently outlined it this way for Scott:

> 1) The chemical industry and manufacture of explosives has to be organized, coordinated and centralized.
> 2) I am aware that the French have got some valuable manufacturing processes for explosives, which we lack and I offered my services to go over and confer with them and establish co-operation.
> 3) The country where Chemistry is best organized, even better than Germany is, is Switzerland and I offered to go over and get over here 2 or 3 of their best men, who would help in establishing the organization as mentioned under point 1).

Weizmann was offering the results of his lifelong itinerary as a kind of Wandering Jew of science, but the thrust of it must have seemed startlingly ambitious to the minister of munitions. Did he want Weizmann to be, in effect, an under-secretary of chemistry? He was not one to begrudge displays of ambition in men of talent, however—as long as they were not his political rivals—and he expressed interest in point 3, asking Weizmann to write up the proposal for him.

Weizmann composed his letter on Wednesday, June 9, and showed it to Scott before sending it on to Lloyd George. He began by saying again that his acetone process was now under the Admiralty's control and that Sir Frederick Nathan could provide information about it. "I need only add," he said, "that in my opinion as much acetone as is needed can be produced by this process." He then moved on to his larger vision. "There are many good chemists in this country," he wrote,

> but not enough for the purpose of reorganizing our explosives industry quickly so as to meet the supreme needs of the moment. We are lacking especially in men with great chemical-technical experience. This deficiency can be made good in two ways. I am aware that the French have command of a great many methods and processes not employed at all, or not employed adequately, here. I take it that they would be anxious, if authoritatively approached, to share their knowledge with us. Cooperation with them ought to be established at once. The Swiss chemical industry is not excelled in skill and organization by any other chemical industry, and in my opinion it is even better than the German. If we are prepared to spend the money, we can secure the services of a few of the leading Swiss industrial chemists.

Expatiating on this last point, Weizmann envisioned these Swiss experts being surrounded by a generation of young British assistants who would be "the foundation of a general chemical industry in this country after the war." But he added that such training also was an immediate necessity, in the face of such German wartime technical developments as poison gas. He ended by reminding Lloyd George of his own past associations with leading chemists in France and Switzerland—going beyond the minister's original request, which referred only to Switzerland—and repeating his offer to go over in person and make the necessary contacts.

Doubtless Lloyd George perceived that Weizmann's zeal to

prove himself as a statesman of chemistry was also, in effect, an ambition to demonstrate the qualities of potential Zionist statesmanship and to win some political gratitude for Zionism from the British Government besides. But nothing in this was contrary to the minister's own purposes, which he was far more willing than Balfour to let overlap. Weizmann's chemical projects were worth a try among the manifold things Lloyd George was energetically trying, and the fact that this also meant having in tow an authoritative consultant on Palestine matters whenever they should arise only added to the chemistry's attractiveness.

At lunch with C.P. Scott the following Wednesday, Lloyd George asked about Weizmann and was told "a good deal." He then brought Scott back to talk about Weizmann with Christopher Addison, the parliamentary under-secretary of the Munitions Ministry. Addison seems to have been less impressed by Weizmann's qualifications than Lloyd George was, but this did not stop the latter from taking the Manchester chemist on. Before the summer was over, Weizmann was to find himself in the employ of both the Ministry of Munitions and the Admiralty.

·14·

THE BEGINNINGS OF
A MIDDLE EASTERN POLICY

"**D**ardanelles," wrote C.P. Scott in his diary for June 16, as he recalled Lloyd George's remarks on the subject at lunch. "Was extremely pessimistic as to prospect. A mad enterprise. His conviction personally was that the Germans in command were simply playing with us, that it suited them admirably that we should go on wasting men and shells, and they would keep us at it, but that when it suited them they could drive us into the sea." Now that Churchill was out of the Admiralty and the burden of conviction about Gallipoli lay on the shoulders of Kitchener and Asquith, Lloyd George, still aspiring to a landing at Salonika if not Haifa as well, was less inclined than ever to believe in this "mad enterprise." Balfour, whose enthusiasm had been for a naval assault only, was with him in this disaffection.

Yet, for all the frustrations of the campaign, Gallipoli was having some salutary side effects upon the Allies' war effort. For one thing, Italy had been brought in on their side at last. Italy had been the outstanding anomaly of the war, in that she was the only Great Power in Europe to have remained outside of it. Allied with Germany and Austria for thirty-two years, her government had decided on August 3, 1914, that they were not required by the treaty to honor either Austrian expansionism in the Balkans or the German invasion of France and had declared neutrality. Virtually from that moment on, however, the Entente Powers had regarded Italian participation on their side as both likely and desirable—although Russia's desire had recently begun to diminish. The Russians feared Italian ambitions in the Balkans, and with reason: the eastern Adriatic, along with Italy's northeastern boundaries, had in fact formed the subject of negotiations between Rome and Vienna in the early part of 1915, and these, had they been concluded successfully, would have brought in Italy on the side of the Central Powers after all. But the Dardanelles campaign had inspired the Italians to try bargaining with the Entente as well, and the result, after nearly two months of negotiations, was the secret London Agreement of April 26. In it, Italy was granted claims not only in central and southern Europe—the latter after some modifications at Russia's behest—but also in Africa and the Ottoman Empire. On May 23 Italy, taking her first step as a belligerent, declared war on Austria.

Another side effect of the Gallipoli campaign was to stimulate the first manifestations of an Allied policy concerning the postwar disposition of the Ottoman Empire. Britain and France, sensing the potential conflicts in their respective claims, had tried to neglect the issue at first, but they were now being forced into a confrontation by the clamors of their allies. Russia had been first; then Italy raised its claims. With regard to Turkey, the Italians had demanded acknowledgment of their claims to sovereignty in the Dodecanese Islands, which they still occupied, and in Libya; they also demanded rights in the southwestern part of the Anatolian Peninsula itself, at the port of Adalia. All this was granted in the London Agreement. About other Ottoman matters there seems to have been some reticence in the London discussions. Palestine was not mentioned in the agreement, even though it could possibly have been a matter of Italian concern in that it greatly interested the Vatican and the London terms guaranteed support of Italian opposition to any participation by the Holy See in peace negotiations. "We never stipulated that Mesopotamia or Palestine should be ours," Sir Edward Grey later said of these discussions: "only that they should not go back to the Turk."

This was prudent, and not altogether disingenuous in the climate of thinking that spring. For Britain's postwar Ottoman policy had still been developed no further than a single general principle, which had already been formulated for the Russians and was reiterated in the London Agreement as Article 12: "Italy declares that she associates herself in the declaration made by France, Great Britain and Russia to the effect that Arabia and the Moslem Holy Places in Arabia shall be left under the authority of an independent Moslem Power." We have seen Grey adumbrating this principle as far back as August 1914, in a letter to his ambassador at Constantinople; there, he stated less ambiguously that an Arabia independent of Turkey was one of the prices the latter would be made to pay if she entered the war. In his March 12 memorandum to the Russian government commenting upon the Constantinople Agreement, this, along with a suggestion that an eight-year-old convention between Britain and Russia dividing Persia into spheres of influence would have to be revised, had been the only basic desideratum of his own Government that he could come up with for the time being. At a March 19 War Council meeting, while Allied ships were making the major attack that was expected to force the Dardanelles, Grey once again stated this principle as basic British policy. It was still vague as to the boundaries of the "independent Moslem Power" at the north of the Arabian Peninsula, and as to the degree of its independence from Turkey, but the principle stood fast as a bulwark against any possible opposition among the Muslims of India and Egypt to war upon the caliph of Islam.

This was no longer enough, however; the time had come for Great Britain and France to begin elaborating their respective positions in the Middle East. The matter had been raised urgently at last on March 23 by Paul Cambon, the French ambassador to London, who conveyed to Sir Edward Grey the feelings of his own foreign minister, Théophile Delcassé. Grey wrote about the conversation to his ambassador in Paris, Sir Francis Bertie:

> M. Cambon informed me today that M. Delcassé had observed that, as the question of Constantinople and the Straits, which was the chief question affecting Russia, had now been disposed of, it was rather for France and Great Britain to discuss other questions respecting Asia Minor. M. Delcassé therefore proposed, that there should be an unofficial discussion, either verbally or in the form of private letters, about French and British desiderata. It might take place either through your Excellency in Paris with M. Delcassé, or between M. Cambon and myself here.
>
> I agreed to this, and said that it would be better that the discussion should be between M. Cambon and myself. The Cabinet here had not yet had time to consider our desiderata, and they would have to be discussed with the Cabinet, and referred to it from time to time. I said that we have already stipulated that, when Turkey disappeared from Constantinople and the Straits, there must, in the interests of Islam, be an independent Moslem political unit somewhere else. Its center would naturally be the Moslem Holy Places, and it would include Arabia. But we must settle what else should be included. We ourselves had not yet come to a definite opinion whether Mesopotamia should be

included in this independent Moslem State, or whether we should put forward a claim for ourselves in that region.

M. Cambon said that the whole subject had better be discussed unofficially in the way now proposed.

No discussions could take place, however, until the British had formulated their desiderata. For this purpose, on April 8, Prime Minister Asquith appointed a Committee on Asiatic Turkey, made up of representatives of the Foreign, India, and War offices and of the Admiralty and the Board of Trade, "to consider the nature of British desiderata in Turkey in Asia in the event of a successful conclusion of the war." It was placed under the chairmanship of Sir Maurice de Bunsen, an assistant under-secretary at the Foreign Office, but formerly the ambassador to Vienna down to the outbreak of war and a one-time secretary to the British embassy at Constantinople. The de Bunsen Committee held thirteen meetings between the middle of April and the end of May, and presented its report on June 30.

"Early in March last," the report begins,

the Russian Government, anticipating an early and successful issue to the operations which had been started at the Dardanelles, communicated to the allied Governments its claims in regard to Constantinople.

These claims are summed up. "In return," it continues,

Russia promised scrupulously to respect the special interests of France and Great Britain in the area claimed, and to view with sympathy the claims which those Powers entertained in regard to other regions of the Ottoman Empire.

There follows a summary of Sir Edward Grey's March 12 memorandum to the Russians, including its preliminary desiderata that the 1907 Anglo-Russian Agreement regarding Persia be revised and that Arabia and the Muslim Holy Places "remain under independent Moslem rule."

"The French Government," the report goes on,

were more precise in announcing their counter-claims to Russia. They demanded Cilicia and Syria, in which latter term they included Palestine and the Christian Holy Places, though they did not specify the precise form of their claim—whether annexation or protectorate or sphere of interest. It would appear that Russia is ready to accede to the French claim to Cilicia and Syria proper, but will demur strongly to the inclusion of Palestine.

Russia at any rate agreed to the British stipulations so far as they went—adding that the caliphate, along with the Arabian Holy Places, should perhaps be removed from Turkish hands altogether—and it remained only "for His Majesty's Government to formulate their definite desiderata in Asiatic Turkey." This, then, is the task of the report—with the understanding, however, that "any attempt to formulate them must as far as possible be made to fit in with the known or understood aspirations of those who are our Allies today, but may be our competitors tomorrow." As to the nature of these aspirations,

> France has already given a fairly clear indication of what she will claim; Russia's geographical position, accentuated by the possession of Constantinople, makes it possible to assume with some confidence the essential lines of her development in Asiatic Turkey; Italy demands a field for enterprise around Adalia; and Greece has dreams of expansion in Asia Minor, which her participation in the war may yet convert into reality.

Germany's long-standing aspirations, on the other hand, may be set aside, since the entire report is based upon presumption of an Allied victory, in which case "Germany will not be in a position to intervene, either to assert fresh claims or to maintain her existing privileges."

Before moving on to its formulation of the British desiderata themselves, the report makes one final point about the principles that are to limit them: these include not only the claims of Allied countries already mentioned, but also "the necessity of maintaining a just relation between the prospective advantages to the British Empire by a readjustment of conditions in Asiatic Turkey, and the inevitable increase of Imperial responsibility." We have already noted the reluctance of many Liberals to contemplate any extension of British imperial commitments, and this had remained true of Grey and Asquith in particular, even though they had by now granted that justice demanded their claiming some share of "the carcase of the Turk." Taking this view into consideration, the report at this point seeks to define the essential principle whereby a British claim can be considered valid.

To be so, the report says, it must spring

> from one of the cardinal principles of our policy in the East, our special and supreme position in the Persian Gulf. From that principle, and from the developments, often unconscious, of the policy necessary to maintain it, other claims and aspirations have arisen; but therein lies their justification.

In other words, the British Empire and its interests remain essentially what they always have been: India, her frontiers, and the sea routes leading there—in principle, nothing more. The India Office representative on the committee must have been quite gratified at seeing the old view from Delhi prevail like this. There is no mention of Egypt here, or anywhere else in the report, as a valid and essential principle of empire. Furthermore, as we shall see, the report finds it possible to make the Persian Gulf principle serve any of the claims that Egypt might have served. In this way, the report implicitly gratifies both Liberal sensibilities still worried about Britain's occupation of Egypt, and India Office people who did not want to see major territorial commitments anywhere but in areas affecting their own particular concerns.

Now the report moves on to the desiderata. There are nine in all, and of these the first six are based squarely upon the Persian Gulf principle and its direct ramifications in terms of interests and responsibilities. They call for full "recognition and consolidation" of the British position on the gulf, for the maintenance of British markets there and throughout the present Ottoman Empire, for security with regard to major undertakings such as dam construction and oil drilling in the area, and for continuance of Britain's strategic position in both the gulf and the eastern Mediterranean. One of the points calls for development of the grain supply "which an irrigated Mesopotamia is expected to provide, and of a possible field for Indian colonization"—a point that had often been discussed since the Shatt-al-Arab had come to be occupied by Indian soldiers. Point 3, which is of special interest, calls for the fulfillment of pledges "given, or under consideration" to various chiefs and peoples along the Arab shores of the Persian Gulf and their hinterlands, as well as to those adjacent to the British base at Aden:

> to the Sheikhs of Koweit and Mohammera, the Emir of Nejd (Bin Saud), the people of Basra (Persian Gulf region), Said

Idriss, Imam Yahya, and Sheikh Mavia (in the Yemen); and, generally, maintenance of the assurances given to the Sherif of Mecca and the Arabs.

These are matters to which we shall recur in the next chapter.

Points 7, 8, and 9 of the list of desiderata move on from the realm of interests and treaty obligations dealt with in the first six to that of larger moral responsibilities—a traditional and indispensable justification to Englishmen for their imperial appetite. They are:

(7.) To ensure that Arabia and the Moslem Holy Places remain under independent Moslem rule. Dependent upon this, we should seek for a settlement which will appeal to, or at least not antagonize, Indian Moslem feeling, and will provide a satisfactory solution of the question of the Khalifate.

(8.) A satisfactory solution of the Armenian problem.

(9.) A settlement of the question of Palestine and the Holy Places of Christendom.

These last three desiderata, the report goes on to point out, are matters that would have to be discussed with the Great Powers even if Britain made no claims at all in Asiatic Turkey. But in the meantime, as we shall see, Palestine will make its way back into the discussion in another context entirely.

"It is comparatively easy to formulate our desiderata," the de Bunsen report goes on; "it is very difficult to lay down how to shape the opportunity now at hand for attaining them." A discussion of the possible overall solutions for the disposition of Ottoman Asia by the Great Powers is about to begin, but first the report rejects two out of hand: a system of protectorates whereby, as with Egypt (which is still unmentioned), sovereignty remains theoretically in local or in Ottoman hands and is not surrendered to the occupying power; and a scheme of overall internationalization. Both of these, the report says, would lead to confusion and strife among the occupying powers.

Four possible solutions are then spelled out: (A) the limitation of Turkish sovereignty to the Anatolian Peninsula and the outright partition among the powers of the rest of an extinct Ottoman Empire; (B) the maintenance of the Ottoman Empire as a nominally independent state, but divided into zones of political and commercial interest in which the various powers would have effective control; (C) the maintenance of the Ottoman Empire as it was before the war;

(D) the maintenance of the Ottoman Empire with modifications de-centralizing it along federal lines. Any one of these four schemes would of course be subject to the territorial and political modifica-tions already dealt with—the independent Muslim sovereignty in Arabia, the Palestine question, Armenian and Greek claims, and so forth.

Each of these schemes is then explicated and analyzed at length; but the greatest length is given to course A. This certainly had its faults, as the report points out—it was the course that would frankly turn Allied war policy into one of annexation and that would as-suredly keep the Turks in the fight even if Constantinople were con-quered. But we may observe that, in this era before the concept of "mandate" had evolved, it was the only course that could be seriously considered under all the given circumstances. We shall therefore con-fine ourselves to a consideration of course A among the four. We may also note that the points in the report that concern us the most in the context of this narrative remain fairly well the same throughout the four schemes.

Course A, pursuing the ramifications of the basic British de-siderata, leaps from the Persian Gulf into Mesopotamia as swiftly as the Indian army did. "When war broke out with Turkey," the report reads,

> His Majesty's Government gave assurances to the Sheikhs of Koweit and Mohammerah and to the Emir of Nejd that Basra would never again be allowed to be subject to Turkish authority. Moreover, the inhabitants of the town of Basra itself had been given a formal assurance by the Viceroy of India that "the fu-ture will bring them a more benign rule" than that of the Turk.

Basra, then, must remain in British hands. But, with Russia and France to the north and northwest of it, what would be its defensible frontier? "The Committee have carefully considered a note by the Viceroy" of India, the report goes on,

> wherein His Excellency would limit the acquisition of territory to sovereign rights in the Basra vilayet,* and a protectorate over Bagdad, as well as a further Note by the Political Secre-tary, India Office, pointing out that Basra by itself is untenable and that Bagdad commands it.

* A vilayet is a Turkish administrative district.

Baghdad should therefore be included in the British claims—and, under the terms of course A, by annexation rather than protectorate. Even then, however, a defensible frontier would not have been attained, and so the report's argumentation pushes northward and does not stop until Mosul has been included in the British sphere. All this is based upon a confidence derived from continuing reports that, among foreign suzerainties, the people of the area would prefer that of the British to any other.

The security of a British Mesopotamia, however, would not begin at the borders of Mesopotamia itself in the west. "In the event of an invasion of Mesopotamia by Russia," the report observes,

> it is unlikely that India would be able to spare troops for its defense, while in such an emergency the difference between success and disaster may well lie in the rapidity with which reinforcements can reach the threatened area. From this consideration it becomes a military necessity to provide a back door into Mesopotamia from the Eastern Mediterranean.

We come, then, to the question of Alexandretta versus Haifa, which by now had been thoroughly discussed not only in cabinet circles but in the various ministries themselves.

"The most natural choice," we read,

> would apparently be Alexandretta which is the best harbor on the coast of Syria and is already connected with the Bagdad railway system. Its annexation would have the double advantage of giving us the facilities we require for reinforcing Mesopotamia from the Mediterranean, and of denying to foreign Powers the only harbor in Syria which is susceptible of being developed into a naval base.

But the French "would hardly welcome" the resultant wedge of British territory "cutting their own zone in half," and under such circumstances "could not be refused the southern part of Syria, which would bring her frontier into Arabia, a situation which we could scarcely tolerate." Once again, Egypt is not mentioned at a crucial point. "In these circumstances," the argument concludes,

> it appears desirable to exclude Alexandretta from the limits of British interests and to replace it by Haifa, which, though not

such a good natural harbor as Alexandretta, is capable of development into a sufficiently good port, and of connection by railway with Mesopotamia.

The matter of a railway is then considered at length, and arguments are offered as to why a line connecting Haifa with the Euphrates, Mosul, and Baghdad would have to be entirely within the British zone. The conclusion is a projected northern boundary to British claims in the area that would begin in the west at Acre, on the northern side of Haifa Bay, and form a great arc eastward, running up through Tadmor (ancient Palmyra) to Al Mayadin on the upper Euphrates, and thence past Mosul to the Persian border at Rowanduz. The southern boundary would be drawn so as to leave an independent Arabian Peninsula. This geographical scheme, the report observes, only

> entails one serious international difficulty: it removes Palestine from the French, only to include it in the British sphere. Suggestions for the actual settlement of the intricate problem of the sacred places scarcely come within the scope of the Committee's labors, but as regards this particular difficulty they think that His Majesty's Government should be prepared to make no claim themselves to the possession of the Holy Places, and to leave their future to be decided as a separate question, in discussion with those who stand for the national and religious interests involved.

The "separate question" of Palestine—at least of its Holy Places—has thus made its way into the British sphere after all, by way of the Mediterranean "back door." The authors of the report themselves seem almost startled at having made this suggestion, for though they subsequently express the hope that "we may count on Russian support in return for sympathy for Russian views in regard to Palestine"—views making it likely that the Russians would prefer even exclusive British control of Palestine to having the French there—they retreat a little at the end when they come to a full discussion of the last three of the nine desiderata, those concerning Arabia, Armenia, and Palestine. "Still less," they write, after disclaiming any qualifications to put forth concrete suggestions about the Armenian question,

> do the Committee desire to offer suggestions about the future destiny of Palestine, but since that territory has been included

within the geographical limits assigned to the British sphere in the two schemes, of partition, and of zones of interest, they desire to repeat that they see no reason why the sacred places of Palestine should not be dealt with as a separate question. They have felt free to deliberate on the assumption that the French claim will be rejected, since they are convinced that the forces opposed are too great for France ever to make that claim good but for the same reason they consider that it will be idle for His Majesty's Government to claim the retention of Palestine in their sphere. Palestine must be recognized as a country whose destiny must be the subject of special negotiations, in which both belligerents and neutrals are alike interested.

The gist of this irresolute position seems to be: if we cannot have Palestine, then neither can anyone else—but really, we should have it. The whole thing tends toward an argument favoring effective British control under the guise of internationalization—which was, indeed, to be the formula concerning Palestine that would be tried in the coming months.

But can it be that this position evolved out of geopolitical considerations alone? When the report refers to the "national and religious interests involved" in the Palestine question, may we not take this formula as intended to include Zionist and Jewish, as well as French and Catholic, Russian and Orthodox, Arab and Muslim, Armenian, Ethiopian, and other such interests? Most likely we may, since, judging from Admiral Fisher's letter of April 29 to Herbert Samuel, the latter's proposals regarding Palestine had apparently been made known to the committee. Indeed, the interest in Palestine that we have detected at the Admiralty seems to have been well represented by their man on the committee, Admiral Sir Henry Jackson. In March, Jackson had been one of the prominent advocates of Alexandretta as the British port in the Levant, but the records of the de Bunsen Committee show that sometime during its sessions he submitted a memorandum favoring Haifa instead.

Furthermore, we may note a highly suggestive change of emphasis in the final report over an earlier statement made at one of the committee's sessions by the man who was probably its single most influential member. Indeed, readers of his prose in general are likely to suspect that his pen was the crucial one in the writing of the final report for the de Bunsen Committee. This was Lieutenant Colonel Sir Mark Sykes, whom we have already met as a prewar traveler and observer in Ottoman Asia, and who was now an adviser at the War Office and Lord Kitchener's personal representative on the de

Bunsen Committee. During the session of April 17, Sykes had spelled out for the committee what he thought to be the six essential problems where Asiatic Turkey was concerned. These were: "(1) economic development; (2) the question of the Khalifate and the Arabian question; (3) the Armenian question; (4) the status of Christian holy places; (5) the interests of the Entente Powers; and (6) the interests of the neutrals."

There is nothing here about *national* interests, in Palestine or anywhere else—neither the Armenian nor the "Arabian" question was yet being thought of precisely in national terms—nor is there any reference to Palestine other than the oblique one in point 4 about the Christian Holy Places. Evidently a new awareness regarding Palestine was arrived at by the committee sometime between April 17 and the final report—or shall we say between April 17 and April 29, the date of Admiral Fisher's letter to Samuel? The contrast is all the more striking in that the earlier statement of position, relatively weak as it was concerning the status of Palestine, is seen here coming from a man who was soon to become one of Zionism's most enthusiastic supporters in Government circles.

Not that the Zionists would have been happy with the de Bunsen Committee report had they been able to see it. In keeping with a reticence that was to remain in official statements, however secret, until early the following year, there was no *explicit* mention in it of Jewish interests—national, religious, or otherwise. Indeed, there is no reason to suppose that the committee thought of Zionism as any more than one of a number of interests making claims in Palestine. The report did make a bid for the idea of British control of Palestine so dear to English Zionists, but then retracted it. Worst of all, however, from a Zionist point of view, was the northern boundary of Palestine as arrived at in the report: for it cut off the entire northern Galilee, historically part of the Land of Israel and the site of a number of Jewish settlements.

One important fact remained, however: the question of Palestine had been set apart as a separate one in this first formulation, however tentative, of British policy in the Middle East.

·15·

THE ARABIAN SWEEPSTAKES

The de Bunsen report, like most previous official statements on the subject, remained ambiguous regarding the nature and extent of the "independent Moslem rule" that was being specified for Arabia and its Holy Places. To be sure, this meant that, with certain traditional British exceptions along the northeastern and southeastern coasts, there was to be no European control of the peninsula. But the possibility of some kind of continuing Turkish sovereignty was not being entirely abandoned—though it was understood that this possibility, if applied after an Allied victory, would only be on condition of an Arabian autonomy even greater than had prevailed before the war. That principle of autonomy was not yet based, however, on any commitment to Arab nationalism, which was still only dimly perceived at the Foreign and India offices. Ideas in their midst regarding some greater Arab entity tended at this time to be confined to the Arabian Peninsula alone or to include only a limited and tentative area to the north of it.

Within these limits, however, Sir Edward Grey, for his own part, continued to hope that the outcome would be a truly independent and sovereign Arabia. "You should inform Wingate," he had written on April 14 to his high commissioner in Cairo, telling him to relay the message to the British governor general in Khartoum, "that I authorize him to let it be known, if he thinks it desirable, that His Majesty's Government will make it an essential condition in any terms of peace that the Arabian Peninsula and its Moslem Holy Places should remain in the hands of an independent Sovereign Moslem State." And this was sufficiently unambiguous for him to want to add prudently: "Exactly how much territory should be included in this State it is not possible to define at this stage." The British authorities at Cairo and Khartoum, who were alert to signs of Arab nationalism around them, were bound to be pleased with this; but the fact that the whole thing was easier said than conceived was fully recognized by the new high commissioner in Cairo, Sir Henry McMahon, who wrote back a few weeks later: "Term 'independent sovereign State' has been interpreted in a generic sense because idea of an Arabian unity under one ruler recognized as supreme by other Arab chiefs is as yet inconceivable to Arab mind."

The fact was that, in the history of the Arabian Peninsula, unity was as rare as was full subjection to any outside power. Since at least the tenth century, this homeland of the Islamic religion and the Arabic language had been politically divided among an array of rival princes whose allegiance to the succession of political authorities emanating from Baghdad, Cairo, or Constantinople usually was tenuous at best. Only once, for a few decades at the end of the eighteenth century and the beginning of the nineteenth, had there been anything approaching unity for the entire peninsula, and this had been under circumstances representing a grave threat to Ottoman rule there.

The situation had arisen out of an alliance between the Muslim theologian Muhammad ibn Abd al-Wahhab, founder of a puritanical Sunni religious revival, and Muhammad ibn Saud, the emir of Nejd in the heart of the peninsula. Fired by their newfound Wahhabi faith, Ibn Saud and his successors embarked upon a series of campaigns that achieved its initial success in 1773 with the conquest of Riyadh—which was to remain their capital—and culminated in an invasion of Iraq in 1802 and the occupation of Mecca a year later. The Ottoman sultan responded to this danger in 1811 by delegating to Mehemet Ali, the new strong man of Egypt, the task of reconquering Arabia for the empire. In the next eight years, Egypt won a succession of victories over the Saudis that ended in their being effectively confined once again to their Nejd homeland. The immediate result was not an Ottoman triumph, however, but hegemony for Mehemet Ali over the Red Sea coast of Arabia. This was brought to an end at last with his defeat in 1840, and the nominal Ottoman rule was once again in force on the peninsula.

But that rule continued to be compromised in a variety of ways. For one thing, British concern with the route to India and with the Persian Gulf inevitably extended to the southeastern and northeastern coasts of Arabia. Starting in the late eighteenth century, the East India Company had entered into a series of special arrangements with some of the semiautonomous sheikhdoms along those coasts. Then, with the occupation of Aden by Great Britain in 1839, a more formal pattern was begun. This culminated in a series of agreements, concluded by the government of India between 1880 and 1899, in which the sheikhdoms of Bahrain, Muscat and Oman, and Kuwait surrendered to Great Britain the right to conduct their foreign policy. Of these "veiled protectorates," Kuwait in particular, under the resolutely anti-Ottoman Mubarak ibn Sabah, had become a stronghold of British influence by 1914.

Meanwhile, the interior and the west of the peninsula had continued to be dominated by rival princes who enjoyed, in effect, varying degrees of independence from Ottoman rule. The irrepressible Saudis had become a major force again, but this time they had a formidable rival for control of the interior in the dynasty of Ibn Rashid, located at Hail in the Jebel Shammar to the northwest. Indeed, in 1891 Muhammad ibn Rashid actually conquered Riyadh and forced Abdul Rahman ibn Saud to flee with his family, taking refuge in Kuwait; but eleven years later Abdul Rahman's son, Abdul Aziz, recaptured the traditional Saudi capital in a surprise attack. By the end of 1906, Abdul Aziz ibn Saud had established control over all of desert Arabia and had even done battle with Turkish troops. In May 1913, he took his next major step and captured the province of Hasa, the only foothold the Turks had been able to maintain on the Persian Gulf coast of Arabia amid the chain of British suzerainties there. With the outbreak of war in 1914, Ibn Saud and not Turkey was the only power besides Great Britain on the Arabian shore of the Persian Gulf.

In the west of the peninsula, the principal autonomous power was that of the Sherif Hussein* in the Hejaz, the province that formed the entire northern half of the Red Sea littoral and included Medina, Mecca, and the one railway in Arabia. Just to the south of the Hejaz on the Red Sea coast was the province of Asir, ruled by the Idrisi, Sayid Muhammad; the scion of a dynasty of religious teachers originating in Morocco, he had received arms and money from the Italians during the Tripolitanian War of 1911-12. And south of Asir was the Yemen, which was itself just north of British-controlled Aden, and was under the domination of the Imam Yahya, who in 1911 had led a full-scale revolt against the Turks, which failed.

These, then, were the starters in November 1914 in what one eminent British traveler in Arabia was to call "the big race: the

---

* Though his proper princely title was emir, he was popularly known in the West as the Sherif (or Grand Sherif) of Mecca.

Arabian Stakes!" The possible prizes included control of the peninsula and possession of the Muslim caliphate; but the sponsor was Great Britain, now the enemy of the Turkish overlord. It was a difficult choice, between the call of *jihad* and Muslim solidarity—albeit represented by a hated Turkish bureaucracy—and the call of ambition, gratification for which was being offered by the one European people to have somehow made themselves liked in Arabia. The more urgent question, of course, was: which side was going to win?

Meanwhile, we may pause a moment to wonder what it was that had made the English, of all the Western nations, the most ardent wanderers in Arabia. "The theory," offered a celebrated Sinai traveler of the 1840s, Alexander Kinglake,

> is that the English traveler has committed some sin against God and his conscience, and that for this the evil spirit has hold of him, and drives him from his home like a victim of the old Grecian furies, and forces him to travel over countries far and strange, and most chiefly over deserts and desolate places, and to stand upon the sites of cities that once were, and are now no more, and to grope among the tombs of dead men. Often enough there is something of truth in this notion; often enough the wandering Englishman is guilty (if guilt it be) of some pride or ambition, big or small, imperial or parochial, which being offended has made the lone places more tolerable than ball-rooms to him a sinner.

Whether originating in guilt or not, the impulse seems to have been felt in common by aristocratic wanderers such as Lord Byron, who felt the pull of the East, and who wrote,

> *Is it not better, then, to be alone,*
> *And love Earth only for its earthly sake?*

and such a spokesman of a more bourgeois outlook as Thomas Hughes, who ruminated in *Tom Brown's School Days* on "the consciousness of silent endurance, so dear to every Englishman—of standing out against something and not giving in."

Sir Richard Burton, when he started out on his celebrated pilgrimage to Mecca in 1853, four years after leaving Indian army service, wanted among other things "to ascertain how much a four years' life of European effeminacy had impaired my powers of endurance." As for the desert itself, he wrote, "to the solitary wayfarer there is an interest . . . unknown to Cape Seas and Alpine glaciers, and even to the rolling Prairie,—the effect of continued excitement on the mind, stimulating its powers to their pitch." Charles M. Doughty, the most mystical of English travelers in Arabia, found the desert in its scorching vastness and silence to be a teacher of the primal. "As for me who write," he said in his *Travels in Arabia Deserta*, "I pray that nothing be looked for in this book but the seeing of an hungry man and the telling of a most weary man; for the rest the sun made me an Arab, but never warped me to Orientalism." Gertrude Bell, the most celebrated wanderer of the Middle East on the eve of the war, wrote of a kind of timeless oriental paradise upon reaching the Jebel Shammar in February 1914:

> So here we are, camped in red gold sand among broken hillocks of red sandstone, with all the desert shrubs gray green and some even adventuring into colorless pale flowers. They smell sweet and aromatic. "Like amber," said Ali, sniffing the wind as we came into camp this afternoon. And the camels have eaten their fill. We march slowly, for they eat as they go, but I don't mind. I never tire of looking at the red gold landscape and wondering at its amazing desolation. I like marching on through it and sometimes I wonder whether there is anywhere that I am at all anxious to reach.

But if the rather Elizabethan Sir Richard Burton loved the excitement of the surge to Mecca and the truly fin de siècle Miss Bell loved a seemingly undriven serenity, what they and other English travelers in the desert had in common was a profound sympathy for the people there in preference to those of the villages and towns. "In practice the Englishman," T.E. Lawrence was to write, "and especially the Englishman of family, finds the tribes more to his taste than the villages"; it is among the former that he can experience what Lawrence calls "the test of nomadism, that most deeply biting of all social disciplines." " 'Arabs' we call them east of Jordan," Gertrude Bell wrote of the Bedouin, "they being the Arabs par excellence."

As for the *fellahin*, the peasants of Syria, on the other hand, one member of the Palestine Exploration Fund expeditions of the 1870s saw fit to describe them as, "all in all, the worst type of humanity that I have come across in the East . . . totally destitute of all moral sense." Miss Bell, who wrote elegiacally about the steady encroachment of cultivated land upon the desert—the two basic conflicting elements in Arab civilization, according to the fourteenth-century philosopher Ibn Khaldun—said that "the Syrian merchant is separated by a wider gulf from the Bedouin than he is from the Osmanli [Ottoman Turk]." Burton even thought the gap was to be found in the matter of personal hygiene. "One point struck me at once," he said of the various pilgrim groups making camp at Mecca, "the difference in point of cleanliness between an encampment of citizens and of Badawin. Poor Mas'ud sat holding his nose in ineffable disgust."

Doughty did not necessarily see notable cleanliness in the Bedouin he lived among, but he was not talking about real dirt either when he said with particular reference to them: "The Semites are like to a man sitting in a cloaca to the eyes, and whose brows touch heaven." The purity for him was in that special relationship with heaven: "Like to this," he writes of the Bedouin tents and clay houses,

> was Moses' adorned house of the nomad God in the wilderness. Also the firmament, in the Hebrew prophet, is a tabernacle of the one household of God's creation. These flitting houses in the wilderness, dwelt in by robbers, are also sanctuaries of "God's guests," *theûf Ullah,* the passengers and who they be that haply alight before them. . . . "Be we not all, say the poor nomads, *guests of Ullah?"*

And he completes his ruminations upon this godly hospitality by adding:

> Such is the golden world and the "assurances of Ullah" in the midst of the wilderness: traveled Beduins are amazed to see the sordid inhospitality of the towns;—but where it were impossible that the nomad custom should hold.

Can we see in this preference for nomad custom, then, another form of that Old Testament passion so widespread among Englishmen? It is to be found in Doughty and some others, at any rate, if not in Gertrude Bell. To dwell in tents like those of Moses—here was an appropriate fulfillment for descendants of the Puritans! It was no wonder that, as it seems, the Arabs of the peninsula and the region just north of it liked Englishmen as much as did the Zionists, those other wilderness wanderers—and disliked the French as much, too. The French were more at home in the New Testament world of northern Syria, among a landed peasantry like that from which Jesus had come, and there they were liked better, too. As France and England made their first moves to begin dividing the Arab world of Ottoman Asia into their respective spheres of influence, they seem to have been guided as much by appetites of the spirit as by considerations of political and economic geography.

"Syria, especially Southern Syria, where Egyptian prosperity is better known, is exceedingly pro-English." So wrote Gertrude Bell—who was sensitive to Arab nationalism and to the possibilities of a Greater Arabia extending northward of the peninsula itself—on September 5, 1914, in a report that the director of military operations had asked her to prepare on the basis of her journey from Damascus to Hail to Baghdad the previous winter and spring. "Last autumn," she went on, "an additional impulse was given to this sentiment by the dislike of growing French influence. This dislike is universal. Germany does not count for much either way in Syria." As for Mesopotamia, she wrote, "we weigh much more heavily in the scale than Germany because of the importance of Indian relations—trade chiefly. The presence of a large body of German engineers in Baghdad, for railway building, will be of no advantage to Germany, for they are not popular." Speculating that Mesopotamia would probably not take any active part in a war by Turkey against England, she thought that the Turks would turn for support, in the event of such a war, "to Arab chiefs who have received our protection. Such action would be extremely unpopular with the Arab Unionists who look on Sayid Talib of Basra, [on] Kuwait, and [on] Ibn Saud, as powerful protagonists."

Of these three Arab leaders in the Persian Gulf area, whose cooperation was indeed solicited by Turkey after its entry into the war, Ibn Saud was the only one whose potential loyalties remained uncertain in November 1914. The other two were staunchly anti-Turk and friends of the English. As for Ibn Saud, though he had spent his adult life—he was now thirty-four—asserting his independence from Turkey, he had not been given by the English any reason for liking them. In July 1913, the Foreign Office had negotiated a treaty with the Turkish government regarding British rights on the Persian Gulf coast of Arabia, but had omitted all mention of Hasa, taken by Ibn Saud two months before: the effect was that the province was still being regarded by Britain as Turkish. On March 9, 1914, the British and the Turks had signed another treaty dividing the Arabian Peninsula into respective spheres; in it, Britain was acknowledged everything southeast of a line running from Qatar to Aden, while the Nejd, among other areas to the north of the line, was treated as a Turkish province. Ibn Saud himself, on the other hand, had tried as far back as 1904 to establish relations with the British through their political agent at Kuwait, but had been rebuffed. Now that Turkey was in the war, however, and all the old treaty arrangements were obsolete, the British—and the Indian government in particular, with its residents in the gulf area—were forced to recognize the potential value to them of Ibn Saud's friendship.

Gertrude Bell's journey just before the war had taken her no further south than Hail, where she had been entertained by Ibn Saud's rival, Saud ibn Rashid. But while she had been making that journey, another one through Arabia—and including Riyadh—was being made by a British traveler who had in recent years established a close relationship with Ibn Saud. This was Captain W.H.I. Shakespear, the new political agent in Kuwait, who had visited Ibn Saud for the first time in 1911 and had then had no choice but to turn down the emir's request for British sympathies regarding his ambitions in the Hasa. On his journey in the winter and spring of 1913 and 1914—a feat of endurance and exploration which took him from Kuwait to Aqaba—Shakespear had stopped at Riyadh with the official task of placating Ibn Saud over the Anglo-Turkish agreement then being negotiated, which would have made the emir a mere governor of a Turkish province. Shakespear seems to have been as opposed to that agreement as was Ibn Saud, and he had come away from the meeting determined to persuade the Foreign and India offices that the future of Arabia lay in Ibn Saud's hands.

Certainly by the fall of 1914, as Turkey's pro-German stance became increasingly evident, the British were convinced that Ibn Saud was at least one of the people in whose hands that future lay, and Shakespear was called back from England and sent to make contact with him. The two men met at the end of December at Ibn Saud's war camp at Khufaisa, where the emir was preparing once again to do battle with his old rival Ibn Rashid. Shakespear had brought along a letter from Sheikh Mubarak of Kuwait, urging Ibn Saud to throw in his lot with the British. Ibn Saud recognized that his own future lay in this direction, but he was still indignant about the Anglo-Turkish agreement of the preceding March, and he insisted that a formal treaty be negotiated as a condition for his cooperation.

Shakespear stayed on at the camp to continue the discussions.

"Dear Miss Bell," he wrote on January 5, 1915, to the fellow Arabian traveler whom he had never met in person, but with whom he had occasionally corresponded:

> I am in camp here with Bin Saud, and having the luxury of being halted for a few days am banging off some letters. I can't remember when I last wrote but think it must have been before I went down to Aldershot . . . just as that got going nice and smoothly the India Office wired for me and fired me out here "to get into personal touch" with Bin Saud. It was a weary long voyage out . . . I had got as far as Karachi when war with Turkey was announced. . . . Here I find immense relief that we have turned the Turks out of Basra and not a trace of any fanaticism or of feeling against the British. Bin Saud is as pleased as possible. He is making preparations for a big raid on Ibn Rashid with a view to wiping him out practically and I shouldn't be surprised if I reached Hail in the course of next month or two as BS's political adviser!

But this was not to be: Shakespear, conspicuous in his British army uniform, was killed during the indecisive battle that finally was joined between Ibn Saud and Ibn Rashid on January 24. The result was to slow negotiations with the Arabian leader upon whom the India Office had begun to place its principal bets.

The others were still very much in the running, however. From the standpoint of the Aden resident, who also represented the Indian government, the Arab chiefs whose positions in the war were of greatest concern were the Imam Yahya and the Idrisi Sayid. They were in a state of war with one another, complicating the situation; furthermore, the Idrisi, though he was the more anti-Turk of the two, had shown strong pro-Italian leanings beginning with the Tripolitanian War, and Italy's position was not yet defined early in 1915. Nevertheless, the Idrisi had approached the Aden authorities at the time of Turkey's entry, and they were very much in favor of him. "Idrisi's approaching us," wrote the Aden resident to a still uncertain Foreign Office on March 15, 1915,

> has caused immense impression in this quarter of Arabia and has inspired Arabs generally to anticipate death blow to Turkish misrule in the Yemen. Idrisi's agent carries high credentials from Egypt where he is known to be eminently pro-British. To give him the cold shoulder or appear to doubt sincerity of his

hatred of the Turks defeats our policy, viz., the expulsion of Turks at Arab hands; and may even throw Idrisi into Italian hands as before.

The text of a treaty with the Idrisi was finally drawn up on April 30, four days after Italy had joined in with the Entente. In it, the Idrisi agreed "to attack and to endeavor to drive the Turks from their stations in the Yemen and to the best of his power to harass the Turkish troops in the direction of the Yemen and to extend his territories at the expense of the Turks." It was further specified that the Idrisi would "abstain from any hostile or provocative action against Imam Yahya, so long as the latter does not join hands with the Turks." In exchange for this, the British Government agreed to safeguard Asir against all attacks by sea, to guarantee independence to the Idrisi within his own domain, and to adjudicate at the end of the war between his claims and those of the Imam Yahya or any other rival.

The draft text of the treaty also added: "The British Government has no desire to enlarge its borders on Arabian soil but wishes solely to see the various Arab rulers living peacefully and amicably together, each in his own sphere, and all in friendship with the British Government." But the wording here troubled the Indian government at Delhi, who were not sure what was to be considered the line delimiting "Arabian soil" to the northeast, and they wrote to the India Office in London: "The only point that appears to require definite qualification is the expression 'Arabian soil' in article 6, as this scarcely falls in with our position in Mesopotamia. If the words 'Western Arabia' were substituted for 'Arabian soil,' this objection would be removed, and our intentions would be sufficiently defined in the treaty." There was hesitation, however, over this proposed change at the Foreign Office, to which it had been duly sent on for approval. Sir Edward Grey still was not ready to assume outright an annexationist position regarding Mesopotamia. At last he accepted the emendation on grounds that a small extension of the Aden protectorate might become strategically necessary at the war's end.

The treaty with the Idrisi was signed on June 21, with the effect that hope for cooperation with the Imam Yahya in the Yemen was being all but abandoned. "Arabia for the Arabs," the Imam had said, "with an Arabian Khalif at Mecca"—but now he was out of the running for that prize. From the moment of Turkey's entry into the war, the British had suggested that they were ready to see a defeated Constantinople surrender the caliphate into Arab hands—

though they had always declared this a matter in which they could not interfere and which only Muslims could settle. This did not mean, however, that they were above trying to fix the race, intimately related as it was to the political one.

The only problem for the British approach was that two rival groups were placing their bets: on the one hand, the Indian government, represented in London by the India Office, and on the other, the Foreign Office, which was receiving more and more initiatives from Cairo* toward a Middle Eastern policy of its own. If the India people—who traditionally had regarded the entire Middle East as their own province—were backing Ibn Saud as their candidate for political control of the peninsula and (since Ibn Saud was not interested in the caliphate) the Idrisi as their candidate for religious control, the Foreign Office and, above all, Cairo had other ideas. Indeed, Cairo, upon receiving word of the impending treaty with the Idrisi, promptly sent a report to London that denounced him as a troublemaker and referred to him as the "Mahdi of Asir." That was certainly a turn of phrase for Kitchener to ponder when the report was sent on to him, and he, with Cairo still in his heart, minuted on the folder: "This is quite a possibility.—There will be several claimants for the Arab Khalifat but the Sherif of Mecca will be the winning horse." Then, between "will" and "be" he inserted "I think."

Kitchener had been given the opportunity to begin considering his own bet even before the war. At the beginning of February 1914, when he was still the British agent and consul in Egypt, he had received a visit from the Emir Abdullah, second son of the Sherif Hussein of Mecca, who was passing through Cairo on a trip to Constantinople. Officially Abdullah was visiting the khedive, whose guest he was at the Abdin Palace, and was simply paying Lord Kitchener a courtesy call; but in fact he wanted to discuss political matters. His father was not sitting easily in the emirate of Mecca; it was the Turks who had put him there, and it was they who now—in a quarrel centering on the Hejaz railway—were threatening to depose him. What Abdullah wanted to know was, would the British Government be prepared to intervene in his father's favor? Kitchener could give no definite reply until he had consulted with London, but he suggested that it would probably be negative, since Britain's policy still was to support Turkish interests.

* Egypt, though it had just become a protectorate, was still under Foreign Office jurisdiction.

Abdullah departed with no further protest, but then returned to Cairo in the middle of April on his way home from Constantinople. By this time, tensions had grown worse between his father and the Turkish government. The Hejaz railway, covering the pilgrimage route from Damascus, had been built by Sultan Abdul Hamid II on subscriptions collected from all over the Muslim world, but had reached only as far as Medina when the Young Turk revolution of 1908 put a stop to construction. Now, in the spring of 1914, the Young Turk government wanted to resume and extend the tracks to Mecca; but this was causing consternation in the Hejaz, where the camel trade that was thereby being threatened was an important source of revenue. The Turks even were offering 30 percent of the railway's revenue to compensate for the loss of trade, but the Sherif did not find this adequate.

His position therefore was in some danger. Since the Saudi conquest in the early nineteenth century, the emirate of Mecca—though it remained within the Hashimite family, who had founded it in the tenth century—had been weak. It was now under the control of the Turks to a large extent. For three generations, emirs from the same family had been appointed at the will of the Porte, which had placed Hussein in power in 1908 after he had been held in detention in Constantinople for fifteen years. Now about sixty years of age, Hussein was—perhaps under the inspiration of Ibn Saud's example—groping his own way to some kind of autonomy or independence.

On this second visit in April 1914, Abdullah was more discreet than he had been in February and asked to see not Kitchener but the latter's oriental secretary, Ronald Storrs. Essentially appointed for fluency in Arabic, the oriental secretary, in Storrs's own words, was someone "who must anyhow be the eyes, ears, interpretation and Intelligence (in the military sense) of the British Agent, and might become much more." The thirty-two-year-old Storrs, son of an eminent clergyman and a first in classics from Pembroke College, Cambridge, was a man of considerable culture and linguistic accomplishment, and proud of it; as such, he was a most suitable choice both as oriental secretary and as Abdullah's go-between.

"I visited him in the Abdin Palace," Storrs was to write of the meeting that took place at 9:15 on the evening of April 18, "and . . . was astonished and delighted at the range of his literary memory. He intoned for me brilliant episodes of the Seven Suspended Odes of Pre-Islamic poetry, the Glories and the Lament of Antar ibn Shaddad, during which we must have accounted for whole quarts of the rich Khedivial coffee." Such a rapport could not have been achieved by Kitchener with his more perfunctory Arabic, not to mention his less affable personality. Storrs, whose blond moustache perhaps gave a hint of dilettantism in the way it curled up slightly at the ends, had fallen completely under the spell of this Arab prince who was the same age as he and looked younger. "Short and thick built," is the way Abdullah was described at around this time, "apparently as strong as a horse, with merry dark brown eyes, a round smooth face, full but short lips, straight nose, brown beard. In manner affectedly open and very charming, not standing at all on ceremony, but jesting with the tribesmen like one of their own sheikhs." In his noble Arab dress he presented himself as the real thing; and though he apparently knew some French and English, and was fluent in Turkish, he would not speak to Storrs in anything but Arabic, in all its desert richness. "I think it's rather a triumph," Gertrude Bell had once written home excitedly of one of her earliest desert encounters, "to have conducted so successful a piece of diplomacy in Arabic, don't you?" For the English Arabist, all such moments were colored by a sense of jubilation at handling a language that made one's school Greek seem easy.

"Traveling by a series of delicately inclined planes," Storrs's account continues, "from a warrior past I found myself in the defenseless Arab present." Abdullah proceeded to tell Storrs how, in his recent interview with the grand vizier in Constantinople, he had learned that "the extension of the railway was regarded by the Porte as essential." In response, Abdullah had "pleaded strongly that without the development of quays etc. at Jeddah [the port of Mecca on the Red Sea], and mining and other industries in the interior this extension would mean the economic death of the camel-owning population of Arabia. But the Grand Vizier, hinting darkly at the possible intervention of certain Powers, declared that the project was a strategic necessity. The Sherif [Abdullah] then asked him point-blank which Power or Powers he meant. The hands of France were already over-full; Germany's share was known to be far distant, and by its position to exclude all danger from Russia; Italy was preoccupied elsewhere; and Austria had never pretended to any interests in fields so remote. Did His Highness therefore allude to Great Britain? The Grand Vizier, while agreeing to the Sherif's exposition of the case, refused to be precise or to mention names.

"The Sherif then continued that if, as seemed fairly clear, Great Britain was the Power indicated and had the intention of cooperating in an Arab revolt, the railway could avail the Turks little or nothing. The Arabian ports could be occupied, a stream of arms poured in, and the advance of Ottoman forces attacked on either flank. He implored the Grand Vizier to reconsider his decision, but the latter remained firm." It was owing to this intransigence that Abdullah was now approaching "His Britannic Majesty's Agent in Cairo with a view to obtaining with the British Government an agreement similar to that existing between the Amir of Afghanistan and the Government of India, in order to maintain the status quo existing in the Arabian Peninsula and to do away with the danger of wanton Turkish aggression." In 1905, the British Government, while still safeguarding Afghanistan's border with Russia, had agreed with its Amir not to interfere in the internal affairs of his country.

Abdullah concluded the conversation by assuring Storrs that "the Arabs were concentrating and solidifying, that Ibn Saud, the Idrissi, and even the Imam Yehia would before long be in complete unity with each other and with the Sherifate." Storrs went back to the British Agency to report on this conversation and then returned to see Abdullah first thing the next morning.

Storrs "informed him (under instructions) that he should not expect any encouragement from the British Government; that it was more than possible that the Porte did not really intend to carry out their threat; that in any case we should want to hear how the latest developments were received at Mecca before communicating the Sherif's desire to the Foreign Office; that we had in principle not the smallest wish to interfere in the government or the administration of the Holy Cities, which only concerned us in so far as they affected the safety and comfort of British [colonial] pilgrims."

Abdullah had to accept this; he changed the subject, giving Storrs a description of the political scene in Turkey. He concluded by saying that Enver Pasha—the former Enver Bey—had seen him off from Constantinople with a gift of two rifles and two pistols; "and he left me in very little doubt," Storrs later reported of Abdullah, "as to the direction in which he would like to discharge these pieces should the occasion arise." Abdullah left Cairo for Mecca by the 11:00 A.M. train.

After the war began, but even before Turkey's entry into it, the question of the Sherif of Mecca's attitude was no longer to be dismissed in London and Cairo. Confidential reports arrived that feelings in the Hejaz were pro-German and pro-Turkish; but could this really represent the outlook of the very men who had approached

Kitchener and Storrs in February and April? Storrs did not think so, and he persuaded his superiors in Cairo to send a letter to Kitchener in London suggesting it was time to reestablish contact with Hussein and his family. Kitchener's reply was relayed by the Foreign Office in a telegram sent to Cairo on September 24, 1914:

> Tell Storrs to send secret and carefully chosen messenger from me to Sherif Abdullah to ascertain whether "should present armed German influence at Constantinople coerce Khalif against his will and Sublime Porte to acts of aggression and war against Great Britain, he and his father and Arabs would be with us or against us."

Storrs thereupon "prepared a letter for Abdallah and a suitable gift, and chose for secret messenger X, the father-in-law of my little Persian agent Ruhi, who accompanied him as far as Suez." Messenger X sailed from Suez on October 5 and reached Jeddah in three days. From there he rode by donkey to Mecca, where he performed the rites of pilgrimage and discovered that Hussein and his family were away in Taif. When they returned more than a week later, messenger X obtained permission to be among the first to visit the Sherif and kiss the hem of his garment. At the palace, Abdullah "took X into a small room and asked him for the letter, which he gave. Sharif Abdallah then said that in his opinion Mr. Storrs was a Moslem, to which X tactfully agreed. He was convinced of that by reason of Mr. S.'s numerous quotations from the Koran, and alluded to him as his brother."

The messenger was "then taken into a very large and magnificent room in which he ate with the Sharif and his four sons. This from the morning until two in the afternoon. Shortly after this the Sharif Abdallah bade him take his ease, refresh himself, and with many compliments said he would give him a letter to take to Mr. S. In a few minutes he found himself alone; upon which a servant came and took him to a much finer room on the very top of the house in which he found seated by himself the Grand Sharif of Mecca." Until this moment, polite form had required that Abdullah, the one member of the family who had dealt personally with Storrs, be the receiver of the latter's message. This was why the white-bearded Hussein began by saying to the messenger: "My son, though I am as one uninvited in this matter I will yet speak."

Then, as he paced up and down the room—insisting that the

messenger remain in his seat—he began: "The Ottoman Empire has rights over us and we have rights upon her. She has made war upon our rights, and I am not responsible before God if she has made war upon our rights; nor am I responsible before God if we have therefore made war upon hers." With this, he stretched out his arm and threw back the sleeve, saying, "My heart is open to Storrs even as this." And he concluded with a grand gesture: "Stretch forth to us a helping hand and we shall never at all help these oppressors. On the contrary we shall help those who do good. This is the Commandment of God upon us: Do good to Islam and Moslems—Nor do we fear nor respect any save God. Give him my greeting, fitting to him and to his country."

"To hear is to obey, O my Lord," replied messenger X, who then was given Abdullah's written reply to Storrs and escorted back to Jeddah by the Sherif's four sons, as well as by "150 pilgrims with arms and music." He was back in Cairo on October 30, the day after Turkish ships had bombarded Russian ports on the Black Sea.

Sir Milne Cheetham, Kitchener's temporary successor as British agent in Cairo—after the declaration of the protectorate, Sir Henry McMahon was to arrive as high commissioner—wired to London the next day a brief summary of the results of the mission:

> Messenger has returned from Mecca with letter from Shereef Abdalla. Communication is guarded, but friendly and favorable. Desires "closer union" with Great Britain, but expects and "is awaiting written promise that Britain will abstain from internal intervention in Arabia and guarantee Emir against foreign and Ottoman aggression."
>
> Shereef himself in a secret conversation with messenger, expressed himself more freely and openly, saying "Stretch out to us a helping hand and we will never aid these oppressors."
>
> Messenger was received and treated with great consideration. It should be noted that Shereef Abdalla is only repeating without any additions proposals he made to His Majesty's Agency on [April 18].
>
> Reply is being prepared subject to your approval disclaiming all intention of internal intervention and guaranteeing against external aggression only, independent of Shereefate.
>
> Messenger must leave Monday morning [November 2] or week will be lost. Please instruct me at once.

Kitchener wasted no time writing his reply, which was cabled out at 6:35 P.M. the same day:

Following from Lord Kitchener.

Lord Kitchener's salaam to the Shereef Abdalla. Germany has bought the Turkish Government with gold notwithstanding that England, France and Russia guaranteed integrity of the Ottoman Empire if Turkey remained neutral in this war. The Turkish Government have against the wish of the Sultan through German pressure committed acts of war by invading the frontiers of Egypt with armed bands followed by Turkish soldiers which are now massed at Akaba to invade Egypt. If the Arab nation assist England in the war that has been forced upon us by Turkey England will guarantee that no internal intervention takes place in Arabia and will give the Arabs every assistance against external foreign aggression.

It may be that an Arab of the true race will assume the Caliphate at Mecca or Medina and so good may come by the help of God out of all evil which is now occurring.

Upon the arrival of this message in Cairo, Storrs and his Persian-born Arabic translator Ruhi went to work composing a reply to Abdullah on the basis of it. Their message went as follows, according to the English rendering that they made for Government files:

To: H.H. The Sherif Abdalla (Titles)

After compliments and thanks. We have understood your reasons and acknowledge the justice of your request. So we have sent to Lord Kitchener (titles) who has replied as follows:

Salaams to Sherif Abdalla (titles). That which we foresaw has come to pass. Germany has bought the Turkish Government with gold notwithstanding that Great Britain, France, and Russia guaranteed the integrity of the Ottoman Empire if Turkey remained neutral in this war. The Turkish Government have against the wish of the Sultan and through German pressure committed acts of war by invading without provocation the frontiers of Egypt with armed bands followed by Turkish soldiers which are now massed at Akaba to invade Egypt so that the cause of the Arabs, which is the cause of freedom, has become the cause also of Great Britain. If the Amir (titles) and Arabs in general assist Great Britain in this conflict that has been forced upon us by Turkey, Great Britain will promise not to intervene in any manner whatsoever whether in things religious or otherwise. Moreover, recognizing and respecting the sacred and unique office of the Amir Hosayn (titles) Great Britain will guarantee the independence, rights and privileges of the Sherifate against all external foreign aggression, in particular that of the Ottomans. Till now we have defended and befriended Islam in the person of the Turks: henceforward it shall be in that of the noble Arab. It may be that an Arab of true race will assume the Khalifate at Mecca or Medina, and so good may come by the help of God out of all the evil which is now occurring. It would be well if Your Highness could convey to your followers and devotees, who are found throughout the world, in every country, the good tidings of the Freedom of the Arabs, and the rising of the sun over Arabia.

The reader will note here a tendency, which we have not seen for the last time, to flesh out with Cairo enthusiasms the bones of London formulas.

By the time this letter reached the family of the Sherif Hussein, England and Turkey were at war, and the *jihad* had been proclaimed. It was a moment for caution, and caution was the spirit of Abdullah's reply. "Respectable and Powerful Friend," it ran:

After paying due respects, yours of the 12th Zil Hoga has been received with due honor and reverence, and we have taken it as a basis for action and a reference for the present and the future. In accordance with it, and in view of its fidelity and accord, our country has come to hold most conscientiously to your suggestions, and has undertaken to carry out faithfully what we said in our previous letter and what we confirm in the present one; and has avoided since our foregoing letter all that affects unfavorably your material and moral interests. Yea more, we are endeavoring to discourage any man who seeks to harm these interests—any one of those who are outside the pale of the Hedjaz colony.

If you could perceive our critical position in undertaking the matter you would know that we are doing that which is more important than the performance of that which is naturally imposed upon us, regardless of whether or not these negotiations take place, and whether or not an agreement is arrived at. It is so because religion which justifies it and which is the sole foundation of action, prevents us from working at once. But when the time shall come, and it is not far distant, we can not but accomplish it, even though the Ottoman Empire be not occupied and even though it should muster against us all its army.

In closing, I would remind you that we act upon the words of him who said, perform ye the promise ye make to God when ye pledge yourselves. We then pay to His Highness and yourself our best regards, requesting you to keep this correspondence secret until the right time should come.

Disappointingly evasive and ambiguous as this letter was, however, it was accompanied, as the preceding one had been, by conversational remarks made by the Sherif to the messenger that were somewhat more committal. "Ali Bey," he had told the messenger—the *X* of the previous journey—

> please impart my best salaams, faithfulness and friendship to Mr. Storrs, and my acceptance of what his great Empire has on another occasion proposed. Ali, do your best to make Mr. Storrs understand that he should not consider my answer as a breaking up of relations.
>
> It simply came late, and if she [the British Empire] had granted our demand when we made it, things would have been better. The day will come when we will demand more of her than she is now preparing for us, and perhaps soon.
>
> Ali, inform Mr. Storrs that I am using all my political and material influence in spreading the British policy in my country as well as in that of al-Imam Yehia, as he is my friend and never acts against my advice.
>
> Ali, Turkey is weighing down heavily upon us, beyond the power of our endurance. We therefore oppose the execution of its commands and plans. . . . And perhaps causes might spring up which would break these relations [of ours with Turkey] even before you arrive at your country; and it might come to pass that the thing would be delayed some three or four or six months. . . .
>
> Our relations with the [Ottoman] Empire are waning, dying, even as a flickering lamp whose oil had run out.

Hussein then proceeded to explain what were the things preventing his rising up against the Turks at that moment, and also to dispose of them. He was bound, he said, by three ties—the religious tie, the caliphate, and the debt of gratitude he owed the Ottoman ruling house for having bestowed the emirate upon him. As for the first of these—by which he meant his obligation to keep the peace at the Holy Places and on the pilgrimage routes—he pointed out that "religious matters have become lax. Therefore we are no longer bound to obey them." As for the second tie, it "concerns our obedience to the Caliphate, but there no longer exists a Caliphate, and that for various reasons, among others that their rule projects plans and deeds which are all contrary to religion. The Caliphate means this, that the rules of the book of God should be enforced (and this they do not do)." And as for the third tie, concerning the Ottoman ruling house, "the reins of power have passed from this family," Hussein observed. The Turkish government, he said, "has come to be nothing more than Enver and his clique. We therefore are no longer bound to them by any tie.

"Notwithstanding this," Hussein concluded,

> I am of opinion that it will be better now to put off action. This is due to the reasons explained here above and to the fact that it will be in our interests that this delay be.

It would be good, Hussein suggested, if Great Britain could in the meantime help the Hejaz obtain grain, which had become woefully short since the beginning of the war. But that was all for now:

> Say, Ali, are you satisfied? Yes, Sir.

And thus ended the messenger's report.

Nothing more was heard from the Sherif until July, when a correspondence of historic import began.

·16·

PROMISING LANDS

I n January 1915, the Sherif Hussein received a young bodyguard sent to him by courtesy of the Turkish army. But Fauzi
al-Bakri, as it turned out, had maneuvered his way into this
assignment for other reasons than courtly distinction. The offspring
of a prominent Syrian family, he was a newly sworn member of al-
Fatat, a secret Arab nationalist organization that had been founded
in Paris in 1911 and was now centered in Damascus. The leaders of
this society of some two hundred Muslim and Christian members
had instructed him to ask the Sherif if he would be willing to lead,
not just a local rebellion, but a general Arab revolt against the
Turks.

Arab nationalism was a new phenomenon; there had been
scarcely any signs of its existence as a distinct idea prior to the last
decade of the nineteenth century. Arabism had been mainly a uni-
versalist concept, linked historically with the birth and spread of
Islam. As such, it had been uncomfortable neither with the lax regime of the Turks—a Muslim people, after all, who were fairly respectful of the Arab culture that was a principal source of their
own—nor with the strong traditions of localism and tribalism that
had given rise to systems of warring chieftains, all of whom at any
rate worshiped Allah and read the same Koran. But by the end of
the nineteenth century, European nationalist themes had inevitably
penetrated to Egyptian and Syrian intellectuals, finding a particular—though by no means an exclusive—resonance among Christian
Arabs, who had naturally been immune to the ideals of Islamic uni-
versalism and were especially susceptible to political ideas coming
from France.

It was the Young Turk revolution of 1908 that quickened the
incipient currents of Arab nationalism. In September of that year,
an Ottoman Arab Fraternity was founded to seek cultural and some

degree of political autonomy within the framework of the empire. But its aims were soon frustrated under the emerging repressiveness and Turanian (i.e., pan-Turkic) nationalism of the Committee of Union and Progress. Some Arab leaders went on hoping for a solution under the Ottoman Constitution and, in 1912, founded an Ottoman Decentralization Party, which sponsored an Arab congress held in Paris the following year. But others responded to the repression by forming secret societies such as the Jamiyat al-Arabiya al-Fatat (the "Young Arab Society"), which sought complete independence from the Turks even before the war, and which had sent Fauzi al-Bakri on his special mission to the Sherif of Mecca.

Why had they turned to Hussein to be their leader? One can only speculate as to the reasons. In Syria itself, Djemal Pasha was beginning a dictatorship that was even more zealously opposed to any signs of Arab nationalism than it was to Zionism; indeed, this opposition was soon to prove murderous. Furthermore, large numbers of able-bodied Syrian Arabs had been conscripted into the Turkish army and were therefore unlikely material for an organized revolt. Syrian Arab nationalists felt impelled to look elsewhere for the leadership and personnel of an uprising, and their eyes naturally fell on Arabia. Not only were the Arabian chiefs more autonomous than their equivalents in Syria and Mesopotamia—even the Sherif Hussein, though less independent of the Turks than Ibn Saud was, had complete control over conscription within his territory and had in fact kept the young men of the Hejaz out of Turkish military service—they also were traditionally the objects of a particular admiration within the Arab world.

One of the early theorists of Arab nationalism, Abd al-Rahman al-Kawakibi, a native of Aleppo, had listed just before his death in 1902 twenty-six reasons for the excellence of the people of Arabia. These range from their special relationship with the language and religion they originated to such traits—which appealed to the English as well—as their chivalry, their generosity, and the fact that, of all Muslims, they "are the best able to bear hardships in order to attain their aims, and to undertake travel and residence abroad because they have not succumbed to the servile habits of luxury." On top of all this was the luster that surrounded the name of the Sherif of Mecca, the guardian of the Holy Places of Islam and, in the view of most Sunni Arabs, the proper claimant to the caliphate.

Fauzi al-Bakri presented his message to the Sherif "in a whisper," we are told, and the latter, "too cautious to countenance a plot before a stranger, made no reply and asked nothing, but stared out of the window as though he had not heard." Within a few weeks, however, he had arranged a mission for his third son, Feisal, who was Abdullah's younger brother and still only in his late twenties. Ostensibly, the purpose of the journey on which Feisal set out in the middle of March was to bring to Constantinople some complaints about the Turkish governor of the Hejaz; its real purpose was to make personal contact with the leadership of al-Fatat in Damascus. He arrived there on March 26 and stayed four weeks, entertained by Djemal Pasha and his entourage and also by the members of the Arab secret societies. Feisal met the leaders not only of al-Fatat, but also of al-Ahd ("the Covenant"), an organization of Arab officers in the Turkish army that had been founded just before the outbreak of war.

Feisal journeyed on to Constantinople, where he stayed almost a month, and where he was told by Enver, Talaat, and others that they were likely to become more sympathetic to the grievances of his father once the latter had declared himself openly in favor of the *jihad*. The Sherif's excuse for not doing so was that his proximity to Egypt would, in the event of such a declaration, leave him open to severe reprisals from the English. When Feisal at last headed home, he stopped again in Damascus on May 23. There he was presented by the secret societies with a program of Arab nationalist desiderata that they had drawn up during his absence.

The Damascus Protocol, as it came to be called, was a statement of the conditions under which these nationalist societies were prepared to cooperate in a defensive alliance with Great Britain against the Turks. It called for the "recognition by Great Britain of the independence of the Arab countries" within frontiers that were then defined in detail. These took in all of Arabic-speaking Ottoman Asia north and east of the Sinai Peninsula, including Mesopotamia, as well as all of Syria and Palestine. The political character envisioned for this vast entity was not specified, but under the circumstances it was clear that the Sherif of Mecca was being offered the possibility of rule over an empire. Feisal brought home a prospect that his father could not but seek to act upon.

"A North African or near eastern vice-royalty," Ronald Storrs wrote in March to Colonel Oswald FitzGerald, Kitchener's military secretary, "including Egypt and the Sudan and across the way from Aden to Alexandretta would surely compare in interest and complexity, if not in actual size, with India itself." Storrs's vision adds not only Egypt and the Sudan, but also out-and-out British rule, to the plan of the Damascus Protocol; but the idea from Cairo and the one from Damascus weighed more heavily with what they had in common than with the differences between them. The Arab version recognized the desirability, if not the necessity, of some kind of British sponsorship or even tutelage; and as for the British version, one need only recall Storrs's enthusiastic embroidering of Kitchener's already ardent appeal to "the Arab nation" by way of the Sherif Hussein the previous November to perceive the depth of feeling on this subject among Cairo officials.

Cairo itself had, in fact, long been a center of nationalist thought and activity in the Arab world, and since the beginning of the war the British authorities there had been feeling the force of that fact. As early as August 24, 1914, Sir Milne Cheetham, the acting British agent and consul in Cairo, had sent to London a report on Major Aziz Ali al-Masri, one of the founders of al-Ahd and, though a native Egyptian, an authoritative spokesman for that society's branches in Mesopotamia. Al-Masri, Cheetham wrote,

> is deputed by a central committee at Baghdad to ascertain the attitude of the British Government towards their propaganda for forming a united Arabian state, independent of Turkey and every other Power except England, whose tutelage and control of foreign affairs they invite.
>
> ARABIA is defined as the land of Arabic speaking people, bounded on the north by the line Alexandretta-Mosul-Persian Frontier.
>
> The movement is totally independent of religion and therefore distinct from Pan Islamic and Arabian Khalifate movement.

After Turkey's entry into the war, al-Masri offered to start a revolution in Mesopotamia with British help, but the India Office put a stop to this matter potentially within its jurisdiction, arguing that it was enough to concentrate on Ibn Saud. Here was an early case of wartime confrontation over Middle Eastern issues between the India Office—which was opposed to Arab nationalism as a potential irritant to the loyalty of Indian Muslims—and Cairo, steadily feeding its Arab nationalist enthusiasms to the Foreign Office back home.

These enthusiasms had obtained further support since the end of December with the arrival of the first high commissioner of the newly proclaimed Egyptian protectorate, Sir Henry McMahon. Appointed at Kitchener's recommendation, and with the understanding that he was to be in Cairo only until Kitchener was ready to return there, McMahon had come prepared to assume the war secretary's point of view. Ironically, McMahon had been born in India and had spent twenty-seven of his fifty-two years—his entire adult career since graduation from the Royal Military College at Sandhurst—in the Indian service. But this seems only to have provided an additional stimulus to the eagerness with which he proceeded to try creating a counterweight to Indian power at the other end of the Middle East. By February, he had obtained the consent of the Foreign Office to his request that the affairs of the Hejaz be placed specifically under the jurisdiction of Cairo rather than of the government of India, hitherto the sole British authority on the Arabian Peninsula.

To be sure, in his first months of office McMahon was really more concerned with his Sherifian horse than with Arab nationalism. For him, the Sherif was the preeminent candidate for the caliphate and a potentially strong ally for Great Britain in western Arabia—but probably no more than that until the summer of 1915. McMahon had a highly personal example before him of what he wanted to do: for it was he who had led the negotiations demarcating the frontier between Afghanistan and Baluchistan from 1894 to 1897, and in the process he had won the undying friendship of the Amir. Among the most personable—if also, in the opinion of some of his colleagues, one of the slower witted—of colonial officials, he clearly was ambitious to make the Sherif Hussein his new Amir of Afghanistan.

But there was no lack of voices surrounding McMahon at Cairo to influence his pro-Sherifian enthusiasms in the direction of the Arab nationalism for which the Sherif was about to become spokesman. The British headquarters in that city had become a virtual college of Middle East scholars by the middle of 1915. First of all there was Storrs, in whose hands McMahon seems to have been quite willing to leave the principal management of Arab affairs. T.E. Lawrence and Leonard Woolley both were there, too, working in military intelligence—as was their old mentor, David G. Hogarth, serving as a naval commander and in and out of Cairo while doing duty in the eastern Mediterranean. Two young members of Parliament, now in uniform—George Lloyd and Aubrey Herbert—were often there; and Ronald Graham, one of the most gifted younger members of the diplomatic corps, had been in Cairo since 1907. Among these men was a considerable degree of sentiment favoring whatever signs of Arab nationalism they perceived.

This sentiment was perhaps strongest of all at the Cairo head-quarters itself in the man around whom, as T.E. Lawrence put it, "nearly all of us rallied"—Colonel Gilbert Clayton, the director of military intelligence. The forty-year-old Clayton, an accomplished Arabist, had first come to Egypt as an army officer in 1900, but had then gone to the Sudan and entered civilian government service there. And it was during his years in Khartoum—from which he had been sent to Cairo as its agent and director of military intelligence at the beginning of the war—that he had fallen under the influence of the man who was, since Kitchener's departure, the most commanding British personality of all in northeastern Africa: Sir Reginald Wingate, the governor general of the Sudan.

Born in 1861, Wingate had gone to the Royal Military College at Woolwich in an era when service to the empire still above all meant India; but he served in that country in a moment when Egypt and the Sudan became a new frontier for young men with imperial appetites. By the time of the British occupation of Egypt in 1882, Wingate was in Aden, where he embarked upon the study of Arabic. In 1883 he joined the Egyptian army and two years later was serving along with young Kitchener in the ultimately unsuccessful expedition to relieve General Charles Gordon at Khartoum. In 1898 he was with Kitchener in the reconquest of Khartoum and succeeded him as governor general the following year when the latter went to South Africa to command the British army in the Boer War.

Organizing public services, building schools and roads, policing the country to eliminate the slave trade, Wingate governed the Sudan in the same spirit of benevolent autocracy as had characterized Cromer's tenure in Egypt. A dashing colonial figure with his waxed moustaches, fez, and British army uniform, he drew upon his accomplished Arabic to make himself a vivid and forceful presence among the Muslim elements predominant under his authority. Speaking forthrightly to them, he did not hesitate to represent decisively the views of the empire, even when he had not been fully apprised by London of what those views officially were.

And no one serving near or under Wingate could doubt where he now stood, even though he had supported Britain's generally pro-Ottoman stance in the prewar years. "I—who so warmly supported the Turk on utilitarian grounds—" he was to write in the fall of 1915, "now espoused the Arab cause with still greater warmth and with more real sympathy." One of his tasks was to try and see to it that the Government back in London saw these matters as clearly as he did in Khartoum. Indeed, it was in response to a communication from him that Sir Edward Grey wrote his letter of April 14 declaring the goal of "an independent Sovereign Moslem State" to be British policy.

Geographically closer to Mecca than any other British governing authority, Wingate was highly responsive to the prospects of the Sherif Hussein for general Arab leadership. These were represented to him vigorously by the foremost Arab religious dignitary in the Sudan, Sayid Ali al-Mirghani, who by the spring of 1915 had become an unofficial liaison between Khartoum and Mecca and had begun to sound out the Sherif on prospects for further cooperation on his part with Great Britain. On May 15, Wingate sent to the Foreign Office a translation of an interview with al-Mirghani, in which the latter affirmed his belief that the Sherif Hussein was "the most suitable man" for the caliphate, and Great Britain "the most competent Power" to render him support. In his covering letter, Wingate went beyond the caliphate idea stressed by al-Mirghani to the vision of statehood adumbrated in Grey's April 14 letter. "I am well aware," he said,

> that it may be considered futile to talk of the formation of a New State without territory, without [a] Capital and without ruler—but—however Utopian it may be, there can be no doubt that, when the psychological moment comes, all Moslem eyes will be turned to Great Britain to whom they look for support in this—perhaps the supreme crisis—in their religious and national existence.

By the spring of 1915, then, Cairo and Khartoum had together formed not only a formidable rival to the India establishment as a generator of Middle Eastern policy, but Britain's advance guard into the complex realm of Arab nationalism, the caliphate, and Sherifian ambitions. None of these were things the India Office would touch or could approve of anyone else touching, and responses from there and from Delhi grew more and more vehement as Cairo became bolder. In June, the India Office wrote—in the name of its new secretary of state, Austen Chamberlain, who had replaced Lord Crewe in the cabinet upheaval in May—a letter to the Foreign Office protesting against the position Wingate had taken with respect to the al-Mirghani interview. "Mr. Chamberlain is inclined to think," it ran, that the policy of His Majesty's Government should be to encourage the Grand Sharif by all possible means short of military intervention to throw off the Turkish yoke, and to support him against Turkey (subject to the same limitations) as independent ruler of the Hedjaz, using their* good offices with other Arab chiefs whom they can influence (such as the Idrisi Saiyid and the Amir of Nejd) to recognize him in that capacity. If, when he has asserted his independence, he claims the Khalifate it would be for Saiyid Ali el Morghani and others to acclaim him as such. Whether the various Arab rulers will do so will doubtless depend upon what the claim imports for them, and how far, if it implies political sovereignty over territory which they at present rule, they are willing to subordinate themselves and their subjects to him. In Mr. Chamberlain's opinion it would not be politic for His Majesty's Government to give the Grand Sharif more than diplomatic assistance.

But even as the India Office had prepared this cold douche, Cairo was creating a new issue to exercise them. At the beginning of June, still responding to Grey's April 14 letter—and to his written consent on May 19 to their wish to formulate its contents as a public pronouncement—the men at British headquarters had printed a leaflet (the India people, when they found out about it, called it a "proclamation") and rained it by airplane over western Arabia. Much of the text was devoted to explaining why England was fighting against the Turks and to deprecating the notion of *jihad* as applied to the present conflict; but there was a final paragraph that said:

> The Government of His Majesty the King of England and Emperor of India has declared when this war ends it shall be laid down in the terms of peace as a necessary condition, that [the] Arabian peninsula and its Mahometan holy places shall remain independent. We shall not annex one foot of land in it, nor suffer any other Power to do so. Your independence of all foreign control is thus assured, and with such guarantees the lands of Arabia will, please God, return along the paths of freedom to their ancient prosperity.

Upon seeing this, Lord Hardinge, the viceroy of India, wrote that it could be open to misinterpretation, since it seemed to imply the pos-

---

* That is, His Majesty's Government's.

sibility of withdrawal from Aden. The Foreign Office agreed, and the document was not circulated in Mesopotamia as McMahon had wished.

Cairo and Khartoum had thus provided a good deal of encouragement to the various aspirations of the Sherif Hussein by July 14, when he and his son Abdullah at last renewed the correspondence that had been broken off in November. The form they used was the already established one of a letter from Abdullah to Storrs, but enclosed with it this time was a long letter from the Sherif himself to Sir Henry McMahon. This was delivered to Storrs by messenger on August 18.

Abdullah's covering letter to Storrs said, among other things: "Do not trouble to send aeroplanes or warships to distribute news and reports as in the past: our minds are now made up." But apart from a broad hint or two, he said nothing more about the fundamental issues, and went on to make a renewed request for grain shipments. It was Hussein's letter to McMahon that came right to the point, speaking from its opening sentence of the "Arab nation," and moving on to its basic terms for an understanding with Great Britain. These were basically a reiteration of the Damascus Protocol.

The first and most important of the demands Hussein made was the territorial one, which ran as follows:

> Great Britain recognizes the independence of the Arab countries which are bounded: on the north, by the line Mersin-Adana to parallel 37°N. and thence along the line Birejik-Urfa-Mardin-Midiat-Jazirat (ibn 'Umar)-Amadia to the Persian frontier; on the east, by the Persian frontier down to the Persian Gulf; on the south, by the Indian Ocean (with the exclusion of Aden whose status will remain as at present); on the west, by the Red Sea and the Mediterranean Sea back to Mersin.

Further provisions repeated the Damascus Protocol's call for the abolition of the Capitulations, for the granting of economic preference to Great Britain, and for a defensive alliance with her. Hussein also added a provision of his own: "Great Britain will agree to the proclamation of an Arab Caliphate for Islam." The letter concluded with a call for speed and a hint at dire alternatives:

> Therefore, since the entire Arab nation is (God be praised!) united in its resolve to pursue its noble aims to the end, at what-

ever cost, it requests the Government of Great Britain to return
an answer, whether negatively or in the affirmative, within
thirty days of the receipt of this message, in default of which it
reserves the right to complete freedom of action, just as we will
consider ourselves absolved from the letter and the spirit of the
declaration which we made earlier through Ali Effendi.

Hussein's sudden transformation from an Arabian chief favored among others to a demanding spokesman for the entire Arab
nation was bound to be startling even to the men at Cairo headquarters. "He knows," wrote Storrs the day after receiving the letter, "he
is demanding, possibly as a basis for negotiation, far more than he
has the right, the hope, or the power to expect." McMahon, wiring a
summary of Hussein's letter to the Foreign Office on August 22—a
full translation was sent out by diplomatic pouch—said: "His pretensions are in every way exaggerated, no doubt considerably beyond
his hope of acceptance," and added, "but it seems very difficult to
treat with them in detail without seriously discouraging him."
McMahon then proposed a reply which would express gratification at
the Sherif's identification of Arab with British interests and reiterate the sentiments of Lord Kitchener's communication of the
previous fall, but which would deem "premature" any detailed discussion of boundaries.

Sir Edward Grey was inclined to agree with McMahon's suggested reply, but before writing back he referred the matter to the
India Office. Its answer came on August 25: "Mr. Chamberlain
agrees that the terms proposed by the Sherif, which appear to be
dictated by extreme Pan-Arab aspirations, are obviously unacceptable as they stand, and probably incompatible with the rights and
interests of other Arab chiefs with whom His Majesty's Government
have arrangements." The note added Chamberlain's suggestion that,
since Hussein evidently wanted something more definite than what
McMahon proposed to reply, a request might be added that he send
his son Abdullah to Cairo in order to negotiate a preliminary agreement. This suggestion was in the spirit of the India government
approach that had already brought about a treaty with the Idrisi and
was in the process of making one with Ibn Saud.

As for the caliphate, Chamberlain's view still was that Hussein,
like any other candidate, should consult with his fellow Muslims
about the matter; it was not Britain's affair. In an August 25 telegram conveying his own and Chamberlain's views to McMahon, how-

ever, Grey was inclined to place the matter of the caliphate in a more distinctly pro-Sherifian light: "if the Sherif, with the consent of his coreligionists, is proclaimed Khaliph," the foreign secretary wrote, "he may rest assured that His Majesty's Government will welcome the resumption of the Khalifate by an Arab of their race, as already indicated in Lord Kitchener's communication of last November."

McMahon, still opting for prudence, demurred at both of the suggested additions to his own proposed reply. "The moment in my opinion has not arrived," he wrote back to Grey, "when we can usefully discuss even a preliminary agreement, and it might at this stage injure the Sherif's chances of the Khalifate to advertise his dealings with us by sending a son or other notable to treat with us." He said that he also was not going to make any mention, in his reply to Hussein, "of the Sherif as the future Khalif as the terms of my message will be sufficiently clear to him on this point." He feared that explicitness on this point would limit the usefulness of his letter as a document that Hussein could show to others.

With that, McMahon—whom Grey had advised to accept or reject the proposed additions at his own discretion—went ahead and wrote a reply to Hussein along the lines he had originally suggested and sent it back with the Sherif's messenger on August 30. In it, he expressed the sentiments he had outlined to the Foreign Office, promised to send grain, and declared "once more that the Government of Great Britain would welcome the reversion of the caliphate to a true Arab born of the blessed stock of the Prophet"—a formula that was, in effect, all but explicitly naming Hussein as the British candidate. "As for the question of frontiers and boundaries," Mc-Mahon wrote, however, "negotiations would appear to be premature and a waste of time on details at this stage, with the War in progress and the Turks in effective occupation of the greater part of those regions." In an effort to bring the point home, McMahon went on to stress that, after all, a great many of the Arabs of Syria and Mesopotamia were fighting on the Turkish side.

Hussein wasted no time about replying to this. "We received your note of the 19th Shawwal, with gratification," he wrote on September 9, "and have given it the fullest consideration, notwithstanding the obscurity and the signs of lukewarmth and hesitancy we descried in it in regard to our essential clause." By this he meant

that your statements in regard to the question of frontiers and boundaries—namely that to discuss them at this stage were unprofitable and could only result in a waste of time since those regions are still occupied by their sovereign government, and so forth—reflect what I might almost describe as reluctance or something akin to reluctance, on your part.

"The fact is," Hussein went on to argue,

that the proposed frontiers and boundaries represent not the suggestions of one individual whose claim might well await the conclusion of the War, but the demands of our people who believe that those frontiers form the minimum necessary to the establishment of the new order for which they are striving. This they are determined to obtain; and they have decided to discuss the matter, in the first resort, with that Power in whom they place their greatest confidence and reliance, and whom they regard as the pivot of justice, namely Great Britain.

So much for those who may have imagined that Hussein had been speaking in the name of anything less than the entire Arab people. "It should be noted," he further pointed out, "that, in drawing up their proposed delimitation, they have not outstepped the bounds of the regions inhabited by their race." As for McMahon's rash argument regarding the many Arabs who were still fighting for the Turks, the Sherif easily turned it into a weapon of his own by saying

that the people of all those countries, including those of whom you say that they are zealously furthering German and Ottoman designs, are awaiting the result of the present negotiations, which depend solely upon whether you reject or admit the proposed frontiers, and upon whether or not you will help us to secure their spiritual and other rights against evil and danger.

There were the dire alternatives again! Furthermore, lest there be any mistake about the priorities in Hussein's letter of July 14, he now wrote: "As for the caliphate, God have mercy on its soul and comfort the Moslems for their loss!" Even the caliphate issue, the Sherif was now saying in effect, was secondary to that of territorial boundaries.

Cairo had shown a judicious resistance to Hussein so far; but it was, after all, being pressured by him into a position for which sentiments were not lacking there and in Khartoum. On August 25, Wingate had written a note to both the Foreign and India offices in which he said: "In the present confusion of ideas and policies . . . I am increasingly drawn to an attempted solution on Pan-Arabian lines." This, he argued, would have in it the "germ of an arrangement which might wean Sunnite Islam from the aggressive Pan-Islamism of the Ottoman school." Here was an authoritative formulation of an idea that had been in the air for a while: since Germany and Turkey, building upon the foundering principle of *jihad*, were trying to depict their cause as a truly pan-Islamic one, Great Britain might best reply to this by consolidating the special position she held with regard to Arab national feeling. The Arabs, Wingate wrote, were the "only effective counterpoise to Ottoman influences," which were growing increasingly Anglophobe. He therefore proposed fostering an Arab Union.

"I am under no delusion," he wrote,

> regarding the practical difficulties in the way, or the elusive character of Arabian political conceptions, but I conceive it to be not impossible that in the dim future a federation of semi-independent Arab states might exist under European guidance and supervision, linked together by racial and linguistic bonds, owing spiritual allegiance to a single Arab Primate, and looking to Great Britain as its Patron and Protector.

For Wingate, seeing the matter in terms of a Sunni "revivalist" movement, the vision of an "Arab Primate" was a way of dealing simultaneously with his own inclinations in favor of the Sherif and with the problems implied in any attempt to achieve Arab unity on a purely *political* level.

One important question remained, however: to what extent could the Sherif really claim to speak for the Arabs of Syria and Mesopotamia? Coincidentally—or perhaps not—an answer came at around the time Hussein's second letter reached Cairo. On August 20, a young Arab officer serving with the Turkish army in Gallipoli had surrendered himself to the British and asked to be taken to Cairo. The twenty-four-year-old Muhammad Sharif al-Faruqi, a native of Mosul and a direct descendant of Caliph Umar, one of the Prophet's immediate successors, said he was a spokesman for the Arab officers' nationalist movement al-Ahd and that his credentials could be confirmed in Cairo by Aziz Ali al-Masri. He was granted his request after questioning, and was in Cairo being interviewed by Colonel Gilbert Clayton on October 11.

"He is, according to his own statement," Clayton reported, "a prominent member of the Young Arab party (Military) and his contention is borne out by the fact that his family is one of some eminence among the Arabs, and also by Aziz Bey Ali El Masri, himself a sworn member of the same party and now in Egypt." Al-Faruqi told Clayton that his party had "now come to the conclusion that the moment is approaching when action is imperative. They have therefore decided to approach England with the offer of active cooperation in return for a guarantee that England will support them in their attempt to secure independence." Al-Faruqi said that his party and al-Fatat had proclaimed allegiance to the Sherif of Mecca, and that they had heard he "was in communication with the High Commissioner in Egypt, and the English are willing to give the Sherif the necessary arms and ammunition for the attainment of his object." They also had heard that "the English have given their consent to the Sherif establishing an Arab Empire, but the limits of his Empire were not defined."

Neither of these last two pieces of information was quite accurate as regards McMahon's letter of August 30, which had not specifically dealt with an Arab Empire or said anything about arms and ammunition. Indeed, it had not even been written at the time of al-Faruqi's surrender; the young Arab officer must have been drawing from sources that did not base their conclusions on the correspondence alone. There are, in fact, grounds for assuming that potential points of agreement between the British and the Sherif had already long been discussed by Wingate with Sayid Ali al-Mirghani, who had conveyed them to Hussein. In any case, the fact that al-Faruqi was so well informed helped him to make a considerable impression upon Clayton, who from this moment on does not seem to have doubted the strength and influence of the Syrian nationalist movement, even though there were good reasons for doing so. Clayton's respect for al-Faruqi's authority came to be shared by his colleagues at Cairo headquarters.

As for the boundaries of a Greater Arabia, al-Faruqi was as firm as Hussein had been about the need to establish them as soon as possible. In the north, he said, they should reach to the "Mersina-Diarbekr" line, which was even beyond the thirty-seventh parallel; "a guarantee of the independence of the Arabian Peninsula [alone] would not satisfy them," Clayton reported, "but together with the institution of an increasing measure of autonomous government, under British guidance and control, in Palestine and Mesopotamia would probably secure their friendship." As for Syria, it was, Clayton remarked in his report,

> of course included in this program, but they must realize that France has aspirations in this region, though El Farugi declares that a French occupation of Syria would be strenuously resisted by the Mohammedan population. They would however no doubt seek England's good offices towards obtaining a settlement of the Syrian question in a manner as favorable as possible to their views and would almost certainly press for the inclusion of Damascus, Aleppo, Hama and Homs in the Arab confederation.

The territorial issues being discussed here require closer examination. Hussein had drawn his map of a projected Arab entity without modifications, doubtless assuming that the British would suggest some that could then be negotiated. But al-Faruqi, in the give and take of conversation, had already begun to consider modifications. The principal challenge to the aspirations he and Clayton shared for Arab autonomy under British tutelage was, as they saw it, French claims in Syria, and al-Faruqi clearly was ready to acknowledge that the French could not be kept out of the Lebanon. This was why he placed special stress on a line eastward of it to which they must not be allowed to penetrate. This north-south line of towns and cities— Aleppo, Hama, Homs, and Damascus—was to be an important element in the discussions from now on, though why it was chosen as the sine qua non of Syrian Arab aspirations is not at all clear. The idea for the particular configuration seems to have been a British one, and there is a theory that it may have been inspired by a passage in Chapter 58 of *The Decline and Fall of the Roman Empire*: "the Latins reigned beyond the Euphrates," Gibbon writes of the conquests of the First Crusade, "and the four cities of Hems, Hamah, Damascus, and Aleppo were the only relics of the Mohammedan conquests in Syria." The Englishman in Cairo most likely to have indulged in such a display of literary culture under these circumstances was Ronald Storrs, who probably was present at the interview.

Outside of this division of northern Syria, however, Clayton and al-Faruqi do not seem to have discovered any substantial differences between themselves. Mesopotamia was not a problem: on the one hand, al-Faruqi expected some form of British tutelage there, and on the other, Clayton—in the prevailing spirit of his colleagues in Cairo, Khartoum, and the Foreign Office, though not of those in the India government and office—was not annexationist regarding that region.

Nor was there any apparent disagreement between them about Palestine, even though Clayton certainly knew the recommendations of the de Bunsen report, which had been conveyed to Cairo headquarters in July by Sir Mark Sykes in person. Wiring Cairo's reactions back to London on that occasion, Sykes had said that McMahon thought "the Palestine portion of British territory should be included in the domains of the Sultan of Egypt. Jerusalem would thus nominally remain under a Moslem ruler, while the nature of its local self-administration could be adapted to meet international interests under British protection." And General Sir John Maxwell had suggested, according to Sykes, that both Mesopotamia and Palestine could be "under the nominal suzerainty of the Sherif of Mecca but under our protection."

Neither of these suggestions, which adhered solidly to the principle of Arab autonomy under British tutelage, was incompatible with the spirit of the discussion between Clayton and al-Faruqi. But Clayton also knew that France and Russia would not acquiesce in even nominal Arab control of the Christian Holy Places. His mentor Wingate had stressed in his August 25 note envisioning an Arab Union that "Palestine might be the subject of a special arrangement in which Russia would participate." Yet there is no evidence that Clayton specified to al-Faruqi any kind of exception for Palestine. Perhaps he looked upon the matter of the Christian Holy Places as too specific and territorially minor to be brought up in this sweeping and tentative discussion—it could be dealt with at its proper moment. And as for the possibility of Jewish claims in Palestine, this clearly had not yet impressed itself upon him as an element in serious projections of the future of the region.

Since Clayton and some of his colleagues in Cairo were to find Zionism an acceptable element in their political calculations in the near future, albeit reluctantly, the evidence that they had given it very little thought up to this moment is all the more striking. Indeed, the only notable exception to this general indifference that the record shows is a portion of a letter written by Ronald Storrs to Colonel FitzGerald in London on December 28, 1914. FitzGerald's preceding letter, which does not survive, had evidently mentioned the possibility of Palestine as a buffer state against the French in the north and may even have relayed some of the talk about a Jewish role there that Herbert Samuel was generating among his cabinet colleagues. "A buffer State is most desirable," Storrs agreed,

> but can we set one up? There are no visible indigenous elements out of which a Moslem Kingdom of Palestine can be constructed. The Jewish State is in theory an attractive idea; but the Jews, though they constitute a majority in Jerusalem itself, are very much in a minority in Palestine generally, and form indeed a bare sixth of the whole population.

Storrs thought Islam in general would be "extremely indignant at the idea," and concluded: "I cannot see India or the Arab world hailing such a denouement with enthusiasm." With that, he seems to have put any further thoughts on the matter effectively out of mind. Nor was there any reason for him to have done otherwise, since no consideration of the Zionist position had emanated from the Foreign Office as yet. In October 1915 it was not a factor that had to be considered while the Sherif and al-Faruqi pressed the men at Cairo for a commitment as to the boundaries of the Arab world.

"It was the most unfortunate date in my life," McMahon was to say a year later, "when I was left in charge of this Arab movement and I think a few words are necessary to explain that it is nothing to do with me: it is a purely military business. It began at the urgent request of Sir Ian Hamilton at Gallipoli. I was begged by the Foreign Office to take immediate action and draw the Arabs out of the war. At that moment a large portion of the [Turkish] force at Gallipoli and nearly the whole of the force in Mesopotamia were Arabs, and the Germans were then spending a large amount of money in detaching the rest of the Arabs, so the situation was that the Arabs were between the two. Could we give them some guarantee of assistance in the future to justify their splitting with the Turks? I was told to do that at once and in that way I started the Arab movement."

Actually, the Foreign Office records for October 1915 show that McMahon and his advisers had become, under the impact of al-Faruqi's arrival and the Sherif's warnings, more importunate than anyone else in calling for an accommodation with the Arabs as soon as possible. The prudence and deliberation they had managed to display in response to Hussein's first letter were now completely swept aside. It was General Sir John Maxwell who first sounded the alarm to London, wiring the War Office the day after Clayton's interview with al-Faruqi:

> A powerful organization with considerable influence in the army and among Arab chiefs, viz: the Young Arab Committee, appears to have made up its mind that the moment for action has arrived. . . .
> If their overtures are rejected or a reply is delayed any longer the Arab party will go over to the enemy and work with them, which would mean stirring up religious feeling at once and might well result in a genuine Jehad.

Kitchener replied in less than twenty-four hours. "The Government," he wrote, "are most desirous of dealing with the Arab question in a manner satisfactory to the Arabs. Please telegraph to me the headings of what they want and discuss the matter with Mc-Mahon. You must do your best to prevent any alienation of the Arabs' traditional loyalty to England." McMahon echoed Maxwell's concern in a telegram to the Foreign Office on October 18, in which he said:

> From further conversation with Faroki it appears evident that Arab party are at parting of the ways and unless we can give them immediate assurance of nature to satisfy them they will throw themselves into hands of Germany who he says has furnished them fulfilment of all their demands. . . .
> Arab party say they cannot longer hesitate because they must act before Turkey receives further assistance from Germany.

Al-Faruqi, it should be pointed out, was at this moment the sole source of these ominous warnings and provided the sole ground for the conviction at Cairo headquarters that they were valid. Such was the state of his credibility and of the credulity of the British authorities in Cairo, among whom a mood of panic seems suddenly to have taken hold.

There was apparently no choice, then, but to formulate a reply for Hussein on the matter of boundaries right away. McMahon, in his October 18 telegram to London, was already able to spell out the terms that, according to al-Faruqi, the Arab movement would find acceptable:

England accepts principle of independent Arabia under British guidance and control within limits propounded by Sherif of Mecca, in so far as England is free to act without detriment to the interests of her present Allies (this refers to French, in regard to whom see remarks on modification of north west limits of Arabia). . . .

In regard to North Western boundaries proposed by Sherif of Mecca, Faroki thinks Arabs would accept modification leaving in Arabia purely Arab districts of Aleppo, Damascus, Hama and Homs, whose occupation by the French they would oppose by force of arms.

He also accepts the fact that British interests necessitate special measures of British control in Basrah Vilayet.

The Foreign Office, in a letter presumably written by Sir Edward Grey himself, replied to this on October 20:

You can give cordial [changed from "warm"] assurances on the lines, and with the reserve about our allies, proposed by you. . . .

There is no difficulty in speaking without reserve about Arab peninsula and Holy Places. The general reserve you propose is however necessary more especially for North Western Boundaries.

As regards Mesopotamia, proposed sphere of British control, namely, Basra Vilayet, will need extension in view of special interests in Bagdad province and area actually in our occupation. Our treaties with Arab chiefs will of course stand.

But the important thing is to give our assurances that will prevent Arabs from being alienated, and I must leave you discretion in the matter as it is urgent and there is not time to discuss an exact formula.

The simplest plan would be to give an assurance of Arab independence saying that we will proceed at once to discuss boundaries if they will send representatives for that purpose, but if something more precise than this is required you can give it.

It was now entirely up to McMahon and his staff to formulate a statement of British policy regarding the Arab Middle East.

The reply to the Sherif Hussein was dispatched at last on October 24. "I regret to find," McMahon wrote, "that you inferred from my last note that my attitude towards the question of frontiers and boundaries was one of hesitancy and lukewarmth. Such was in no wise the intention of my note. All I meant was that I considered that the time had not yet come in which that question could be discussed in a conclusive manner." But owing to the urgency with which the Sherif evidently regarded it, McMahon said, the question was referred to the British Government, and a reply could now be given. McMahon then went right to the boundaries question, in a passage he never could have imagined was to echo through decades to come:

> The districts of Mersin and Alexandretta, and portions of Syria lying to the west of the districts of Damascus, Homs, Hama and Aleppo, cannot be said to be purely Arab, and must on that account be excepted from the proposed delimitation.
>
> Subject to that modification, and without prejudice to the treaties concluded between us and certain Arab Chiefs, we accept that delimitation.
>
> As for the regions lying within the proposed frontiers* in which Great Britain is free to act without detriment to the interests of her ally France, I am authorized to give you the following pledges on behalf of the Government of Great Britain,

and he proceeded to spell out the terms by which His Majesty's Government would recognize "the independence of the Arabs," safeguard the Holy Places against external aggression, and advise and assist in the establishment and administration of governmental authority. McMahon stressed that "it is understood that the Arabs have already decided to seek the counsels and advice of Great Britain exclusively." As for the "vilayets of Baghdad and of Basra," McMahon called for Arab recognition that "Great Britain's established position and interests there will call for the setting up of special administrative arrangements." He concluded with yet another hearty assertion of Great Britain's sympathy with Arab aspirations to become free of the Turks.

A copy of this fateful letter was not sent to the Foreign Office until two days after it had been dispatched to Hussein. In the immediate aftermath, the principal British objections to it came from the India Government and Office, where the feeling was that it had not provided sufficiently for a British Mesopotamia and had given too much weight to the claims of Hussein and to the Arab potential for

---

* George Antonius, whose translation is being used, has placed a comma at this point—a tribute to the muddledness of the letter's Arabic prose, but a clear violation of McMahon's intent. See below, page 253.

unity. The India Office also noticed that the letter had not dealt adequately with Palestine. "The problem of Palestine," minuted Sir Arthur Hirtzel of that department on November 9, "has not been expressly mentioned in these negotiations. Jerusalem ranks third among the Moslem holy places, and the Arabs will lay great stress on it. But are we going to hand our own holy places to them without conditions? Whatever may be the attitude of western Christianity on this subject, the very strong feeling of Russia will have to be reckoned with."

Yet there apparently were no other criticisms on this point. Certainly there was none from the Foreign Office, probably because officials there thought that the language arrived at by McMahon and his advisers in Cairo—albeit rather tortured and mystifying—*had* adequately dealt with Palestine. Didn't the bewildering formula "cannot be said to be purely Arab" for "portions of Syria" on the Levantine coast imply that Palestine was being excluded from the projected Arab entity? Palestine, after all, was less "purely Arab" than any other region on the coast.

But why, then, the peculiar formulation "lying to the west of the districts of Damascus, Homs, Hama and Aleppo"? A glance at any adequate map will show that even the southernmost of these places, Damascus, is still considerably to the north of Haifa, and on a line not reached even by the small northern tip of what could then be construed as Palestine. This casual geography may have seemed good enough under the circumstances to the men at the Foreign Office, but from the standpoint of a somewhat pedantic common sense, and of the general meaning of the word "district" in English, it was going to be possible to argue that McMahon had not excluded Palestine after all.

In the controversy about McMahon's meaning that arose a few years later, there was to be much discussion of the word "districts." The Arabic *wilayah*—used in its plural, *wilayat*, in the letter sent to Hussein—does not only mean "district," however; among other things, it is the same word as the Turkish *vilayet* and its original historically. Now, since a vilayet was an Ottoman administrative district, this sense of the word yields a possible construction of McMahon's language that would have him indeed excluding Palestine from the Arab entity: for Damascus was the capital of a vilayet that extended all the way south to Aqaba and whose western boundary was the Jordan-Dead Sea-Arabah line. All of Cis-Jordanian Palestine was west of this vilayet. It was therefore to be the official

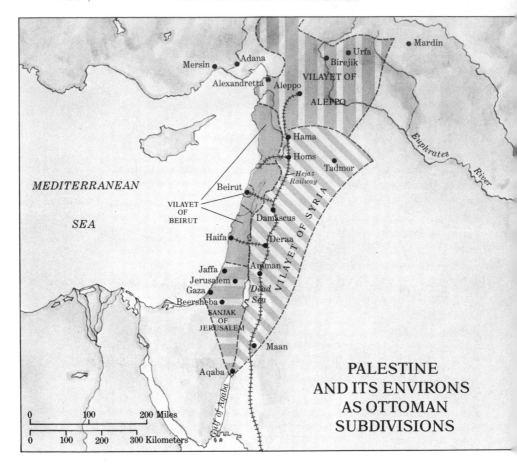

PALESTINE
AND ITS ENVIRONS
AS OTTOMAN
SUBDIVISIONS

British Government position in years to come that "vilayet" was the sense of McMahon's *wilayah*—as rendered by Storrs and Ruhi—in this context.

But the weaknesses of this construction readily present themselves. The name of the administrative district of which Damascus was the capital was the Vilayet of Syria, not the Vilayet of Damascus. Why, then, the odd locution? Furthermore, though there was a Vilayet of Aleppo, there were no "Vilayets" of Homs or Hama: those towns were included with Damascus in the Vilayet of Syria. In other words, if we accept the official interpretation of the text, we are to conclude that the McMahon-Storrs-Ruhi *wilayah* meant "Vilayet" of Syria in the case of Damascus, "district" in the case of Homs and

Hama, and "Vilayet" of Aleppo in the case of Aleppo—incredibly sloppy language for the experts in Cairo, particularly since they go on in the letter to use the term "vilayet" quite precisely in the case of Baghdad and Basra. To be sure, sloppiness of terminology was quite common at this time among British officials in the Middle East, few of whom were as accomplished in Arabic as they would have liked. The Storrs-Ruhi Arabic of this correspondence has become notorious for its faults among historians qualified to judge. Nevertheless, the "vilayet" construction raises vexing problems of internal consistency regarding this and other letters exchanged by McMahon and Hussein and is quite contrary to the spirit in which the four towns of the "Gibbon line" were regularly referred to in the correspondence between Cairo and the Foreign Office during this fall of 1915. There must be some better explanation of what McMahon, his advisers, and his translators had in mind.

McMahon himself—who was to state publicly more than twenty years later "that it was not intended by me in giving this pledge to . . . Hussein to include Palestine in the area in which Arab independence was promised"—offered an explanation of the letter's language a few years after the war that in no way resorts to what was to become the official one. "My reasons," he wrote confidentially to a Government colleague in 1922, "for restricting myself to specific mention of Damascus, Homs, Hama and Aleppo in that connection in my letter were: (1) that these were places to which the Arabs attached vital importance and (2) that there was no place I could think of at the time of sufficient importance for purposes of definition further south of the above." The argument that those four towns and nothing south of them were a particular focus of attention in Cairo at the time, for Arabs and British alike, is certainly borne out by the documents. McMahon's point, therefore, that his mention of them was not meant to be restrictive in the north-south sense—that he meant *all* of those "portions of Syria" (i.e., of Greater Syria) lying to their west, even those southward of a line through Damascus—is not unreasonable. But the question remains: if he "intended" to exclude Palestine from the Arab area, why couldn't he have found a less bewilderingly ambiguous way of doing it?

We may come closer to an answer if we examine the letter he wrote to the Foreign Office on October 26, 1915, explaining the reply he had sent to the Sherif two days before. "I have been definite in stating," he explained, "that Great Britain will recognize the principle of Arab independence in purely Arab territory, but have been equally definite in excluding Mersina, Alexandretta and those districts on the northern coast of Syria, which cannot be said to be Arab, and where I understand that French interests have been recognized." The terms "districts on the northern coast of Syria" and "French interests" both are quite compromising to McMahon's assertions of later years that he intended to exclude Palestine from the Arab area. Palestine is not even mentioned in this letter; but whereas it is true that Palestine also was never explicitly mentioned in the correspondence between McMahon and the Foreign Office leading up to his October 24 "pledge" to Hussein, the term "North Western Boundaries" was emphatically used in it more than once.

Now, the context of Foreign Office statements using this discreet term—in lieu of the more forthright position on Palestine that it was not yet prepared to take—indicate clearly that what they meant was the *entire* northwest of the area outlined by Hussein's July 14 letter, including Palestine as well as northern coastal Syria. But McMahon obviously was not taking it in this sense when he referred in his explanatory letter to "districts on the northern coast of Syria." He and his advisers in Cairo simply misunderstood the diplomatic language of the Foreign Office on this point and, through their misunderstanding, arrived at a conception of the proposed Arab territory that did *not* intend to exclude Palestine from its boundaries. In the light of this letter of October 26 to the Foreign Office, the formula "lying to the west of the districts of Damascus, Homs, Hama and Aleppo" must be taken in its restrictive sense after all.

This is not to say that McMahon and his colleagues neglected altogether to think of the possibility that Palestine might have to be excluded from the area of the "pledge" to Hussein. But the only perspective from which they contemplated it was that of "French interests." They were not thinking seriously about a Zionist claim— nor were they, for that matter, pondering "a country the size of Wales." In terms of their concerns of the moment, Palestine was essentially a stretch of southern Syria across which the line dividing French from British interests still had to be drawn. To be sure, the Christian Holy Places required some form of international control, perhaps even a "Jerusalem enclave," but no one in Cairo seems to have thought of this as significant enough a compromise to Arab desiderata to be worth mentioning. Hussein and al-Faruqi both were probably quite aware of it, anyway. As for whatever part of Palestine would fall under British control, it was already understood between Clayton and al-Faruqi that this would be autonomously

Arab in the same sense as Mesopotamia would be. In McMahon's eyes, then, there was no principle upon which Palestine was possibly to be excluded from the Arab area other than that of the still undefined extent of French claims in southern Syria.

Indeed, French claims were the rub, and not just in Palestine. "I am not aware of the extent of French claims in Syria," McMahon continued in his explanatory letter of October 26,

> nor of how far His Majesty's Government have agreed to recognize them. Hence, while recognizing the towns of Damascus, Hama, Homs and Aleppo as being within the circle of Arab countries, I have endeavored to provide for possible French pretensions to those places by a general modification to the effect that His Majesty's Government can only give assurances in regard to those territories "in which she can act without detriment to the interests of her ally France."

In other words, McMahon regarded the tortured phrasing of his letter to Hussein as having satisfactorily equivocated even on the "Gibbon line," ostensibly the sine qua non of Arab claims in Syria! Caution regarding the French was inducing the men at Cairo headquarters to promise, in the guise of nearly everything, practically nothing at all.

"Luckily," Clayton was to write to Wingate the following spring of the correspondence with the Sherif, "we have been very careful indeed to commit ourselves to nothing whatsoever." He was still thinking of the proviso about French claims, but he may also have been inadvertently revealing something about the atmosphere within which the McMahon "pledge" had been generated in October. After all, what kind of commitment in the name of the British Government could one presume to have made in that season of precipitate haste, unilateral and ultimately unauthorized policy formulations, ill-considered judgments, misunderstood terminology, and bad Arabic translations? Perhaps the men in Cairo had in fact maintained a proper perspective on themselves—although this would have meant that they had been very cynical indeed. That December the viceroy of India, Lord Hardinge, reported to Austen Chamberlain that he had written to McMahon complaining of his having offered to give Iraq away to the Arabs "without reserve." Whereupon, Hardinge told Chamberlain, McMahon had replied,

> in a very curious letter, recognizing the justice of our complaint, by implying that the negotiations are merely a matter of words

and will neither establish our rights, nor bind our hands in that country. This may prove eventually to be the case, especially if the Arabs continue to help the enemy, but I do not like pledges given when there is no intention of keeping them.

What, after all, was the status of this vague and hasty "pledge"? It certainly was not a treaty: McMahon had no authority to make one, nor did Hussein have any legitimate claim to represent the entire Arab world in a binding contract. "I cannot decide here what weight attaches to information as to Arab feeling collated in Egypt," Chamberlain wrote in his first angry response at seeing the McMahon letter,

> but my information is that Grand Shareef is a nonentity without power to carry out his proposals, that Arabs are without unity and with no possibility of uniting and I disbelieve in reality and efficacy of suggested Arab revolt in Army and elsewhere. . . . The next step should be to make clear to them that promises made by McMahon are dependent on immediate action by them in sense of their offers and will not be binding on us unless they do their part at once.

The argument was well taken. Protesting in his reply to McMahon's letter of October 24 that "your advocacy of speedy action seems to us to entail risks as well as advantages," Hussein made it clear that the British would have to wait a while for an Arab revolt after all.

The disastrous haste in Cairo had been to no purpose. The British were to wait seven months for the Sherif to rise up against the Turks in the Hejaz, and there never was to be a revolt in Syria and Mesopotamia at all. All this could have been considered sufficient grounds for release from any obligations thought to have been incurred by the McMahon "pledge"—that is, if any obligations other than the general moral one to endorse Arab independence from the Turks were considered definitive at the time. But the fact was that Hussein, in his responses to McMahon, displayed the same apparent feeling as his British counterpart that nothing final had been decided in the matter of boundaries, anyway. It was only after the war, in an atmosphere of vindictiveness and in a reversal of positions they had taken previously, that Hussein's family was to remember the McMahon "pledge," note its apparent failure to exclude Palestine, and invoke it as a binding obligation.

Sheer inadvertence had thus conspired with overhasty and irresponsible initiative to create an embarrassment for the British Government that was to last a generation. In light of the many blunders committed by McMahon that were fully recognized at the time by his peers in London and Delhi, it is particularly ironic that he left his most disastrous legacy in an area that hardly anyone was thinking about at that particular moment. And this condition was soon to change: in scarcely more than four months, there was to be a good deal of thinking about Zionism and Palestine, both in Cairo and at the Foreign Office.

·17·

M. PICOT PRESENTS TERMS

The day before McMahon's October 24 letter to the Sherif Hussein, Sir Edward Grey had written to Ambassador Paul Cambon suggesting that their governments begin the discussions about Ottoman Asia that Cambon had first proposed in March. At that time, the grounds for urgency had been the Dardanelles campaign and Russia's claim to Constantinople once the Turks had been defeated; now—with Gallipoli beginning to appear a lost cause—the pressure came from the Sherif's demands and the promise of an Arab revolt. How free were the English to treat with the Arabs regarding Syria, and what were the geographical limits of whatever freedom they had? These questions could be answered only after a definite agreement had been made with France as to the extent and limitations of her claims.

On November 13 the Foreign Office received from Cambon a letter announcing the appointment of François Georges-Picot as the "délégué chargé d'établir, d'accord avec les représentants du Gouvernement britannique, les frontières de la Syrie." At this time first secretary at the French embassy in London, Picot had for some years been consul general in Beirut. The past summer, he had been on a mission to Cairo, apparently in order to groom himself for the very task to which he was now being appointed. On the day Cambon's letter was received, a preliminary meeting was held by a newly appointed interdepartmental Committee to Discuss Arab Question and Syria, made up of representatives from the Foreign, India, and War offices, to decide upon the points they would raise when they got together with Picot. The committee's chairman was Sir Arthur Nicolson, the permanent under-secretary of state for foreign affairs. At sixty-six, he was one of the most seasoned members of Britain's diplomatic corps; indeed, he had been designated to succeed Sir Francis Bertie, who had wanted to retire, at the embassy in Paris just at the moment when the war intervened to delay all such moves. Along with his son Harold, also at the Foreign Office, Nicolson remained a source of skepticism toward the Sherif, whose political claims he described at this meeting as incoherent and unreal. On the other hand, Cairo's enthusiasms for the Sherif—which, after all, were Lord Kitchener's as well—were strongly echoed on the committee by Lieutenant Colonel A.C. Parker, one of the War Office representatives, who was Kitchener's nephew and had served in Egypt.

"It was decided," the committee reported of this November 13 meeting, "that, when discussion was opened with M. Picot, he should be told of the negotiations with the Sherif of Mecca and the disposition of the Arabs in the Turkish army, as stated by El Farughi. The danger of the present situation should be made clear, and the fact that all promises to the Arabs depended on the Arabs at once giving serious proof of their break from Turkey. And the French Government should be asked to resign their immediate hopes of Damascus, just as we were ready to give back Basra etc., if the Arabs came in."

These last words in particular indicate to what extent, despite the presence of two India Office representatives, the modest or all-but-nonexistent imperial appetites of Sir Edward Grey's Foreign Office were still predominating on the committee. Grey himself underlined this fact when he minuted on the report:

> Make it clear that we have told the Arabs we cannot make promises about Syria irrespective of the interests of our Allies; that we have no intention of standing in the way of the French there or pushing claims of our own; that our sole object is to detach Arabs from Turks and unless this is done Egypt or Soudan may be endangered and the trouble will extend to the whole of North Africa.

In other words, as far as Grey still was concerned, Picot was being asked to consider French interests in Syria solely in terms of the Arab presence; Britain's role there was hardly more than that of the Arabs' earnest advocate. Grey undoubtedly was sincere in thus holding to a prewar Liberal ideal that had remained unshaken in him even by the de Bunsen report; but the fact remained that he was thereby establishing a weak bargaining position with the French, who now had only to dispute Cairo's contentions about what was happening in the Arab world.

Picot met with the interdepartmental committee, gathered at the Foreign Office, on Tuesday, November 23. The British expounded for his benefit their position and its history. "Our case for doing all that was possible to win over the Arabs to the side of the Allies," according to Sir Arthur Nicolson, "was fully explained to M. Picot—and the grave embarrassments which could ensue were the Arabs to take sides against us were also pointed out to him."

But Picot, who had just spent a month in Paris preparing his position, was not ready to give the English satisfaction on this first day of negotiations. He replied firmly "that no French Government would stand for a day which made any surrender of French claims in Syria. Asked what those claims were, he said possession . . . of land starting from where the Taurus Mountains approach the sea in Cilicia, following the Taurus Mountains and the mountains further East, so as to include Diarbekir, Mosul and Kerkuk, and then returning to Deir Zor on the Euphrates and from there Southwards along the desert border finishing eventually at the Egyptian frontier"—in other words, all of Greater Syria including Palestine, as well as some of Anatolia and Mesopotamia to the north and northeast. Whatever discussions of territorial boundaries in Syria may have gone on between London and Paris before this, M. Picot was, as the French say, setting out again from zero. All he conceded was that France might be willing "to throw Mosul into the Arab pool," if the British did the same with Baghdad.

Picot applied a Cartesian skepticism to the various arguments offered by his British colleagues against his position. With respect to the supposed Arab preference for the English over the French, he "observed that when he was lately in Cairo the same Arabs who begged our [British] officers to come to Syria to preserve them from the French, went on to him, to say how they were longing for the arrival of French troops and the establishment of French supremacy." As for the promised Arab revolt, he "did not believe in any but a few Arab tribes joining us, no matter what we promised, for the Germans could not only always outbid us [in money and supplies], but could also use the religious cry [of *jihad*], from which we were debarred." But he really doubted altogether "the Turks and Germans being able to stir up any religious Mohammedan movement. And he asked for proofs as to the strength of the Arab and Syrian racial [sic] movement, which he suggested was much exaggerated by the Cairo authorities." In any case, however, he thought that "though an Arab union with Turk and German might be very awkward for [the British] in Egypt and India, the French were quite happy about Algeria and Tunis."

The committee also tried to persuade Picot that, whatever the extent of territory ultimately held in Syria by France, she should be prepared to offer some measure of independence to its inhabitants. But he "held out *no* hopes whatever" for this. "It was further urged on him that though the Arabs desired a considerable portion of Syria, they were willing to concede to the French a monopoly of concessions, ample security for their educational and other establishments, and they had also intimated their willingness to admit French advisers." All this had come from al-Faruqi, relayed in a message from Cairo by Sir Mark Sykes just three days before. "In the circumstances," Picot was told, "France would practically have a great influence in Syria, and would be able in a very short time to hold a predominating influence. In short her position with an Arab rule would be far better established than under the present Turkish regime. It would, in fact, develop into a French protectorate." But "these considerations," Nicolson added in his report, "did not shake M. Picot's view that nothing short of a French annexation of Syria would be admitted by the French public."

The meeting had ended in an atmosphere of gloom from the British point of view. "M. Picot is to submit a report to his Government for their observations," wrote the committee's secretary, Sir George Clerk, "and though there is little hope of any modification of this attitude, I suppose we must await them." To Sir Arthur Nicolson, Picot "intimated his readiness to proceed to Paris to explain personally our views and the Arab desiderata," but Ambassador Cambon dampened any of the optimism this might have aroused by saying that his colleague "would not be well received at the Quai d'Orsay were he to carry with him such unpalatable proposals as we had suggested." Picot went to Paris anyway, leaving the impression in London that the only point he would discuss with his own government was how to accommodate the Sherif as far as possible in terms of a Syria claimed entirely by France. His Majesty's Government had no choice but to wait. "The Arabs will not now be gained by promises" that could not be guaranteed, Grey glumly observed, "and it is hardly worth while to pursue the subject. I suppose," he added, "it was made clear to M. Picot that we have no designs in Syria and can promise nothing about it . . . unless the French agree."

The reaction at the War Office was more combative. Colonel Parker was furious and he sat down to write a "Note on the Arab Movement" which summed up his own version of the arguments that had to be reiterated to the French to make them understand. The arguments went:

From information, the sources of which (Cairo and Constantinople*) are not available to the French, it is known that the Arab and Syrian racial movement has great force, given the opportunity.

There is a chance, though it is every moment becoming fainter, of using it as a powerful weapon against the Turks.

There is the certainty that, if proofs are not given of the sympathy of the French and British with the movement, it will range itself on the Turkish side and that, provided the Turks play their cards cleverly, it will become solid against the Allies.

Consequent upon the above there is the most imminent danger that the Germans and Young Turks will succeed in what it has been their constant endeavor to achieve from long past, namely the military cooperation of the whole Mohammedan world in a religious war against the Allies.

Then the threat is made explicit:

From the above considerations it should be pointed out to the French that the refusal to act as we wish may endanger all British possessions in the East, and may thus necessitate the removal of a very large part of the British army from France, thus weakening the Allies in the French theater dangerously; also, that the French themselves may be faced with serious embarrassment and danger in North Africa.

This is followed by a quick return to sweet reasonableness:

The French must allow that we have studied the matter carefully and honestly. They must allow that no opportunity of damaging the enemy, however slight it may seem, should be neglected.

Even supposing, as suggested by the French representative, that our premises are incorrect, the French are liable to no drawbacks, except possible sentimental ones, in making the offers suggested, since these offers are only conditional on the action of the Arabs against the Turks.

But Parker, unable to lay aside his sword just yet, was moved to add that

if other means fail, it may be desirable to put to the French that: since their refusal to consider sympathetically our sugges-

---

* "Constantinople" in this context can only mean the American embassy, which was still representing British interests there.

tions will, in our opinion, consolidate the Arabs and the Syrians against the Allies, the result of which would chiefly be felt in Egypt by us, we must therefore reserve to ourselves the right to entirely reconsider the whole Syrian question.

It was, after all, the English and not the French who had an army in Egypt: how forbearing was one to be in the eagerness to show consideration to an ally? Indeed, Parker and some of his colleagues at the War Office had not completely renounced Kitchener's old idea of a British landing at Alexandretta, and they thought that, if one occurred, it should not stop short of the taking of Aleppo. What then would be the French position in Syria?

Parker reported the new developments to Clayton in Cairo, and the reaction there was an anger similar to his. Picot was remembered in Cairo, and Clayton wrote back his opinion that negotiations with the French would get nowhere if he were not replaced. McMahon wrote to the Foreign Office on December 10:

> Selection of Picot as the representative on recent committee on this question is discouraging indication of French attitude. Picot is a notorious fanatic on Syrian question and quite incapable of assisting any mutual settlement on reasonable common sense grounds as situation requires. It is unfortunate that adviser of French Government here, de France, is man of similar type. Notwithstanding recent assurances to me I am informed that he sent a few days ago for a leading Arab notary of Damascus now in Egypt and told him as follows: "You can tell all your friends here from me and I tell you this in my capacity as representative of French Government that Syria shall never be part of Arab Empire. Syria will be under protection of France and we shall shortly send an army to occupy it but we shall govern it in the way which most suits its people of all races and religions."

McMahon was particularly vexed because he was at this moment trying to formulate a reply to the Sherif's letter of November 5, which had objected to the fact that the vilayets of Aleppo and Beirut had not been included in their entirety in the proposed Arab entity—which had been done out of consideration for the French. For McMahon, the upshot of the meeting with Picot in London was that he could tell Hussein only that the British Government had "fully understood your statement in that respect and noted it with the greatest care. But as the interests of [our] ally France are involved in these two provinces, the question calls for careful consideration." He could only add that he would communicate again on this subject, "at the appropriate time": it was a case of the very paralysis signaled by Grey in his own response to the November 23 meeting with Picot.

"M. Picot is now in Paris, nominally trying to get his Government to agree to the very anodyne reply to the Sherif which Sir H. McMahon proposed about Syria," observed Sir George Clerk at the Foreign Office,

> and the most favorable issue I expect is that the French Government will make us the "great concession" of agreeing, if we will definitely recognize the French claim to the whole coast from Egypt to Mersina. Of the two alternatives, I prefer by far to risk the Arab danger, but the question is so serious that I think it must be treated between Government and Government, and no longer between M. Picot and this Department. This is a matter for consideration by the War Committee and I would venture to urge that that body should hear the views of Sir Mark Sykes, who is not only highly qualified to speak, but who understands the French position in Syria today—and in a sense sympathizes with it—better probably than anyone.

To this Sir Arthur Nicolson added: "We can await the return of Picot from Paris and see what he brings back with him—I have no doubt Sir Mark Sykes could give valuable information to the War Committee if they wished to call him."

·18·

THE TRAVELS OF SIR MARK SYKES

On November 19, 1915, Sir Mark Sykes had wired the following message from Cairo to London:

> I am waiting here for an opportunity of seeing General Officer Commanding [Sir John Maxwell] and the High Commissioner [Sir Henry McMahon] in accordance with your instructions. By the favor of Sir M. Cheetham I have seen correspondence relating to Arab movement and Sheriff. Two difficulties strike me. (a) Arab want of confidence in our might; (b) difficulty of making arrangements with Arabs, inoffensive to French susceptibility based on financial interests and historical sentiment.

Sykes, now a lieutenant colonel on special assignment with the War Office, had been traveling all over the East since June, expressly for the purpose of explaining the de Bunsen report to British authorities in Egypt, Aden, the Persian Gulf, and India; at the same time, he was gathering information that had by now made him one of the most knowledgeable of Englishmen about current Middle Eastern questions. Just arrived in Cairo for his third sojourn during the present tour, he was about to begin turning his knowledge into an instrument for decisive political influence.

Sykes had been a Middle Eastern traveler all his life. The only child of a wealthy Yorkshire baronet, Sir Tatton Sykes—who had a considerable reputation as a donor to the building of churches—he was first taken to the East by his travel-loving father in 1886, when he was seven years old. From then on, the return trips—interspersed with travel to other parts of the world, including America—were repeated every few years. Even during his two years at Jesus College, Cambridge, he took off during the Lent terms to travel in the East, and out of these journeys came a book instead of a degree: *Through Five Turkish Provinces*, published in 1900.

In general, Sykes was a man of whom it could be said that travel had been his university, and if the result was a rather brilliantly unconventional turn of mind, this was true to the spirit of his early education and upbringing. At the age of three, he had been converted to Catholicism along with his mother, Lady Jessica; the highly intelligent and strong-willed daughter of a member of Parliament, she was partly of Irish extraction and had fallen under the influence of Cardinal Manning and the Oxford movement. As a result, Sykes had spent his boyhood as something of an outsider among others of his age and class, undergoing a very different educational route from theirs: first, private tutors, then the Jesuit school near Windsor, Beaumont College (the "Catholic Eton"), followed by schools at Monaco and at Brussels, where he acquired fluent French. His subsequent impatience with Cambridge and unreadiness to finish seems to have been a natural outcome of this restless and colorful background. Even in his Arabic studies with the great E.G. Browne, he showed flair rather than application, and he never was to come near men like Storrs or Lawrence in his capacity to handle that language. His best talents in the university years were displayed in nonacademic pursuits: acting and drawing—or rather, cartooning, for he was a caricaturist of mordant cleverness.

Upon entering young manhood, Sykes may even have been in some danger of becoming an aimless if charitable eccentric like his father. He was spared this, however, not only by his enormous energy and high spirits, but also by the Boer War, in which he served as a lieutenant in the Yorkshire Militia, and which seems to have awakened in him an ideal of public service. After the war, he traveled in the Middle East again and produced another book about it— *Dar ul-Islam*—in 1904; then he spent the year 1904-05 in Dublin as assistant to George Wyndham, the Irish secretary in Balfour's cabinet. By this time he was married. His wife, Edith, was the daughter of an outstanding public servant, Sir John Eldon Gorst, who had been one of the members of Parliament for Cambridge University when Sykes studied there. Edith's brother was Eldon Gorst, Lord Cromer's successor in 1907 as British agent and consul in Egypt (Kitchener did not succeed to that post until Gorst's premature death in 1910). Sykes and his wife went on to spend the years 1905 to 1909 in Constantinople; there, he served as an attaché to the British embassy. More journeys in the hinterlands of Ottoman Asia ensued during these four years, often with Edith along as companion, and the eventual outcome was *Five Mansions of the House of Othman*, published in 1909, and *The Caliphs' Last Heritage*, begun in this period but not completed until 1915.

After his return from Constantinople, Sykes decided upon a parliamentary career and became the Conservative candidate for the Buckrose division of the East Riding in Yorkshire. But he lost twice there and did not win a seat until he stood for nearby Central Hull in 1911. Two years later, his father died, and Sir Mark succeeded him as the sixth baronet of Sledmere, settling down there with Edith to raise their six children.

By the outbreak of war, Sir Mark also had organized a reserve battalion of the Yorkshire regiment, mainly consisting of tenants on his own estates, with which he held the rank of lieutenant colonel. Sykes, though still the MP for Central Hull, was prepared to go with his regiment to France whenever it was sent. But, from the outset, he also recognized the possibility of Turkish entry on the side of the Central Powers and he felt that his knowledge of Ottoman affairs might be put to good use. It looked to him, he wrote in a letter to Winston Churchill on August 24, 1914, as if "the Germans are straining every nerve to involve Turkey," thereby to create "a Pan-Islamic diversion against us" and "a Caucasian complication for Russia." He went on:

> I know you won't think me self-seeking if I say all the knowledge I have of local tendencies and possibilities is at your disposal. . . . If operations are to take place in those parts I might be of more use on the spot than anywhere else. My Battalion is practically willing for foreign service, i.e. 85%, and with my personal knowledge of its possible antagonist in the regions I mention, I could make it serve a turn, raise native scallywag corps, win over notables or any other oddment.

Churchill replied with the hope that "we shall avoid a rupture with Turkey, though the situation is not good with those people," and said nothing more about the suggestion. But Sykes pursued it after Turkey's entry, this time with the War Office, which at last gave him an assignment in London. He was separated from his battalion, which—despite his earlier fond hopes, and not without some raised eyebrows as a result—subsequently went off to France without him.

Sykes's fertile mind, constantly abounding in detailed analyses and plans of action, soon impressed itself upon Lord Kitchener, who placed him on the general staff for Eastern service by the end of the year. When the naval assault on the Dardanelles began, Sykes could not resist giving Churchill the benefit of his knowledge and lively reflections regarding the Turks. "I see by the papers," he wrote to the first lord on February 26,

> that there has been liveliness in the vicinity of the Dardanelles, though what it portends I know not, but as you bore with me the last time, I venture again to write of certain things passing through my mind. . . .
> I feel that the blow delivered there should be hard, decisive, and without preamble. Morally speaking every bombardment which is not followed by a passage of the Dardanelles is a victory in the eyes of the mass of Turkish troops around the Marmora. It is worth considering that the Turks are accustomed to thinking in terms of passive defense—Plevna, Erzerum, and Chatalja* each make Turks think a long resistance or repulsed attack all that can be wished for. Therefore do I think that "reconnaissance" and "harassing" are things to be used as sparingly as tactical requirements will allow. Turks always grow formidable if given time to think, they may be lulled into passivity, and rushed, owing to their natural idleness and proneness to panic, but they are dangerous if gradually put on their guard.
> During the Balkan war, they were at one moment ready to abandon Constantinople but in 18 days they had recovered and were ready to fight to their last man.

If Sykes often presented observations such as these in conversation with his War Office colleagues during the Dardanelles campaign, they must soon have recognized that he was a young man of vivid and often very sound perceptions. Lord Kitchener seems to have chosen Sykes without hesitation to be his personal representative on the de Bunsen Committee. During its deliberations in April and May, as the minutes show, he made himself one of its guiding voices. He was a natural choice to embark on a journey East to explain the findings of the committee to British leaders and spokesmen, as well as to gather information on the general situation there.

Sykes left on June 1, accompanied by his secretary, Sergeant Walter Wilson. After stops in France and Italy, he was in Athens by June 11, discussing the de Bunsen recommendations with Sir Fran-

---

* These are all examples of tenacious Turkish defense during the Russo-Turkish War of 1877–78.

cis Elliot, the British ambassador there. By June 28 he was in Sofia, and from there he went on to Salonika, to Lemnos—where he conferred with Sir Ian Hamilton—and to Egypt; by July 14 he was in Cairo, staying at Shepheard's Hotel. There he spoke not only to the British authorities—eliciting written critiques of the de Bunsen recommendations from Sir Henry McMahon and from General Sir John Maxwell—but also to Egyptian and Arab nationalist leaders. The sultan of Egypt told him that Syria should be made part of the Egyptian government after the war—an idea in which McMahon concurred at that moment. Muhammad Rashid Rida, one of the pioneer intellectuals of Arab nationalism, expressed his opinion to Sykes that the British were afraid of Islam. The Sherif's letter of July 14 had not yet arrived in Cairo, but Sykes could already see "that it is important that Great Britain and France should come to some understanding as soon as possible with regard to Syria."

In one of the reports he cabled to the War Office, Sykes went on to express his belief—based on what he had heard about Picot's recent mission to Cairo—"that the French will give up the coast to the South of Akka: this indeed is essential to our position in Mesopotamia. I further believe that possibly we might obtain Damascus from them." Whatever Frenchmen Sykes may have been speaking to, they were representing a more conciliatory position than Picot himself was to assume in November. Sykes was sure at this point that it would be possible to persuade the French to give up all their political claims in Syria in return for compensation elsewhere and for commercial and railway concessions in Syria itself. The three Syrian vilayets of Beirut, Aleppo, and Syria (Damascus) "could then be under the government of the Sultan of Egypt and the spiritual dominion of the Sherif of Mecca. Worked as one unit these three regions are united by language and financially self-supporting." Sykes was for the moment completely captivated by the vision, upheld by Storrs and others, of a British suzerainty over all of Greater Syria emanating from Cairo.

Sykes, who sailed to Aden and then was back in Cairo before moving on to India in mid-August, made a strong personal impression upon his colleagues in Egypt. A rather large man, with blue eyes and blond hair and moustache, he tended to dominate a room with his abounding vitality the moment he entered it. "He was one of those few for whom the House of Commons fills," Ronald Storrs recalled many years later. "As a caricaturist and political cartoonist he could have imposed his own terms upon the evening Press," his drawings, according to Storrs, being "struck off instantaneously, at white heat, upon the nearest scrap of paper, with rich gurgling at each evocation."

T.E. Lawrence, writing at a time when he could no longer view Sykes with friendly equanimity, saw the underside of these same gifts. "He would take an aspect of the truth," he wrote of Sykes years later, "detach it from its circumstances, inflate it, twist and model it, until its old likeness and its new unlikeness together drew a laugh; and laughs were his triumphs. His instincts lay in parody: by choice he was a caricaturist rather than an artist, even in statesmanship. He saw the odd in everything, and missed the even. He would sketch out in a few dashes a new world, all out of scale, but vivid as a vision of some sides of the thing we hoped."

India, which he had never visited before, brought out the caricaturist in Sykes when he viewed the daily work schedule of the typical British civil servant there, which he deemed "not convenient for anyone in a hurry." He summed it up this way in a letter home in early September:

6.30.—Breakfast—ride, swim, sleep, idle.	2.30 to 4.30.—Sleep, I think.
	4.30 to 6.30.—Go about.
9.30.—Breakfast.	6.30 to 8.0.—Hang about club.
10.45.—Go to office.	8.0.—Dress for
12.30.—Break for Tiffin [lunch].	dinner.
1.30.—Tiffin.	9.0.—Dinner.

But it was also in India that Sykes's political sense of the conflict with Turkey began taking on a new authoritativeness, as he interviewed large numbers of the Arab soldiers in Turkish service who had been taken prisoner in Mesopotamia and were being held in the British detention camp at Sumerpur. Through these contacts he became one of the first to conclude—along with Sir Reginald Wingate—that the warring principles in the Middle East had become pan-Islamism versus Arab nationalism, the former supported by Germany and Turkey, the latter by Great Britain. By late September Sykes was in Basra, and there an idea that had come to him in India for an anti-*jihad* committee ripened in his mind. "As the result of my tour of the whole Eastern theater," he cabled to the War Office on October 9,

I am impressed by the necessity for the coordination of our policy in regard to the Ottoman Empire, Arabian people and the

Mahometan opinion in the British Empire. A means of ame-
liorating the position which suggests itself to me would be to
authorize me . . . to complete my mission by establishing in
Cairo a Bureau under your department which should receive
copies of all telegrams giving available information regarding
our enemies, Islamic propaganda and methods and effect
thereof, as well as tendency of popular opinion, from intelligence and political officers in Mesopotamia and Persian Gulf,
Indian Criminal Investigation Department, Soudan Intelligence
Department, Chief Intelligence Officer Mediterranean Expeditionary Force, Intelligence Officer Athens. I could then from
time to time transmit to you for the use of the Cabinet a general
appreciation. I suggest Egypt as the place for the Bureau owing
to its central situation and the local touch with the Islamic
world.

This proposal was soon to have results, although Sykes was not
to have his wish fulfilled of presiding over the bureau in Egypt himself. Meanwhile, it was clear that he had become even more solidly
identified than before with the Cairo outlook on Middle Eastern affairs. "I believe that the moment has now come," he wrote to the
War Office from Basra on October 23, "when His Majesty's Government might profitably consider the future attitude of Great Britain
towards Arab peoples within the area of British interest," and he
went on strongly to oppose the idea of Indian colonization of Mesopotamia.

On November 15, sailing for Egypt on the Red Sea, Sykes wrote
a memorandum that, when it reached London, was considered important enough to be printed for cabinet distribution. The fruit of
five and a half months of travel, inquiry, and reflection, it was an
attempt to formulate the essentials of a British policy in the Middle
East. Sykes, who had last left Cairo before the arrival there of Hussein's July 14 letter, did not yet know of it or of the ensuing correspondence with McMahon. "I suggest that our ultimate goal should
be: in Arabia—," he wrote,

(1) Recognition of the independence of the Hejaz under the
Sherif.
(2) The conclusion of peace between Idrisi and Imam Yahya,
and the fixing of their territories, compensating Yahya in the
Aden hinterland and Hadhramaut, if necessary, in return for
the expulsion of the Turks from Yemen.

(3) Declaration of an external protectorate* over the Arabian littoral from Koweit to Hodeidah.

(4) Declaration of a British internal and external protectorate over an area in Southern Syria and Mesopotamia to be agreed upon with France and Russia.

Declaration of a French internal and external protectorate in an area north of the British area.

(5) An agreement between the Entente Powers which would ensure political and military cooperation without prejudice to the future status of certain territories, thus permitting the use of British, French, Italian, or Russian troops in any area.

(6) If possible to stimulate an Arab demand for the Caliphate of the Sherif.

On reaching Cairo, Sykes was shown the McMahon-Hussein correspondence and was in general satisfied with it. He does not seem to have been troubled by its inadequacies, regarding Palestine or anything else; but it is clear from his subsequent statements and actions that he, too, regarded it as all highly tentative. Indeed, on November 19, in the first flush of his enthusiasm upon seeing the correspondence and hearing about the conversations with al-Faruqi, Sykes cabled to London a whole new set of ideas regarding the present and future of Syria, not all of which were consistent either with his memorandum of November 15 or with McMahon's letter to Hussein of October 24. For the sake of an arrangement with the newly outspoken Arabs that would be "inoffensive to French susceptibility," he proposed that all of Syria become "independent Arab territory" after the war, and that the French be granted special—in some places exclusive—economic concessions in northern Syria. With this proposal—which reflected his thinking of the previous July—he was putting aside his own of a few days earlier for French and British protectorates; he was also, in effect, ignoring McMahon's suggestion that parts of the Syrian coast could not "be said to be purely Arab."

Sykes was also nonchalant about other points that some might have considered to be already established. The problem of Arab want of confidence in British power, he suggested, could be dealt with by a blockade of the Cilician gates and an occupation of the whole borderline between Turkish-speaking and Arabic-speaking territory. Though he did not explicitly say so, this clearly was a reiteration of the old plan of invasion at Alexandretta, which had been

---

* An external protectorate would control only foreign policy; an internal one, domestic affairs.

supported with special ardor at Cairo and probably had originated there, and which had been rejected by the de Bunsen Committee as an unnecessary provocation to the French.

Sykes had begun committing ideas to the telegraph virtually as fast as they came into his head; and it seems to have been in a euphoria of ad hoc improvisation that he spoke to al-Faruqi the next day, November 20. "I saw Faruki," he wired London, "and anticipating French difficulty discussed the situation with him with that in view. Following is best I could get but seems to me to meet the situation both with regard to France and Great Britain. Arabs would agree to accept as approximate northern frontier Alexandretta Aintab Birijik Urfa Midiat Zakho Rowanduz." This was a modification to the southward, both of the line proposed by Hussein in his July 14 letter and of that proposed by al-Faruqi himself in his October 11 conversation with Clayton. Sykes and al-Faruqi were again starting from the beginning.

"Arabs would agree," Sykes went on, "to convention with France granting her monopoly of all concessionary enterprise in Syria and Palestine." The idea of compensating France with economic concessions for her relinquishment of political claims in Syria had already appeared in Sykes's telegram of the day before, and there is no reason for supposing he was not its originator now, since the idea bespeaks a different approach to the problem of the French than had been taken by al-Faruqi and Clayton in their conversation of October 11. It also bespeaks—once again—a readiness on the part of Sykes and al-Faruqi to ignore the details of the McMahon-Hussein exchanges.

"Hedjaz Railway as far South as Amman could be sold to French concessionaire," Sykes went on in his report of the al-Faruqi interview. "Arabs would further agree to employment of none but Frenchmen as advisers and European employees in this area. . . . Arabs would agree to all French educational establishments having special recognition in this area." As for the British sphere, "Arabs would agree to identical convention with Great Britain with regard to remainder of Greater Arabia viz. Irak and Jazirah and Northern Mesopotamia." In the south, "Arabs would agree to Basrah town and all cultivated lands to the South being British territory." The French compensation for this was that "Arabs would agree to any territory North of Greater Arabian frontier being French possessions under French flag." These were the suggestions that Sir Arthur Nicolson's committee was to present to Picot on November 23.

All of this, Sykes proposed, could form elements in a treaty that the Arabs "would be prepared to make" with the Entente—though he does not specify who the authority qualified to make such a treaty would be. Meanwhile, al-Faruqi had insisted that any such formal agreement would be

> dependent on Entente landing troops at a point between Mersina and Alexandretta and making good Amanus Pass or Cilician gates. He further stipulated that Sherif could not take action until this had been done. I agree that any other course is out of the question and that to call on Sherif or Arabs to take action until we had made above mentioned passes secure would be impossible. Faruki also urged necessity for immediate adequate action in the Gulf of Alexandretta.

These were Sykes's own ideas again; but he had gone so far in his enthusiasm of the moment that he was endorsing conditions far stiffer than Hussein's and really untenable. If the Allies were to stage so ambitious a military operation as was here being proposed, they certainly would not have done so merely on the basis of a shaky guarantee by al-Faruqi or the Sherif that the Arab nation would rise up to support it. Furthermore, if the landing could have been brought off successfully before getting open Arab support—as al-Faruqi here seems to be demanding—then what would have been the point of bargaining with the Arabs from a weaker position in the first place?

As for Palestine, Sykes—who, unlike his colleagues in Cairo, was acquainted with the Herbert Samuel memorandum—seems to have mentioned something to al-Faruqi about the possibility of Jewish claims there, although he gave no indications of this in his reports from on the spot. A few months later, however, in another context, he was to wire London that when he was in Cairo al-Faruqi and another Arab nationalist leader, Dr. Faris Nimr—though their views were poles apart in other respects—both told him "that Arabs, Christians and Moslems alike, would fight in the matter to the last man against Jewish Dominion in Palestine." Sykes was to regard this problem as soluble, but doubtless he saw no reason during this November 20 conversation with al-Faruqi to press any further a matter that was inflammatory to his listener and about which the British Government had not yet come up with a policy. Al-Faruqi may have been especially difficult on this question, anyway, since he had told Clayton in October that, whereas Christians, Druses, and other religious minorities would have "the same rights as Moslems" in the proposed Arab state or federation, "Jews will be governed by a special law." Clearly, he was not the Arab with whom to be discussing the prospects for Zionism.

The day after his interview with al-Faruqi—which he was ready to take as the "basis of our arrangements with Arabs"—the indefatigable Sykes wired to London a set of preliminary recommendations for any such future arrangements. "With regard to France and Arabs," he wrote, "our task is to get Arabs to concede as much as possible to French and to get our Haifa outlet and Palestine included in our sphere of enterprise in the form of French concession to us." For the moment at least, he was remaining consistent with the switch he had made from the idea of protectorates in Syria to that of mere European economic preference there—although now he was back to acknowledging that the British had claims against the French in Palestine. As for the Arabian Peninsula itself, Sykes did not think that "proposed Arab movement affects our position with regard to various Gulf and Red Sea interests. Gulf and Aden treaties will hold good and I am confident that suzerainty of Shereef in Arabia proper will be in practice purely honorary." This note of skepticism about the extent of the Sherif's potential influence is also sounded in Sykes's remark that the British should retain political authority in Baghdad and Basra because these cities "are divided from Arabia by schism"—meaning they were predominantly Shiite, as opposed to the Sherif's Sunni authority—"and are too disorderly and rancorous for newborn state to govern. . . . Arab nationalism has little influence and the Khalifate none south of Bagdad in the cultivated area." Sykes went on to offer specific consolation to the India Office that "the suggested Arab state cannot become a formidable power in itself so long as it is protected from German and Turkish influence by France and ourselves." And he concluded with a warning: "In the event of our letting this opportunity go Arabs in Syria and northern Mesopotamia will, I believe, fall in with the Turks in order to get the best terms for nationalist aspirations from those whom they would then regard as certain winners."

This seems to imply that Sykes shared the Cairo view of Arab support in Syria and Mesopotamia as being the factor that could tip the balance of victory in the direction either of Turkey or of the Entente. Yet he says something rather different eight days later, on November 29, in a telegram warning that if the Arabs were to throw in their lot with the Turks the latter would massacre Christians in Syria "on the Armenian scale." This was a reference to the terrible new round of Armenian massacres that the Turks had begun in

April, a revival of those that had shocked the world from 1894 to 1896. Such a massacre, Sykes went on, would compromise Muslim Arabs permanently, since it would eliminate the "last center of uncontrolled intellectualism from [the] Ottoman Empire" and eradicate the sources of French support. "I submit," he concluded, "that this would be fatal to French prospects in Syria."

This last point seems to have been the main one in this message that was incidentally so compromising to the claims of Arab nationalism. Indeed, the underlying point that could have been derived by a reader in London from the bewildering and often contradictory variety of messages Sykes had been sending over the past month was that the position Picot had taken on November 23 was untenable. And Sykes—with his vivid knowledge of all the factors involved—was thereby demonstrating that he might be the man who could deal with the French regarding claims in the Middle East.

·19·

SYKES AND PICOT
ARE BROUGHT TOGETHER

Sykes had no sooner returned from his long journey than he was invited to appear on December 16 before the cabinet's War Committee, which was the current incarnation of the supreme councils that had been directing war policy since August 1914. After the cabinet upheaval and formation of the coalition Government in May, the former War Council had been reorganized as the Dardanelles Committee, the very name of which indicated where wartime policy had to be made from one day to the next at that time. The political decisions that then needed to be made for the stagnant western front were few and far between. But the Dardanelles, after another major attack in August and a new landing at Suvla Bay, had proved as hopeless as France and Flanders after all, and an evacuation of the British forces on the Gallipoli Peninsula was about to begin. In a new reshuffle in early November, the Dardanelles Committee had been replaced by the War Committee.

Consisting of only five members, the War Committee included Asquith, Lloyd George, and Balfour, all three of whom had been on both the War Council and the Dardanelles Committee. The other two members were Andrew Bonar Law, leader of the Conservative opposition and there to represent the principle of coalition, and Reginald McKenna, Lloyd George's replacement in May as chancellor of the Exchequer. Neither Grey nor Kitchener was on the committee—apparently by choice—but they were in regular contact with it. The most significant change had been the departure of Winston Churchill, who had remained on the Dardanelles Committee even while holding the minor cabinet post of chancellor of the Duchy of Lancaster. The Dardanelles vision was now a thing of the past, and with it had gone its foremost exponent; his political career seemingly at an end, Churchill had gone over to France on November 18 to join the regiment with which he held a reserve commission.

Kitchener, along with other representatives of the War Office, came to the meeting at 10 Downing Street to hear Sykes testify. Kitchener had recently returned from a visit to Gallipoli that had led him to agree that the British positions there—at least those at Suvla and Anzac—had to be evacuated. He had also been to Paris twice, once at the end of November on his way back from Gallipoli, and again on December 5, when he, Asquith, and Balfour had discussed with the French leaders the landing their troops had jointly made at Salonika at the beginning of October. Also present to hear Sykes were members of the Foreign and India offices, including Austen Chamberlain and Lord Crewe, Chamberlain's predecessor as secretary for India and now lord president of the council. Crewe was coming, however, not in either of those capacities, but as acting foreign secretary. Since June, Sir Edward Grey had been taking more and more frequent respites from work on account of his failing eyesight, and Crewe had been standing in for him.

Asquith opened the proceedings by asking Sykes to sum up his recent itinerary. Sykes did so, and said that the fruit of the observations he had made during the course of it was his shipboard memorandum of November 15, with its six-point proposal about the future of the Middle East, including the idea of French and British protectorates. Upon his return home, Sykes's shifting thoughts on the subject had returned to this position after all. He added his view that, since November 15, "subsequent events have altered anything one had to say on military questions, though, I think, the political questions remain as they were before." He evidently meant by "subsequent events" both the failure of the Gallipoli campaign and the possibility of active Arab intervention on the British side. "With regard to the Arab question," he went on, "the fire, the spiritual fire, lies in Arabia proper, the intellect and the organizing power lie in Syria and Palestine, centered particularly at Beirut."

After several exchanges of questions and answers, Sykes got to his point that "if matters are allowed to slide . . . the Sherif, I think, will be killed," and a nominee of Constantinople would be put in his place at Mecca. Sykes expounded his view of the German ambition to dominate a "Turco-Arabia" held together on pan-Islamic principles. To counter this, Britain, he said, had to back the Arabs, coordinate its Eastern operations, and organize a powerful army in Egypt that would not merely guard the canal but be "capable of taking the offensive." The major obstacle in the way of all this was the French:

"practically all the Arabs," Sykes observed, "are pro-English and not anti-French, but frightened of the French. . . . They like the French and they like French culture, but they are frightened of French methods." Sykes therefore urged that "we ought to settle with France as soon as possible, and get a definite understanding about Syria."

Balfour took his lead and asked, "What sort of an arrangement would you like to have with the French? What would you say to them?"

"I should like," replied Sykes, "to retain for ourselves such country south of Haifa as was not in the Jerusalem enclave. . . . I think it is most important that we should have a belt of English-controlled country between the Sherif of Mecca and the French."

Prime Minister Asquith, perhaps a bit hazy about the contents of the de Bunsen report all these months later, was startled at the extent of Sykes's proposed belt of English-controlled country. "You mean," he asked, "the whole way from the Egyptian frontier to Haifa, except the enclave?"

"I think it could be argued to the French," Sykes said, "that they were not giving up very much, assuming the enclave is large enough to contain the head of the Dead Sea and enough of the Jordan for the pilgrims to go into." After some more questions, Sykes elaborated on this. "They are only giving up what lies between Acre and the beginning of the Jerusalem enclave, which will be about twenty miles."

This, it should be noted, is the first indication we have been given of anyone's notion as to the extent of the proposed Jerusalem enclave. What Sykes has just sketched out is a territory extending well northward of the Jaffa-Jerusalem pilgrimage route that would have to be comprised within such an enclave by even the most minimal conception. As for its southern frontier, Sykes obviously envisions nothing intervening between the enclave and the British-controlled Sinai. His conception of the whole enclave clearly was larger in territorial scope than that of most of his colleagues and suggests he may already have had in mind some consideration of Zionist claims. Certainly he knew that, as conceived, the area was potentially one of de facto British suzerainty, even under an official regime of international control.

Balfour asked Sykes where he wanted, then, to make the division between French and British claims in the Middle East, and the latter replied, "I should like to draw a line from the 'e' in Acre to the last 'k' in Kerkuk."

After a few more exchanges, Sykes was asked what he thought might be done to get good terms from the French. "I think that we have . . . two assets," he answered. "I think that we can play on the French colonial if we work it well: get it into the French colonial's head what a Committee of Union and Progress Sherif means and put out what they have done in India [to stir up pan-Islamic feeling against the Entente] and what they might do elsewhere." As for the other asset, it was that "the French clerical is quite capable of being influenced by reason of the danger to his one asset in Syria"—this being a reference to the possible slaughter of Syrian Christians that Sykes had mentioned in his November 29 letter from Cairo. The result would be that, having thus robbed "the occult French financial force of its two agencies [in Syria], then, I think, you are on the high road to a settlement." Sykes pointed out that the French authorities he spoke to in Egypt, though they would begin by demanding almost everything in Syria, would end by admitting that "giving up to Acre is giving up very little—only that small strip. It must be remembered that the desert does not end with the Egyptian frontier; the desert comes right up to Hebron." And deserts, after all, were for nomads and Englishmen.

Austen Chamberlain was sufficiently impressed with Sykes to suggest that he might be sent to Paris to deal directly with the French government and bypass the obstacles presented by Cambon and Picot. Lord Crewe agreed to write for advice on this point to Sir Francis—now Lord—Bertie, the British ambassador in Paris.

Crewe wrote Bertie the next day. "I do not know whether you ever met him," he said of Sykes. "He has traveled a great deal in Asia and learnt much about the people, knowing, I think, both Turkish and Arabic. He is certainly a very capable fellow, with plenty of ideas, but at the same time painstaking and careful."

Crewe then summed up the British Middle Eastern position of the moment, no doubt hoping that Bertie would convey some of it to his French colleagues and thereby aid the cause of bypassing Picot. He began by hinting that the defense of Egypt ought better to be turned into an offensive, as Sykes had urged: the Suez line did not "seem to be a particularly defensible position in itself," and "if the Turks advance unchecked, everything behind them will be either won over or destroyed." Now, if such an advance extended to Arabia,

it means that all hopes in which we have indulged of exploiting the Arab dislike of Turkey, and perhaps of creating an Arab Federation under the Shereef of Mecca, go by the board. The

Shereef, who is friendly to us and tolerates the French, will either be put to death or have to fly for his life. If the Committee of Union and Progress get control of Mecca, they might be able to declare a regular Jehad, probably affecting Afghanistan and giving serious trouble in India.

This was why it was desirable to forgo a passive defense of Egypt, and why "every stage further back, whether it be Palestine or Syria, or right up to Asia Minor, at which we could attack in force, would be so much to the good."

This, then, Crewe went on, was what had brought Great Britain

up against French susceptibilities and claims, and any discussion becomes exceedingly delicate, because the French always seem to talk as though Syria and even Palestine were as completely theirs as Normandy. Only today, when Cambon was here, he talked at length about the way his Government have been kept in the dark concerning conversations with the Shereef of Mecca. These were carried on, as I may tell you for your private information, without great wisdom by McMahon in Cairo. I was able to reassure Cambon that we had no intention of arranging that a new Arab State, if one could be formed, would include the Lebanon or any part of the world to which the French could lay distinct claim. I added, however, that his Government would be wise to consider the situation in all its bearings, because, if Arabia should be won over by the Young Turks, the Syrian Christians, man, woman, and child, would undoubtedly enjoy the fate of the Armenians during the last few months.

Bertie replied on December 21, saying he did not think Sykes's appearance in Paris would be useful. Annoyed at the way his own Government had handled the matter so far, he could not resist commenting: "When the French pegged out absurd claims at Alexandretta, Syria, etc., we ought to have objected; and when we disclaimed any political aspirations for ourselves in Syria, the French took it that they might have them although we did not say so."

But otherwise, Bertie's letter contained an optimistic note that caused the Foreign Office to print up this exchange between him and Crewe for cabinet circulation. "I met a few weeks ago," he wrote, "a M. Victor Bérard, a traveler and writer, who knows Egypt, Syria, and Palestine well." Bérard was a distinguished classical scholar whose specialty was Homer, but who in recent years had done a good

deal of writing on current Near Eastern affairs. A friend and informal adviser to several leading statesmen, he was a true French re-
publican secularist, even in regard to Syria, where he considered his
country's claims to be primarily Catholic and hence incompatible
with its principles as he understood them.

Bérard's own sympathies in Greater Syria were not so much
with Christianity there as with Arab and Jewish nationalism.
Though not a Jew himself, he had recently joined a Comité de
Propagande Française auprès des Juifs Neutres ("Committee for
French Propaganda Among Jews of Neutral Countries"), the purpose of which was to persuade the neutral Jewish communities—
especially that of the United States—that the Allied cause was theirs
in spite of the participation in it of anti-Semitic Russia. Not all the
members of the comité were persuaded that the Allies should adopt
a Zionist policy to prove the point, but Bérard seems to have been
one who was. At any rate, he was in friendly contact with Baron
Edmond de Rothschild and had in early December taken part in a
conversation in Paris that included the baron, Chaim Weizmann, and
Lord Bertie. Indeed, it is quite likely that this was the very occasion
to which Lord Bertie was referring in his letter to Crewe.

According to Bertie, Bérard had described a recent luncheon
meeting between himself and the two previous French prime ministers—Gaston Doumergue, who had held the office from December
1913 to June 1914, and René Viviani, who had held it from the outbreak of the war until the past October, when he was replaced by
Aristide Briand. "To them," Bertie wrote, Bérard

> had argued in favor of an Arab empire under the protectorate of
> England, with an Anglo-French convention for the protection of
> French religious and educational establishments, etc.; and he
> put it to M. Viviani that France could only claim to exercise any
> authority as a Roman Catholic Power, which would be incom-
> patible with a Republican Government with the Church sepa-
> rated from the State; and that the French Republican
> Government would not have the real sympathies of the Catho-
> lics and other Christians, and would have all the Mussulmans—
> viz., the majority of the population—against them; whereas
> England is the Power which can obtain the sympathies of Mus-
> sulmans and yet be impartial between Christians.

These were powerful arguments to two men whose lifelong political
commitment had been to the separation of church and state. "M.
Viviani said that he would pass a law to separate Church and State

in Syria, etc.!" Bertie went on, and added: "M. Bérard hoped to convert M. Paul Cambon and the Ministers here to his views. I told him that I regarded such a crusade as hopeless." But clearly he did not.

The story now takes a startling and mystifying leap. On December 21—the very day on which Bertie was composing his letter to Crewe—Picot met in London with Sir Arthur Nicolson's interdepartmental committee for the first time since their disastrous encounter of November 23 and with an entirely different position to present. He suddenly was prepared to limit the area of French annexation or direct control entirely to Turkish-speaking areas in the north, beginning roughly at the northernmost line of Arab preponderance that the British had arrived at in their exchanges with Hussein and al-Faruqi. Everything south of this line, he proposed—with the exception of a Jerusalem enclave, "its boundaries yet to be defined," and of some other modifications—was to be part of an Arab state, to be divided between Great Britain and France into spheres of commercial interest. The French claim to the Lebanon and to coastal Syria as far south as Beirut was to be satisfied by the right to police and protect that area and to nominate its governor. Only two basic points were set aside in Picot's proposal for further discussion: the "allocation of the Mosul Vilayet" and the "position of Haifa and Acre as outlets for Great Britain on Mediterranean from Mesopotamia."

From the omnivorous stance of November 23, Picot had gone to the other extreme that Sykes had adumbrated in his hasty November telegrams from Cairo. Had some of Sykes's arguments penetrated to him and his colleagues in Paris after all? Sykes certainly seems to have known where they were prepared to relent: as far back as July, in the wake of Picot's mission to Cairo, he had gathered the impression from the French there that they would be ready to "give up the coast to the South of Akka." In retrospect, this seems to have been quite accurate: Picot's hard line of November 23 had surely only been one from which he intended to start bargaining. But now, without any signs of bargaining having yet occurred, Picot has gone beyond mere relenting all the way to renunciation. How did this happen? We can only speculate.

Sykes's arguments may somehow have been conveyed to the French government by this time, in spite of Bertie's opposition to a personal mission by him. Perhaps Bertie had relayed some of Crewe's points to the right French circles, after all. Victor Bérard's warnings probably had their influence, too. But Picot and his colleagues seem to have been struck in the meantime by something more forceful than these—by arguments with the power, let us say, of those presented by Colonel Parker of the War Office in the memorandum he wrote on November 29 responding to the first meeting between Picot and the committee. Could these stern warnings have made their way to Paris? It is worth noting that Parker's uncle and mentor, Lord Kitchener, had arrived in Paris from Gallipoli on the very day they were written, when he had lunch with President Poincaré, Prime Minister Briand, Generals Joffre and Galliéni, and other notables. Whether or not Kitchener had the gist of his nephew's remarks—which even reached as far, we may recall, as a hint at substantial British withdrawal from the western front—to convey to his French colleagues, his mood of the moment certainly was in favor of retrenchment on British commitments and possible overcommitments in the war.

It is known, in fact, that what Kitchener remained particularly troubled about now that Gallipoli was being terminated was the current Anglo-French expedition in Salonika—which was to be the main topic of conversation when he returned to Paris on December 5 with the prime minister and the first lord of the Admiralty. This operation in an unrelentingly neutral Greece to save a Serbia that had since gone under anyway had never been to Kitchener's liking: it was the French who had ardently desired it, along with Lloyd George at home—another reason for the war secretary to take a dim view of it. In Paris on December 5, the British leaders had urged withdrawal. In the sequel, withdrawal did not occur—but in the course of confrontations such as this, how could Kitchener have refrained from making it clear that the British army, though acquiescing over the Balkans, alone called the tune in the Arab Middle East?

But whatever had been said to cause them to change their position, Picot and his French colleagues surely also knew that by assuming their new stance of sweeping renunciation they had called what was in effect a British bluff. Sir Edward Grey's increasingly solitary protestations to the contrary notwithstanding, the British really wanted a bit more for themselves in Syria than a zone of economic concessions. Direct control of the Haifa port was becoming indispensable in their eyes, and Picot had placed them in the position of having to make offers in exchange for it—in northern Syria, for example.

It now was left up to Sykes to complete the affair. "After the Committee under the presidency of Sir A. Nicolson had met M. Picot twice," Sykes was to report, "it became apparent that there were so many details which required separate consideration that either more time would have to be devoted to the work by the committee than the press of other business on its various members would permit, or that negotiations would be prolonged, which, in view of the military and political situation in the Near East, was undesirable. Sir A. Nicolson therefore suggested that M. Picot and I should examine the whole question so as to clear the ground of details and collaborate with him in drawing up a memorandum which would correlate the various factors of the general problem." The final bargaining was about to be done.

·20·

TRIALS AND ERRORS OF
A CHEMIST AT WAR

Chaim Weizmann had received his two Government appointments by the end of September. At the Admiralty he was
temporary honorary technical adviser on acetone supplies, with a
grant of £2,000 a year for two years, and at the Ministry of Munitions he was chemical adviser for one year at £1,500. In the case of
the Admiralty, this was confirmation of a status he had achieved
with the trials he had been authorized to undertake in May. In July,
Nicholson's gin distillery in the southeast London borough of Bromley had been commandeered by the Admiralty for Weizmann, and
there—commuting often between Manchester and London, where he
stayed at hotels or at the home of Ahad Ha'am in Hampstead—he
had undertaken his first attempt at the large-scale manufacture of
acetone by his process. There had been difficulties at first—at one
point, the bacterial culture he brought with him from Manchester
became infected and he had to start a new one in London—but by
September he seemed ready to produce acetone in quantities of
about two thousand gallons at each fermentation.

This was not yet very much in terms of wartime needs; but the
Admiralty, whose functions in the immediate production of explosives for the war were now being superseded by the Ministry of
Munitions, was thinking as much of long-term requirements as of
immediate ones when it took on Weizmann. "The Admiralty decided
not to concern themselves about supplying the country with acetone," Weizmann wrote to Ahad Ha'am at the time of his appointment. "They decided to build a plant for *their own* needs, now and in
time of peace; they have now started work on the plans, and will
build a model factory according to all the rules of bacteriological and
chemical science."

The factory was to go up at Poole, near Wareham, in the vicinity of the Royal Naval Cordite Factory already existing at Holton Heath; meanwhile, it was in the latter plant that further large-scale trials of the Weizmann acetone process were begun. The Admiralty also provided Weizmann with a London laboratory, at the Lister Institute in Chelsea. By the end of September, having taken a leave from the university, he was living in temporary quarters in Chelsea at 3 Justice Walk, which he soon was to be sharing with Vladimir Jabotinsky. Vera Weizmann, who had just been appointed chief medical officer for all of Manchester's lying-in clinics, was going to have to give up her post and join her husband in finding a London home.

It was now up to the Ministry of Munitions to take over the work at Nicholson's and whatever other distilleries it decided to commandeer—Lloyd George must have taken special delight in converting vats from the service of Drink to that of the War—for the purpose of immediate acetone production by the Weizmann process. Furthermore, Weizmann was brimming over with ideas for the useful application of the large quantities of butyl alcohol—in a proportion of about two units to every one of acetone—that his process inevitably had to produce. He had other projects in mind as well. But though he was most eager to begin this work, he suddenly found himself forced to proceed at the ministry with a slowness that was not accidental. Nor was his chemical work itself the only area in which a delay had set in: as far back as August, Weizmann had been expecting to depart before the end of that month on the scientific mission to France and Switzerland he had first proposed to Lloyd George in June. Yet even as November approached, nothing was coming of that plan, either. Weizmann was on the payroll of the Ministry of Munitions, but he had not yet really begun doing anything directly for it. What had happened?

It will be recalled that, from the beginning, some skepticism at the ministry about the value of Weizmann's work had been shown by the parliamentary under-secretary, Christopher Addison. By now, however, Addison's resistance to Weizmann had come to be shared by an even more formidable figure, the ministry's director general of explosive supplies, Lord Moulton. Born a parson's son in Shropshire in 1844, John Fletcher Moulton had gone on to prove himself one of the more remarkable Englishmen of his generation. He had first pursued an academic career and was an outstanding Cambridge University mathematician. Then, in 1873, he had given that up and gone to London to read for the bar, subsequently to become one of

Britain's foremost patent lawyers. He had received a life peerage upon being appointed lord of appeal in 1912.

After the outbreak of war, the War Office had made special acknowledgment of Moulton's talents by appointing him chairman of its Committee of High Explosives, of which he was the only civilian member. As far as Lloyd George was concerned, Moulton was the last man to be considered responsible for the War Office's inadequacies in munitions production. "He was one of the subtlest brains in England," Lloyd George wrote of him years later. "As usually happens his subtlety caused distrust and misunderstanding amongst blunter minds. He was not only one of the greatest lawyers of his day, he was also a man of distinguished scientific attainments." When Moulton transferred from the War Office, the minister of munitions—himself a man of no scientific attainments—was most assuredly glad to have him.

Weizmann had met Lord Moulton for the first time on July 12, 1915, a month after the meeting with Lloyd George that led to his Munitions Ministry appointment. On that occasion, after making a detailed presentation on the progress of his Admiralty experiments, Weizmann had again brought up the idea of his going over to make contact with scientists in France and Switzerland, and Moulton had seemed receptive: "he agreed both with my criticism of the present situation," Weizmann wrote to C.P. Scott a few days later, "and with the proposal to bring over the chemists from Switzerland." But then he stated a qualification that may well have sounded ominous in Weizmann's ears. "He limited it to French Switzerland. I stated that I shall be able to go in a month. But I am still skeptical about the actual carrying out of the proposal as Lord Moulton—I gather—changes his mind often."

If Weizmann had already sensed that relations between himself and the distinguished lawyer-scientist, who was thirty years his senior, were not starting out well, he also had been given clear sign of one of the sources of the trouble in Moulton's exclusion of German Switzerland from his itinerary. Weizmann was still, after all, a foreigner in most Englishmen's eyes, and one with distinct German associations at that, both in his personal background and in his Zionist connections. It would be uncharitable to suppose there was more than a touch of anti-Semitism in Moulton's attitude; chances are that if Weizmann had been an English-born, non-Zionist Jew—like Sir Frederick Nathan—Moulton would have had no qualms about him. But, as it happened, later in that week of his first meeting with Moulton, Weizmann received a telegram from Bern, Switzerland, that would have caused the older man to feel quite justified in his suspicions, had he known about it.* Sent by two old Zionist colleagues—one of whom, Berthold Feiwel, had been born in Austrian-dominated Moravia and now lived in German-dominated Strasbourg—the telegram asked Weizmann if and when he could meet in Bern two other colleagues from the World Zionist Organization. One of these was Julius Simon, who, though stationed in The Hague, was German by birth and citizenship. Such contacts were no longer quite desirable for a man engaged in war work for the British Government. Weizmann soon was prudently to abjure them for the duration of the war; but, though it is not clear whether he actually replied to this telegram, he seems to have been ready to take part in the proposed meeting should he obtain authorization to make his trip.

Apparently, he did obtain it. On Friday, July 16, the day after the telegram from Bern, Weizmann received a letter from Lord Moulton confirming his consent to the journey. Weizmann was prepared to leave in a month—and even six weeks later, on Friday, August 27, he felt able to write to Ahad Ha'am: "I think that I'll leave for France on Tuesday or Wednesday." But this did not happen, and the weeks of delay turned into months.

The problem clearly was Moulton. On October 4, during one of his visits to London, C.P. Scott asked Lloyd George what was happening with Weizmann at the ministry, and Lloyd George said he was soon going to see both Weizmann—for the first time since June—and Sir Frederick Nathan about the matter. "I think," Scott noted in his diary, "from the extremely candid way in which he responded to some observations of mine about Lord Moulton that Lord M. may shortly be superseded—none too soon." But the munitions minister was perhaps not being as candid as the editor thought.

Scott was concerned as much about the delay in Weizmann's experiments as about that in his trip to France and Switzerland. In another visit on October 14, he brought up to Lloyd George "the question of chemical munitions on Weizmann's and Sir Frederick Nathan's behalf—Weizmann's plan for manufacture of toluene, for which he has perfected [a] new method, benzine of which there is [a] prospective shortage, owing to our having promised to part with half our supply to France. George admitted vital importance of both and

---

* Perhaps he even did get to know about it. Certainly he would have if England were policed anywhere near as thoroughly in 1915 as most Western democracies have come to be since that time. But there is no way of knowing if this was the case.

said [he] would deal with the matter as soon as the political crisis was over." Lloyd George was at that moment engaged in a battle with his own Liberal colleagues over the issue of conscription, which he advocated. "I gathered," Scott went on, "that he would borrow Sir Frederick Nathan from Admiralty and give him and Weizmann a free hand. That is Weizmann's ardent desire."

Lloyd George finally saw Weizmann on Tuesday, October 26, and the chemist was able to write on Friday that all his plans of work at the ministry "will be set into motion next week." Yet the trip abroad was still not so imminent as he may have supposed—even though new reasons quickly arose to make it seem more urgent. "I saw the French Naval Attaché yesterday," Weizmann wrote on November 10 to Madame Dorothy de Rothschild. "The French Govt. would like to take up the acetone process and he wrote to Paris that I should be asked to go over there and most probably I shall go at the beginning of next week." Weizmann must have known that this was too sanguine an expectation, however; on Friday, November 12, he drew up a memorandum spelling out the reasons why he should be allowed to go abroad right away. It began with the French naval attaché's interest in acetone, and went on to say that a visit to Paris "would enable me to get into touch with one or two French chemists and we would discuss the problem of synthetic production on a large scale of benzol and toluol." Then he reiterated his old reasons for wanting to go to Switzerland as well.

On Monday, November 15, C.P. Scott, again in London, had lunch with Lloyd George and brought up the case of Chaim Weizmann on two fronts. "My object in seeing him," Scott recorded, "was mainly to secure an interview for Weizmann on the Palestine question and to get leave for him to accept the invitation of the French naval attaché to go to Paris to start his acetone process there for them. He said he should be interested to see Weizmann on the first and asked me to come with him to lunch on Wednesday. The moment I spoke of the second he seemed alarmed and said, 'Don't let him settle anything about that till he has seen me.' It is quite plain they don't really trust Weizmann and that there is a settled resolution not to let him go outside this country if they can help it. I fancy Lord Moulton is at the bottom of this. Shall take first opportunity of challenging."

C.P. Scott had fully taken on the role of Weizmann's champion, both in Zionism and in chemistry, by the previous June. That was when he helped Weizmann obtain the Munitions appointment, and it also was when the *Manchester Guardian* made its first explicit pronouncement in favor of the Zionist cause—in the form of a leading article entitled "Jews and the War," which appeared on Friday, June 25. "Among the many tremendous reactions of a war which is destined in one way or in another to change the whole current of European civilization," the article began, "is the effect—little noticed in the clash of arms and the struggle of nations—which it is having and is destined to have upon the Jewish people." The article proceeded at first to talk about the grim lot of the Jews of Russia and Poland. This, so far, was an orthodox Liberal approach to the Jewish question, a treatment of what was its principal wartime manifestation in the eyes of Englishmen of goodwill. But then it took a less orthodox turn:

> Jews are fighting in all the armies. They are fighting, therefore, against men of their own race; often they are fighting against their own vital interests, whether as members of one of the warring states or as Jews pure and simple. For the Jew everywhere, scattered as he is among many nations, is obliged to fight the battles of the State in which he lives, even though it stand to him in the relation only of oppressor, and there exists as yet no Jewish State which can claim his undivided loyalty.

There followed a discussion of the aims of the Zionist movement, which used as its acknowledged source a recent pamphlet by Weizmann's friend Leon Simon, *Zionism and the Jewish Problem*. The conclusion was that the future of Palestine was, from this point of view, "a matter of pressing capital importance." There was no discussion of Britain's relation to Palestine in the present or in the immediate future; nor was there any mention of Jewish statehood as an immediate aim. For the moment, the *Guardian*'s pages simply stood on the ground of general endorsement of Zionist aims. This was significant enough.

Who had written the article? Probably not Scott himself, though he undoubtedly watched closely over it; this was the kind of subject matter he usually turned over to experts, either on the staff or near at hand. A good possibility for its authorship was Weizmann's young friend and colleague Harry Sacher, who had lost his job at the *Daily News* on June 9, just a little over two weeks earlier, on account of an overly vigorous leader he had written criticizing Russia—Britain's ally after all—for its harsh treatment of Jews. Sacher, who had previously been at the *Guardian* from 1904 to 1909, was now to rejoin its staff in August 1915; but he had begun contributing to the paper almost immediately after his dismissal from the *Daily News,* and this could have been one such occasion.

Yet Sacher was by no means the only possible author. It also could have been Leon Simon himself, who was to appear from time to time on the *Guardian*'s pages as a contributor on Jewish and Zionist subjects. Still another possibility was Alfred Zimmern, a Board of Education inspector whose great reputation as a scholar still lay ahead of him, and who was at this time associated with an influential Liberal-imperialist journal, the *Round Table.* Of German-Jewish extraction on his father's side, Zimmern had become a warm friend of Zionism without actually affiliating with the movement and was to express himself to this effect from time to time in the pages of the *Guardian* and elsewhere. He and Sacher had been friends since their student days together at New College, Oxford.

The influence of Harry Sacher's Zionism in and around the *Guardian* had been significant, and it had not stopped at his fellow Jews. In his earlier stint there, he had also won the sympathies of two slightly older non-Jews who were among the elite of its staff: W.P. Crozier, who was news editor from 1912 onward, and Herbert Sidebotham, who, since August 1914, had been adding new luster to a reputation already earned during the Boer War as author of a twice-weekly series of military analyses signed "A Student of War." A winner of two firsts at Oxford, Sidebotham had developed a technique of analyzing the sparse materials on military operations available to the public that was penetrating enough for even men in the Government to want to check their knowledge regularly with the "Student of War."

The enthusiasm for Zionism with which Sidebotham had become imbued through contact with Sacher was largely founded in the "Student's" geopolitics. He knew perfectly well what a Jewish-administered and British-protected Palestine would mean for the security of the Suez Canal and of any new foothold in Mesopotamia. In the months following Sacher's return to the staff and Scott's conversion to Zionism—even though he and the editor were not always on the best of terms—Sidebotham was increasingly to feel a commitment to its idealistic aspects as well; but his polemical strength in its cause continued to lie in his ability to muster strategical arguments in its favor. He gave his first demonstration of this in a leader he wrote on "The Defense of Egypt" that appeared in the *Guardian* on November 22, 1915, just eight days after Scott's latest plea to Lloyd

George on Weizmann's behalf. In the course of a careful analysis of its mainly military subject, the article advocated a Jewish Palestine. "The main line of supply for the Turkish armies now in Palestine," it said,

> runs east of the Jordan, and if this line were to remain in the possession of a possibly hostile Power it would outflank the natural line of defense for Egypt. Moreover, we are in Mesopotamia engaged in operations which seem likely to give us a new province, which ought not to be separated from Egypt by hostile territory. If Palestine were now a buffer state between Egypt and the north, inhabited as it used to be by an intensely patriotic race, friendly as it was in the past to Egypt because that Power was less aggressive as a rule than the great military Empires of the north, the problem of Egypt in this war would be a very light one. It is to this condition that we ought to work.

The resources of Scott's newspaper, as well as his own personal influence, were beginning to be mobilized on Weizmann's behalf.

The luncheon meeting with Scott and Weizmann that Lloyd George had proposed for Wednesday, November 17, had to be canceled when the munitions minister made a sudden trip to Paris. But, after his return, Scott wasted no time about arranging a new date. "Saw Lloyd George's Secretary [J.T.] Davies on way through London ... November 25," Scott wrote in his diary, "and asked him to make appointment if possible with Lloyd George for Weizmann and me for following day. Arranged for lunch."

When Scott and Weizmann arrived at the ministry on the 26th, a Friday, they found Herbert Samuel also there, invited by Lloyd George to join them. Samuel had been appointed earlier that month to the chancellorship of the Duchy of Lancaster upon Churchill's resignation: that bottom rung in the ladder of cabinet posts had switched from being the locus of Churchill's last stand in his descent to Samuel's first step in a political return. On this occasion, Samuel clearly was serving a dual purpose for Lloyd George, who was more eager to have the proposed conversation on Palestine with Scott and Weizmann than to discuss the obstructions of Lord Moulton at the ministry, but who also clearly did not like to talk Zionism to Weizmann without an intermediary. Samuel would serve both as that intermediary and as assurance that the conversation would hew closely to the subject of Palestine.

Scott saw the point and managed to get in briefly to Lloyd George alone before rejoining Weizmann and Samuel at the dining table. Scott "put it to him," as he writes, "whether he had any mistrust of Weizmann, or whether the persistent and unaccountable opposition to his being allowed to leave the country for important business in furtherance of his work and of the supply of essential materials originated with Moulton, or whether there was any mistrust of Weizmann on the ground that he might give valuable information to Germany, or whether it was just jealousy on Moulton's part of any independent initiative." There was no slithering away from this assault. Lloyd George, according to Scott, "absolutely repudiated" any mistrust of Weizmann for his own part. "When I trust a man," he said, "I trust him altogether. It's no use trusting by halves."

Lloyd George went on to explain to Scott that he had just appointed Weizmann's old Admiralty sponsor, Sir Frederick Nathan, to the Ministry of Munitions, precisely so that Nathan could "act as a check on Moulton." But Scott said Weizmann already had told him that Nathan "found he could do very little against Moulton's opposition." Lloyd George replied by claiming he "had had a great fight with Moulton in order to bring Nathan in, and that finally he had had simply to over-ride Moulton's opposition in such a way that he thought Moulton must have resigned—but he didn't." This reply had not really dealt with Scott's objection; but Lloyd George concluded, at any rate, by assuring Scott that during lunch he was quite free to raise "the question of Weizmann's going to Paris at once on the urgent request which he had just received from the French authorities."

By the time the four men sat down to lunch, Lloyd George was eager to get on to the Palestine question, but Scott was still too hot with indignation at Moulton to be able to do so right away. Apologizing to Samuel, Scott at first returned to that subject, speaking freely about Moulton, "his incompetence, vanity and obstructiveness." Like a father interceding with a hitherto heedless schoolmaster, Scott asked Weizmann "to explain why it was urgent for him to go to Paris and why to Switzerland." But all this was most indiscreet in front of Samuel, and even Scott soon recognized that "we could not get very far under the conditions, and the conversation soon passed on to the War and then to the question of Palestine in which Samuel, as a good Jew—he has become a Zionist—is deeply interested."

Lloyd George must have breathed a quiet sigh of relief, and he took advantage of the respite to hold forth for a time in his usual manner—passing on even to a short discourse about Russia, which he thought might be in imminent danger of revolution. "As to Palestine," Scott noted with some annoyance, "the conversation did not go very deep, turning chiefly on the railway question." This turn had no doubt been inspired by Sidebotham's *Guardian* leader that Monday, the 22nd. "Samuel remarked that the Hejaz Railway was not in itself a menace to Egypt, as it ran a good way east of Palestine, but that the Turco-Germans [*sic*] were constructing, or had constructed, a connection from Damascus through Palestine . . . to the Egyptian frontier of the Sinai Peninsula." Samuel at that point managed to reintroduce his old basic position by saying it was against the danger of an invasion along this line of approach "that a mediatized Palestine under British protection could guard."

Lloyd George, having heard the hard-line French position on Syria that had been expounded by Picot just three days before, protested to Samuel, who was not privy to the Picot negotiations, "that France would probably object and wanted Palestine for herself, and all this of course on the assumption that the war ended in our favor and the Turkish possessions were at our disposal—that, moreover, there would be no objection in this country to such an extension of our responsibilities." Lloyd George liked to obtain reinforcement for positions he himself favored by taking up the objections to them in front of their advocates.

Scott countered with the old suggestion "that if France got [northern] Syria that should satisfy her, and that Russia would certainly object to a Catholic power holding the Holy Places and would much prefer a Protestant one as being quasi-neutral, in the religious question." He added that, when it came to the extension of responsibilities, "we had already the responsibility of defending Egypt and that it was only a question of how that could best be done in face of the new danger." But Lloyd George continued to present some resistance to the claim for British control and gave it as his opinion that "a condominium of the three Powers might be proposed." This provoked objections from both Weizmann and Samuel, who "agreed that from their point of view this would be the worst solution"—and Scott thought it also was "not good from ours."

At this point, Lloyd George asked Weizmann "how many colonists the Jews expected to be able to supply and Weizmann said he thought half a million in 50 years. George evidently thought this a very small number"—and, indeed, it was small even in relation to other estimates Weizmann had given out since the war began: he had, for example, projected a million settlers in fifty years for Israel Zangwill's benefit in October 1914. Perhaps he thought the present context of conversation called for modesty in his estimate. He went on to defend the low figure by pointing out that "this kind of colonization was extremely expensive (it had cost so far about £200 per family, or per holding)." Lloyd George suggested that there might be a rapid immigration of Jews from Russia, encouraged by the Russian government, "but Weizmann said Palestine could offer no solution to the Jewish question in Russia with its 6 million Jews." Samuel also pointed out, as he had done in his memorandum, that Palestine was not large enough to accommodate all of Russian Jewry. Weizmann thought that the Russians would welcome a Jewish Palestine anyway, but "as a means of seeming to do something for its Jews while not really doing anything." As for the British public's response to a protectorate in Palestine, Samuel thought the idea would be popular, "as giving us something tangible as a result of the war. Otherwise, while France might get Alsace-Lorraine, and Russia the fulfillment of some of her ambitions in the East, we should have nothing to show."

Much of this was old ground, and Scott at least was eager to return to the subject of Weizmann at Munitions. "When Samuel had gone," he writes, "Weizmann got about 5 minutes straight talk." Weizmann entered into a critique of the organization of Moulton's department, arguing "that everything necessary could be done and all the materials needed produced easily in quantity if there were an efficient organization, but that with Moulton at the head of the Department, delays were endless and results more than doubtful." Weizmann confirmed what Scott had said about Nathan's problems with Moulton. Lloyd George, Scott records, "was obviously troubled and impressed and finally said he must see Nathan that afternoon and would ask him to meet us afterwards—at 5:30 at the Munitions Office." It can scarcely be believed that Lloyd George really was persuaded by one amateur outsider—however distinguished an editor he was—and one young reader in biochemistry from the provinces—however forceful a spokesman for Zionism he was—that Lord Moulton might not be competent at his task in the Munitions Ministry. But he certainly must have been troubled at all this dissension among talented men in his charge and eager to find some way to conciliate them. That afternoon, he spoke to Moulton before seeing any of the others.

Scott arrived for the appointment before Weizmann did, and found Nathan still waiting to have his own preliminary conversation with Lloyd George. Nathan was now director of the Department of Propellant Supplies at the ministry. He and Scott had time for a short conversation, in which Nathan reiterated his old high opinion of Weizmann, "but seemed to think he was a little difficult to work with." Nathan, one suspects, had been busy since his transfer to Munitions trying to conciliate both Moulton and Weizmann and tending to agree to criticisms of the other for the benefit of whichever one he happened to be conversing with. Moulton had not welcomed his arrival, which was so obviously intended to strengthen Weizmann's position among other things; but Nathan was not necessarily of a temperament to go on having conflicts with the great man in the name of a young chemist he once had sponsored, but whose brashness and volatility evidently were beginning to try even his patience a little.

Scott, unruffled by this hint of possible disaffection, spoke to Nathan frankly about Moulton, saying he ought to go "and that it was absurd that the claims of one man should over-ride those of a great state department." This view was undoubtedly Weizmann's, but it probably was not shared wholeheartedly by Nathan. However, Nathan "did not dissent, but said he thought things had gone too far—the whole department (inherited of course by George from the War Office), was now [fully] manned and organized, and it would be difficult to upset this, even though it had been all done wrongly." Scott took it for granted that Nathan was merely giving the "official" view. "I don't think he held it very strongly," the editor added in his diary, and said that he expressed his disagreement to Nathan.

But whether the somewhat vacillating Nathan held this view strongly or not, he certainly was—for the time being, at least—to fall in line with Scott and Weizmann at the end of the few minutes he now spent alone with Lloyd George while the other two waited outside. There is no record of what Lloyd George said to him, but the tenor of it could not have been favorable to Moulton. Since Lloyd George was to express such appreciation for Moulton years later, we must therefore assume that whatever aspersions he may have cast upon him in this moment were attributable either to a passing mood or to a desire to keep Nathan in Weizmann's camp, even at the expense of an honest expression of his feelings—perhaps a little of both. If, after all, Lloyd George liked having Weizmann in the ministry whatever his failures or successes as a chemist may have been, then it was important that the latter have allies among his colleagues there.

Scott and Weizmann were summoned at last, and there ensued "a curious conversation," as the *Guardian* editor put it, "Lloyd George evidently feeling strongly and frankly admitting the difficulty of his position as a non-expert at the head of an expert department." That afternoon, the minister said, Moulton had "talked his head off," and had "eloquently demonstrated that everything was right." Lloyd George had apparently found nothing to say in reply.

"It's his business to talk," Nathan commented ironically, thus rising to the occasion.

Lloyd George said the only person Moulton had spoken well of was his chief assistant, an engineer from South Africa named K.B. Quinan—with whom, the minister significantly added, he had himself had "a severe contest as to Nathan's appointment, and who had threatened resignation but unfortunately* not persisted in it when he found it would certainly be accepted." The implications here are that a direct rivalry had arisen between Quinan, with Moulton backing him, and Weizmann, who presumably was to be backed by Nathan. Lloyd George pointed out that Quinan "was said to have produced great quantities of dynamite in the South African War."

"A thing anybody could do," Weizmann interjected, "if he had the well-known materials supplied to him—not a chemical problem at all."

Lloyd George thereupon mentioned "some other important chemical on the production of which, as a scientific problem, this gentleman was said to be engaged."

"As simple as this pencil," retorted Weizmann. "It is all in the textbooks. You might have had thousands of tons by this time, and I have been amazed to know that you hadn't."

"Well," the Minister replied, "he ought to be quite good. He's getting £5,000 a year!" Lloyd George then made some remarks implying that even shell production itself was going slowly under Moulton. "They've sent me a lot of photographs," he said, "but they mean nothing to me. Perhaps you can make something of them," he suggested, turning to Nathan and handing him a large bundle.

Nathan made another sally into the fray by recalling that Moulton had promised Winston Churchill that a certain factory "would be turning out stuff in August." But, he said, nothing had yet been produced there.

* The "unfortunately" may, of course, be entirely Scott's own in his paraphrase of Lloyd George's remarks.

"Is that in writing?" Lloyd George asked of Moulton's promise. Nathan said that it was and that he would obtain a copy of it.

Scott observed in his diary that "it appeared that Lloyd George has absolutely no competent scientific chemical adviser on the problems of synthetic or bio-chemistry on which everything depends." Nathan contributed to these reflections by saying at one point, to everyone's surprise, "I am not a chemist"—Lloyd George seems to have stimulated him into making a contest of amateurist protestations. "He meant apparently," Scott reasoned in his diary, "that discovery was not his business, but installation, as he was Nobel's manager before he went to the Admiralty." This, too, led Scott to the inexorable conclusion: "So it all comes back to Weizmann."

The conversation at last made its way to the matter of Weizmann's proposed trip abroad. Lloyd George suggested that Weizmann not wait any longer but just go, saying if challenged that he had the munitions minister's authorization.

"But don't be away for long," he told Weizmann. "I shall want you for another conference in a few days, and don't go beyond Paris."

This was a more diplomatic method than Moulton's of telling Weizmann not to go to Switzerland after all. Lloyd George perhaps did not share Moulton's fears of what Weizmann might say to German acquaintances in a neutral country, but by providing this one limitation he could at any rate placate the eminent jurist regarding Weizmann's trip. He told Weizmann to summon to Paris any Swiss scientists he wanted to see, offering them expenses.

Weizmann and Scott left with the impression that Weizmann would leave for Paris Sunday morning—soon enough to be back in time for a department conference that Lloyd George projected for the following Thursday, December 2, just six days away. The conference, Scott believed, was nominally to be "on some question of Munitions installations, but really to go into the whole question of the supply of essential chemicals—Moulton to be then faced with Nathan and Weizmann. Lloyd George evidently wants to press things to an issue." Nathan stayed behind to discuss matters further with the minister.

"Just like them," Weizmann observed of Moulton and his allies as he and Scott walked away together. "They are asked for shells and they send photographs."

Scott returned to Manchester that weekend confident, no doubt, that he had finally won the victory for Weizmann; but the moment had not quite arrived, after all. On Thursday he received a letter written the day before by Weizmann, who had yet to leave. "Dear Mr. Scott," it said:

> Please don't be surprised to get a letter from me from Chelsea. I fully intended to leave on Sunday morning, but, I found on inquiry that I could not get through with the passport until Monday, which would mean leaving London only on Tuesday morning, as there is only one train a day to Paris. In that case it would be impossible to get back here for Thursday and after having consulted Sir F. Nathan we decided to postpone my journey until Friday or Saturday, until after the conference with Mr. Ll. George.

But this had not been the worst of it. "You remember," he went on,

> that last August Lord Moulton agreed to my going to France and Switzerland; he wrote me a letter to that effect. At that time Major Bagot [also of the Ministry of Munitions] offered to get my documents for the journey in order and for that purpose I gave him my . . . passport, which he proposed to "viser" at the Consulates. Since then he kept my passport. Today I called in and asked for my passport and Major Bagot told me that he cannot give me my passport, that Lord Moulton strongly objects to my going to France, that Lord M. saw Mr. Lloyd George and that I am *not* to go.

Nor was this the end of the troubles Weizmann had to relate. "I understand," he continued,

> that Mr. Nicholson, the distiller, on whose premises I am working, gets instructions from them to carry out new experiments, that a man who had nothing to do with the work, which has cost me five years of labor and which I have placed unreservedly at the disposal of the country, an amateur, who has no notion of the whole thing, who is not a chemist or a bacteriologist, is apparently entrusted with *my* process.

Weizmann therefore thought that his position was

> becoming untenable. I've broken up my home in M/C [Manchester], I've established my laboratories here and it seems to me, that it is impossible for me to go on a day longer if matters are

not definitely settled. Not only for the sake of the cause, but also for my personal sake I must again trouble you and appeal to you.

Scott responded to the appeal without hesitation. "I am afraid," he wrote to Lloyd George that very day, enclosing a copy of Weizmann's letter, "that unless a change can be made Weizmann will say it is useless for him to try to carry on." This time Lloyd George—who, meanwhile, had postponed the conference originally scheduled for Thursday—took action, and Weizmann was at last able to leave for Paris the following Sunday, December 5. He was there until Friday the tenth.

Weizmann does not seem to have achieved anything in particular for the Munitions Ministry on this trip, but at any rate a point had been proved. Scott was able to write triumphantly in his diary for December 15 of the breakfast he and Weizmann had that morning with Lloyd George. After a detailed exposition by Weizmann of his plans for the synthetic production of various vital chemicals, Lloyd George had given "an amusing account of his encounter with Lord Moulton and his chief assistant [K.B. Quinan], Sir F. Nathan being also present. He had been furious about the withholding of Weizmann's passport, which he had handed them to be visaed and which they then refused to return, told them it was monstrous to treat a distinguished scientific man who was giving his best service to the country in that way, and ended up by saying, 'If you offer me your resignation I shall accept it,' but they didn't offer it. What evidently had enraged him particularly," Scott went on to observe, "was that they should treat Weizmann, as a Jew and a foreigner, in a way they would not venture to treat a man in a different position. That is the generous side of Lloyd George."

There were other signs of improvement in Weizmann's situation. A few days later, on Sunday, December 19, Weizmann was able to write Scott that Lloyd George's proposed conference had finally taken place and that, as a result of it, a distillery in Belfast had been placed at his disposal. He was leaving that night to inspect it and was also going to Stirling to look at another distillery for possible conversion to Munitions use. Moulton, he said, "battled hard against it, but the decision went against him." Sir Frederick Nathan now was satisfied "that he will be able to work properly, and I am happy to say that there is every chance of my coming under his jurisdiction." Weizmann concluded his letter with a tribute to Scott's efforts on his behalf. "Once more you settled a point and it was high time that you should settle it, as the importance of it cannot be underrated. In the opinion of everybody at this meeting every drop of acetone will be needed."

That same day Weizmann also wrote to Herbert Samuel, describing a meeting he had had with Baron Edmond de Rothschild in Paris that, in relation to the Anglo-French negotiations then going on—of which Weizmann, of course, knew nothing—was even more significant than he realized. Also present at the meeting had been Lord Bertie and Victor Bérard. Weizmann described the latter as

> a distinguished *homme de lettres*, who has devoted a great deal of time to the study of Near Eastern problems, and whose word carries great weight in influential quarters. Mr. Bérard said, that with the exception of some ardent Catholic politicians, the French statesmen attach *no* value to Palestine or even Syria. On the contrary, in the opinion of Mr. Bérard it would be rather a dangerous adventure for France to follow out the Catholic program or ambition. It would involve her in religious strife in France itself, in political difficulties with Russia and perhaps with this country, and as a territory Palestine has no value to the French at all. Sir Francis [Lord Bertie] concurred and said, that as far as he knows England would view with dissatisfaction any predominance of another great power in Palestine, although may not be inclined to take it for herself.

Bertie knew just what he was talking about. As for Bérard, we have already noted that he seems to have said other significant things about the Middle East at this meeting, which, through Bertie, were perhaps to have some influence on the Anglo-French negotiations. The progress of these in the next few weeks was to prove Weizmann incorrect about the immediate facts of the situation when he concluded this letter by saying, "I think one can dismiss the rumors about a settlement or agreement concerning Palestine as without foundation." But his longer view was, as usual, instinctually accurate when he added: "and again the situation is such, that the center of this problem is in this country." As a Zionist, at least, Weizmann had made something significant of his latest trip to Paris, whatever its importance may or may not have been for the chemistry of Munitions. One is again inclined to suspect that Lloyd George considered this to be value enough.

PART THREE

·1916·

·21·

SYKES COMES TO TERMS WITH PICOT, AND THE BROWN AREA EMERGES

O n January 5, 1916, some two weeks after they had been brought together to complete negotiations, Sykes and Picot presented their memorandum on Ottoman Asia. It began by describing the general background of the problem and the various desiderata they had had to consider. "The main problem to be solved is to discover a middle course which will harmonize with the requirements of the various parties," it said, and then proceeded to spell these out.

France required

a settlement which (1) while compensating her for the inconvenience and loss attendant upon the disruption of the Ottoman Empire, will (2) safeguard her historic and traditional position in Syria, [and] (3) assure her of full opportunity of realizing her economic aspirations in the Near East.

As for the Arabs, what they required was:

(1) recognition of their nationality, (2) protection of their race from alien oppression, and (3) an opportunity of reestablishing their position as a controlling factor in the world's progress.

And Great Britain required

(1) to assure her position in the Persian Gulf, (2) opportunity to develop Lower Mesopotamia, (3) (a) commercial and military communication between the Persian Gulf and the Mediterra-

nean by land, (b) influence in an area sufficient to provide the
personnel engaged in Mesopotamian irrigation work with suitable sanatoria and hill stations, and containing an adequate native recruiting ground for administrative purposes, (4) to obtain
commercial facilities in the area under discussion.

A final proviso in this opening section was made for "the conscientious desires of Christianity, Judaism and Mohammedanism in regard to the status of Jerusalem and the neighboring shrines."
Nothing resembling *national* interests was mentioned in this
context.

A middle section of the memorandum developed the arguments
for the claims of the various parties involved and presented—in
order to demonstrate the necessity for all-round compromise—what
would have been the *ideal* solution for each of them. A summary of
the French historic, economic, and cultural role in Greater Syria ends
with the conclusion that,

> on the hypothesis that there were no other circumstances to be
> considered, the French Government might be expected to desire
> commercial and political predominance in an area bounded on
> the south by a line drawn from El Arish to Kasr-i-Shirin, and on
> the north by the main ridge of the Taurus and anti-Taurus, be-
> ginning in the vicinity of Cape Anamur and ending about
> Koshab,

in other words, the entire area of Picot's demand of November 23,
drawn in the widest sense. As for the Arab leaders, their ideal

> would be to establish a confederation of states under the aegis
> of an Arabian prince, roughly corresponding to the Arabian
> Peninsula plus the Ottoman provinces of Basra, Bagdad, Jerusa-
> lem, Damascus, Aleppo, Mosul, Adana, and Diarbekir, with its
> littoral under the protection of Great Britain and France.

It was obvious that some compromise had to be made between this
ideal and that of one of the protecting powers, France.

Compromise was even required with British desiderata, though
these—not surprisingly in this document which bears the earmarks
of the prose style and thought processes of Sir Mark Sykes—appear
as the most modest among those of the three main parties:

> The ideal solution for Great Britain would be to have
> administrative control and priority of enterprise in an area

bounded by the line Acre, Tadmor, Ras-ul-Ain, Jeziret-ibn-Omar, Zakhu, Amaida, Rowanduz,* combined with the possession of Alexandretta, with a suitable hinterland connecting the Euphrates Valley with the Mediterranean, and rights of railway construction connecting Alexandretta with Bagdad. Further, that Great Britain should have a veto on irrigation schemes likely to divert water from Lower Mesopotamia.

In the light of the British thinking on the subject by this time, it is clear that Alexandretta was there purely for bargaining leverage.

A final look is taken in this middle section at "International Religious Interests" with regard to Jerusalem and the Holy Places. These were:

> (*a.*) The Latin and Orthodox religions require equal consideration in Palestine. (*b.*) The members of the Jewish community throughout the world have a conscientious and sentimental interest in the future of the country. (*c.*) The Mosque of Omar represents, next to Mecca, the most holy and venerable shrine in Islam, and it must be a *sine qua non* that the Mosque of Omar itself should be under the sole control of the Moslems, and that the chief of the Arabian confederation should have an equal voice in the Administration of Palestine.

This passage suggests that, whatever considerations may have existed in Sykes's mind regarding possible Zionist claims in Palestine, they did not form part of his negotiations with Picot. The proviso about "a conscientious and sentimental interest" on the part of world Jewry appears only in the context dealing with Jerusalem and the Holy Places, and every indication here and to come is to the effect that Picot did not think of this interest in potentially political terms, even though Sykes almost certainly did.

These, then, were the terms upon which the two parties had negotiated; and even the way they are stated suggests the lines of the tentative agreement they arrived at, which are spelled out in the final section of the memorandum. The entire region in question, north of the Arabian Peninsula and west of Persia, was to be divided into five sectors. Of these, two were designated for annexation or direct control by the negotiating powers respectively. France was to have the northwesternmost sector—colored *blue* on the map drawn up to illustrate the agreement—which took in coastal Syria, including

---

* This is, with slight variations, the line prescribed by the de Bunsen report.

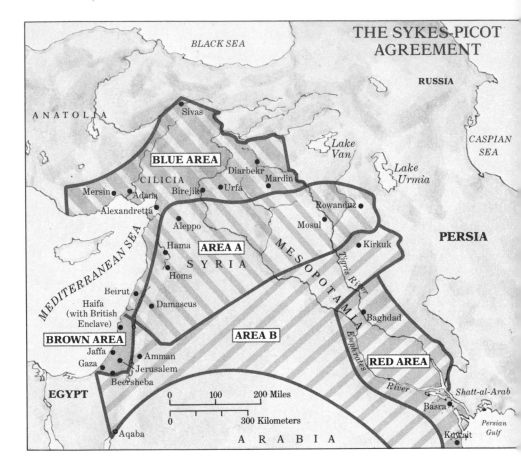

Beirut, down through Tyre and a great triangular portion of Anatolia from west of Mersin and Adana to east of Diarbekr and to the
north above Sivas. Great Britain was to have a sector in the southeast—colored *red* on the illustrating map—that in effect constituted
the vilayets of Baghdad and Basra. Between these Blue and Red
areas was to be the "confederation of Arab States," divided into
areas A and B, which would be, respectively, French and British
spheres of interest. Each of the two powers in its sphere "should
have priority of right of enterprise and local loans" and "should
alone supply advisers or foreign functionaries at the request of the
Arab confederation."

The fifth section—colored *brown* on Sykes's and Picot's

map—was Palestine from Acre down through Gaza and from the Mediterranean to the Jordan, a somewhat expanded version of the "Jerusalem enclave." The text stated that in the Brown Area "there should be established an international administration, the form of which is to be decided upon after consultation with Russia, and subsequently in consultation with Russia, Italy and the representatives of Islam."

Further provision was made for the ports of Haifa and Acre, which were to be accorded outright to Great Britain, even though they were surrounded by the Brown Area. Britain was granted the right to build and be the sole owner of a railway connecting Haifa with the B Area in which her interests were to predominate. The matter of Haifa and its links inland had been the crux of the negotiations, and Picot certainly realized that he had allowed a door to be left open to eventual British predominance in Palestine. But he had obtained a good deal in compensation. Alexandretta, though it was to be a free port for British goods, was firmly within the French-controlled Blue Area, along with Beirut; and if Damascus, Homs, Hama, and Aleppo indeed belonged to the Arab confederation according to this scheme, they were at any rate within the French-dominated A Area. So also was Mosul, a prize given up altogether too easily by Sykes, who had thought little of it when he traveled there some years before. The fact that oil deposits were now known to be there does not seem to have troubled him: commerce was not his vein.

This agreement—which, with amendments, was to be approved by the interdepartmental committee on February 4 and ratified by the French government four days later—conformed to a large extent to the plan Picot had presented on December 21, but with significant variations. The essential variation was that of the two areas—northern coastal Syria for the French, Haifa and its railway connections for the British—into which the two powers had extended their direct control, respectively, from Anatolia and from Mesopotamia. These clearly had been a quid pro quo—as also, probably, were the two other principal variations, namely, the inclusion of Mosul in the French-dominated Area A, and the Brown Area, which was virtually all of western Palestine except Hebron, the Negev, and northern Galilee.

The Brown Area was a "Jerusalem enclave" conceived even more broadly than the substantial one intimated by Sykes before the War Committee on December 16. For his part, it represented a triumph in the negotiations, for it was a fulfillment of the optimum aspirations of the de Bunsen report: a Palestine as British as possible, but at any rate international rather than French. Surely it was in appeasement for this that he had conceded the Mosul Vilayet to Picot. The result was that, for the first time in the history of British and Allied policy since the beginning of the war with Turkey, Palestine had been set aside by international agreement as a territorial entity whose future could be separately considered.

"I must confess," wrote Major General Sir George Macdonogh, the director of military intelligence, upon reading the draft agreement between Sykes and Picot, "that it seems to me that we are rather in the position of the hunters who divided up the skin of the bear before they had killed it." The compulsion to start submitting claims upon "the carcase of the Turk" had first been experienced in the spring of 1915, which now was another era. Since then the Dardanelles campaign had dribbled away into failure; the final withdrawals from Cape Helles were to occur within two days of Macdonogh's memorandum. The Anglo-French troop landing at Salonika in October had ended in another stalemate, whereupon Bulgaria had finally come into the war on the side of the Central Powers and helped to defeat Serbia. Even the Mesopotamian campaign had suffered serious reverses: an overly optimistic advance upon Baghdad in November had ended in an indecisive battle at Ctesiphon and a British withdrawal to Kut-el-Amara, which was now under a Turkish siege.

As for the Arab revolt, in the name of which the Sherif Hussein had extracted such far-reaching promises from the eager Sir Henry McMahon, it showed no sign of materializing anywhere just yet. Syria—where Djemal Pasha had recently rounded up and jailed some of the leaders of the secret societies—was utterly silent in this respect, as was Mesopotamia. The Sherif himself was giving no indications of hurry: "We are only waiting for an opportunity in consonance with our situation," he had written to McMahon on January 1, but there was no way of knowing what would be deemed such an opportunity or when it would arise. "We cannot afford to waste any time," General Macdonogh went on in his comments upon the Sykes-Picot memorandum. "It is essential that we should get the Arabs to side with us at once, otherwise they may first incline to the one party, then to the other, and finally join the Jehad, which the Germans are trying to raise in the Near East." In particular, he thought any further advances by the Turks in Mesopotamia and Persia "would be very difficult if opposed by the Arabs, and correspondingly easy if assisted by them."

But the Admiralty had already grown skeptical of the prospects held out jointly by Hussein and by al-Faruqi, who was now together with the Sherif in Mecca. "The Arab question seems now to have entered into a new phase," wrote Captain William R. Hall, the Admiralty's director of intelligence, in his own response to the January 5 draft agreement. "A few weeks ago it seemed possible that there might be an 'Arab movement' in favor of the Allies. Now (as in the case of Bulgaria) the question has become one not of inducing the Arabs to join us, but of preventing them from joining the enemy." Hall also thought that Sykes's and Picot's preliminary statements of requirements and ideals had erred in the direction of implying too strongly an Arab desire for unity. What the Arabs wanted, he said, was independence. "They will never be united."

Then, somewhat gratuitously using it as a stick with which to rap at Arab nationalist claims, Hall suddenly introduced the Zionist element into the picture. "Opposition must be expected," he wrote, "from the *Jewish interest* throughout the world to any scheme recognizing Arab independence and foreshadowing Arab predominance in the southern Near East. This objection, however, will hold against all schemes which are based on a desire to conciliate or enlist pan-Arabism, and not especially to the one under discussion." It is not clear how Hall arrived at this rather extreme view of the Jewish attitude toward Arab nationalism, but it at any rate served him as a preliminary to coming to the point about Jewish involvement in the area under question. "Jewish opposition," he went on, "may be partly placated by the status proposed for the *Brown area.*" Then he stressed that "the Jews have a strong *material,* and a very strong *political,* interest in the future of the country." This evidently was meant in deliberate contrast to Sykes's and Picot's weaker and somewhat evasive formulation of a "conscientious and sentimental interest in the future of the country" on the part of Jews throughout the world. In his final summary, Hall made the point even more explicit by saying: "In the *Brown area* the question of Zionism, and also of British control of all Palestine railways, in the interest of Egypt, have to be considered."

Although there are signs enough that it had been used in word-of-mouth discussions before this, the word "Zionism" is here making its first appearance on the written record of officially evolving British policy for the Middle East. Captain Hall sounds for all the world as if he had been reading the *Manchester Guardian* on Zionism, Palestine, and the defense of Egypt. In any case, it is not suprising that this initiative should have come from the Admiralty, which had given indications in the past of favorable sentiments about Zionism. Balfour was now first lord, and Admiral Fisher was back at the Admiralty as chairman of an "Inventions Board" for "coordinating and encouraging scientific effort"—a position that probably brought him into occasional touch with Weizmann. Surely the Admiralty representatives on both the de Bunsen Committee and the interdepartmental committee that had begun the negotiations with Picot had raised the matter in discussions before; but if they had, it would have seemed merely academic until now. The designation of the Brown Area had changed the whole picture.

·22·

ZIONISM AT THE FOREIGN OFFICE, I: A YEAR OF INDIFFERENCE

Even the Foreign Office was ready to begin explicitly considering the Zionist position in the Middle East. This was a wholly new departure, for whatever sympathetic expressions Sir Edward Grey may have offered in his conversations on the subject with Herbert Samuel in November 1914 and February 1915, there are no signs of his ever having let them affect Foreign Office business before now. Indeed, he himself seems for a long time to have ignored all efforts other than Samuel's to present a Zionist case.

As for Grey's associates, they did not know about Herbert Samuel's proposal, but they were similarly cool toward other such ideas. They received one from a Jewish private citizen in January 1915 that had claims to serious consideration but was not accorded it. This had been written by a lawyer named Norman Bentwich: he was the son of Herbert Bentwich, who also was a lawyer and had been a co-founder both of the Maccabaeans and of the English Zionist Federation. The younger Bentwich, thirty-one years old, had been in Egypt since 1913, serving there as a commissioner of courts and a lecturer at the Cairo Law School, and had traveled extensively in Palestine. After admitting to being a Zionist and therefore prejudiced in his view of Jewish achievements there, Bentwich set out in his memorandum to demonstrate a special relationship between England and the Jewish settlement in Palestine by outlining the history of the latter. He spoke of Palmerston and consular protection, of Disraeli, Montefiore, George Eliot, and "a wayward and brilliant Englishman of letters, Laurence Oliphant." He also spoke of Herzl, El Arish, and East Africa, of Colonel Goldsmid, and of the Anglo-Palestine Bank.

Bentwich also mentioned the Zionist canvass taken at the 1906 general election and the favorable response to it among English statesmen; and he made a point of disparaging any notion of a special relationship between Zionism and Germany.

Bentwich did not even advocate a political program, such as a protectorate or British sponsorship of a Jewish state, though he did provide some names of people to contact for further information should the Foreign Office have any such ideas in mind. Essentially, he was doing nothing more than presenting a set of historic facts relevant to current events, to be placed on file for whatever use might be made of them. Indeed, one Foreign Office official minuted on Bentwich's memorandum that "it may be useful to have it registered or noted by the Library"—a response as modest as the paper itself. Another official there responded more vividly—and more negatively. "I wonder whether Mr. Bentwick [sic]," wrote Lancelot Oliphant, "has greater justification for his hopes of the future of Zionism than had my 'wayward and brilliant' namesake and relative. I fear not."

It is possible that this same Oliphant feared seeming susceptible to Zionist blandishments precisely on account of his name—although it was not he, but one of his colleagues, who later that month turned down a request for an interview that had come from Yehiel Tschlenow and Nahum Sokolow. Oliphant's name did appear significantly in this respect, however, some two months later. That spring, the U.S.S. *Vulcan*, the first American relief ship for Palestinian Jews since Turkey's entry into the war, was preparing to sail, and the Foreign Office found itself handling a request for free passage through the British-patrolled Mediterranean. This was eventually granted, but until it was, many supporting letters came in from Jewish leaders and organizations. One of these was from Leopold Greenberg, writing on *Jewish Chronicle* stationery, and this letter was minuted by Oliphant with a strong suggestion that all correspondence with Greenberg be avoided. Doing otherwise, he wrote, would "only render less harmonious the relations we have" with Lucien Wolf and the Conjoint Foreign Committee. Here was one basic reason for Foreign Office indifference to Zionism at this time.

The Conjoint Foreign Committee could be described as having been the virtual "foreign office" of the Anglo-Jewish establishment. That establishment consisted essentially of two venerable organizations: the Board of Deputies of British Jews, founded in 1760, and the Anglo-Jewish Association, founded in 1871. Each had been characteristic of the era in which it was born. The Board was made up of the elected representatives of synagogues throughout the land and was founded to advocate the rights of Jews in Great Britain. The Association was entirely secular and based on direct membership; it had been founded shortly after the Alliance Israélite Universelle of Paris and for the same purpose—that of advocating the rights of Jews all over the world. In 1878 the two bodies had established the Conjoint Foreign Committee (CFC), the purpose of which was to devote itself to the problems of oppressed Jewish minorities, especially in Eastern Europe. Its learned members unearthed and published facts and advocated solutions to which the Foreign Office, among others, gave attention. On February 17, 1915, for example, Sir Edward Grey wrote a letter to Leopold de Rothschild—who was Lord Nathaniel's younger brother, a vice-president of the Anglo-Jewish Association, and a member of the CFC—assuring him that he would give "careful consideration" to any matters brought up by the CFC "that might come within the purview of the Foreign Office." To put the matter another way, the CFC and the two organizations it represented were at that time virtually the only Anglo-Jewish entity the Foreign Office recognized. The fact that these organizations, since the vast influx from Eastern Europe that had begun in the 1880s, were no longer representative of the majority of British Jews had not yet made an impression at Whitehall.

If the CFC enjoyed privileged access to the Foreign Office, then, the voice above all representing it there was that of Lucien Wolf. Born in London in 1857, Wolf was the son of a political refugee from the 1848 revolution in Bohemia and the grandson, on his mother's side, of a Viennese banker. Educated in Brussels and Paris, he had gone into journalism as a specialist in foreign affairs, distinguishing himself with a weekly column called "The Foreign Office Bag" in the *Daily Graphic*, where he had become an editor in 1890, and with a succession of essays in the *Fortnightly Review* which he signed with the pen name "Diplomaticus."

Yet, for all the cosmopolitanism in his background and professional milieu, Wolf had devoted himself to Jewish matters throughout his adult life. His very first job as a journalist, taken when he was seventeen, was with the *Jewish World*. He was an ardent researcher and writer in the field of Anglo-Jewish history—publishing a biography of Sir Moses Montefiore in 1884—and he had been the founding president, in 1893, of the Jewish Historical Society of England. He also had been an active member of the Anglo-Jewish Association since at least 1886, and had become a member of the CFC in 1888. In it, he distinguished himself as a specialist in the problems of

East European Jews, visiting Russia in the wake of the Kishinev pogrom in 1903 and becoming editor of a journal called *Darkest Russia*, which was founded in 1912 and published weekly until the outbreak of war, when discretion demanded that it stop appearing. Since then, Wolf had been elected to the Board of Deputies of British Jews and appointed director of a special branch of the CFC "for dealing with the Jewish questions in connection with the eventual reconstruction of Eastern Europe," and "for watching subsidiary Jewish questions arising out of the War." Wolf, who had begun having severe difficulties with his eyesight, thereupon gave up his journalistic work and was now devoting all his time to the CFC.

Completely unreligious, Wolf was a secular Jewish intellectual of the type who, in that generation, often had felt the attraction of Zionism; indeed, he had briefly felt it, too, but then had resisted. He was not unfavorably disposed toward Zionism at the time of his interview with Theodor Herzl for the *Daily Graphic* in 1896. But by the end of 1903—the year in which both he and Herzl had made separate trips to Russia in the wake of the Kishinev pogrom—he had become hostile to it, perhaps out of anger that Herzl had been willing to treat with such men as Witte and von Plehve for Zion's sake. Wolf genuinely feared that Zionism had become a threat to the Russian Jew's aspiration to equal rights; the claim of separate nationhood, he believed, would only cause the tsarist authorities to respond by telling the Jew to go to Palestine if he wanted freedom. This possibility troubled him more than the one—important to so many of his anti-Zionist associates—of losing status as an Englishman as a result of Jewish nationalist claims. The fact that Zangwill's Jewish Territorial Organization laid stress upon refuge for persecuted Jews rather than on national identification doubtless was why Wolf gladly supported that organization when it was founded in 1905. In any case, by the time of the war, Wolf's anti-Zionism stood solidly alongside his concern with oppressed Jews in the world to qualify him as an authentic spokesman on both these issues for the Anglo-Jewish establishment. Lancelot Oliphant and others at the Foreign Office did not have to go farther than to Lucien Wolf to be persuaded on good authority that the Zionists had no case.

In spite of his negative view of Zionism, however, Lucien Wolf was politician enough to know that it was a force to be reckoned with. He was troubled by the split it represented in British Jewry, which he hoped would be able to speak in a single voice at any postwar peace conference. That is why he did not respond unfavorably when Harry Sacher had begun approaching him in November 1914 about the possibility of some kind of understanding between the CFC and the Zionists. Weizmann thought he had been haughty on that occasion, but actually Wolf welcomed the chance to deal with other Zionists than those of the Cowen-Greenberg faction, which had been—with the help of Greenberg's *Jewish Chronicle*—especially vociferous in their criticisms of him and the CFC. When Weizmann saw him in London that December, Wolf made his view quite plain "that it might be possible under certain conditions to establish an entente between the nationalist section of Jewry and their former opponents, so as to appear before the powers as a united body."

Wolf also had been one of the Jewish leaders with whom Herbert Samuel conferred in February 1915 while revising his memorandum, and he had satisfied Samuel by saying he supported the Zionists' cultural policy in Palestine—even, perhaps, the plan for a Hebrew university—as well as their desire for free immigration and facilities for colonization there. In other words, Wolf was perfectly willing to take a "territorial" approach to Palestine as a land of Jewish refuge—even as a special one, with facilities for Jewish culture and communal organization—under the protection of powers or a power, preferably Great Britain. But he would hear nothing of Jewish nationality, statehood, or special rights in relation to the surrounding population. If only these latter elements were omitted from the discussion, he felt it was possible to come to some kind of understanding with the Zionists.

Sacher's overtures finally brought results on April 14, 1915, when a formal meeting was held between spokesmen of the Zionists and of the CFC. Among those present for the CFC along with Wolf were Claude Montefiore, president of the Anglo-Jewish Association, and David L. Alexander, president of the Board of Deputies of British Jews. Leopold de Rothschild was unable to attend "owing to indisposition." Of the five Zionists present, only Joseph Cowen stood for the English Zionist Federation; Herbert Bentwich was there to represent the Maccabaeans, and Moses Gaster, Yehiel Tschlenow, and Nahum Sokolow stood for the World Zionist Organization—an indispensable presence in the eyes of the CFC even though none of these latter three were native Englishmen and two of them were not British subjects at all. Chaim Weizmann was not present, but there was no reason why he should have been. He was indeed by now the foremost spokesman for Zionism in certain high places, but this fact carried no official status; technically, he was outranked by all the Zionists at this meeting—even by Gaster, whose position as *haham*, or chief rabbi, of the Sephardic community gave him special status as the Zionist who held the highest position in the Anglo-Jewish institutional structure.*

At the start of the meeting, there evidently was genuine optimism on Wolf's part that it could produce "a working understanding on the basis of a scheme from which the larger political aims of the Zionists should be provisionally excluded." Tschlenow, a conciliator by nature, opened the proceedings with a long speech stressing both the practical need for unity between the two groups—he made several references to the future "Peace Congress"—and the possibility of attaining it. As an expert in Russian-Jewish affairs, he insisted that the realization of the Zionist program would not hinder the achievement of Jewish rights in Russia but would, on the contrary, help it. He also gave his authoritative opinion that Russia would not stand in the way of Jewish aspirations in Palestine and would be willing to let its political future be determined by England and France.

On the other hand, he thought that hopes were dim for a solution of the Russian-Jewish problem in the immediate future and he proposed the Zionist solution as a way of helping to alleviate it as soon as possible. Even this final qualification may not have been too irritating to the CFC representatives, who realized that it would take some time before the Jews of Eastern Europe could become "as indistinguishably Russian or Polish as their co-religionists in this country or in France are British or French." But then Tschlenow yielded the floor to Zionist colleagues who were far less willing than he to leave their "larger political aims" out of the discussion. Gaster insisted upon the point that the Zionists would be satisfied with nothing less than a Jewish commonwealth. Sokolow, who wanted Palestine to be a British protectorate, offered his wish—shared by Cowen—that a chartered company be formed under which the Palestine Jewish community could be expanded and organized for the eventual creation of a commonwealth. These notions were totally unacceptable to the gentlemen of the CFC.

As far as Wolf was concerned, the mere fact that the Zionists took these positions—not to mention the possibility of their realization—"is itself a serious danger, for, if it were admitted in any responsible Jewish quarter, or by any large section of Jewish opinion, it would at once relieve persecuting countries of much of their pres-

---

* Dr. Joseph Hertz, the Ashkenazi chief rabbi since 1913, was, unlike his predecessor Hermann Adler, favorably disposed toward Zionism, but he was not affiliated with the movement as Gaster was.

ent incentive to pursue a policy of emancipation. This danger," he went on in his report of the meeting,

> is aggravated and may be vastly extended by the Nationalist postulate of the Zionists. The idea of a Jewish nationality, the talk of a Jew "going home" to Palestine, if he is not content with his lot in the land of his birth, strikes at the root of all Jewish claim to citizenship in lands where Jewish disabilities still exist. It is the assertion, not merely of a double nationality—a doctrine which is just now in extremely bad odor—but of the perpetual alienage of Jews everywhere outside Palestine.

As for the charter idea, Wolf insisted it would violate British traditions since it implied preferential treatment on a "religious basis." And he added: "How could we continue to ask for equal rights for the Jews in Russia and Roumania if we claimed special rights for the Jews in Palestine?" Wolf reiterated the position he had taken with Herbert Samuel in February, concluding his report with the assertion that the CFC would be ready to cooperate with the Zionists on this basis if the latter agreed to an "*ad hoc* elimination of Nationalism and exclusive rights from their program." The report was submitted to the Foreign Office and read sympathetically there. Lancelot Oliphant minuted on the folder: "An interesting sidelight on Zionism, showing how hopelessly unpracticable the Zionists are."

The meeting had come to nothing, even though the Zionists must surely have known that a successful understanding with the CFC would have given them access to the Foreign Office. No doubt they—Gaster in particular—believed that their special relationship with Herbert Samuel would be effective enough as a political instrument when the time came. This was all the more reason why Samuel's loss of his cabinet status in the May crisis must have grieved them greatly. But for Samuel, they were without a strategy.

Only Chaim Weizmann, carrying on his customary freelance diplomacy, continued to find other means of access than the conventional ones to men of power in the country. In August 1915—through the good offices, as was so often the case, of Dorothy de Rothschild—he added the name of Lord Robert Cecil to his list of such contacts. A son of the great Lord Salisbury and Balfour's first cousin, Cecil had followed the family tradition of statesmanship by entering Parliament in January 1906, winning a seat as a Conservative against the Liberal flood tide. Zionism was not new to him: in that election, he had responded to Sir Francis Montefiore's letter to the candidates by saying: "I am in agreement with the objects of your [English Zionist] Federation, and, indeed, with the whole of your circular on the subject."

When Weizmann went to see him at the Foreign Office on August 18, Cecil had just been appointed parliamentary under-secretary for foreign affairs. "He was anxious," Cecil later reported of his visitor, "to interest me in the restoration of Palestine to the Jews. He thought the most desirable way of doing it would be to put Palestine under a British protectorate for the avowed purpose of encouraging the Jewish colonization of that country." Weizmann stressed the importance Palestine would have for British interests, mentioning not only the security of Egypt but also the link between the Mediterranean and Baghdad. He touched upon the Russian-Jewish problem, but characteristically spoke of the Zionist solution in terms not of a rescue from persecution but of an alternative to the "present anomalous national position" of the Jews, the true source to their woes.

"He said with great truth," Cecil acknowledged, "that even in this country a Jew always had to give an explanation of his existence and he was neither quite an Englishman nor quite a Jew, and that the same thing was equally true with much more serious results in other countries." This was essentially the argument Weizmann had used with Cecil's cousin, the present first lord of the Admiralty, and it was having a similar effectiveness. With it, Weizmann was able to outflank all the "Russian" arguments of the Anglo-Jewish establishment and offer the Wolfs and the Montefiores themselves as the problem in need of a solution. "It is impossible to reproduce in writing," Cecil noted, "the subdued enthusiasm with which Dr. Weizmann spoke, or the extraordinary impressiveness of his attitude, which made one forget his rather repellent and even sordid exterior."

Repellent and sordid? Weizmann would no doubt have been startled to know he looked that way in Cecil's eyes, but he might also have appreciated the honesty of the response. Cecil had no doubt rarely seen men who looked and sounded like Weizmann outside of certain shops or neighborhoods, where they perhaps had proclaimed their wares too stridently or performed their services too obsequiously for his taste. Here, on the other hand, was a Jew from Pinsk who had a heavy accent and a way of arguing points with the ungentlemanly intensity of a true believer, and who was as proud as a lord of being what he was. No "105 percent" Englishman he, but he could debate about the things that counted to him with the subtlest minds in the realm. "Perhaps a phrase he used," Cecil added in his report, "may convey something of the impression which he made. He said, 'I am not romantic except that Jews must always be romantic, for to them the reality is too terrible.'" Too repellent and sordid, perhaps: Cecil was now absorbing some of the romance of Chaim Weizmann.

It may be said, then, that by the fall of 1915 Zionism had won some degree of sympathy among three personages at the Foreign Office: Cecil, Grey himself, and Lord Crewe—the last now standing in so frequently for Grey, who needed rests on account of his failing eyesight, that the foreign secretaryship may be considered as virtually a dual office at this time. Among other officials there, the feelings toward Zionism seem to have ranged from indifference to outright hostility; but some of these were men of the type whose outlook can always be considerably affected by the winds of authority. None of them is likely to have known—as Grey, Crewe, and probably Cecil, did—of Herbert Samuel's memorandum, and consequently, of the serious consideration being given to Zionism by at least some members of the cabinet. The Zionist idea had simply not yet been fed into the machinery of Foreign Office policy making.

Coincidentally, strong new incentives to begin taking the Zionist claim seriously arrived at the Foreign Office at almost the very moment when Sykes and Picot were bringing the Brown Area into being. Their ultimate sources were the United States of America and its 2 million Jews. The American attitude toward the war had been a major concern of Englishmen from the beginning, often second only to events on the battlefields themselves as an ongoing theme in the British press. "There are signs," had run a typical and prominent item in *The Times* of November 23, 1914,

> that the Germans are again planning to make a bid for American sympathy by peace talk. The *New York Times* publishes a long interview with Mr. Jacob Schiff, one of the leading German-American bankers, and a close friend of the German official representatives in the United States, which shows clearly that their line of attack is to secure a lasting peace. . . .
> The moderation of Mr. Schiff's brief for Germany, his lamentation over the misery of the war, annotated as it is by accents of suffering Flanders, his appeal to the humanitarian instinct of the American people, to their sympathies with the under-dog, to say nothing of his other points, all show a consid-

erable advance of the Teutonic grasp of the American point of view.

As far as many Englishmen were concerned, the American point of view ought to have been innately Anglo-Saxon, and until the United States was ready to throw in its lot with England and France in the present conflict, something that seemed at times to border on a law of nature was being violated in their eyes. But clearly, as they saw it, the problem was that there had come into being a pronounced Germanic element in American society, which had a significant voice in the nation's affairs and which harbored natural sympathies for its ancestral homeland. In 1914 and early 1915 it was apparently this element in particular that tended to endorse Germany's argument that she had gone to war to defend herself against the threatened aggression of Russia, allied with France, and that what she really wanted was peace as soon as possible. *The New York Times* itself, in the course of the November 1914 interview article on Jacob Schiff, asserted that it did "not want to see Germany crushed." Though this was a position then still being held in private by some Englishmen, including David Lloyd George, it looked far different when printed in a context of American neutralism. The fury of the official Anglo-French crusade against German militarism had simply not yet been felt by Mr. Schiff and the publishers of *The New York Times*—and the fact that these gentlemen were not only of German extraction but also were Jews was not missed by knowledgeable Englishmen.

The association made in many English minds between Jews, Germans, and pro-German feelings was one of those delicate myths about Jews that have some basis in reality but become inflated out of all proportion to it. There can be no doubt that, through the course of the nineteenth century, German had become the definitive language of European high culture and learning among a substantial portion of the educated Jews of Central and Eastern Europe, and that Jews elsewhere tended to feel the pull of it—as also did a good many learned Protestants in that epoch. Also undeniable was the fact that, among American Jews, it was not only those of German extraction who tended to sympathize with the Central Powers during the early months of the war; so also did a great many of the East European Jews—though not so much out of fondness for Germany as out of extreme hatred for tsarist Russia. Englishmen who were aware of these feelings did not necessarily know that the strongest political sentiment of all among American Jews, whatever their countries of origin, was a passion for liberal democracy—a trait that could ultimately make them susceptible to the historic claims of Great Britain, and even of France, in spite of the Dreyfus affair (the wrong of which had been righted by 1914).

On the contrary, many Englishmen of culture were so persuaded of an innate link between Jewishness and Germanism that they regarded the Jews and Dunmeh* of Salonika as having been a major cause of Turkey's entry into the war. "Berlin and Vienna inspired the soldiers," wrote *The Times* in a purported analysis of the event on November 28, 1914, and "Jewish Salonika, hoping, perhaps, for revenge on the Greek: perhaps—who knows—plotting the complete capture of the Turk in the interests of Judaeo-German finance, had close relations with the civilian extremists." Sir Reginald Wingate, for one, was so taken with this way of looking at the matter that, in an address to a gathering of Sudanese sheikhs the following month, he had readily placed some of the blame for events upon a "syndicate of Jews, financiers, and low-born intriguers" at Constantinople. The fact that the only member of Enver's ruling circle who was of Jewish extraction—Djavid Pasha, a Dunmeh from Salonika and Turkey's minister of finance—had resigned in protest when Turkey went to war on the German side, does not seem to have abashed the enthusiasts of this viewpoint. The tendency to identify all Jews—and especially Zionists—with Germanism was one of the most formidable problems English Zionism had to face.

To be sure, this was an identification that did not trouble German Zionists, who were as patriotic as their British counterparts and as convinced as they that the future of the cause lay with their own country's victory. In a book called *Die Juden der Türkei (The Jews of Turkey)*, published in 1915, the German Zionist Davis Trietsch developed a vision of what would be the Jewish place in an Ottoman pan-Islam under German sponsorship. Theorizing that "in a certain sense the Jews are a Near Eastern element in Germany and a German element in Turkey," he pondered the "possibilities in a German protectorate over the Jews as well as over Islam." In November 1915, the German Zionist leadership—who still regarded the Berlin office as the headquarters of the worldwide movement, and who presided

---

* The Dunmeh are the descendants of those followers of the seventeenth-century pseudo-Messiah Sabbatai Zevi who had, like him, converted from Judaism to Islam. They have remained a distinct group with certain quasi-Jewish customs down to the twentieth century, and they were, along with the Jews of some parts of the Ottoman Empire—especially Salonika—a strong source of support for the Young Turk revolution.

over the branch at Constantinople, which still had crucial control over Palestinian Jewish affairs—succeeded in getting the German government to instruct its consuls in the Ottoman Empire that it looked favorably upon "Jewish activities designed to promote the economic and cultural progress of the Jews in Turkey, and also on the immigration and settlement of Jews from other countries." This was still a step short of an endorsement of Zionism, but German Zionists believed the next step would soon be taken.

German propagandists in the United States readily exploited such developments, and American Zionists were keenly aware of their import. Starting in particular with Turkey's entry into the war, both Zionists and non-Zionist Jewish philanthropists in America were concerned that the position of worldwide Zionism should be uncompromisingly neutral, lest anything be done to offend the powers controlling the destinies of Palestine Jewry. This attitude was still very much in force in November 1915, when Louis D. Brandeis, chairman of the Provisional Executive Committee for General Zionist Affairs—the central body for American Zionism at this time—announced: "This Committee maintains a strict neutrality towards the nations now at war, as is demanded by Jewish interests." The view was not by any means pro-German in itself, but the fact that some Zionist leaders in America did have distinct German sympathies, along with the presence of names of Central European origin among those American Jews who spoke loudest for neutrality, suggested to English observers that this was a sector of American life in which German propaganda was enjoying considerable success.

The problem was felt with growing acuteness by the last weeks of 1915, as the war pushed on to its second New Year's Day with a record of stalemate after stalemate and no end in sight. The yearning by the Allies for American participation on their side was greater than ever—and now there even were hopeful signs regarding this. Since the sinking of the British liner *Lusitania*, with 128 Americans on board, by a German U-boat in May, President Wilson had adopted a distinctly harsher tone in his exchanges with the German government. Nor had he yet obtained satisfaction in his demand for the cessation of unrestricted submarine warfare on the Atlantic when, in the fall, discoveries were made that German agents were committing acts of sabotage on American factories producing war materials for shipment to the Allies. The German military attaché in Washington, Captain Franz von Papen, was recalled home in an atmosphere of suspicion and scandal; and each new rumble of anger among the American public was recorded jubilantly in the British press. Perhaps the time was coming when the Americans could be won over to the cause after all. And as Englishmen pondered this prospect, some of them again turned to thoughts of what the Jewish role might be in either hindering it or helping to bring it about.

English observers of American public opinion tended to make two significant assumptions about Jews at this time. First, they considered the Jews of America to be a powerful force in the nation's political life. Though this notion was greatly exaggerated, it certainly was not groundless. In 1915 the American Jewish community was already on its way to becoming one of the most articulate, cohesive, and intellectually and financially gifted subgroups in the American body politic. Some of the country's greatest newspapers were owned by Jews. The presence of Jews among President Wilson's advisers—above all, of Louis D. Brandeis, who was to be appointed to the United States Supreme Court in January 1916, just as the Foreign Office was pondering these very questions—was also quite noticeable. And if Englishmen perhaps had too great a tendency to look upon Jacob Schiff as a kind of American Rothschild, they nevertheless were right if they recognized that they had nothing at home to compare with the Jewish population of New York as a body generating political ideas, influence, and voting power, for all the poverty still prevailing in its midst. The British had legitimate grounds for assuming that the political sentiments of 2 million American Jews counted for more than a little as their country entered a presidential election year.

The other prevailing British assumption about American Jews was that they were overwhelmingly Zionist. Indeed, this would probably have been found true if one could have plumbed their sentimental depths, though it was not yet so in any formal sense. Zionists had still been only a small minority among them in 1914 if one considers the term strictly in the sense of organizational membership, which was about 130,000. In fact, until almost the eve of war, the main thrust of American-Jewish political thinking had been decidedly anti-Zionist. The Reform establishment—made up mostly of Jews of Central European extraction—which had dominated American-Jewish life for the entire second half of the nineteenth century, was as vehemently assimilationist and opposed to Jewish nationalism as its British counterpart. As for the East European masses who had rapidly become the Jewish majority group since the 1880s, their intellectual life—centered in its secular aspects upon the Yiddish press—had to a large extent been influenced by Socialism and Bundism, which were devoutly anti-Zionist.

But something had happened within both these groups in their confrontation with one another and in response to the chemistry of American soil. A Reform Jew from Louisville, Kentucky, Louis D. Brandeis was of a type that ought to have seemed destined for assimilation, for example. But his work during the Progressive era as a lawyer crusading for urban reform had brought him into daily contact with the immigrant Jewish masses of New York, and the experience had awakened in him a sense of peoplehood. There were others like him in his generation, and once he had lent his great moral authority to Zionism by affiliating with the movement in 1913, there were to be more.

As for the immigrants from Eastern Europe, the development of Jewish nationalist sympathies—whether accompanied by Zionist affiliation or not—was to some extent perfectly natural among those who followed the prevailing trend in America away from Old World orthodoxies, whether in religion or in radical politics. Chaim Weizmann had, as usual, grasped a significant trait of the Jewish psyche when, in his Geneva debating days, he had aimed in particular at Bundists as potential converts to Zionism. The further the immigrant moved up the ladder of American middle-class life, the weaker became the grip of the old attitudes, with the result that his or her instinctual ethnocentrism was freer to express itself in terms of a national ideal. Even the once rabidly anti-Zionist *Jewish Daily Forward* of New York, the most widely read Yiddish newspaper in the world, was soon to find itself speaking with fondness of the Jewish settlement in Eretz-Yisroel. In 1915, this trend had been manifesting itself in a movement to organize an American Jewish Congress, which was to reflect the new social structure of American Jewry more accurately than such organs of the old German-dominated establishment as the American Jewish Committee and was to be decidedly Zionist in orientation. On the issue of incipient Zionism, then, the British judgment of American-Jewish attitudes was not so much sound as prophetic.

This was the atmosphere within which, in the first half of December 1915, the Foreign Office received a memorandum that had been passed along a chain of contacts by its author Horace Kallen, a prominent American Zionist and a professor of philosophy at the University of Wisconsin. "I have made in the last few months," Kallen wrote,

a pretty thorough study of Jewish public opinion as that is reflected and expressed by the Yiddish press in New York and
elsewhere. I find a number of my initial beliefs which I thought
were based on fact rather falsified by the data. Though it is true
as I had supposed that the sentiment of the community was
largely anti-Russian, and that this anti-Russian feeling got emphasized in pro-German ways, I was interested and pleased to
find that the pro-Germanism was not a natural or spontaneous
fact, even among the writers in those papers which seemed most
violently to glory in German victories.

Suggesting not only that this superficial pro-Germanism was the
result of the influence of German agents, but that the Yiddish papers might even have been receiving some German financial support
for their enthusiasms, Kallen went on to say:

> I think it a pity that the Allies have not also taken a hand in
> the matter, the more so as I am convinced that a statement on
> behalf of the Allies favoring Jewish rights in every country
> (analogous to the Teutonic announcements), and a very veiled
> suggestion concerning nationalization in Palestine would more
> than counterbalance German promises in the same direction,
> and would give a natural outlet for the spontaneous pro-English,
> French and Italian sympathies of the Jewish masses.

Kallen concluded with the hope that the Foreign Office might "see
its way to sending agents to New York to oust the German agents."

The letter was bound to make a strong impression at that moment, particularly since there also arrived at the Foreign Office, not
more than a week later, a major communication to the same effect
from Lucien Wolf. A good deal had happened in recent weeks to
persuade Wolf that it was urgent to try once again building the
bridge to the Zionists that he had sought the previous spring. Writing directly to Lord Robert Cecil, he sent two enclosures with his
letter. One was a note to him from Jacques Bigart, the secretary of
the Alliance Israélite Universelle, telling him of the formation of the
long-discussed Comité de Propagande Française auprès des Juifs
Neutres. The French, too, had become worried about German propaganda among American Jews, and the organization they created to
do something about it had the highest official sanction: its president
was Georges Leygues, chairman of the Foreign Affairs Commission
of the French Chamber of Deputies. The comité's membership—

which was composed of Jews and non-Jews alike—included Emile Durkheim, the illustrious sociologist, and Victor Bérard, the writer we have seen discussing Middle Eastern affairs with Messrs. Viviani and Doumergue, as well as with Baron de Rothschild, Lord Bertie, and Chaim Weizmann, just a short time before this. The affiliation of Anatole France was also expected soon.

"The specific object of this Committee's activities," said Bigart's letter to Wolf,

> is to send to the Jewish newspapers of neutral countries—above all to the Yiddish newspapers of the United States—factual material favorable to the Allies with respect to Jewish questions: for example, the promotion of a Jew to the rank of General in the French army, his photograph, the citations and decorations Jews have received, etc., perhaps newsreels of events in which Jews play an outstanding role; and on the other hand, materials showing the German attitude on the Jewish question. . . . The Committee will publish brochures both in French and in Yiddish . . . dealing with the following questions: what the Jews of Switzerland owe to France; the character of anti-Semitism in Germany as compared with that in France and in England; Russia is not anti-Semitic, only its bureaucracy is, etc.

There was nothing about Zionism, however, in Bigart's letter: the French were demonstrating once again that their thoughts did not readily run in that direction.

In his covering letter to Cecil, Wolf expressed his very sound doubts "whether our French friends are proceeding on the best lines." Among other problems, he pointed out that "it is necessary to speak to the American Jews in English as well as Yiddish." But despite its faults of perception, the comité had vitality, and before the end of December it had dispatched to the United States one of its members, Victor Basch, a lecturer at the Sorbonne. Basch, a Jew born in Budapest, was a Socialist with strong Zionist sympathies— Weizmann had once described his outlook as "Rachmones Zionism."[*] He apparently spoke good Yiddish, and was to spend a good deal of time during his American stay investigating the Yiddish press and coming to much the same conclusions as Horace Kallen had.

Wolf's second enclosure, obviously inspired by the first, was a memorandum setting out his own "suggestions for a pro-Allies pro-

---

[*] *Rachmones* is Yiddish for "pity" or "compassion," and here has a tinge of irony.

paganda among the Jews of the United States." Wolf began it with the observation that, since the sinking of the *Lusitania*,

> the unsympathetic attitude of the Jews of the United States towards the cause of the Allies has become much softened, and this tendency has of late been markedly accentuated by the growing prospect of conflict with the Central Powers, which would necessarily deprive the American Jewish citizens of their present freedom of choice. Nevertheless, the situation still leaves much to be desired, and this is in no small degree due to the fact that hitherto there has been no systematic propaganda intelligently adapted to the various national origins of the American Jews and their consequent varied psychology. That such a propaganda would be very useful is evidenced by the fact that in the United States the Jews number over 2,000,000 and their influence—political, commercial and social—is very considerable.

Wolf then proceeds to give his Foreign Office readers a brief historical portrait of American Jewry in its various national origins. First, he lists the Jews "of British, Spanish and Dutch extraction," that primarily Sephardic community, who "number among them the oldest Jewish families in America." They represent no problem, Wolf says, because "their sympathies are even more uncompromisingly English than those of the American non-Jew." But their numbers are small.

"A very much larger group," Wolf continues,

> is that of the Jews of German extraction, now in their second or third generation. They are perhaps the most influential section of American Jewry. Hitherto their tendency has been pro-German. This tendency is, however, purely superficial, and is due largely to the fact that they have not been approached by the Allies in a proper way.

Wolf describes them as descendants of Liberals of "the Heinrich Heine type"—he does not feel the need to remind his learned readers that that great German-Jewish poet spent most of his life in French exile and was an admirer of English political institutions—among whom "political doctrine stood higher than patriotism." Wolf is no doubt thinking here of his own father. "It should not be difficult to reawaken these tendencies in their American descendants," Wolf observes. On the other hand, he says, the more recent German-Jewish immigrants, "largely influenced by the Bismarckian tradition" and taking pride in German unity and power, "could not be influenced by our propagandists." This one small group Wolf concedes to the Germans.

"The fourth group," he goes on,

> is that of the Russian and Polish Jews. They are for the most part in moderate circumstances, but they are more numerous than any of the other groups. They are almost entirely fugitives from Russian oppression, and belong more particularly to the Pogrom and May Laws era, which began in the early eighties. They are, of course, bitterly hostile to Russia, and they are disposed to resent the Alliance of Great Britain and France with that country as a betrayal. But, they know nothing of modern Germany, and very little of the changes that in recent years have come over Russia, which to them is still the unreformed and unrelieved despotism of Alexander III. Consequently they offer hopeful material for an intelligently directed propaganda.

Wolf, who was personally acquainted with Russian Liberals, was himself not ready to give up the hope—upon which his life's work was based—that Russia would become better. But if Russian Jews were likely to be skeptical on this point, he also had other things for them in his repertory of persuasion, which now followed.

Continuing his memorandum, Wolf proceeded to outline a proposed propaganda campaign among American Jews under three headings. The first was "Propaganda on General Lines," which, he said,

> should be similar to the scheme adopted by the new French Committee, but should accentuate more largely and definitely the essential difference between the reactionary foundations of modern Germanism, of which anti-Semitism is an integral and inseparable part, and the fundamental Liberalism of British, French and Italian life.

Wolf maintained that "liberal concessions" in Germany were always incomplete, "because the dominating influence is an exclusive racialism, which necessarily seeks its inspiration and justification in the more brutal traditions of medieval life." This was not the case in the countries in which "Liberalism is fundamental, modern and instinctive," where the "occasional relapses into a wild Nationalism and anti-Semitism are necessarily accidental and ephemeral." The victory of the Allies, therefore, "would make for the liberation of the Jews everywhere, because it could not do otherwise."

This inevitably led to the second heading, "The Russian Question." Wolf evidently was having difficulty with this, and it shows in his formulations. "In this connection," he writes, "efforts should be made to obtain fairer treatment of the Jews during the war, and a promise of reforms when peace is restored." No one would have quarreled with this; but what does the essential fact implied here—to wit, that Russia treats Jews unfairly—do to the argument that the Allied cause is the better one for the Jews? Wolf maintains weakly that "the prevailing misconceptions of Russia should be dealt with. We take our picture of Russian life from the Court, the Government, the Bureaucracy, and the Black Hundreds, and leave out of account 150,000,000 of Russians and Russian subordinate nationalities who are all longing and striving for freedom on the British, French and Italian models." He is again speaking for some hoped-for better Russia of the future, but not for the actual one that is part of the cause he is asking Jews to support. Delivering a few blows against Stephen Graham and the vision of what he calls a "Germanized Russia"—that is, a vision based on notions of racial purity—Wolf concludes this section with startling naïveté:

> The great bulk of the Russian people is on the side of the Allies, and all they stand for. It is consequently the duty of every foreign Jew to support them, as the Russian Jews themselves are supporting them. Any other course will merely play into the hands of Russian Reaction and anti-Semitism, which are the natural Allies of Germanic Reaction and anti-Semitism.

With such arguments, Wolf must inevitably have realized that something more had to be offered to the Russian Jews of the United States to win their favor. And so, on his own initiative—and despite the unresolved differences between the CFC and the Zionist leadership in England—he now proposed "Zionism" as heading number three. "I am not a Zionist," he fervently states at the outset,

> and I deplore the Jewish National Movement. To my mind the Jews are not a nationality. I doubt whether they ever have been

one in the true sense of the term, and I am certain that to bottle them up in a single national life would be tantamount to a renunciation of all their most sacred ideals, and would retard their political assimilation in the lands of their present dispersion, where the bulk of them must remain, and where they can have no other than the local nationalities.

Having perforce gotten that off his chest, Wolf was ready to move on:

> Still, the facts cannot be ignored, and in any bid for Jewish sympathies today, very serious account must be taken of the Zionist movement. In America the Zionist organizations have lately captured Jewish opinion, and very shortly a great American Jewish Congress will be held virtually under Zionist auspices. This is the moment for the Allies to declare their policy in regard to Palestine.

This statement, though it was now about to be qualified by Wolf's stand regarding the Jews and Palestine that the Zionists had thought insufficient, was in itself rather momentous, coming as it did from the spokesman of the foreign policy organ of the Anglo-Jewish establishment. From the Foreign Office standpoint, it was as *official* a statement of the Jewish view of the matter as they had ever received. Wolf, after observing shrewdly that Germany and Austria, "with their Turkish attachment, cannot well say much on this subject," went on to spell out what he meant:

> The Allies, of course, cannot promise to make a Jewish State of a land in which only a comparatively small minority of the inhabitants are Jews, but there is a great deal they can say which would conciliate Zionist opinion. If, for example, they would say that they thoroughly understand and sympathize with Jewish aspirations in regard to Palestine, and that when the destiny of the country comes to be considered, those aspirations will be taken into account, and that in addition to equal rights with the remainder of the population they would be guaranteed reasonable facilities for immigration and colonization, for a liberal scheme of local self-government for the existing colonies, for the establishment of a Jewish University, and for the recognition of the Hebrew language as one of the vernaculars of the land, I am confident they would sweep the whole of American Jewry into enthusiastic allegiance to their cause.

Wolf concluded that "what the Zionists would especially like to know is that Great Britain will become mistress of Palestine," but he thought—since he of course knew nothing of the negotiations with Picot—that this would be difficult owing to French claims. He recommended that there be propaganda committees in London, Rome, and Petrograd along the lines of the one in Paris to handle the matters dealt with in his memorandum.

Not quite ready to deal with Wolf's recommendations, the Foreign Office forwarded a copy to the British ambassador in Washington, Sir Cecil Spring-Rice. In January, Spring-Rice replied with a despairing outcry about the state of American public opinion. "All the enemies of England have been marshaled against us," he wrote, "and the Irish have lent their unequaled power of political organization to Jews, Catholics and Germans." The Zionist element in Wolf's memorandum had not yet caught the imagination of the makers of Great Britain's foreign policy, but it was to do so within a matter of weeks.

·23·

ZIONISM AT THE
FOREIGN OFFICE, II:
THE AWAKENING

E arly in February 1916, Edgar Suarès, the president of the
Jewish community of Alexandria, held a far-reaching conversation with an Englishman who seems to have been connected
with the organization providing relief for the Palestinian Jewish
refugees in that city. In the course of it, Suarès presented his views
about Great Britain and Palestine and about their relation in terms
of the present struggle.

Suarès thought the British had not succeeded in winning "the
sympathy of the Jewish Race," whose indifference or hostility, he
feared, had been a "deadweight" against them so far and would
"continue to retard every step" they took toward victory. This he
attributed to the fact that "British policy had not been more encouraging to the Jews" in regard to Palestine. He was himself an anti-
Zionist, he stressed, but nevertheless "he was anxious that Palestine
should be open to such Jews as wished to go there, and that the
management of its internal affairs should be in the hands of Jews
and under British protection." Apparently alluding to the American-
Jewish organizations now active in providing relief for the Palestinian Jews in Alexandria, Suarès hinted that, "given the sympathy of
the British Government today," he himself could exercise influence
in securing for England "the support of the whole Jewish and German-Jewish Community in America within perhaps one month; and
at most three." It was just a matter of "a stroke of the pen, almost,"
with which "England could assume to herself the active support of
the Jews all over the neutral world."

Suarès had evidently had a strong hunch that these remarks

would reach British governing circles, and he was right: a report of the conversation was sent by the man with whom he held it to Sir Henry McMahon in Cairo, and McMahon promptly sent it on to the Foreign Office. The first person to read it there, on February 23, was twenty-nine-year-old Harold Nicolson, who was inclined to respond in the conventional Foreign Office way. "I fear," he wrote, "that for H.M.G. [His Majesty's Government] to announce publicly their determination to support Zionist aspirations in Palestine would be a course of more difficulty than M. Suarez appears to imagine, and that it is doubtful whether the favor which this move would find with *some* (but by no means *all*) Jews, would be worth it."

But despite Nicolson's echoing of the traditional line, feelings about this question had undergone considerable changes at the Foreign Office in recent weeks. This transformation was due in part to the kind of intelligence about American and world Jewry lately received from Horace Kallen and Lucien Wolf, as well as to the fact that the French government had by now agreed to the terms arrived at by Sykes and Picot, which included a viable Brown Area in Palestine. Furthermore, there had by this time been a quiet shift in the weight of Foreign Office opinion in the direction of those men who were inclined to view the Zionist case sympathetically. With Grey surrendering more and more of his work on account of failing eyesight, Crewe and Lord Robert Cecil—both more persuaded of the Zionist case than Grey had ever really been—were taking on greater influence. There also were two new arrivals to the Foreign Office upon whom the claims of Zionism had made a strong impression. These were Lord Eustace Percy, son of the Earl Percy who had listened sympathetically to the young Chaim Weizmann's arguments back in 1904 and himself recently returned from service with the embassy in Washington, and Hugh J. O'Beirne, former counselor and chargé d'affaires at the embassies in Saint Petersburg and Sofia. Irish-born and educated at Beaumont—like Mark Sykes after him—and at Balliol College, Oxford, the forty-nine-year-old O'Beirne had been in Bulgaria until its entry in the war the previous October on the side of the Central Powers.

O'Beirne had recently been talking to his fellow Catholic in the diplomatic service, G.H. Fitzmaurice, who had been the chief dragoman at the embassy in Constantinople from 1907 to November 1914. Fitzmaurice—whom Mark Sykes had thought to be perhaps the last Englishman still interested in maintaining the Ottoman Empire—was one of those who were outspoken in their conviction that the Jewish and crypto-Jewish element was a strong and dire influence on the politics of the Young Turk movement. But he also was a man whose dislike of Jews was of such a nature as to predispose him to look with some interest upon Zionism when he heard about it. And he seems to have heard more than a little about it at the Admiralty, where he had been working for some months. In fact, he had had an interview there on February 16 with Moses Gaster, a contact he undoubtedly had made through Herbert Samuel. The upshot was that Fitzmaurice, with his own highly respected knowledge of the politics of Constantinople, had come up with solid reasons of his own in support of Zionism. These had made their way to O'Beirne, who responded to the Suarès proposal at the Foreign Office on February 28 with a short but significant memorandum.

"It has been suggested to me," he began, alluding to his recent discussions with Fitzmaurice, "that if we could offer the Jews an arrangement as to Palestine which would strongly appeal to them we might conceivably be able to strike a bargain with them as to withdrawing their support from the Young Turk Government which would then automatically collapse." Fitzmaurice and O'Beirne were by no means the only men in the British Government to add this particular belief to the myths of world Jewish power, but they seem to have been the first to use it as an argument in favor of Zionism. "The tremendous political consequences of such a deal," O'Beirne went on, "are quite obvious. I am told that notwithstanding the indifference or hostility of a great many Jews to the Zionist idea an arrangement completely satisfactory to Jewish aspirations in regard to Palestine might nevertheless have immense attractions for the great body of Jews."

O'Beirne developed his ideas about what kind of arrangement regarding the Jews and Palestine might be feasible. "The Zionists are opposed to an international protectorate and would wish for a British protectorate, which seems impracticable," he said, and then mentioned an idea that here makes its appearance in the record for the first time. "I understand," he said, "that the idea has been put forward that there might be an American protectorate which would probably appeal intensely to the very influential body of American Jews." From this moment on, the idea was to be a persistent one, a hopeful variation—along with that of an Anglo-American protectorate—on the theme of exclusive British control of Palestine. Its origin can only be guessed at; but there may well be significance in the fact that Colonel Edward M. House, President Wilson's special envoy to the Entente Powers, had just been in London and that the future of the Ottoman Empire had been discussed with him during a dinner at

Lord Reading's home on the evening of February 14, attended by Asquith, Lloyd George, Grey, and Balfour.

"While there would necessarily be an international administration of some kind in Jerusalem itself," O'Beirne went on,

> it is conceivable that in the rest of Palestine the Jews could be given special colonizing facilities which in time would make them strong enough to cope with the Arab element, when the management of internal affairs might be placed in their hands under America's protection. Meanwhile Palestine outside Jerusalem might possibly be left under the administration of some neutral nationality if the United States would not agree to undertake the administration themselves.

O'Beirne concluded by disclaiming any competence, for his own part, to say whether any of these schemes was feasible. He admitted that "the difficulty of Jewish colonists displacing any large proportion of the 6-700,000 Arabs in Palestine, or growing strong enough to administer them, seems to me almost insurmountable." And his last words were: "I would suggest that we might consult Mr. Fitzmaurice."

No memorandum originating at the Foreign Office itself had yet spelled out so fully and so favorably the possibilities of a pro-Zionist policy in Palestine. O'Beirne's colleagues responded with a minor eruption of conflicting opinions. Sir Arthur Nicolson evinced a skepticism similar to that of his son. "I am not clear," he wrote the following day, "as to the strength of the Zionist movement among the Jews. I was under the impression the Zionists were in a considerable minority. As we are proposing to Russia, in conjunction with France, the placing of Palestine under an international administration we cannot advocate another scheme." Lord Eustace Percy, filled with his own Washington-gathered impressions of what world Jewish opinion might be, took a very different position, urging the Foreign Office to tell Ambassador Paul Cambon "that it has been suggested that Jewish feeling which is now hostile and favors a German protectorate over Palestine might be entirely changed if an American protectorate was formed with the object of restoring Jews to Palestine." He added that "there would have to be international control of Christian Holy Places," evidently feeling that this would be sufficient to satisfy the requirement of international administration mentioned by Sir Arthur Nicolson.

Sir Arthur went ahead and tried out the idea in conversation with Cambon, and the result was negative. Cambon said "he was sure that his Government would not be disposed to entertain the proposal, and he had very great doubts if Russia would either. I would suggest leaving it alone," Sir Arthur concluded; but strong voices differed with his. Lord Crewe, in charge again for the moment, wrote on March 3: "It is a vexed question, because even Jewish opinion is by no means unanimous upon it, but no doubt it embraces remarkable possibilities. I will take an opportunity of also speaking to M. Cambon." And Lord Robert Cecil added: "I do not think it is easy to exaggerate the international power of the Jews."

In the meantime, the Foreign Office had been hearing again from Lucien Wolf. He had been to Paris, where Victor Basch had returned with his report on American-Jewish opinion. Wolf and his colleagues on the Comité de Propagande Française auprès des Juifs Neutres—who, in common, were more concerned with the Jewish problem in Eastern Europe than with the Palestine question—had worked out a list of recommendations to make to their respective governments, and Wolf came with these on Thursday, March 2, to Lancelot Oliphant at the Foreign Office.

They began by discussing a seeming disparity between the French and the British official views regarding Jewish rights in Russia and Rumania. Wolf had the distinct impression that the French government, "so far from being unwilling to raise the subject at Petrograd," as he told Oliphant, "were prepared to make representations in case of need. The motive for this was their desire to secure the support of the American public." Oliphant challenged the correctness of Wolf's impression, but at any rate made it clear to him that the British were indeed reluctant to make such a move. Wolf and the French comité had even hoped something could be done right away to force the Russian government to grant concessions to its Jewish subjects; but Oliphant let him know that His Majesty's Government—ever mindful of the sensitivities of the unpredictable ally in the East—thought any such move at the present time "would be unwise."

For the time being, then, there were no prospects of realizing the part of Wolf's and the comité's program that dealt with Jewish rights in Eastern Europe. That left only the Zionist part. Wolf reiterated for Oliphant's benefit his view that "any tangible announcement by the British and French Governments with regard to the future of Palestine would have a most far-reaching effect in the United States." By now, even Oliphant was ready to listen sympa-

thetically to an idea that had come to assert its presence at the
Foreign Office so resoundingly of late. The upshot was that Wolf
agreed to submit a formula for a possible public declaration by the
British Government regarding Palestine.

By the next day—Friday, March 3—Wolf had composed his "Suggested Palestine Formula" and he sent a copy of it to Oliphant,
along with a draft of the letter he proposed sending with it to the
comité in Paris. He requested approval of both the formula and the
letter. The formula went:

> In the event of Palestine coming within the spheres of in-
> fluence of Great Britain or France at the close of the war, the
> Governments of those powers will not fail to take account of the
> historic interest that country possesses for the Jewish commu-
> nity. The Jewish population would be secured in the enjoyment
> of civil and religious liberty, equal political rights with the rest
> of the population, reasonable facilities for immigration and colo-
> nization, and such municipal privileges in the towns and colonies
> inhabited by them as may be shown to be necessary.

"The formula as regards Palestine," wrote a chastened Harold
Nicolson on Monday, March 6, "appears perfectly moderate and acceptable." His father, too, saw "no harm in the proposed 'formula,'"
but he thought that "before giving an imprimatur to it we should
consult the French Government—or in any case that we should inform M. Cambon and ask for his views." O'Beirne disagreed with
this, however, pointing out that the draft letter by Wolf to the comité "only says that the 'formula' has been submitted to the Foreign
Office for approval. So that in approving the draft reply we do not
approve the formula." O'Beirne therefore thought they could tell
Wolf to go ahead. But Sir Arthur Nicolson stood his ground, saying,
"I still think we ought first to consult the French—if we approve the
draft letter we practically imply that we see no objection to the
'formula.'" With that, Lord Crewe suggested, "Perhaps Sir A. Nicolson will speak to M. Cambon." Yet Crewe knew as well as everyone
else that such a consultation with Cambon the week before had
merely brought frustration on virtually the same issue. Was it to
become stalemated once again?

This time, however, Lucien Wolf was eager to provoke an outcome as soon as possible. He and the Conjoint Foreign Committee
(CFC) were being subjected more severely than ever to criticism
from the larger Jewish community—especially in the pages of the

Jewish Chronicle—on account of the continuing unrepresentativeness of his organization in the face of the world crisis. The CFC was in fact about to respond to this and enlarge its membership, and Wolf, who was beginning to fear possible loss of credibility as a Jewish spokesman, wanted to present a political achievement to the public. He made this clear in yet another letter to Oliphant, written on Monday, March 6. "Dear Mr. Oliphant," he wrote:

> On the chance of the F.O. doing anything with the suggested formula on Palestine that I sent you last week, I should like to let you know that a great Mass Meeting of Jews is to be held under my presidency, in the East End, next Sunday. Its object will be to promote a closer union in the community in face of the international crisis, and to impress, especially upon the foreign element, the necessity of making every possible sacrifice for the cause of the Allies, with which all Jewish hopes are bound up. It has occurred to me that if Sir Edward Grey entertains any suggestion of a public statement on Palestine, next Sunday's Meeting would be a good opportunity for giving it to the world. The Meeting has the support of all the leading members of the Jewish community.

Wolf was adding a significant new inducement for acceptance of his formula. Starting in January the British Government, for the first time in its history, had begun introducing conscription: as the war dragged on, the Kitchener volunteer system was proving no longer adequate in supplying recruits. But immigrants who had not been naturalized were not subject to conscription—although now, under another reversal of British tradition, they were eligible to volunteer for military service. However, as anyone involved in Jewish questions was keenly aware, there was considerable resistance among Russian-Jewish immigrants to a war effort in which the tsar was an ally. The East End was still populated by a noticeable number of able-bodied young men who neither would volunteer nor were eligible to be conscripted. No one doubted the patriotism of British Jews in general: seventeen thousand of them out of a total of a quarter of a million had volunteered by the end of 1915, many had died in battle, and three had won the Victoria Cross. But that record seemed in danger of becoming compromised when *The Times* could see fit to write in December: "There is, of course, a residuum [among young British men in general] which nothing but compulsion could possibly secure. Certain classes of young Jews in East London are among this type of men." Vladimir Jabotinsky, still agitating for a

Jewish legion, was beginning to make himself heard at the War and Foreign offices partly on account of the growing concern over this question.

Wolf's new letter arrived at the Foreign Office on March 7, just as his suggested formula on Palestine had seemed about to be put on the shelf along with his December memorandum. Its effect was to provoke a renewed sense of urgency. Lancelot Oliphant, following Wolf's lead in Jewish matters as ever, warned his colleagues in response to it that "the intangible nature of any reply returned hitherto by His Majesty's Government is arousing the suspicion of the Jews." He admitted that the French still had to be consulted before a position could be taken, but he pointed out something significant about them that Wolf had told him—namely, that the Chamber of Deputies' Foreign Affairs Commission, presided over by Georges Leygues of the comité, was more pro-Jewish and more influential in these matters than the French Foreign Ministry. He was hinting that a direct approach to Paris, and to ears there that were likely to be friendly regarding this question, was preferable to any further dealings with Ambassador Cambon in London. "Should we consult Paris," he asked, "and so inform Mr. Wolf?"

Among Oliphant's colleagues were men even more eager than he had now become to reach some conclusion on this question, but unlike him, they would not be hurried along by the personal urgencies of Mr. Lucien Wolf. "We should inform Mr. Wolf," O'Beirne told Oliphant, with Lord Crewe's approval, on Wednesday, March 8, "that his suggested 'formula' is receiving our careful and sympathetic consideration, but that we must consult our allies and that that must take time." Oliphant was to write Wolf precisely to that effect the next day, but in the meantime, O'Beirne produced another short but major memorandum on the subject.

"The one ruling consideration, as it seems to me," he wrote,

> by which we should be guided in the present stage of this matter is to be found in the answer to the question whether any of the suggestions mentioned in my minute [of February 28, in response to the Suarès proposal], or any alternative suggestions that can be put forward, would appeal powerfully to a large and influential section of Jews throughout the world. If that question is answered in the affirmative, and I believe it is so answered by good authorities, then it is clear that the Palestine scheme has in it the most far-reaching political possibilities and we should, if I may be allowed to say so, be losing a great oppor-

tunity if we did not do our utmost to overcome any difficulties that may be raised by France and Russia.

The methods, he thought, had been too halfhearted:

> So far we have confined ourselves to sounding the French Ambassador, and Monsieur Cambon, I understand, has pooh-poohed the whole idea. It was rather to be expected that Monsieur Cambon would take this attitude, but is it not possible that the result might be completely different if we placed the whole scheme in a favorable light before the French Government, explaining fully to them the political object which we hoped to attain by turning in our favor the Jewish force in America, the Near East and elsewhere, which is now largely if not preponderantly hostile to us? And would it not be possible to take steps to make use in some way of the Foreign Affairs Committee of the Chamber in Paris, which we are given to understand by Mr. Wolf would be likely to interest itself warmly in the scheme? I would suggest that we should telegraph to Lord Bertie on these lines.

O'Beirne added, with a hardheadedness equivalent to that of the India Office in its responses to the McMahon-Hussein exchanges, that "in any communications which we may address to Mr. Wolf or any other representative Jew we should be careful to make it clear that we do not propose to give the Jews a privileged position in Palestine for nothing, but that we should expect whole-hearted support from them in return."

These suggestions had a decisive impact—even upon Sir Arthur Nicolson, whose only objections to them were the aspersions they cast upon his contacts with Ambassador Cambon. It was the Suarès proposal that Cambon had pooh-poohed, he pointed out, "not the general assurance asked for by Mr. Wolf of which M. Cambon has, as yet, no knowledge." The Suarès proposal had been for a British protectorate of Palestine, "modified by us to an American protectorate," and Nicolson thought it should be excluded from any discussion of Wolf's formula with the French government. Regarding Wolf's formula, he said, "we must clearly consult our allies—especially in view of the fact that we are discussing the future of Palestine at Petrograd." Here he was referring to the mission of Sykes and Picot, who were at that moment in Petrograd explaining the terms of their accord to the Russian government. Part of their agenda there was a discussion of the envisioned political nature of the Brown Area. "I think we might ask Paris and Petrograd," Nicolson went on, "whether they see any objection to the formula, pointing out to both the advantages which could be caused to the Allies by having a sympathetic attitude on the part of the Jews as outlined in the O'Beirne minute."

Lord Crewe concurred in this entirely. "I am quite clear," he said, "that this matter ought not to be put aside, and I think Sir Edward Grey is of the same opinion. It is a difficult question, because Jewish opinion is considerably divided about it," he observed once again, echoing his remarks of the previous Friday, and this time adding, "and Mr. L. Wolf cannot be taken as the spokesman of the whole community." Crewe knew both poles of the community on this subject—at least through his wife, whose mother had been a Rothschild, and who in recent months had become friendly with Chaim and Vera Weizmann. He had himself responded favorably to Dorothy de Rothschild's presentation of Weizmann's views to him in November 1914, and he knew perfectly well that Lucien Wolf could not be taken seriously as a spokesman for Zionism, whatever some of his associates at the Foreign Office may have felt on that subject.

His feelings in this respect were shared by that other scion of nobility in their midst, Lord Robert Cecil, who was to respond to Crewe's remarks less than a week later by saying: "May I add that if and when we are allowed by our allies to say anything worth saying to the Jews it should not be left to Mr. Lucien Wolf to say it?" Wolf, who had been producing a steady stream of letters to Cecil as well as to Oliphant in recent weeks, had perhaps overplayed his hand. "I quite approve of the proposed reply," Crewe wrote of O'Beirne's suggestion to Oliphant that he send a standoff to Wolf's letter of Monday, March 6, which had started this present round of discussion, but which Crewe was ready to put aside indefinitely now that it had made its point. "But we ought to pursue the subject," he went on, "since the advantage of securing Jewish goodwill in the Levant and in America can hardly be overestimated, both at present and at the conclusion of the war. And we ought to help Russia to realize this."

Lord Crewe himself then prepared the draft of a letter about Palestine to be sent to Lord Bertie and Sir George Buchanan, the British ambassadors in Paris and in Petrograd. "It has been suggested to us," he wrote, that if we could offer the Jews an arrangement in regard to Palestine completely satisfactory to Jewish aspirations, such an offer might appeal strongly to a large and powerful section of the Jewish community throughout the world, although it is true that a considerable number of Jews are known to be indifferent to the idea of Zionism. If the above view is correct it is clear that the Zionist idea has in it the most far reaching political possibilities, for we might hope to use it in such a way as to bring over to our side the Jewish forces in America, the East and elsewhere which are now largely if not preponderantly hostile to us.

Crewe went on: "The following definition of Jewish aspirations in regard to Palestine has been submitted to us by Mr. Lucien Wolf," and he proceeded to give the formula word for word. At the end he added that it "seems to us unobjectionable but we have confined ourselves to telling Mr. Wolf that it would receive our sympathetic consideration and that we must consult our Allies about it."

Then comes a remarkable paragraph:

We consider, however, that the scheme might be made far more attractive to the majority of Jews if it held out to them the prospect that when in course of time the Jewish colonists in Palestine grow strong enough to cope with the Arab population they may be allowed to take the management of the internal affairs of Palestine (with the exception of Jerusalem and the Holy Places) into their own hands.

But for the lack of nationalist rhetoric, this was out-and-out Zionism, going far beyond anything Lucien Wolf had cared to consider. Where had it suddenly come from? Clearly it had been produced by the combination of Crewe, Cecil, and O'Beirne that was now taking the initiative on the Palestine issue at the Foreign Office. All three had shown a tendency to disparage Lucien Wolf's claims as a spokesman on the issue, and O'Beirne had formulated the essence of this crucial paragraph by Crewe in his own memorandum on the Suarès proposal less than two weeks before. As for Cecil and Crewe, there is every reason to assume that they had been strongly influenced by the ideas of Chaim Weizmann.

Crewe, unlike Cecil, had not met Weizmann personally, but his wife had done so the previous June and had seen the Weizmanns socially from time to time since the beginning of the year, when they had resettled in London. At the time of their first meeting Weizmann had subjected Lady Crewe to another of his ardent discourses on Zionism and had followed it up with an equally ardent letter that her husband undoubtedly read. The effect this had on Lady Crewe was to be recorded by Vera Weizmann in her diary on March 20, 1916—some nine or ten days after this letter by Lord Crewe with its Zionist paragraph. According to the entry, Dorothy de Rothschild told of having overheard a conversation about Zionism between Lady Crewe and Lord Robert Cecil. Madame de Rothschild said that Lady Crewe had, in the course of it, asked Lord Robert whether the time was ripe to start a Zionist campaign, and had observed: "We are all 'Weizmannites' in this house." There is no way of knowing whether this conversation took place before or after Lord Crewe's letter to Bertie and Buchanan, but it certainly was at about the same time, and it vividly bespeaks the climate of feeling—on the part of both Crewe and Cecil—within which the letter was written.

But what about Sir Edward Grey? What role was played by the foreign secretary himself in the formulation and dispatch of this letter? Crewe wrote it between March 8 and 11—the latter being the day it was wired, in its final, corrected form, to Paris and Petrograd—but though the draft contains a marginal comment by Sir Arthur Nicolson, there is nothing on it to indicate it was read or commented upon by Grey. Indeed, though the record shows Grey to have been present at the Foreign Office the following week, when the responses from Paris and Petrograd were to begin coming in, there is no sign of his having been present during this crucial week of March 6 through 11, which began with the arrival of Lucien Wolf's formula and ended with Lord Crewe's pro-Zionist amendment to it. The fact that March 11, the day of the final redaction and dispatch of the letter, was a Saturday, makes it all the more likely that Grey was simply not around as this development took place.

Would it have occurred had he been there? One can only guess; but everything about Grey's extremely cautious relation to Zionism from the time of his first conversations about it with Herbert Samuel suggests that he probably would have preferred to stop at Wolf's formula and go no further. Possibly he might not have felt ready to send the formula out at all.

Sir Arthur Nicolson, in his comments on Crewe's draft, had nothing to say about the Zionist-leaning amendment, which therefore remained intact. Nicolson took issue only with a subsequent paragraph in which Crewe, suggesting that some influential Jewish opinion would be opposed to an international protectorate, had mentioned the idea of a possible American one over Palestine instead.

Nicolson thought the American reference was more than was necessary for the moment, and Crewe obligingly deleted it, writing in its place that "we do not desire to state a preference."

The first response to the letter, which was wired at 7:00 P.M. on Saturday, came on Tuesday, March 14, from Sir George Buchanan in Petrograd. Foreign Minister Sazonov, he wrote, "raises no objection to the scheme in principle, but sees great difficulties in the way of its execution. Though Russian Government would welcome migration of Jews to Palestine, he doubts whether any considerable number of them would care to settle there. He will send me answer after a thorough examination of the question." Buchanan was to follow this up the next day confirming the Russian government's sympathy with the proposal, provided that the Holy Places were definitely excluded from the scheme and placed under international control. But meanwhile, a more vivid response to Crewe's letter had also come from Petrograd; cabled out on Tuesday night, it arrived at the Foreign Office at eleven the next morning. It was a long letter from Sir Mark Sykes.

·24·

SYKES DISCOVERS
A NEW ENTHUSIASM

After their draft agreement had been ratified by the French government on February 8, Sykes and Picot faced as their next major task that of explaining it to the Russians. They were to be in Petrograd at the beginning of March. Meanwhile, Sykes, established in a London town house opposite Buckingham Palace, went to work developing possibilities out of the agreement that were not explicitly in the text. Captain Hall's Admiralty memorandum, with its insistence that the Zionist factor had to be considered in regard to the Brown Area, clearly had made an impression upon him, for he now got together with Herbert Samuel.

Since his return to the cabinet as chancellor of the Duchy of Lancaster in November, Samuel had been back in the ascendant. In January he had been appointed home secretary, replacing Sir John Simon, who resigned in protest when conscription was introduced. Presiding over the office that dealt with the affairs of aliens, Samuel now had to deal with the delicate question of the Jewish immigrants and military service. No doubt he recognized the potentially significant connections between this question and his Palestine memorandum of the previous March.

In their conversation toward the end of February, Samuel gave Sykes a fresh copy of the memorandum; Sykes surely had seen it in his days on the de Bunsen Committee, but his memory of it would have needed refreshment by now. "I read the memorandum," he subsequently wrote to Samuel on February 26, "and have committed it to memory and destroyed it—as no print or other papers can pass the R[ussian] Frontier except in the F.O. bag." Evidently he foresaw the possibility of discussing the Zionist question in Petrograd, though he had not yet received any authorization to do so. Some aspects of the question as he had discussed it with Samuel were still on his mind. "There is one suggestion which I forgot to mention to you," he went on in his letter, recalling something Picot had urged in January, "at least I did not put it properly, that is that Belgium should assume the administration [of Palestine] as the trustee of the Entente Powers. I have no personal opinion on the merits of this, but I believe that it might be more acceptable to France as an alternative to an international administration." Samuel must have pressed hard his old arguments against international and in favor of British control, but Sykes knew better than anyone how hard the French would resist this, and he was in search of alternatives. The American alternative about to start appearing in Foreign Office memoranda two days later had not yet reached him—but perhaps it had not yet surfaced at the Foreign Office, either.

Samuel and Sykes evidently had devoted a good part of their discussion to the boundaries of the Brown Area, with Samuel noting how far short they fell of the traditional limits of Palestine. In the east, its frontier was the Jordan, even though the Palestine Exploration Fund had devoted an entire volume to an eastern Palestine that began on the other side of that river and extended roughly to the line since marked by the Hejaz railway. In the southeast, its boundary with the British-influenced Area B curved upward from the Egyptian frontier below Gaza to the northwest corner of the Dead Sea in such a way as to exclude Hebron, one of the traditional Holy Cities of Judaism. But "I think on the whole," Sykes insisted in his letter,

> that the boundaries as marked are more favorable than if they were wider. By excluding Hebron and the East of the Jordan there is less to discuss with the Moslems, as the Mosque of Omar then becomes the only matter of vital importance to discuss with them and further does away with any contact with the Bedouin, who never cross the river except on business.

Surely Samuel had also pointed out that the northern boundary of the Brown Area cut off the Jewish settlements of the northern Galilee; but that again brought up the problem of the French. For the moment, Sykes could not bring himself to deal with the boundaries question any more. "I imagine," he went on hopefully, "that the principal object of Zionism is the realization of the ideal of an existing center of nationality rather than boundaries or extent of territory." And he concluded: "The moment I return, I will let you know how things stand at P[etrogra]d." He left on February 29.

Sykes was to keep his promise to Samuel, for Lord Crewe's telegram of March 11 to Petrograd suddenly turned the Zionist issue into one of the major ones preoccupying him. His reply of March 14 was an outburst of Sykesian intellectual energy that was bound to cause a stir at the Foreign Office, not least of all because of its revelation that he had described the contents of Crewe's message to Picot. "M. Picot," he wrote, "on hearing the sense of telegram made loud exclamations and spoke of pogroms in Paris." Picot then had calmed down, but had gone on maintaining that "France would grow excited." Sykes had tried to urge upon him the "inestimable advantages to Allied cause of active friendship of Jews of the world, force of which he reluctantly admitted." But Sykes added in his telegram to the Foreign Office that the Zionists "should, I submit, give some demonstration of their power; accentuation of German financial straits and glow of pro-Allied sentiment in certain hitherto anti-Ally neutral papers would be sufficient indication."

Sykes then developed his thoughts on the whole subject. "In ascertaining," he went on,

> what Zionists will accept and what refuse, I am guided by your telegram coupled with my memory of Mr. Samuel's memorandum to the Cabinet in March 1915. Telegram says international regime unacceptable, memorandum says French dominion equally unacceptable. As against this, French (if Picot represents them correctly) would never consent to England having temporary or provisional charge of Palestine; not even if we offered Cyprus as a gift and appointed French Governors for Jerusalem, Bethlehem, Nazareth and Jaffa. They seem hardly normal on this subject and any reference seems to excite memories of all grievances from Joan of Arc to Fashoda.

He then mentioned the possible Belgian solution, which Picot had brought up again in their Petrograd conversation about Palestine, this time suggesting that the Belgian monarch have the title of king of Jerusalem. "I deem this opens Arab difficulty," Sykes commented, "that is, alien Christian King introduced into Arab land."

Sykes now addressed himself to the "Arab difficulty," remembering how, in Cairo the previous fall, al-Faruqi and Dr. Faris Nimr both had told him that "Arabs, Christians and Moslems alike, would fight in the matter to the last man against Jewish dominion in Palestine." He speculated that the

> Shereef will be in the position to say to us, "You propose to introduce idolatrous Indians into Mesopotamia to oust Moslem Arabs, impose French rule in Syria to Frenchify Arab Christians, and now decide to flood Palestine with Jews to drive out Arabs whether Moslems or Christians. Turks and Germans are preferable."

But he quickly added: "I only mention these matters to demonstrate difficulties and dangers. I deem problem soluble and think there is room for compromise."

Having reached this point, Sykes would have violated his exuberant nature had he stopped short of formulating a possible solution. And so he offered one, in detail:

> Following seems to me to go some way in all directions.
> 1. Arrange with Shereef to appoint one of sons of Abdul [Kader?]* or one of his own sons independent Sultan of Palestine.
> 2. Russians to agree to France and Great Britain being guarantors of independent Sultanate.
> 3. Incorporation [in constitution of] new State of privileged chartered Company, purchasing land for the purposes of [Zionist] colonization including settlement of terms under which Company's colonists become citizens of State and cease to be alien subjects, thus covering Wolf's demands.
> 4. Agreement satisfactory to Russia and France in regard to administration and status of Holy Places.
> 5. That Great Britain should be arbitrator in any question arising between land Company and Palestine Government.
> 6. That France should be arbitrator in any question arising between administration of Holy Places and Palestine Government.

"I regret complicated problem requires complex settlement," he added, "but under above, France gets a position in Palestine, Russian demands are satisfied, Arabs have a Prince, Zionists get consti-

---

* Here and in paragraph 3 I have offered guesses where the text was garbled in the telegraphic transmission. Abdel Kader, whose ancestor and namesake was the hero of Algerian resistance to French rule, had settled in Damascus and become a spokesman for Syrian nationalism.

tutional position and have British protection, which I understand
they desire."

The men at the Foreign Office were not taken in by this vision
of a Jewish state being allowed to grow like a cuckoo within the nest
of an Arab principality. "It is clear," wrote Harold Nicolson, the first
to read the message, "that the chartered Jewish Company suggested
by Sir M. Sykes would very soon gain complete administrative, financial and executive authority in the new state, but our real object
in raising the question is to find something with which to dazzle
Jewish opinion—and I much doubt whether an Arab Sultanate would
have that effect." Oliphant went a step further, saying, "I believe
that in execution the Arab Sultan would certainly wreck the
scheme." O'Beirne offered the most authoritative of the minutes. "In
the first place," he wrote, "put out privately to Sir G. Buchanan that
the matter should not have been discussed by Sir M. Sykes with M.
Picot." Then he took care of Sykes's Palestine sultanate by dismiss-
ing it without mention: "It is evident," he wrote,

> that Jewish colonization of Palestine must conflict to some ex-
> tent with Arab interests. All we can do, if and when the time
> comes to discuss details, is to try to devise a settlement which
> will involve as little hardship as possible to the Arab population.
> We shall then of course have to consult experts, but meanwhile
> we cannot enter into a discussion with Sir Mark Sykes at Petro-
> grad on the subject.

This led Sir Arthur Nicolson to conclude: "There is no necessity at
this moment to reply to these observations." Sir Arthur also noted in
the margin his agreement with O'Beirne that Buchanan should be
reminded of Sykes's indiscretion, and this provoked Sir Edward
Grey himself to add: "and also ask Sir G. Buchanan to tell Sir Mark
S. to obliterate from his memory that Mr. Samuel's Cabinet Memorandum made any mention of a British protectorate. I told Mr. Samuel at the time that a British Protectorate was quite out of the
question and Sir M. Sykes should never mention the subject without
making this clear." Back at his post this week, Grey also was back to
his old position on Palestine, to wit: what will the French say? Cling-
ing resolutely to this concern, he seems almost to have been oblivious
to the previous week's outburst of Zionism at the Foreign Office.

The appropriate message was sent to Petrograd, but Sykes in
the meantime had not ceased pondering the Palestine question and
putting his ideas to the telegraph. Wiring on the night of March 16

that the French and the Russians were in nearly complete agreement on the limits of their respective claims in Anatolia, he could not resist adding:

> As regards Arabs and Zionists greatest caution is now requisite as a slip in either direction might imperil scheme.
> Dangers in regard to Zionists are (1) they may make a premature move . . . (2) they may dislike suggested settlement and overthrow project, which is in their power to do. I suggest that Zionists be carefully sounded and kept in hope of sympathetic decision. I believe we can get them full colonizing facilities coupled with their rights in an enlarged Palestine. We cannot get them either political control of Jerusalem within the walls of the city nor any scheme tending thereto.

O'Beirne, for one, was beginning to find all this creative exuberance on the banks of the Neva a bit trying. "I hope that our telegram of March 16 will have had a quieting effect on Sir Mark Sykes," he wrote, and added: "As regards his reference to the Zionist scheme, it need only be said that nobody proposes to give the Jews 'political control' of Jerusalem, and that to speak of the Zionists 'making a move' of any kind seems quite premature."

The next day, Sir George Buchanan sent to London the outlines of the Russian accord with the agreement between Sykes and Picot, which included this acquiescence in the newly introduced Zionist factor: "As regards Palestine, Russian Government agree to any proposal which should assure to all Orthodox establishments in the Holy Land free exercise of their religion and maintenance of their acquired rights and privileges, and they have no objection in principle to the admission of Jewish colonists to the country." Two hours later, Buchanan also forwarded Sykes's reply to the chastening message that had been sent to him on the sixteenth. "My informal discussion of Zionism with Picot unavoidable," Sykes said, "owing to M. de Sazonov showing French Ambassador and Picot Embassy memorandum embodying your telegram [of March 11]." Furthermore, he maintained, the subject "did not come as a surprise to Picot as when we were in London I told him to expect Zionists to move in London when they knew he and I were at Petrograd." This was a startling notion, since there was not a single Zionist at this time who could have known of the secret agreement between Sykes and Picot, much less that they were going to Petrograd to discuss it. Sykes probably meant Herbert Samuel—not precisely a Zionist, but the closest thing to one Sykes had yet encountered. But all Samuel did while Sykes and Picot were in Petrograd was to circulate, on March 16, copies of his old memorandum "to those Members of the Cabinet who did not then belong to it"—something he felt impelled to do "in view of the discussions now taking place on the subject of Palestine."

Sykes concluded his defense by addressing himself to Sir Edward Grey's criticism of him, saying: "I have never mentioned Palestine to Picot without making it clear that His Majesty's Government have not idea [sic] to protect Palestine, but I could not keep [from] discussing difficulty arising out of Zionists' known desire for British protection clashing with French susceptibilities." It was with this difficulty in view, he went on, that "Picot and I jointly and informally sketched solution suggested by my telegram of March 14." Sykes further pointed out that he and Picot had discussed the matter again that morning, and that Picot was quite satisfied with point 3 of the plan—the one regarding the Zionist chartered company. As for point 5, granting Britain special status in relation to the chartered company, Sykes said that Picot "hesitates but admits he might get French Government to fall in with it on the ground that it might materially help in the war." By now, French troops were fully engaged in the frightful slaughter at Verdun and were more than ever in need of an English ally whose public had begun to evince scattered protests at continuing in the war at all.

This was Sykes's last communication from Petrograd. He left that afternoon, traveling to Moscow and thence to Tiflis and Baku, probably to interview more Turkish army prisoners. But he had not finished devoting a great deal of thought to Palestine.

Sykes had found a new enthusiasm; but what within his nature had given rise to this interest in Zionism? On the surface of it, the record of his utterances on the subject of Jews until now was of a character that some would even have called anti-Semitic. Indeed, like that other recent convert to Jewish nationalism, David Lloyd George, he had found justification in the Boer War for occasional outbursts against Jews. "British colonists are liars or Jews," he had written in one angry letter to a friend while serving in South Africa in 1900; and to his fiancée Edith Gorst he wrote, momentarily despairing that the militia would ever be sent home again, even after the war's end, "O dear no! They will find the Militia so useful, probably, in building farms for the returned prisoners, or, if there is a dearth of Kaffir labor, to dig the mines for the Jews at Johannesburg!" Another, rather "literary," letter from South Africa listed with resentment the ways in which this world of colonial adventures was not at all like the one Kipling had described: "and as for the speech of women talking to men," he added, "if it gives pleasure to some to see sleek, fat Jews and their womenkind talking to one another, I am not one of those."

Among the vast array of cartoons that Sykes had dashed off in the course of his life so far, there inevitably were those depicting Jews in the spirit of that last remark. One entitled "The Diaspora" seems to have been meant as a scathing rendition of what some of Sykes's contemporaries might have, in moments of extreme anti-Semitic lunacy, referred to as the "Judaization" of Britain: it shows, lined up as though in the lobby of the House of Commons, "A Boy of the Bull-Dog Breed," "An Earnest Christian," "A Sinn Feiner," "An Ulster Loyalist," and "A Welsh Nationalist"—all in full-nosed "Jew-ish" profiles and front views that in our day too readily recall the cartooning styles of the Nazi era. Such types recur, with similarly heavy-handed intent, in other Sykes cartoons.

The ever-present spirit of the cartoonist can even be found in this passage in Sykes's 1904 travel book, *Dar ul-Islam*, when he described the Jews of a community he had visited in northern Meso-potamia:

> The Jews at Nisibin form a large and important Israelite colony: their origin is only noticeable in their large unshapely hands and long flat feet; and their appearance is much improved by oriental costume, in which any man with thick nose, dark hair, full beard, and Semitic lips looks noble and dignified. It is indeed a pity that their brethren at home have assumed Euro-pean attire. Imagine how picturesque and interesting a walk in the City near the Stock Exchange would become; what a blaze of color Chapel Court would be if the children of Israel retained their ancient and handsome dress!

The point had thoroughly captured his pictorial imagination, and he could not resist the temptation to elaborate on it:

> Young Salmon, the outside broker, canoeing on the river with Lewis McTaggart, in red Kaffieh and green garments, would be a much more pleasing spectacle than those gentlemen now present in ill-conceived blazers and striking flannels. I trust that the Uganda Zionists will adopt my suggestion.

Indeed, some of the Zionist friends whom Sykes was soon to acquire, eager to explain away his early follies on the subject of Jews, were to see the incipient Zionist in a passage like this, with its preference for a true Hebrew—albeit romanticized—over the "105 percent" Englishmen of the stock exchange.

There was even some truth to this view of the early Sykes. A true Tory radical, Sykes was a great admirer of Disraeli—"that mighty genius," he once called him—and wrote to a friend upon reading *Tancred* in 1907: "It is very wonderful. I suppose you have read it superficially; it is 'the fatal fascination of the East and all that sort of thing,' but there is a vast deal behind it. The true backbone of it is, of course, the Semitic and the nature-worshiper. But with all the glory . . . Dizzy grasped the Syrian, the Levantine and the Bedawi." Sykes had grasped some of the essential elements of the Zionist romance; yet this had made him in no way sympathetic to it before the war. As late as 1913, in the course of another of his scathing summaries of the mistakes of the Young Turk regime, he had written: "Zionism was backed because it was bad cosmopolitanism and finance."

Perhaps one way to understanding the contrast between Sykes's prewar jeering at Jews and the sympathy with their national ideals that began arising in him in 1916 is to ponder the well-known playfulness of his nature. "His instincts lay in parody," T.E. Lawrence has already told us, and in his younger days these instincts notably applied themselves to many of the things that ultimately were to concern him the most. They dominated his early perceptions of the peoples of the Middle East no matter whom he wrote about. When, in his 1900 book of travels, *Through Five Turkish Provinces*, he described his part-Cypriote dragoman Isa Kubrusli as saying of the Jews, "dis man is more vile more dirty more beas'ly from all de world because he dirty like Rooshan and robber like Armenian," the twenty-one-year-old author was allowing himself to be amused at everyone's expense, including that of Isa with his funny "Henglish." In this passage, Sykes also is making fun of Russians and Armenians—indeed, the irreverent young man was worst of all on the subject of Armenians, another people to whose national cause he was to devote himself during the war, and about whom he saw fit to write in this book: "I feel such an intense prejudice against Armenians that I am certain that anything I might say would only be biassed and therefore not worth reading, and I think anyone who has had dealings of any kind with this abominable race would probably be in the same position. . . . Even Jews have their good points but Armenians have none." Sykes wrote this only a few years after the Armenians had suffered the first of what was to be a long series of terrible massacres at the hands of the Turks, but for him this seems only to have reinforced an impression of "cowardice," of "senseless untruthfulness," and of depth of "intrigue" on the part of the victims.

Nor did the Arab—the third of the trio of peoples whose aspirations would occupy Sykes's attention during the war—escape the occasionally vitriolic outlook of the caricaturist in those early days. Evidently, his callowness was as irrepressible as his gifts in those days, and he was satisfied to be most indiscreet in the formulation and free expression—even for publication—of his instinctually parodic view of things. He also directed some of his barbs at Englishmen of his own class, but the differences in vulnerability between them and Jews or Armenians do not seem to have greatly impressed themselves upon this privileged young man. As a Catholic in England, he saw everything around him with the eye of an ironic outsider; but as the heir to vast estates and tenant rolls, his irony seems to have taken on a special tinge toward those he saw below him in the social or ethnic hierarchy.

The war changed him, as it changed everyone. The callowness had begun to depart years before—perhaps from the moment he entered Parliament—and by 1916 the superciliousness had gone, too. As far back as the Boer War, Sykes had learned to respect the ordinary English soldier, and the fact that men of this sort were sacrificing their lives by the tens of thousands on the soil of France and of Flanders was bound to affect him with new realizations about social justice, as it did all men of conscience. Two qualities remained of the boyish wanderer and anthropological caricaturist of his early days, but deepened and raised onto a new level at the same time. One was the genuine acuteness of his perceptions of human groups and their capacities to respond to given situations, present or to come. This was the mark of a caricaturist turned statesman and social observer; by 1916 the youthful irreverence veering over into occasional nastiness that once had accompanied it was, if not overcome completely, at least pushed back into its proper place among the darker recesses of his character. The other quality was the capacity for enthusiastic and brilliantly creative, if at times overimpulsive, outbursts. This trait could be trying, but even in its more outlandish moments—and despite T.E. Lawrence's enduring dislike of it—it never ceased serving as the fuel driving Sykes himself and others around him in the direction of some bold and ultimately lasting realization.

The touch of the privileged boy was still there; indeed, Sykes had already begun treating the Middle East as if it were simply some vaster, more exotic Sledmere for him to administer. But the passion to make his estate a repository of justice and human fulfill-ment to be admired by all mankind had grown great in him. He seems to have wanted to reinstate upon the rolls of landed nobility the very peoples of the Middle East whom he, and history, had lately scorned. He became a supporter of their nationalisms the way many another man of privileged background became a Socialist, doubtless sparked by more than a touch of guilt toward the very people who had once been the objects of an unthinking, childish snobbery on his part.

Sykes was traveling in the interior of Russia on March 22, when Lord Bertie's reply finally came to Crewe's letter of the eleventh. It showed the French government to be a little less acquiescent in the matter than Picot had been in Petrograd. "Ministry for Foreign Affairs considers it is a question," Bertie cabled,

> whether scheme would really have the influence on Jewish com-munity which is anticipated, as attitude of those of community who are hostile to Allies is inspired by motives which have noth-ing in common with Zionist aspirations, realization of which would not remove those motives.

In Victor Basch's report on American-Jewish attitudes, which had unquestionably been seen at the Quai d'Orsay, stress had been laid almost exclusively upon labor organizations and the Yiddish Social-ist press, where Zionism hardly was rife. Waving aside all suspicion that the Yiddish papers were receiving German money, Basch had pointed out that such a man as Abraham Cahan, editor of the *Jewish Daily Forward,* was "nettement pro-German par sentiment juif." Such people, he said, would become pro-Ally when Russia did some-thing to alleviate the lot of its Jews.

M. Briand and his colleagues also had suddenly begun thinking about the Arab aspect of the question. "Moreover," Bertie went on,

> solution of problem as set forth presents serious difficulties and establishment of such a scheme would run particular risk of awakening susceptibilities of Arabs whom it is advisable to

treat with caution; and to this point President of the Council desires to draw very special attention of British Government, and he is of opinion that consideration of scheme could not be usefully taken up until after question of creation of Arab Empire has been solved.

At the Foreign Office, this letter caused Lancelot Oliphant to revert to his old uncertainty about Zionism and to his tendency to endorse Lucien Wolf in all Jewish-related matters. "The view herein expressed in paragraph 1," he minuted on Bertie's letter, "appears to me to have much force. Certainly Mr. Wolf and his gang [sic] are bent on more material amelioration of Jews in European countries, rather than on Zionism."

But Wolf was now being studiously ignored by Oliphant's colleagues, and O'Beirne minuted once again in terms of his wonted pro-Zionist position. "The first paragraph of the French reply," he wrote,

> seems to me rather to beg the main question at stake. If it is the case that the Zionist scheme does not appeal to any large and influential section of the Jews throughout the world, who are now antagonistic to our cause, then I agree that the whole scheme had better be dropped. But our information so far as I know is not to that effect.

French and British intelligence simply differed on this point, and that was to be that from now on. It must be added that if the American mission of M. Basch, speaking French, Yiddish, German, and only a little English, was an example of how French intelligence was working on the subject, then the British had good reason to prefer their own.

As for the Arab question raised by the French prime minister, this, O'Beirne went on,

> appears to have more force in it. It must be admitted that if the Arabs knew we were contemplating an extensive Jewish colonization scheme in Palestine (with the possible prospect of eventual Jewish self-government), this might have a very chilling effect on the Arab leaders. The difficulty ought not, however, to be regarded as insoluble, and a good deal depends on the value which we attach to the military cooperation which the Arabs are likely to give us in the war. I had always assumed that this value must be placed very low.

Indeed, there are signs that London had by now given up altogether on the prospects of an Arab revolt. This was one of the reasons why the possibility of worldwide Jewish cooperation in recognition of a pro-Zionist policy had come to be so strenuously considered in recent weeks. It represented an alternative way of gaining strength for Great Britain in the Middle East. "I hope," O'Beirne concluded, anticipating the Grand Council meeting between the French and British premiers, foreign ministers, and other high officials that was due to take place in a few days, "we shall be able to talk over the whole Palestine question with the French when in Paris." O'Beirne himself was to accompany Sir Edward Grey to this meeting.

For the time being, then, though Sykes and Picot were no longer quite the plenipotentiaries they had been at the beginning of the year, they alone carried on whatever Anglo-French discussion there was of the Palestine question. Sykes was now as determined to make this a matter of his personal initiatives as he had been in November with respect to the Arab national movement. Within twenty-four hours of his arrival in London on April 10, he got in touch again with Herbert Samuel.

·25·

SYKES AND GASTER:
AN INTERLUDE

"**H.** Samuel rang up," Dr. Moses Gaster recorded in his diary for Tuesday, April 11, 1916. "Important changes foreshadowed in our Palestine work. Asks whether I could come with Waizman [*sic*] Friday or Sunday. I suggested Sokolow to him and he willingly agreed. Hearing of my illness he offered to come here. I thanked and rang up Sokolow."

Having just heard from Sykes, freshly returned from Russia with his plan for Palestine, Samuel now wanted to relay that plan to his Zionist contacts. Significantly—though he seems to have called Weizmann too—he had turned to Gaster right away. As ever, the Zionist leader to whom Samuel felt closest and into whose hands he was most ready to place important considerations was Gaster, even though the latter remained a solitary figure within English Zionism and was not particularly trusted either by the controlling Cowen-Greenberg faction of the English Zionist Federation (EZF) or by the ascending Weizmann group. What Gaster continued to have was the prestige of being the Sephardic chief rabbi of Great Britain and—owing to his youthful contacts with Laurence Oliphant in Rumania, his early embracing of Herzl, and his one-time incumbency as president of the EZF—the authority of a Zionist elder statesman. Now sixty years old, he was an imposing figure of a man, with a great white prophet's beard and a grandiose rabbinical platform style; he was an effective speaker and a profuse writer, whether of polemics or of learned historical discourses. Samuel was not the only British statesman still inclined to feel that Gaster perhaps was naturally the man—or at least one of the men—to assume the leadership of Zionism at whatever moment the Allies might be ready to treat with that movement as a legitimate political entity.

Gaster, who clearly also foresaw this possibility for himself, did not, however, wish to have any rivals who were British, whether born as such or naturalized. He was as eager to keep Weizmann down as he was to undermine the claims of Cowen and Greenberg, and he kept his activities as secret from Weizmann as Weizmann kept his own activities from the chief rabbi. The one viable link between them was Sokolow—who, since Tschlenow's permanent return to Russia the previous summer, was the highest official representative of the worldwide Zionist organization in England, and who had the additional virtue of not being a British subject and hence not too serious a rival to either Weizmann or Gaster. Now settled in the newly opened Regent Palace Hotel in Piccadilly Circus—his friends took to calling it the "Regent Palestine"—Sokolow was quietly carrying on work as best he could, addressing Zionist meetings, doing research in the British Museum, and seeing men of influence whenever it was possible to do so. In fact, he had just made contact with the Foreign Office when Samuel called Gaster to arrange a meeting over Sykes's proposal.

Sokolow's contact was with Henry A. Cumberbatch, who had been consul general in Beirut from 1908 to the outbreak of war with Turkey and had since come to work at the Foreign Office. Cumberbatch had met Sokolow in the winter of 1913-14 when the latter was visiting Palestine and Syria; the introductions had been made by the Beirut branch manager of the Anglo-Palestine Company. Cumberbatch's impression of Sokolow on that occasion had been favorable, and when Sokolow came to see him at the Foreign Office at around the beginning of April, he made a note about the matter for his colleagues. He suggested that, if "enquiries at the Russian Embassy show that Mr. S. is what he appears to be, a respectable and important person," he might be someone to provide "information as to anything that may be going on in Jewish circles."

Harold Nicolson responded by suggesting that Sokolow's "views might be interesting in connection with the question of the proportion of Jews who have Zionist aspirations, about which we and the Russian Government appear to have divergent views"—this last being a reference to Sir George Buchanan's response of March 14 to Lord Crewe's proposal about Palestine. Lancelot Oliphant proposed that Cumberbatch ask Sokolow for a memorandum, and Cumberbatch replied on April 6: "I will see Mr. Sokolow and ask him for a

Memorandum on the proportion of 'Zionists' in Palestine"—which was not what the younger Nicolson had in mind. An estimate of the number of Zionists or potential ones in the world would have been far more useful to the Foreign Office, though extremely difficult—if not impossible—to make.

On Thursday, April 13—two days after Samuel's telephone call to Gaster—Sokolow submitted to the Foreign Office a handwritten summary on the Jews of Palestine and their political outlook, along with a typewritten memorandum on "England as the Protective Power for Palestine." The handwritten report divided the Jewish population of Palestine into two roughly equal-sized parts: (1) "The old inhabitants of the country, the strict orthodox Jews (Ashkenazim and Sephardim)," and (2) "the new element who arrived during the last generation (from Russia, Poland, Roumania) and the young generation of the old inhabitants." The first class had no influence on the country's future, Sokolow said, but the second was politically important and represented "the Jewish masses who aim at immigration to Palestine." They "are the men of the future and they are as one in the desire of establishing a Jewish Commonwealth, with preference of an English protectorate."

The second memorandum, which evidently had been in Sokolow's drawer awaiting its moment, pursued that last point, so dear to its author's heart—for Sokolow, with a disregard for his supposed neutrality as a member of the Zionist executive equal to that of his counterparts in Berlin, was now emerging as the most passionate of Anglophiles. "The Jewish population of Palestine," it began, "has ever considered England to be, from the Jewish point of view, the best Protective Power for Palestine," and then it proceeded to explain why. England is the country that has shown herself able to administer dependencies "in a sensible and generous spirit," the country that "protects and does not oppress" and that carries out in her colonies "the same principles which made the mother country so good and so powerful." Furthermore, he wrote, turning to the themes of some of his current research and writing, "it was England's noble and far-seeing sons who dreamed, spoke and wrote of restoring the Jewish land to the Jewish people long before the modern Zionist movement arose in the Jewish people itself."

Lest ideals not seem enough, however, Sokolow also listed the "material and political" values that would accrue to Britain if she had Palestine within her orbit. This soon-flourishing province would strengthen Britain's position on the Mediterranean, and the great commercial houses certain to be established in it would bring advantages to Britain first among outside nations. Sokolow also did not neglect to mention the effect British protection of a Jewish Palestine would have upon influential Jewish opinion all over the world, especially in America. Reverting to geopolitics, he mentioned the protection that would be afforded the Suez Canal and the "separating wall" that would be formed "between the Arab population of Asia and Northern Africa," which could not fail to be of significance "for a Power that possesses Arab subjects." Finally, he said, the "Jewish element, through the introduction of European civilization, will contribute to the elevating and strengthening of these peoples and provinces, in accordance with British ideals." He ended with a brief historical summary of the Anglo-Jewish relationship in Palestine, including mentions of Palmerston, Moses Montefiore, Consuls Young and Finn, and the Anglo-Palestine Company.

Cumberbatch passed on these two memoranda at the Foreign Office and attached a note. "Mr. Sokolow has shown me," he wrote,

> the manuscript for a book he proposes to publish on the whole Zionist question. It appears to be practically a history of the Palestinian Jews and of the Zionist movement. Its purpose is to further the object of the movement under British auspices and to work up the Jews of England and America to favor and assist it. But before handing the manuscript over to the publisher Mr. Sokolow thinks it advisable to obtain the sanction of His Majesty's Secretary of State [for Foreign Affairs], and with this object in view he is willing to submit the manuscript to anyone delegated by the Secretary of State in order that he may read it and report as to the general matter of the contents, whilst also helping him in a way by revising his compositions, as he does not feel very sure of his power to express himself in English.
>
> I am ready to assume this work if my services are not needed elsewhere at present.
>
> If, before deciding, Sir Arthur Nicolson would wish to have more particulars as to the scope of this publication, I would suggest that he should accord Mr. Sokolow a short interview at as early a date as may be convenient to him.

Cumberbatch had been won over by the Sokolow powers of persuasion, but he was going a bit too far in Sir Arthur's estimation. "Seen by Sir A. Nicolson," another hand minuted on the folder, "who has informed Mr. Cumberbatch that circumstances render it inadvisable to pursue matters with Mr. Sokolow." No doubt, "circumstances" simply meant that it was hardly the moment for the Foreign Office to become coauthor of a Zionist project. Indeed, the Palestine issue had not been mentioned during the sessions of the Grand Allied Council in Paris at the end of March, in spite of O'Beirne's hope that it would be. Sokolow's day at the Foreign Office had not come just yet.

"Sokolow, Waizman and Herbert Samuel," wrote Moses Gaster in his diary on Sunday, April 16, after the meeting that morning in his home at 193 Maida Vale. "Before H.S. came, Sokolow told me Waizman had informed him that H.S. had phoned to *him* to see him and that *I* was asked [to] be there. Of course piece of his blustering." The Gaster-Weizmann rivalry was only to be exacerbated by confusions of this sort.

"H.S.'s meeting of far-reaching momentous importance," Gaster went on. "It practically came to a complete realization of our Zionist program. We are offered: French-English condominium in Palestine, Arab Prince to conciliate Arab sentiments, and, as part of the Constitution a Charter to Zionism for which England would stand guarantor and which would stand by us in every case of friction. We insisted on: national character of charter, freedom of immigration, internal autonomy, and the same full rights of citizenship [illegible] in Palestine."

Gaster does not say what Weizmann's and Sokolow's reactions were to the plan, and since his diary is the sole record of the meeting that has survived we can only guess at them. It is not likely that either Weizmann or Sokolow ever thought of a modified Arab principality as "practically" a "complete realization" of the Zionist program—Gaster's formulation doubtless was a product of enthusiasm stemming from his special relationship with Samuel—and they probably were rather negative after their respective fashions. In Sokolow's case, this negativity must have been muffled by diplomatic politeness and the respectful demeanor of a foreigner eager to stay on good terms with a British cabinet minister. Samuel did not mention Sykes's name and could therefore only have been vague about the provenance of the scheme. He probably represented it as at least partly his own, and this would have been all the more reason for Sokolow to remain outwardly noncommittal.

Weizmann may have been a little more outspoken in his disagreement. By this time, between his scientific work and the social connections Dorothy de Rothschild had established for him, he was in frequent personal contact with at least two other cabinet members—Lloyd George and Reginald McKenna—and had met or was known to other men highly placed in the Government as well. He certainly no longer had to feel that his political position hung on a thread dangled by Herbert Samuel, and a remark he had made in a letter to his wife two days before this meeting suggests even a certain skepticism regarding the home secretary: "I shall be seeing Samuel on Sunday," he wrote, "and it will be interesting to hear what song he sings." Gaster and Sokolow must have been struck at the meeting by a rather independent attitude on Weizmann's part.

They had a chance to discuss it a little over a week later. "Sokolow for dinner," writes Gaster in his diary for Monday, April 24. "Serious talk on situation. He is surprised at Weizman's [joviality?] and Zabotinski's dangerous activity causing more trouble for Russian Jews here." Jabotinsky, with the ardent assistance of Colonel Patterson, was now fully at work agitating in high places—including the Foreign Office—for a Jewish legion and was not hesitating to use the matter of the Russian-Jewish immigrants and their attitude to military service as a means of forcing the issue. Jabotinsky claimed that the same East End Jews who were resisting the call to arms at present would gladly serve in a Jewish legion assigned to liberate Palestine from the Turks. Gaster, who had frequently been in touch with Herbert Samuel on the problem of the immigrants and military service, was vehemently opposed to a Jewish legion and thought Jabotinsky's agitation was only exacerbating an already difficult and delicate situation. Sokolow entirely agreed with him—it was one of the few positions, as it happened, that they and other Zionists held in common with Lucien Wolf, out of fear that the lot of the Jews in Turkish-dominated Palestine would be jeopardized by such a clear identification of Zionism with the Allied cause. Weizmann, on the other hand, was one of the few prominent Zionists who supported Jabotinsky. "He now begins to understand," Gaster added in his diary entry about dinner with Sokolow, "my doubts about Weizman's [illegible]."

But the chief rabbi was now to have his own chance at direct access to the men who were making the basic decisions about Palestine, for within the next two days Sir Mark Sykes told Samuel he would like to see Gaster. Sykes, whose father-in-law, Sir John Eldon Gorst, had died on April 4, while Sykes was on his way back from Russia, had just had another upsetting experience within the past week or so. A scurrilous sixpenny pamphlet called *The Armenians*, by a man named C.F. Dixon-Johnson, was being circulated among members of Parliament. In it were quoted several of the more unfortunate remarks on the subject that Sykes had made in his early writings, and the impression was given that he had in some way endorsed the book. Sykes had responded by writing a letter to *The Times*, which appeared on Thursday, April 20; in it, he took

> the opportunity of stating that I have the very deepest sympathy with the unfortunate Armenian peoples, whose millennium of martyrdom is, I hope and believe, reaching its final stage, and that the horrible sufferings which they are now enduring are but a part of that profound darkness of the dying Eastern night which heralds the sudden and glorious dawn.

It was time to do more to hasten that dawn, and—perhaps it now occurred to Sykes more vividly than ever—to show what he wanted to do in the cause of peoples about whose condition he had been careless in the past. This certainly was the season to reconsider such oversights: for on that very Easter Monday, April 24, a long-frustrated Irish nationalism rose up in the streets of Dublin to remind a Liberal England of how such questions remained unresolved even close to home. Ironically, the man who led the British troops putting down the rebellion was Sir John Maxwell, just back from Egypt, where he had been one of the champions of the cause of Arab nationalism.

Sykes had doubtless asked Samuel to recommend a Zionist leader, and Samuel, in naming Gaster, had shown where his natural preference still lay. "Dear Dr. Gaster," Samuel wrote on April 26:

> The suggestion about which I came to see you a few days ago originated with Colonel Sir Mark Sykes, Bart., M.P., 9 Buckingham Gate, who is in very close touch with the Foreign Office and who has recently visited Russia in connection with the subject. As the matter should be kept absolutely confidential, I think it would be better for him to see you alone, at all events in the first instance. Would you mind writing to him direct to arrange an appointment saying that I have written to you on the subject?

In his eagerness to be discreet, Samuel did not spell out the name of the "subject," though he might better have done so. "I thank you very much for your letter of yesterday's date," Gaster replied on Thursday, the 27th:

> I am writing at once to Sir Marcus Sykes (M.P.) for an appointment. Of course you can rely on my absolute discretion, but I should like to inform you that Mr. Zabotinsky, with the irresponsibility of the journalist agitator, has been going about the country for some time past, and has created among the masses in London and the Provinces a profound irritation, which we are now striving to allay. I will keep you informed of the result of my interview with Sir Marcus Sykes. I sincerely trust that a way may be found to satisfy our demands and at the same time win the hearty cooperation of the Jewish masses.

The reference to Jabotinsky was bound to be confusing to Samuel, and the last sentence may have seemed downright alarming. What did Jabotinsky have to do with it, and why on earth was Gaster raising the prospect of propaganda among the Jewish masses at this delicate moment that required the utmost secrecy? But it may at last have occurred to Samuel that another "subject" he and Gaster had recently been discussing was the Russian Jews and military service. "Dear Sir," Gaster had written to Sykes after finishing his letter to Samuel:

> I write at the suggestion of Mr. Herbert Samuel, the Home Secretary, to ask you for an interview concerning the question of recruiting Russian subjects. I should feel obliged if you could make it possible either to call on me tomorrow, Friday, or Saturday afternoon between 4 and 6 o'clock, as I am still suffering from a virulent attack of lumbago, or if you prefer, I will call on you Tuesday or Thursday afternoon at any time agreeable to you.

There is no way of knowing what Sykes made of Gaster's reference to the recruiting of Russian subjects—it must have been quite mystifying to him—but at any rate he had his man, and his only concern now was to have the appointment. "My Dear Rabbi," he replied on Friday, the 28th, "If it would be equally convenient for you, I should be glad if I might call upon you, at 4.30 on Tuesday." Gaster wrote back on Sunday, agreeing to the suggestion.

"Lt.-Col. Sir Mark Sykes," wrote Gaster in his diary for Tuesday, May 2, seeing it all now with triumphant clarity. "Very long interview. He is the man who made the proposal to H. Samuel. Sgt. Wilson with him. Had seen Sazonoff, whom he won over to Zionism problems. Saw there dispatch of English Foreign Office and *aidemémoire* presented by Lucien Wolff."

One of the main problems Sykes and Gaster discussed was the resistance of the French to the Palestine idea. Sykes said he had discussed the matter with Picot in Petrograd, though he could not have divulged anything to Gaster of their real reason for being there together. "After long wrangle," Gaster continues about Sykes in his entry, "got his French colleague Georges Picot to see the point of Jewish help. He first stood against. Then agreed condominium." But Sykes made it clear to Gaster that this did not yet constitute agreement on the part of the French government itself, which still resisted Zionist claims. He told Gaster he was going to see Picot again soon, and no doubt asked for advice as to the line he should take with him.

"I put the case clearly," Gaster says. "Weizman was against France and even prefers to have German condominium as latter's interests *not* in Egypt." This was a most unlikely summary of Weizmann's views, and a potentially damaging one under the circumstances. In fact, there are grounds for believing that the inclination to consider the possibility of an Anglo-German condominium in Palestine really was Gaster's own. But the chief rabbi must have felt a certain embarrassment at making the suggestion; why else would he have attributed it to Weizmann?

Gaster continues in his diary that Sykes wanted him "to influence *Daily Telegraph* and then work on America." They were back to the subject of Jewish opinion and its influence in the world. Gaster wisely suggested that what was needed to win Jewish opinion was some kind of fait accompli in Palestine. "He answers to occupy Jerusalem—I, *not* by Jews, but by *English* soldiers." Gaster did not miss his opportunity to disparage the Jewish legion idea, after all. He was in effect rehearsing for the following day, when he was to see Colonel Patterson and tell him off.

After Sykes left, Gaster phoned Sokolow and reported to him on the conversation. Sokolow in turn told Gaster about the Victor Basch mission and about a promise the latter had received from the French government to do something about his recommendations. Gaster and Sokolow agreed that the French plan for a Jewish propaganda was all too vague and simply "not helpful." They were more troubled by the evident French diffidence on the subject of a Jewish Palestine than by the prospect that France was to be at all involved in it. "We must get something tangible," they decided, and without further consultation—certainly without saying anything to Weizmann—Gaster wrote to Sykes the next day. "I write now," he said, "to ask you to let me see you before you meet your French colleague. I have some information to communicate to you which bears on the meeting, and which may be of interest to you."

Sykes came to see him the next day. "Told him about French maneuvers," Gaster recorded, evidently meaning the Basch mission, the French government's response to it, and the feeling shared by himself and Sokolow that the French were trying to sidestep the Zionist issue. "He saw it as well as my point for [some?] written statement, even if in the form of conventional arrangements. Fulfillment depended on action both sides." There is every reason to suppose that it was Sokolow who had come up with the idea of seeking a written agreement from the French, but he remained judiciously out of the picture. Sykes concluded the conversation by promising to bring about a meeting between Picot and Gaster.

This took place the following Wednesday, May 10. "Sir Mark and Picot," Gaster writes in his diary for that day. "Long interesting conversation. I believe I made them, especially Picot, see importance of Jewish [Administration?] in Palestine as the ideal for which the [French] Republic is at war, and this result if carried out will benefit mankind and bring true civilization to the East. Told him of reverence for memory of Napoleon among Jews. *His* idea of Jewish Kingdom in Palestine." This was the kind of orating in which Gaster could be at his most impressive; but he also did not neglect the practical side of the argument. "Against *positive* assurances," he told Picot, "we would do our best for creating public opinion favorable to France."

Picot evidently was impressed, for he was to come back to Gaster for further discussion some weeks later. Sykes also was impressed enough to open some doors for Gaster in the coming weeks, when the chief rabbi was to have another interview with G.H. Fitzmaurice and one with Lancelot Oliphant: he had become the Zionist of the moment at the Admiralty and the Foreign Office. As for Sykes himself, he wrote again to Gaster on May 23, less than two weeks after introducing him to Picot, about a disturbing item that had appeared in that morning's *Times*. It said that Henry Morgenthau, who had resigned his post as American ambassador to Turkey earlier in the month, had just given a speech in Cincinnati in which he "disclosed the fact that he had recently broached to the Turkish Ministry the advisability of their selling Palestine to the Zionists after the war." He claimed that the Turkish ministers had eagerly approved of the idea, that figures had been discussed, and that they were ready to grant concessions now for the building of harbors and hotels. The Turkish government was eventually to deny this story, but not before it had caused some alarm among British Zionists and their friends.

Sykes enclosed a clipping of the news story with his letter. "My Dear Rabbi," he wrote, "I was very grieved to see enclosed in today's *Times*. Nothing could be more unfortunate or dangerous, than for a person in Mr. Morgenthau's position to take such an action, just as certain persons are beginning to improve." Gaster was swift to offer a peculiar consolation. "Dear Sir Mark," he wrote the next day. "Never mind. Things may have taken their proper course. You probably remember that I hinted at possibilities from other quarters, and that I suggested eventually a different combination for a possible condominium." Gaster may have been referring to the often discussed possibility of an Anglo-American condominium; but it is more likely that he was talking about the idea of an Anglo-German one he had mentioned to Sykes three weeks before, attributing it to Weizmann. Sykes could hardly have been impressed by it. In any case, though Gaster concluded this note with the expressed hope of further discussing the matter in person, there is no sign of Sykes's having taken the bait. Sykes was at this moment being assigned to the Foreign Office—he had been officially at the War Office until now—and placed in charge of a variety of interdepartmental functions relating to the Middle East; he was now, in effect but without title, His Majesty's secretary for the affairs of that region. But though Gaster was to see Picot in July and write several notes to Sykes in the ensuing months, the latter was not to resume personal contact with the rabbi until November.

Had Gaster annoyed Sykes with a hint at a possible Anglo-German condominium for Palestine? Perhaps so; but in any case, there had been an irrelevant quality to Gaster's latest response that may also have perturbed Sykes. For wasn't Gaster showing here the same tendency his letters and diaries suggest for the entire first month of contact between them—a touch of absentmindedness, a way of seeming now and then to miss the point? Gaster was a learned and noble-spirited man, but the ability to take firm grasp of hurtling everyday political realities may not have been among his gifts. He does not even seem to have fully grasped the import of the awesome responsibility that had been dangled in front of him during these weeks. Sykes may by now have suspected that, when the time came, Great Britain might have to find a more forceful candidate to stand for Zionism as its historical moment drew near.

·26·

DR. WEIZMANN'S
TRIALS CONTINUE

January 1916 had opened a season of new beginnings for Chaim Weizmann. Vera had just given up her position in Manchester and come with the eight-year-old Benjamin to London. For a short time, they all went on living in Chaim's "bachelor" quarters at 3 Justice Walk, with Vladimir Jabotinsky still in residence; then the Weizmanns found a temporary residence in Kensington, at 41 Campden Hill Road. They had not quite burned their bridges—Chaim was still technically only on leave from the university, and they had not yet sold their Manchester home—but the elements of risk and disruption were threatening enough. "On my arrival in London," Vera was to write years later, "I promptly fell ill with 'flu and Chaim was left to look after Benjy, which he did with his usual patience and good humor." Destiny begins at home; and destiny, for the moment, was exhausting.

But the difficulties were more than made up for by the fresh turn in their lives. Things seemed for the moment to be going well for Chaim Weizmann in both his careers. His Zionism was moving in the direction of a growth of his strength on the English scene, with a concomitant loosening of his old ties abroad. As late as December, his German colleague in The Hague, Julius Simon, had still sought a meeting between them in some neutral country. But Weizmann—along with Englishmen in general—had changed considerably in circumstances and outlook since July, when such a meeting had first been broached to him and he had been able at least to consider it. On January 16 he wrote to Simon, protesting at first that he was too busy. "Besides," he went on, suddenly coming to the point, "I don't think that the meeting of Zionists at present could do any good. We can do very little for Palestine and for the Jewish cause in general as long as the political situation remains as it is. One has to wait patiently." It was a fairly discreet way of endorsing on a personal level the state of war that existed between their two countries, but it was no less decisive than an outright declaration of war would have been. Weizmann was in effect pronouncing what the nature of his Zionism had come to be since the moment the war began: an Allied and a British cause.

Indeed, it was in this very month that British Zionism in general showed signs of awakening from its torpor. Until now, the movement in Great Britain had consisted, on the one hand, of the tepid discussion society presided over by Joseph Cowen and endorsed in the pages of Leopold Greenberg's *Jewish Chronicle,* and on the other, of the freelance and uncoordinated diplomacy conducted separately by Chaim Weizmann, Moses Gaster, Vladimir Jabotinsky, and Nahum Sokolow. On January 23, however, at the instigation of Cowen and Weizmann, a meeting of twelve Zionist leaders was held at the Hotel Great Central in London to review the situation and take some kind of action to improve it. Among those present were Cowen, Greenberg, Weizmann, Sokolow, Jabotinsky, Leon Simon, Herbert Bentwich, and Ahad Ha'am: this was a conciliatory get-together between the Cowen-Greenberg faction that officially ran the English Zionist Federation and the Weizmann-Sokolow group that now represented effective Zionist influence in the country. Gaster—as ever, maintaining the Olympian aloofness that was his own way of bidding to be all or nothing in British Zionism—did not attend, though he had been invited. The upshot of the meeting was the appointment of an official "Zionist Executive for England"—the very name was a declaration of independence from the old Zionist executive in Berlin and Copenhagen—consisting of Cowen, Weizmann, Sokolow, Bentwich, Gaster (in spite of his absence), and Tschlenow (though he had returned to Russia the previous summer). This was the first step in a reorientation of British Zionism in the direction of what had become its real leadership.

The general atmosphere of promise for Weizmann seemed to manifest itself also at the Ministry of Munitions, where a kind of January thaw set in among his relationships. "Sir Frederick is already installed in office," he had been able to write to C.P. Scott at the end of December of Nathan's long-awaited appointment there as director of propellant supplies, "and things move quite differently now. All is well so far." Lord Moulton's opposition had quietened, at least for the time being, in the wake of Weizmann's trip to Paris, and meanwhile, Lloyd George had evinced interest in the progress of the acetone trials for the Admiralty at Poole. And as for those, "you will be interested to know," Weizmann wrote happily to Dorothy de Rothschild on January 14, "that the second big experiment in Poole went off beautifully and what is more important in just *half* the time than it usually takes. It means we can double the output. That is very satisfactory."

Confident of success in this vein, Weizmann began pressing at Munitions for other projects he had conceived. Speaking to Lord Moulton on January 20 about the problems in the production of toluol, one of the ingredients of TNT, Weizmann offered his own method for producing it and got a rebuff that at least was not too severe. "He told me that lots of people were working at it," Weizmann wrote Madame de Rothschild, "but that they were not successful. From the little he mentioned about their ways of tackling the problem, I'm not surprised to hear that they failed. I gave a few indications." But he did not have to try cajoling Moulton; he had a tried and true method for dealing with opposition at the ministry. "To London by night train," C.P. Scott recorded in his diary for January 27 and 28, "primarily in order to see Lloyd George about Munitions. Weizmann having achieved complete success in large-scale production of acetone, essential ingredient for cordite (projectile), eager to push on with experiments in production of toluol, essential for high explosives. Some expense involved. Lord Moulton obstructive." Lloyd George was "keenly interested," Scott thought, and he "promised to act" on the matter. Scott reported to Weizmann that afternoon.

But if C.P. Scott was still regularly intervening at the ministry in Weizmann's cause, this did nothing to break down the continuing resistance to him among some of his colleagues. On the contrary, that resistance began mounting again in February. A first sign of its renewal had come on the twelfth—a glum enough date for Weizmann, for it was then that he received news of the failure of a major acetone trial at Wareham. Later that day, he was told by Sir Frederick Nathan of a Government decision to take over most of the distilleries in the country for acetone production. Weizmann could not but have treated this as good news; but he must also have wondered why he had not been consulted in the matter. He also was not consulted in the days that ensued.

That particular danger signal was still muffled, however, and the next time C.P. Scott came to town the main concern was still the obstruction Moulton had begun making to Weizmann's interest in other materials as well as acetone. On the morning of February 23, Scott met Weizmann at the National Liberal Club, then "took him to Munitions Office to see Lloyd George. Saw [Lloyd George] alone first. He was due at Cabinet, but stayed half an hour. . . . I then told him of Weizmann's brilliant success, within the last few days, in producing synthetic toluene, and his confident expectation that he could do the same for picric acid, and asked him if he would like to see him. [Weizmann] came in and explained the matter himself. Lloyd George greatly pleased and sent him on to his assistant, Dr. Addison, with intimation that he could have any money he liked for further experiments." Weizmann, assuming that this meant large-scale trials, suggested that they could be set up in the nearly completed new Admiralty factory at Poole. That day he wrote confidently to the supervisor in Wareham telling him he had his choice whether to put the new line of trials "entirely under the auspices of the Admiralty or whether you would like me to provide the funds from the Ministry of Munitions, the latter could be done very easily if necessary."

But Scott was only an outsider after all, and despite Lloyd George's protestations of support, the evidence suggests that the munitions minister was not at this moment prepared to go against a decision that seems to have been made by Moulton and others to keep Weizmann away from all the sites of large-scale production. Far from being able to start work on new materials, he was even to be deprived of access to places where his own process was in use. This could only have been due to a continuing fear of Weizmann's foreign connections; but it also no doubt had been stimulated by temperamental difficulties. Too many associates of the self-confident and stridently assertive Weizmann at the ministry were finding him hard to get along with—perhaps all the more so on account of C.P. Scott's frequent interventions on his behalf.

On Saturday, February 26, Weizmann, sensing that things were once again going wrong, had an interview with Sir Frederick Nathan to try to ascertain what was happening. Nathan suggested that Weizmann write, in the form of a letter to him, a memorandum summing up his work so far and reviewing his present position. Weizmann did this the following day. The letter opened with a brief review of his entire relationship with Munitions and the Admiralty, beginning with the approach Nathan had made to him in April 1915. He told of the first trials at Nicholson's Distillery and of the decision in the fall to move them to the Royal Naval Cordite Factory in Holton Heath. "The trials there," he said,

began about the 1st of January 1916 and the results were satisfactory. The Admiralty then decided to proceed with the construction of a factory which would produce about 2,000 tons of
acetone yearly and also about 4,000 t. of Butyl alcohol. The process has also been adopted by the Indian Government.

Weizmann then described how the Ministry of Munitions decided to interest itself in his process, but "only after all the trials in
Bromley were considerably advanced" and "after a great amount of
discussion and delay." He stated the conditions of both his appointments, at the Admiralty and at Munitions, and then moved on to a
discussion of his work at the Lister Institute. Enumerating the problems that had been worked out there in September, he pointed out
that his benzene and toluene process in particular "promises to be of
great military value." Another of his Lister Institute processes—that
of the conversion of butyl alcohol into methyl ethyl ketone, another
solvent—was, he said, considered valuable by the Admiralty "for the
Air Craft Department."

So much for history; Weizmann had now arrived at the present
situation that was the reason for the letter. "About a fortnight ago,"
he went on,

> you were good enough to inform me that the Government has
> decided to take over most of the distilleries in Britain and to
> adapt them for the purpose of making acetone. I understand
> that the quantity of acetone to be produced is about 30,000 tons.
> To face a problem of such magnitude it becomes necessary to at
> least [increase] the size of my present laboratories, to train up a
> large number of men, to make provisions for [supplying] all the
> factories with good ferment, to supervise the setting up of labo-
> ratories practically all over the country and to control the scien-
> tific side of the process. All that involves already at present and
> certainly will still more involve in future heavy responsibilities
> and duties, which come in addition to my research work.
>
> I venture to submit, that when we began work in Septem-
> ber we scarcely realized that it will grow out to such huge
> dimensions.

But despite this sudden awesome transformation in scale, Weizmann
was still ready to assume hopefully—for the purposes of this letter at
least—that the now-resistant doors of the distilleries would open for
him after just a little pushing. In the next two paragraphs, Weizmann expatiated on the virtues of his acetone process, just to make

sure that the ministry knew what it was apparently taking so lightly.

This was not quite the end of Weizmann's plea. The problems he was having at the ministry had reminded him of the fact that his professional security in general was now standing on shaky ground. His Admiralty appointment had another year to go, but he was half-way through his Munitions appointment, and in fact had to inform the University of Manchester in just a few weeks whether he planned to return in the fall. "Somehow," he said, "I remain a temporary and anonymous worker, and it is in the interests of the important work I have to perform that this state of things should be altered and my authority strengthened." Meanwhile, he went on,

> the present arrangements I had to make for my family and myself are necessarily very costly and unsatisfactory. I had to take temporarily a house here without giving up my house in Manchester. My wife gave up a very good medical municipal post in Manchester and is unable to take any work here as we are not settled. All that involves a considerable amount of discomfort, which interferes with work.

"I have tried," the letter concluded, "to place the case before you in as concise a manner as possible and I trust that it will be possible for you to soon find a way how to improve and regularize the status and position of myself and of my laboratories."

C.P. Scott reentered the fray the following week. "Another by-work," he wrote in his diary of the few days he spent in London between Tuesday, February 29, and Friday, March 3, "was to see Weizmann and, on his behalf, Dr. Addison and Sir F. Nathan in order to try to remove or mitigate the difficulties in the practical working and organization on the great scale of his acetone process which were preying upon him and destroying his working power. Spoke also to Lloyd George as to need for giving him a more permanent and assured position." But if the latter need was something Lloyd George could satisfy without too much difficulty, the former could not be met without bucking an alignment of forces that were by now more important to the ministry than the virtually solitary Weizmann.

Meanwhile, however, for all his frustrations at the ministry, Weizmann was enjoying a triumphant personal life in London. In March, Vera, pregnant with their second child, began a diary to record the round of exhilarating engagements their social life was becoming. "Chaim was invited to lunch at the Astors' in Saint James's Square to discuss Zionist problems," she writes in her first entry, that of Wednesday, March 15. Waldorf Astor, scion of one of the great American fortunes, and his Virginia-born wife, Nancy, both British subjects, had made their London home a prominent political salon. Chaim Weizmann had just been introduced into their circle, as he had been into others of social eminence, by Dorothy de Rothschild. Among those invited to the March 15 lunch were Alfred Zimmern and Arthur James Balfour, "whose professional occupations," according to Mrs. Weizmann, "prevented him from being present. But he rang up and expressed the wish to meet Chaim next Sunday evening." That meeting did not materialize either, but the Astors were to invite Balfour to dinner for the twenty-fifth of the month, along with both Chaim and Mrs. Weizmann. It was a long way from evenings at the Dreyfuses.

On March 16, the Weizmanns were at Dorothy de Rothschild's home for lunch. Among the guests were Lady Crewe and Reginald McKenna with his wife. McKenna, who had been first lord of the Admiralty before Churchill's accession to that office in 1911, was at this time rising to new influence in the Liberal party and was a strong rival of his predecessor at the Exchequer, Lloyd George. Indeed, he had been a rigorous opponent of the conscription measures that, championed by Lloyd George, were now coming into law, and he fumed about them at lunch—though apparently without mentioning Lloyd George, no doubt out of consideration for Weizmann, whose work at Munitions he knew about through C.P. Scott. Instead, he focused his anger upon Lord Derby, the administrator of the conscription. "He said they have already over 400,000 men and don't need any more," according to Vera Weizmann's diary, "and called Lord Derby an idiot."

After the ladies retired, McKenna drew Weizmann into conversation, asking him if it was possible to make nitric acid from the air, as the Germans were said to be doing. Weizmann, Vera writes, "answered that he thought it possible, though it was not in his line, but he did not see why it couldn't be done, if the Germans could do it." McKenna then displayed his knowledge of Weizmann's activities by asking him "if English students are a good material for scientific research," and saying that "Chaim has now a lot of new things, which could be the nucleus of the chemical industry after the war. He was well informed on Chaim's last discoveries of acetone and benzol and toluene etc." McKenna must have felt that Lloyd George was not sufficiently appreciative of Weizmann's work at Munitions, as depicted by C.P. Scott.

Weizmann replied that, though he thought the human material in Great Britain was excellent for potential scientific research, "the whole English system is wrong; they are not encouraged to do research and therefore don't get the same chance as the Germans. To that McKenna replied, that as long as he lives, he will keep up the laboratories started now and will make them national companies; he asked Chaim to call at the Treasury any time to discuss it."

After Lady Crewe and the McKennas had left, the Weizmanns lingered to discuss the afternoon's events with Dorothy de Rothschild. Their hostess explained of Lady Crewe that she "is not as snobbish or mondaine as she looks; she is very good-hearted, serious and a very brilliant woman, but her manners are so objectionable that she puts everybody at a distance and people generally feel shy in her presence." But it was only four days after this that Vera Weizmann was able to record Madame de Rothschild's report of the conversation overheard between Lady Crewe and Lord Robert Cecil, in which Lady Crewe had reported that they all were "Weizmannites" in her house. Perhaps Lady Crewe's restraint at lunch was the product of some schooling in the art of political discreetness. Her husband, in his March 11 letter to the Paris and Petrograd embassies, had just performed the greatest service for Zionism by a British statesman since Herbert Samuel's memorandum of a year before; under the circumstances, she may well have felt that the less said to the Weizmanns at this time the better. As for McKenna, a few days later Madame de Rothschild was to warn Chaim Weizmann to be "very discreet and careful" with the chancellor of the Exchequer, "who is ready to wring Lloyd George's neck."

It was on Saturday evening, March 25, that the Weizmanns went to dinner at the Astor home. In addition to Balfour—whom Weizmann was seeing for the first time in a year—the guests included some American journalists and Philip Kerr, the thirty-three-year-old editor of the *Round Table*. It was good for Weizmann to meet the influential Kerr, who doubtless knew a good deal about him already through Alfred Zimmern. As for Balfour, he and Weizmann must both have felt a certain relief at this chance to get together under purely social circumstances. In Whitehall, Balfour still seems to have wanted to keep Weizmann at a distance, but the opportunity to see him in Saint James's Square was one he had gladly taken when Mrs. Astor presented it. Unfortunately, their notoriously straightforward hostess compromised the occasion by creating a moment of embarrassment between them. "Mrs. Astor tried with success," Vera Weizmann records, "to bring the conversation with Balfour round to Zionism. She very indiscreetly then said to Balfour, 'you really must speak about Zionism to Dr. Weizmann,' and made the situation rather awkward." She of course had no idea how involved in the subject together Weizmann and the first lord had already been.

The rest of the evening reverted to standard political gossip, mainly about the prime minister, whose popularity in the country was rapidly waning.

But at the Ministry of Munitions, Weizmann's isolation continued to grow. If the chemist from Manchester had not yet noticed in February that he was beginning to lose the support even of Sir Frederick Nathan—brought in ostensibly to be his protector—the fact certainly became obvious when he and Nathan got together on April 4 for their first important meeting in many weeks. "I had a long interview with Sir Frederick," Weizmann wrote to Scott in consternation the following day,

> and the chief point of the discussion was the ways and means of how to carry on the work in the distilleries. The distillers apparently object to my interference in their work. I would like nothing better than not to have anything to do with the distilleries, as it is certainly not my class of work, but until the things run smoothly it is my duty to see that the alteration of the distilleries is carried out in a proper manner and that no risks be taken in simplifying the thing and jeopardizing the process itself.

Weizmann described how he had visited a recently commandeered distillery in Hammersmith and "found the place in a hopeless condition." He had offered the opinion that the plant was in such a state that "nothing will be proved if the experiment does not go and it will be a mere fluke if the experiment does go through." This remark had upset the chief engineer on the premises, who had promptly complained to the ministry; the upshot was that Sir Frederick had now told Weizmann that he, Nathan, "is responsible for the process and my responsibility finishes with the Lister." In fact, on the very day Weizmann was writing this to Scott, Nathan composed a note telling Weizmann he had been officially appointed "Superintendent of the Lister Institute Government Laboratories"—so much for the regu-

larization of his status—and that large-scale production in the distilleries had been placed under a separate branch of the Department of
Explosive Supplies.

Weizmann, in his letter to Scott, went on to speak of his "severe
disappointment" at the position Sir Frederick had taken in the
whole matter. Moreover, he added,

> it seems to me that the process is getting entirely out of my
> hands, the cultures and the knowledge will be spread all over the
> country and unless my position is cleared up completely in the
> next few days I shall consider it impossible to do any further
> work. I have mentioned all this to Mr. Lloyd George who was
> very sympathetic and promised to look into the matter care-
> fully.

But this was not the end of the disappointments Nathan had provided. Sometime during the preceding weeks, Lord Moulton had
asked Sir Frederick Nathan to take over the supervision of Weizmann's benzene and toluene process; Weizmann at the time had
thought this to be a development in his favor. But in the previous
day's meeting with Sir Frederick, he now wrote,

> I was suddenly informed that the premises which I have taken
> over for a factory should not be used for this purpose and the
> process should be handed over to Professor Hewitt who is the
> head of a new research department established by Lord Moul-
> ton, and Professor Hewitt whom I have never met has had abso
> lutely nothing to do with this process of mine. I of course flatly
> refused to comply with Lord Moulton's request, and Sir Fred-
> erick then told me that of course he cares nothing about the
> process, as there is any quantity of benzene and toluene in the
> country and they are giving away large quantities of it and this
> process could just as well "go down the drain."

Weizmann's dismay at this second and more extreme display of Sir
Frederick's disaffection is all but audible. "I am quoting his very
words," he writes, and then points out: "I could say nothing to a
statement like that but the same evening I heard both from Mr.
Lloyd George and from his secretary the contrary."

Since it was becoming evident that Lloyd George's expressions
of concern were far more forthcoming than his readiness to take
action, Scott and Weizmann decided that, in the matter of regulariz-
ing the latter's uncertain status, they would try using some of the

political leverage they had obtained in their common acquaintance-ship with Reginald McKenna. They had already discussed this possi-bility by the time of Weizmann's April 5 letter to Scott, in which he said:

> I do not think I ought to approach Mr. McKenna until I hear from Mr. Lloyd George as perhaps Mr. Lloyd George may object to outside interference, although he mentioned to me yesterday that he had a talk with the Chancellor of the Exchequer about regularizing my position.

After all, this was to some extent a question of funds, and therefore represented a chance for the chancellor of the Exchequer to undercut Lloyd George in a small matter of patronage.

Nevertheless, McKenna proved cautious about any possible in-fringement on Lloyd George's territory. When he saw Weizmann on Tuesday, April 11, he told him, according to a letter Weizmann wrote later that day, that he was "quite prepared to make an arrangement with me but he cannot do it unless he is approached by one of the Departments, either the Admiralty or the Ministry of Munitions. He also expressed the opinion that he would much rather deal with the Admiralty as it is a permanent institution." McKenna said he was in fact going over to the Admiralty that afternoon, "and he promised to raise this point there." By now, the aim had subtly shifted from one of providing a stable position for Weizmann at the Admiralty or Munitions Ministry, which had been the predominant one before McKenna came into the picture, to that of providing Weizmann at least with a permanent award for his services and discoveries on the Government's behalf. There no longer was any way he could stop the forces that sought to exclude him; but on the other hand, no one seems to have doubted that he was entitled to a just compensation for his efforts.

Three days later he was able to write to Vera, who was vacation-ing with Benjamin in Brighton, that

> Mr. Scott was most confident that everything will be settled. He asked me what amount I would like. I said £2,000 a year, i.e., a capital sum which would give such a return. This would be in addition to a professorship, and also in addition to all the patent rights in all countries, which would remain mine. He found this demand reasonable, and said that all this will be arranged.

The matter of Weizmann's award had now definitely been taken up by the Admiralty; it therefore was in Balfour's jurisdiction. In the next few days, Scott saw McKenna and spelled out Weizmann's terms. McKenna found them acceptable and relayed them to Balfour, who also thought them provisionally satisfactory.

Things were not to be rushed along, however. On May 9, nearly a month later, Scott was still pressing McKenna for the outcome. The chancellor told him "he had seen Balfour twice on the subject. He was personally willing, but Lord Moulton and Sir [Frederick] Nathan both advised delay." About two weeks later, Scott again approached McKenna about the matter, and this time saw Balfour as well. Scott records that he even received a promise from Balfour "that he would then and there send in [a] requisition to [the] Treasury for full amount of £50,000." But Scott footnotes this in his diary: "I clearly so understood him, but received a note next day from his secretary which indicated hesitation." Scott had also obtained Lloyd George's consent to this sum. On the morning of May 25, Scott brought Weizmann to breakfast with Lloyd George, and they explained to the minister the "latest remarkable developments of the work and the difficulties and delays caused by Lord Moulton. Lloyd George"—in what ought to have been an overly familiar litany by now—"at once determined to call on Moulton and the head of explosives and propellant departments to meet him and Weizmann and have the matter out." Since Lloyd George had just received a request from the prime minister that, on top of his other duties, he conduct an inquiry into the Irish crisis, it is not likely that he was ready to give much attention to Weizmann's problems at this moment.

In the meantime, Lord Moulton and Sir Frederick Nathan, now solidly aligned against Weizmann, had been finding additional grounds for their resentments toward him. The King's Lynn factory of the Synthetic Products Company—which, it will be recalled, had been producing acetone through the fermentation of potato mash since 1912 and was under contract with the War Office in the early months of the war—had been commandeered in March by the Ministry of Munitions. It would seem that the propellants department had decided from the outset to use the Weizmann process there instead of the old Fernbach one involving potatoes. In any case, the entire move obviously had caused chagrin at the Synthetic Products Company, and the upshot was that questions began being raised there about Weizmann's patent. Wasn't this really the same process as that developed by Fernbach in 1912—when Weizmann had worked as his assistant—and patented in England in partnership with Edward Strange of Synthetic Products?

Sir Frederick Nathan had called in Weizmann on April 27 and queried him in the matter. Whereupon Weizmann had compiled a list of all the relevant patents dealing with fermentation processes, as well as descriptions of the specific patents taken out by Fernbach and Strange, and submitted it all to Nathan. "It can easily be seen," he stressed in his covering letter,

> that the conditions under which they work are materially different from ours, moreover as you mentioned yourself this morning Strange has admitted that they could not carry out their fermentation on maize, a fact which has been confirmed over and over again in the laboratory here by various workers, a vigorous culture of the fermenting bacteria gives scarcely any trace of oil in 48 hours.

In spite of these arguments, by the middle of May Fernbach and the Synthetic Products Company had sent a letter to the ministry stating the case for their view that their patents had been infringed by the Weizmann process. Without consulting Weizmann, Moulton and Nathan thereupon went ahead and held a meeting with representatives of the company. Moulton explained to them that the Department of Explosive Supplies had no authority to adjudicate claims; they replied by suggesting that the matter could be settled by arbitration. Moulton finally apprised Weizmann of all this in a letter written on May 26. Weizmann replied on the thirtieth, pointing out that the grounds for the claims against his process had not been made clear. "Prof. Fernbach and the Synthetic Products Co.," he wrote, "certainly have no rights to my inventions, and the process adopted by the Government is different from anything Prof. Fernbach and the Synthetic Products Co. have done or been able to do." Weizmann also expressed surprise that they had known enough about his process to be able to make their claims against it, since it was supposed to be a Government secret.

On Saturday afternoon, June 4, Weizmann had a crucial interview with McKenna. The chancellor told him things were going well at the Admiralty factory in Wareham, and that Weizmann's process would therefore be used for acetone manufacture at the new Admiralty factory nearby, which was to be ready in August. "He further informed me," Weizmann wrote the next day, "that the Admiralty has decided to take up the processes for the conversion of Butyl alcohol into aromatic Hydrocarbons and into Methyl-Ethyl-Ketone and that the large scale tests of these processes will be completed by July." He therefore urged Weizmann to wait until then in the matter of his award, about which he was remaining in consultation with the Admiralty.

Weizmann said he was "quite satisfied to wait until July, that I am not at all anxious to have my money at once, but I am anxious that my position should be made clear, that I should not be worried by intrigues of all sorts." Then he showed the chancellor Moulton's letter of May 26 and his reply to it. McKenna expressed approval of Weizmann's reply "and recommended not to worry about those things and go on working." But then he admitted that he had heard about the Fernbach claim already and that he thought the possibility of an infringement having been committed was not out of the question. "He told me," Weizmann writes, "that the people claim to be able to ferment maize, but by a more expensive method and he gave me the following reasoning: supposing there is a patent x which can produce an article at a price of £500 per ton and a patent x + y which can produce same article at a price of £200 per ton, there is a possibility that x + y may be an infringement of x. I pointed out to Mr. McKenna emphatically that this reasoning does not hold good in my case, as my process is perfectly independent of theirs and that so far they have not been producing any acetone from maize even by their 'expensive' method although they had their works for more than three years. I could not go into details as the Chancellor was pressed for time having had an appointment with the Prime Minister." Weizmann was in any case not going to bite too hard the hand that was about to feed him. McKenna closed the conversation by suggesting that Weizmann's forthcoming award would be granted on the basis of his production of butyl alcohol rather than of acetone anyway, since his acetone work had been given free to the nation at the beginning of the war.

By Tuesday, June 6, Weizmann had been informed that he would be assigned to supervise personally the work of adapting the King's Lynn factory to his process. This was a direct show of confidence from Lloyd George, and Weizmann could not but be deeply grateful for it after all that had happened. But he had been stung, and he warily wrote to the munitions minister that "as I have heard within the last few days that Professor Fernbach and [the Synthetic Products] company are, without the slightest foundation, alleging that they have some rights to my process, I hesitate to go to King's Lynn and in the presence of their workpeople put my process into practice, unless I can feel sure that they have failed entirely to produce acetone from maize."

Lloyd George gave his answer to this to C.P. Scott in person a few days later, when the *Guardian* editor mentioned the problem again.

"I don't care whose process it is," he said. "Weizmann has given his invention to the State and the State means to have it. Tell Weizmann if he has any further trouble from these people simply to refer them to the Minister for Munitions."

And that was the end of it for the time being. The situation had been stabilized: Weizmann had his constituencies in King's Lynn and the Admiralty works as well as the promise of just compensation, the patent question had been put on the shelf,* and Moulton and Nathan had been outmaneuvered after all. This was just in time for both Weizmann and Lloyd George, as it turned out: for two major events had occurred that week, indeed, on the same day—one a disaster in the North Sea, the other a fresh start in the Middle East— that would ultimately have major effects upon the occasionally intertwining destinies of the minister and the chemist and that were beginning to result in sharp shifts in their attentions even now.

---

* It was not to be resolved until 1926, when, in the case of *Commercial Solvents Corporation* v. *Synthetic Products Co., Ltd.*, the decision finally was made in Weizmann's favor.

·27·

THE REVOLT IN
THE HEJAZ

The Anglo-German naval competition that had been the source of so much friction before the war finally came to full-dress battle on May 31 and June 1, 1916, in the North Sea off Jutland. Vera Weizmann reflected the mood of the British public in general when, on June 2, she recorded in her diary "news of a great Naval battle with heavy English losses. We were all frightfully depressed, and were afraid that it was the beginning of the end." Later she granted that this had been "an over-pessimistic assessment." Indeed, the result had been a standoff and therefore, though her losses were greater than Germany's, even a victory for Britain in a sense: for her navy emerged still in control of the North Sea, continuing the blockade of Germany.

It was not until four days later that the most severe German blow of the battle landed. On June 5, at approximately 7:40 P.M., the cruiser *Hampshire*, sailing west of the Orkneys on the first leg of a journey to the Russian port of Archangel, struck a German mine. Within fifteen minutes the ship sank, bringing down with her all but about a dozen survivors. One of those drowned was the secretary for war, Lord Kitchener, who had been on a diplomatic mission to the tsar.

Kitchener's departure on this journey had been another sign of his declining prestige within the cabinet: for by now even Prime Minister Asquith, long a stout supporter of the hero of Khartoum and still unwilling to request his resignation, was ready to take every opportunity to have him out of London, and the minor invitation from the tsar had presented as good a one as any. Kitchener had remained popular in the country at large, but among his political colleagues the failures not only in the Dardanelles but also at Loos in

France the previous fall were laid largely at his door. Kitchener's one-man, secretive approach to the making of War Office policy had become more disturbing than ever to close observers, and there had been times when he did not even seem to have grasped essential information at his disposal. A month or so after Kitchener's drowning, C.P. Scott told the Weizmanns frankly that the war secretary "could not have done better than to have gone down, as he was a great impediment lately."

This surely was also the view of Lloyd George, Kitchener's foremost critic and the man immediately recognized, by cabinet and country, as his likeliest successor at the War Office. Lloyd George was appointed secretary for war on July 6, his position thereby confirmed as the most vigorous war leader in the Government now that Kitchener and Churchill both were out of the way.*

Arab affairs now leaped back into the news: on June 5, the very day Kitchener died, the Sherifian revolt he had done so much to encourage got under way. That morning, Hussein's eldest son, Ali, and third son, Feisal, rode out through Medina's Damascus Gate to the tomb and mosque of the Prophet's uncle, Hamza, some four miles away. Awaiting them there were about fifteen hundred men who had been recruited by their father. When they arrived, according to the historian of the event, they "proclaimed the independence of the Arabs from Turkish rule, in the name of the Sherif Husain, Lord of Mecca. Then they galloped away, followed by the recruits, and joined the tribesmen at the appointed place to the south-east of Madina. The Arab Revolt had begun."

The men at Cairo headquarters, unlike most of their colleagues in London, had never ceased to believe in the imminence of this outcome, even though the Sherif had not written to McMahon since February 18 and his last letter had contained some discouraging elements. For one thing, it had urgently requested £50,000 in gold and considerable supplies of food and ammunition, but without hold-

---

* There was also an ironic side to the relation between Lloyd George's destiny and the sinking of the *Hampshire*, for he had thought of going with Kitchener to Russia until Asquith persuaded him to lead the inquiry into the Dublin uprising instead. "This escape, at least," Lloyd George was to write, "I owe to Ireland."

Along with Kitchener and his aide Colonel FitzGerald, yet another man significantly concerned with the future of Ottoman Asia was aboard the *Hampshire* and was drowned: Hugh J. O'Beirne of the Foreign Office, who was to have brought his long experience of Russia to bear as an adviser. There is every reason to wonder what would have been the outcome in the Middle East if the *Hampshire* had not gone down or if Lloyd George had been aboard when it did.

ing out the hope of any immediate return. On the contrary, it had contained an intimation that in Syria, at any rate, the Arab nationalist uprising may have been nipped in the bud. "We had informed your Excellency," the Sherif wrote,

> that we had sent one of our sons [Feisal] to Syria to command the operations deemed necessary there. We have received a detailed report from him stating that the tyrannies of the Government there have not left of the persons upon whom they could depend, whether of the different ranks of soldiers or of others, save only a few, and those of secondary importance.

And in case this had not sufficiently dampened Cairo's Syrian expectations, Djemal Pasha had staged a large round of executions that April and May, hanging twenty-two leaders of al-Ahd and al-Fatat in the public squares of Beirut and Damascus.

That certainly had been the low point for Cairo, a far cry both from its own euphoria of October and from the successful conclusion the India Office had achieved on December 26, when a treaty had been signed with Ibn Saud at last. No sweeping pan-Arab promises had to be made to *him*—hardly anything more, rather, than guarantees of his territorial claims in central and eastern peninsular Arabia and a relatively modest grant of financial support.

It was clearly as a gesture of self-defense that McMahon had, in April, sent to the Foreign Office a summary of all the negotiations that had taken place so far between Hussein and himself and of the commitments that had and had not been made. "It should be observed," the high commissioner pleaded in his covering letter,

> that no guarantees which could give rise to embarrassments in the future between ourselves and the Allies, or ourselves and the Arabs, have been given by us to any of the Arab parties. Realizing that the present stage of military operations in the Ottoman Empire is transitional, but daily declaring itself more and more in our favor, we have made every attempt to avoid definite commitments for the future.

Among the Foreign Office minutes placed on this communication was an outburst of impatience from Sir Edward Grey, who wrote once and for all: "We have gone far enough in promises to the Sherif and he has as yet done nothing—we may give him arms & money but no more negotiations* till he has done something."

* Instead of "promises," which is struck out.

Always sure that he *would* do something, Cairo headquarters had meanwhile expanded its operations in the self-appointed role of midwife to the birth of Arab independence. This role had become institutionalized early in the year with the creation of the Arab Bureau, a direct product of the proposal Sir Mark Sykes had made the previous fall for such a body, "which should receive copies of all telegrams giving available information regarding our enemies, Islamic propaganda and methods and effect thereof, as well as tendency of popular opinion, from intelligence and political officers" in various parts of the Middle East. This proposal had been formally submitted to the cabinet by Sykes on December 23, after his return to London and the start of his negotiations with Picot, and it was accepted by an interdepartmental committee on January 7, two days after Sykes and Picot had presented their memorandum. Sykes had suggested the name "Islamic Bureau," but the committee changed this to "Arab Bureau," recommending that it should be organized "as a section of the existing Soudan Intelligence Department in Cairo [under Colonel Gilbert Clayton], and that it should make its report through the High Commissioner of Egypt to the Foreign Office."

Opinions on Sykes's proposal had been solicited from Cairo, where Clayton had already in effect been running such a bureau since November, when Sykes had been there and they had begun developing the idea together. McMahon wired back his enthusiastic approval on January 9, stressing that the bureau had to be in Egypt, though granting that "it should have agency in London and liaison members in India and Mesopotamia." He also urged that the bureau have the services of Sykes and D.G. Hogarth. But Sykes—however disappointing this may have been to him—was not to be available, since his work with Picot and his emerging status as a coordinator of Middle Eastern policy made it necessary that he be based in London.

As for Hogarth, who as a lieutenant commander in naval intelligence had already sojourned frequently in Cairo over the preceding year, he seems to have been recognized from the outset as the man most naturally qualified to run the bureau there. Even Clayton was ready to acquiesce in this choice, though he might have preferred a less imposing personality in this post that was ostensibly under his supervision. In his own response to the proposal about the bureau, which he sent to Sykes on January 14, there are hints that he foresaw considerable autonomous power for it. "I agree in general to your suggestions," he wrote, but only as a guidance for a scheme of work and future reorganization. Details and exact scope can only be decided as work goes on and experience is gained.

I can start immediately with a personality now here, but I shall be glad of Hogarth's help when available. . . .

In my opinion the Bureau should be nominally under the Foreign Office, but only in so far as it will be under the control of the High Commissioner.

The India Office, already facing a loss of status in Middle Eastern affairs by the mere fact of an Arab Bureau's existence in Cairo, sensed the danger of this last paragraph when the letter reached London, and registered its protest, saying it would cooperate only if the bureau were "effectively under the control of the Foreign Office." The committee had included this stipulation in its recommendations, though this was not in fact going to prevent the bureau from steering its own course to a large extent, in the Cairo tradition.

Clayton's reference to "a personality now here" was a reminder of how rich Cairo was in potential staff for such an operation. Which of the many possibilities did he have in mind? He could not have meant Storrs, who had his own power base and a heavy round of duties as oriental secretary, or Ronald Graham, who was about to return to London and the Foreign Office. Possibly he meant Lieutenant T.E. Lawrence, who was soon to assume an important role in the bureau's work, though in January he was just beginning to make his mark and was not to be officially appointed to the bureau until the fall. Another possibility was Kinahan Cornwallis, a thirty-two-year-old captain who had been in the Sudan Civil Service before the war and was in Cairo making a strong impression with his knowledge of Arabic and Arab affairs; he was, in fact, to replace Hogarth in August as chief of the Arab Bureau. There also were two civilians, either of whom Clayton could have had in mind. One was Philip Graves, for many years the *Times* correspondent in Constantinople, and now making his services freely available for intelligence work in Cairo; he was soon to be commissioned as a captain in military intelligence. The other was Gertrude Bell, the most famous Arabist of them all. In Cairo since November at the request of Hogarth and Admiralty intelligence, she was at work writing assessments of various Arab tribes and sheikhs. But by the end of January, upon Hogarth's arrival to take up his new post, she was on her way to India and thence to Basra, where she would take up the position of oriental secretary to the political resident, Sir Percy Cox.

Hogarth's work at the bureau that winter and spring may occasionally have had the air of a university seminar. With the help of, among others, his former students Lawrence and Woolley—the latter occasionally coming down from Port Said, where he was in charge of military intelligence—Hogarth supervised the preparation of such reports as the one in April summarizing the negotiations with the Sherif, and of handbooks. By the beginning of June, two of the latter had been published, one on Asir by Cornwallis and one on the Hejaz by Hogarth himself. Lawrence suggested that the bureau publish a recurring report of Middle Eastern news for British Government officials the world over, and the *Arab Bulletin* soon got under way. But the bureau—which significantly adopted the telegraphic code name "Intrusive"—also did not hesitate to move beyond the mere collecting and disseminating of information to the beginnings of a more activist role.

Indeed, if it is true—as some historians have suggested—that, ever since the days of digging and of observing the German railway builders at Carchemish, Hogarth had been presiding over a more or less informal spy ring, in which Lawrence was one of the star disciples, then it was being triumphantly revived in Cairo in 1916. After the Russians, for example, had begun an offensive in Armenia early in the year, Lawrence had been able to put their intelligence in touch with anti-Turkish Arab officers in Erzerum: this may possibly have aided them in the capture of that city on February 16. In late March, Lawrence was sent to Kut-el-Amara, where the ten thousand British troops who had retreated after failing to take Baghdad in November were still under siege, to see if he could ransom them from the Turkish commander. He raised the offer from £1 million to £2 million while there, but he was refused, and found himself taking part in the negotiations for the surrender of the garrison on April 29. Allowed to leave, he was soon again "nailed within that office at Cairo—the most interesting place there is till the Near East settles down," but as eager as his colleagues to play a role in the imminent Arab revolt. As it happened, the first issue of the *Arab Bulletin*, in which he was prominently involved, came out the day after Ali and Feisal had proclaimed the revolt outside Medina.

For Ali and Feisal, the proclamation on the morning of June 5 was the climax of a journey that had begun with their departure from Mecca at the end of the previous year. By then Djemal Pasha was planning another attack on the Suez Canal, and the Hashimites ostensibly were playing a role in the preparations for it. While Hussein had stayed in Mecca with Abdullah and his youngest son Zaid to recruit a promised fifteen hundred soldiers, Ali had gone to Medina and Feisal to Damascus. From the Turkish point of view, Ali's task in Medina was to prepare to take command of the battalion raised by his father; but his real purpose, according to his family's historian George Antonius, was "to watch the Turkish governor and instruct the neighboring tribal chiefs who were to be let into the secret." As for Feisal, he had placed himself in the midst of Djemal's entourage "with the settled purpose," Antonius writes, "of fomenting a revolt of the Arab divisions in the Turkish army and a mass rising of the population, on a signal from his father. Accompanying him were a picked retinue of some forty determined men, several of them members of the Sharif's clan, who were to form his personal bodyguard and who, like him, were carrying their life in their hands. To Jemal, he justified their presence by representing them as an advance-guard of the force which the Sharif had been asked to raise in the Hejaz, and the pretext had been taken at its face-value and welcomed."

Djemal's suspicions against Feisal were slow to be aroused, perhaps because there was little harm left for him to do in Damascus. Djemal had already taken the precaution of transferring a large part of the Syrian officer corps, with its complement of such potential rebels as al-Faruqi, to other fronts. With troops returning from Gallipoli, a second attack upon the Suez Canal was being prepared. As for the Arab nationalist leadership remaining in the country, Djemal now ferreted them out. One execution took place in April; twenty-one more were scheduled for the first week in May. Feisal was in a delicate situation. He "moved heaven and earth," Djemal was to recall, "to secure a pardon for the condemned men. He came to see me every day, and always brought the conversation round to the question of pardon." Antonius confirms that Feisal "pleaded with Djemal in person" on behalf of the accused, although it is hard to see how he was able to do so without arousing suspicion against himself. Lawrence claims that "it took the intercessions of his Constantinople friends, chief men in Turkey, to save him from the price of these rash words," but no inkling of this is to be found in Djemal's or Antonius's account. Perhaps Djemal assumed that, since the condemned men's offenses had not yet been publicly announced, Feisal was making a merely sentimental display of Arab solidarity in their favor. Djemal writes that when the facts making clear "how shameless their treason was" were at last published on the day of the twenty-one executions, Feisal came to him and said:

"I swear by the memory of my ancestors that, had I known how heinous was the offense of those criminals, I should not merely have refused to intervene for them. I should have asked them to be torn limb from limb to prolong their sufferings. God's curse be upon them!"

These words may have quelled any suspicions felt by Djemal. They were in marked contrast to the ones Feisal had uttered that morning, according to Antonius, when news of the mass execution had been brought to him at the home of friends a few miles outside Damascus. Then he had leaped to his feet, thrown his *kefiyeh* to the ground, trampled upon it, and cried: "Tab al-maut va 'Arab!" ("Death [for the sake of our ideals] is sweet, O Arabs!") Antonius, here acknowledging that Feisal had indeed "gone beyond the bounds of prudence in pleading with Jemal for the lives of the Arab patriots," adds significantly: "Whatever doubts may have lingered in his mind as to the wisdom of breaking with the Turks were now swept away in a passionate revulsion of feeling, and the cry which escaped him on hearing the news of the executions became the battle cry of the Arab Revolt." Lingering doubts? Here is another possible element in the story. Djemal may simply have been giving Feisal the benefit of *his* doubts until now.

For the dictator of Syria shows himself to have been troubled for some time by the behavior of the rest of Feisal's family, at any rate. Both Hussein and Ali were now openly quarreling with the Turkish governors in Mecca and in Medina, respectively, and were in general showing the old Hashimite insubordination to Constantinople. Djemal, who had cabled a reprimand to Hussein in February or March, writes that he finally called in Feisal in May and told him that "your father is beginning to show separatist inclinations, while your brother, Ali Bey, is pursuing a line of conduct which is in harmony with your father's claims." According to his account, he even intimated that he thought they had rebellion in mind, but Feisal had protested passionately and said he would bring his brother Ali to kiss Djemal's hand. Djemal depicts himself as growing suspicious of all of them, but unable under the circumstances to do anything about it. "At that time I had no documentary evidence of the criminal designs of these people," he says. In Antonius's version, Djemal was at this point still completely deceived by Feisal, who "played his cards with consummate skill."

Certainly the most accomplished deception of all was only now about to come, if we are to believe T.E. Lawrence, who, at this particular moment in the narrative, rivals Antonius for the role of Feisal's uncritical historian. It was time for Feisal to rejoin Ali in Medina and take charge of the fifteen hundred troops their father had raised. Their purpose was revolt; but Feisal persuaded Djemal to let him go there on the pretext that he would personally lead these recruits into Syria for the new Sinai campaign, which had already begun late in April with a successful Turkish assault upon the Katia oasis, some twenty-five miles east of the Suez Canal. But Djemal, in giving his consent, had added that he and Enver Pasha were going to follow Feisal to Medina and inspect the troops Hussein had gathered. Feisal, upon hearing this, had to swallow his dismay. He had planned, according to Lawrence, "to raise his father's crimson banner as soon as he arrived in Medina, and so to take the Turks unawares; and here he was going to be saddled with two uninvited guests to whom, by the Arab law of hospitality, he could do no harm, and who would probably delay his action so long that the whole secret of the revolt would be in jeopardy!"

And so the charade was played out, "though the irony of the review was terrible," Lawrence writes. "Enver, Jemal and Feisal watched the troops wheeling and turning in the dusty plain outside the city gate, rushing up and down in mimic camel-battle, or spurring their horses in the javelin game after immemorial Arab fashion. 'And are all these volunteers for the Holy War?' asked Enver at last, turning to Feisal. 'Yes,' said Feisal. 'Willing to fight to the death against the enemies of the faithful?' 'Yes,' said Feisal again"; though, in another moment, one of the Arab chiefs who had come up to be presented drew the young Hashimite aside and whispered, "My Lord, shall we kill them now?" "No," Feisal replied, "they are our guests."

Lawrence says that the sheikhs protested against this stand, and that Feisal had to go out of earshot with them to "plead for the lives of the Turkish dictators, who had murdered his best friends on the scaffold. In the end he had to make excuses, take the party back quickly to Medina, picket the banqueting hall with his own slaves, and escort Enver and Jemal back to Damascus to save them from death on the way. He explained this labored courtesy by the plea that it was the Arab manner to devote everything to guests; but Enver and Jemal being deeply suspicious of what they had seen, imposed a strict blockade of the Hejaz, and ordered large Turkish reinforcements thither." Actually, the thirty-five hundred Turkish troops at that moment heading by rail to Medina under the command of Khairy Bey had been sent under the initiative of Baron Othmar von Stotzingen, one of the German generals in Turkey, for the ostensible purpose of establishing themselves in the Yemen. It apparently was intended that they menace Aden from there and possibly provide reinforcement to troops fighting in German East Africa. Another of their purposes may have been to keep the Sherif in line—in which case, Djemal and Enver may not have been so naïve after all. Whatever the purposes of this military force, however, Hussein certainly saw its impending passage through Mecca as a threat to himself, and we are told that this was why he pushed up the date of his revolt to early June, instead of August as he originally had planned.

As for Feisal, Lawrence writes that Djemal and Enver wanted to detain him in Damascus after he had escorted them there; "but telegrams came from Medina claiming his immediate return to prevent disorder, and, reluctantly, Jemal let him go on condition that his suite remained behind as hostages." However it came about, Feisal was back in Medina by June 1 and found the city full of Turkish troops, all under the command of Fakhri Pasha, who had achieved worldwide notoriety by slaughtering Armenians. Four days later Feisal was in the desert with his brother Ali. "When he raised the Arab flag," as Lawrence was to see it, "the pan-Islamic supranational State, for which Abdul Hamid had massacred and worked and died,* and the German hope of the co-operation of Islam in the world-plans of the Kaiser, passed into the realm of dreams."

As early as May 23 Hussein's supporters at Cairo headquarters had word that the long-awaited event was in the offing. On that day, they had received a message from Port Sudan on the Red Sea coast, a regular point of communication with Asir and the Hejaz across the water. "Sharif's son Abdallah urgently requires Storrs to come to Arabian coast to meet him," it read. "Movement will begin as soon as Faisal arrives at Mecca." Storrs departed from Cairo on the evening of May 28, accompanied by Hogarth and Cornwallis and carrying £10,000 in gold. Sailing from Suez the following morning, they made several stops on both the African and the Arabian coasts of the Red Sea—where the British navy was in control—picking up at one port Storrs's assistant, the Persian agent Ruhi, and at another, a

---

* Actually, Abdul Hamid II, in exile since 1909, was still alive and would be for another two years.

message from the Foreign Office approving payment of £50,000 more to the Sherif, but "only in return for definite action and if a reliable rising takes place." On June 5, the day of Feisal's and Ali's proclamation outside Medina, Storrs and his companions were anchored off Jeddah, "a fine town," as Storrs described it, "with four and even five-storeyed houses and one minaret nearly as much out of the perpendicular as the leaning tower of Pisa." There they had expected to meet Abdullah, but were handed three messages instead.

The first was signed by the Sherif Hussein, though Storrs could tell that it was in Abdullah's handwriting. "Honorable and respected," it read, "I deeply regret my inability to send Abdallah for an urgent reason which bearer will explain: but his brother [Zaid] will represent him with one of his cousins, Sharif Shakir, Amir of the Ataibah, of the same degree as himself." The second note was an unsigned slip, which said: "Please order by wireless immediately 500 rifles of same pattern as those already sent us. Details of consignment from our sons Zaid and Shakir and also 4 machine guns, both with ammunition." The third letter was written and signed by Abdullah. "To the most honored and respected Mr. Storrs," it said: "I deeply regret I am unable to meet you personally, but an urgent need has called me and taken me, so my brother will come to you with all news. My own request of you is to start operations in Syria to the best of your ability. God is our guide. Later will be our real meeting."

The reference to "operations in Syria" was an expression of the Hashimite family's undying hope that the British would yet stage a landing at Alexandretta. As for Abdullah's absence, this was explained by the messenger as being due to his departure for Taif, to which he and his troops were going to lay siege: this was the first the Englishmen had heard to the effect that the revolt actually was in progress. The messenger told them that the date set for military action was next Saturday, June 10. "He said the movement would be initiated simultaneously at Medina by Feisal and Ali; at Mecca by the Grand Sharif: at Tayif by Abdallah, and at Jedda by Sharif Mohsin, Amir of the Harb tribe." Storrs sent a telegram explaining all this to McMahon in Cairo.

The next morning the English ship was anchored outside a village near Jeddah, about two miles from shore. Storrs and his companions got into a small boat at 5:30 A.M. and headed for land, until they broke their rudder on a reef. "With me," Storrs later reported, "were Hogarth, Cornwallis, Oraifan [the messenger], Agent Ruhi, £10,000 and two sacks of al-Haqiqa ["The Truth," Cairo headquarters' Arabic propaganda newspaper] besides light refreshments for the party we expected ashore. Soon a canoe shot towards us directed by Shaikh Ali, who takes consignment of our munitions embarked from Port Sudan. He guided us through the reef to a dhow half-full of sacks of dura—maize—where, there being no sign of Zaid upon the beach, we tied up and sat for over an hour whilst the mariners hauled across a sail as an awning and spread their shawls over the sacks, making us fairly comfortable.

"At length a bunch of ten camels appeared on the horizon and descended to the shore where Oraifan, who had meanwhile prepared a tent of honor, awaited them. He soon came off in his canoe, announcing that Zaid wished me to land and see him alone." Storrs set off in Oraifan's canoe, and ten yards from shore was picked up and carried the rest of the way by two slaves. Zaid and Shakir came up to him and exchanged greetings; then the three of them retired to the tent and sat down on rugs. Storrs noted that Zaid, "the youngest son of the Sharif by his second wife, a Circassian of good family, is and looks about 20 years of age. I tested him later in Turkish and found he spoke it well and fluently. He is about five feet five in height, fair in complexion, with fine eyes and the round face and Greek profile characteristic of Circassians. He is evidently attempting to encourage the growth of a somewhat backward beard." As for Shakir, he was "two inches taller and perhaps ten years older," with hair plaited in several long thin tails.

Zaid then confirmed Oraifan's report of the day before that the rising had been fixed for the coming Saturday. Storrs asked him what his family's specific plans were, and he replied: "We will summon the Turks to surrender and shoot them if they refuse. If they surrender we will imprison them until the end of the war. We intend to destroy the Hejaz railways as far north as Medain Salih, which will be our advance post." Zaid then asked for still more money—another £20,000 beyond the £50,000 that the British Government had just pledged—and also urged a British landing on the Syrian coast, at Alexandretta or elsewhere. Storrs put him off regarding both these matters and asked him about the Muslim pilgrimage from India, which had not been possible in the last two years owing to the war. Zaid assured him that this fall it would be possible.

After coffee, Storrs proposed that they visit the English ship. "Leaving our own refreshments for the guard," he writes, "we were carried with much splashing to the boat where I presented Hogarth and Cornwallis." They reached the ship at about 9:15 A.M. and had breakfast. After a shipboard tour and a session of posing for photographs, the two young Arabs left by steam launch at about 12:30 P.M., escorted as far as the dhow by Storrs and Cornwallis. "Here they took leave of us with very cordial farewells," Storrs writes, "carrying with them, rather to our alarm, the £10,000 and the two bundles of *al-Haqiqa*; I sending after them from the ship 1000 cigarettes for Faisal and Ali, the only smokers in the family, at Medina." Storrs had already given his own wristwatch to Zaid.

Storrs and his companions were back in Egypt on June 10, and only then did they learn of the death of Kitchener. "Al-Lurd, al-Lurd mat," one sheikh kept saying, "Allah yirhamu!" ("The 'Lord,' the 'Lord' is dead, may God have mercy upon him!") Storrs was greatly shaken by the loss of his "dear old chief," but wrote and submitted his report right away. The next day McMahon wired London:

> Storrs returned yesterday and I dispatched his report by bag yesterday.
> He met Zaid as arranged on June 5th. Outbreak was to commence on June 4th [*sic*] at Medina under Sherif's [sons] Faisal and Ali. Risings elsewhere to take place on June 10th that is at Mecca under Sherif, at Taif under Abdullah, and at Jeddah under . . . Abdel Mohsin. Railway was to operate as far as Medisaleh where their advanced posts will be.
> Owing to youth and inexperience of Zaid it was impossible to obtain very detailed information, but appreciation of the situation formed by Storrs and Hogarth is that revolt is genuine and inevitable but about to be undertaken with inadequate preparations in ignorance of modern warfare. Both in organization and armament of forces too much has been left to the last moment and to luck. Success will depend on their overwhelming numbers. It is evident that we should assist them by all means possible at our disposal. Success also will raise problems demanding our assistance.

Meanwhile, neither Cairo nor London had word yet about what had happened the day before—about whether the revolt had enjoyed any success or even whether it had taken place at all.

It had indeed taken place. The first shots of the revolt had been heard in Mecca at 3:30 A.M. on Saturday, June 10, when troops loyal to the Sherif opened fire on several Turkish barracks and the main government building. Because it was summer, when large numbers of the Turkish soldiers in the garrison were sent up to Taif on a relatively cool inland plateau, not many of them were in Mecca at that moment. But they possessed one major advantage that the Arabs lacked—artillery. The Arab attack was soon answered by a barrage of shells from the Jiyad fortress, high on a hilltop just south of the city. The Sherifian palace was hit, though apparently no one in it was injured. In response to a telephone call from the officers commanding the garrison, the Sherif sent a delegation to discuss the situation with them. The delegation announced that the country had declared its independence and asked the Turks to lay down their arms. The request was refused, and the exchanges of fire were resumed until nightfall.

The results of the other Arab attacks that day were equally indecisive. At Jeddah, a force of some thirty-five hundred Harb tribesmen led by Sherif Mohsin attempted to force entry into the town, which was garrisoned by only fifteen hundred Turkish soldiers; but they too were held off by artillery fire. At Taif, Abdullah's forces did not attack until midnight. "The Turks had fortified the walls of the town and dug trenches," he later was to recall. "Our attack was made with great violence. In the center our riflemen made a raid and returned with some prisoners and loot. At sunrise the Turkish artillery began to shell us heavily." By evening Abdullah's thirsty and exhausted troops, their ammunition used up, had to withdraw to positions well outside the city. The situation at Medina was the worst of all. Unable to cope with Fakhri Pasha's overwhelming force, Feisal and Ali had withdrawn, respectively, to Yenbo and Rabegh on the coast.

In the days of sometimes sustained, sometimes desultory fighting that ensued, the first Arab success was at Jeddah, where the Turkish garrison surrendered on June 16. This had happened because that coastal and consular city was not, in contrast to the inland holy districts of Mecca and Medina, off limits to non-Muslims and their military capacities. Compensating for the Arab lack of artillery, British warships had shelled the Turkish positions, and British seaplanes had dropped bombs. Muslim contingents from the Egyptian army, with Muhammad al-Faruqi in their midst, also had landed there. These same reinforcements, along with fresh supplies of ammunition, enabled the Sherif's men at Mecca to subdue the Jiyad fortress at last on July 4, though not before the Holy Kaaba—the most sacred spot in the Muslim world—had been hit by its shells. Similar aid made it possible for Abdullah—who did not risk a second assault—to maintain a siege at Taif until it capitulated on September 21. But even siege tactics could not bring about the surrender of Medina, the southern terminus of the Hejaz railway, so long as the

railway itself—well within territory still controlled by the Turks—
remained intact.

The British public first received word on June 22 of what had
happened in the Hejaz. *The Times* gave a rather sanguine report.
"GREAT ARAB REVOLT," ran the headline, "MECCA TAKEN FROM THE
TURKS"—nearly two weeks before the fact—"MEDINA BESIEGED."
"Authentic news has been received," the article ran,

> that His Highness the Grand Sherif of Mecca, supported by the
> Arab tribes of West and Central Arabia, has proclaimed Arab
> independence of Turkey and of Ottoman rule, under whose mal-
> administration and inaction the country has so far suffered.
>
> Operations began about June 9 and have resulted in the
> signal success of the Sherif's forces.
>
> Mecca, Jeddah, and Taif have been captured [*sic*], and the
> garrisons have surrendered, with the exception of two small
> forts at Taif, which are said to be still holding out.
>
> The numbers of the troops who surrendered at Mecca and
> Taif are not yet known, but at Jeddah 45 officers, 1,400 men, and
> six guns were captured.
>
> Medina, according to the latest news, is closely besieged,
> and all communications to the Hejaz are in the hands of the
> Sherif.
>
> The fact that Jeddah is in secure possession of the Grand
> Sherif now makes it possible to reopen communications by sea,
> and trade to the Hejaz port can now be resumed. It is, therefore,
> confidently expected that the difficulties which have attended
> the annual pilgrimage to the Holy Places during the past two
> years will now be removed.

Continuing jubilation over triumphs in the East could have been
a much-needed tonic for a people who were about to enter into yet
another hopeless and devastating round of slaughter on the western
front. For the Battle of the Somme—British repayment for the mass
French immolation that was approaching its end at Verdun—began
nine days later, on July 1, and by nightfall nearly sixty thousand
British soldiers had died, been wounded, or taken prisoner there. It
is generally held that on the Somme then and in the days that followed, the "Kitchener armies"—the masses of volunteers who had
responded to that strong face calling out from the poster Your Country Needs *You*—died their final death: it was to be the new conscript
army fighting for Britain from now on. The Kitchener era had
passed—except perhaps in the Middle East, where his star had risen

in the first place. Even now, some Englishmen may have been stirred by the old dreams of colonial glory there—of dramatic victories in the desert to make up for the frustrations of Flanders and France. But soon the summer passed and, for the time being at any rate, there was no more good news from the Middle East either.

"However it was," T.E. Lawrence writes, "things in the Hejaz went from bad to worse. No proper liaison was provided for the Arab forces in the field, no military information was given the Sherifs, no tactical advice or strategy was suggested, no attempt made to find out the local conditions and adapt existing Allied resources in material to suit their needs." Lieutenant Colonel C.C. Wilson of the Sudan Political Service had been sent over to Jeddah as the British representative to the Sherif's new sovereign authority, and a French mission under Colonel Edouard Brémond established itself there in September. These, and the Egyptian Muslim troops that now were stationed between Medina and Mecca to prevent any Turkish advance upon the latter, were what the Allies had provided—along with money and supplies—to the Arab revolt so far; direct interference was something that London and Paris had long ago pledged to Hussein they never would make. Furthermore, in a major engagement in the Sinai at Romani in August, British troops had decisively repelled the second Turkish threat to the Suez Canal. This helped bring about a lessening of military pressure in the whole region.

Nevertheless, Lawrence—and no doubt some of his Cairo colleagues along with him—thought that what had been done so far with regard to the Hejaz revolt was even worse than unhelpful. The French mission, he believed, "was permitted to carry on an elaborate intrigue against Sherif Hussein in his towns of Jidda and Mecca, and to propose to him and to the British authorities measures that must have ruined his cause in the eyes of all Moslems." Lawrence, who had been one of Cairo's most ardent advocates of a British landing at Alexandretta, was by now quite convinced that French ambitions in Syria were the great stumbling block in the way of Arab national hopes. He could only conclude, at least in retrospect years later: "The Arab Revolt became discredited; and staff officers in Egypt gleefully prophesied to us its near failure and the stretching of Sherif Hussein's neck on a Turkish scaffold." Eager to prepare the way for such an eventuality, the Turks had appointed a new emir of Mecca, Ali Haidar, who had been waiting in Medina since July for the day when he would replace Hussein.

Lawrence himself had spent the summer working on the preparation of maps and of the *Arab Bulletin* and designing postage stamps for the independent Hejaz. "I'm going to have flavored gum on the back," he had written home in July, "so that one may lick without unpleasantness." But the urge for action on the part of this brilliant and slightly eccentric young man—who was known at Cairo headquarters for his rumpled uniform and generally unmilitary demeanor—was growing strong. Two of his four brothers had been killed fighting in France during 1915. Writing about this to a friend, he had observed that "they were both younger than I am, and it doesn't seem right, somehow, that I should go on living peacefully in Cairo." Furthermore, by the late summer of 1916 the military intelligence section in Cairo, to which he was technically still attached, had become uncongenial to him. Clayton had been transferred to other duties by the new commander in chief, Sir Archibald Murray—who was far less favorably disposed to the Arab nationalist movement than his predecessor Sir John Maxwell had been—and had been replaced in that position by Colonel Thomas Holdich, who shared his general's views. It was in response to this that Lawrence had managed to get himself transferred officially to the Arab Bureau by the end of September. But then he promptly arranged another assignment for himself, the outcome of which was to make him a legendary figure.

At the end of September, Storrs had made another trip to Jeddah, in an attempt, which proved unsuccessful, to make personal contact with the Sherif. Then, as he writes, "I had hardly returned to Alexandria when we received a telegram from . . . Abdullah begging me to run back to Arabia and have a few words with him." And so, in early October, Storrs prepared to make his "third descent to the Hejaz"—but on this occasion, unlike the second, he was not to leave Cairo alone. Lawrence, at boiling point in his antagonisms with his immediate military superiors, "took this strategic opportunity," he writes, "to ask for ten days' leave, saying that Storrs was going down to Jidda on business with the Grand Sherif, and that I would like a holiday and joyride in the Red Sea with him. They did not love Storrs, and were glad to get rid of me for the moment. So they agreed at once." Lawrence wrote home on October 12, "I am going off tomorrow for a few days. I hope to be back in about a fortnight or less." Later that day, Storrs found himself on "the train from Cairo little Lawrence my super-cerebral companion."

Sailing from Suez in the company of Aziz Ali al-Masri—who,

after two years in Cairo representing the Arab nationalist cause to the English, was to try taking command of the Sherif's armed forces—Storrs and Lawrence reached Jeddah on October 16. Storrs promptly rode out with Colonel Wilson for a preliminary conversation with Abdullah—whom he was seeing in person for the first time since the spring of 1914—at the latter's camp; but the main discussion was held for Abdullah's return visit to the consulate that afternoon. "Abdulla, on a white mare," Lawrence was to recall, "came to us softly with a bevy of richly-armed slaves on foot about him, through the silent respectful salutes of the town. He was flushed with his success at Taif, and happy. I was seeing him for the first time, while Storrs was an old friend, and on the best of terms; yet, before long, as they spoke together, I began to suspect him of a constant cheerfulness." As the conversation went on, Lawrence writes, "I became more and more sure that Abdulla was too balanced, too cool, too humorous to be a prophet: especially the armed prophet who, if history be true, succeeded in revolutions." If the atmosphere of Destiny pervading these words is being breathed more by the author of the *Seven Pillars of Wisdom* than by the young subaltern of October 1916, we may nevertheless perceive that keen and eager mind at work even then, perhaps making observations somewhere along these lines.

Abdullah complained at length of the insufficient help he thought the British to be giving the Arab cause, but the conversation remained friendly. Lawrence, joining into the Arabic dialogue, showed such a detailed knowledge of the situation in the Hejaz that at one point Abdullah turned to Storrs in amazement and asked: "Is this man God, to know everything?" The afternoon culminated in a telephone call from the sherif himself in Mecca, behind whom could be heard a military band playing. In another day or two, while Storrs stayed on in Jeddah for further conversations, Lawrence sailed north to Rabegh, now determined to find out on his own as much as he could about the Arab revolt. On the ship he met Lieutenant Colonel A.C. Parker, who had been so critical of Picot back in November when he was still at the War Office and who was now working out of Egypt as the British liaison officer with the Sherif's eldest son Ali. Parker, who doubtless was pleased to find a man as suspicious as himself of the French role in the Arab world, arranged that Lawrence be introduced to Ali and through him to Feisal. "To Ali himself I took a great fancy," the historical Lawrence was to write, though noting that he was too much "the prey of any constant companion, and too sensitive to advice for a great leader." He concluded that if

"Feisal should turn out to be no prophet, the revolt would make shift well enough with Ali for its head."

But Lawrence seems already to have made up his mind that Feisal, whom he had still to meet, would prove to be the best of the Hashimites. It was already known in Cairo that he was the most imposing personality among the Sherif's sons, and the most capable military commander. For Lawrence, Feisal's anticipated luster was now to be added to by his first taste of the Arabian desert, the true homeland of the culture he had studied for so long: for Feisal's headquarters were at the village of Hamra on the Wadi Safra, some seventy-five miles across the sands to the north of Rabegh.

Setting out on camel-back with a guide, Lawrence soon rediscovered the world celebrated by Burton and Doughty. "My camel was a delight to me," he found, "for I had not been on such an animal before. There were no good camels in Egypt; and those of the Sinai Desert, while hardy and strong, were not taught to pace fair and softly and swiftly, like these rich mounts of the Arabian princes." In those few days he learned something more of the beauty and the lore of the desert, the rivalries over its watering places, and its special hardships. At the end of one day he observed how the long ride had "tired my unaccustomed muscles, and the heat of the plain had been painful. My skin was blistered by it, and my eyes ached with the glare of light striking up at a sharp angle from the silver sand, and from the shining pebbles. The last two years I had spent in Cairo, at a desk all day or thinking hard in a little overcrowded office full of distracting noises, with a hundred rushing things to say, but no bodily need except to come and go each day between office and hotel. In consequence the novelty of this change was severe, since time had not been given me gradually to accustom myself to the pestilent beating of the Arabian sun, and the long monotony of camel pacing."

At length they came to Hamra, with about a hundred houses, forded a stream, went up a walled path, and made their camels kneel alongside a low house. The guide spoke to a slave, who thereupon led Lawrence to an "inner court, on whose further side, framed between the uprights of a black doorway, stood a white figure waiting tensely for me. I felt at first glance that this was the man I had come to Arabia to seek—the leader who would bring the Arab Revolt to full glory. Feisal looked very tall and pillar-like, very slender, in his long white silk robes and his brown head-cloth bound with a brilliant scarlet and gold cord. His eyelids were dropped; and his black beard and colourless face were like a mask against the strange, still watchfulness of his body. His hands were crossed in front of him on his dagger."

Feisal guided Lawrence into a room that "held many silent figures," gazing steadily at the Englishman or at their leader. Lawrence has told posterity that Feisal, after commenting on the speed of his journey, then asked him, "And do you like our place here in Wadi Safra?" and that he replied: "Well; but it is far from Damascus." This remark, he writes, "had fallen like a sword in their midst. There was a quiver." Whether or not Lawrence had begun in that moment to assume leadership of the Arab revolt—indeed, whether or not he was ever really to assume it—he was at any rate no longer eager to hurry back to Cairo.

·28·

THE ADVENTURES OF
AARON AARONSOHN

Around the time Lawrence met Feisal, a man from Palestine who also had been doing undercover work for the British arrived in London at the end of a long and tortuous itinerary. It had begun in the first week of July at his home a few miles from the settlement town of Zichron Ya'akov, south of Haifa. Traveling at first by mule cart, he had journeyed for a week from Haifa to Beirut and then Damascus. At Damascus he obtained a travel permit from Djemal Pasha in person, boarded a troop train headed into Anatolia, and reached Constantinople on July 22. He stayed a month in the Turkish capital, leaving at last on August 19 on a train going via Bulgaria to Berlin. After a short sojourn there, he went on to Hamburg, from which he sailed to Copenhagen on September 16. In the capital of neutral Denmark it took him a month to establish discreet contact with the British consular authorities and make the arrangements he sought, but on October 19 he was able to embark on the *Oskar II*, bound for New York. At Kirkwall in the Orkneys the ship was intercepted by a British naval patrol, which, after a seemingly routine interrogation of the passengers, "discovered" the stowaway Aaron Aaronsohn and removed him. In London by October 24, Aaronsohn was ready to provide military intelligence there with a good deal of useful information.

The forty-year-old Aaronsohn, stocky, energetic, and a master agriculturist, had been among the finest fruits of the first generation of Jewish pioneering in the Holy Land. Born in Bacau, Rumania, he had emigrated at the age of six with his parents and a younger brother to Palestine, where they formed part of the group that founded Zichron Ya'akov in 1882. Four more children had then been born to Ephraim and Malkah Aaronsohn, but Aaron, as the eldest, tended to assume moral leadership among an unusually close-knit and energetic group of brothers and sisters. At eighteen, after several years of working under the agricultural administrators sent to the colony by Baron Edmond de Rothschild, Aaron was invited by that benefactor to go to France and study at the agricultural college in Grignon. He spent two years there, then returned to Palestine and became an instructor at the newly founded colony of Metullah, in the northernmost Galilee; but within a year he had run afoul of the baron's administrators and was dismissed. Quickly finding work as the manager of a large farm in Anatolia, he stayed there the next two years, learning the language and customs of the Turks as well as deepening his knowledge in his own field.

Back in Palestine just before the turn of the century, Aaronsohn began a period of thrashing about in search of his true calling that was to last several years. In 1901 he was one of three young men—the other two were, respectively, an agronomist and an engineer—who founded a bureau to make agricultural and technical surveys of Palestine for potential Jewish settlement. In 1904 he participated in a geological expedition around the Dead Sea led by the German professor, Max Blanckenhorn. The following year he was part of a survey along some of the route of the future Hejaz railway, and the year after that was on a botanical exploration of Palestine with Professor Otto Warburg of Berlin. By this time, Aaronsohn was an expert in Palestine geology and knew more about the country's flora than anyone else alive. Encouraged by the German botanists with whom he had worked, both in Palestine and on two visits to Berlin, he began a search for wild wheat—for the natural prototype of the common wheat known only in its cultivated form for centuries, which was in need of being strengthened through cross breeding with that primitive counterpart—and found it in the Upper Galilee in the summer of 1906.

On the basis of this discovery, Aaronsohn acquired a worldwide reputation. After participating with Blanckenhorn in another Dead Sea expedition, he was invited to visit the United States in 1909 by the Department of Agriculture. There he spent a pleasant year writing a department bulletin on "Agricultural and Botanical Explorations in Palestine" and giving advice in the western states on wheat cultivation. He even received an invitation to stay and teach at the University of California, but, owing to the contacts he made with prominent American Jews during his stay, he was able instead to return home and carry out a project that would be the proper fulfillment of his life's work.

Since 1904 the Zionist organization had been planning to set up an agricultural experimental station in Palestine, where the fruits of the land's future could be developed and tested. Otto Warburg, who was not only one of the world's foremost botanists but a leading Zionist as well, was particularly interested in this project, and through his own intimate contacts with American Jews was able to arouse interest among them in the potential of this young man who had become one of his protégés. The result was that a group of American friends, led by the Chicago philanthropist Julius Rosenwald, provided Aaronsohn with the funds to establish such a station. Returning to Palestine in 1910, Aaronsohn persuaded one of his younger brothers, twenty-two-year-old Alexander, to return to the United States in his place and carry on his work at the Department of Agriculture.

Aaron Aaronsohn chose a site at Athlit on the coastal plain at the foot of Mount Carmel, about nine miles north of Zichron Ya'akov and alongside the ruins of a Crusader fortress. He began there "a type of experimental agriculture which would be epoch-making" in the opinion of his friends at the U.S. Department of Agriculture. In Palestine itself his work became legendary, even among the younger generation of Labor- and Socialist-oriented settlers who had begun to arrive in the wake of the Kishinev pogrom and who resented him for employing Arabs at the station instead of self-made workers from their own ranks. One of them who eventually got to work for him by not asking for wages, Rahel Yanait,* was to describe his achievements with great admiration, writing, for example, of one of the station's departments:

> It was a marvelous tree nursery. Aaronsohn was proud of the improved genus of fig tree he had imported from Smyrna, and explained the process of its maturation. He had meticulously tended mulberry trees taller than a man, their trunks white-washed—the latest types from California. There were trees from the world over, even Japan. Aaronsohn had studied dry-farming in Utah, which resembled Palestine in soil quality and sparse rainfall.

Of his geological work, she noted that he "could read the fossils as a pious Jew reads the Scriptural portion of the week."

The Agricultural Experimental Station became a stop virtually

* Later Rahel Yanait Ben-Zvi, whose husband was to be the second president of the State of Israel.

required for distinguished visitors from abroad, especially the United States. Indeed, it was in some ways a touch of America itself: in 1912 Aaronsohn imported Palestine's first motor car from there and built from the station to the main highway the only really good stretch of macadamized road in the country. In 1913 he joined his brother in the United States for another extended sojourn, giving lectures and fund-raising talks and meeting, among other notables, Louis D. Brandeis, who wrote of him: "As a talker, he is one of the most interesting men I have met." Alexander, who had applied for his first citizenship papers in the United States, returned with Aaron to Palestine to take photographs and film footage for further lectures. He was there when the war broke out and soon found himself—an American in speech, aspirations, and outlook, but still technically an Ottoman subject—conscripted into the Turkish army.

As for Aaron, his American connections combined with his own talents and achievements to place him in a position of considerable importance in wartime Palestine. From the moment the *North Carolina* arrived with $50,000 in gold at the end of September 1914, he was one of the administrators of the American relief funds and supplies that soon were arriving with some regularity. Together with Arthur Ruppin, the Zionist organization's chief representative in Palestine, he took part in a renewed effort to coordinate the affairs of the country's hitherto loosely organized Jewish community. He did not hesitate to complain to Djemal Pasha during the latter's persecutions of Jews in the winter of 1914-15, but this does not seem to have harmed his status under the Turks. On the contrary, he soon was given an important new responsibility by them. That spring, after Djemal had relented in his treatment of the Jews, the country fell under a scourge even greater than himself: a plague of locusts. "Airborne swarms of locusts darkened the sky," Arthur Ruppin was to recall; "the young ones, still unable to fly, crawled out of their eggs and formed processions thirty to fifty meters wide and several kilometers long and devoured the corn and the greenery on the trees." Djemal assigned Aaron Aaronsohn to apply his scientific skills to combating the scourge.

It was to the hatching eggs on the ground—the flying locusts were a hopeless target—that Aaronsohn devoted his efforts after Djemal had given him several thousand Arab soldiers to help in the task. But discovering and destroying all the eggs required the cooperation of farmers, many of whom were not educated to the awareness needed, and after two months the surviving eggs had hatched and a new swarm covered the land. "Not only was every green leaf devoured," Alexander Aaronsohn was to recall, "but the very bark was peeled from the trees, which stood out white and lifeless, like skeletons. The fields were stripped to the ground, and the old men of our villages, who had given their lives to cultivating the gardens and vineyards, came out of the synagogues where they had been praying and wailing, and looked on the ruin with dimmed eyes. Nothing was spared. The insects, in their fierce hunger, tried to engulf everything in their way. I have seen Arab babies, left by their mothers in the shade of some tree, whose face had been devoured by the oncoming swarm of locusts before their screams had been heard. I have seen the carcasses of animals hidden from sight by the undulating, rustling blanket of insects." By fall the swarms had gone—to be immediately followed by a typhoid epidemic—but Aaron Aaronsohn remained permanently on assignment to deal with the locust problem.

It is not clear exactly when and under what circumstances Aaron Aaronsohn decided to begin conveying sensitive information to the British authorities at Cairo—an activity in which he had become fully engaged by the beginning of 1916. On the surface of it, he had no reason not to share the neutralist outlook of his American friends or even to sympathize with the hopes of those German and Austrian Zionists who—in Constantinople and Jerusalem as well as at home—were so zealously watching over the wartime welfare of Jews in Palestine. But it would seem that Aaronsohn, who had visited England on each of his journeys to and from the United States and who had always spoken French as his principal language, was genuinely convinced that the future of the Jews of Palestine lay with the Allied cause. Furthermore, his political outlook had by this time become dominated by a fierce hatred of the Turks. For this feeling, he had no need to draw upon anything more than his own bitter experiences; but it must also have been greatly nurtured by the passions of some of those who were closest to him—notably his brother Alexander.

A few months in the Turkish army had been a nightmare for Alexander Aaronsohn. An experienced soldier—after returning to Palestine just before the war, he had organized a Jewish farmers' self-defense organization called the Gideonites—he had done well in training; but nevertheless, he was soon rounded up along with other Jewish and Christian recruits to be part of a labor battalion. "We were disarmed," he was to recall bitterly; "our uniforms were taken away, and we became hard-driven 'gangsters.' I shall never forget

the humiliation of that day." Soon he decided to follow an old Ottoman tradition and bribe his way out of the army. On his way home,
in an Arab village he saw a Turkish soldier help himself to a piece of
fruit from an elderly street vendor without paying; when the old
man protested, the soldier beat him unmercifully. An officer came
along, found out what had happened, and turned to the vendor and
said: "If a soldier of the Sultan should choose to heap filth on your
head, it is for you to kiss his hand in gratitude."

Later, when Alexander toured the country to examine the effects of the locust plague for his brother, he found that a scourge
called "military requisitions" had been "even more desolating" than
the locusts in some places. In Beirut, where he visited his sister
Rivkah—the youngest member of the family—who was staying at
the American college, he was struck by the contrast between what
works the French and the Americans had achieved there and what
the Turks, at that moment trying to take over the college, had done
or left undone. Returning home to Zichron Ya'akov, he found that
his old widower father and other Jewish farmers were being threatened by a gang of pillagers under the leadership of an otherwise
feckless young Turkish nobleman, Fewzi Bey; but when he complained of this to Djemal Pasha, the dictator dealt with the situation
by giving Fewzi a commission in the militia. Leading the Gideonites
against Fewzi's depredations, Alexander soon was in danger of his
life—a danger heightened when the Turks were able to discover most
of the arms and ammunition he and his men had stored in Zichron
Ya'akov. He decided to leave the country, and by the end of the
summer of 1915 he and Rivkah were sailing from Beirut, carrying
papers that identified them as a married couple from neutral Spain.

Alexander and Rivkah were to end up in the United States, but
not before sojourning a short time in Cairo. There Alexander made
contact with the British authorities and tried to persuade them that
he could organize an anti-Turk rebellion in Palestine. But the men of
Cairo headquarters—by then in contact with the Sherif Hussein and
hoping to achieve an Arab revolt through him, and furthermore still
inclined to regard all Palestinian Jews as pro-German—did not
choose to trust him. He also proposed to them—again without success—an intelligence service from Palestine, something he had already discussed with his brother and friends.

Another strong force in Aaron Aaronsohn's life at this moment
was Absalom Feinberg, the twenty-five-year-old Palestine-born son
of two of the original settlers of Rishon le-Zion. His family had been
living a number of years in nearby Hadera and had become friendly

with the Aaronsohns: in fact, the tall, handsome, and rather dashing Absalom had formed a particularly strong relationship with the two youngest members of the Aaronsohn family, the sisters Rivkah and Sarah. Absalom had become engaged to Rivkah by the time she fled with Alexander to the United States. But in that same summer her elder sister Sarah, who had been married since March 1914 to a Bulgarian Jew and living in Constantinople, returned home to Zichron Ya'akov from a husband she did not love. Sarah and Absalom, who were the same age, once again became close; and it was within this isolated little world of spouseless brothers and sisters and passionate friendships that the idea came into being of spying for the British.

Absalom, who was Aaron's assistant at the station, seems to have been the first to realize that—between the vast information-gathering facilities they now possessed on account of their antilocust operations and other activities, and the location of their station on the coast of the British-patrolled Mediterranean—they were in a unique position to convey intelligence to Cairo. Aaron and subsequently Sarah accepted this suggestion eagerly, and Absalom, carrying forged papers, soon was making his way by boat to Egypt to present the scheme. This was not long after Alexander had tried without luck; but Absalom made the felicitous choice of going not to Cairo but to Port Said, where the Intelligence Bureau was being conducted by Lieutenant Leonard Woolley. Unlike his colleagues in Cairo, who, he was to write years later, "were very suspicious of Alex [Aaronsohn], and thought he might probably be an enemy agent," Woolley was impressed by Absalom's proposal and decided to try it. Absalom made his way back to Athlit, and some two weeks after that a British ship paused while passing the station in the dark of night and sent a sailor ashore to retrieve the first parcel of information the Aaronsohn circle had prepared.

The spy work at Athlit had begun in an almost casually adventurous way, but by the beginning of 1916 it was taking on a new intensity. The British failure and withdrawals at Gallipoli had affected the mood of the Aaronsohn circle, and as preparations for a new Suez attack with Ottoman troops released from the Gallipoli front took place before their eyes, they found themselves all the more eager to do what they could. Aaron began keeping a diary, in which details about the movements of troops and guns were meticulously set down, but always—in case it should be discovered by the Turks—under the guise of observations made by an Ottoman scientific official who had his own work to do.

To compound the feeling of crisis during the first half of 1916, early in the year a ship carrying Leonard Woolley was torpedoed, and Woolley was taken prisoner by the Turks. Communication with the British became more difficult, and by June, Aaron had decided that he would get to them with his diary in person. Knowing nothing of the Zionist activity in London, he also was determined to persuade the British Government to take a position in favor of a Jewish Palestine and to invade the country. It was doubtless because he was so well known that he did not try Alexander's and Absalom's method of sneaking to Cairo with false papers, but chose rather to get to England by way of Europe and in his own identity. The first phase of his journey—which was to Damascus—was routine: he was often there to confer with Djemal, as was Absalom, who now met him there with new information gleaned from the vicinity of El Arish. Aaronsohn then persuaded Djemal that he had to go to Constantinople and thence to Vienna in connection with his work. The degree of confidence he had achieved with the Turks is well indicated by the readiness with which his request was granted. He traveled as far as Constantinople in the company of another of his assistants at the station, but from there on made his way alone.

In Berlin, Aaronsohn met two American Zionists who were there in connection with Jewish relief work, Alexander Dushkin and Rabbi Judah Magnes, but it is not clear whether this was prearranged or by accident. He seems to have persuaded them he wanted to return with them to the United States, but he is not likely to have let them know that such a trip was to be a cover for an effort to get to England, since Magnes was a prominent pacifist and had pro-German leanings. In any case, Magnes—who was one of the founding trustees of the Agricultural Experimental Station—was among Aaronsohn's warm supporters, and he agreed to help him obtain the desired passage once they got to Copenhagen. Aaronsohn then used the influence of his scientific colleagues in Berlin to get permission to visit a seed-breeding center in Stockholm, apparently as a cover for his trip to Copenhagen. He did indeed make a trip to Stockholm, but then stayed on in the Danish capital making arrangements that included—according to his secretive diary—a promise from the British consul *not* to detain him at Kirkwall in the Orkneys. This evidently was a code for a decision precisely to the opposite effect.

The *Oskar II* arrived at Kirkwall very early on Sunday, October 22. Aaronsohn later wrote in his diary: "The English examining officers begin on the ship at 10. First they go through the Americans, then the Scandinavians, then the rest. . . . When my turn comes, the officer is a bit surprised, but he looks at me in such a way as to make me realize that the instructions regarding me have arrived.

"A few moments later, the same officer says he will talk to me after lunch.

"At about 2:30 they call me and send me to one of the cabins. Suddenly, right behind me comes Captain Alfred Deware. He is not in on the thing, but I explain to him that he has to take me prisoner and he agrees.

"The comedy is carried out. They hold over me a whole range of evidence, informing the captain of the ship that my cabin is 'full of German stuff,' and after I part from Magnes I am taken prisoner at 4 in the afternoon. My fellow passengers are astonished."

Aaronsohn was brought to London on Tuesday evening, October 24, and checked into the First Avenue Hotel in High Holborn. The next morning a series of interrogations began at Scotland Yard. In the ensuing days his main interrogator was Major W.H. Gribbon of military intelligence, and the sessions took place at the War Office. But he was not treated as a prisoner. As an Ottoman subject he was issued papers under the category "alien enemy," which technically carried a curfew of 9:00 P.M.; but he was allowed an extension to 11:30 and spent many an evening at the theater—seeing, among other things, the popular comedy about two Jewish businessmen, *Potash and Perlmutter in Society*, by Montague Glass, an American-Jewish writer who had been born in Manchester. During the daytime, when he was not being interrogated, Aaronsohn played the eager tourist, often walking fifteen miles a day through the London streets.

It was on October 27 that Sir Mark Sykes met with him for the first time. During about an hour's conversation, Sykes knowledgeably asked him about his Jewish political position—whether he was "closer to Gaster's outlook, or to that of Lucien Wolf." Aaronsohn, though he had attended an occasional Zionist congress and often had worked closely with the organization's representatives, was not an affiliated Zionist, was far from orthodox in his outlook, and indeed was usually at odds with the official Zionist leadership. He therefore evidently provided what was very much his own answer to Sykes's question; for the report on him submitted to the War Office a few days later said:

> The informant is a partisan of a particular school of Zionists. The Zionists may be said to fall into three distinct schools:
> (i) The Zionists who desire to promote unity among Jews

throughout the world and by concerted action improve the lot of Jews in those countries where they still labor under disabilities.

(ii) The Zionists who regard religion as of more importance than nationality and desire the acquisition of the Temple site and the reestablishment of the Jewish people and Palestine as an independent sovereign state.

(iii) The Zionists who regard nationality as of greater importance than religion and for the present confine themselves to endeavoring to obtain freedom for colonization in Palestine.

The informant belongs to the latter category.

This seems to be Sykes's own formulation, drawn up in the give-and-take with Aaronsohn. The first "school" is that of Lucien Wolf, whom Sykes here still sees as some kind of Zionist. The third "school" is Sykes's notion of that of Gaster—still the only full-fledged, affiliated Zionist he knew. The second category is reserved for all others, whoever they may be, who clamor for too much, too soon, without in the meantime being of any help.

Aaronsohn saw Sykes again at the latter's residence at 9 Buckingham Gate on Monday, October 30, at 9:30 in the morning. G.H. Fitzmaurice also came, and the conversation does not seem to have been about intelligence matters at all, but was primarily about what Aaronsohn now regarded as his principal mission in England: to persuade the Government to invade Palestine and support a Jewish state. Sykes said he hoped the British would soon be in a stronger position to do something along these lines, but stressed that "it requires work." Aaronsohn, who saw Sykes again the following Monday for what was to be the last time during that London sojourn, thought he had not made much of an impression upon the Englishman. "From the diplomatic point of view, fiasco," he was to record of his efforts during this stay; but he was probably wrong. He seems in fact to have made a strong impression upon Sykes, if one may judge by the contacts to occur between the two men the following year. In general, this settler who also was a scientist of rare intellectual gifts made a deep impression upon Englishmen who had never seen or even dreamed of Jews like him. Weizmann had been impressive enough to many; but here was a Weizmann with a farmer's physique who could claim a lifetime in the Land of Israel.

A British campaign in the Sinai aimed at Palestine was to begin within a month, and Aaronsohn seems to have made a contribution in helping to bring it about. Major Gribbon's thirty-four-page typewritten report of the interviews he held with an "Inhabitant of Athlit"—as the informant, left nameless, is always called in the official papers—was filled with information under such headings as: "Supplies in Syria," "Transport," "Communications," "Coasting Vessels," "Troops," "Relations Between Germans and Turks," "Enemy Appreciations and Plans," "Economic Situation in Syria," and "Political Situation in Syria." Aaronsohn was able to provide information on epidemics in scientific detail, but also to point out that "Kressenstein lived in a tent for 14 months sooner than be in contact with Jemal," and that the Turkish soldiers resented the Germans for the better comforts they enjoyed. He could describe how Muslim Indian soldiers taken prisoner were courted for the *jihad*, and how the basic Turco-German plan against the British seemed to be to concentrate first on retaking Basra and then to direct an assault against Egypt. The attack on Katia in the Sinai in April, he said, had been designed to catch the British napping and to get heavy guns within range of the canal at least long enough to cause several months' worth of damage there. "The attack," he said, "would only be the prelude to a greater attack which would depend on success in Mesopotamia." It all was an argument for an offensive approach by the British, both in the Sinai and in Mesopotamia once again.

Aaronsohn's knowledge and connections clearly pointed to his being sent to Cairo to work with military intelligence there. He did not attempt to refuse when this idea was presented to him, although he seems to have been disappointed at it. He had envisioned a larger political task for himself. In the United States, his brother Alexander, who had been lecturing at Zionist meetings since his arrival there with Rivkah the previous October, had recently moved on to a more pointed form of propaganda activity. He had written his memoirs, which first had appeared in relatively abbreviated form in the July and August issues of the *Atlantic Monthly* and were being published in the fall as a book entitled *With the Turks in Palestine*. It must have shocked the more cautious of the American Zionists who had taken Alexander and Rivkah in hand upon their arrival, for it minced no words in its denunciation of Turkish rule in Palestine and Syria. The stages of its publication may have been coordinated with Aaron's activities: the articles, appearing when their author's brother was still in Ottoman and German hands, say almost nothing about him, whereas the book shows him, like Alexander, vigorously opposed to the Turks. But there is, of course, nothing in either version about the espionage work.

Aaron had wanted to proceed to the United States to join his brother in speaking out against the Turks, but not before he had made a propaganda conquest in England. In this the almost anchoritic sage of Athlit was being rather naïve. If it is understandable why he could not have known much about the progress English Zionism had been making since 1914 while he was living under the Turks, it is, on the other hand, quite remarkable how little he did to acquaint himself with the situation during his month in London. At one point in his diary, Aaronsohn says he wants to find out where Ahad Ha'am lives; but this is dropped after a single inquiry among some people who turn out never to have heard of the Hebrew philosopher. One evening he went to hear a lecture by "that idiot named Sokolow." Standing outside the hall, he let Sokolow brush by him without recognition; then he left before the lecture was over. He made no attempt to see Weizmann, who once had written to Judah Magnes, of all people, that Aaronsohn's views "on Palestinian matters are not altogether the right ones." As for Gaster, he turned out to be the one Zionist in England to know of Aaronsohn's presence, but that was because of Sykes, who had contacted him to find out what he knew about the visitor from Athlit. "I told Sir M.," wrote Gaster in his diary for November 14, "that I do *not* trust Aaronsohn. An ambitious man." Living incognito in London under the assumed name of William Mack, Aaronsohn did not at this time make his influence felt either within these circles or within the political arena where they were active.

But, in his own way, he was making his influence felt all the same. He left for Egypt on November 24.

·29·

A GATHERING OF FORCES

The Anglo-Zionist movement about which Aaron Aaronsohn knew little and cared less was, even during his stay in London, steadily moving from strength to strength. By now the significant initiatives within the movement were entirely those of Chaim Weizmann's circle. In particular, the Anglo-Zionist history of the last six months of 1916 seems to have been dominated by Harry Sacher and others associated with him in the Manchester that Weizmann was leaving permanently behind him. It was in July that Sacher finally published the volume of Zionist essays he had begun planning more than a year before. He had in the meantime been the general editor of a series of pamphlets on the subject; but the present volume, *Zionism and the Jewish Future*, was more ambitious in its contents than the pamphlets had been, comprised a more distinguished list of contributors, and was more clearly intended to present the case to a wide audience of Jews and non-Jews alike. Included among its essays were a review of the previous hundred years of Jewish history by Sacher himself, a study of anti-Semitism by Albert M. Hyamson—the author of the influential *New Statesman* article of November 1914 on "The Future of Palestine"—a description of the modern Hebrew revival by Leon Simon, a history of Zionism by Professor Richard Gottheil of Columbia University (who was English-born), and an economic and technological view of Palestine's future by Norman Bentwich.

Of special note were the contributions by Weizmann, Gaster, and Sokolow. In "The New Jew: A Sketch," Sokolow went back to the type of feuilleton journalism that had been a specialty not only of his own during the many years in which he had edited the Warsaw Hebrew newspaper *Ha'tsefirah*, but also of other Zionist intellectuals—most notably Herzl himself and Jabotinsky. In the form of a memoir, Sokolow describes several encounters over a period of years

with an uprooted young East European Jewish intellectual, unhappy
and in search of himself until he at last finds fulfillment as a farmer
in Palestine. Gaster's essay, "Judaism as a National Religion," argues the essential paradox that Jewish nationality is defined not by
any of the criteria applying to other nationalities but by the religious tradition alone—and that the Jewish religion is utterly national in character. "The conception of a mere religious confraternity," he writes,

> which has been put forward as a definition of the Jews, or, to
> put it in a different way, the claim to be Englishmen of the
> Jewish persuasion—that is, English by nationality and Jewish
> by faith—is an absolute self-delusion. . . . For the Jew, faith is
> not a mere profession of spiritual truths or of dogmatic princi-
> ples detached entirely from the historical evolution of the Jew-
> ish people as a nation; the Jewish faith is a profession of
> national and religious unity in the past and in the future.

The argument was a blow aimed directly at the sensitive jaw of the
Anglo-Jewish establishment.

Weizmann, in his introductory essay, "Zionism and the Jewish
Problem," went even further in the assault upon Anglo-Jewish assimilationism, arguing at one point that "the position of the emancipated Jew, though he does not realize it himself, is even more tragic
than that of his oppressed brother" in Eastern Europe. For the Jew
in the Russian pale at least has his great spiritual traditions intact—
indeed, Weizmann argues, it is there that the inner life of the Jewish
people was maintained for centuries in its greatest purity. "It is
therefore no exaggeration to say," he goes on, "that East European
Jewry has been for some centuries the real center of Jewish life, and
that its disruption, not accompanied by the establishment of another
center, would threaten the very existence of the Jews as a people."
Emancipation in the West was no solution to this particular problem,
since it tended to break up the solidarity of Jewish cultural life. In
fact, Weizmann says, modern secular culture is a threat to the continuity of Jewish traditions without a national center in which Jews
can absorb that culture on their own terms, as any other people does
in its own country. "When the aim of Zionism is accomplished," he
concluded, "Palestine will be the home of the Jewish people, not
because it will contain all the Jews in the world, but because it will
be the only place in the world where the Jews are masters of their
own destiny, and the national center to which all Jews will look as

the home and the source of all that is most essentially Jewish."

The public, preoccupied at this time with the agony of the Somme, responded to the book modestly but with respect: some three thousand copies were sold. The *Manchester Guardian* was prompt about reviewing it. "Of all the constructive ideas which the war seems likely to further," wrote the paper's anonymous reviewer in the July 31 edition, "none can compare in intrinsic importance and nobility with that of Zionism, the faith which is working for the restoration of Jews to Palestine under a polity which shall give them freedom of national development." Stressing the strong element of idealism that pervades the volume, the reviewer saw the book as "a useful corrective to the vulgar idea of the Jews as a race given over wholly to the materialistic view of life. But the one idea that is common to all the essayists in this volume is that a spiritual and intellectual idea cannot flower as it should unless it has the support of a genuinely national state." The *Guardian* was giving its usual solid support to the idea.

The most important review to appear was one by Lord Cromer in the August 12 issue of the *Spectator*. It was nine years since Cromer's retirement as British agent and consul general in Cairo, but since then he had achieved some literary distinction as a commentator upon Middle Eastern affairs: just a few months earlier, he had published a monumental two-volume work, *Modern Egypt*, which combined historical narrative with personal observation. Cromer's view on the Palestine question was bound to carry weight; and the fact that he was first cousin to the foreign secretary—who had just been named Viscount Grey of Fallodon—also was not to be ignored.

Cautious in his support of the book, Cromer devoted more of his review to the Jewish question than to the more delicate one of Palestine. "In England," he declared,

> there has never been any "Jewish question" properly so called. This is due partly to the fact that religious toleration, both in the letter and the spirit, has established a firm hold on English public opinion, and partly to the further fact that the relatively small number of Jews in the United Kingdom—there are at present only some two hundred and forty-five thousand—has prevented them from exercising so commanding an influence over national life as has been the case in some other countries. There is not, as in Austria, a Jew moneylender in almost every village in the country, who often holds the future welfare of the noble in his castle and of the villager in his cottage in the hollow of his hand.

Having got that point off his chest, Cromer proceeded to give a sympathetic accounting for the desire of Jews to maintain their identity even under favorable conditions, quoting Weizmann, Gaster, and even Ahad Ha'am—who was not one of the contributors to the volume—along the way. "It would be both premature and presumptuous," he at length concluded,

> to attempt to forecast the future of the Zionist movement. . . . Enough, however, has been said to show that, although possibly the Jewish question will not mature quite so quickly as some of the more enthusiastic Zionists consider probable, it is rapidly becoming a practical issue, and that before long politicians will be unable to brush it aside as the fantastic dream of a few idealists.

As for that Anglo-Jewish establishment so severely challenged by Sacher's book, it made no significant response at first. Then, in November, there appeared in the venerable *Fortnightly Review* an article called simply "Zionism" and signed by "An Englishman of the Jewish Faith." This was probably Lucien Wolf, who is known to have been particularly offended by Weizmann's remark that the position of the emancipated Jew was "even more tragic" than that of his brother in Eastern Europe. At no point does the article explicitly address itself to *Zionism and the Jewish Future*, but its arguments all are implicit responses to the book. It begins with the question of religion and nationality. "When the Jews in England were granted full political rights," the writer says, "what were the arguments used to justify the gift? The main argument of the Jews was that it was only certain religious doctrines and practices which separated them from their Christian fellow-citizens. A Jew, resident in England, was an Englishman of the Jewish faith, just as a Jew, whose home was France, was a Frenchman of the Jewish faith." But now, the writer maintains, "a very dangerous movement" has arisen among Jews "which, unless checked, may hinder their emancipation in countries where this emancipation is yet to seek, and even imperil its continuance (in the spirit, if not necessarily in the letter) in countries where that emancipation has already been attained." With the utmost confidence, the author pronounces the origin of "this strange and retrograde movement" to be "entirely due to anti-Semitism," claiming as his source for this view a conversation he once had had with Herzl himself. But, the writer asks, "how can a man belong to two nations at once? How can he be a Frenchman, or an Italian, and something else as well?" The conclusion is that there is only one salvation for Jews: "the uncompromising maintenance of the old emancipation point of view. No separate nationality, no national language; only a religious community, the members of which can be the devoted citizens, or 'nationals,' of all the countries in which they make their home, and in which full civic and political rights are assigned to them."

The *Jewish Chronicle*, which had for the past half year—since Lucien Wolf's reforms in the organization of the Conjoint Foreign Committee (CFC)—been hopefully devoting itself to the building of a bridge between the Zionist and non-Zionist segments of the Anglo-Jewish community, responded to this article in a mood bordering on hysteria. "What evil genius," its November 3 leader ran, "can it be who ventured at this moment upon a cruel, bitter, and venomous attack upon the Zionists?" And its columnist "Mentor"—who usually was Leopold Greenberg himself—devoted a long critique to this "perilous article," as he called it: in fact, his commentaries were to continue for the next three issues. "Mentor's" anger at the anonymous anti-Zionist author reached its height in his November 17 column, which ended with reflections on "the foulness of the blow he has dealt—at this moment of all others—at Anglo-Jewry in particular and at Jewry in general. God forgive him! His offense is such that to pardon it none less than a Power with attributes Divine is capable. Humanly speaking, it is unforgivable." In December the *Fortnightly Review* was to placate such feelings by carrying refutations written by the elder Bentwich and by Dr. J.H. Hertz, the chief rabbi of Great Britain and the Empire.

Harry Sacher had responded to the challenge three days after the initial reaction in the *Jewish Chronicle*, and in the pages of the *Guardian* at that—though in the discreet form of a letter to the editor. "An article in the current 'Fortnightly Review' on Zionism," he wrote,

> seems to us likely to do such injury to this country that we ask you to assist us in immediately checking the spread of the mischief. How deeply it has wounded Anglo-Jewry on its religious side may be gathered from the Anglo-Jewish press, and it is not necessary to add anything to what is there said on that head. On the broad political aspects of the matter, however, the attack is no less injurious.

Sacher then took up what he saw as the two main contentions of this writer whose identity—for him, unlike the *Jewish Chronicle*—was "not concealed by a pseudonym." The first was the notion that there had been an emancipation "contract" between Great Britain and its Jews, in which the latter had renounced their nationality. There had been no contract, argued Sacher—the recipient of a first in history at Oxford—and the Jewish struggle for civil equality in Great Britain, won in 1858 with Lionel Rothschild's entry into Parliament, had been a religious and not a national issue.

"The writer's second point," Sacher went on,

> is that a man cannot both aspire to Jewish nationalism and be a loyal subject of the British Empire. This principle, if accepted, would be the grossest libel on the subjects of the King, and betrays a false, one had almost written Prussian, conception of what empire really is. *Imperium cum libertate*, which is our proud boast, means nothing at all if an Australian can be a good subject only by ceasing to be a good Australian. . . . It is the distinction of British imperialism that a man does not become a better subject of the King by being a worse Australian, Canadian, or South African.

And this brought Sacher to the point at which he could make some propaganda of his own. "So far from Zionism detracting from the loyalty of Jewish subjects," he concluded,

> it is a desirable and even necessary completion. In the opinion of the British Palestine Committee, on whose behalf I am writing, the inclusion of Palestine within the British Empire is essential to British Imperial interests, and only by our allying ourselves with Jewish nationalism can we assure that a British Palestine will be a strong, free, self-supporting dominion.

It is not hard to hear in Sacher's words the participating voice of Herbert Sidebotham, the "Student of War," now fully aroused to the idea of a Jewish Palestine as a British imperial necessity. It was Sidebotham and Sacher together who had just formed the British Palestine Committee, with the participation of Chaim Weizmann's two other young Manchester friends, Simon Marks and Israel Sieff. This was in some ways a family affair: Marks and Sieff were married to each other's sisters, and earlier in the year Sacher had become the third in a trio of brothers-in-law by marrying another Marks sister, Miriam. They also represented a rising new challenge, on the part of a generation born of immigrants from Eastern Europe, to the economic and social domination of the old Anglo-Jewish establishment: Marks had just inherited from his father the mercantile establishment of Marks and Spencer, Ltd., which he and Sieff were eventually to build into a chain-store empire. They were an important initial source of funds for the British Palestine Committee, which was soliciting members, both Jew and Gentile, throughout the country and preparing to issue publications propagandizing for the cause. In London the committee was represented by other members of the Weizmann circle: Leon Simon, Albert M. Hyamson, and a Belgian Zionist named Samuel Tolkowsky, who had fled to London in 1915 and was another contributor to *Zionism and the Jewish Future*. Weizmann himself remained officially detached from the committee, but it was in effect another base for his growing power within the Zionist movement.

For Weizmann, the latter half of 1916 had been marked by a combination of personal and political triumphs with a steady fizzling out of his Government work as a chemist. His Munitions Ministry appointment came quietly to an end on September 30, and with Lloyd George no longer there to be pressured by C.P. Scott, it was not renewed. To be sure, his work in the Admiralty laboratories—relocated on Point Pleasant in Wandsworth—continued, and the French and Italian governments still showed some interest in his acetone process; for this reason, he even made a trip to Paris early in September. In fact, at the end of the summer, Auguste Fernbach had failed in a test demonstration in Paris intended to show that his process worked with maize just as well as Weizmann's did. But Fernbach was not to drop his claim that Weizmann's process was his own, and in the meantime, things were not going perfectly well where that process was in use. There had been setbacks at the Bromley distillery, and, owing to transportation difficulties, a shortage of maize was looming on the horizon. All in all, acetone production had been far below the mark originally set for 1916, and the difference had been made up only by an improvement in the American market and the adoption of a new form of cordite, RDB, which was manufactured with ether alcohol as a solvent instead of acetone. As for the butyl alcohol produced in such large quantities as a by-product of Weizmann's process, the sale of which was to help pay for the acetone work, the market for it had proved to be poor. Little remained for Weizmann to do but wait for the final terms of his award, which were still not forthcoming in spite of the protestations of McKenna and Balfour the previous spring.

In contrast to this dim history of his scientific work in these months was the palpable emergence of Weizmann as a figure of importance on the Anglo-Jewish scene, and not only in Zionist matters. For most of 1916, the foremost Jewish issue in Great Britain had been that of the "Russian" aliens and military service. This had reached a point of crisis during the summer. In response to growing clamors, Herbert Samuel—who, as home secretary, was responsible for the disposition of aliens—had announced in the House of Commons on June 29 that Russian subjects of military age residing in Britain would be expected either to enlist or to return to Russia to do military service there. The suggestion had a surface logic: now that all native-born or naturalized Englishmen from eighteen to forty-one were being called up, whether they were married or single, it was only fair that the subjects of an Allied government should also be made to do their duty in this respect. Indeed, the idea had been expressed in some quarters that aliens of military age ought to be conscripted, which could well have solved the whole problem; but the Government refused to perform what seemed a possible violation of international law. Instead, the concession had been made—in a reversal of British traditions—that the aliens were eligible for enlistment in the army (not the navy, however), and this was soon followed by the guarantee that military service would result in virtually automatic naturalization.

The whole issue, involving a few thousand potential recruits—many of whom spoke English poorly and were still (like their contemporaries in Ireland, who were exempt from conscription) not convinced that this war was really theirs—had taken on a certain coloration owing to the fact that almost all of them were Jews. Certainly there were anti-Semites pure and simple among those who had raised the clamor against them; but there was also a noticeable Jewish presence among those who subsequently joined in. The *Jewish Chronicle* became as loud as anyone in decrying the "slackers" and "shirkers," and, when the threat of possible deportation to Russia was made, proceeded to rationalize it after a hard swallow. The religion of the home secretary, who was suddenly more vindictive in the matter than many of his non-Jewish Liberal colleagues, was noticed by all. "Mr. Samuel," the *Manchester Guardian* wrote, "seems to have thought it somehow incumbent on him to display austerity towards the Jewish immigrant." He also felt called upon at times to display his ardent support for tsarist Russia: on August 1, when a Liberal colleague speaking in the House of Commons on the aliens' behalf suggested that the British alliance with Russia was a "tainted" one anyway, Samuel had demurred. "What a doctrine to express in the House of Commons," he said, "in view of the glorious deeds and the immeasurable services that were being rendered by Russian armies! [Cheers]"

Opposition to the threat of deporting the aliens was a view Weizmann held firmly in common with Gaster—indeed, it brought them closer together than they had been in more than a year—and together they exerted their influence upon Samuel to persuade him to modify his position. "I saw S[amuel]," Weizmann wrote to Ahad Ha'am on July 24, "spoke to him for a long time about our cause, and don't know whether I have convinced him that his statement was out of place." At that point, the promise of facilitating naturalization for aliens who volunteered had not been made, and Weizmann had urged Samuel to give it serious consideration. Weizmann's arguments may also have influenced other concessions made by Samuel in the ensuing weeks, such as his agreement not to deport "political" refugees (it was promptly suggested to him that *all* Jewish immigrants from Russia could be considered "political" refugees), and his hint that intransigents might be sent to America instead of Russia. But palpably significant in influencing Samuel's attitude was a committee of British Jews of Russian extraction, organized by a banker named Gregory Benenson, which Weizmann had joined by the end of July. Hitherto, the only Jewish group lobbying on the question had been the Jewish War Services Committee, an organ of the old establishment. Now, Russian-Jewish organizations were being heard from; Benenson's was not the only one, though it was the most prominent.

"I have been approached by a responsible committee of leading Russian Jews," Samuel said in the Commons on August 22, "who have expressed their willingness to carry on an active recruiting campaign in London and in other centers with a view to securing the voluntary enlistment in the British army of Russian subjects living in this country who are eligible for military service. I have agreed that until the results of this campaign are seen the question whether those who do not enlist should be repatriated shall remain in abeyance." The campaign, he said, would be tried until September 30, after which "the question of repatriation will again be considered, as will also the question whether the advantage of the special arrangements for naturalization should still be open to those who have not yet presented themselves for enlistment." A statement to this effect was then published, and in it the "odious" question of deportation—as Weizmann called it in a letter of August 24 to Ahad Ha'am—was for the time being omitted. "Our Committee," Weizmann went on in the letter to Ahad Ha'am,

> is to meet tomorrow to discuss details for the first time. Gaster has also joined. Sokolow is having a talk with [some East End Jewish] representatives today, while Benenson is calling at the Ministry again to discuss some details; we would like, for example, to put off the date to October 15th instead of September 30th.

The deadline was in fact to be extended to October 25; but in the meantime, a moment occurred in which the whole matter reentered Weizmann's life from another direction, and with a special irony. For on August 31, he himself received a letter calling him up for military service. He was, after all, only forty-one and a British subject. Furthermore, in transition from the temporary quarters at Campden Hill Road to a new home being readied in Kensington, Weizmann and his family were spending the summer in a Surrey suburb; and it was there that a local military board, not knowing of his work, sent him the conscription notice. Weizmann hastily wrote back saying he was "badged"—employed in essential war work and therefore militarily exempt—and adding that, besides, he was going to be forty-two on November 27. That proved to be the end of it: this "Russian," at least, would not have to jump to the commands of a British sergeant.

At the same time another "Russian," a friend and colleague of Weizmann's, was eagerly seeking his opportunity to do so under the right circumstances. Since the summer of 1915, Vladimir Jabotinsky had been in London, separated from his wife and small son in Petrograd and eking out his living as correspondent for the *Russkiye Vyedomosti*. His idea of forming a Jewish legion was almost universally unacceptable to official Zionists—in the Allied countries, in the neutral countries, and in Germany and Austria—because it represented the possibility of too open an identification of the Zionist cause with one side in the war, and hence among other things a danger to the Jews of Turkish-dominated Palestine. In England, Sokolow, for all his Anglophilia, was opposed to it, as was Gaster and, for antinationalist reasons, Lucien Wolf. The two notable exceptions to this opposition were Joseph Cowen, who had been advocating a separate Jewish unit since the start of the war, and Jabotinsky's sometime roommate Chaim Weizmann. But Weizmann was unwilling to jeopardize his own position in English Zionism by openly campaigning for the legion, though he had promised to stand by Jabotinsky when the time was ripe.

In the meantime, Jabotinsky had gone about making his own connections among Englishmen of influence and power with a skill—considering that he represented virtually no Jewish constituency in the country—that must be ranked equal to Weizmann's. In some cases, Weizmann seems to have made the connection for him, as in that of C.P. Scott, who, by December 1915, was writing a letter to Lord Robert Cecil introducing "my friend Mr. Jabotinsky." But another important friendship materialized for Jabotinsky in that moment: Colonel John Henry Patterson. Back in London from Gallipoli, Patterson was eager to turn his Zion Mule Corps—which was then being disbanded—into the nucleus of a Jewish legion. On Trumpeldor's advice, Patterson had looked up Jabotinsky and then introduced him to a brilliant if eccentric member of Parliament, Leopold Amery, who had just seen military service in Flanders, the Balkans, and Gallipoli, and was a figure of growing eminence on the extreme right wing of the Conservative party. Born in India of an English father and a Hungarian mother who had escaped her native country after the failure of the 1848 revolution, the forty-two-year-old Amery had enjoyed outstanding simultaneous careers as a scholar, a journalist, a soldier, an athlete—though he was notably short of stature—and now as a parliamentarian whose supernationalist views were, in a time of all-out war, no longer the obstacle to his advancement they once had been. There were obvious temperamental affinities between him and Jabotinsky, and the two men took to one another, Amery becoming a warm supporter of Zionism.

In January and February 1916, Lord Robert Cecil found himself subjected to something of a Jewish legion campaign at the Foreign Office, receiving, among other things, a long letter from Jabotinsky on the matter and personal visits from both Amery and Patterson. This was around the time when the predominant form being taken by the Jewish question at the Foreign Office was that of how American-Jewish opinion could be made more favorable to the Allied cause. Jabotinsky and his friends took the view that, since the British Government was not yet in a position to give any open promises regarding Palestine, it could in the meantime win Jewish sympathies throughout the world by establishing "a Jewish legion for service in the East." Cecil was interested in the proposal, but his colleagues insisted that it was purely a War Office matter. And the War Office—that is to say, Lord Kitchener—was at that time unwilling even to consider it.

The whole matter took on a different coloration, however, in the summer and fall, after Kitchener's death, when the issue of the "Russian" aliens and military service became prominent. Jabotinsky had always been keenly aware of the East End problem: "Healthy, replete, well-dressed young men," he was to write, "thronged its broad sidewalks, restaurants, tea-rooms, movies and theaters every night: a separate isle inside England, divided from it by another and even deeper Channel." But he also sympathized with their problem, unlike his supporter Cowen, or the British Liberal MP to whom he once explained the "vast difference between your boys and those East End boys. Your boys are British; if Britain wins their people is saved. Ours are Jews; if Britain wins, millions of their brothers will still remain in purgatory. You cannot demand equal sacrifices where the hope is not an equal one."

Jabotinsky's solution to this problem was ready to hand: a Jewish legion, determined to fight in Palestine and help liberate it from the Turks should the occasion arise, but meanwhile prepared to be organized for home defense. He proposed a recruitment campaign that would be called—half in English and half in Yiddish—Home and *Heym*, the latter word also meaning "home," but suggesting a specifically Jewish one. With a small but growing group of supporters, and with funds that Cowen was able to obtain, Jabotinsky began collecting signatures from Jewish immigrants who promised to enlist should the prospect of a Jewish unit be made available to them. By this time Trumpeldor and the other veterans of the Zion Mule Corps were in England, having reenlisted as British soldiers after the disbanding of their unit, and they joined in to help Jabotinsky's campaign. Herbert Samuel's sympathetic attention was won to the idea, and on August 23 the *Manchester Guardian* published a leader advocating it. Samuel even called in Jabotinsky to ask if the Home Office could be of any help, but demurred when he was asked for a statement openly advocating a Home and *Heym* regiment—that was, after all, a cabinet matter.

Lacking such a guarantee, Jabotinsky's campaign was not greatly successful in the short run. But it had won national attention, and the idea of a Jewish unit was now firmly fixed in the public mind.

Yet another important development in the politics of English Zionism had occurred in August, when Weizmann and Lucien Wolf were brought together for a personal meeting. The two men had known one another from a distance, but Weizmann had not hitherto been a direct party to any of Wolf's more or less official attempts to talk terms with the Zionists. If Wolf was now acknowledging that Weizmann was, above all, the Zionist in England with whom he should talk, this was because of the intercession of James de Rothschild—a fact that also was a tribute to Weizmann's triumphant if unorthodox diplomacy, with its many personal conquests of notables on both sides of the Channel. Baron James, back in London after a prolonged convalescence from injuries incurred in a driving accident at the front, and soon to be transferred from French to British military service, was now taking up his share of the role established by his wife, Dorothy, as go-between for Weizmann with leading members of Anglo-Jewish society. It was his father, Baron Edmond, who had urgently desired a meeting between Weizmann and Wolf, and James arranged for it to take place at his London home and in his presence on August 17.

Essentially, what Wolf sought from Weizmann was the acquiescence he had failed to obtain from the latter's Zionist colleagues in the meeting of April 14, 1915. But this time he could put his position on Palestine more concretely, for he now had the "formula" he had composed in March. And in this connection, he thought he had a trump card in his hand, for though he presented the formula to Weizmann, he did not tell him he had submitted it to the Foreign Office. What Wolf did not know was that the Foreign Office had seen fit to amend his formula with a statement leaning more strongly than his to the Zionist position and that the officials there were losing faith in him as a spokesman for the Jewish point of view.

Weizmann could not have known any of this, but with the unerring instinct that comes with absolute confidence in one's own destiny, he proceeded to treat Wolf and his views as utterly without consequence. He told Wolf that he did not think the British Government would necessarily go on communicating with the CFC about Zionist matters and that the charter so desired by the Zionists and so opposed by Wolf had already been discussed by members of the Government—who, Weizmann added, saw no objections to it in principle. This last, somewhat startling assertion apparently was based on the April 16 meeting at Gaster's home, in which Herbert Samuel had relayed Sykes's plan of the moment for Palestine. It also doubtless had received support in the many conversations Weizmann had been having over the past year with men in or near the seats of power. But Wolf afterward was to claim that Weizmann had used the name of Lloyd George in this connection, which Weizmann denied. Wolf was to persist in the belief that Lloyd George had already made some kind of "Zionist promise," though the record shows no evidence for this. On the other hand, it is likely that Lloyd George had at times indulged in rhetoric with such listeners as Weizmann, C.P. Scott, or Herbert Samuel that could have taken on this tenor to their ears. It also is possible that James de Rothschild, who was friendly with Lloyd George, had made a remark during the conversation that suggested this conclusion to Wolf.

As for Wolf's principal concern—the Jewish problem in Eastern Europe—Weizmann had no help to offer. He gave it as his opinion that, so far as Russian Jews were concerned, this was essentially a Russian internal matter and that "no satisfactory result can be brought about by outside interference." He also stressed that this problem was "entirely independent of the Palestine question and the two things have no connection." Wolf later reported of this part of the conversation that "Dr. Weizmann showed no disposition to come to terms with us either on the subject of nationality or special rights."

Wolf came away from the meeting convinced that "vital and irreconcilable differences of principle and method" remained between the CFC and the Zionists. The main problem, as he reported it in a subsequent letter to James de Rothschild, was Weizmann's "assertion of a Jewish nationality," which Wolf thought had found particularly grievous expression in his remark about the "tragic" position of the emancipated Jew in *Zionism and the Jewish Future*. Wolf wrote that he regarded this view as "a capitulation to our enemies" and "a repudiation of the solemn pledges by which the Jewish communities of the western world obtained their emancipation"—language that goes further to suggest that he may indeed have been the anonymous author of the article entitled "Zionism" to appear two months later in the *Fortnightly Review*. As for the Zionists' professed desire to obtain a chartered company for the colonization of Palestine, Wolf declared in his letter to Baron James that any attempt on their part to do so would be opposed by the CFC "tooth and nail."

Neither James de Rothschild nor his father were happy at this latest demonstration of irreconcilability between the Zionists and the Anglo-Jewish establishment, but they also knew that some prominent members of the English branch of their family were leaning toward Zionism all the same. James also considered that the moment had arrived for Weizmann and his friends to make an official statement of position, for presentation both to Government and to Anglo-Jewish leaders. In effect, the younger Baron and some of his powerful English friends were "electing" Weizmann to the leadership in Zionism that he had long been effectively assuming. It is hard to imagine that Lloyd George was not somehow involved in this. After receiving Wolf's report at the end of August, Baron James passed it on to Weizmann and his friends and asked them not only to reply to it, but to formulate a fully wrought though concise statement of the Zionist program. At a September 30 meeting, the Zionist Executive for England assigned Nahum Sokolow, who already was drafting the reply to Wolf, to prepare such a statement.

Sokolow worked throughout October and November, presenting drafts to his colleagues for revision at various intervals. By the beginning of December, this collaboration had produced a "Programmatic Statement" and an accompanying memorandum explaining the Zionist position. The "Programmatic Statement" ran as follows:

1. *Basis of Settlement.*
Recognition of Palestine as the Jewish National Home.
2. *Status of Jewish Population in Palestine Generally.*
The Jewish population present and future throughout Palestine is to possess and enjoy full national, political and civic rights.
3. *Immigration into Palestine.*
The Suzerain Government shall grant full and free rights of immigration into Palestine to Jews of all countries.
4. *The Establishment of a Chartered Company.*
The Suzerain Government shall grant a Charter to a Jewish Company for the colonization and development of Palestine, the Company to have power to acquire and take over any concessions for works of a public character, which may have been or may hereafter be granted by the Suzerain Government, and the rights of pre-emption of Crown Lands or other lands not held in private or religious ownership and such other powers and privileges as are usual in Charters of Statutes of similar colonizing bodies.

5. *Communal Autonomy.*

Full autonomy is to be enjoyed by Jewish communities through-out Palestine in all matters bearing upon their educational, religious or communal welfare.

Summary.

Palestine is to be recognized as the Jewish National Home. Jews of all countries to be accorded full liberty of immigration.

Jews to enjoy full national, political and civic rights according to their place of residence in Palestine.

A Charter to be granted to a Jewish Company for the development of Palestine.

The Hebrew language to be recognized as the official language of the Jewish Province.

Along with this statement—which came to be known among the Zionists as "the Demands"—Sokolow prepared a memorandum of twenty-seven typewritten pages explaining the history of the Jewish question and of Zionism.

There was an air of expectancy surrounding the preparation of these documents, of an imminent moment of realization. On November 15, Baron James presented drafts of them at a Rothschild family luncheon. Present were Lady Emma Louisa, widow of the first Lord Rothschild, and her two sons Charles—long a friend of Weizmann's—and Lionel Walter, the present Lord Rothschild; Herbert Samuel also was there. At this time, little yet was known of the views on Zionism of the second Lord Rothschild, who was forty-eight years old and more inclined to spend time with his vast zoology collection at Tring than to mix either in politics or in the family banking business. But it was becoming clear to some that Lionel Walter was—even as his father seemed to have become again in the last moments of his life, and as his brother certainly was—favorably inclined toward Zionism. A new generation's viewpoint was now taking shape in the family, leaving that of Uncle Leopold far behind.

No clear signals came from the Rothschild family of London just yet, nor was there any sign of change from the Government until December; but in the meantime Chaim Weizmann gave evidence of preparing himself for a new and more statesmanlike role. In October, he, Vera, and Benjamin had at last settled into permanent London quarters at 67 Addison Road in Kensington, where their second son, Michael, was born on November 16. Anyone who still thought of Chaim Weizmann as a provincial academician of modest means was likely to have been surprised at the splendid town house in which he now made his home. It was a sizable three-story villa with a front

portico, gardens in front and in back, and a semicircular driveway
running between two separate gateways from the street. This was a
home suitable for important receptions. Vera was no longer employed as in Manchester, but stayed home to run the household. The
first important social event at the house was Michael's circumcision
on November 23, which was attended by the James de Rothschilds as
well as some Zionist notables. Weizmann diplomatically asked Gaster to be the *sandak* ("godfather") for the occasion.

·30·

THE NEW GOVERNMENT

I t was on Monday morning, December 4, that the newspapers carried the first indication that a historic turning point was arriving for Great Britain, for the war, and inevitably for Zionism. An official statement had been issued by the prime minister at 11:45 the previous evening which said: "The Prime Minister, with a view to the most active prosecution of the war, has decided to advise His Majesty the King to consent to a reconstruction of the Government." At first it was not clear—not even to Asquith himself—that the new crisis was to result in his definitive resignation after eight and half years of office; but this was what had happened by Tuesday night. From the time of the outbreak in 1914, questions had been raised— even among the greatest admirers of his mastery of the processes of cabinet and parliamentary government in peacetime—whether Asquith was the right leader for all-out war. His long-recognized proclivity for dealing with problems by letting them resolve themselves in due course had now come to seem in many eyes a basic inability to take the initiatives required to defeat an enemy. He was perhaps too urbane and diffident a man for the task; it also seems that some last reserve of strength for the battle may have gone out of him in September, when he had received word of the death of his eldest son, Raymond, at the Somme.

Meanwhile, political consensus had been joining forces with chance and personal ambition to single out the man who—with Kitchener gone and Churchill, though back from the front and again in Parliament, still in bad odor—alone seemed forceful, determined, and ruthless enough to guide the nation victoriously through the war. Lloyd George, at the War Office since July, had been gathering allies within the coalition Government in the manner of a man who had become a maverick in his own party. It was above all in alliance with the Conservative leader Bonar Law that the war secretary had begun exercising strong pressure upon the prime minister in No-vember. Lloyd George demanded changes in the structure of the War Committee that would have given him effective control of the Government's war policies. Asquith wavered for a time, then ac-quiesced, and announced on the night of December 3 that the Gov-ernment would be reconstructed. Then he changed his mind, thereby provoking an all-out confrontation with Lloyd George, who resigned from the cabinet. Asquith then himself resigned as a maneuver, thinking that neither Bonar Law nor Lloyd George could success-fully form a government. But Lloyd George was able to do precisely that, even though he had virtually no support from his own party, which remained largely loyal to Asquith. His true base of support was the nation and the press. "It was," in the words of one eminent historian of the period, "a revolution, British-style." As Lloyd George was to put it, "there had never before been a 'ranker' raised to the Premiership—certainly not one except Disraeli who had not passed through the Staff College of the old universities."

One of Lloyd George's master strokes was to offer the Foreign Office to a man who was very much a representative of that old staff college and a former prime minister himself: Arthur James Balfour, who accepted. This was the climax of a personal and political relationship between Balfour and Lloyd George in which public acrimony had with growing frequency been interspersed with a strangely warm mutual admiration over some two decades. Weiz-mann and his circle could not but have been struck deeply by the significance of having a prime minister who had often enthused over the idea of a Jewish Palestine and a foreign secretary who once had all but wept at it. This was a long way indeed from the scoffing of Asquith and the diffidence of Grey.

Soon after the formation of the new Government it had become evident that the British military strategy in the Sinai Desert was shifting from a defensive to an offensive one. The roots of this change had been planted through the course of the preceding year. General Sir Archibald Murray, who in March had succeeded Sir John Maxwell as commander in chief for Egypt, had from the outset thought the defensive posture at the canal itself to be wrong. In his opinion, the first line of defense against the Turks should have been in the Sinai outposts that British troops had vacated at the begin-ning of the war. Setting his own sights upon El Arish, about eighty miles east of the canal along the Mediterranean coast, Murray had begun construction of the two indispensable elements for the establishment of such a position—a railway and a freshwater pipeline (the latter being the very thing Cromer had refused the Zionists thirteen years before)—by the time the Turks made their attack at Katia on April 23. After that setback, construction had proceeded, and the railway and pipeline had reached Romani by August 4, when the British and Anzac troops won a decisive victory there against a Turkish assault.

Murray then resumed construction of the railway and was able also to extend the pipeline after the arrival on September 24 of five thousand tons of twelve-inch piping from the United States. He intended to occupy El Arish in the winter, explaining his views in a letter to the War Office on November 12:

> I intend as soon as possible to occupy El Arish and there to protect Egypt and clear the province of Sinai. I also propose, while having due regard to my primary duty of defending Egypt, to harass the Turks in Syria with my mobile forces to the full extent of my strength. I thus hope to attract to myself Turkish forces which would otherwise be engaged against the Sherif, or the Russians, or in Mesopotamia. I hope by acting on the defensive-offensive to gain full value from my Egyptian army field force which a purely defensive role would not achieve.

At this time, there was talk in the cabinet and at the War Office of sending a division from Egypt to Rabegh, on the Red Sea coast of Arabia, to form part of an Anglo-French force that would help the Sherif in his revolt; but Murray was strongly opposed to this, as was the Sherif himself. Another difficulty in Murray's way was the fact that General Sir William Robertson, the chief of the Imperial General Staff, was an ardent "Westerner" who was reluctant to divert troops from France and Flanders. Murray had four divisions and wanted a fifth for an advance upon El Arish, but Robertson would not grant it.

Murray found new moral support, however, with the formation of the Lloyd George Government in December. The new prime minister was as enthusiastic an "Easterner" as ever. His idealism regarding Palestine in particular still was strong, and he also felt that a campaign there, "like that in Mesopotamia, was one especially suited to the special abilities and experience of British generals. It was the kind of warfare in which our army excelled." This was a keen and significant observation from the man who had been one of the most ferocious opponents of a colonial war in Britain's history.

But Lloyd George's newly formed five-man War Cabinet included— in addition to himself and the two Opposition leaders, Bonar Law and the Labour party's Arthur Henderson—two of the most eminent recent proconsuls of the empire: Lord Curzon, former viceroy of India, and Lord Milner, high commissioner for South Africa during the Boer War and one of Lloyd George's most hated enemies at that time. The moment of reconciliations for maximum national strength had arrived.

The first meeting of the Lloyd George War Cabinet, held at 10 Downing Street on Saturday, December 9, 1916, came up with an endorsement of Murray's position. The sending of troops to Rabegh was discussed, but no conclusion about that was arrived at for the time being. Instead, Lloyd George made a special point of stressing to Robertson, who was present, the desirability of making the operations in the Sinai "as successful as possible." Robertson promptly wired Murray, urging upon him the "importance of achieving big success on Eastern front." Murray wired back the next day, announcing that he intended not only to take El Arish, but to advance from there the additional twenty-five miles to Rafah, right at the border between the Sinai and Palestine. Nor was that to be the end of it. "My action subsequent to reaching Rafah," he went on, "must naturally be dictated by situation at moment, and by main consideration that the enemy must be defeated in the field. My idea, however, if circumstances permit, is to advance from Rafah to Beersheba, where enemy's main concentration appears to be. Occupation of this place would, moreover, have advantage of placing me on a railway." Taking advantage of the sympathetic hearing he now clearly was getting in Whitehall, Murray went on to ask for two divisions from Mesopotamia, realizing that any from France "may be out of the question."

For Murray, Beersheba would be a vantage point from which to guard the Sinai and provide assistance to both the Mesopotamian campaign and the Hejaz revolt. He did not necessarily see it as the beginning of a British conquest of Palestine. Lloyd George, on the other hand, was likely to have seen it as that above all. Robertson wired back on December 12 that Murray's message had "been seen by Prime Minister, who wishes you to make the maximum possible effort during the winter." But Robertson, who clearly was beginning to have second thoughts about all this enthusiasm for a sideshow, and who also foresaw political difficulties with the French arising out of a British campaign in what they still regarded as southern Syria, said that no troops could be sent from Mesopotamia until the spring.

Any reinforcements, he pointed out emphatically, would have to be drawn from either France or Salonika. At what stage, he prodded, would Murray need the two divisions—for Rafah or for Beersheba? (He did not even mention El Arish in this context.) And could he water as large a force as he envisioned?

Murray took the hint. "In my first appreciation," he wired back, referring to his communication of November 12,

> I said that an additional division, making five in all, would be necessary to hold and operate from Arish. I still consider this necessary in order to ensure security, though I shall do my best to push forward from El Arish to Rafah without it, commencing about 15th January. For my further advance from Rafah to Beersheba, I feel justified in asking for a second division, but this would not be required until about 15th February.

This concession on Murray's part, however, alarmed Robertson all the more. Robertson could not have conceived of sparing troops from Europe during the winter, the most agreeable season for campaigning in the Sinai and the Negev. And Murray now was displaying an intention to go on campaigning into the spring, when a new offensive was being planned in the West. The brainchild of General Robert Nivelle, the new French commander in chief appointed to replace Joffre after Verdun, this planned new offensive had won the vigorous support even of Lloyd George. Robertson therefore wired back on December 15:

> In order that any possibility of misunderstanding may be removed, I wish to make it clear that notwithstanding the instructions recently sent to you to the effect that you should make your maximum effort during the winter, your primary mission remains unchanged, that is to say, it is the defense of Egypt. You will be informed if and when the War Office changes this policy.

Robertson went on to urge Murray to take El Arish, but suggested that any further advances would be up to him; meanwhile, no additional troops could be made available.

That there were now political as well as military grounds for Robertson's display of reticence is shown by the fact that on December 15, the day of his latest message to Murray, the War Cabinet pondered a memorandum he had written the day before which said:

Operations will shortly be begun in the Sinai Desert with the immediate objects of occupying El Arish, thence a further advance on Rafa is projected. Subsequent operations must depend on circumstances, and we desire to have liberty to follow up any success we may achieve.

If our advance is continued beyond Rafa, the international sphere as defined by the agreement entered into by the French, Russian and British Governments in the spring of this year would become part of the theater of operations. It would therefore seem desirable that the French Government should be informed, with the utmost secrecy, of our intentions, otherwise the reason for the operations may be misunderstood by them in view of their well known susceptibilities in regard to Syria.

The French might also be informed that our sole object is to defeat the Turks, and that we should welcome their political cooperation both in the international sphere and in any negotiations which may become necessary in the French sphere of direct control and in that of commercial and political interest. We should, however, do our utmost to avoid the association of any French troops with our own, as a mixed force is, for many reasons, political and military, always objectionable.

For a discussion of matters in this campaign touching upon what had come to be known in governing circles as the Sykes-Picot Agreement, Sir Mark Sykes himself was present at the War Cabinet that day. Along with Leopold Amery, Sykes had just been appointed a special under-secretary to the War Cabinet secretariat. At the meeting, he explained that "if the forthcoming operations proved successful, it was possible that the tribes east of the Medina [i.e., Hejaz] Railway would rise, and, as the headquarters of these tribes were in the French sphere, as defined by the Agreement . . . , it was important to secure the French political cooperation." The War Cabinet decided to inform the French government, "with the utmost secrecy, of our intentions, that our sole object is to defeat the Turks, and that we should welcome their political cooperation." It also was decided that a telegram would be sent to Wingate authorizing him to inform the Sherif, "if he thought it prudent to do so, that the Sinai offensive would take place immediately, and to indicate to him the assistance which might result from this, especially if the Arab tribes in Southern Palestine could be induced to rise against the Turks."

On the night of December 20—the British railhead having been brought to within twenty miles of the town—the advance guard of the British forces on the eastern frontier of Egypt, known as the Desert Column, moved out to take El Arish. Consisting of an Anzac cavalry division and a Camel Corps brigade as well as of two infantry divisions, the Desert Column encountered during its night journey an environment wholly new to it in this war: patches of cultivated land. "As they rode in the darkness," writes the official historian, "the men, to their delight, felt their horses pass from the sand which they had known so long to firm soil. And with morning light, though sand-dunes mile on mile lay to south and east of them, their eyes were gladdened by green patches of cultivation, with wheat and barley just sprouting, and many palms." They were in fact at the edge of one of the world's great barley-growing districts, a prominent point of origin for English beer. But this was not the only pleasant surprise that awaited them: for as they carefully approached and surrounded El Arish on the morning of December 21, the realization gradually dawned upon them that it was empty of Turks.

"As our troops were not strong enough to defend the town of El Arish," General Kress von Kressenstein was to write years later, "which was unhappily situated and exposed to the fire of British warships, we were obliged in December to evacuate this place also." Not that the British were thereby deprived of an armed confrontation, however; for, while part of the Turkish force had retired to Rafah, the rest had moved twenty miles southeast up the Wadi El Arish to the oasis of Magdhaba. It was upon the latter location, which was discovered by reconnaissance flights, that the British decided to make an assault.

On the night of December 22, Lieutenant General Sir H.G. Chauvel, an Australian, set out with his Anzac cavalry division—less one brigade, which had been withdrawn for a rest—and the Camel Brigade along the dry bed of the wadi, followed by a column of water-carrying camels. At about 8:00 A.M. on the twenty-third, the Anzac cavalry began surrounding the Turkish redoubts on both sides of the wadi. It was intended that the Camel Brigade would charge to the center of the enemy position at the right moment. The fighting proved difficult, however, and at 2:00 P.M. Chauvel pondered withdrawal. But news arrived from a troop of engineers who had been sent to dig wells nearby that no water was available outside Magdhaba itself. This was potentially a great problem for the men and a disaster for the horses, so the attack was continued. Finally, at about 4:30 P.M.—just before darkness fell—a key Turkish position was taken, and soon the British had won. More than 1,200 Turks were taken prisoner and 97 lay dead; the British had suffered 146 casualties: 22 dead and 124 wounded.

General Murray's troops were now securely established in an area that had once been considered for Zionist colonization under British auspices. Then, and now, it was perceived as the gateway from the Sinai to Palestine itself.

PART FOUR

·1917·

·31·

PALESTINE: MAKING A BEGINNING

Sir Archibald Murray wasted no time after the El Arish victory in preparing for an attack upon Rafah, twenty-five miles beyond. Work was resumed on the railway, and it had reached El Arish by January 4, 1917. At 4:00 P.M. on the ninth, Major General Sir Philip Chetwode rode out with the Anzac and British cavalry, the Camel Brigade, and a Light Car Patrol that consisted of six Fords, each carrying a machine gun. There were no real roads in the area, but these cars were usable on desert tracks. A bivouac was established at the village of Sheikh Zowaid along the way. At dawn on the ninth, the British began surrounding Rafah itself and the main Turkish position, which was some two miles south of it at El Magruntein.

The town itself was easily taken—among the 45 prisoners were some Germans, as well as Turks and armed Bedouin—but the position at El Magruntein proved surprisingly tough. As at Magdhaba, it looked for a moment as if the day would end without a decision. At 4:30 P.M., General Chetwode, hearing of the advance of Turkish reinforcements from Shellal and Khan Yunis to the east and the northeast, respectively, was about to call for a withdrawal; but at that moment the Anzac cavalry came through once again. One brigade of it suddenly took the main Turkish redoubt, and the entire enemy position soon fell. Detachments of cavalry were then sent off to deter the oncoming Turkish reinforcements. Over 1,600 Turks were taken prisoner, while another 200 lay dead; the British casualties were 71 killed and 415 wounded. The British were now on the very threshold of Palestine.

Aaron Aaronsohn, in Egypt since December 12, had not had a

great deal to do until this moment, other than strive to establish terms with the British authorities there and demonstrate his good faith. At one point Norman Bentwich, now a lieutenant in the Camel Transport Corps, was called back from El Arish to interview him and verify his claims. Bentwich, who had visited the Agricultural Experimental Station more than once before the war, was able to give him a hearty recommendation.

Otherwise, there appears to have been a good deal of frustration for Aaronsohn in his efforts to make his way past an array of minor officials who did not know precisely what to do with him. The captures of El Arish and of Rafah were surprises to him; he had had nothing directly to do with either. But by the time of the latter victory, things were beginning to change. On January 9, he was put into the charge of a gifted new member of the Arab Bureau, Major William Ormsby-Gore, the thirty-one-year-old eldest son of the third Baron Harlech and himself a member of Parliament since 1910. This proved the beginning of a relationship founded in a strong mutual respect and one that was to have a significant impact upon Ormsby-Gore, who became an increasingly enthusiastic supporter of Zionism from this moment on. Aaronsohn was put to work by the aristocratic young Welshman writing intelligence reports, the significance of which could not have escaped him: for on January 11, the day he heard about Rafah, he was assigned to develop a map of southern Palestine. The value of Aaronsohn's services was being recognized at the moment the Palestine campaign was about to begin in earnest.

This was not the only Jewish offering in regard to Palestine that could now be perceived as valuable. Back in London, Jabotinsky was at last obtaining serious consideration for his Jewish legion idea. Leopold Amery, who owed his appointment as a cabinet under-secretary to a close personal connection on his part with Lord Milner, had quickly seen to it that Jabotinsky's scheme was brought to Milner's attention. Milner was interested: the idea was now winning some popularity on account of the recent publication of Colonel Patterson's enthusiastic memoir of the Zion Mule Corps, *With the Zionists in Gallipoli*. Amery asked Jabotinsky and Trumpeldor to prepare a memorandum on the subject. They did so, submitting it—with Amery's corrections—to the cabinet on January 24, 1917. A few days later, Jabotinsky took what seemed the inevitable next step. Trumpeldor and a number of his comrades from the disbanded Zion Mule Corps had reenlisted in the British army and were now with the Twentieth Battalion, London Regiment. Training at Hazeley Down, near Winchester, they hoped they were the nucleus of a future Jewish regiment to serve in Palestine. Jabotinsky hoped so, too, and enlisted for service with the Twentieth Battalion at the end of January.

In general, if 1916 had opened in an atmosphere of weariness and frustration, the beginning of 1917 was permeated with a sudden enthusiasm for the various ideals that were coming to be considered the aims of the war effort. In December, within a week of the formation of the Lloyd George Government, Germany had sent, through the good offices of the American chargé d'affaires in Berlin, a proposal for peace negotiations with the Allied Powers. President Wilson, just reelected as the man who had kept his country out of the war, had taken this as an opportunity to send out a peace note requesting statements from the belligerents on their terms for a settlement. Arthur James Balfour, speaking for a cabinet that regarded the German overtures with the utmost suspicion, had on January 10 replied with a note calling for sweeping reforms in international affairs. These included the liberation of minorities still under Hapsburg and Ottoman rule and a general reorganization of Europe on the principle of nationalities. Whereupon Wilson delivered before the Senate on January 22 a speech calling for a new world order based on an "organized peace." This became celebrated throughout the world, though its call for "peace without victory" did not sit well with the Allies, who showed no inclination to stop fighting—especially when, at the end of the month, Germany made known her decidedly annexationist terms.

The first issue of *Palestine*, the weekly organ of the British Palestine Committee, appeared on Friday, January 26, and it was in keeping with the idealism of the moment. A modest eight-page bulletin without a cover and priced at two pence, it proclaimed its purpose in capital letters just under the masthead: "THE BRITISH PALESTINE COMMITTEE SEEKS TO RESET THE ANCIENT GLORIES OF THE JEWISH NATION IN THE FREEDOM OF A NEW BRITISH DOMINION IN PALESTINE." This was followed by a quote from an 1882 issue of the *Spectator*: "If he [Lord Beaconsfield] had freed the Holy Land, and restored the Jews, as he might have done, instead of pottering about with Roumelia and Afghanistan, he would have died Dictator." Most of the ensuing pages were devoted to an essay, unsigned but probably written by Harry Sacher, called "England and Palestine," which invoked the traditional idea that special affinities existed between

Englishmen and Jewish aspirations for revival in the Holy Land. "It is sometimes asked," the essay ran,

> why Jews, who are at once of all nationalities and of none except that of their age-long dreams, should turn to England to recover for them their ancient birthright. To this question the answer that Jews all over the world would make is that they turn to England because she alone has known how to combine Empire with liberty. In the British Empire, the better Australian, or Canadian, or South African a man is, the better subject of the King he is, and of no other Empire could this be said with truth. Jews turn to the British Empire because they know that under it, provided that there is loyalty to the common ideal, they are free to develop their own nationality, and, indeed, that the better Jews they are the better British subjects they will be.

There then followed a historical survey summing up the relevant works of such British notables as Palmerston, Shaftesbury, Disraeli, George Eliot, Sir Moses Montefiore, and Laurence Oliphant, and of such institutions as the British consulate at Jerusalem and the Palestine Exploration Fund—with special mention, in the latter case, of Conder and Kitchener. Also mentioned were Joseph Chamberlain and Lord Lansdowne—the latter still alive in January 1917 and the foremost spokesman for peace initiatives in the House of Lords—in connection with the East Africa offer to the Zionists. "Not often," the writer concluded,

> has a small society like the British Palestine Committee been able to claim a line of such distinguished ancestors in politics. . . . The mere list of names of our sympathizers is a résumé of much that is best in English life for the last century. This is no new movement disconnected with the life of England. On the contrary, it has floated down the broad stream of our politics and our philanthropy for nearly a hundred years.

This did not mean, however, that the paper was settling down entirely to the level of idealistic invocation. Things were happening, after all, in the Middle East: General Sir Stanley Maude, now commanding in Mesopotamia, was recovering lost ground and moving back upriver toward Kut-el-Amara; and General Murray was surely not going to stop in the flush of victory. Among a series of short items at the end of the first issue of *Palestine* was one on "General Murray's Campaign." Speculating that "a forward move into Turkish territory has been decided upon," the article warned that it was still early "to estimate the full extent of General Murray's intentions." But it did not hesitate to conclude: "Doubtless he will express himself once again, with swift, skillful, and heavy blows." These words clearly had been written by Herbert Sidebotham, who was preparing to contribute the major article to the next issue on his well-established theme: "Our Military Interest in Palestine."

The moment seemed dominated by a confluence of currents flowing, respectively, out of peace initiatives, war aims, the aspirations of national minorities, and victories in the Middle East; this also manifested itself that Friday morning at Lloyd George's breakfast table. On this occasion, the prime minister had two guests. First to arrive was C.P. Scott, coming to breakfast with his erstwhile comrade in pro-Boerism for the first time since the latter's assumption of the highest office. Later they were joined by Neil Primrose, the thirty-four-year-old younger son of former Prime Minister Lord Rosebery and his wife Hannah, the daughter of Mayer Nathan Rothschild. Primrose, who had preceded Lord Robert Cecil as parliamentary under-secretary of state for foreign affairs in 1915, was now chief whip for the Lloyd George Government.

Moving through a succession of current topics—including the growing threat of revolution in Russia—the conversation came momentarily to rest on President Wilson's peace initiatives. Lloyd George said he had not minded the Senate speech of January 22; he thought that in essence it corresponded not only to Balfour's note of January 10 but also to ideas he had himself outlined for Colonel House during the latter's visit in February 1916. What had bothered him was Wilson's earlier peace note; he thought it had been too pro-German. Scott had in fact written about the matter to his fellow journalist Walter Lippmann, one of Wilson's advisers, who replied— as Scott had reported to Lloyd George in a letter of December 24— "that pro-Germanism has nothing whatever to do with the note, as Wilson owes nothing, unless it be resentment, to German-Americanism in politics which the election effectually disposed of." This, however, had not satisfied Lloyd George, who now insisted that the president's peace note had been "a pro-German move" made "in fulfillment of a definite pledge given during the course of the recent Presidential election to certain pro-German Jews in exchange for cash for the Elections Fund which was running very low." He claimed that the British Government "had positive evidence of this."

A few significant words relating to the subjects of Palestine and

Zionism also were exchanged at breakfast. At one point Scott mentioned Weizmann, and Lloyd George said there were "several things he wanted to talk to him about." This could not have been acetone business, which the prime minister had put far behind him. At another point Primrose raised the subject of Palestine.* "Oh!" Lloyd George said. "We must grab that; we have made a beginning." Over the weekend Scott was to see further signs of that particular beginning.

* Primrose was to be killed in action on the Palestine front in November.

·32·

SYKES MEETS THE ZIONIST LEADERSHIP

"Saw Weizmann in morning about Palestine question," C.P. Scott wrote in his diary for Saturday, January 27, the day after his breakfast with Lloyd George. "Sir Mark Sykes deputed by FO to deal with it. He [Weizmann] and Lord R[othschild] and James [Rothschild] and others to see him. Memorial was being prepared on whole question. Very important to obtain American Jews' support. It would be unanimous if they could be assured that in the event of a British occupation of Palestine the Zionist scheme would be considered favorably. Now was the moment for pressing the matter when British troops were actually on Palestine soil."

Now clearly had also been the moment for Sir Mark Sykes to become known to Chaim Weizmann, James and Lord Rothschild, and others who shared their outlook. Sykes's well-established role in Middle Eastern affairs was taking on new dimensions and a greater urgency than ever before. At the beginning of the month Ambassador Paul Cambon had announced that France intended to participate in the administration of whatever parts of Palestine the British were going to occupy. For this purpose, his government had chosen as its representative François Georges-Picot, who had thereupon come to London for preliminary discussions before going on to Egypt. In the meantime the War Cabinet had decided that a political officer would have to be attached to General Murray's staff to act as a British counterpart to Picot. This position almost inevitably fell to Sykes, who consequently had to be prepared to leave for Egypt before long.

There were important questions to iron out with the Zionists. To this end, Sykes had put himself in touch with Gaster again and seems to have had a personal meeting with him on January 8; but he must have realized that Gaster alone was no longer enough. Undoubtedly he also was seeing Herbert Samuel, who, having along with other loyal Liberals refused an invitation to join Lloyd George's cabinet, was again devoting himself to the promotion of his Palestine memorandum. Indeed, it could not have been anyone but Samuel who spread the word about Sykes to Weizmann and the two Rothschilds. Gaster was still not ready to share his secret; and as for Sykes himself, though he surely intended to contact them soon regarding Palestine, he had not yet done so when Scott saw Weizmann on Saturday morning, January 27. Rather, it was James de Rothschild who turned out to have taken the initiative and made an appointment with Sykes for later that very day. The two men knew one another socially and had a common interest in the breeding of racehorses; but this proved to be their first discussion on Zionism.

Scott met with James de Rothschild and Neil Primrose still later that day at the Reform Club. Reporting on the conversation he had just had with Sykes, Rothschild said that "France was competing hard for Palestine. Her face might be saved by giving her the policing of Jerusalem, but he did not see how we could go beyond that. Sir Mark Sykes was being consulted as the expert on the whole question of the Near East. He was at present engaged in examining what is 'Armenia.' When I suggested," Scott adds in his diary, "that in addition to Syria France might have Damascus as a sop for resigning any pretension to Palestine, R[othschild] said that Sykes designed to include it in the new Arab Kingdom, as its commercial capital—a strange idea." Scott did not yet know that the British Government's conception of an Arab kingdom took in somewhat more than just the Arabian Peninsula.

Rothschild's remark about Armenia suggests that this had been the question preoccupying Sykes for the moment. As far back as his de Bunsen Committee days, he had considered the fate of the Armenians to be among the essential problems of Ottoman Asia, and he had since added their national movement to the roster of those for which he proposed to seek fulfillment in the postwar world. If he had been a bit tardy in contacting other Zionists besides Gaster, this may have been because he was pondering ways in which he might present the Armenian cause to them as linked with their own.

Over the past year, Sykes had established a relationship with the London representative of the International Armenian Committee, James Aratoon Malcolm, a Persian-born Armenian businessman with an Oxford education and an Anglicized name. Malcolm was a lively organizer of public activities and personal connections and had a circle of acquaintances that even included Leopold Greenberg. He had met the *Jewish Chronicle* editor in 1915 when he was collecting signatures for an organization called the Russia Society, which sought to promote better relations between Great Britain and the ally with whom she was the least comfortable. Malcolm regarded Russia as the destined protector of an Armenian national entity; Greenberg, who had signed the petition, regarded Russia as an ally in spite of everything and Lucien Wolf as a nuisance.

Sykes, in his conversation that Saturday with James de Rothschild, does not seem to have mentioned the possibility of a political alliance between the Zionists and the Armenian nationalists. But clearly he had already discussed such an alliance with Malcolm, who had immediately gone to Greenberg and asked for the names of Zionist leaders to whom he might propose it. Greenberg had complied, giving prominence on his list—whether out of unbiased realism, ungrudging respect, or a touch of malice, one cannot say—to Chaim Weizmann and Nahum Sokolow. Rothschild's meeting with Sykes may then have given new fuel to the idea, for it was later in the same day that Weizmann heard from Malcolm.

What they discussed was described by Weizmann the next morning to C.P. Scott, who called on him to talk over questions relating to acetone patent rights in America. Scott found himself listening to "a curious story about an Armenian enjoying the name of 'Malcolm' who appeared to be on intimate terms with Sykes and who approached Weizmann with a view to gaining Zionist support for 'stable' i.e. bureaucratic and reactionary—Government in Russia, alleging parallel between Russian protectorate in Armenia and British in Palestine. Apparently the idea was that if Zionists gave their support to the Russian protectorate, Russia would not make difficulties about a British protectorate. Weizmann replied that Armenia was completely outside the sphere of Zionist interests."

It was an embarrassment. Scott as an eminent Liberal editor was at least, unlike Weizmann, ready to concern himself with other national questions besides the Jewish one—and the Armenian one was of major importance. But he obviously agreed that it was an unnecessary and possibly disruptive entanglement for the Zionists. Furthermore, the character of Malcolm—Sokolow was to call him a *brasseur d'affaires*; in America today he might be called a wheeler-dealer—was not such as to inspire confidence among everyone who knew him. On the other hand, both Scott and Weizmann knew that the last thing any Zionist wanted was to offend Sykes. They must have decided that Weizmann ought to get in touch with Sykes right away; perhaps Malcolm had also suggested this the day before. At any rate, Weizmann called Sykes that morning and asked for an appointment later in the day.

Sykes must have known a good deal by now about Weizmann and his pivotal role in English Zionism: he ought to have wanted to see him about that alone. But the idea of an Armenian connection evidently still had Sykes in its grip, and he seems to have agreed to see Weizmann that afternoon believing it was to be the main subject of conversation. There can be no other reason why Sykes proposed, as he did, that Weizmann come over with Leopold Greenberg—who no doubt had been urged upon Sykes by Malcolm as another Zionist he ought to see. The fact that Greenberg was the editor of the *Jewish Chronicle* could have made it seem to outsiders that he was of some consequence within the Zionist movement, which he had long ago ceased to be. The upshot was that when Weizmann arrived at 9 Buckingham Gate that Sunday afternoon, he had Greenberg as his unlikely companion. This was enough for the *Jewish Chronicle* editor—between whom and Weizmann there was little warmth—to be able, in years to come, to claim "the honor of bringing Dr. Weizmann and Sir Mark Sykes into touch with one another."

From the little we can learn of what transpired during that afternoon's conversation, we may readily conclude that Sykes saw with sudden clarity what he had been missing all these months by dealing with Gaster instead of Weizmann. As it happens, virtually all that is known comes from Gaster's diaries—for Weizmann, having been informed by Sykes of the long association between him and the Sephardi chief rabbi, had wasted no time about calling the latter when he got home that evening. "Message from Weizmann, wants to speak to me," Gaster records. "He rings up. . . . He had met Sir Mark Sykes and found out that he was an old friend of mine and that he referred W[eizmann] and Baron James to me. . . . He realized that the whole problem rested now in Sir M.'s hands and that he was the man on whom our Zionist hopes hang." Gaster's game was up: it must have been above all to let him know this that Weizmann was so quick to get in touch with him. First, Gaster had concealed Herbert Samuel; then, Sir Mark Sykes. But all that was over now.

Gaster seems to have been genuinely dismayed. He wrote to Sykes the next day. "One of my co-workers," as he put it, "told me last night of the interview which he had with you and of the various suggestions which you have made." Evidently perceiving that the chief rabbi had to be consoled, Sykes invited him to come to Buckingham Gate the day after that, Tuesday, January 30, to discuss what had taken place. "*Went to Sykes,*" Gaster recorded afterward. "Long conversation. Told me the whole history. On Saturday note from Baron James to meet him. S[ykes] thought it was about horses, one of which he had bought from him. To his surprise, it was about Zionism." Sykes took the opportunity to tell Gaster how impressed he was by this demonstration in contradiction to "Picot's statement that French Jews would *not* help"—not realizing that James de Roth-schild was now, in effect, as English as Gaster or Weizmann.

"I asked him about W.'s visit," Gaster continues, "and I learned that it was *not* Baron James at all who introduced him. Sykes had told Baron James to come to *me* and did not hear of another name. W. had rung him up on Sunday and came together with Greenberg!" At this, Gaster's mood shifted to all-out indignation. Weizmann was one thing, but Greenberg was too much, and he told Sykes how little he thought of him. But Sykes did not need to be convinced on this point. "Dr. Weizmann had made a more favorable impression," Gaster records. "He was earnest in his plea for Zion. They then learned from S. that *I* had been in constant communication with S. S. had not entered upon many details, but, as I learned from him, he had repre-sented it as urgent that steps should be taken to formulate pro-posals, to prepare for some machinery." Sykes explained to Gaster that by this he meant that the Zionists should be ready to help "put into immediate practice some of the principles of local Government and administration, to define our activity, to have men on the spot when the English entered Jerusalem so as to take effective part in the administration of at least the Jewish section of the population."

Gaster may by now have felt appeased as to the continuing importance of his own role with Sykes, although he had to record at the end of the same entry: "I then learned that W. had another appointment with him that evening." Who but Gaster could then have doubted that Weizmann had made his conquest? The chief rabbi went on seeing to it, however, that he was kept abreast of everything that happened. "I hope to see Dr. W. this afternoon," he wrote to Sykes on Wednesday, "and I shall probably hear from him the result of his visit to you last night." Weizmann kept his word, coming to Gaster's home and describing both his conversations with Sykes. "Had been introduced, as he alleged, by the Armenian Gal-man [*sic*]," writes Gaster, having been given the least perturbing and, in a sense, the most literal version of how it all had come about. "He said that Sykes wanted a meeting with Herbert Samuel and other representatives." Well, Gaster would certainly have his part in that. It was he who, that same day, sent Sykes copies he had requested of the Zionist Memorandum and Demands drawn up the previous fall.

The next few days consisted not so much of a power struggle between Gaster and Weizmann—the latter now with Sokolow securely by his side—as of an often quarrelsome confrontation in which Gaster tried to assert the authority he thought he had and Weizmann sought to keep him in place while humoring him at the same time: this was not the moment for open and disruptive splits. On Thursday, February 1, Weizmann, Sokolow, and Gaster convened at the rabbi's home to plan the forthcoming meeting with Sykes, and the discussion became acrimonious. "Gaster thinks that he has got the monopoly now," Weizmann wrote two days later to Israel Sieff. "He was laying down the law last Thursday night, and I had to tell him off once or twice." Gaster had reported the results of that discussion to Sykes by letter, but it is clear that Weizmann and Sokolow also were in touch with Sykes at this time. On Monday, February 5, they kept an appointment—described in a note by Weizmann to Sokolow the previous day as "very important"—with James Malcolm at the latter's club, the Thatched House, in Saint James's Street off Piccadilly.

The Zionist meeting with Sykes was set for Wednesday, February 7, at Gaster's home, with Gaster as chairman; but this apparent triumph for the chief rabbi seems to have been a deliberate appeasement planned by Weizmann and Sokolow with Sykes's collusion. Sykes had probably begun having doubts about Gaster as far back as the end of the previous May, after the euphoria of their very first encounters had passed. Gaster had actually gone on to have an interview alone with Picot in July 1916, but nothing of concrete importance appears to have come out of it, and Picot was to claim years later that he had subsequently asked Sykes to find a Zionist with a more realistic grasp of the situation. Sykes certainly had done so by now. He was to explain it all to Aaron Aaronsohn two months later when they got together in Egypt. Gaster had originally assured Sykes, according to Aaronsohn's summary in his diary,

> that he was capable of setting all of Zionism in motion. Sykes let himself be won over and ended by perceiving that Gaster was on the decline. . . . He then turned to Weizmann and Sokolow through the Armenian Malcolm as intermediary. These two impressed him. But it was a question of not offending Gaster; so Sykes suggested a meeting at Gaster's house which he, Sykes,

would attend as a private individual, and at which two representatives would be chosen to deal directly with him.

On February 6, the day before the meeting, Weizmann suggested to
Gaster that Sokolow be appointed to carry on discussions with Sykes
after that, but Gaster "hotly resented" the idea. The matter was left
for decision at the meeting itself.

The most important event to date in the progress of English
Zionism took place as scheduled in the chief rabbi's home at
193 Maida Vale, on Wednesday, February 7, 1917, at 11:30 in the
morning. Present besides Gaster, Weizmann, Sokolow, and Sykes
were Herbert Samuel, James de Rothschild, Lord Rothschild, Harry
Sacher, Herbert Bentwich, and Joseph Cowen. Sacher's presence,
Gaster felt, had been "forced upon" him by Weizmann and Sokolow,
but he had compensated for this by ringing up Cowen and the elder
Bentwich early that morning; they had not otherwise been invited.
In a sense they were declining powers, like Gaster himself: Bentwich's Maccabaeans were no longer a force to be reckoned with, and
Cowen had just announced that he would not seek reelection to the
presidency of the English Zionist Federation at its forthcoming annual conference on Sunday the eleventh. Instead, Weizmann was
going to run and there could be little doubt as to the outcome.
Gaster, in the chair, opened the meeting by stating the aims of
the Zionists in general terms. These were twofold. First, he said,
"there must be no condominium or internationalization in Palestine,
as that would be fatal." Zionists wanted a British protectorate. The
vehemence of this assertion was due to the impression gathered by
every one of those present who had spoken to Sykes over the past
week and a half, beginning with James de Rothschild, that an Anglo-French condominium was what was mainly being considered by
the governments involved. If Sykes had said this in so many words,
he certainly had misrepresented the arrangement still being envisioned, which was that of the international Brown Area. But what he
surely had done was lay stress upon the French as being the principal obstacle in the way of a purely British Palestine. In this he would
have been correct, and by doing so he had inevitably aroused what he
undoubtedly had sought: a hearty Zionist endorsement of British
suzerainty alone. The second of the two Zionist aims spelled out by
Gaster was of no particular concern to Sykes at this moment. It
called for the recognition of the Jews of Palestine as a nation: using

the term traditionally applied by the Turks to national and religious minorities within the Ottoman Empire, Gaster demanded that the Jews be recognized as a *millet*.

Gaster then opened the floor to statements. The first to speak was Lord Rothschild, who pronounced his full sympathy "with the development of a Jewish state in Palestine under the British Crown." He was thus endorsing what had, in effect, always been his father's position through its many permutations: if Zionism meant Jews living as citizens of a *British* Palestine, then he was for it. He was, according to Sokolow's minutes, "irreconcilably opposed to any form of condominium." The condition for the support of the lay leader of British Jewry had thus been made quite clear. Lord Rothschild did concede, however, that he was prepared to see the control of the Holy Places put into the hands of another nation besides Great Britain "should that be thought necessary," except if it were Russia. "It would not be fitting," he said, "that the officials of a nation which was oppressing the Jews should exercise authority in Palestine." Lord Rothschild favored the establishment of a Jewish chartered company to develop Palestine.

Herbert Samuel, who spoke next, agreed with the statements made by Gaster and Lord Rothschild and stressed his long-standing opposition to a condominium. He explained, however, that the arguments against internationalization did not apply to the special matter of the Holy Places. On the contrary, an international arrangement for these would be advantageous to world Jewry "because there would be no fear that the Jews would obtain control over the Holy Places and no antipathy to Judaism arising out of any such expectation." But he was troubled—perhaps as a result of conversations with some of his assimilationist friends and relatives—by the unqualified use of the word "nation." He thought that "care must be taken to explain the sense in which the term was used, because there was much misunderstanding among Jews of the West and some fear owing to that misunderstanding that a Jewish state in Palestine might be incompatible with their loyalty. So long as it was plain that by 'nation' is meant an organized community well and good,"—this was, in fact, the sense of the term *millet* that Gaster had used—"but it might be misunderstood as meaning that the Jews in Great Britain, for instance, would constitute as a result of a Jewish Palestine a separate nation in the same sense as the British are a nation. That did not mean that the Jews in Palestine itself may not have all the attributes of a nation in the largest sense of that term. There may in time come to be a Jewish nation in Palestine." Samuel concluded with a suggestion that Jewish immigration to Palestine should be a right unrestricted by the suzerain power, but that the chartered company might be authorized to regulate it when that seemed necessary.

Sokolow, Weizmann, and Sacher then spoke in succession, offering some of their well-established views. With his ever-burgeoning Anglophilia, Sokolow again described the Jewish veneration for the British, which would inevitably become even greater once they annexed Palestine and fostered Zionist goals there. He also insisted that the immigrants to Palestine would not be just poor Eastern Europeans, but would also be middle class and occasionally come from America as well. Weizmann emphasized "that the Jews who went to Palestine would go to constitute a Jewish nation and be 100% Jews, not to become Arabs or Druses or Englishmen," and "that the Suzerain authority should not put any restriction on Jewish immigration into Palestine." Sacher provided a discourse on the distinction between a nation and a state: "Jews in Palestine would be members of the Jewish state and owe it political obligation. Jews outside Palestine would be members of the Jewish nation and owe Palestine such respect or reverence as they thought fit, but would owe it no political obligation." Samuel thought this would be like Catholics and Rome.

Sacher then added some significant remarks about the United States and Justice Brandeis. In the little more than two weeks since Wilson's Senate speech, the American vision of world peace had been delivered a severe blow. On January 31 the German government had announced, in defiance of the president's many pleas, that it would begin a campaign of unrestricted submarine warfare in the Atlantic the following day. On February 3, the United States had responded by severing diplomatic relations with Germany; and from that moment on there was widespread expectation that America would enter the war against Germany any day.

"If the United States entered the war," Sacher observed, "that Power would be deeply interested in the question of Palestine. President Wilson's adviser in Jewish matters was Justice Brandeis, the head of the Zionist movement in America.* Mr. Brandeis was in favor of British annexation of Palestine and utterly opposed to a condominium." James de Rothschild, speaking next, added his assurance that "Mr. Brandeis desires a British protectorate and is op-

---

* Brandeis actually had resigned all his official Zionist functions upon his appointment to the Supreme Court a year earlier; but one certainly could say that his influence in American Zionism had remained preeminent.

posed to a condominium." He thought, in fact, that the Jews of America and of Russia ought to be "encouraged to send petitions exhorting the British Government to take over Palestine." Joseph Cowen capped this by asserting that "every German Zionist would welcome a British Suzerainty over Palestine," though he did not offer any authority for this astonishing remark.

After Herbert Bentwich took his turn to say a few words and Herbert Samuel and Lord Rothschild offered some additional remarks, the floor was at last yielded to the man whose presence was the reason everyone else was there. Stressing, as he had planned to do, that he had come in his private capacity, Sykes went on to say that British soldiers would probably soon be in Palestine and that there were consequently some pressing questions to be dealt with. He began by surveying the viewpoints on Palestine of the several nations involved other than Great Britain and the Jews. First, there was Russia: describing his conversation in Petrograd with Sazonov—then foreign minister, now Russian ambassador in London—Sykes concluded that Russia's interests in Palestine were only religious and implied that she would not oppose a Zionist entity there. Then, the Arabs: Sykes spoke of the growing Arab national movement and of Hussein's role in it. "One would have to go very carefully with the Arabs," he admitted, mentioning that Hussein's official organ, *al-Kiblah*, had published in November an article criticizing Zionism and that he had issued word through Cairo expressing strong disapproval of any further expressions of this sort. "Still the Arabs could be managed," Sykes insisted, "particularly if they receive Jewish support in other matters."

Passing quickly over the Italians as representing no great problem, Sykes got to France, which, he said, "was the serious difficulty." He professed to be unable to understand French policy. "The French wanted all Syria and a great say in Palestine. What was their motive? Was it sentimental, that is clerical or colonial ambition?" He did not think it was the railway interests, but rather "nationalist and clerical pretensions" that were chiefly behind the French attitude. "We ought to discuss the matter with the French very frankly," he said. "We have given them no pledge in Palestine." This was not true, of course, and James de Rothschild, who knew enough people in high places to have heard otherwise, spoke up, pressing Sykes for assurances on this point. "The French have no particular position in Palestine," Sykes replied, "and are not entitled to anything there." He then suggested that the Zionists should directly approach the French representative dealing with this question, M. Picot, who was now in London, and persuade him of their position.

This last suggestion, one of the principal ones Sykes had come to make, was presented as if it had not already been decided upon by himself, Weizmann, and Sokolow. It took some of the others by surprise, however, and provoked objections. Samuel said that dealing with the French was the business of the British Government. James de Rothschild said that "if the Zionists approached the French Government, that Government would probably try to get the French Rabbis to say that they wanted a French Palestine." Gaster said nothing, surely seeing himself as the natural choice to continue the discussions with Picot that he had begun the previous year.

Before that point was brought to a conclusion, however, Sykes raised another crucial one: that of the boundaries of proposed Jewish settlement. He proceeded to describe them as he understood them—which were those of the Brown Area—and the effect upon his listeners was like that of a bombshell. Someone pointed out to Sykes that his suggested frontier would exclude much of the Galilee, among other things. Samuel, for whom Sykes's map was nothing new, made himself the most emphatic of those present in driving home objections on this issue. He said that the French "had no claims whatsoever in Palestine," and that it should be sufficient for them that they were going to get, after victory, "one-third of Africa, Alsace-Lorraine and Syria." Lord Rothschild, taking Sykes's word for it that no pledges had been made to the French, protested that it would be absurd to open negotiations with them by offering extensive concessions in advance. Gaster, as if deliberately seeking to lower the sword that already hung over him, asked "what would happen if the Jews, rather than see Palestine cut up, suggested a French Palestine?" Sykes disingenuously replied that the Foreign Office "would not be greatly concerned."

As the meeting drew toward its conclusion, Herbert Samuel stressed, as he had done earlier, his old argument about the strategic importance of Palestine for Great Britain—an argument that had gained reinforcement from Sidebotham's piece in the previous week's issue of *Palestine*. Sykes claimed that the military leadership was not impressed by this argument. Then James de Rothschild, absolutely unconvinced by Sykes's assurances to the contrary, asked once again whether any pledge had been given to the French about Palestine. Sykes suggested that Mr. Samuel might be able to answer that, but Samuel protested that he could not reveal cabinet business.

Sykes then simply repeated ambiguously that "the British Government had managed to keep the question of Palestine open." It certainly was still open as far as he and the Lloyd George Government were concerned.

Sykes ended by asking that the conference appoint someone "to put the Jewish views before M. Picot and to continue negotiations with himself." James de Rothschild, according to the minutes, thereupon "indicated Mr. Sokolow, who could speak for the Russian Jews also, as the proper person. This was seconded and agreed to by the Conference and readily accepted by Col. Sykes. It was thereupon arranged that Mr. Sokolow should be introduced by Sir Mark Sykes to M. Picot on the following day." The whole thing had been accomplished almost before there was time to think about it. Two days later, Gaster was to write to James de Rothschild asking him why he had thus chosen Sokolow, and Rothschild would reply in terms of Sokolow's qualifications; but there can be little doubt that Baron James, feeling the force of Sykes's, Weizmann's and Sokolow's wishes, had been persuaded in advance to make this nomination.

The meeting ended at 1:45 P.M., two and a quarter hours after it had begun, and Gaster was free to confide an intimate overview of the event to his diary. "The most important meeting ever held concerning Zionism," he wrote, "was held *here*, under my chairmanship. . . . Proceedings most satisfactory, but I played against a direct attack. It will however not succeed." But it *had* succeeded. Gaster's brief career as the diplomat of British Zionism was at an end.

·33·

THE POLITICAL EMERGENCE OF
SOKOLOW AND WEIZMANN

"In our Palestinian affairs an important step, I hope, was taken yesterday," wrote Weizmann on February 8 to Private Vladimir Jabotinsky at Hazeley Down. "A conference was held at Gaster's. . . . We talked to Sykes, before whom we put our demands and have seriously discussed everything. I shall tell you in greater detail when we meet, but I regard this conference as an historic one."

That same day, Sokolow went to 9 Buckingham Gate, where Sykes introduced him to Picot. Sykes said among other things that Sokolow was the editor of *Ha'tsefirah*, "an important Hebrew daily formerly published at Warsaw." This prompted Picot to ask Sokolow if he thought the independent Poland envisioned at the war's end "would of its own accord grant equal rights to Jews." Sokolow said he thought a new Polish government would feel honor-bound not to revive anti-Jewish discrimination, although "this could not be relied on with safety." The Entente Powers, he went on, would have to guarantee it. But Sokolow had not come to discuss this; though, as he later reported, he "perceived a desire on the part of M. Picot to discuss the rights of Jews in Russia and Poland rather than the subject of Zionism." It was a matter of quietly manipulating the conversation in the desired direction.

Picot seemed to provide an opening in his next question: he asked "whether, in the event of Jews obtaining equal rights in Russia and Poland, the Jewish question would still remain?" Sokolow said it would, pointing out that it was still acute in Austrian Galicia despite official emancipation there, and that it was just as bad in Poland as in the rest of the Russian Empire, even though the anti-Jewish legislation there had not been as harsh. The reason for this,

Sokolow went on, was that the Jews of Eastern Europe had been prevented—either by legislation or public opinion or both—from developing a normal class structure ranging from agricultural and industrial to professional and bureaucratic. A reorganization of that Jewish society was needed, and the "only solution of the problem was the Zionist solution along national lines."

But Picot did not take the bait. "If the Jews obtained equal rights in Poland and Russia," he asked, "why should not the Jews settle on the land in those countries, the land being bought for them, if necessary?" Furthermore, since land purchase was permitted for Jews in some areas, why had they not already settled on the land?

Sokolow replied that this had been tried in Galicia some twenty years before, when Baron de Hirsch had put up 12 million florins for the purpose. "There was no legal obstacle at all," he stressed. "Nevertheless, the Polish population of Galicia were violently opposed to the project. They created a strong and hostile opinion in press and public, and made the scheme impossible." The same thing happened in Russian Poland when a similar scheme was proposed there, "and even the most philosemitic Polish writers took up the agitation with the motto, 'The Polish land for the Poles.' Jews might do anything they liked but they must not own the land."

Why, then, Picot asked, did not the Jews of Poland "become Poles, just as the French Jews became Frenchmen and the English Jews Englishmen?" This was playing right into the hands of Sokolow, who explained that the situation of Jews in Eastern Europe was quite different than in England or France. In Russian Poland there were 2 million Jews among a total population of 10 million. They were not, as in England or France, "a very small minority in an environment which had attained a high degree of culture, making it a comparatively simple matter for them to be absorbed in and by their environment." The Jews of Poland differed from the surrounding people "in traditions, in language, in manners and customs, in religion, in intellectual and spiritual aspirations and ideals." From the cultural standpoint as well, their problem could only be solved on national lines, "by restoring to them the land which they lacked."

Picot now had little choice but to ask what these separate aspirations and ideals were, and how they manifested themselves. Sokolow replied with a discourse on the Zionist view. He pointed out that in former times "the Jewish spirit had found expression in a specific religious life, that it had produced great Rabbis and laid stress on a highly specialized form of education. In modern times it had manifested itself in the revival of the sense of continuity of the Jewish people, in the revival of the Hebrew language, in the new Hebrew literature and in the return to Palestine of a portion of the people. It (the nationalist revival) had progressed from the literary to the spoken language (Yiddish) and given rise to a great development of Yiddish literature." But this creative surge was "out of harmony" with its environment, and needed a center in which it could develop and join "the stream of civilization," Sokolow concluded; the gates of Palestine had to be opened for the Jews.

Picot complimented Sokolow on this exposition. Then he asked how the Jews proposed to organize themselves as a nation in Palestine. Sokolow said they would start by establishing themselves on the land as farmers, as the French and the English had done in Canada. Picot expressed his approval, saying he once had thought that Jews could not do this, but personal experience of the settlements in Palestine had changed his mind. *"Ce que j'ai vu là-bas est merveilleux,"* he said; Sykes intervened to say that he, too, thought the achievements of the Jewish colonists had been "most wonderful."

Sokolow had now brought the discussion exactly where he wanted it. Pointing out that these results had been achieved under adverse conditions largely due to Turkish misrule, he asserted that lack of faith in the Turk was one reason why many Jews had remained aloof from Zionism. "If Palestine came under the control of a great civilized power," he said, "this opposition would disappear and offers of men and money would be forthcoming."

Picot asked which power Mr. Sokolow had in mind.

Well-versed in the subject of the affinities between Great Britain, the Jews, and Zionism, Sokolow proceeded to expound it. Jews, he said, recognized that for many years Great Britain "had championed their cause and distinguished herself by benevolence towards them." Zionists considered that Great Britain had "a great and noble mission in the East," that she had special gifts in colonial enterprise, and that she allowed the nationalities under her rule "freedom of development" without making any effort to "hamper or suppress their individuality." Sokolow was careful to add that, as to France, "Jews had always recognized the great contribution which it had made to civilization and in common with all civilized people looked upon it as the center of the idea of liberty and equality in Europe and the world." Nevertheless, the predominant feeling among Jews was to favor British suzerainty in Palestine.

"Mais, Monsieur," Picot objected, *"vous devez savoir, comme politicien, que c'est l'affaire de l'Entente."*

Sokolow agreed, but added that the Entente could not govern Palestine.

Sykes broke in, and for a few moments he and Picot discussed some of the understandings they had arrived at regarding Palestine. Sokolow, who knew nothing yet of the Sykes-Picot Agreement, was able to gather "that at one time the idea had been entertained of the internationalization of Palestine," but he had the impression that both men were now against it, especially Sykes.

Picot then told Sokolow that by "Entente" he meant not only Great Britain and France, but also Italy and Russia. Sokolow, who had long known about the Russian attitude through contact with Tschlenow and had by now been told something by Sykes as well, was able to say that Russia had only religious interests in Palestine and would not object to British suzerainty there. Picot wondered what Sokolow's sources of information were, but the latter would not divulge them. As for Italy, Sokolow said he thought there would be a good deal of sympathy for Zionist aims there, especially on the popular level. The question, then, came back to being essentially one between Britain and France.

With that Picot evaded the issue no longer and declared that in his opinion "there was no possibility of France renouncing completely its aspirations in Palestine in favor of Great Britain. Ninety-five percent of the French people," he insisted, "were strongly in favor of the annexation of Palestine by France." But he promised he would do his best at home to make known the Zionist aims. Sykes then proposed that, however Palestine was administered, its colonization might be placed in the charge of an English chartered company. Picot objected to this.

The French diplomat ended the discussion by asking Sokolow what the Jewish attitude would be "to the other peoples of Palestine, more particularly the Arabs, to the Christian sects and to the Holy Places." Sokolow replied that "Palestine was not the national center of the Arabs, so that they would have no cause for ill will against Jews on that account." He said he understood that "the Arabs would be given opportunities to develop a national center of their own. As to the Holy Places the Jews were determined not to interfere with them in the slightest." The same applied to the Christian sects in Palestine.

The conversation ended there, and Picot took his leave. Sykes assured Sokolow of his "great pleasure in listening to the discussion," and of his satisfaction at the way the meeting had turned out. He suggested that Sokolow call on Picot the next day to resume the conversation, and this was arranged.

A natural affinity seems to have developed between Sykes and Sokolow that afternoon. The man with the most cultivated intellect as well as the widest diplomatic experience—with, in the strictest sense, the *only* diplomatic experience—among the Zionist leadership in England, Sokolow had qualities of worldliness and even of dilettantism that were destined to make a strong appeal to Sykes. Sokolow could discuss literature and music as well as history and politics with depth and wide knowledgeability, and could do so with facility in at least seven languages. One of his literary achievements had even also become a contribution to history: for the title he had given to the Hebrew translation he had made of Herzl's *Old-New Land* was *Tel-Aviv*,* and this had inspired the naming of the Jewish suburb of Jaffa that was founded in 1909 and was eventually to grow into a great city in its own right. Wearing like Weizmann—who was fifteen years his junior—the moustache and goatee of the East European *intelligyent*, he also had an easygoing Warsaw sophistication and a touch of Bohemianism about him that were not to be found in his younger colleague in Zionism. Indeed, though he and Weizmann, recognizing each other's strengths in this crucial moment, had suddenly made a firm alliance, there remained a natural opposition of qualities between them that would never cease threatening to turn into outright antipathy.

A man of scientific single-mindedness and essentially bourgeois instincts, Weizmann was always to remember with a certain distaste his youthful visits to the home of the well-known editor in Warsaw—where Sokolow's wife and children were still living and enduring the war—filled with groups of students and admirers coming and going at all hours, awaiting Sokolow who would make his first appearance of the day in the afternoon, in his dressing gown, giving little sign that he had anything else to do. Weizmann also never forgave Sokolow for abstaining in the "Uganda" vote at the Sixth Zionist Congress; an ardent admirer of Herzl, Sokolow had simply held fast

---

* "Then I came to them of the captivity at Tel-abib, that dwelt by the river of Chebar" (Ezekiel 3:15). It is not known exactly what place this is—it appears only this once in the Bible—but the literal meaning of the term is "Mound of Spring." Since "tel" implies archaeological antiquity, "Tel-Aviv" is a rich rendering of "Old-New Land."

to the position initially taken by Weizmann and subsequently renounced by him, to the effect that the offer should not have been
rejected out of hand but turned over to some entity other than the
Zionist organization. "The world will not go under if you yield an
inch," Sokolow would say to his colleagues; "and it makes life a little
more bearable."

This was the outlook that had helped make him, in effect, the
virtual foreign secretary of the Zionist executive through a succession of posts prior to the war, visiting Russia's Count Witte in 1905
and some members of the British Foreign Office in 1913. And though
his earlier links to the Foreign Office seem to have dissolved by the
time of the war, his diplomatic experience and skills were able to
impress themselves whenever he succeeded in making a new contact,
as with H.A. Cumberbatch in April 1916. The impression Sokolow
now made on Sykes was enough to place him at the very center of
Zionist endeavor in the crucial months to come.

Sokolow kept his appointment of Friday, February 9, with Picot,
calling upon him at the French embassy. Picot greeted him warmly
and began by noting that, in the previous day's discussion, they had
neglected to talk about what was to be done in the immediate future.
Sokolow, who had obtained the impression from Picot's remarks the
day before that there were considerable "misunderstandings and
prejudices" in France regarding Zionism, suggested that public
opinion there should be informed about the matter. But Picot
thought such a move was not immediately necessary and might even
provoke a violent counteragitation. Rather, he would see to it
that "the facts about Zionism were communicated to the proper
quarters."

Then they returned to the central question: the Zionist preference for Great Britain over France in Palestine. Picot protested
that France had taken a special interest in the cause of small nationalities ever since the day when she "first became the champion of
European liberty." But with this he had once again played into the
hands of Sokolow, who expressed satisfaction that "the Jews were
considered in France as one of the smaller nationalities which were
now struggling for liberty." Picot had to retreat, knowing that the
last way to deal with the Jewish question in France was to depict it
as the cause of a small nationality. As such, he said, "it would meet
with considerable opposition, more perhaps from French Jews than
from true Jews [sic, in Sokolow's minutes]." Sokolow then graciously
commented that this was, after all, only a theoretical point, "and

that when a good practical scheme for the colonization of Palestine by Jews was put forward all opposition would vanish, including the opposition of the French Jews."

They moved on, and Picot reiterated his objection to a chartered company "with special privileges." He said the result would be that "the other nationalities of Palestine would ask for similar privileged companies" and "this would almost certainly lead to grave complications." Sokolow acknowledged that the question was a difficult one, but insisted that "the mere granting of equal rights to the inhabitants of Palestine was insufficient to build up a flourishing colony in that country. Naturally," he stressed, "there would be no discrimination against any class of the population when Palestine was governed by a great civilized power; but it would be a profound error to make the application of this principle a reason against the establishment of a Company." Sokolow said this was not the time to work out the details of such a scheme; the matter could be handled when the time came, particularly if France's benevolent participation could be assured.

Picot assured him that the Zionists could feel confident of this, but noted that it "would be of great use to their cause if the Jews would make their devotion to the Entente more evident and more publicly known." Sokolow replied that it hardly was necessary to prove the devotion of Jews to the Entente when three-quarters of a million of them were fighting for Russia in spite of everything. As for those of France, Great Britain, and Italy, their ardent patriotism was well known. Even in the neutral countries "many were on the Entente side and many were on the other. To win the sympathies of all the Jews for the Entente," he went on, shifting the burden of proof back onto Picot's shoulders, "the simplest way would be to show them clearly that the cause of Jewish liberty was intimately bound up with the success of the Entente." Mentioning the prospects for such propaganda in the United States, he referred to Victor Basch's mission. Picot tried to disparage this, but Sokolow protested that he had heard that Basch "had done his best."

Sokolow then repeated the question of whether there was anything to be done immediately. Picot favored waiting a little longer before making any public move. It remained to be seen what the Americans would do in regard to the war. As for Italy—which, as Sokolow could not know, had yet to ratify the Sykes-Picot Agreement—Picot suggested that there might be reason in the near future to call upon the Zionist influence in that country. But in general,

Picot said, there was no need to do anything more until either he or Sykes informed the Zionists that the time had arrived for it. With that, the conversation ended.

On the following day, Saturday, February 10, Sokolow joined Weizmann and Sykes at the latter's residence to discuss where they now stood. Sykes said he thought the results of the conversations were going to be "very satisfactory." He agreed with Picot about awaiting events with regard to Italy and America, though he thought the Zionists would be doing no harm if they in the meantime entered into correspondence "with friends in those countries." Sokolow and Weizmann asked if they could have special facilities—in effect, the Government telegraphic services—for communicating with colleagues in those countries and in Russia. They were particularly eager to obtain the signatures of Tschlenow in Russia and Brandeis in America for the Zionist Memorandum and Demands. Sykes promised to arrange this right away. Sokolow and Weizmann were achieving something like official status.

Sokolow then asked Sykes if he thought the moment was opportune to start a Zionist propaganda campaign among non-Jews in Great Britain. This was mainly in reference to the British Palestine Committee, which had put out three issues of *Palestine* by now, bearing the same masthead slogans advocating British control. Sykes saw no objection to "a purely pro-Zionist propaganda," but he thought it was necessary "to keep the idea of a British suzerainty in the background for the time being as it was likely to intensify the French opposition." He expressed his concern about the journal *Palestine*, which he regarded as "much too emphatic in its exposition of the British interests in Palestine." He feared that this open emphasis was going to make the achievement of that very object more difficult.

Discussing some of the political questions relating to the eventual British role in Palestine, Sykes returned to an idea he had raised in the meeting at Gaster's house about the chartered company. He thought the company approach might be tried out at first in a limited area, which could be expanded when the method proved successful—a prudent, piecemeal arrangement. At the Wednesday meeting, the two Rothschilds had been the most vehement in objecting to this idea, on grounds that it would be tantamount to treating sales of real estate as transfers of political allegiance. Weizmann and Sokolow now objected that this scheme would be to reduce the creation of the company "from an event of great political importance and attractive power to the smaller dimensions of a mere colonization undertaking." As such, it "would almost certainly fail to fire the imagination and win the wholehearted support of the mass of the Jewish people."

Sykes retreated, saying he had made the suggestion simply because "in the limited form the scheme would meet with less opposition from the other Powers interested in the future of Palestine." Sokolow and Weizmann replied that they were confident in the power and influence of Great Britain to remove whatever difficulties might arise in the way of the realization of Zionist aims. Sykes seems to have raised no objection to this way of putting things.

The meeting concluded with a discussion of the areas to be colonized and of the proposed boundaries of Palestine. Sokolow promised to prepare data on these matters and send them to Sykes. Weizmann and Sokolow then took their leave, doubtless filled with the realization that their moment and Zionism's was now rapidly arriving.

The next day Sykes rang up Sokolow to tell him he had already taken steps to facilitate Sokolow's and Weizmann's communication with Russia and America.

Weizmann was duly elected president of the English Zionist Federation that Sunday morning, February 11, and after a round of tributes to the outgoing Joseph Cowen, began firmly placing the stamp of his leadership upon the conference. Two resolutions were presented and defeated that afternoon. The first came from a delegate of the West London Zionist Association, proposing: "That the Conference resolve that it be an essential part of any Peace settlement that full rights, economic, political, religious and cultural, be secured for all peoples and individuals in every State coming within the purview of the Peace Conference, whether self-governing or otherwise." This kind of broad, vague humanitarianism was typical of the Cowen era, though on this day it received a few adverse criticisms from the floor. It was the tough-minded new president, however, who effectively disposed of it by saying that the EZF "might be in sympathy with the principles of the resolution," but that he himself "saw some danger in the vagueness of the wording. It would ... be better not to come forward just now with such a motion." It was withdrawn.

The second resolution, an effort to be more precise, was made by a rabbi from Newcastle: "That the Executive Council of the English Zionist Federation take steps immediately to organize and convene, as soon as the time shall be ripe, a representative Congress of the

Jews of the United Kingdom for the purpose of formulating the claims which the Jewish people should raise at the expected Peace Congress."

This was too much for Weizmann, who now launched into an extended discourse. According to the *Jewish Chronicle*, he said "there were two questions that had to be considered separately. The first was the question of Palestine, and the second was that of political rights. He was going to make a statement regarding the question of Palestine. From certain information in their possession—information of a very reliable nature—they had every reason to hope that they were standing appreciably nearer the realization of their cherished aims. Whether that realization would be the maximum of the Jewish wishes or not depended entirely on the Jews themselves. For they could not withhold from the highest quarters the most humiliating fact that there were many Jews who were opposed to Palestine becoming the home of the Jewish people. They had to be quite decided about one point, namely, that they were not going to water down Zionism by putting forward such claims as Jewish rights.

"That, of course," he went on, "was not to suggest that Zionists were not concerned about Jewish rights. The Zionists, however, had taken up the question of Palestine, and by that program they had to stand or fall. He knew they would be reproached for neglecting other Jewish work, but they were not to be frightened by such a charge, because they, as Zionists, believed that the acquisition of Palestine was the only radical solution of the Jewish question. . . . It was quite clear that although Zionism had always been regarded as a dream, it was now easier of achievement and was much simpler than emancipating the Jews. The question of emancipation was an internal question and depended largely on the general conditions of the particular country where Jews lived. The Peace Congress would, therefore, have little to say about such matters. The Palestine question, however, was of a quite different character; the issue was quite plain. They had a definite program and that was their advantage. They must adhere to that advantageous asset and not confuse it with any other issue. They were standing at a critical moment and now, more than ever, was it necessary for them to concentrate all their energies for their definite Zionist purpose."

Weizmann sat down amid applause. The old voice of the Russian polemicist of Geneva, rigorously opposed to involvement in side issues and palliatives, had taken on the additional authority of a man who had been moving in high Government circles for the past two years. There could be no controverting it; the second motion also was withdrawn.

That evening the conference opened itself to the public, at a hall on Alie Street in Aldgate, and made its position resoundingly unambiguous. The essential motion was presented by Rabbi Samuel Daiches: "That this mass meeting of Jews reaffirms the necessity for the creation of a publicly recognized, legally secured home for the Jewish people in Palestine, as the only solution of the Jewish question." This was a restatement of the Basel Program, formulated at the First Zionist Congress in 1897, and still the fundamental aim of the movement. Then Sokolow spoke at length, insisting once again that "Jewish rights" as such not only was not the central concern of Zionism, but was not even possible to deal with as a general issue. If "Jewish rights" meant the removal of the disabilities of Russian Jews, he said, that was a matter for Russia itself. The only general solution to the Jewish question was "to be found in a home in Palestine." This was greeted by cheers.

While Weizmann and Sokolow presented their case to Jews, the British Palestine Committee continued reaching out to present it to Englishmen in general. From its first issue, *Palestine* had been provoking vivid public responses. A notable one had come right away from Josiah Wedgwood, heir to the chinaware fortune and an outstanding Liberal member of Parliament, who had served as an officer in Gallipoli and there become an admirer of Joseph Trumpeldor and the Zion Mule Corps. Wedgwood had met Weizmann at a Lloyd George breakfast sometime in 1916. On February 1, a letter by him had appeared in the correspondence column of the *Manchester Guardian*. "Sir," it said:

> At a time when Palestine is to the front of men's thoughts many besides myself must have been reading the new organ of the British Palestine Committee.
>
> Both those two immortal charters of the liberties of small peoples—Mr. Balfour's Note to President Wilson and President Wilson's speech to the American nation—appeal to that idealism latent in the Puritan, liberty-loving spirit of Americans and Englishmen. They between them have raised the whole tone of the war, which was tending to become materialistic.
>
> Now, among the small peoples for whom we are fighting let us not forget the Jews. Syria has suffered atrociously from the Turks, hardly less evilly than Armenia. The Turks and their

masters must go. Do let our statesmen consider betimes the possibility and bounds of an autonomous Jewish State, under the protection of a Great Power. Though an Englishman, I venture to urge that that Power should be the United States of America and not England. Let me put it quite bluntly. Such a solution would both implicate America in European politics and provide a buffer State to Egypt, Arabia, and possibly India.— Yours, etc.

Josiah C. Wedgwood

House of Commons, January 29

A vividly controversial response to *Palestine* appeared in the Liberal weekly the *Nation* in its issue of February 17—but in opposition only to the "British Dominion" idea rather than to the essential one of Jewish statehood. "It is to be regretted," the *Nation* leader went,

> that a section of the Zionist movement has adopted as its formula a Jewish community in Palestine with the status of a "British Dominion." The less contentious and more natural plan would be a neutral Jewish State under international guarantees. Such a State would be the proper flank and buttress of the Suez Canal, which is legally (a fact too often forgotten) a neutral, international highway.

This was grist for the mill of Herbert Sidebotham, who replied in a letter to the editor of the *Nation* that appeared the following week. "Why should we regret, as you did last week," he wrote,

> that a section of the Zionist movement should wish Palestine to become a British Dominion? It seems to me one of the greatest compliments ever paid to this country and to its liberal traditions, for this prejudice (if you will) in favor of the British allegiance is not confined to the Jews of this country but, before the war at any rate, was shared by Jews all over the world, including Germany.

Repeating some of the arguments he and his associates had made familiar in the pages of *Palestine* as to why Jews preferred British suzerainty and what were the geopolitical advantages to Britain of such an arrangement, Sidebotham went on to urge:

> Let us beware of making the mistake of the mid-nineteenth century politicians who regarded every fresh extension of terri-

tory as an increase of responsibility that ought to be avoided. Quite a different standard of judgment has to be applied to increases in the family and increases in the rest of the establishment. The Dominions, as this war has proved, have brought no fresh responsibility but greatly increased strength; so it will be in the future of the British Dominion of Palestine. And the increase of strength will not be direct only, but indirect, by reason of the headship of Jewry that Jerusalem, as a city of the British Empire, would confer upon us.

Sidebotham, at least—and doubtless his colleagues on the British Palestine Committee as well—had evidently decided that not even Jerusalem was to be international, whatever may have been the views on the matter of Zionism's friends in the British Government. Indeed, there was a rambunctious quality to this little group in Manchester, who had already worried Sykes and who were now showing a tendency to take policy matters into their own hands even in defiance of Weizmann. In its issue of February 15, *Palestine* had carried an article on "The Boundaries of Palestine" that projected the Jewish state far enough northeastward to include even Damascus. Sykes had promptly complained to Weizmann about this. "Dear Nahum Osipovich," Weizmann wrote to Sokolow on Sunday, the eighteenth, "Sir M. invited me today to tell me that he is very displeased with the latest issue of *Palestine*. It was most unpleasant and I tried very hard to pacify him, in which I hope I succeeded. I wrote to the Manchester people and I hope that they will be careful." Weizmann had written to his dear friend Israel Sieff and thereby created a rare moment of tension between them. Sieff replied on Monday, expressing the opinion that Sykes was more concerned with the Arabs than with Zionism and that the committee should not give way to him but rather combat the threat of "an Arab Palestine." He suggested that Weizmann "diplomatically hint that you are not responsible for the hot-headed youths of the B.P.C.," and that objections should be made directly to them. A furious Weizmann responded to this with a telegram: "Letter received. Disagree completely, your attitude renders further efforts here useless, we therefore decide to resign everything on Thursday." A meeting in London between Weizmann, Sokolow, and the leaders of the British Palestine Committee had been scheduled for that Thursday, but Weizmann was saying that he and Sokolow would wash their hands of the committee and that, as he put it in a follow-up letter, "you can do what you please but you must remember that you and you alone are responsible for the consequences." Sieff backed down and wired back that, for the sake of "discipline and unity," the forthcoming issue of *Palestine* would "contain a Jewish article which will meet with the wishes of Sir M."

The issue appeared on Thursday, February 22, nearly three-quarters of it devoted to a harmless history of "Jewish Self-Government in Palestine," and the rest to small feature items. That same day the scheduled meeting was held, at which Weizmann said that nothing less than the "Foreign Office" had been displeased at the boundaries article. Sidebotham admitted that he had been responsible for suggesting the inclusion of Damascus. In the ensuing discussion, he relented both on this and on the proposed inclusion of the Hejaz railway in the Jewish state—although everyone present still assumed a boundary to the east of the Jordan River. Only Harry Sacher refused to relent on anything. It was finally agreed that Sidebotham and Samuel Tolkowsky would themselves try to obtain an interview with Sykes on the boundaries question. Evidently Weizmann and Sokolow did not divulge that Sokolow had already discussed or was about to discuss this matter with Sykes that very day.

This was not quite an end to the tension. Sidebotham's letter to the *Nation*, appearing two days after the meeting, was another defiance of Sykes's wish that the committee not overplay the issue of British control. "I read Sidebotham's letter in *The Nation*," Weizmann wrote to Tolkowsky on February 28, "and did not like one or two remarks there; we shall have to institute a more effective control over the B.P.C. if it is at all possible." Weizmann could no longer brook any compromises with his own authority within English Zionism.

·34·

SYKES PONDERS THE
QUESTION OF CONTROL

If Sir Mark was sensitive at this moment to every Zionist effort to wave the Union Jack in public over the map of Palestine, it was above all because Picot was still in London. Picot was clearly not ready to acquiesce in the idea of British suzerainty, and Sykes did not want this issue to get in the way of the more pressing one—the validity of Zionist claims in the first place. The French had not yet agreed even to this; but if British or Entente armies—for the French still hoped to participate militarily—were soon to begin occupying Palestinian soil, it was urgent to establish what the Jewish status under that occupation was going to be. Sykes does not yet seem to have had a clear notion himself of the suzerainty he ultimately desired for Palestine—except that he, like almost any Englishman in a position of responsibility, did not want it to be exclusively French. But he rightly perceived that this was a matter that would in a sense take care of itself once the Zionist claim was officially acknowledged by the Entente. To the extent that he desired British control, he would then have the Zionists themselves to stand up for it. There would also be the element of a fait accompli once the British army had begun to occupy Palestine—for in any case the French participation would perforce be insignificant. In the meantime, the strategy he decided upon was to persuade Picot of a Zionist Palestine entirely within the framework of the agreement they had concluded a year ago.

For this reason, Sykes was particularly anxious to have the report Sokolow had promised to give on the boundaries of Palestine and proposed areas of colonization as foreseen by the Zionists. He spoke to Weizmann on Friday, February 16, and asked if Sokolow had the material ready, in which case he wanted to see him the following day. Sokolow was not yet ready; but he was able to get a handwritten report to Sykes early the following week, and they met at Buckingham Gate on Thursday the twenty-second to discuss it in detail.

One focus of their conversation was on the vexed question of the northern boundary. The Zionist claim extended well into the area that was to be directly under French control according to the Sykes-Picot Agreement and where Sokolow and Weizmann, though of course ignorant of the agreement itself, had been given to understand that French claims would be the strongest. Sykes asked about the condition of the Jewish settlements in the north and whether they were within the boundaries of ancient Palestine. Sokolow said they were and pointed to the success of the northernmost of the modern Jewish colonies, Metullah, which had been bought from the Druses. Sykes asked if there was any bitterness toward the Zionists on the part of the Druses, and Sokolow replied that, on the contrary, relations between the two groups were quite good—an assertion to be proved correct time and again through years to come. Sykes received this with evident mixed feelings: he was pleased, of course, but he also clearly hoped for some reason to claim that the Jews ought to back down from the northern Galilee. Agreeing that there was not likely to be trouble with the Druses, he nevertheless expressed the view that "there is no possibility of any considerable development in the neighborhood."

Unwilling to be trapped by this, Sokolow admitted that Zionist authorities agreed that "a *considerable* development in the northern direction is not to be aimed at." But, he added, there were many good possibilities just to the south and the east of Metullah—for example, the swampy Lake Huleh, which, if drained, would bring to light a tract of considerable fertility.* Sokolow then described in detail the entire region of streams surrounding the Huleh that form the sources of the Jordan, Sykes listening and asking questions in fascination. Sykes finally suggested that details of this sort could be discussed at a later time, and this part of the conversation ended with Sokolow evidently having won his point about the north. This, however, was not what Sykes was ready to discuss with Picot, and the conversation seems to have moved on to other matters that Sokolow—perhaps out of regard for the sensitivities of Zionist colleagues who would be reading it—did not choose to include in his report.

---

* The Huleh basin has since been drained by the State of Israel and is indeed a fertile tract.

By the time he wrote to Picot on February 28 concerning his interview with Sokolow six days before, Sykes had again let the whole question sprout freely in his fertile imagination. Out of regard for French susceptibilities, he had sternly put down all Zionist attempts to tout British control in public; but by now it had occurred to him that perhaps, if the north of Palestine were conceded to the French, they might be persuaded to allow a system of control to the rest of the country that would in effect be, not British, but Anglo-American. "You will notice," Sykes wrote to Picot of the maps he had enclosed, which showed the existing Jewish settlements, "that with a few exceptions North of Haifa these are almost wholly in the area which is generally regarded as Palestine." The "few exceptions" were in France's Blue Area.

Using his accompanying maps, Sykes divided the Zionist claims in Palestine—excluding those in the northern Galilee—into five sectors. Three of these—in the south, in districts east of the Jordan, and in the northern part of the Brown Area—were in areas of British preponderance according to the Asia Minor Agreement, a fact that Sykes left unstressed but that he and Picot both perfectly understood. Instead, he wrote in his letter that he had told Sokolow "these were areas in which Great Britain and France had a special secular and political interest, as apart from other powers, and that provided a just understanding could be come to with the Arabs, I apprehended that there need be no great difficulties in the way. In this I felt sure you would agree." Pointing out that these three sectors added up to about two-thirds of the region claimed by the Zionists as well as the likeliest field for colonization on account of the paucity of inhabitants now in them, Sykes said he had asked Sokolow if they would not suffice. Sokolow, he wrote, had replied that this scheme was sufficient from a material point of view but not from a sentimental one, since it excluded what had been the main area of Zionist aspiration and settlement for forty years. Excluded, of course, was the entire Jerusalem enclave taken in its widest sense—which meant not only Jaffa and Jerusalem and everything between them, but also a swath across Palestine some sixty miles wide.

"This I agree is an important point," Sykes commented in sly understatement about Sokolow's response, "since it is no use trying to satisfy Jewish aspirations which depend so much for initial impetus on sentiment, tradition, and hereditary impulse, unless the fundamental traditions, sentiment, and hereditary longings are given outward prominence."

"This brought us to the knotty point of the problem," Sykes went on. His maps divided this "knotty point" into two sectors: one, a relatively small sector taking in Jerusalem and Bethlehem and extending in a line eastward to the Dead Sea and the Jordan up to Jericho; the other, all the rest of the broadly construed Jerusalem enclave. Regarding the Jerusalem-Bethlehem sector—the main concentration of Holy Places—Sykes wrote that there "should not be any difficulty in establishing a special administration on which the powers interested in the affairs of Christendom and Islam could agree at leisure." Rather, the main problem was the remainder of the enclave, the largest single sector of all the five being discussed and the one most crucial to Zionist aspirations. This was the heart of the Brown Area, but Sykes was now at last coming to a point over which he was going to suggest a revision in the agreement. It had to do with suzerainty.

Joint or international control in this sector was out of the question, Sykes wrote. This would be problem enough in the Jerusalem sector, but in as large an area as the one under consideration now, he felt it was untenable. As for proposing that it be either British or French, he hastened to say, this was "to my mind only asking for trouble, leaving a sense of vexation in the public mind of the power which conceded to the other, even if such a proposal is acceptable to the remaining powers." Sykes went on to say that he and Sokolow had then discussed the possibility of introducing "some power not directly interested in the surrounding territories, not especially identified with any one of the various religious or racial problems involved." If Sokolow really had done this, he had entered into what his closest colleagues in Zionism would have regarded as heresy; but it is quite possible that he may have agreed with Sykes that the matter had to be put this way to Picot.

"Here our choice," Sykes went on, "is really limited to Belgium, Switzerland and the United States." Belgium, of course, had already been discussed between him and Picot a year before; but Sykes now rejected it, arguing that Russia might object because it was predominantly Latin, and offering his own low opinion of Belgian functionaries and what they might do in Palestine. As for Switzerland, he thought the German element was too preponderant there for it to be eligible under the circumstances. That left the United States. "I believe," he wrote,

that if the U.S.A. could be induced to agree to accept the responsibility of the provisional administration of this area, on the invitation of the Entente Powers, . . . we should be somewhere near a solution not only of our immediate but our future difficulties. I submit that such an arrangement would not affect the international equilibrium as regards the Entente in the Holy Land.

On the other hand, the offer of such an arrangement, he thought, "would give a very strong impetus to the Entente cause in the U.S.A."

To what extent Sykes took this complex plan seriously—even, for that matter, to what extent it had actually been discussed and agreed upon in the conversation with Sokolow the previous Thursday—is impossible to say. There is no evidence to show that he may have been discussing it elsewhere. Sykes, with characteristic enthusiasm, may indeed for a moment have thought he had come up with a viable solution for the control of Palestine.

Whatever the explanation of Sykes's letter to Picot of February 28, there is at any rate no resemblance between the picture it draws and the one Sykes sketched out the very next day for C.P. Scott. To be sure, Scott—who undoubtedly had been urged by Weizmann to look up Sykes on this occasion—was not the man in whom Sykes would want to confide either state secrets or proposals likely to upset his Zionist friends. Yet there is an air of disarming candor pervading Sykes's remarks to Scott that day as recorded in the latter's journal.

"An interesting person," Scott wrote of Sykes, "and one of the best of the progressive Tories. Employed by FO as adviser on questions relating to nearer Asia through which he traveled. An [enthusiastic?] believer in the future of the Arab race whose language is spread over vast regions from the Persian border to the Mediterranean and along the whole of Northern Africa. The true center focus of the whole region at present under the sovereignty of Turkey was Cairo with its great university and 15,000 students. Syria, on the breakup of Turkey, might go in full possession to France and she might exercise a protectorate over the hinterland—i.e. the upper region of the Tigris and Euphrates—while we should exercise a protectorate over Palestine and Mesopotamia and give support to the new Arab Kingdom which would include the Arabian Peninsula and extend as far north as, and include, Damascus."

Here was essentially the Sykes-Picot Agreement with revisions in suzerainties and their character. This formulation provides for a purely British Palestine. Surely this was at least one of Sykes's ideal solutions, and he was to refine it in a moment. But first he stressed for Scott that the center of this arrangement would be Cairo and not India—a point he had recently made to Lord Curzon, the former viceroy of India and now a member of Lloyd George's War Cabinet, who "had been extremely haughty about it and quite immovable. When he was Viceroy of India he had sent his gun-boats to the Persian Gulf—that was enough." Sykes thought that Arabs and Indians were "absolutely antipathetic and the manners of the Anglo-Indians repellent to Arab feeling. The Arabs of the Persian Gulf district were the riff-raff of the race—people who had been expelled or fled from the Peninsula or the more settled regions of Mesopotamia. But the Arabs as a whole were a fine people who could rise to the European level and even now should be treated by us as, for instance, we would treat Italians. The Turks, with all their misgovernment, recognized them as equals and Arabs held high positions in both the Turkish army and administration."

Then Sykes returned to the question of Palestine and French claims there. He said he was "rather inclined to compromise. Said France was very insistent in pressing her claims to something like condominium (he is a Catholic and, though apparently a very unprejudiced one, this may make him more open to approach). That would not do as we must have military control over the country—except as regards the Holy Places and perhaps the railway from Jaffa to Jerusalem, which might be internationalized and policed by the French—but he thought we might secure all we wanted if we acted as the 'mandatories' of the powers, i.e. exercised a delegated authority."

With that, Sykes had helped bring a significant new word—here certainly making one of its earliest appearances with this meaning on record—into the vocabulary of international relations. Where and how it had come to him in the past few days is not clear, but it certainly represented as serious a notion on his part as the checkerboard Palestine with American protectorate that he had spelled out to Picot the day before. On top of all this, Sykes concluded for Scott's benefit, "it would make a great difference, when we came to the Peace Conference, if we were already in military possession of the country, the invasion of which we had already begun." Once again, the big battalions were to be the strongest argument of all.

·35·

WALLS TUMBLING DOWN

The transition from winter to spring in 1917 was accompanied by eruptions destined to alter not only the long, weary course of the war but the history of the world. On March 8, a wave of strikes and riots in Petrograd began what proved to be the long-anticipated revolution in Russia, confirmed two days later by a general mutiny of the soldiers garrisoned there. A provisional government headed by liberals and moderate socialists was established on March 12, and on the fifteenth Tsar Nicholas II abdicated. It was on the following day that news of the event began to reach the outside world. "REVOLUTION IN RUSSIA," *The Times* proclaimed in London. "ABDICATION OF THE TSAR—FIRST NEWS FROM PETROGRAD—REVOLUTION COMPLETE."

Englishmen of goodwill could at last feel relieved about the character of the ally they thought they would go on having. They also were able to hope that the Russian contribution to the war would be more effective from now on. "The new Government," wrote the *Manchester Guardian*'s "Student of War" on March 17, "will be much keener about the war than the old bureaucracy which has been overthrown, but the mess will not be cleared up quickly." C.P. Scott wrote in his diary of Lloyd George, whom he visited with a Russian friend on March 17: "At tea he did most of the talking, rejoicing in the great change and discoursing on the extreme difficulties he had encountered in his dealings with the fallen Government. . . . Now all would be different."

Things would also be different in the eyes of Jews the world over. "That which has long been awaited has finally come," was the comment on March 16 of the *Jewish Daily Forward*, the New York Yiddish newspaper whose anti-Russian and hence rather pro-German attitude had worried Victor Basch and other Jewish friends of the Entente. "A revolution in Russia," it went on, "a free Russian people, a free Jewish people in Russia! Is this a dream?" And after three more days of similar euphoria, a banner headline in the *Forward* of March 20 proclaimed: "JEWISH TROUBLES ARE AT AN END." That same day Chaim Weizmann wrote to C.P. Scott: "Yes, the events in Russia are tremendous and it is certainly the very best thing which could have happened." Then, with characteristic realism, he added: "let us hope that the situation will soon clear itself and not get out of the control of the provisional government." How the Zionist cause was to be affected remained to be seen.

In the meantime, the British campaigns in the Middle East were providing more immediate prospects to be pondered by Zionists and their friends. It was generally expected that General Murray's troops would move on into Palestine any day; but this was part of a two-pronged thrust, and the first news of an important victory arrived from the Mesopotamian front. Since the middle of December, the British public had been following reports of the advance along the Tigris led by Major General Sir Stanley Maude, who had succeeded Townshend as commander in chief in that theater after the latter's capture at Kut-el-Amara. On February 23, Maude had retaken that town, avenging the British defeat there of the previous spring, and had not stopped his northward progress. On Sunday, March 11, the eagerly anticipated event took place: Baghdad fell to the British.

In his "Student of War" column on Tuesday the thirteenth, Sidebotham did not fail to note the significance of this victory in relation to the Palestine campaign. Mentioning that Enver Pasha was now visiting Palestine, he asserted that the Turks would "rather lose Bagdad than Jerusalem," since they wanted the prize of Egypt above all as justification for going to war against England. Therefore, he went on, "if they have to choose between a campaign for the recovery of Bagdad and one for Southern Syria they would choose the second. There is some reason to think that the advance from Egypt has diverted to Syria reinforcements that would otherwise have gone to Mesopotamia."

That evening Chaim Weizmann—unaccompanied by Vera, who was ill—had dinner at the Astor home; not only was Balfour there, as he had been when Weizmann last attended an Astor gathering a year before, but also the prime minister himself. Lloyd George had not seen Weizmann since Ministry of Munitions days, and he had no sooner entered, according to Vera Weizmann's diary account (evidently obtained from her husband's descriptions) "than he asked Chaim in the presence of everybody if he liked the situation and the campaign in the East." Knowing Baghdad was not enough for the Zionist leader, he euphorically mentioned Palestine, too; Mrs. Weizmann records that he confidentially "informed Chaim that British troops were already in Gaza," which was decidedly not the case. "He said he must see Chaim to discuss Eastern affairs, and when Chaim remarked that he was afraid to take up his time, L.G. simply said that Chaim must come and inflict himself upon him."

The way Weizmann was to describe it to Scott two days later, Lloyd George had said that he could not make an appointment with him and that instead, "You must take me by storm. Just come and if Davies says I am engaged don't be put off, but insist on seeing me." But he indicated to Weizmann that the time was ripe for the Government to make definite plans regarding Palestine. He told him that the Hejaz railway would in any case have to remain in Arab hands, but that the Jews would be able to build a parallel one in Palestine. Once the British protectorate was established, he said, the Jews "would form a great development company and get ahead." Lloyd George then left early, and the rest of the evening Weizmann discussed Zionism with Balfour, "merely academically," according to Vera Weizmann, but to the thrilled fascination of their listeners.

At breakfast on Friday, March 16, Scott had a chance to hear more of what the prime minister's thoughts on Palestine were in this moment between the victory at Baghdad and an imminent attack upon Gaza. At one point in the conversation, Lloyd George named "the destruction of the barbarous domination of the Turk" as one of the main objects of the war. This destruction "was in course of accomplishment," he added. "We were already at Gaza in the land of the Philistines which the Turks—appropriately—were defending. As to the future of Palestine," he went on, "once we were in military possession it would make a great difference." This clearly was meant with reference to France. "The French had an eye to it," he said with considerable understatement. He told of how a prominent Frenchman, not a believing Catholic, had approached him to say that France wanted Palestine. "I protested," writes Scott. Lloyd George "agreed that it was not to be thought of."

Weizmann surely was receiving whatever was Scott's latest word about Lloyd George all the time, but he nevertheless was eager to have a meeting of his own with the prime minister and discuss matters under better circumstances than the Astors' dinner party had provided. He was all the more eager for this because Sykes, who had recently come up with the idea that Weizmann accompany him to Egypt in readiness to do propaganda work and diplomacy in Palestine once it was occupied by the British, had not been inspiring him with confidence of late. Israel Sieff's protest that Sykes was more concerned with Arab than with Zionist aspirations had made its mark upon him, and this found occasion to be aggravated when he read the newspapers on Monday morning, March 19.

What appeared in them was a proclamation General Maude had issued to the people of Baghdad over the weekend. It was an inspirational address in a highly poetical language intended for translation into Arabic, which told its listeners that "our armies do not come into your cities and lands as conquerors or enemies, but as liberators." Reviewing the centuries of oppression under the Turks, Maude had said that Britain and its allies now wanted the people of the city to "prosper even as in the past, when your lands were fertile, when your ancestors gave to the world literature, science, and art, and when Baghdad city was one of the wonders of the world." Then, referring to the example of Hussein and the Hejaz, the proclamation went on to express the hope "that the Arab race may rise once more to greatness and renown among the peoples of the earth, and that it shall bind itself together to this end in unity and concord." Maude concluded with the wish "that you may be united with your kinsmen in North, East, South, and West in realizing the aspirations of your race."

These words had been composed by Sir Mark Sykes in the spirit of the appeals to the Arab nation that had begun coming from Kitchener and Cairo as early as the fall of 1914; Baghdad was a long-awaited fulfillment. There was only one problem: of the roughly 200,000 inhabitants of Baghdad, some 80,000—well over a third—were Jews, many of them descended from forebears who had been in Mesopotamia even before Arab civilization had arrived there. Were they to receive no words of encouragement? Even some of the British on the spot had noticed this lack in the text, issued to them from London on March 12, and they had responded on the sixteenth: "Proclamation is addressed to people of Baghdad only, and predominant element of population in that city is Jews. Possibilities foreshadowed, therefore, by announcement would greatly disturb and unsettle minds of inhabitants who have seen British flag hoisted with fervor and relief." Other objections had been registered in the note, but three days later the proclamation was issued without alterations.

The *Manchester Guardian*, in a leader published on March 20, was quick to fill in the gaps left by the proclamation. "The Arabs are, with the Jews, the sole survivors of the great Semitic family," it said, and then continued:

> The proclamation of General Maude speaks of a union be-
> tween Arabs, north, south, east and west of Bagdad. This is no
> time to ask what will be the precise extent of an Arab State
> with boundaries so vague as these; but we may suppose that
> these vague words are used to give the widest possible scope for
> the new state or, it may be, confederation of states. The Arab
> race is distributed from Syria to the Indian Ocean and the
> shores of Northeast Africa, and from as far west as Morocco to
> the borders of Persia; but there is in the area of the old Semitic
> civilizations between the Mediterranean and the Persian Gulf a
> region wide enough, and under good government rich enough, to
> satisfy the amplest ambitions. In a portion of this region, that
> which lies south of Damascus and west of the Hejaz Railway,
> the Jews have the prior political claim, and it is one which we
> cannot, by the very reasoning which makes one anxious to re-
> vive the political existence of the Arab State, deny to them.
> They are both Semites; there is a close resemblance between
> their languages; and though their religion is different the one
> people has never had the smallest difficulty in understanding the
> virtues of the other. Both in Bagdad and in Spain the Jews and
> Arabs always got on well together; indeed, the Jewish colony in
> Bagdad is the oldest in the world, and in the great days of Arab
> culture and prosperity was one of its chief sources of strength.
> So it will continue to be. Two conditions there are of cooperation
> in the great work of regenerating the ancient Semitic world
> which seems destined to fall to the Arabs and to the Jews. One
> is a continuance on both sides of that wise toleration and sym-
> pathy which has usually marked their relations in the past. The
> other is that the larger unity of the Arabs and the smaller unity
> of the Jews should both alike have full freedom of economic
> expansion. We say nothing at this stage of the effect that the
> restoration of two such ancient and noble civilizations will have
> on our own position in the East, except that it cannot but be
> beneficial and strengthening. For the present the great thing is
> that English people should understand the splendor of the politi-
> cal ideals that are now put forward by this country.

Weizmann evidently had not yet seen this leader—probably written by Sidebotham—when he wrote that same day to Scott, describing how things stood with Sykes. "The Zionist negotiations with Sir Mark Sykes are entering upon their final stage," he said, referring to the conversations about boundaries and the problem of French claims that Sokolow had been having with him. "I do not think," Weizmann went on,

> that anything absolutely definite can be arrived at at the present moment simply because the military and political situation in Palestine may change from day to day. I understand that the French people have not yet fully formulated their claims, they have not yet said whether they would limit their claims to Syria only or whether they would press some claims for the north of Palestine.

This last was a point on which Sokolow was by now more likely to have been informed than Weizmann; for Sokolow—who may even have been informed of the Sykes-Picot Agreement—was now being led by Sykes into the rarefied atmosphere of international diplomacy. "Sir Mark is of opinion that this may still adjust itself," Weizmann went on, relaying at least the outlook that had correctly been conveyed to him,

> and I am perfectly convinced that it could be easily arranged if the British assert their claims, which I think they will do, with some force when the country is occupied by British troops. After the occupation of Gaza the military events may develop much more rapidly.

Then came his reservations, partly based on the Baghdad proclamation, which he knew had been written by Sykes. "At the same time," he said,

> although Sir Mark is very keen on the Zionist scheme I cannot help feeling that he considers it somewhat as an appendix to the bigger scheme with which he was dealing—the Arab Scheme. Of course I quite understand that the Arab position at present is much more important from the point of view of the immediate prosecution of the war than the Jewish question which requires rather a long view to appreciate its meaning, but it makes our work very difficult if in all the present negotiations with the Arabs the Jewish interests in Palestine are not well defined.

Now he came to the point that the *Guardian* had dealt with that very morning. "I was rather unpleasantly struck," he wrote, by the manifesto which was issued at Baghdad. This manifesto has been written by Sir Mark and I think Baghdad possesses the biggest Jewish community in Asia. Not a word has been said about them in this manifesto. It is true that Baghdad is an Arab center of great importance but in this manifesto there was a splendid opportunity of saying a good word to the Jews and holding out to them some hope that would have been helpful both to us and to the people in Baghdad. The Jews lived fairly happily under Turkish rule; what their life under Arab rule will be is not known and in the interest of everybody it would have been important to say a word or two to the Jews who form the overwhelming majority of the population in Baghdad. That that has not been done is not in itself a great misfortune but I regret it chiefly as a symptom.

Weizmann went on to say that this was why he thought "our negotiations," as he now often put it, should "be placed very soon on a more definite practical basis." He alluded, as an example, to the journey he assumed he would soon be making with Sykes to Egypt, for the purpose of entering there

> into negotiations with the leading Arabs from Palestine and see what can be done almost immediately in the way of acquisition of land in the Palestinian territory already occupied by the British.

The Zionists had to be there as soon as possible, he said, in order to show that they meant business. This was particularly urgent in light of the most recent historic events. "With the present change in Russia," he observed,

> the Zionist organization there will become a very great power. Although we may lose some adherents who built up their Zionism on the theory of oppression we shall on the other hand be strengthened by the fact that we can work freely there organizing and collecting funds in a way which was impossible to this time. But in order that we should be able to begin our work properly in Russia and America it is essential that our negotiations with the Government which hitherto have been semi-official should assume a definite character and I think that my going to the East would be a sign that things are becoming more tangible.

The idea of his going on a mission to the East represented the prospect of an entirely new role for Weizmann. But in the meantime, there was a good deal he could do in his old one to begin transforming his hitherto semiofficial relationship with the Government into one that promised to have a more definite character. Within the next two weeks he was to call upon both the foreign secretary and the prime minister in his capacity as a Zionist leader. Outside of a few social occasions, it was to be his first audience with Lloyd George since the days when the chief subject of conversation between them was supposed to have been munitions chemistry, and his first with Balfour in two years.

The one with Balfour, sought by Weizmann since their encounter at the Astors' dinner party on March 13, took place at the Foreign Office on Thursday, March 22. There had been a time when Balfour could be moved to the brink of tears when Weizmann spoke to him of the Jews and Palestine; but that was before he was foreign secretary. On this occasion, Balfour assumed the mask of diffidence that he had worn with mastery so often in his career. "Mr. Balfour," Weizmann later reported to Scott, "did not at first see the importance of the Zionist claim from the British point of view." The fact was that there had just been a War Cabinet meeting at which Zionism was discussed; and it was either at this meeting or at one only a few days later that Balfour had expressed himself "freely in favor of Zionism," according to one eyewitness. But it was in particular toward the vehement Zionist preference for British suzerainty that Balfour felt he needed to apply his classic circumspection.

"I think I succeeded in explaining that to him," Weizmann told Scott regarding the matter of Britain and Palestine, "and he agreed with the view but he suggested that there may be difficulties with France and Italy." Weizmann, still in the dark about the Sykes-Picot Agreement, thought that this view was "of course the usual one and . . . not based on any new facts except on the usual claim of the French." Nevertheless, his feeling was that "Mr. Balfour does not attach very much importance to the French claim and certainly does not attach any value to the French holding Palestine, on the contrary he would not think it advisable to hand Palestine over to the French and he would have to resort to the internationalization of this part of the world as an extreme measure. He suggested that in case no agreement can be reached between England and France it would be advisable to bring in the Americans and have an Anglo-American Protectorate over Palestine." Sykes's Anglo-American idea—a revival of a notion that was a year old and that may very well have been discussed in February 1916 by Lloyd George and others with Colonel House—was clearly making its way around in cabinet circles. Weizmann, evidently now hearing the idea for the first time, thought it had attractive aspects though "it is always fraught with the danger that there are two masters and we do not know yet how far the Americans would agree with the British on general principles of administration."

Balfour, resorting to diffidence again, protested to Weizmann that "the practical aspect of the subject was not very familiar to him." However, he mentioned to Weizmann "confidentially" that there had been some talk about this question at a recent cabinet meeting, and that "Mr. Lloyd George took a view which was identical with the view [Weizmann] laid before Mr. Balfour, namely that it is of great importance to Great Britain to protect Palestine." Balfour evidently did not say what his own views had been at that meeting. Instead, he told Weizmann he ought to see Lloyd George about the matter in person and added: "You may tell the Prime Minister that I wanted you to see him." Weizmann, still hoping that Scott would arrange such a meeting, added emphatically in his letter: "I thought you would be interested to hear about that."

Weizmann went away from this interview delighted at the realization that he and Balfour had discussed Zionist matters in a *practical* way for the very first time. To Brandeis a little over two weeks later he was to write: "I have no hesitation in saying that the Secretary of State for Foreign Affairs is in full sympathy with our aspirations and I am sure that we may reckon on his support." Now he was all the more eager for a meeting with Lloyd George.

The long-awaited attack on Gaza began at dawn on March 26. This was from the outset a more difficult operation than the ones at the Wadi El Arish and at Rafah had been. Gaza was an ancient fortress city, located on a commanding height and surrounded by rough terrain; it also had a substantial garrison. Since the element of surprise was all-important for its capture, General Murray had not extended his railhead and pipeline beyond Rafah. The British had to make their attack across desert with supplies good only for twenty-four hours or until the capture of the city, which had abundant wells. The crucial importance of the time element was made more acute by the plan of attack: the city was to be surrounded to the north and to the east by cavalry, forming a cordon to protect the planned infantry assault from the south.

Any delay was likely to be disastrous; and the first threat of disaster struck with dawn itself, when a fog rolled up from the sea over the advancing British troops and did not clear until 7:00 or 7:30 A.M. The cavalry reached their positions shortly after that, having ridden all night; but it was not until almost noon that the Fifty-third Division, in action for the first time since Gallipoli, could begin its infantry attack. Their progress was again slowed down, however, when they came to the dense fields of cactus hedges that formed a natural barrier—almost equivalent to barbed wire—just south of the city.

The infantry clearly was not going to make it by nightfall, and early in the afternoon the mounted troops in the north were ordered to attack. The order was slow to reach them, however, and they did not begin their assault until 4:00 P.M. Nightfall came shortly after six; nevertheless, by then the cavalry had been able to take a series of commanding ridges to the east of the city. (It was learned later that the Turkish garrison had been ready to surrender at that point. But this news came too late.) In the meantime, the British field commanders—General Murray was in Cairo—concerned about the problem of supply once the sun had set, had ordered all troops, including the cavalry, back to their bivouac in the Wadi Ghuzze five miles south of the city. They tried again at dawn, but by that time Turkish reinforcements had arrived, and the British were repulsed.

In his official report, General Murray made it sound like a victory anyway: the British, after all, were now securely in Wadi Ghuzze, on Palestine soil. "We advanced our troops," he wrote, "a distance of 15 miles from Rafa to Wadi Ghuzze (Gaza), five miles south of Gaza, to cover construction of railway." He said that on the twenty-sixth and twenty-seventh, British forces were "heavily engaged in the neighborhood with a force of about 20,000 of the enemy"—an estimate considerably larger than the one made by the field commanders and even slightly larger than the one to be given after the war by Kress von Kressenstein. "We inflicted very heavy losses," Murray went on, "and have taken 900 prisoners, including General Commanding and whole Divisional Staff of 53rd Turkish Division." This was sufficient for the ardently patriotic Lord Northcliffe to proclaim a "Victory in Palestine" in his newspapers, and for *The Times* to carry a leader that began: "Sir Archibald Murray has won a victory near Gaza which seems no less complete than Sir Stanley Maude's triumph at Baghdad."

Even the War Cabinet was sufficiently satisfied with this version of the outcome to wire Murray on March 30 that he should now regard Jerusalem as an immediate objective. Only the "Student of

War" noticed that something was wrong. "The dispatch about the Battle of Gaza, in the form in which it is published in this country," he wrote, "is a veritable scandal." As Murray made preparations for another assault, there may also have been some who were beginning to notice a disadvantage in the fact that, since becoming commander in chief in Egypt, he never had himself directed operations in the field.

By the time Weizmann was brought by Scott to breakfast with Lloyd George, on Tuesday morning April 3, the atmosphere was alive with the prospect of yet another historic occurrence. Just the day before, after the sinking by German submarines of four more American merchant ships during the month of March, President Wilson had asked Congress to declare that Germany had "thrust" a state of war upon the United States. The congressional response was still being awaited as Scott, Weizmann, and several other guests gathered at the prime minister's table.

The conversation eventually made its way to Palestine, Lloyd George and Weizmann "doing most of the talking" at that point, as Scott confided to his diary. The prime minister, repeating an old view, said Palestine "was to him the one really interesting part of the war." To Weizmann's relief, he went on to say that he was absolutely opposed to a condominium with France. But then he asked Weizmann: "What about international control?"

The Zionist leader thought this would be even worse than an Anglo-French condominium, since it would mean confusion and intrigue—a view that already had been solidly represented in governing circles by Sykes and Herbert Samuel.

"What about joint control with America?" Lloyd George pressed.

Weizmann, who had had time to think about this idea since his conversation with Balfour, said he could accept it. The two countries, he thought, would pull together.

"Yes," commented the prime minister, "we are both thoroughly materialistic peoples."

Scott, evidently amused by this last remark, commented that it was "obviously dictated by the conscious superiority of the Kelt." He records nothing further in his diary of the exchange on the control of Palestine between Lloyd George and Weizmann, yet the latter was to feel able to write to Sokolow the following day that the prime minister "was very emphatic on the point of British Palestine."

The conversation at breakfast moved on to the problem of the aliens and military service, which had still not been resolved, and which was drawing attention again on account of the Russian revolution. Weizmann spoke of the great change that event was bringing about in the feelings of Russian Jews in England. He was sure, according to Scott, that "he could get a couple of thousand volunteers from among the 30,000 Russian Jews in London. George said there could be no question now that they must be compelled either to serve in the British army or else be sent back to Russia. Weizmann said he could not agree that the refugee who could not make England his home was under equal obligations with the native born, but he did not dispute that the Russian Jews ought now to fight. They ought to be sent to Palestine," he added. "That will go far to reconcile them."

By this time Jabotinsky and Trumpeldor, still in training at Hazeley Down, had been making considerable inroads with the six-page proposal for a Jewish regiment that they had presented to the cabinet late in January. Sykes had seen it and written to Jabotinsky saying he did not think the scheme should be pressed for the moment, but should be kept alive for when the right time did come. Weizmann had subsequently relayed an appeal to him from Jabotinsky when it looked as if the Twentieth London Battalion was going to be sent to France. How can the scheme be kept alive, Jabotinsky had asked, "if the bearers of the idea are lost in France?" Especially now that a front was opening in Palestine, that was where they should go.

At breakfast, Lloyd George agreed with Weizmann's last remark about sending the Russian Jews to Palestine, but added that the effect upon public opinion of the Jews' claim to that country would be very bad if it turned out that "they were not willing to fight for it." Weizmann retorted that "they would fight and fight well. They were no cowards." Reminding Lloyd George of the outstanding service performed at Gallipoli by the men of the Zion Mule Corps, he pointed out that 120 of them were at that moment serving with the Twentieth London Battalion in Winchester. "They had implored the War Office to send them to join the army in Palestine but had so far been steadily refused and might at any moment be sent off with their battalion to France." This, despite the fact that they knew the languages of Palestine, as well as "every road and every village and every village Arab sheikh" there.

Hearing this, Lloyd George "was furious and said they were the very men wanted, whose local knowledge would be invaluable, and he would see that very day that they should go. They would be precious too for 'spying out the land,' as in Joshua's day."

The spirit of this indignant protest may have been all too familiar to Weizmann. But, though they were not going to get to Palestine so quickly, Jabotinsky and Trumpeldor were to be able to present their case to the new war secretary, Lord Derby, within the next few days. And their unit was not sent to France.

·36·

SYKES AND SOKOLOW
IN PARIS AND ROME

The time had come for Sir Mark Sykes to make his journey to
Egypt, and there also was work to do in Europe along the
way. Indeed, so far as Palestine was concerned, until a substantial
part of the country was occupied by British troops, the main problems were those to be resolved in Paris and Rome. In Paris, though
there was still no chance of winning acquiescence in a British Palestine, the more fundamental issue of French acceptance of the
Zionist claim still had to be settled. In Rome, the problem was essentially the same, though at once more delicate and less serious. Italians had been ruffled by the Sykes-Picot Agreement, since it did not
deal with any of their claims formulated in London in April 1915.
Italy wanted another conference at which these claims would be
given guarantees in the manner of the Sykes-Picot Agreement. To
make matters worse, neither the Italian government nor the Vatican
had yet been consulted about the disposition of the Holy Land.

Foreseeing the possibility of dealing with some of these problems on his way to Egypt, Sykes had arranged to have at his side the
man who had become his unofficial Zionist diplomatic representative,
Nahum Sokolow. In fact, Sokolow had already gone to Paris before
Sykes's departure. "In accordance with an understanding between
Sir Mark and M. Picot," Sokolow had written to Herbert Samuel on
March 30, "I am leaving tomorrow evening for Paris, where I am to
meet M. Picot and others, and acting on the desire of both these
gentlemen, a common friend of theirs, Mr. Malcolm, who is in sympathy with the Zionist cause, is accompanying me on this trip." Neither Sokolow nor Weizmann was happy about Malcolm's presence,
viewing it as a sign not only of Sykes's continuing desire to link the
Zionist and Armenian causes, but also of his and Picot's evident

belief that such a linkage could have a particular impact in Paris at this moment. Clearly, France was to assume a new prominence in the Armenian question now that the situation in revolutionary Russia was in doubt; Malcolm must have wanted from Paris the guarantee he hitherto had sought from Petrograd. He, Sykes, and Picot seem to have had it in mind to propose to the French government—which, since March 19, had been under the premiership of Alexandre Ribot—an extension of its Middle Eastern sphere to include all of Armenia, in compensation for withdrawing its claims to Palestine.

For the first four days of April, Sokolow—staying at the Hotel Meurice on the rue de Rivoli—carried on negotiations in Paris without Sykes. It is not clear if he saw anyone during that time besides Picot himself, who was in close contact with colleagues at the Quai d'Orsay, but in any case he was receiving impressions from the French government that put him in a despondent mood. The French were determined to have the whole of Palestine for themselves, he wrote back to Weizmann, and will give the Jews "rights" there but not autonomy or a charter. He had similar impressions from Baron Edmond de Rothschild, who like his son favored a British Palestine, but who thought it impossible to work for this in Paris. Yet Sokolow was not completely discouraged. "This work is very difficult but not impossible," he wrote to Weizmann on the 4th; "many points in our demands will be accepted here." Evidently the French were taking their by now familiar position of starting with a stone wall and then gradually showing the openings in it.

The atmosphere improved substantially when Sykes arrived to join Sokolow on the 5th. Two days earlier, Sykes had met with Lloyd George and Lord Curzon, and they had reiterated to him "the importance of not prejudicing the Zionist movement and the possibility of its development under British auspices." The prime minister in particular had stressed the importance, "if possible, of securing the addition of Palestine to the British area," and was opposed to making any concession. Indeed, Lloyd George even thought "we could take care of the Holy Places better than anyone else," but the Catholic Sykes took issue with him on this point. The following morning, Wednesday the fourth, Sykes had met with Scott and Weizmann and reported some of the substance of this conversation. He took his leave of them assuming that Weizmann would follow him to Egypt in a week or ten days.

By Friday April 6, Sykes was able to send back to the Foreign Office a glowing report from Paris on Sokolow's progress. "After five days' negotiations," Sykes wired, he has reached the following points: that tomorrow or day after he is to submit to French Government Zionists' desiderata in regard to facilities of colonization, communal autonomy, rights of language and establishment of Jewish chartered company. French Government are likely to concur in admitting justice of these demands. Sokoloff is of opinion that admission by France of principle of recognition of Jewish nationality in Palestine will be step in advance, and I agree.

Whatever the complexities of this question for Jews in France, Sokolow was having success in persuading the French government that the Jews in Palestine were to be legitimately regarded as a nationality: the days of Lucien Wolf's influence were as much over at the Quai d'Orsay as they were in Whitehall. Sokolow must have persuaded his French listeners of the extent to which his view represented world Jewish opinion; and the fact that the United States had officially entered the war against Germany that very day seems to have made the French no less eager to be certain that American-Jewish opinion was definitely on their side. Moreover, they were concerned about the pacifist movement in revolutionary Russia and what they considered to be the Jewish influence upon it.

As for the question of British control of Palestine, Sykes went on in his April 6 telegram,

I have seen M. Picot and have impressed on him the importance of meeting Jewish demands, and expressed my opinion strongly that it would be advantageous to prepare French mind for idea of British suzerainty in Palestine by international consent. I pointed out to him that our preponderant military effort, rights of trans-Palestine railway construction, rights of annexation at Haifa, coupled with general bias of Zionists in favor of British suzerainty, tended to make such a solution the only stable one. I further urged such a solution would facilitate cooperation between British and French in gaining for France her desiderata in Armenia, Syria and Area A.

Actually, Picot, who had himself learned a good deal about Jewish and British realities regarding Palestine by now, was not the person with whom these points had to be argued—at least he did not present himself as such to Sykes. "M. Picot," Sykes said,

was personally less hostile to such an idea than I had anticipated, but pointed out that gross ignorance prevailed in circles formative of political opinion in France, and that the average politician regarded Palestine as being the greater part of Syria instead of one-seventh, and that it would be impossible to prepare the ground until French public were interested in Syria proper by military action or by visible signs of Arab movement in Blue Area or Area A.

Sykes, at Picot's urging, went to see the new French prime minister the following day. He had not intended to raise the Palestine question, but wanted only to make it clear to Ribot that the French would need British assistance in establishing friendly relations with Muslims in their sphere of interest: this was a plan for winning compliance in advance for British desiderata. The question of Palestine did not come up, and this was a sign that Ribot, a Protestant, was not prepared to raise strong opposition to the British stance. The upshot was that Sykes could report back to London later that day that "things here are not so bad as I expected." His conversation with Ribot had only confirmed his feeling that British strength in the matter lay in the facts that "the French cannot make good with the Arabs except with our help, that their interests and opportunities are immense outside Palestine, and that if there is not accord between us they will lose immense opportunities. I try to drive this home as much as I can." He went on to sum up what he thought to be the situation all parties were approaching:

i. British occupation of Palestine as a fait accompli.
ii. British granted Haifa, Acre, and a trans-Palestine railway.
iii. Half the Jordan Valley granted as in the British sphere of interest.
iv. French recognize Jewish national aspirations.

Points two and three were already a fact of the Asia Minor Agreement; points one and four were expected imminently. "With such a case," Sykes concluded, "we should be able to go into a Peace conference fairly well equipped."

Not all interested parties were inclined to be so sanguine. Lord Bertie, still British ambassador in Paris despite his increasing illnesses, was to report a few days later on the conversation between Sykes and Ribot and express some reservations regarding its implications for Palestine. "In dealing with the question of Syria and Palestine," he wrote, it must be remembered that the French uninformed general public imagine that France has special prescriptive rights in Syria and Palestine. The influence of France is that of the Roman Catholic Church exercised through French priests and schools conducted by them; and the Government of France is anti-clerical and for the most part free-thinking. Monsieur Ribot is of the French Protestant faith, which in the eyes of the French Catholics as a body is abhorred next unto the Jewish faith. Even if M. Ribot were convinced of the justice of our pretensions in regard to Palestine, would he be willing to face the certain combined opposition of the French chauvinists, the French uninformed general public, and the Roman Catholic priests and their flocks?

Sykes was certainly not unaware of these problems. During his short stay in Paris, he obtained a report from an English friend living there about a group of French notables and political leaders who had come to be referred to as the "Syrian party." This group—which even included Georges Leygues of the Comité de Propagande Française auprès des Juifs Neutres—regarded Picot as "a fool who had betrayed France" and insisted upon French control of "the whole of the Mediterranean littoral down to Arish, and the Hejaz railway as far south as Maan." It conceded that "a small international enclave of Jaffa, Jerusalem, and Bethlehem might be arranged, in which France should predominate, but might act with the assistance of a board of advisers. For the rest, the country should be absolute French territory as far east as the Euphrates. England might, if she insisted, be granted the port of Gaza—but Haifa, never." Sykes also knew that not much support could be expected from the Jews of France, no matter what their feelings. "The Parisian Jews," he wrote in his report of April 7, "are very weak in the matter of Z[ionism], chiefly on account of the fear they have of raising hostility against themselves; though they won on the Dreyfus case in appearance, they felt the odium very much, and are shaken and easily terrified; though at heart they are Z[ionist] they dare not say so."

It was another instance of the gap that occasionally arises between the public opinion of a country and the realities of foreign policy its government must face. In the meantime, the French government moved a step closer to acquiescence in the realities of Palestine on Monday, April 9, when Sokolow paid an important visit to the Quai d'Orsay to discuss the memorandum on Zionist desiderata that he had submitted in the previous two days. It was an important moment, and its outcome was awaited with great excitement by Sykes, who had driven in early that morning from a visit he made to the front the day before. He and Sokolow had worked together in his room at the Hotel Lotti on the rue Castiglione, around the corner from the Hotel Meurice, for several hours, preparing the material for presentation. He was to wait at the hotel for Sokolow's return from the French Foreign Ministry just across the Pont de la Concorde. "But," Sokolow was to recall, "as I was crossing the Quai d'Orsay on my return from the Foreign Office I came across Sykes. He had not had the patience to wait. We walked on together, and I gave him an outline of the proceedings. This did not satisfy him; he studied every detail; I had to give him full notes and he drew up a minute report. 'That's a good day's work,' he said with shining eyes."

Sokolow had spoken to a group that included—in addition to Picot—Paul Cambon, the French ambassador to London; his brother Jules Cambon, secretary general of the French Foreign Ministry; and Ribot's chef de cabinet. Sokolow had managed to dodge the question of who was to be the future suzerain power in Palestine, and the discussion had focused upon Zionist aspirations there. Jules Cambon stressed two areas in which Jewish influence was of concern to the French government: in Russia, where it was hoped that Jewish influence was being thrown into the scale against the pacifists, and in Italy, where Jewish influence might work toward "consolidation of the Entente." Sokolow felt able to reassure Cambon about these matters. The result was that Sokolow was assured of French acceptance of the principle of Jewish nationality in Palestine. There was nothing in writing as yet, but Sokolow nevertheless—with Sykes's support and doubtless some urging as well—telegraphed Brandeis in the United States and Tschlenow in Russia that evening: "After favorable results in London and Paris I was received with goodwill by Ministry for Foreign Affairs here. I have full confidence allied victory will realize our Palestine Zionists aspirations."

Sykes left the next day for Rome, where he again set to work preparing the ground for Sokolow. For the enterprising Sykes, this meant venturing into an area that he and Sokolow—who now was planning to see members of the Italian government—had not even discussed: the Vatican. Making contact right away with Count J. de Salis, the British envoy to the Holy See, Sykes arranged to see Monsignor Eugenio Pacelli,* assistant under-secretary for foreign affairs

* Later, Pope Pius XII (1939-1958).

there. Sykes and de Salis had their audience with Pacelli on Wednesday, April 11. "I told him," Sykes later reported to the Foreign Office, "that I was going to act as Political Officer to General Murray and that a French Commissioner was also accompanying the army into Palestine. I was exceedingly careful to give no hint as to any arrangements that had been come to between the Powers, and I also told him that I was acting entirely on my own responsibility in seeing him." Monsignor Pacelli observed that the high position Great Britain had accorded to Sykes, a Catholic, was "a signal example of the toleration which existed" in that country.

Sykes then got to the point, speaking of "the immense difficulties which surrounded the question of Jerusalem, the Arab Nationalist movement, the Moslem Holy Places, Zionism, and the conflicting interests of the Latins and Greeks, besides the aspirations of the various powers." He spoke of the possibility that orthodoxy might reassert itself in Russia in spite of the revolution, and therefore of the possible renewal of the old conflict between Russian and French Christians in the Holy Places. Sykes noted that the monsignor, "by certain turns of speech, let it be easy to see that the idea of British patronage of the Holy Places was not distasteful to Vatican policy. The French I could see did not strike him as ideal in any way."

Sykes moved on to the matter of Zionism, explaining its purposes and ideals, and even making the suggestion that the monsignor should see Sokolow when the latter came to Rome. "Of course," Sykes explained in his report, "one could not expect the Vatican to be enthusiastic about this movement, but he was most interested and expressed a wish to see Sokolow." Realizing that the main concern was the Holy Places themselves, Sykes "was able to give full assurances that the Zionists had no aspirations in that direction."

After meeting with Pacelli, Sykes did not see any reason to stop with that success; on Friday, April 13, he had an audience with Pope Benedict XV himself. The pope seemed ill, and the interview lasted only some ten or twelve minutes. "With regard to the work which I had to do," Sykes reported, "His Holiness observed that my office was a great responsibility for so young a man as myself, and that he realized the many complex problems which had to be dealt with. I asked His Holiness whether he would give me some message for the Catholic Chaplains with the Egyptian Force, and he gave me 15 sacred medals with his effigy on the reverse." Sykes thought that, in spite of the little that transpired, "in event of Jerusalem being taken . . . it will be of a great advantage to have had this audience, as we shall have to deal not only with the Latin Patriarch but also the

Custodian of the Holy Places, and it will make the authorities in Rome much more accommodating, in event of our having to remove German or other enemy clerics we may find."

But Sykes evidently also felt that something of value for the Zionist cause had taken place between himself and the pope, as is suggested by the letter he composed for Sokolow the next day. "My Dear M. Sokolow," it ran:

> I visited Monsignor Pacelli and was received in audience by His Holiness. On both occasions I laid considerable stress on the intensity of Zionist feeling and the objects of Zionism.
>
> I was careful to impress that the main object of Zionism was to evolve a self-supporting Jewish community which should raise, not only the racial self-respect of the Jewish people, but should also be a proof to the non-Jewish peoples of the world of the capacity of Jews to produce a virtuous and simple agrarian population, and that by achieving these two results, to strike at the roots of those material difficulties which have been productive of so much unhappiness in the past.
>
> I further pointed out that Zionist aims in no way clashed with Christian desiderata in general and Catholic desiderata in particular in regard to the Holy Places. I mentioned that you were coming to Rome, and I should strongly advise you to visit Monsignor Pacelli, and if you see fit have an audience with His Holiness.
>
> Count de Salis the British representative at the Vatican can arrange this if you will kindly show him this letter. . . .
>
> Yours very sincerely,
Mark Sykes

Leaving the letter at the British embassy in Rome, Sykes wired the Foreign Office to tell Weizmann to wire Sokolow that it was awaiting him there. In another few days, after seeing Pacelli again in the company of Picot and Cardinal Gasquet, the French envoy to the Vatican, Sykes resumed his journey to Egypt.

Before Sokolow left Paris for Rome, some historical events intervened that, though they did not have any evident direct impact on his present mission, were bound to affect the climate within which it was carried on. On the morning of April 17, the second battle of Gaza was begun. Since the element of surprise had been lost—General Murray's railhead was now only some eight miles south of the city—it was no longer possible to envelop Gaza with a cordon of cavalry as had been done the first time. What was planned was a direct assault in two stages, the first of which was successfully accomplished on the seventeenth, when two divisions established themselves just south of the city. But that was the end of success; for Kress von Kressenstein had fully prepared his Turkish garrison and enlarged it. The situation was, for the first time in the Sinai campaigns, something like that on the western front, with one side entrenched and virtually immovable while the other hurled itself into a hopeless attack. The British made their assault on the 19th, and by the end of the day, their objective unattained, sixty-five hundred of them had fallen dead or wounded—three times the number of Turkish casualties.

This had happened within a renewed atmosphere of military frustration in the west. Under the eager prodding of General Robert Nivelle, the new joint offensive planned for that spring had already been begun at Arras on April 9 by the British Third Army under General Sir Edmund Allenby. Canadian troops had made a brilliant capture at Vimy Ridge, and in general the British were making a definite if limited advance. But the French part of the offensive, which was begun on April 16 at the Aisne and in the Champagne, quickly proved to be a disaster. At the Chemin des Dames, the only position taken by the time the offensive was exhausted a month later, there were 120,000 casualties at the end of the first two days of the attack. It was to cost Nivelle his command. Under the circumstances, it was natural that a frustrated Lloyd George War Cabinet, which had put considerable faith in Nivelle against the better judgment of the War Office, should begin to ponder a replacement for General Murray in Egypt and Palestine.

There also were problems to be settled with the Italians. The war against Austria at the Isonzo had been frustratingly without results, and now, to compound the disillusionment, the Italian government was annoyed at having been left out of the Sykes-Picot Agreement. Steps to correct this situation had been undertaken in January, and on April 9 the British Foreign Office had agreed to allow a small detachment of Italian troops—not exceeding some three hundred men—to participate in the invasion of Palestine. Then, on April 19, Lloyd George and Ribot met with Paolo Boselli and Baron Sidney Sonnino—the Italian prime minister and foreign minister, respectively—at the Alpine village of Saint Jean de Maurienne to arrive at final terms for Italian participation in the Asia Minor Agreement. The terms concluded in the next two days granted Italy the port of Smyrna in addition to the rights in the Dodecanese and in Adalia—the latter now somewhat expanded—that had been accorded her in the London Agreement two years before.

Regarding Palestine, or the Brown Area, the Sykes-Picot provisions were amended to read that Italy would be party to the consultations on the form of international administration to be established there. Lloyd George was continuing to pay lip service to a set of understandings that had preceded his prime ministry and that he no longer wholly accepted.

The Foreign Office was becoming aware of the growing contradictions of this policy. Particularly disturbed about the matter was Sir Ronald Graham, the former adviser to the Egyptian Ministry of the Interior, who had returned to England a year earlier and was now an assistant under-secretary of state at the Foreign Office, in charge of Palestine affairs. Ever since he had attended at the birth of the Zion Mule Corps in the spring of 1915, Graham's sympathy for Zionism had steadily grown, and he was now one of its ardent supporters in governing circles. But he feared that the unrelenting tension between commitments to the Allies regarding an internationalized Palestine on the one hand, and desire for British control on the other, was going to tear the situation apart. On April 21, the day the Saint Jean de Maurienne Agreement was concluded, he confided some of his thoughts about the matter in a memorandum addressed to Lord Hardinge, the former viceroy of India and now the permanent under-secretary of state for foreign affairs. Balfour had just left on a visit to the United States, making Hardinge the ranking person at the Foreign Office at this moment.

"His Majesty's Government," Graham began,

> are now committed to support Zionist aspirations. Sir Mark Sykes received instructions on the subject from the Prime Minister and Mr. Balfour and has been taking action both in Paris and Rome. He has been assisting to the best of his ability M. Sokoloff, the well-known Zionist leader. At the present moment I am obtaining leave from the Admiralty for Mr. Weizmann, another prominent Zionist, to relinquish his official work for a couple of months and to proceed to Egypt to join Sir Mark Sykes who has urgently asked for his help.

So far so good; but here was the problem, as Graham saw it:

> However remarkable the Zionist idea may be and however rightly anxious His Majesty's Government are to encourage it, there is one aspect of the situation to which attention should be drawn. Every Zionist with whom I have discussed the question, Baron James de Rothschild, Dr. Weizmann, Mr. Sidebotham of

the "Manchester Guardian," etc., etc. (and I believe that Sir Mark Sykes and others who have had similar discussions have enjoyed the same experience), insists that the Zionist idea is based entirely on a British Palestine. They are unanimous in the opinion that their project would break down were Palestine to be internationalized.

Graham went on to refer to the Asia Minor Agreement and its provision for an international administration in the Brown Area. "We cannot," he wrote,

of course, inform the Zionists of this Agreement, but are we justified in encouraging them in so great a measure when the prospect of Palestine being internationalized is distinctly stronger than the prospect of the country coming under our protection? I know that the Prime Minister insists that we must obtain Palestine and that Sir Mark Sykes proceeded on his mission with these instructions. But those who are best qualified to gauge French opinion, including Lord Bertie, are convinced that the French will never abandon their sentimental claims to Palestine.

Graham concluded by wondering

whether we are justified in going so far in our encouragement of the Zionist movement, which is based on a British Palestine, without giving the Zionists some intimation of the existing arrangement with France in regard to Palestine. I feel that if in the end the French refuse to give way, and the attitude of Italy and Russia on the subject is also uncertain, the odium of the failure of the Zionist project to which we shall have given so much encouragement will fall entirely upon us.

Hardinge was in any case not one of Zion's enthusiasts at the Foreign Office. "I cannot help feeling," he replied,

that this Zionist movement and its consequences have not so far been sufficiently considered. It appears that it is inseparable from a British Palestine, and this seems at present unrealizable. Are we wise in giving encouragement to a movement based on a condition which we cannot enforce? Failure, when it comes, will be laid at the door of the F.O., and not without reason.

This response, which implies reservations going beyond the particular ones raised by Graham, was certainly not in the spirit of the absent Balfour. But Lord Robert Cecil, who on the whole shared his cousin's outlook regarding Zionism, and who was acting foreign secretary in the latter's absence, also saw the memorandum, and wrote on it: "I quite recognize the very great difficulty of carrying out the Zionist policy involving as it does a strong preference for a British protectorate over Palestine. That seems to me to make it the more desirable to get France to join us in an expression of sympathy for Jewish Nationalist aspirations." Cecil had put his finger on it and no doubt knew quite well that Nahum Sokolow was at that moment very close to eliciting such a statement.

It may have been the belief that such a statement was imminent that caused Sokolow to stay on in Paris another two weeks after the April 9 meeting at the Quai d'Orsay—although he certainly found other things to do, speaking to French Jewish groups and striving to break down the resistance to Zionism that was widespread among them. Most of this time he had by his side James Malcolm, who—inadvertently encouraged by Sykes—was at this moment still apparently envisioning himself as the necessary link between the Zionists and governing circles in both London and Paris. When Malcolm finally returned to London on April 20, Sokolow ventured an evaluation of him in a letter to Weizmann. "I must say," he wrote,

I did not like to have a stranger in the center of our work. But, as you know, he was thrown upon us. The chief [Sykes] thought that he had connections here and demanded his participation.

Sokolow nevertheless was ready to acknowledge Malcolm's virtues:

He is a business man of the "brasseur d'affaires" type, with a vivid imagination, an ardent Armenian patriot. He has great sympathy for Zionism (not for the Jews in general), is endowed with an esprit of a goyish kind, is very adroit and somewhat conceited. . . . I am sure I would have achieved what I did without him, but I must say he worked well and behaved tactfully.

But Sokolow concluded with the suggestion that, though he had had no choice but to keep Malcolm informed of what was happening while they were in Paris together,

I would not initiate him into any confidential things in London.
. . . We had to accept his cooperation, but I would not like to have
him *à la longue* in the center of our activities.

Soon after his arrival in London, Malcolm saw Graham and reported
on Sokolow's activities in Paris; but little more was to be heard from
him in connection with Zionist matters from then on.

Sokolow arrived in Rome around April 23 and found Sykes's
letter of April 14 awaiting him. It took him by surprise. He had
come, as he was to tell Weizmann in a letter, "for the definite purpose of getting the most reliable information about the attitude and
the intentions of the Italian Government with regard to Palestine
and Zionism," and now a new element had suddenly entered his
program. "It never crossed my mind before that I should approach
the Vatican."

He approached both governments, but it was with the Vatican,
through the good offices of Count de Salis, that he was able to get his
first appointments. On April 29 he saw Monsignor Pacelli, who dwelt
upon the question of the Holy Places and insisted that they would
have to be clearly defined. Sokolow thought that "in spite of the
extraordinary courtesy shown . . . the interview was somewhat
strenuous." Things went more pleasantly two days later, when he
had an audience with Cardinal Gasparri, the papal secretary of state.
Gasparri also stressed the Holy Places and offered a startlingly
broad definition of them that included Nazareth and Tiberias as well
as Jerusalem, Bethlehem, and Jericho, but he went on to give a
hearty endorsement of Zionist aspirations. Pleased by the interview,
Sokolow came away from it with the impression that Gasparri preferred British to French suzerainty in Palestine.

The best interview of all was with the pope himself, on May 6.
Benedict XV was an ardent Liberal who had been deeply perturbed
by the persecutions of Jews in Eastern Europe. From the beginning
of the conversation he made clear his sympathy with Zionism.

"What a turn of destiny!" he said. "Nineteen hundred years ago
Rome destroyed your homeland, and now, when you wish to rebuild
it, you have chosen the path that leads to Rome."

"I am deeply moved by such historical memories," Sokolow replied. "And may I be permitted to add that that Rome which destroyed Israel was appropriately punished. Rome fell shortly
afterward, whereas the people of Israel still live. They are so alive
that now they even desire that their land be returned to them."

"Yes," said the Pope. "It is Providential. God has willed it."

In this atmosphere, it was easy for Sokolow to explicate fully the aims of Zionism in both the larger and the immediately practical senses. He spoke of the preference for British control, and the pope seemed to agree with this. When the pope mentioned the Holy Places, Sokolow remarked that they would surely be better off under the British than they had been under the Turk, and elicited a smile. When Sokolow concluded by asking for the moral support of the Holy See for Zionist aspirations, the pope said: "Yes, yes, I trust we shall be good neighbors," and repeated this several times.

"Have been received by Pope in special audience which lasted three-quarters of an hour," Sokolow jubilantly wired Weizmann through the British embassy in Rome. "Pope attentively listened to my report," he went on,

> and remarked that although had report from Cardinal Gasparri welcomes opportunity of receiving more particulars. Pope declared Jewish efforts of establishing national home in Palestine met sympathetically. He sees no obstacle whatever from the point of view of his religious interests concerning only Holy Places which he trusts will be properly safeguarded by special arrangement. I declared we Jews will be most careful respecting Christian religious properties and sentiments. He replied he receives these declarations with confidence and wishes realization of our program. His declaration culminated in saying repeatedly "we shall be good neighbors." He spoke almost sympathetically of Great Britain's intentions. The whole impression of honoring me with a long audience and tenor of conversation reveal most favorable attitude.

Sokolow now renewed his efforts to see Italian government officials, with less glowing results than at the Vatican. Using the good offices of Angelo Sereni, president of the Italian-Jewish community, he tried to see Baron Sidney Sonnino, who had been prime minister and was now foreign minister, but was rebuffed. Sonnino, who was of partly Jewish origin himself, later explained to the British ambassador in Rome, Sir Reginald Rodd, that he was sympathetic to Sokolow's ideas but "did not wish to treat the matter in any way officially." This suggests that he was hesitant, given his high position, to offer any public intimations of what some would have called a "racial" preference; but the fact that Sokolow had already been to the Vatican also seems to have had something to do with it. The Vatican, Sonnino added in his explanation to Rodd, "would no doubt be all the better pleased at knowing that they were approached first in Italy and that the Italian Government had not been." But, whatever the grounds for his refusal to see Sokolow, he was to relent, and Sokolow was to see him before returning to Paris later in the month.

Meanwhile, with Sereni by his side, Sokolow went to see Prime Minister Paolo Boselli on Saturday, May 12. The visitor had some difficulty bringing the subject of discussion around to Palestine and Zionism. Boselli was at first eager to talk about any other aspect of the Jewish question than that one—especially about the Jews of Italy, the good treatment they received, their good relations with their fellow Italians, and their important services to the state. Finally Sokolow brought him to the point, and he replied that it was a matter in which Italy could not take the initiative, but would offer its support should a move be made in favor of Zionism by the Allied Powers more closely involved. This was an assurance that had already been given to Sokolow four days earlier by Di Martino, the secretary general of the Italian Foreign Ministry. But Boselli now added the qualification that Italian support would be "within the limits of the possible." He reiterated the sympathy of the Italian government for Zionism, however, and as a further mark of goodwill, sent out instructions to Marquis Imperiali, the Italian ambassador in London, to give Sokolow a hearing.

Sokolow now even hoped to have an audience with King Victor Emmanuel III, but this was not to be.

·37·

WEIZMANN CARRIES ON AT HOME

When Sokolow left for Paris at the end of March, he had done so under no illusions about what the French might be willing to concede. They could be persuaded to agree to Jewish national aims in Palestine, but not to British suzerainty. It is possible that Sykes may even have intimated something of the fact of the Asia Minor Agreement to Sokolow, who certainly would have seen in that moment the imprudence of sharing such a piece of knowledge with Weizmann. For Weizmann, long in favor of exclusive British control of Palestine, had by now become as obsessed with the idea as were his friends on the British Palestine Committee. "Here last week," he had written to Sokolow on Wednesday April 4, "practically every paper wrote about Jewish Palestine under British Protectorate: the *Daily Chronicle, Evening News, Manchester Guardian*, the Liverpool papers and even the *Morning Post* and the *Times*. There can be no doubt that the feeling here is very strong and, of course, much more concrete than it was a fortnight ago."

This summary of opinion in the press was in fact a bit too sanguine. The *Times* leader of March 30 on "The Victory in Palestine," had said nothing more to the point than: "For the Jews and the Arabs, who form the majority, the Allies are carrying on a real war of liberation." As for the *Guardian*, it confined itself on this occasion to a critique of General Murray's report—although its overall record in favor of Weizmann's views certainly was beyond reproach. The other papers had indeed responded as Weizmann described. "Once more I emphasize," he added at the end of the letter after covering several other matters, "that there is a strong feeling for Jewish Palestine under a British Protectorate in this country and you may point it out to our friends on the other side."

Even the idea of American participation in the administration of Palestine, in which Weizmann had expressed a passing acquiescence, was not something he really could contemplate for all its attractiveness. On that same Wednesday as his letter to Sokolow, he wrote a note to Josiah Wedgwood—now the most celebrated British exponent of the idea of American suzerainty—asking for an appointment. Weizmann had met Commander Wedgwood at a Lloyd George breakfast about a year before and had the greatest respect for his pro-Zionist enthusiasms, but on this occasion wanted to disagree with him. In London at the moment was a prominent American journalist and friend of Brandeis and President Wilson, Norman Hapgood; he had long interested himself in Jewish affairs and had recently written an article advocating a Jewish commonwealth in Palestine under American protection. He seems to have been a friend of Wedgwood's too, and the result of Weizmann's letter was a meeting on Friday or Saturday which included not only Hapgood, Wedgwood, and Weizmann, but also Herbert Samuel, Neil Primrose, and James de Rothschild. In a letter to Brandeis on April 8, Weizmann felt able to mention this meeting, along with the same British newspaper articles he had mentioned to Sokolow, and other things besides, in support of "our position," as he put it, which is described elsewhere in the same letter as "a Jewish Palestine under a British Protectorate." Brandeis was not one who was inclined to disagree with this formula.

Indeed, the only threat to the complacency of this view within the circle of Weizmann's friends and close associates seemed to be Sokolow. The old distrust between Weizmann and Sokolow had survived in spite of the firm alliance that political necessity had sealed between them, and it was now being reawakened in Weizmann by the combination of Sokolow's traditional secretiveness and known ability to compromise with his newfound intimacy with Sykes and the vexing distance of Paris from London. "I was very anxious about the absence of news from you," he had written in his April 4 letter to Sokolow, only four days after the latter's departure, "but this very minute I received your letter, which, although it gives no facts still conveys some idea about the state of things on the other side." It was a grudging response to what was in fact an unilluminating report, but things were not to improve much on either side in the coming days.

Sokolow sent a long report on the fourth, but this was a summary of general impressions the day before Sykes's arrival, and from then on his communications became laconic again as obviously important occasions came and went. "Important progress," he wired Weizmann on April 8, the day before his crucial meeting with the two Cambons at the Quai d'Orsay. "Will be received tomorrow. Will perhaps be obliged to go to Rome a few days before returning to London. Telegraph Moscow Washington good prospects. Prepare your voyage Egypt be ready when the chief wires. Details letter." But all that followed this rather cryptic report was a similarly cryptic one wired on the tenth: "Result official interview quite satisfactory. We all must continue work. Decided going Rome about Saturday [April 14]. Malcolm returning Saturday London will give you details. Send by wire some money." Weizmann could barely contain his exasperation in his reply the next day. "Dear Nahum Osipovich," he wrote:

> Heartfelt thanks for your kind letters and telegrams. I am, of course not satisfied and should love to know all the details as soon as possible, but I understand perfectly well that you are busy and shall, therefore, wait patiently. Here, we are of course unable to understand the sudden change in your tone, as your letter [of April 4] was so pessimistic and suddenly telegrams in a completely different mood started to arrive. And knowing you—knowing that you are not likely to be carried away and are not exaggerating—we are delighted at the changed mood. I shall be waiting impatiently for M[alcolm]'s arrival.

Having sent the desired money the day before, Weizmann may very well have been struck by a feeling that he was becoming some kind of errand runner to the traveling exploits of Sokolow and Sykes, especially as, on Saturday, April 14, he received word from the Foreign Office that Sykes wanted him to tell Sokolow about the message waiting at the British embassy in Rome. Finding a way to speak for both Sykes and himself very succinctly, Weizmann cabled: "Expect urgently detailed letter from yourself please call British embassy Rome for letters." But it was four days since Sokolow had been heard from, so Weizmann, like a parent calling other parents in search of the child not yet home for dinner, sent a telegram to Gaston Wormser, Baron de Rothschild's private secretary in Paris: "Anxious absence news Nahum. Important decisions held up. Please telegraph details your impressions his work also his present address. Impossible prepare my journey Egypt without knowing details results obtained by Nahum." On the fifteenth Weizmann finally received a telegram that Sokolow had sent on the eleventh, the day after his last brief communication; but this only said: "Continuation work all right. Wired yesterday my movements. Awaiting your wires." This was hardly satisfactory, and on April 17, with no further messages and Malcolm yet to be heard from, Weizmann discharged his feelings in yet another wire: "Very anxious absence all news from you ignorance result your efforts paralyzes all work Maccallum [*sic*, for Malcolm] not arrived telegraph immediately." It was not until the nineteenth that Sokolow replied: "Myself and friends [that is, Sykes to the Foreign Office and Baron de Rothschild to his son] already wired most successful results no reason anxiety or any suspense your work Malcolm arriving Saturday [April 21] report particulars myself Saturday evening leaving Rome."

At that point, communications improved somewhat. "Only yesterday Malcolm arrived," Weizmann reported to Harry Sacher on Sunday the 22nd,

> and he brought me some news and also two letters from Sokolow. The position of affairs there is briefly the following. They had a series of discussions with the French Authorities and they have eliminated from these discussions all questions relating to the political fate of Palestine, I mean to say the question of the suzerain power has been left alone. Sokolow tried to give the French authorities a clear idea of what the Zionist Movement means and stands for. As you know public opinion and official circles in France knew very little of Zionism and scarcely reckoned with this. In the opinion of Sokolow and also of Baron Edmond who wrote to James, they have succeeded in impressing the French with the importance and the value of our movement and I think that the work as far as it goes in that respect is valuable, although I would not like to overestimate it. The French agreed to this view and agreed to all the Jewish national claims as expressed in our Demands, without reference of course as to who is going to be the Suzerain Power in Palestine.

There was the rub as far as Weizmann was concerned. "Sokolow is particularly happy about this success," he went on, with a slight touch of scorn in the emphasis,

> so is Baron Edmond. The latter wrote in that sense to James but he added that in his opinion the bride is too beautiful and he foresees difficulties.

And in Weizmann's opinion? "I need not say," he went on,

that I do not share the great optimism of Sokolow; the only thing which I would consider valuable is if Sokolow will be able to convince the French that Palestine belongs to the English, a role which of course he could not play. On the other hand as a result of these negotiations I foresee a danger that it may be possible that the French will use these negotiations as an argument vis-à-vis the English in telling the English that they also agree with the Zionists and would do for the Zionists all the English are prepared to do. We are in a way covered against this danger by the fact that Sokolow went to Paris with the knowledge and consent of the British Government on the suggestion of Sir Mark Sykes and reports of his visit have been lodged with the Foreign Office here. He left for Rome yesterday and he intends to make a lengthy stay there. I do not know what he will be doing there but he seems to attach great value to his journey to Rome.

It was a truce; things were all right for the time being, but they were not to stay that way for long.

By now the inevitable had occurred: without getting the names of the Frenchman and the Englishman who had drawn it up (how would he have responded, in this bewildering moment, to the label "Sykes-Picot" now regularly attached to it by those who knew about it?), Weizmann had learned at last of the Asia Minor Agreement and its disposition of the Brown Area. It was C.P. Scott, who, having heard from a French colleague the viscomte Robert de Caix, foreign editor of the *Journal des Débats*—that France was to have northern Palestine down to the Acre-Tiberias line and that the rest of the country was to be internationalized, conveyed this information to Weizmann in a letter of April 16. "This was startling information indeed!" writes Weizmann in his autobiography. "Chaim and all those in the inner circle of British Zionist affairs," Vera Weizmann was to recall, "were in a state of consternation over the position."

In his letter of the sixteenth, Scott had gone on to urge Weizmann not to leave for Egypt until he had a definite formulation of the Government's policy regarding Palestine. He also thought Weizmann should not leave until the matter of the award for his Government scientific work—which was still pending, despite the air of imminency that had surrounded it fully a year earlier—was settled once and for all. When he came down to London on the evening of

April 18, Scott was ready to look personally into some of these matters. He saw Weizmann the next morning and then visited Sir Edward Carson, the new first lord of the Admiralty, to discuss Weizmann's award and the obtaining of leave for him to go to Egypt. On Friday the twentieth, Scott had tea with Lord Milner—celebrated or notorious as the high commissioner for South Africa during the Boer War and now, by one of history's ironies, a member of Lloyd George's War Cabinet—and Palestine was one of the things they discussed. "As a member of the War Cabinet I thought he might have views about Palestine," Scott recorded in his diary, "but he was rather vague about it."

This vagueness probably was a personal strategy in the manner of Balfour, however, since Herbert Samuel had sent Milner a copy of his Palestine memorandum in January and Milner had responded vividly in a letter agreeing that British control "certainly appears to me the most attractive" of the alternatives presented. Scott wrote that Milner "seemed to think" Palestine would have to be internationalized, and that he "evidently knew nothing of the Zionist view that this would be fatal for Zionism and therefore for our whole policy in Palestine. Spoke of the French assertiveness in regard to it and of 'unfortunate engagements' entered into a year ago. I said Palestine was a small thing compared with the vast territory we were overrunning in Mesopotamia, but that it was the thing which mattered."

Scott reported on this conversation to Weizmann, who decided to seek clarification about any Anglo-French understanding over Palestine from men closer to the source. On Tuesday, April 24, he went to see Herbert Samuel in the morning and Sir Ronald Graham in the afternoon. Samuel, as Weizmann later described it to Scott, said he could not disclose "the nature of the arrangement made because he was a member of the Cabinet at that time but he could say this much, that the arrangement was not satisfactory from the British point of view." But Samuel went on to say that he saw no objection to this question being reopened, particularly now that the British army was actually on Palestine soil. He strongly advised Weizmann to go to Egypt and watch events there carefully, making it clear to the Foreign Office that he was going there "with the definite purpose of working for a British Palestine and mobilizing Jewish opinion both in and outside Palestine" to that end. Weizmann told Samuel he was "quite willing to go out but the Foreign Office and the British Government must give me the possibility of doing this work and they must make up their minds what they intend to do with Palestine." In conclusion, Weizmann asked Samuel to arrange a meeting about the matter between themselves and Lloyd George, and Samuel agreed to do so.

"On the same day in the afternoon," Weizmann continued in his report to Scott, "I saw Sir Ronald Graham at the Foreign Office to whom I repeated these facts giving him also the report of my interview with Mr. Samuel." Weizmann told Graham, according to Vera Weizmann's diary, that "he couldn't go to Egypt unless he has a definite mandate to raise public Jewish opinion for British Palestine." Graham replied that he was most sympathetic, that he had learned of the Anglo-French arrangement over Palestine only after he had come to the Foreign Office the year before and that he did not consider it satisfactory. The position it had created was ambiguous, he said, "nothing is clear and he himself has presented a minute to the Secretary for Foreign Affairs demanding that the position should be made clear" before Weizmann left for Egypt. Graham was referring to the memorandum he had sent to Lord Hardinge just three days before, in which he had then seen the problem as compounded by the fact that the Zionists could not be told of the Asia Minor agreement. That element of the problem no longer existed, however, and Graham now proposed that Weizmann discuss the whole matter with Lord Robert Cecil, still the acting foreign secretary while Balfour was in America. An interview was arranged for the following day.

Weizmann came to Cecil that Wednesday afternoon fully prepared to give a systematic exposition of the Zionist viewpoint on suzerainty over Palestine. He proposed to review the three possibilities, of a British protectorate, an Anglo-French condominium, and internationalization, each in its turn. Starting with the British protectorate, Weizmann spelled out the reasons why Zionists regarded this as the most desirable solution, invoking the by now standard Zionist argument regarding the wisdom with which Britain has governed her colonies in all their diversity and adding a new Jewish twist. "Under British rule," he said, "great and flourishing Jewish communities have been established all over the world like the communities in Canada, South Africa and Egypt and even the American community has been established under an English speaking race which is imbued with the same spirit of justice and fairness as the

British race. The fact that England is a biblical nation accounts for the spiritual affinity between them and the Jews."

Moving on to the idea of an Anglo-French condominium, Weizmann insisted that the principle of dual control was "fraught with gravest dangers." History has often shown, he said, that under a dual control one part of the population will be played off against the other. In such a case, Weizmann said, the French would probably rely on "the Syrians and Christian Arabs, that is generally on the Levantines." Now, the Levantine, Weizmann maintained, "is not an attractive type; he has lost the primitive virtues of the Arab and has not acquired the virtues of European civilization; he is covered with a veneer of superficial French polish; he cannot be relied upon as a suitable element with which cooperation would promise good results." In the relations between the two governments, he argued, there would be jealousies, intrigues, and endless wasting of time.

The alternative of internationalization was dealt with more summarily by Weizmann, who said it would present the same difficulties as condominium "but in a still more aggravated form." According to Cecil's brief memorandum of the meeting, Weizmann even said he would prefer that Palestine "be left under Turkish Government, because international government was the worst in the world, involving every sort of interference with liberty without any of the advantages of a strong administration." If Weizmann said this, it surely was in a moment when he was carried away by rhetorical fury.

Cecil now decided to try out Weizmann's views on the question of a purely French control of Palestine. Weizmann at first responded that French control was preferable to dual control or internationalization, but Lord Robert noticed "as he proceeded that he regarded French administration with scarcely less disfavor." Indeed, before the interview had ended, Weizmann was saying that Zionists everywhere would regard French control as "a third destruction of the Temple." He explained that "the French in their colonizing activity have not followed the same lines as the English, they have always interfered with the population and tried to impose upon them the 'esprit français.'" He argued, according to Cecil's report, "that the French Government, who were atheistical at home, were Roman Catholic abroad. Catholicism was, for them, an article of exportation, and, as practiced in French Dominions abroad, it was in the hands of the most intolerant section of the Roman Catholic Church. Apart from that, he regarded the French as incapable of understanding the aspirations of small nations under their administration, and particularly as unsympathetic to Jewish and Zionist aspirations." Weizmann had the impression that Lord Robert saw the force of the argument, and the question was not pursued any further.

The discussion now turned to the Asia Minor Agreement, or rather to that part of it which was the only one Weizmann knew or cared about, regarding Palestine. Weizmann argued that "this arrangement embodies all the faults of an Anglo-French and an international settlement and is moreover aggravated by the fact that Palestine is cut up into two halves [sic] and the Jewish colonizing effort which has been going on before the war for more than thirty years is thus annihilated." Alluding to all the colonies north of the Brown Area's boundary, Weizmann said that region "would certainly constitute a Jewish irredenta."

According to Cecil, Weizmann said that "Galilea and Judea were both parts of the same country, and ought to be kept together. But he did not attach very great importance to that, because he said that it would take some time for the Zionists to colonize Judea; and when they had done so, and desired to extend, they would have a very strong case for 'over-running' (as he put it) Galilea." According to Weizmann's own report, the way he put it was that "we would find a certain amount of compensation in the fact if at least Judea were British, for a generation or two the Jews could work under a British protection in Judea, try to develop the country as much as possible and hope for the time when some just tribunal would give them the rest of Palestine on which they have an historic claim." There is no way of knowing whether Weizmann had discussed with any of his Zionist colleagues this remarkable notion that, for a while at least, they might be ready to accept the loss of the northern Galilee so long as southern Palestine was under purely British control. But if, on the other hand, "Judea instead of becoming British would be simply internationalized," Weizmann argued, "then this partition from a Jewish point of view is a Solomon's judgment of the worst character, the child is cut into two and both halves mutilated."

In the end, though, the matter should be decided not on "strategic considerations," as Weizmann put it, but in accordance with the high ideals that have now become part of the war effort, which include "the settlement of the map of the world on national principles." These are among the principles that "have been proclaimed by the Allies since the beginning of the war and which have lately been so strongly emphasized by America and Russia." On the other hand, he argued, "a Jewish Palestine under a British Protectorate could not be interpreted simply as an annexation of Palestine by Great Britain. In view of the relation of the Jews to Great Britain mentioned before it would be easily understood that Great Britain is, so to say, keeping the country in trust for the Jews."

The conversation ended with an exchange about Weizmann's proposed mission to Egypt and Palestine. Weizmann said "he would go on the clear understanding that he is to work for a Jewish Palestine under a British Protectorate." His account of the conversation goes on to say that "Lord Robert agreed to this view; he mentioned that of course there are considerable difficulties in the way but that it would strengthen the position very considerably if the Jews of the world would express themselves in favor of a British Protectorate." Lord Robert's account does not indicate any such acquiescence on his part; but neither does it show him opposing Weizmann's insistence upon advocating British control. His only expressed concern lay elsewhere. "I was much impressed," he wrote, "as indeed I have been on previous occasions, by the enthusiasm and idealism of M. Weizmann; but of course I am not in a position to express any opinion as to how far he represents Jewish feeling in this matter."

Weizmann had thus effectively aired his feelings about the Asia Minor Agreement to men in positions of power and influence, and the result was some indication of a possible victory over it. Now there remained only the problem of Sokolow and the intimations he seemed to be giving of wooing the French over a Palestine settlement. "All unanimously agree," Vera Weizmann wrote in her diary, "that Sokolow's presence in Paris any longer is dangerous and all connection with the French ought to be severed. Telegram to that effect sent to Sokolow who was then in Rome." Weizmann sent it on Friday, April 27. "Your work in France," it said,

> may be interpreted as negotiations on behalf our movement in favor of French alternative. On no account such impression admissible. You only went on suggestion of Sir Mark to explain Zionist program *à titre d'information.* Have submitted Foreign Office shall only go Egypt with distinct program support Jewish Palestine under British Protectorate. Brandeis Tschlenow informed accordingly. Brandeis apparently agreed as has cabled money asked for. Your presence here absolutely necessary before I leave here middle next month.

Weizmann had been studying carefully the materials Malcolm had brought on Sokolow's activities in Paris, and by this time a subtle but seemingly significant detail had aroused him. It was in the message Sokolow had wired to Brandeis and Tschlenow after his important April 9 meeting at the Quai d'Orsay. "After favorable results in London and Paris," it had run, "I was received with goodwill by Ministry for Foreign Affairs here." According to Malcolm's diary, the first draft of this passage had referred only to London, and the words "and Paris" had been added at Jules Cambon's suggestion. "In other words," Weizmann explicated in a long and stern letter he wrote to Sokolow on May 1,

> the impression conveyed to Washington and Moscow by these telegrams was that you are equally satisfied with the success in London and Paris and you consider the success in both places of equal value. Whereas I am perfectly convinced that you may have put in the word Paris out of politeness, in fact you were not in a position to refuse it, I am very much afraid that in Washington and Moscow they may think that you, as a representative of the Zionist Organization, consider it possible to advocate a French Protectorate or a joint Anglo-French control. I need hardly say that we would all deplore any confusion in the minds of our fellow Zionists abroad on that fundamental point. This is why I do not see any further reason for your staying on in Rome and for making any stay in Paris on your return journey.

Referring to Sokolow's reports on the sudden display of sympathy for Zionism he had obtained from the French on April 9, Weizmann indulged in a spiteful display of suspicion. "The *volte face*," he wrote,

> and the rapid change from an hostile or indifferent attitude to these sympathetic expressions of opinion makes me doubt a little the genuineness of the interest, it is so contrary to all we have heard and known up to now. The only explanation of this attitude is the endeavor of the French to secure the cooperation of the Zionist organization and the Jews at large in the establishment of a condominium over Palestine.

Weizmann concluded this outburst by stressing: "I am speaking on behalf of all our friends and collaborators here in asking you to shorten your stay on the Continent and proceed to London if possible at once."

Sokolow, who received this just after seeing Pacelli and Gasparri and just before his audience with the pope, replied in a telegram on May 4 through the British embassy in Rome. "Astonished fallacious commentaries," it said:

> Acted France strictly "à titre d'information." Closest relations with Sykes. My program were our demands for which enlisted official sympathy without slightest allusion to French alternative or any engagement. Must protest emphatically against misleading interpretations. My ideal solution is naturally British Palestine, for this I am working here also successfully of course with necessary carefulness. Shall return as soon as possible.

This proved to be somewhat chastening, particularly since, by the time Weizmann received it on Saturday the fifth, he had received word from a Zionist colleague in Switzerland of a recent conference in that country held by leading Catholics from Germany, Austria, and Italy, who were determined that Palestine should be internationalized under the auspices of the pope. Furthermore, Weizmann had by now heard from Sokolow about the latter's meetings with Pacelli and Gasparri, and he knew Sykes had been to see these high Vatican personages and the pope as well. Under the circumstances he could not continue to protest against Sokolow's presence in Rome.

Indeed, since it was perfectly clear that Sokolow had only been doing precisely what Sykes wanted him to do—the words "closest relations with Sykes" in Sokolow's telegram must have been particularly galling—and since Weizmann still had no idea that Sykes was one of the authors of that very Anglo-French agreement over Palestine that was exercising him so, Weizmann certainly had to consider himself a poor second to Sokolow for the moment if providing satisfaction to "the chief" was the criterion. Just a few days before, on April 30, Sykes had wired a rebuke to Weizmann from Cairo by way of the Foreign Office, in response to information that Weizmann was apparently saying too much about Sokolow's negotiations to other Zionist colleagues. Two days before that, Sykes had sent another urgent request that Weizmann come to Egypt. This was in the context of a report Aaronsohn had just received—later to prove exaggerated—of a mass evacuation and mistreatment of the Jews of Jaffa.

If ever it seemed urgent that Weizmann be in Cairo it was now. But Weizmann, whose growing round of activities as the fully acknowledged leader of British Zionism was becoming combined with his continuing doubts about the Government's position regarding French claims on Palestine to form a reason for staying home, had just told Scott on Monday, April 30, that he "had finally decided to postpone his departure." Apparently Sir Ronald Graham was also inclined to think he should stay a while, for he wired Sykes on May 4:

> Dr. Weizmann inquires whether in view of existing military situation in Palestine it would not be better for him to postpone his departure for Egypt for a month or six weeks and to continue his propaganda work in Europe and America. He feels that to come out now may prove a waste of time but, if you still press for his immediate services, would be glad to know what use you will be able to make of them.

Sykes replied four days later with a testiness that could make itself heard even through the terseness of telegraphic prose. "I do not know what military situation is," he said,

> assuming that we are either going on or stopping where we are. Weizmann should come out as soon as possible if we are ever going on no matter what the date of our proposed advance. He should be told to drop propaganda if we are going to stop where we are for good, as latter can only add to sufferings of his people who are already beginning to be punished. . . . I propose to use Weizmann to see to Zionist situation in Egypt, easing Judaeo-Arab situation by promoting good feeling and cooperation, assisting in organization of local Zionists and improving such of our intelligence as depends on Jewish information and making plans for political action against our advance. It is the opinion of Aaronsohn that Weizmann should come out, however if Weizmann sees fit to appoint Aaronsohn to act in his place I have no doubt the latter would be ready to do so but he should receive from Weizmann and his friends telegraphic detailed instructions.

That was certainly the last straw: Weizmann did not like the maverick Aaronsohn any more than did almost anyone else in official Zionism. Perhaps Sykes thought he was using this threat as a lever to pry Weizmann away from London, but the only result was that Weizmann neither set out for Egypt nor sent instructions "appointing" Aaronsohn as his replacement. The Foreign Office clearly had overruled Sykes on this one.

In this atmosphere, Weizmann's feelings toward Sokolow's activities on the Continent had softened. "My dear Friend," he wrote to Sokolow on May 8 in response to a complaint about not getting letters, "all your letters from Rome did not offer any occasion for comment, moreover the report about your most important interview [with Cardinal Gasparri] arrived only yesterday and we here on the other hand have no important news and all the information we receive I am sending on by wire to you immediately." After several more placating descriptions of messages being sent, Weizmann offered in implied apology for his recent sharp letters that "what we were concerned about here chiefly were persistent rumors about a suggested arrangement concerning Palestine which has been arrived at by the Powers," and he proceeded to describe it. At the conclusion of the letter he said: "Please continue to send us your valuable reports for which we are all extremely grateful." This was prudent, for in another day he had seen Sokolow's report on the interview with the pope, about which he wired on the ninth: "Your telegram received heartily congratulate brilliant result." The next day he even wired Sokolow a copy of Sykes's complaint from Egypt of May 8, asking for an opinion. A few days later, Sokolow was writing a long letter to Weizmann, fully explaining his activities of the past month and insisting that the question of suzerainty had been left open.

At this very time, Weizmann had been given another reminder that, in spite of everything, he could feel gratified that Sokolow was the only peer he had to contend with in conducting the affairs of Zionism. At the beginning of May he had heard for the first time in a while from Moses Gaster, who wrote asking for a report on recent developments. Weizmann gave one, and in the ensuing exchange behaved with a strict correctness that could only have exacerbated the chief rabbi's wounded feelings at his sudden fall from seeming preeminence. "It is only right," Gaster finally blurted out in a letter of May 10, in which he commented upon the position that had quietly been taken from him since the beginning of February and conferred upon Sokolow, "that I should again mention that up until then it was I who conducted the negotiations for close upon a year, and brought them to that state which it had reached on the day of the meeting in my house."

"Dear Dr. Gaster," Weizmann replied the following day to the man who had held his son for circumcision only six months before:

I beg to thank you for your note of May 10th. As I do not know to what you allude in speaking of the manner of the procedure by which the position has been conferred on Mr. Sokolow I am not in a position to answer this point. Perhaps Mr. Sokolow will be able to do so. With regard to your statement that it was you who conducted the negotiations for close upon a year and brought them to that state which it had reached on the day of the meeting in your house, it is of course a matter of opinion and it is a matter of considerable regret to me that I am unable to share this opinion, but of course it must be left to the historian to give his judgment on it.

What the historian must above all conclude is that the tougher-minded man had won the contest.

·38·

SOME DECLARATIONS

A special conference of the English Zionist Federation was held in London on Sunday, May 20. Since the convening of the regular annual meeting in February, major events had occurred—the Russian revolution, America's entry into the war, the two assaults on Gaza, and the renewal of Turkish persecutions of Jews in Palestine—requiring that the Federation formulate new positions to communicate to its constituent societies. Chaim Weizmann gave the principal speech.

He began by reviewing the situation in Russia. Weizmann had that month published an article on "The Russian Revolution and Zionism" in the first issue of the federation's new journal, the *Zionist Review*. In it he argued that the vast majority of Russian Jews were Jewish nationalists of one form or another and that now that they were free, Zionism would come to play the same role among them as it had among the Jews of the West. An escape from persecution was not the point, nor had it ever been. "Some of us," he observed in his speech before the federation,

> —some of our friends even, and especially some of our opponents—are very quick in drawing conclusions as to what will happen to the Zionist Movement after the Russian Revolution. Now, they say, the greatest stimulus for the Zionist Movement has been removed. . . . Nothing can be more superficial, and nothing can be more wrong, than that. We have never built our Zionist movement on the sufferings of our people in Russia or elsewhere. Those sufferings were never the cause of Zionism. The fundamental cause of Zionism was, and is, the ineradicable national striving of Jewry to have a home of its own—a national center, a national home with a national Jewish life.

526 |

This brought Weizmann to his next essential point: what were the hopes of Zionists at this moment and how did they think those hopes would be realized? He began with an important disclaimer. "One reads constantly in the Press," he said, "and one hears from our friends, both Jewish and non-Jewish, that it is the endeavor of the Zionist Movement immediately to create a Jewish State in Palestine." Weizmann knew that this was a bit of overeagerness that had to be carefully held in check among a friendly but uninformed public—which was why the *Zionist Review* had taken for its masthead slogan the essential formula of the old Basel Program: "The aim of Zionism is to create for the Jewish people a home in Palestine secured by public law." "Strong as the Zionist Movement may be," he now told his audience,

> full of enthusiasm as the Zionists may be, at the present time, it must be obvious to everybody who stands in the midst of the work of the Zionist Organization, and it must be admitted honestly and truly, that the conditions are not yet ripe for the setting up of a State *ad hoc*. States must be built up slowly, gradually, systematically and patiently. We, therefore, say that while a creation of a Jewish Commonwealth in Palestine is our final ideal—an ideal for which the whole of the Zionist organization is working—the way to achieve it lies through a series of intermediary stages.

This led to the second part of the question: how Zionists thought their hopes would be realized. Weizmann did not hesitate to take the position that he, in contrast to his friends on the British Palestine Committee, had eschewed on the masthead of his new journal. "And one of those intermediary stages which I hope is going to come about as a result of this war," he went on,

> is that the fair country of Palestine will be protected by such a mighty and a just Power as Great Britain. Under the wing of this Power Jews will be able to develop, and to set up the administrative machinery which, while not interfering with the legitimate interests of the non-Jewish population, would enable us to carry out the Zionist scheme. I am entitled to state in this assembly that His Majesty's Government is ready to support our plans.

It is not at all clear where this entitlement came from, nor is it even clear whether the "plans" supported by the British Government are the broad Jewish nationalist ones or the specific aspirations for British control. Weizmann at any rate hastened to add that British Government support would be in conjunction with that of the Allied Powers. "Our friend, chief, and leader, Mr. Sokolow," he said, "who, owing to important Zionist duties, is prevented from attending this meeting, has been both in France and in Italy, and from both these Governments he has received assurances of full sympathy and full support." With regard to such a question of international concern as that of the Holy Places, for example, Weizmann spoke significantly of "assurances from the highest Catholic circles that they will view with favor the establishment of a Jewish national home in Palestine, and from their religious point of view they see no objection to it, and no reason why we should not be good neighbors."

Weizmann concluded his speech by turning to the internal conflicts within Jewry itself over Zionism. "Ladies and Gentlemen," he said,

> it is not only a matter of regret, but it is a matter of deep humiliation to every Jew that we cannot stand united in this great hour. . . . It is unfortunate that there still exists a small minority which disputes the very existence of the Jews as a nation.

But he hastened to add that

> if it comes to a plebiscite and a test, there can be no doubt on which side the majority of Jews will be found. And, ladies and gentlemen, I warn you that this test is bound to come—and come sooner, perhaps, than we think.

It was, in fact, coming so soon that one might suppose Weizmann had inside information: for the leaders of the Conjoint Foreign Committee (CFC) had already written a letter to the editor of *The Times* that was to explode in its pages like a bombshell just four days after this speech. In March, Lucien Wolf had made a final attempt to resume the discussions with the Zionist leadership that had broken off the previous fall, writing a letter to this effect to Sokolow. But Sokolow's reply was to repeat the Basel Program slogan as a nonnegotiable basis for the discussions, and Wolf had replied declaring all efforts to resume them to be at an end. During April there had been a strange—in retrospect, ominous—quiescence from the bastions of Anglo-Jewish anti-Zionism, their only manifestation of any note that month being a critical historical study, "The Jewish National Movement," published by Wolf in the April *Edinburgh Review*. Early in May, there even had been an attempt on the part of some of the Zionists who held positions in the Board of Deputies of British Jews and the Anglo-Jewish Association to introduce resolutions either favoring Zionist aims or vowing nonintervention in the case of failure to agree with them. This was simply ignored by David L. Alexander, the Board of Deputies president, and Claude Montefiore, the Anglo-Jewish Association president, who, in their capacities as chairmen of the CFC, were the signatories of the letter sent to *The Times* on May 17.

"In view of the statements and discussions lately published in the newspapers relative to a projected Jewish resettlement in Palestine on a national basis," began the letter, which appeared in *The Times* on May 24, "the Conjoint Foreign Committee of the Board of Deputies of British Jews and the Anglo-Jewish Association deem it necessary to place on record the views they hold on this important question." The writers—who doubtless included Lucien Wolf, even though he was not one of the signatories—then proceeded to give a summary of the special place that, in their view, the Holy Land had always had for Jews. Since their emancipation, Jews "have made the rehabilitation of the Jewish community in the Holy Land one of their chief cares, and they have always cherished the hope that the result of their labors would be the regeneration on Palestinian soil of a Jewish community worthy of the great memories of their environment, and a source of spiritual inspiration to the whole of Jewry." For this reason, the committee "have welcomed with deep satisfaction the prospect of a rich fruition of this work, opened to them by the victorious progress of the British Army in Palestine."

The letter then went on to stress that, for the reasons given, the committee had long shown readiness to support the "cultural" policies of the Zionist organization, aimed at making Palestine a "Jewish spiritual center." As for "larger political questions, not directly affecting the main purpose," these could have been left "to be solved as need and opportunity might render possible." But now, "an agreement on these lines has not proved practicable, and the conjoint committee are consequently compelled to pursue their work alone. They are doing so on the basis of a formula adopted by them in March, 1916."

The "formula" was then described—without, of course, the more Zionistically inclined amendment that Lord Crewe had added to it unbeknownst to its author. "That is still the policy of the conjoint committee," the letter went on solemnly, its authors unaware of the ways in which that policy had become compromised and even superseded in the very quarters for which it had been intended.

"Meanwhile," the letter went on, "the committee have learnt from the published statements of the Zionist leaders in this country that they now favor a much larger scheme of an essentially political character." It was two points in particular of this scheme that the committee regarded as "open to grave objections on public grounds." The first was the "claim that the Jewish settlements in Palestine shall be recognized as possessing a national character in a political sense." In response to this, Claude Montefiore's well-known and long-established arguments were spelled out once again. "Emancipated Jews in this country regard themselves primarily as a religious community," the writers maintained. "They hold Judaism to be a religious system, with which their political status has no concern, and they maintain that, as citizens of the countries in which they live, they are fully and sincerely identified with the national spirit and interests of those countries." The letter also reiterated the significant argument that had been brought up to the Zionists by the committee as far back as April 1915: "The Jewish religion being the only certain test of a Jew, a Jewish nationality must be founded on, and limited by, the religion." But this would mean either "a commonwealth governed by religious tests, and limited in the matter of freedom of conscience," or "a secular Jewish nationality, recruited on some loose and obscure principle of race and ethnographic peculiarity," which, the writers argued, "would not be Jewish in any spiritual sense." This was ever to remain a vexing aspect of the problem.

The second point in the Zionist scheme to which the committee strongly objected was "the proposal to invest the Jewish settlers in Palestine with certain special rights in excess of those enjoyed by the rest of the population, these rights to be embodied in a Charter and administered by a Jewish Chartered Company." The writers thought that this "would prove a veritable calamity for the whole Jewish people." In various countries of the world Jews were still struggling for equal rights, and if they were "to set an example in Palestine of disregarding this principle" they would find themselves "hopelessly compromised" in these struggles. "The proposal is the more inadmissible," the letter went on, "because the Jews are, and will probably long remain, a minority of the population of Palestine, and because it might involve them in the bitterest feuds with their neighbors of other races and religions, which would seriously retard their progress, and would find deplorable echoes throughout the Orient." This touched another chord that was to resound harshly through the decades to come, but the writers resolved it with a note of liberal optimism: "If the Jews prevail in a competition based on perfect equality of rights and opportunity," they wrote, "they will establish their eventual preponderance in the land on a far sounder foundation than any that can be secured by privileges and monopolies." The letter concluded that the CFC would still be prepared to cooperate with the Zionists could any satisfaction be achieved regarding these points.

"A Grave Betrayal," the *Jewish Chronicle* entitled its leader on the Conjoint Foreign Committee letter in its issue coming out the next day; and this was only the beginning. In the next few days, *The Times* was flooded with more letters of protest than it had room for; but the ones it printed resounded all the more as a result. "I do not propose," wrote the chief rabbi of the British Empire, Dr. J.H. Hertz,

> to advance any arguments contesting the extraordinary statement on Zionism and Palestine which you published on Thursday last, signed by Mr. D.L. Alexander, K.C., and Mr. Claude G. Montefiore. But, as Chief Rabbi of the United Hebrew Congregations of the British Empire, I cannot allow your readers to remain under the misconception that the said statement represents in the least the views held either by Anglo-Jewry as a whole or by the Jewries of the Oversea Dominions.

Moses Gaster completed the stance of the headship of the British rabbinate with a letter of protest of his own, leaving only the lay leadership of English Jewry to add its voice to the protests coming from the highest positions in the community. Lord Rothschild filled this gap with a letter sent first to Chaim Weizmann for approval and editing, and published in *The Times* on May 28. "I consider it most unfortunate," wrote Lord Rothschild,

> that this controversy should be raised at the present time, and the members of the Zionist organization are the last people desirous of raising it. Our opponents, although a mere fraction of the Jewish opinion of the world, seek to interfere in the wishes

and aspirations of by far the larger mass of the Jewish people. We Zionists cannot see how the establishment of an autonomous Jewish State under the aegis and protection of one of the Allied Powers can be considered for a moment to be in any way subversive to the position or loyalty of the very large part of the Jewish people who have identified themselves thoroughly with the citizenship of the countries in which they live.

This surely reached the largest audience ever to have heard the second Lord Rothschild say "*we* Zionists," and his letter more than any other must have shown the leaders of the CFC what an utter miscalculation they had made. The prewar social and ideological balance upon which they had based their assumptions was gone, just as the first Lord Rothschild was gone, and the world they now had to face was one in which it was suddenly and dramatically clear that they were no longer English Jewry's preponderant voice.

"It may possibly be inconvenient to certain individual Jews that the Jews constitute a nationality," said Chaim Weizmann, in his own letter published in *The Times* on the twenty-eighth. "Whether the Jews do constitute a nationality is, however, not a matter to be decided by the convenience of this or that individual. It is strictly a question of fact." And he concluded with an expression of regret "that there should be even two Jews who think it their duty to exert such influence as they may command against the realization of a hope which has sustained the Jewish nation through 2000 years of exile, persecution and temptation."

Weizmann had not only British Jewry on his side in the main but also the most influential portions of the British press—whose ranks now were joined by *The Times* itself, with a leader on "The Future of the Jews" that appeared on May 29. Until that moment, *The Times*—occasionally criticized during the war by the Anglo-Jewish press for indelicate remarks about Jews—had never shown any particular interest in Zionism or the Jewish question. But its editor, Geoffrey Dawson, was a member of the *Round Table* group, which favored Zionism, and its foreign editor, H. Wickham Steed, was more than that. As the *Times* correspondent in Vienna from 1902 to 1913, Steed had had considerable opportunity to see the workings of the Jewish question in one of its more sensitive world centers and had become—on grounds as negatively disposed toward the behavior of the assimilationist Jewish middle classes of Vienna as Herzl's had been—a firm believer in the Zionist solution.

Steed had remained silent in the pages of *The Times* over this question until now, but it was he who contributed the May 29 leader under the provocation offered by the CFC. "The important controversy," he wrote,

> which has sprung up in our columns upon the future of the Jews deserves careful and sympathetic attention. The war has given prominence to many questions that seemed formerly to lie outside the range of practical politics. None of them is more interesting than that of the bearing of Zionism—that is to say, of the resettlement of a Jewish nationality in Palestine—upon the future of the Jewish people.

After summing up the contents of the committee's letter, Steed went on to observe:

> It seems to us that in attempting to define Jewish nationality in terms of religion the Committee come dangerously near to begging the question which they raise; and no question can be solved by begging it. As Dr. Weizmann, the President of the English Zionist Federation, observes in the letter which we published yesterday, it may possibly be inconvenient to certain individual Jews that the Jews do constitute a nationality. The question is one of fact, not of argument.

Alluding to the letters of Chief Rabbi Hertz and of Lord Rothschild as well as that of Weizmann, Steed observed:

> Authoritative declarations such as these dispose of the contention that Zionism is not representative of Jewish aspirations. We believe it in fact to embody the feelings of the great bulk of Jewry everywhere.

Steed added his own endorsement to these Jewish feelings.

The Conjoint Foreign Committee's position finally won significant support in the pages of *The Times* on June 1, when a letter written two days before appeared over the signatures of eighteen prominent Jews, including the second Lord Swaythling and Sir Matthew Nathan—Sir Frederick's brother—who had been under-secretary for Ireland until the uprising of 1916. But by then it was too late to prevent damage to the committee. In the days immediately following publication of its controversial letter, there had been three resignations from the committee, and there soon were protests throughout the country from constituent congregations of the Board of Deputies. These led to a special meeting of the board on June 17, in which declarations were passed repudiating the CFC letter and expressing loss of confidence in the committee itself. The committee's days were numbered; furthermore, in the next few days, D.L. Alexander was to resign the presidency of the Board of Deputies, to be replaced by Sir Stuart Samuel, Herbert's brother and not an enemy of Zionism. One of two new vice-presidents was to be Lord Rothschild. Ironically, his uncle Leopold, one of the stalwarts of the CFC and of its opposition to Zionism, had died during the height of the controversy on May 29, at seventy-one years of age.

June 17, the day of the crucial Board of Deputies meeting, was the one on which Nahum Sokolow had finally come back to England, carrying with him the most dramatic result to date of his extended sojourn on the Continent. Sokolow had remained in contact with French government officials his whole time in Rome and had kept them informed of his activities. Evidently satisfied with the results, they had summoned him back to Paris late in May, and on the twenty-fifth he was received for the first time by Prime Minister Ribot. Later that same day he had a long and friendly conversation with Jules Cambon. In both these conversations, he again received firm assurances of French support for Zionist aims, but now he pressed for a statement in writing. That finally came on June 4, in the form of a letter to him from Jules Cambon. "You were good enough," it ran,

> to present the project to which you are devoting your efforts, which has for its object the development of Jewish colonization in Palestine. You consider that, circumstances permitting, and the independence of the Holy Places being safeguarded on the other hand, it would be a deed of justice and of reparation to assist, by the protection of the Allied Powers, in the renaissance of the Jewish nationality in that Land from which the people of Israel were exiled so many centuries ago.
> The French Government, which entered this present war to defend a people wrongfully attacked, and which continues the struggle to assure the victory of right over might, can not but feel sympathy for your cause, the triumph of which is bound up with that of the Allies.
> I am happy to give you herewith such assurance.

It was a milestone—indeed, the most important one in the history of the wartime Zionist effort so far, exceeding in concreteness anything the British had yet done.

One would expect Sokolow to have rushed right back to London with this prize document in his briefcase. But there is a small mystery in the story at this point, for it was nearly two weeks before Sokolow returned to England. There is no evidence as to what his activities or even his whereabouts were during that interval, but it cannot be irrelevant that a highly important gathering took place in Petrograd at the time—the first all-Russian Zionist Congress since the revolution—and that for several weeks it had been anticipated that Sokolow would attend. The concern was growing in Britain as well as in France that pacifist sentiment from the extreme Left was threatening to take over in revolutionary Russia, and it was widely believed that the Jewish presence was significant in it. It was furthermore supposed—quite mistakenly—that Zionism was a crucial sentiment among Jews of the far Left and that a display of sympathy with the Jewish national cause by Britain and France would encourage them to support the Entente cause. In April, Leopold Greenberg had sent a memorandum to the Foreign Office expounding this view and quoting Jabotinsky in support of it. Lord Robert Cecil had even wired Buchanan in Petrograd asking his view of the matter, but the British ambassador had replied that he found "no great enthusiasm for Zionism among Jews in Russia." Word of this reply got to Sykes in Cairo, and he sent a long telegram on April 28, firmly opposing Buchanan's evaluation. By the beginning of June, then, the British Government hoped that Sokolow would go to the Zionist meeting in Russia as its representative.

"Tschlenow wires," Weizmann had cabled Sokolow in Rome on May 14, "all Russian Zionist Conference called Petrograd 6 June new style. Consider your presence there absolutely essential and authorities here share this opinion and will facilitate voyage. Cancel your appointments and leave straight for here. Matter most urgent." Sokolow had even wired back two days later:

> Shall go to Petrograd if authorities consider necessary although I am awfully exhausted. Canceling audience with His Majesty [King Victor Emmanuel III] at the Front. . . . Am leaving Saturday evening arrive Paris Monday. Must see French Government—am wiring prepare quick audience. Hope to arrive London in time. But considering difficulties please wire

Tschlenow urgently postpone meeting week later to be quite sure of my presence.

Weizmann had then cabled Tschlenow, who replied on about May 21 that the possibility of postponement was doubtful. Weizmann informed Sokolow of this, and again urged him to get back to London in advance of the congress. Sokolow went to Paris instead, and by the end of May Weizmann was thinking of sending another delegate—Boris Goldberg, who was not ready to go in time for the conference, but who did subsequently go to Russia as representative of the English Zionist Federation.

There seems to have been no thought that Sokolow might be able to go to Petrograd directly from Paris; yet on June 4, two days before the scheduled opening of the Petrograd congress, Cambon gave Sokolow not only his letter supporting Jewish nationalist aspirations in Palestine, but also one addressed to the French ambassador in Petrograd. After introducing Sokolow and mentioning the support his cause had already received in Paris, London, Rome, and Washington, the letter went on to say: "It is certain that Jewish influence can and should be exercised in Russia in favor of the Allies and for sustaining the forces of resistance on which the Provisional Government seeks to rely. The influence of M. Sokolow, which is considerable, will be used in this sense. I beg you to be good enough to advise M. Sokolow and to give him your support."

This naturally leads to the question: did Sokolow go to the congress after all? If he did so, he never was to tell Weizmann or his other colleagues in the Zionist leadership about it—but secretiveness was, after all, one of Sokolow's trademarks. There also is no sign, however, of his having told the Foreign Office. At the congress, which ran from June 6 to 13, a resolution was passed by the soldier delegates affirming their determination to keep fighting in the Allied cause—which was the main thing the British and French had wanted Sokolow to see to in Petrograd. Presumably the British authorities, and certainly Weizmann, had also wanted Sokolow to try to get a statement of support there for British suzerainty over Palestine; but there is no evidence that any such statement was made at the congress, although there was a reference to British sympathy with Zionist aspirations that was received with acclaim. Tschlenow, in a long address, spoke at greater length, however, about the United States, praising its president, its government, its Jews, and "former Ambassador Morgenthau, that faithful son of the Jewish people, whose services in these hard years Jewry will not forget."

Perhaps Sokolow was relieved at not having to press the British case at Petrograd, which he would have felt required to do had he gone back to London and then to the congress as expected. In any case, only two messages were received from him in London after June 4. One was a long communication on June 6, containing a message from him to be given to the Petrograd congress in his presumed absence. The other was a rather incoherent and uninformative note received by Weizmann on June 11, expressing regret at being unable to return right away on account of "circumstances independent of myself." Was this simply a delayed message, sent in advance of going to Petrograd after all? Quite possibly the whole thing was an arrangement made strictly between Sokolow and the French authorities: if he could go to Petrograd with a written statement of French support, he could certainly encourage the Zionists—who by now represented a clear majority of articulate Jewish opinion in Russia—to support the war. The British aspect would then have to have been deferred until Sokolow's return to London on June 17. But the whole matter must remain a mystery.

Just a little over a week before Sokolow arrived back in England, Arthur James Balfour returned. Balfour had been in the United States and Canada since the middle of April, revisiting them for the first time since his young manhood and now, as foreign secretary, appearing in the name of the grand Anglo-American alliance for world peace about which he had dreamed for years. While there, he saw the president several times, spoke to Congress, and also met Justice Brandeis. "You are one of the Americans I had wanted to meet," he said to Brandeis upon their being introduced at a Washington party just after his arrival. Even that first brief conversation must have touched upon Zionism, for Balfour's private secretary, Sir Eric Drummond, met with Brandeis to discuss this subject on April 24, only two days after the Balfour party had reached Washington.

"I met Mr. Brandeis," Drummond reported afterward, "who is the leader of the Zionist movement in the United States and who, it is stated, has great personal influence with the President, this morning. He was going to see the President with regard to the question of Palestine immediately, and wished to have a talk with me on the subject before doing so." Brandeis told Drummond that he was aiming for "equal rights and opportunities for Jews in Palestine combined with the maintenance of the autonomy which the present

Jewish local institutions enjoy there." This was a somewhat less nationalist formulation than Weizmann and other Zionist leaders were advocating; indeed, it was nothing stronger than the Conjoint Committee formula of March 1916. But, on the other hand, Brandeis proved to be quite in agreement with another point Weizmann had urged upon him by telegram only two days before. "He expressed a strong preference for a British protectorate over the country," Drummond reports, "as he had been most favorably impressed by our treatment of Egypt." Drummond let Brandeis know off the record that such an idea was a possible source of friction with the other Allies and that an international protectorate might therefore be necessary. Brandeis, who knew nothing of the Sykes-Picot Agreement— even President Wilson was only now about to learn of this and the other Allied secret agreements from Balfour in person—agreed with Drummond, "but obviously did not support this solution with any enthusiasm."

This was Drummond's chance to air one of the solutions Balfour had come to favor. "I then suggested to him that if jealousies between European Powers prevented Great Britain from becoming the protecting Power, the same disadvantage would not attach to the United States, and I asked him whether he thought a United States protectorate was a practical proposition." Brandeis proved "by no means averse to the idea, though he preferred the British alternative, but he urged that the present was not an auspicious time to ventilate such a proposition in the United States." He thought that majority opinion in the country was still opposed to war, and therefore would not welcome new obligations abroad. But he also thought "that after some months of war the position might change. He promised to keep the matter in mind." There was no need for him to remind Drummond that the United States was not even at war against Turkey, though the two countries had broken off diplomatic relations four days earlier.

Drummond left the conversation under the impression that Brandeis sought nothing more than equal rights and autonomy for Jews in Palestine. But whatever he actually had said, Brandeis was using the language of the Basel Program by the time he conferred with the president about the matter on Sunday, May 6. Wilson professed himself at that meeting to be "entirely sympathetic to the aims of the Zionist Movement," and "in agreement with the policy, under England's protectorate, for a Jewish Homeland." The president even said he would, at the proper time, make a statement for publication, but first he would "bear in mind the situation arising in France and would exercise his influence in that direction." These formulations suggest that he had discussed the matter with Balfour by now. At the end of the meeting Brandeis cabled James de Rothschild: "We approve your program and will do all we can to advance it. Not prudent for me to say anything for publication now. Keep us advised." Weizmann, who had hoped for an open statement from Brandeis in favor of a British Palestine, was regularly keeping him informed of developments in England.

The next day Brandeis and Balfour got together for the first of two meetings on the Palestine question. "I am a Zionist," Balfour told Brandeis that Monday, and he went on to make clear his admiration and affection for Chaim Weizmann. Balfour then stressed his own preference for an Anglo-American control, though he granted that this would run into French and Italian objections. Brandeis reiterated what he had told Drummond, that there could be at this time no question of American participation and that his own preference was for British control. In this and in the subsequent conversation between them on May 10, "Balfour was powerfully struck with the intellectual and moral distinction of Brandeis," according to the recollection of Felix Frankfurter, who was Brandeis's adviser on Zionist affairs at the time. "Shortly after the meeting between the two men, Lord Eustace Percy quoted Balfour as saying that not only was he impressed with the high moral tone of Brandeis on the Palestinian question, but that in many ways he was probably the most remarkable man he had met on his visit to the United States. Brandeis, on his side, was equally won by Balfour." At these discussions, they agreed that the time was not ripe for an open declaration about Palestine by either the United States or Great Britain. Any such statement from the British, they thought, would be "so qualified as to express less than their desires and intentions."

But this was before Balfour had learned of the Cambon letter and of other developments after his return home on June 9. Just three days earlier, Chaim Weizmann had presented Sir Ronald Graham with evidence of a new revival of German interest in Palestine and in Jewish aspirations there. On May 2, *Der Reichsbote*, a Berlin newspaper known for being an unofficial spokesman for the German government outlook, had printed an article by Gustav von Dobeler, a well-known right-wing publicist, entitled "A Jewish Republic in Palestine." "It cannot be denied," von Dobeler had written, according to the translation Weizmann handed Graham, "that a strengthening of the Turkish State through the influence of Jewish industry precisely on the ardently coveted bridge between Egypt and India, would only be of advantage to the Central Powers, and we ought not to be afraid of promoting such a development." The author, noting that Great Britain was "about to carry out the cleverest political move by the creation of a Jewish Republic," urged that "just as a prairie fire is extinguished by a counter-fire, so can we foil England's latest imperialistic scheme by anticipating her own intention." He ended by observing that "England in the possession of Palestine would signify the isolation of Central Europe, the keystone to [the late] King Edward's policy of encirclement which England will not give up even when she will soon have to regard the present War as lost. Therefore, let us meet the enemy!" The point was brought home to the public as well when the *Jewish Chronicle* printed its own translation of the article in its June 8 issue.

Weizmann called upon Graham again on Monday the eleventh, and two days later submitted to him a long letter summing up new information obtained by the Zionists regarding German overtures. Some six months earlier, Weizmann said, "a distinguished American Zionist" who had been traveling in Germany told him "that the German Government would view favorably attempts made by the Zionists of the world in favor of a peace propaganda." More recently, Weizmann had heard that Victor Jacobson, who had been the Zionist organization's chief representative in Constantinople until 1915 and was now with its bureau in Copenhagen had been approached by the German minister in Copenhagen about the possibility of peace negotiations being initiated by the Zionists. Jacobson had demanded that in such a case Germany would have to stand on the principle of no annexations or indemnities and on a promise to support Zionist claims in Palestine. Nothing more had yet been heard about this, Weizmann wrote, but he reported that recently there had been a spate of articles in the German and Austrian press on the idea of a Jewish Palestine. "It is a policy," Weizmann commented, "which is calculated to influence Jewish public opinion in America and in Russia which will be utilized by German propagandists in both countries against the Entente."

After giving some examples of the unease felt in Germany at the evidence of growing solidarity between Zionism and the Entente, Weizmann went on to spell out the many recent efforts made by Zionist organizations from New York to Moscow to add to that evidence. "In view of the position described above," Weizmann concluded,

I respectfully submit that it appears very desirable from every point of view that the British Government should give expression of its sympathy and support to the Zionist aims and should recognize the justice of the Jewish claims on Palestine, in fact it need only confirm the views which eminent representatives of the Government have many times expressed to us and which have formed the basis of our negotiations throughout the long period of almost three years. I was delighted to hear yesterday that you concur in this view.

Graham, the coauthor with Weizmann of this idea that a public statement by the British Government on Zionism and Palestine should now be sought, promised that he would submit this request "in the proper quarter." That same day, he wrote a long memorandum summing up Weizmann's letter in detail—indeed, closely paraphrasing it—and concluded with these observations of his own: "It would appear that in view of the sympathy towards the Zionist movement which has already been expressed by the Prime Minister, Mr. Balfour, Lord R. Cecil, and other statesmen, we are committed to support it, although until Zionist policy has been more clearly defined our support must be of a general character." Graham went on to stress once again the political advantages that would ensue from British support of Zionism, "especially in Russia, where the only means of reaching the Jewish proletariat is through Zionism to which the vast majority of Jews in that country adhere." As for the situation in England, he said, it was "not so clear, but the balance of Jewish opinion as recently expressed in the Press, appears to incline towards Zionism." Referring to the Jewish Board of Deputies conference of June 17, which was still forthcoming, he said one would be better able to judge after it, for it "may well see a complete defeat of the Conjoint Committee." Graham therefore proposed

that the moment has come when we might meet the wishes of the Zionists and give them an assurance that His Majesty's Government are in general sympathy with their aspirations. This might be done by a message from the Prime Minister or Mr. Balfour to be read out at a meeting, which could be arranged for any time. Such a step would be well justified by the international political results it would secure.

Balfour had returned to his desk at the Foreign Office just in time to ponder this proposal. But Sokolow had not yet returned to London with his note from Cambon, and Balfour was still filled with some of the reservations and preferences he had expressed during his American sojourn. "How can HMG [His Majesty's Government]," he minuted on Graham's memorandum, "announce their intention of 'protecting' Palestine without first consulting our Allies? And how can we begin to discuss dismembering the Turkish Empire before the Turks are beaten? Personally [I] should still prefer to interest the U.S.A. in the protectorate should we succeed in securing it."

Graham was able to apply a many-faceted response to these objections—to all, that is, but the one about the Turks not being beaten yet—by the following week. On Monday, June 18, he had seen Sokolow, freshly returned from Paris the day before with the Cambon letter in hand. He wrote a memorandum reporting on Sokolow's achievements in Paris and Rome, enclosing with it a copy of Cambon's letter, and then went on to describe the demise of the Conjoint Foreign Committee at the previous day's meeting of the Jewish Board of Deputies, enclosing a clipping of a *Times* news article describing the event. The next day, he minuted a response to the comment Balfour had made upon his memorandum of June 13. "I never meant to suggest," it said,

> that the question of the "Protection" should be raised at all. This would be most inopportune in view of French susceptibilities and the Zionists here, who are well aware of the delicate nature of the question, although desiring a British Protectorate, do not ask for any pronouncement on this head. All they ask for is a formal repetition, if possible in writing, of the general assurances of sympathy which they have already received from members of H.M. Government verbally. I only suggest that we should give something on the lines of the French assurance—which would satisfy them—and it is essential we should do so if we are to secure Zionist political support which is so important to us in Russia at the present moment.

Lord Robert Cecil read this and wrote: "I wanted to do this several weeks ago but was deterred by the advice of Sir G. Buchanan." When Balfour got it, he acquiesced, and was able to write later that same day: "I have asked Lord Rothschild and Professor Weizmann to submit a formula." Weizmann described what had happened in a letter he wrote the next day to Harry Sacher, who had just been elected Herbert Bentwich's successor as head of the Maccabaeans:

Lord Rothschild and myself saw Mr. Balfour yesterday and put it to him that the time has arrived for the British Government to give us a definite declaration of support and encouragement. Mr. Balfour promised to do so and he has asked me to submit to him a declaration which would be satisfactory to us which he would try and put before the War Cabinet for sanction. I therefore submit to you that you should draw up a document; I imagine it should be done on the following lines. That the British Government declares its conviction, its desire or its intention to support Zionist aims for the creation of a Jewish national home in Palestine; no reference must be made I think to the question of the Suzerain Power because that would land the British into difficulties with the French; it must be a Zionist declaration. Mr. Balfour expressed his opinion against a dual Anglo-French control and he would be rather in favor of an Anglo-American combination but he thinks that Mr. Lloyd George is strongly against it and the Americans do not favor it either. All this in strict confidence.

·39·

NEW BEGINNINGS IN
EGYPT AND ARABIA

In that season of return journeys, Sykes also had come back to London, on June 14. There had not really been much that he could accomplish in Egypt at this time. He had waited in frustration for Weizmann's arrival; then had decided to treat Aaronsohn as his chief Zionist representative in the occupation of Palestine. But there was not yet any occupation of Palestine to speak of, and during his stay in Egypt Sykes had decided not even to go to El Arish before Gaza was taken. In fact, he was soon to relinquish the post of chief political officer with the Egyptian Expeditionary Force. He had in the meantime worked on Arab affairs, visiting Hussein and his sons at various places along the Hejaz coast and appointing a committee of Arab nationalist representatives in Cairo to deliberate on political matters. Together with Picot, Sykes was able to persuade this committee to accept what were, in effect, the general outlines of the Asia Minor Agreement, as he had done with Hussein and his family, without making it explicit that such an agreement existed. "Further it was agreed by delegates," he wrote in his report, "that Palestine represented too many international problems for a new and weak State such as the Arab must be to assume responsibility for [that area?] but that in the event of Jews being recognized as a Millet or 'Nation' in Palestine they insisted that actual population must have equal recognition." There clearly was no mention of the possibility of a chartered company for the Zionists, but Sykes, who knew that such matters would only cause difficulty for the present, also remained firmly convinced that they would be worked out in the end. "Sir Mark believes," Aaronsohn observed of him right around this time, "that in the unity of Armenian, Jewish and Arab interests a great force can be created in the East."

For Sykes the great problem continued to be the conflict, not between Arab and Jewish claims, but between French and British ones. During this sojourn he had come into personal contact with the French Military Mission, commanded by Colonel Edouard Brémond, that had arrived late in 1916 and ensconced itself at Jeddah. Brémond, determined that France should be left out of none of the advances in the Middle East, continued to favor the project of an Allied landing at Rabegh that the British War Cabinet had shelved in December, and also was thought by some to be planning a French landing—made up of troops brought over from Salonika—somewhere on the Syrian coast. Brémond was one of that school of Frenchmen who regarded Picot as too generously disposed toward the British, and Sykes heartily disliked him. During his own itinerary along the Red Sea coast of Arabia in May, Sykes met the various proconsuls of the French Military Mission there, and in the process lost his once-tolerant view of France's role in the Middle East. In a letter written from aboard ship to Sir Reginald Wingate, the high commissioner in Cairo, he said firmly: "The sooner the French military mission is removed from the Hejaz the better. The French officers are without exception anti-Arab, and only serve to promote dissension and intrigue. . . . They make no disguise that they desire Arab failure." Yet, according to Brémond's account written years later, both Hussein and Feisal had assured him at this very time that they were "grateful to France for her solicitude toward the Arabs."

But Sykes did not have to worry that the French were not disliked enough in the places that counted in Arabian affairs. For even as he left Egypt to return home, the Hejaz was witnessing the decisive emergence of the most remarkable of all the Englishmen to involve themselves in Arab affairs during this war, and a devout enemy of all French ambitions in the Middle East. Captain T.E. Lawrence had—as his new rank indicated—rapidly emerged into prominence since his first visit to Feisal in October 1916. Lawrence had returned to Cairo from that visit in November, expecting to resume his duties at the Arab Bureau, but in a few days Sir Gilbert Clayton—now a brigadier general—had ordered him back to the Hejaz. This enabled Lawrence to take part personally in the first major development in the Hejaz revolt since its outbreak the previous summer: the capture of Wejh, midway up the coast from Yenbo. This was achieved by Feisal's troops on January 23 with the aid of gunfire from British warships.

By the end of winter, then, the position in the Hejaz had become a peculiar one, as Lawrence was well aware. In Mecca, Hussein sat solidly ensconced as the king of the Hejaz—the title that had been agreed upon by the British and French after their negative response to his attempt in the fall to style himself king of the Arab countries. Feisal was in Wejh, some four hundred miles to the north, and between them, with their own respective troops, were Abdullah in the Wadi Ais and Ali still laying siege to Medina. "Out of every thousand square miles of Hejaz," Lawrence was to write, "nine hundred and ninety-nine were now free." All that remained in Turkish hands were the railway and its terminus, Medina: but was it worth the effort to try to take those now that they had become strategically ineffectual? Under English tutelage—first that of Captain H. Garland, a demolition expert, and then spectacularly under Lawrence—a guerrilla campaign was begun by the Hejaz troops against the railway: for the rest of their days in Arabia, the Turks were to be harassed by the disabling explosions of mines laid under tracks. Meanwhile, the possibility had opened up of waging an Arab war of movement outside the Hejaz itself.

The capture of Wejh had caused a number of hitherto undecided sheikhs to come round to supporting the Arab revolt, and among those to enter Feisal's tent one day was Auda abu Tayi, leader of the eastern Howeitat tribe. This "tall, strong figure, with a haggard face, passionate and tragic," as Lawrence describes him, who wore his beard and moustache "trimmed to a point in Howeitat style, with the lower jaw shaven underneath," was effectively in control of one of the major routes of the Arabian desert. The Wadi Sirhan extended in a great northwestward sweep from the Nefud—the stark border region dividing peninsular from continental Arabia—up to the vicinity of Amman, which was on a line just north of Jerusalem and one of the major stops on the Hejaz railway. Access to the Wadi Sirhan, now made possible by Auda's allegiance, meant the possibility of more than just new points of attack northward on the railway: it meant the possibility of a flanking assault upon the Turks in Palestine itself.

Lawrence has told posterity that it was he, while lying in his tent for ten days recovering from an attack of dysentery, who conceived the plan of taking the port of Aqaba, not from the sea as the Turks would have expected, but from the desert. Arab historians have sought to deny his claim and maintain that it was Auda who proposed the idea, and that Lawrence subsequently asked to join him on the expedition. At any rate, it was this campaign, begun on May 9, that was to bring Lawrence his first great experience as an English warrior of the desert and, in its wake, the beginnings of worldwide fame. The military historian Liddell Hart has compared the Lawrence of this undertaking to an Elizabethan privateer—for he did it entirely without consultation with the authorities in Cairo. For Lawrence, it was a pinnacle in his lifelong testing of his powers of endurance. Before the Wadi Sirhan could be reached, it was necessary to cross a stretch of desert known to the Bedouin as El Houl ("the Desolate") and Lawrence not only made this arduous passage without serious difficulty but even at one point, much to Auda's chagrin, turned back and went some distance to pick up a member of the party who had become separated from his camel. When he found himself at the edge of the Nefud, a magnet to English explorers right down to Miss Gertrude Bell, he wanted to make a detour into it, but Auda would not permit this. From Nebk, in the northern part of the Wadi Sirhan, Lawrence left Auda's force and rode up to the outskirts of Damascus on a mission he was to remain secretive about all his life and which seems to have involved making contact with Syrian Arab nationalist leaders.

Lawrence, wearing Arab clothes, was back at Nebk on June 16, and the march down to Aqaba began three days later. Proceeding in a steady southwestward line that took them through Bair and El Jefer and then across the railway tracks below Maan—where they blew up some bridges—Auda, Lawrence, and their companions won skirmish after skirmish with surprised Turkish forces. On July 4 they reached the Wadi Ithm gorge, which descended into Aqaba itself. Lawrence found many of the Turkish soldiers at desolate outposts above Aqaba "most happy to surrender, holding up their arms and crying 'Muslim, Muslim' as soon as they saw us." By this time, Auda's ranks had been swelled by the allegiance of other Arab tribes, so that the problem at each successive small garrison was not so much to defeat the Turks as to get them to surrender before they were slaughtered. As the Arabs rushed in to plunder at one garrison just before Aqaba itself, Lawrence noticed a forlorn "engineer in grey uniform, with red beard and puzzled blue eyes; and spoke to him in German. He was the well-borer, and knew no Turkish. Recent doings had amazed him, and he begged me to explain what we meant. I said that we were a rebellion of the Arabs against the

Turks. This, it took him time to appreciate. He wanted to know who was our leader. I said the Sherif of Mecca. He supposed he would be sent to Mecca. I said rather to Egypt. He inquired the price of sugar, and when I replied, 'cheap and plentiful,' he was glad.

"The loss of his belongings he took philosophically, but was sorry for the well, which a little work would have finished as his monument. He showed me where it was, with the pump only half-built. By pulling on the sludge bucket we drew enough delicious clear water to quench our thirsts. Then we raced through a driving sand-storm down to Akaba, four miles further, and splashed into the sea on July the sixth, just two months after setting out from Wejh."

Lawrence brought the news to headquarters himself. Riding camel-back with a party of eight across the Sinai Desert, he covered 150 miles in a day and a half, reaching the canal near Suez in the afternoon of July 8. In another day, he was in Cairo, urgently re-questing supplies for Aqaba and reporting to a new commander in chief—for the long anticipated replacement of Sir Archibald Murray had occurred. After mounting criticism against him, Murray had lost his credibility entirely when his misleading report of March 28 had been followed by the failure of the second battle of Gaza. The War Cabinet had been pondering the matter since then, and for a time Lloyd George had wanted to give the post to General Jan Christian Smuts, the great Boer leader, who had just conducted a campaign against the Germans in East Africa. But Smuts, who was familiar with the reluctance of Sir William Robertson to lend much support to the Middle Eastern sideshow, turned down the offer and was given a seat on the War Cabinet instead.

The next man turned to was General Sir Edmund Allenby, com-mander of the Third Army in France, who had distinguished himself at Arras in April. Allenby was not asked if he wanted the job. He was simply recalled from France, to his dismay, one day in early June, and did not discover the reason why until he had arrived in London. Deeply attached both to the Bible and to archaeology, he could not have been displeased by the assignment. He arrived in Cairo on June 28 and saw General Murray off a few days later.

A large, formidable man with a bald head and brush moustache whose nickname among those who had served under him was "the Bull," Allenby was a wholly new entity on the Cairo scene. "My word, he is a different man to Murray," noted Colonel Richard

Meinertzhagen, recently arrived in Cairo himself as a senior intelligence officer, in his diary:

> He looks the sort of man whose hopes rapidly crystallize into a determination which is bound to carry all before it. What is most satisfactory is that he means to become active at once and bring new life back into this Army. The Egyptian Expeditionary Force is already awakening from its lethargic sleep under Murray, and I am happy to say the G.H.Q. will shortly move into Palestine and be near troops instead of wallowing in the fleshpots of Cairo.

Within a week of his arrival, Allenby was inspecting the troops at the Palestine front, in advance of setting up his headquarters there permanently. Back in Cairo, he showed the tough side of his nature by demanding an accounting of what everyone was doing and sending home officers who seemed superfluous, and the considerate side of his nature when he gave orders permitting soldiers not in the field to wear trousers instead of breeches and boots—a relief in the summer heat of Egypt and the Sinai.

Lawrence, still wearing Arab dress, was taken in to see Allenby upon arriving in Cairo from Aqaba. "It was a comic interview," Lawrence writes, "for Allenby was physically large and confident, and morally so great that the comprehension of our littleness came slow to him. He sat in his chair looking at me—not straight, as his custom was, but sideways, puzzled. He was newly from France, where for years he had been a tooth of the great machine grinding the enemy. He was full of Western ideas of gun power and weight—the worst training for our war—but, as a cavalryman, was already half persuaded to throw up the new school, in this different world of Asia . . . ; yet he was hardly prepared for anything so odd as myself—a little bare-footed silk-shirted man offering to hobble the enemy by his preaching if given stores and arms and a fund of two hundred thousand sovereigns to convince and control his converts."

Lawrence records that Allenby, who listened and studied the map and said very little, was unable to "make out how much was genuine performer and how much charlatan." The new commander in chief was not nearly so imbued with the romance of the Arab revolt as the man in front of him, but one thing he could see clearly: with Lawrence and the Arabs at Aqaba, only some 130 miles across the desert from the British position just below Gaza, there now were two prongs to the assault on Palestine. Whatever the meaning of the Hejaz revolt was to prove to be, it was a Hejaz campaign no longer, but rather an important asset in his own field of operations.

At the end, Allenby thrust out his chin and said: "Well, I will do for you what I can."

Lawrence was not perfectly sure what to make of this. But in time, he adds, "we learned gradually that he meant exactly what he said; and that what General Allenby could do was enough for his very greediest servant."

·40·

AFTER AN INTERMEZZO,
A DRAFT DECLARATION

I n his letter of June 20 to Harry Sacher describing how Balfour asked for a draft declaration on Palestine to submit to
the War Cabinet, Weizmann had suggested that Sacher prepare the
document. No doubt Weizmann expected to be close at hand for the
revising and correcting of the text, as Sokolow was to be; but when
the moment arrived, he was not. By the end of June, he had left
England and was on his way to Gibraltar to perform an unusual
diplomatic task assigned him by Balfour. What occurred in the next
few days—an unlikely but oddly diverting break from the intense
round of political and scientific activity that his life in London had
become—was to be characterized by him in his autobiography as an
"opera bouffe intermezzo."

The episode had its beginnings in Washington on May 16, when
former Ambassador Henry Morgenthau approached Secretary of
State Robert Lansing with a plan for negotiating a separate peace
between Turkey and the Allied Powers. The United States, although
it had broken diplomatic relations with Turkey, had not entered the
war against that country and had no intention of doing so; indeed, it
had not yet even declared war upon Austria. The idea of removing
both Turkey and Austria from the war by diplomatic means still had
currency in Washington and had even been mentioned by Colonel
House to Balfour a few days earlier. Balfour had acquiesced in
House's suggestion that "certain concessions should be made to
them" were Turkey and Austria to agree to a separate peace; and the
spirit of this exchange may have reached Morgenthau, who had
not lost a certain fondness for Turkey and the feeling that it had
simply been duped by pro-German elements. Morgenthau's plan was
to meet personally in Switzerland with representatives of Talaat

Pasha, the most diffident toward Germany of the Turkish ruling clique, and try to arrive at peace terms that would appeal even to Talaat's more pro-German colleagues.

Lansing obtained President Wilson's consent to his project, and the British Foreign Office was then informed of it. Had Sykes been in London, he would have opposed the project vehemently. But he was still in Egypt, and there was at this time a resurgence of the antique pro-Turkish feeling at the Foreign Office. It was led by Sir Louis Mallet, who had been the ambassador to Constantinople until November 1914. Even in the country at large there were distinct stirrings in favor of now seeking a separate peace with Turkey. The view arrived at was that Morgenthau's mission was not likely to accomplish anything, but that it was worth a try. The prospect that Morgenthau would surely have to concede most or all of prewar Ottoman Asia, thereby abandoning the entire course of British foreign policy for the past two and a half years, does not seem to have been given much thought. The only reservation expressed by the Foreign Office was at the choice of Switzerland as a venue, and it proposed Egypt instead; with that qualification, it gave its consent.

Morgenthau knew that Zionists, particularly in Great Britain, were not likely to be happy about his plan, but this was not the first time he had proposed to take the future of Palestine into his own hands. Perhaps he still thought it could be bought from the Turks once peace had been made. Nevertheless, he knew he would have to reckon with the Zionists, who, he wrote to Lansing, "under the leadership of Brandeis, Dr. Wise and others think that the future of Palestine is primarily their concern." It was apparently out of a desire to pacify them that Morgenthau asked that Felix Frankfurter go along with him as a member of the mission. But another factor to be considered was the necessary camouflage for the mission, which was eventually presented to the public as, in the words of *The New York Times*, "an effort to ameliorate the condition of the Jewish communities of Palestine"—one of Morgenthau's well-established charitable pursuits. By the time Morgenthau sailed on June 21, his entourage included not only Frankfurter and Morgenthau's assistant, Max Lowenthal, but also Eliahu Lewin-Epstein, a prominent New York Zionist.

By that time Chaim Weizmann had got wind of Morgenthau's project. He first heard about it from two disparate sources. One was Brandeis, who, never happy with Morgenthau's idea and only grudgingly acquiescent in Frankfurter's participation in the mission—as Weizmann was to understand it, he was going along "to keep an eye on things"—had sent Weizmann a telegram alerting him to "an American commission" but not saying much more. The other source was the ubiquitous James Malcolm. Early in June, while making his preparations, Morgenthau had learned of the presence in Switzerland of Arshag Shmarvonian, an Armenian who had been a legal adviser to the American embassy in Constantinople, and had asked this ideal "intermediary" with the Turks to join the mission when it got to Europe. Shmarvonian certainly was the original, if not necessarily the immediate, source of the information reaching Malcolm, who recognized the danger Morgenthau's plan represented both to Zionism and to Armenian national aspirations. On June 9, Weizmann and Malcolm brought their complaints about it separately to Sir Ronald Graham, and the next day they went together to William Ormsby-Gore, the former intelligence officer in Egypt who had befriended Aaronsohn and who was now an assistant secretary to the War Cabinet, specializing in Middle Eastern affairs.

In the course of the conversation with Ormsby-Gore, Weizmann—who was under the mistaken impression that a certain prominent group of pro-Turkish Londoners, including a Jewish anti-Zionist named Sir Adam Samuel Block, was being sent to join Morgenthau—urged that "if any Jew is to be sent to meet Mr. Morgenthau, that he, Dr. Weizmann, be sent rather than Adam Block." This suggestion seems to have quickly made its way across the Atlantic, for two days later the Foreign Office received word from Washington that Weizmann was going to be asked to join the Morgenthau mission when it arrived in Europe. The request must have originated with Morgenthau, who no doubt thought he could win from Weizmann the same kind of grudging acquiescence he had obtained from Brandeis and Frankfurter. But Weizmann had made a point of getting Graham to reiterate that it was "axiomatic that no arrangements with Turkey can be arrived at unless Armenia, Syria and Arabia are detached."

By the time he sailed, Morgenthau had made plans to meet with representatives of the French and British governments at Gibraltar in order to coordinate his policies with theirs before moving on to Switzerland or Egypt. No doubt he expected appropriate personages of high Government status, such as Sir Louis Mallet, to be present along with men like Weizmann; but in this he was doomed to be disappointed. As early as June 15, Balfour—now back at the Foreign Office and becoming aware of the can of worms he had perhaps inadvertently helped to open—suggested that there might be no reason to send anyone but Weizmann. But as late as June 26, five days after

Morgenthau and his colleagues had sailed, Weizmann still did not know that he alone had been selected, though he already expected to go to Gibraltar as part of a group. On that day he wrote to C.P. Scott of his own conviction that Sykes, just back from Egypt, should be the British representative. "One would feel absolutely safe with Sir Mark in Gibraltar," he said, "and I am not saying this only from the Jewish point of view but from the British, and I think that if Lloyd George's attention is drawn to this fact, as he may know very little about the whole thing, he would probably insist on Sir Mark's going to Gibraltar and would also get the support of Mr. Balfour." The next day Balfour called in Weizmann and asked him, alone, to be the British representative at Gibraltar.

There were signs that His Majesty's Government was no longer taking the Morgenthau mission seriously. As for Weizmann, he may have begun to sense a summer holiday atmosphere when he found himself departing for Southampton on the afternoon of June 29 in the company of Kennerly Rumford, a well-known singer who now was an intelligence officer and had been assigned to accompany him. Rumford was "a delightful companion," Weizmann found, "though somewhat unsuited for a secret mission. We traveled through France to Spain," his account continues, "and at Irun were met by a lady intelligence officer and conducted to San Sebastian. The lady was very smart, and exceedingly well dressed; she arrived in a big luxury car. From that point on we moved, as it were, with a cortege of German spies. Rumford, though in mufti, looked every inch a British officer; and his methods of preserving secrecy were not exactly subtle. At San Sebastian we took two sleeping compartments for Madrid, and bought up the adjacent compartments on either side. An instant before we started a man boarded the train and claimed loudly and insistently that he had a prior reservation on one of the adjacent compartments. Rumford, losing his patience in the ensuing argument, finally drew a revolver and brandished it in the face of the intruder who, probably unaccustomed to such public demonstrations on the part of a secret-service agent, hastily withdrew."

After a stopover in Madrid, where Weizmann met with the venerable Max Nordau, the unlikely entourage reached Gibraltar on July 3. The Morgenthau group arrived at Cadiz at around the same time, and was in Gibraltar on the fourth. The French representative also arrived that day: it was a Colonel E. Weyl, who had for many years been head of the Turkish tobacco monopoly and was now a member of the French Ministry of Munitions. Evidently a Jew but not a Zionist, Weyl had received no instructions from his government. The nature of its representation suggests that the French government was taking the Morgenthau mission no more seriously than the British, although Weyl gave Weizmann the impression that the French were most eager to conclude a separate peace with Turkey.

The discussions began on Wednesday, July 4, and took up all of that and the following day. "It was midsummer," Weizmann was to recall, "and very hot. We had been given one of the casements in the Rock for our sessions, and the windows were kept open. As Mr. Morgenthau did not speak French, and Colonel Weyl did not speak English, we had to fall back on German. And the Tommies on guard marched up and down outside, no doubt convinced that we were a pack of spies who had been lured into a trap, to be court-martialed the next morning and shot out of hand."

Morgenthau began with an exposition of the present situation in Turkey, in which he was assisted by Shmarvonian, who had been in that country until May 29 and was abreast of developments there. Shmarvonian told of Turkish military weaknesses in troops and supplies, of shortages at home, and of near bankruptcy in the country's finances. He also described the deteriorating relations between Turks and Germans and the growing friction between Talaat and the pro-German Enver Pasha. These were some of the reasons, the members of the mission stressed, why President Wilson had agreed to send them to try and detach Turkey from the Central Powers. They were satisfactory as far as Weizmann was concerned, but, he reported, they were "the only real facts which Mr. Morgenthau was able to communicate to us."

Morgenthau then was asked to present his plans, whereupon, according to Weizmann, "he became very vague, and no amount of discussion and question could elucidate any definite plan or program." Weizmann asked him two questions:

1) "Does he think that the time has come for the American Government, or for the Allies through the American Government, to open up negotiations of such a nature with the Turkish authorities? In other words, whether he thinks that Turkey realizes sufficiently that she is beaten or likely to lose the war, and is therefore in a frame of mind to lend itself to negotiations of that nature?"

2) "Assuming that the time is ripe for such overtures, has he (Mr. Morgenthau) a clear idea about the conditions under which the Turks would be prepared to detach themselves from their present masters?"

Weizmann found it "utterly impossible for us to obtain a definite answer," and records that Morgenthau finally acknowledged that he was "not justified in saying that the time has arrived to negotiate with Turkey." As for conditions, Morgenthau said he had none yet, but when Weizmann gave it as the British position that Armenia, Mesopotamia, Syria, and Palestine had to be detached from the Ottoman Empire, Morgenthau and everyone else present agreed that the Turks would not accept such conditions at the present time.

During the course of the discussions, Weizmann asked Morgenthau "several times why he has tried to enlist the support of the Zionists in his mission. Here again no clear answer was forthcoming, and it was therefore found necessary to clearly state to Mr. Morgenthau that on no account should the Zionist organization be compromised by his negotiations, if such negotiations will be acceded to by the respective Governments: that on no account must the Zionist organization be in any way identified or mixed up even with the faintest attempts to secure a separate peace: that all these negotiations, if ever they are started, must be conducted entirely on behalf of the Governments, and if these Governments should think that the Zionist organization might prove of some use, then it is up to them to say so, but it is not for the organization to take any initiative in a matter like that: that we Zionists feel about this point most strongly, and we would like assurances from Mr. Morgenthau that he agrees and understands this position. This assurance was given."

Morgenthau, who was meeting Weizmann for the first time, perhaps had never had the law laid down for him quite so firmly by a Zionist before. He got the point, and after a brief sojourn in Paris, during which he was informed by a State Department wire that he was not authorized to negotiate for a separate peace with Turkey after all, he was on his way home without the mission having been carried out. His feelings toward Weizmann and toward Zionism were never again to be as friendly as they once had been.

Weizmann, who went on to Paris for a rest and perhaps also to keep an eye on the waning Morgenthau mission, was not to return to London for another two weeks. In the meantime, the drafting of a declaration on Zionism for the British Government proceeded with a swiftness he doubtless had not anticipated. Sacher had begun the process on June 22, when he sent out a draft to several colleagues. It began: "The British Government declares that one of its essential war aims is the reconstitution of Palestine as a Jewish State and as the National Home of the Jewish people." With characteristic eagerness Sacher had gone beyond the Basel Program, and beyond the general lines suggested by Weizmann in his letter of June 20, in two ways: in his specific mention of a Jewish state and in his formulation of Palestine "*as the* National Home" rather than of *a* national home *in* Palestine. These were indeed the ultimate aims of most Zionists; but a state, at least, was not one of the immediate ones sought by the Zionist leadership, and Sokolow in particular perceived it as a troublesome point to raise. On July 5, after Weizmann had gone to Gibraltar, Sokolow presented his own draft version to Sacher and to a group of colleagues that included Cowen and Ahad Ha'am and that soon was to constitute itself as the London Zionist Political Committee. In his version, Sokolow settled for British Government acceptance of "the principle of recognizing Palestine as the National Home of the Jewish People." Like Sacher, Sokolow went on to mention the Zionist organization, but unlike him he did not take up the matter of a chartered company.

"It is not here," Sokolow told Cowen in a letter of July 9, "a question of the 'demands,' which remain as they were. Our purpose ... is to receive from the Government a *general* short approval of the same kind as that which I have been successful in getting from the French Government." But on the same day, Sacher was writing a letter of protest. "I am persuaded," he told Sokolow, "that this matter is of the first importance and that my original idea of asking for as much as possible is the right one. I think my own draft erred in not going far enough, not in going too far." Sokolow replied the next day, pointing out that it was Lord Rothschild who was to present their formula to the Government as a suggestion "in a private way," and that their draft had to meet his approval among other things.* "A good deal of confusion arose with regard to this document," he went on:

---

* This procedure evidently was arrived at in the June 19 conversation between Balfour, Weizmann, and Lord Rothschild, in which Balfour asked for a draft declaration. From then on, it seems to have been understood that the British Government's declaration on Palestine, when and if it became a reality, would be presented in the form of a letter from the foreign secretary, not to a sectarian Zionist organization, but to the head of the foremost Jewish family in Great Britain.

It is not an agreement, neither is it a full program. Such agreement or program we may get from H.M. Government after having presented our demands, but before having handed it over we cannot claim anything in the form of a program. It has, therefore, been suggested that for the time being we should get a *general* approval of Zionist aims—very short and as pregnant as possible.

He concluded with a warning:

If we want too much we shall get nothing; on the other hand, if we get some sympathetic declaration, I hope we shall gradually get more and more.

Sacher was not persuaded, however, and the next day he responded with a new draft version that reiterated his basic opening formula and added: "The definite form of such reconstitution must be an integral Palestine which is a self-governing State." To buttress the point, Sacher enclosed with this draft a version offered by Sidebotham, which essentially repeated his own but added an explanation of what was meant by "A Jewish State": "not a State of which membership is restricted to Jews but a State whose dominant national character . . . will be Jewish in the same sense as the dominant national character of England is English, of Canada Canadian and of Australia Australian." It all had a Manchester sound, and one could say that what had arisen was a small controversy between Manchester and London Zionism. But London was to win.

Sokolow was, for one thing, in daily contact with the Foreign Office, where he and Sykes, assisted by Harold Nicolson, were going over each new draft version: this is the atmosphere conveyed by Sokolow with such phrases as "it has been suggested." For another thing, the London Zionist Political Committee, dominated by the moral authority of that lifelong critic of political Zionism, Ahad Ha'am, was entirely in sympathy with Sokolow's relatively modest though still firmly Zionist approach. Governed by all these factors, Sokolow finally came up on July 12 with a tentative draft to send to Lord Rothschild. It read in full:

His Majesty's Government, after considering the aims of the Zionist Organization, accepts the principle of recognizing Palestine as the National Home of the Jewish people and the right of the Jewish people to build up its national life in Palestine under a protection to be established at the conclusion of peace following upon the successful issue of the War.

His Majesty's Government regards as essential for the realization of this principle the grant of internal autonomy to the Jewish nationality in Palestine, freedom of immigration for Jews, and the establishment of a Jewish National Colonizing Corporation for the resettlement and economic development of the country.

The conditions and forms of the internal autonomy and a Charter for the Jewish National Colonizing Corporation should, in the view of His Majesty's Government, be elaborated in detail and determined with the representatives of the Zionist Organization.

This was sent to Lord Rothschild on the thirteenth with some explanatory comments and the proviso that it would have to be shown to Sir Mark Sykes and Sir Ronald Graham. In the sequel, it was evidently these men who told Sokolow that the draft was still too long and covered too much, and on July 17 he met with members of the Political Committee to do more cutting and revising. "It was feared," Sokolow wrote to Lord Rothschild after the meeting, that "the first declaration was too long and contained matters of detail which it would be undesirable to raise at the present moment. It was thought that the declaration should contain two principles, (1) the recognition of Palestine as the national home of the Jewish people, (2) the recognition of the Zionist Organization." The new version was enclosed. It ran:

1. His Majesty's Government accepts the principle that Palestine should be reconstituted as the National Home of the Jewish people.
2. His Majesty's Government will use its best endeavors to secure the achievement of this object and will discuss the necessary methods and means with the Zionist Organization.

This was succinct indeed, and Lord Rothschild sent it on to Balfour with a covering letter of July 18:

Dear Mr. Balfour,

At last I am able to send you the formula you asked me for. If His Majesty's Government will send me a message on the lines of this formula, if they and you approve of it, I will hand it on to the Zionist Federation and also announce it at a meeting called for that purpose. I am sorry to say our opponents have commenced their campaign by a most reprehensible maneuver, namely to excite a disturbance by the cry of British Jews versus Foreign Jews. They commenced this last Sunday, when at the Board of Deputies they challenged the new elected officers as to whether they were all of British birth (myself among them).

Yours Sincerely
Rothschild

Balfour replied the very next day:

My dear Walter,
Many thanks for your letter of July 18th.
I will have the formula which you sent me carefully considered but the matter is of course of the highest importance and I fear it may be necessary to refer it to the Cabinet. I shall not therefore be able to let you have an answer as soon as I should otherwise have wished to do.

A.J. Balfour

There the matter was to rest for a few weeks.

·41·

THE DRAFT DECLARATION
AT THE WAR CABINET:
THE FIRST SALLY

B y the middle of August, Balfour had prepared a draft declaration that was, except for a modification in the second part
of the second clause, an almost verbatim reiteration of the Sokolow
version presented to him by Lord Rothschild on July 18. It was
couched in the form of a letter replying to Rothschild's, and it ran:

> Dear Lord Rothschild,
>   In reply to your letter of July 18th. I am glad to be in a
> position to inform you that His Majesty's Government accept *
> the principle that Palestine should be reconstituted as the na-
> tional home of the Jewish people.
>   His Majesty's Government will use their best endeavors to
> secure the achievement of this object and will be ready to con-
> sider any suggestions on the subject which the Zionist Organiza-
> tion may desire to lay before them.

The draft was initialed "A.J.B." and was undated; it waited only for
its moment to be brought before the War Cabinet, after which, if
approved, it would be sent to Lord Rothschild for publication.
    The prospects for approval seemed reasonably good. At this
time, the War Cabinet consisted of seven men, including the prime
minister himself. The others were Andrew Bonar Law, leader of the

---

* Grammarians will note with interest the differing views in the various drafts as to
whether "His Majesty's Government" is to be treated as plural or singular. Balfour
always preferred the plural, right down to the final version.

Conservatives; Lord Curzon; Lord Milner (all these were Lloyd George's original appointments in December); as well as George N. Barnes, replacing the outgoing Arthur Henderson as the Labour representative on the War Cabinet; Sir Edward Carson, the recent first lord of the Admiralty; and Jan Christian Smuts, who had been appointed after declining the Egyptian military command. Among the seven, the prevailing outlook was inclined to be in favor of Zionism. Lloyd George's feelings were well known among his colleagues; it was not yet known that General Smuts, the product of an intensely biblical Boer upbringing, was to emerge as much an enthusiast for Zionism as the prime minister was. Milner, Barnes, and Carson all proved warm supporters, though they had not yet done anything to advertise the fact. Only Bonar Law and Curzon were to display mixed feelings. But Balfour—who, though not a member of the War Cabinet, was, as foreign secretary, in frequent attendance at its sessions—could be counted on to give the ardent support for the declaration that was likely to put it through.

The most formidable opposition within governing circles at this moment arose, not within the War Cabinet, but from a man who had been appointed to the regular cabinet the day before Lord Rothschild's letter to Balfour containing the draft declaration. This was the new secretary of state for India, Edwin Montagu, now the only man in the Government who was of the Jewish faith. Herbert Samuel's first cousin and the younger son of that Samuel Montagu, later Baron Swaythling, who had briefly supported Herzl and then repudiated him, Edwin Montagu was a man of some gifts who had struggled hard with both his religious and his political loyalties. After beginning his parliamentary career as part of the Liberal landslide of 1906, he had soon found his way into Asquith's inner circle, and was the prime minister's private secretary for a number of years. In 1910 he served as parliamentary under-secretary of state for India, and became financial secretary to the Treasury in February 1914. After the outbreak of war, he had begun to hold cabinet posts, first as chancellor of the Duchy of Lancaster on two separate occasions and then as Lloyd George's successor at the Ministry of Munitions from July to December 1916. The political crisis of November-December 1916 placed a great strain upon his long and devoted relation to Asquith. Recognizing the strength of Lloyd George's position, Montagu for a time was the most ardent seeker of a compromise arrangement among Asquith's closest confidants—and there was no one in politics closer to Asquith during those arduous few days. In the end he was faced, as he is said to have put it, with a choice "between deserting a sinking ship and boarding one that would not float"—or so he thought. When Lloyd George formed his own Government, he invited Montagu to participate, but the latter had no choice but to refuse.

The ship floated, and, as Lloyd George's strength increased in the ensuing months, Montagu found himself torn again. At thirty-eight years of age he was coming to the peak of his powers, and despite his old loyalty to Asquith he was yearning to serve. He wrote this note to Lloyd George on March 28:

> *As the desert sand for rain,*
> *As the Londoner for sun,*
> *As the poor for potatoes,*
> *As a landlord for rent,*
> *As drosera rotundifolia for a fly,*
> *As Herbert Samuel for Palestine,*
> *As a woman in Waterloo Road for a soldier*
> I long for talk with you.

At the time of his India Office appointment, he wrote to Asquith of "the anguish which separation causes me and the terrible sense of duty which compelled me to come to the rescue of a weak Government, and the sorrow with which I have been forced to fight the temptation to talk it over with you." But Asquith replied: "In view of our past relations it is perhaps not unnatural that I should find it difficult to understand and still more to appreciate your reasons for the course which you tell me you propose to take."

It was not the first time that Montagu's burning personal desires had wounded Asquith. As far back as 1913 this tall, brooding man, then still a bachelor, had proposed marriage to Asquith's dear young friend Venetia Stanley. The beautiful youngest daughter of Lord Stanley of Alderley, Venetia, born in 1887, was the same age as Asquith's daughter Violet and a close friend of hers. The prime minister was fond of sharing political confidences with brilliant young women, and in 1913 Asquith began a correspondence with Miss Stanley that was to assume considerable historical importance. For, whereas the official records of the Asquith cabinet tend to be sporadic and inadequate, the prime minister's letters to Venetia Stanley—written as often as once or even twice a day by the beginning of 1915—have provided historians with a thorough record of what went on during the deliberations of his Government.

Montagu had often been present when Asquith and Miss Stanley were together, but there is little sign that she took him seriously as a suitor before 1915 and a good deal of indication that he was the butt of frequent humorous jibing between herself and the prime minister. In his letters to her, Asquith would refer to Montagu as "the Assyrian"—on one occasion, "fresh from Seville"—and to his house in Queen Anne's Gate as "the Silken Tent." The racial character of the humor is particularly ironic, since Miss Stanley doubtless had known from 1913 onward that any wife of Montagu's would have to be Jewish at least by conversion if he was to go on enjoying the substantial fortune Lord Swaythling had bequeathed, according to a stipulation in the latter's will. "Is it race or religion you care about," she asked him in the spring of 1915, after she had suddenly and surprisingly decided to accept, "or merely the label? If race, then you are debasing it by marrying me, whatever I do. Religion, you know I care nothing about and shan't attempt to bring up my children in. There only remains the label. And will that stick, do you think?" Edwin Montagu cared little about either race or religion and, after Venetia's conversion to the label, the couple was married on July 24, 1915. Asquith, who had been stunned to receive the news of their engagement two months earlier, sent two silver boxes to the bride "with all my love, and more wishes than words can frame for your complete and unbroken happiness." But there were few letters between them after that, and from the beginning of 1916, none at all for years to come.

If Montagu's Judaism meant little to him as race or religion, it meant absolute hostility where Zionism was concerned. As far back as March 1915, when he was chancellor of the Duchy of Lancaster, he had responded to Herbert Samuel's Palestine memorandum with a long letter to Asquith denouncing what he thought would be "a disastrous policy." In the summer of 1916, when he was minister of munitions, his views on Zionism were solicited by the Foreign Office, and he responded with a diatribe against Jewish nationalism, which he called "horrible and unpatriotic" and characterized as "pro-German." Even the views of the Conjoint Foreign Committee, which certainly inspired him somewhat, seem to have been too ethnocentric for him in some respects, for he wrote on this occasion: "I regard with perfect equanimity whatever treatment the Jews receive in Russia." With perhaps special reference to his cousin Herbert Samuel, he stressed that he would have resigned his cabinet post had he been a Jewish nationalist. "Nobody is entitled to occupy the position that I do unless he is free and determined to consider the interests of the British Empire." It comes as no surprise, then, that Montagu reacted with vehemence when, shortly after his appointment as secretary for India, he learned of the recent correspondence between Lord Rothschild and Balfour.

No doubt fully aware by now of the increasing inability of Anglo-Jewish assimilationism to penetrate into governing circles with its views, he decided—albeit without any background in this sort of thing—to appoint himself its representative. On August 23, he presented a lengthy memorandum entitled "The Anti-Semitism of the Present Government."

"I have chosen the above title for this memorandum," he began,

> not in any hostile sense, not by any means as quarreling with an anti-Semitic view which may be held by my colleagues, not with a desire to deny that anti-Semitism can be held by rational men, not even with a view to suggesting that the Government is deliberately anti-Semitic; but I wish to place on record my view that the policy of His Majesty's Government is anti-Semitic in result and will prove a rallying ground for Anti-Semites in every country in the world.
>
> This view is prompted by the receipt yesterday of a correspondence between Lord Rothschild and Mr. Balfour.

Montagu felt that "as the one Jewish minister in the Government" he might be allowed to respond to this. After several lines lamenting the death blow that internationalism had suffered as a result of the war, he got to his central point. "Zionism," he wrote,

> has always seemed to me to be a mischievous political creed, untenable by any patriotic citizen of the United Kingdom. If a Jewish Englishman sets his eyes on the Mount of Olives and longs for the day when he will shake British soil from his shoes and go back to agricultural pursuits in Palestine, he has always seemed to me to have acknowledged aims inconsistent with British citizenship and to have admitted that he is unfit for a share in public life in Great Britain, or to be treated as an Englishman.

He had hitherto always assumed, he went on, that Zionism was meant as one solution to the Jewish problem in Russia, yet even as

Jews there were now being "given all liberties," Mr. Balfour was about to endorse a declaration calling for the reconstitution of Palestine as the national home of the Jewish people. "I do not know what this involves," Montagu said,

> but I assume that it means that Mahommedans and Christians are to make way for the Jews, and that the Jews should be put in all positions of preference and should be peculiarly associated with Palestine in the same way that England is with the English or France with the French, that Turks and other Mahommedans in Palestine will be regarded as foreigners, just in the same way as Jews will hereafter be treated as foreigners in every country but Palestine. Perhaps also citizenship must be granted only as a result of a religious test.

Montagu then laid down four principles "with emphasis." The first was: "I assert that there is not a Jewish nation." Montagu mentioned his own family as an example—in England for generations and in his view no more of the same nation as Jews in other countries than were Christian Englishmen of the same nation as Christian Frenchmen. As for the vague ties of race, he indulged in a play of irony. "The Prime Minister" he said, "and M. Briand are, I suppose, related through the ages, one as a Welshman and the other as a Breton, but they certainly do not belong to the same nation."

The second principle was that

> when the Jews are told that Palestine is their national home, every country will immediately desire to get rid of its Jewish citizens, and you will find a population in Palestine driving out its present inhabitants, taking all the best in the country, drawn from all quarters of the globe, speaking every language on the face of the earth, and incapable of communicating with one another except by means of an interpreter.

Here Montagu had sounded some genuinely ominous notes, but compromised them with his apparent ignorance of the Hebrew revival. Resorting to irony again, he gave it as his understanding that the reuniting of the Jews as one people in Palestine

> would require Divine leadership. I have never heard it suggested, even by their most fervent admirers, that either Mr. Balfour or Lord Rothschild would prove to be the Messiah.

But after conceding the role of Palestine in a messianic era, Montagu went on as his next principle to deny that "Palestine is today associated with the Jews or properly to be regarded as a fit place for them to live in." It was at Sinai, he pointed out, that the Ten Commandments had been delivered, and if Palestine had subsequently played an important role in Jewish history, it had gone on to play such a role in Christian and Muslim history as well. His last principle was a suggestion that Gentile support for Zionism in England was based on anti-Semitism, on a desire to get rid of Jews and send them to Palestine, which would thereby become "the world's Ghetto."

After touching on a few more points, Montagu concluded with his belief

> that the Government are asked to be the instrument for carrying out the wishes of a Zionist organization largely run, as my information goes, at any rate in the past, by men of enemy descent or birth.

He then recommended that Lord Rothschild should be told

> that the Government will be prepared to do everything in their power to obtain for Jews in Palestine complete liberty of settlement and life on an equality with the inhabitants of that country who profess other religious beliefs. I would ask that the Government should go no further.

Even Lucien Wolf's formula had asked for more; but this was the proposal with which Montagu was prepared to go before the War Cabinet when the Palestine issue came up on its agenda.

One further matter that Montagu had raised in the final paragraphs of his memorandum was that of the proposed Jewish legion, which seemed about to become a reality at last. On July 28, *The Times* had carried this announcement, made by the War Office:

> Arrangements are now nearing completion for the formation of a Jewish regiment of infantry. Experienced British officers are being selected to fill the higher appointments in the unit, and instructions have already been issued with a view to the transfer to this unit of Jewish soldiers, with a knowledge of the Yiddish or Russian languages, who are now serving in British regiments.

It is proposed that the badge of the regiment shall consist of a representation of King David's shield.

Further information as to the conditions of enlistment and service will be issued shortly as soon as the necessary legal powers have been obtained.

This was the triumphant outcome of the campaign conducted by Vladimir Jabotinsky, about to graduate as a British army sergeant at Hazeley Down, but also a political spokesman who had made himself known to the leaders of the nation and had personally persuaded Lord Derby, the present secretary for war, of the validity of the Jewish legion idea. The idea seemed to make sense as a way of dealing with the problem of the Russian-Jewish aliens and military service in Britain. A form of compulsory military service for aliens had been put into law at last: an agreement had been signed with Russia promising the return of those of its subjects in Britain who did not enlist. An ideological as well as a practical incentive to enlist was being provided for them, it was felt, if they were put into units of their own, destined for the Palestine campaign. The idea also presented itself in principle as a just corollary to a declaration on Jewish national aspirations in Palestine, a counterpart not only to the existing troops of King Hussein, but also to an Arab legion that Sykes had begun proposing at Whitehall since his latest return from Egypt. The fact that Weizmann was entirely in favor of a Jewish regiment and that Sokolow had, in a reversal of his previous position, begun to support it as well, certainly had helped give force to Jabotinsky's claims in cabinet circles.

But there were forces among British Jewry opposed to the idea that were even more formidable than those opposed to Zionism; for this issue was more visceral and cut across Jewish class and political lines. Jews had been fighting and dying on all fronts since the beginning of the war; was their record now to be subsumed under the character and performance of a single unit marked "Jewish"? The head Jewish chaplain of the British armed forces, the Reverend Michael Adler, had vehemently opposed all talk of separate Jewish units since the fall of 1914, and he continued to do so. The fact that even *The Times* endorsed the Jewish regiment idea, emphatically saying so in a leader by Wickham Steed published on August 23, did not at all sway the partisans of this viewpoint. Indeed, at a superficial glance, the plan, as presented by the War Office announcement at the end of July, could easily have looked like nothing better than the kind of segregation into separate units that was being practiced upon Negroes by the United States Army. As for Edwin Montagu, he summed up the prevailing feeling aptly in his memorandum. "I am waiting to learn," he wrote sarcastically,

> that my brother, who has been wounded in the Naval Division, or my nephew, who is in the Grenadier Guards, will be forced by public opinion or by Army regulations to become an officer in a regiment which will be mainly composed of people who will not understand the only language which he speaks—English. I can well understand that when it was decided, and quite rightly, to force foreign Jews in this country to serve in the Army, it was difficult to put them in British regiments because of the language difficulty, but that was because they were foreigners, and not because they were Jews, and a Foreign Legion would seem to me to have been the right thing to establish. A Jewish Legion makes the position of Jews in other regiments more difficult and forces a nationality upon people who have nothing in common.

This view was shared, not merely by leaders of the Anglo-Jewish establishment, but by Jews who held high ranks in British Government and society—most notably, the lord chief justice, Lord Reading, who had never taken a stand against Zionism despite his mixed feelings about it, but who became one of the leaders of a group determined to oppose an explicitly *Jewish* regiment. The Russian embassy, under whose jurisdiction the Russian-Jewish aliens still technically remained, also opposed that ethnic formula even though it had supported their conscription into the British army. C.P. Scott had a glimpse of both these forces of opposition on August 29, when he visited in turn Constantine Nabokov, the Russian chargé d'affaires in London, and Lord Derby, the secretary for war.

A member of one of Russia's great Liberal families, Nabokov—uncle of the future novelist Vladimir—breathed the essence of that provisional government which was still holding on for dear life in faction-torn Petrograd. He told Scott that he feared the opposition of the increasingly powerful Soviets to the idea of a specifically *Jewish* regiment; their representatives in London, he said, "had indeed already objected." If their objection were ignored, he went on, they would make representation to Ambassador Buchanan in Petrograd. He would reply, he told Scott, that under the terms of the Anglo-Russian convention recently drawn up regarding this matter, "there were no restrictions, and that the War Office could put the Russians who had not opted to go back to Russia in any regiment it liked. Then there would be friction. There were in fact no restrictions," he pointed out. "The convention was badly drawn. He had not been consulted." Nabokov seemed to be shrugging his shoulders at the whole thing, but one could scarcely doubt that he had made his feelings known to the War Office.

Scott saw Lord Derby at the War Office that afternoon. Derby had met personally with Jabotinsky in April, and these two men, so vastly different in background and personal appearance, had hit it off well. Jabotinsky had immediately warmed up to that "country squire of the grand ancient style, florid and tall and generously built, the classical . . . John Bull type with the 'county' mannerisms of droppin' his g's; and quite jolly and friendly." As for Derby, he had, after a few questions, immediately begun discussing with Jabotinsky plans for the Jewish unit that was indeed subsequently announced at the end of July. But Scott, upon meeting with him now, found that "he had completely changed his mind. There was, he said, to be no Jewish regiment, but only a 'Foreign Legion.' A deputation of very influential Jews (Lord Reading and others) was to wait on him next day to protest against the formation of any Jewish regiment, or such, whatever. Evidently he had been overborne." Scott agreed that there should be complete liberty of choice in the matter, but why, he asked, "should there not be a Zionist battalion for the Zionists who fought all the better if they could be appealed to on the religious and racial ground? He said he agreed, but the deputation would say just the opposite and I must excuse him if he found he had to give way."

Scott found him most kind and genial about the matter, but was surprised to discover him this helpless. "Everything moves in a circle," Derby said to him, "and you come back to where you started." Scott gathered his present position to be "that only English, i.e. naturalized, and English-speaking Russians were to be allowed to enter British regiments and all [other] aliens were to be put together in the Foreign Legion. No conditions could be accepted as to where this should serve, but as a matter of fact it would no doubt be sent to Palestine. The whole matter was of consequence only in respect of good relations with the Government of Russia."

If Derby had yielded to Jewish pressure on the highest levels, he must have been all the more ready to do so in face of the fact that Jabotinsky's project did not even have the support of the Zionist leadership. The two exceptions, Weizmann and Sokolow, were indeed notable ones; but Sokolow, characteristically, showed no signs of willingness to compromise his other Zionist work by doing battle for the Jewish legion idea, and as for Weizmann, this particular controversy on top of everything else turned out to be the last straw that almost did him in. Weizmann clearly was exhausted: there can be no other explanation for his having lingered on in Paris after the Gibraltar conference while the most important Zionist work to date—that of drafting a declaration for the British Government—was being carried on in London under Sokolow. Since February, he had been writing letters and telegrams, giving speeches, attending meetings, and making organizational decisions—the English Zionist Federation was in the process of moving its headquarters to a formidable and well-staffed new location at 175 Piccadilly—at a punishing rate. His scientific work—he was still connected with the Admiralty laboratories—had necessarily abated, but the strains it caused were scarcely less than they had been. A shortage of maize had curtailed the workings of his process and he was trying horse chestnuts instead; furthermore, the matter of his final monetary award had still not been settled, more than a year after it had first been broached, although Scott found out for him early in August that a decision had in fact been reached* but for some reason had not yet been conveyed to him—another palpable source of tension.

Something like a breakdown finally occurred for Weizmann at a meeting of the Executive Council of the English Zionist Federation on August 16, when the question of the Jewish regiment was discussed. Despite the Government announcement, some of Weizmann's closest friends and associates—including Leon Simon and, above all, Ahad Ha'am—remained firmly opposed to it, and this proved more than he could bear. Suddenly, he offered his resignation as president. The next day he wrote to Sokolow:

> My very dear Friend,
>   I wish to inform you that after very careful consideration and after having weighed all the consequences I came to the inevitable conclusion that it is impossible for me to continue to serve either on the Executive of the E.Z.F. or on the Political Committee. I have accordingly placed my resignation from the Presidency of the E.Z.F. in the hands of the Council and I beg leave to sever my connection with the P.C. It is a matter of great regret to me that it is impossible out of technical reasons to resign from the A.C. [the Actions Committee, or worldwide Zionist executive].

---

* According to his autobiography, what Weizmann finally received was "a token reward . . . amounting to about ten shillings for every ton of acetone produced, a total of ten thousand pounds."

I shall be grateful to you if you would be good enough to inform the P.C. of my decision.

I need hardly assure you that this step is not dictated by any feeling of animosity towards you or towards anyone else with whom I have been working for the last three years. I am deeply grieved at the fact that it will be impossible for me to cooperate with you and I take this opportunity to express my full admiration for you and your work.

With very kind regards,
Yours sincerely,
Chaim

The last paragraph suggests that a touch of resentment at all Sokolow had recently achieved without his presence may have been part of what drove Weizmann to take this drastic step. That the Jewish regiment question was not alone the reason for it was made clear enough by him in a letter to another colleague, Samuel Tolkowsky, on August 21, in which he said,

believe me, my dear friend, the "Jewish regiment" is simply a special case which shows the state of heart and mind of our Zionists and of our entire people. After three years of arduous effort, I am compelled to admit that we have all the time been working for a people without a name, which is not yet ready to wage the tremendous struggle necessary for the establishment of a Jewish society. The war came too early for us. . . . My decision—I need not assure you—was not motivated by any ill will, but it was just my mood that was responsible.

At another meeting of the EZF Executive Council the next day, he complained again of having received only meager support from the Jewish masses for his work. But after a calmer discussion of the Jewish regiment idea, he withdrew his resignation at least for the time being.

The fit of self-destructiveness was not quite over. On September 5, Weizmann wrote another letter to Sokolow resigning from all his Zionist functions and complaining that the atmosphere surrounding him had been "full of suspicion, envy and a certain fanaticism." That same day he wrote to Ahad Ha'am of his decision, saying regretfully that this might mean the end of their friendship. Ahad Ha'am wrote back to him protesting that his resignation from the Zionist leadership at this point would be "an act of treason" and

"from a personal point of view . . . would be moral suicide." C.P. Scott
put it more gently a few days later when he wrote Weizmann in
response to a rumor that "you were resigning your position as head
of the Zionist Organization in this country. That would be a real
misfortune. So far as I can judge and my experience goes, you are
the only statesman among them." Greatly placated by now,
Weizmann responded in terms of Russian political matters that
Scott also had raised in his letter. "I am afraid," he wrote,

> that even if Kerensky succeeds now in establishing a semblance
> of order it will only be of a very short duration. . . . The so-called
> Maximalist tendencies have demoralized not only Russia but
> threaten to undermine the state of things even outside Russia. I
> felt that in a minor degree in my own organization. Being con-
> stituted as it is chiefly of Russian Jews they began to introduce
> Soviet tactics into the Zionist movement and my only answer to
> that was that not desiring to take the responsibility for the
> consequences I would leave them to continue the work if they
> can. This has had the effect of sobering them down and hence
> the rumors of my resignation.

To this Scott replied: "I'm glad that you are only keeping your people
in order—à la Kerensky!—and not leaving them leaderless." Perhaps
for a moment Weizmann had felt the despair of seeming a Kerensky. Ironically, in years to come, casual observers were often to
note a physical resemblance between himself and Lenin.

Actually, the seemingly certain victory had been deferred and
perhaps compromised at the War Cabinet meeting of Monday, September 3, when both the Jewish regiment and the Zionist declaration came up on the agenda. Oddly enough, neither Lloyd George nor
Balfour was present: both were away on holiday, Balfour in Scotland, Lloyd George in Wales—and the prime minister's stay there
was to be prolonged by an attack of ptomaine poisoning. But Lord
Robert Cecil was on hand to take Balfour's place, and perhaps it was
felt that the matters to be discussed and their prospective outcomes
were firmly enough established that no rescheduling was necessary.
The matter of the Zionist declaration had already been delayed unnecessarily, owing to bureaucratic errors, and its time seemed long
overdue.

The Jewish regiment came up first. Derby was present, and he
reported that "a very influential deputation of Jews" had come to

him and objected to the title "the Jewish Regiment." The deputation, he said, had pointed out to him that some forty thousand Jews
had served with distinction in the British armed forces by now, "and
that it was not fair to them to stake the whole reputation of English
Jews as fighters on the performance of this regiment." Derby therefore proposed to abandon the title "the Jewish Regiment," and simply to give the regiment a number for the time being, "leaving open
the question of adding any further designation which might express
the particular character or aspiration of the regiment, but which
would not involve the fighting reputation of Jews in the army generally. He also insisted that he could not guarantee to keep the regiment, or even a particular battalion of it, filled up with recruits who
all shared the Zionist aspirations."

The war secretary said he hoped eventually to form four battalions, mainly composed of foreign Jews. Some English Jews in
uniform had already volunteered to function as instructors with the
unit. At the end of the cabinet discussion, it "was generally agreed
that there was a close connection between this subject and the question of the attitude to be taken up towards the Zionist movement as
a whole." The discussion was closed with this resolution:

> That for the present the battalions to be formed from Jew-
> ish recruits should receive numbers in the ordinary way, and
> without any distinctive title, without prejudice to the recon-
> sideration of the question of the distinctive title if a definite
> demand in favor of the change were substantially established
> and circumstances favored such a policy.

For the time being, there was to be no Star of David insignia, either.
But in the coming months, the Jewish unit was to have its own
badge and name and to enjoy fulfillment of its wish that it be sent to
fight in Palestine.

The moment now came for consideration of a declaration on
Palestine. The members of the War Cabinet who were present had
three documents before their eyes: the proposed Balfour note to
Lord Rothschild, the Montagu memorandum, and an alternative
draft to the Balfour document that had been devised about two
weeks earlier by Lord Milner. In May, Milner had received a visit
from Claude Montefiore, who had obtained the impression that
Milner's views stood somewhere "between our formula and the full
Zionist scheme." By the middle of August, Milner evidently had con-

cluded that the Balfour draft declaration, based so closely as it was
on Sokolow's document, was a bit too strongly Zionist. He therefore
drew up a proposed declaration that followed the basic lines of the
Balfour draft, but hedged the language in some significant places.
Milner's version read:

> His Majesty's Government accepts the principle that every
> opportunity should be afforded for the establishment of a home
> for the Jewish people in Palestine, and will use its best endeav-
> ors to facilitate the achievement of this object, and will be ready
> to consider any suggestions on the subject which the Zionist
> organizations may desire to lay before them.

The most significant substitution was "every opportunity should be
afforded for the establishment of a home for the Jewish people in
Palestine" instead of Balfour's "Palestine should be reconstituted as
the national home of the Jewish people." Affording every opportunity for something is not the same as acknowledging that it should
be, nor is establishing something in a place the same as reconstitut-
ing that place as something. Ironically, in the latter case, this modification was even more of a reversion to the language of the Basel
Program than Sokolow's text had been. Milner was proposing, as the
Basel Program did, *a* home *in* Palestine rather than Palestine *as the
national* home for the Jewish people. This language represented a
significant retreat from that of Balfour and Sokolow, but the fact
that it stood solidly on the Basel formula—as Milner doubtless knew
well by now—gave it formidable validity. For the rest—Milner following a suggestion that had originally been presented by Ormsby-
Gore, who regarded it as inappropriate that a Christian power
should appear to be "forcing" the realization of Zionist aims—the
major change was the replacement of "facilitate" for "*secure* the
achievement of this object." His pluralizing of "Zionist organiza-
tion(s)" may have been an intentional warning that the Lucien
Wolf-Claude Montefiore group would still have a voice, or it may
have had no real significance.
Edwin Montagu was personally present at the cabinet meeting,
but he seems to have had nothing to do with a suggestion made from
the outset that "a question raising such important issues as to the
future of Palestine ought, in the first instance, to be discussed with
our Allies, and more particularly with the United States." This was a
rather abrupt intrusion of a point that some would have regarded as

settled: Balfour in May and Sokolow in June had obtained assurances, from the American and French governments respectively, of support for Zionist aspirations in Palestine. There was nothing in any of the proposed drafts about the still unsettled question of suzerainty, and as for the decision to make a public declaration, this surely was the prerogative of the one Allied Power—French and Italian token forces notwithstanding—whose army was in Palestine. There is no sign that Balfour himself regarded any further consultation with the Allies in this matter to be necessary. On the contrary, he seems to have become impatient with the growing delay in the outcome and might very well have opposed this suggestion had he been present. It seems above all to have been a delaying tactic, and it was therefore most likely a suggestion made by Bonar Law—acting chairman in the prime minister's absence—who is known to have regarded the time to be not yet ripe for a declaration on Palestine. Bonar Law was well known as a procrastinator, and probably felt that a clear military decision in Palestine was needed before such a step could be taken.

"On the question of submitting Lord Milner's draft for the consideration of the United States Government," the cabinet minutes read, "Mr. Montagu urged that the use of the phrase 'the home of the Jewish people' would vitally prejudice the position of every Jew elsewhere and expand the argument contained in his Memorandum." It is not clear why the Milner document was at this moment being singled out over the Balfour one—if indeed it was—for submission to Washington, nor is it clear how Montagu arrived at the wording "the home of the Jewish people," which is in neither version. There is perhaps a hint of summertime carelessness at this session attended by only four of the seven War Cabinet members—Milner, Smuts, and Carson were there in addition to Bonar Law—and lacking the two personages, Balfour and Lloyd George, without whom a decision about a Palestine declaration might be regarded as not entirely valid.

But with the presence there of Cecil, Smuts, Carson, and even Milner, a pro-Zionist resolution certainly had its defenders. Against Montagu's argument, then, "it was urged that the existence of a Jewish State or autonomous community in Palestine would strengthen rather than weaken the situation of Jews in countries where they were not yet in possession of equal rights, and that in countries like England, where they possessed such rights and were identified with the nation of which they were citizens, their position would be unaffected by the existence of a national Jewish community elsewhere. The view was expressed that, while a small influential section of English Jews were opposed to the idea, large numbers were sympathetic to it, but in the interests of Jews who wished to go from countries where they were less favorably situated, rather than from any idea of wishing to go to Palestine themselves." Retreating to a defensive position, the declaration's defenders had reverted to the old idea of Palestine as an asylum for Jews in distress.

"With reference to a suggestion that the matter might be postponed"—again, most likely having come from Bonar Law—Lord Robert Cecil "pointed out that this was a question on which the Foreign Office had been very strongly pressed for a long time past." On the matter of duress, Cecil surely was protesting too much, but he evidently saw this as a useful tactic against the sentiment in favor of delay. "There was a very strong and enthusiastic organization, more particularly in the United States," he went on with significant emphasis, "who were zealous in this matter, and his belief was that it would be of most substantial assistance to the Allies to have the earnestness and enthusiasm of these people enlisted on our side. To do nothing was to risk a direct breach with them, and it was necessary to face the situation."

This was to no avail. Sitting in the chair, Bonar Law was determined upon a delay, and he had discovered grounds for one that could not readily be challenged. It was resolved in the end that:

> The views of President Wilson should be obtained before any declaration was made, and [the War Cabinet] requested the Acting Secretary of State for Foreign Affairs to inform the Government of the United States that His Majesty's Government were being pressed to make a declaration of sympathy with the Zionist movement, and to ascertain their views as to the advisability of such a declaration being made.

Cecil had no choice but to carry this out. The sequel was to prove as much a fiasco of absentmindedness and evasion of the issue as this particular cabinet deliberation had been.

·42·

THE DRAFT DECLARATION
AT THE WAR CABINET:
THE SECOND SALLY

R ight after the September 3 cabinet, Lord Robert Cecil sent off the prescribed message to Colonel House in Washington. "We are being pressed here," he wrote, "for a declaration of sympathy with the Zionist movement, and I should be very grateful if you felt able to ascertain unofficially if the President favors such a declaration." It does not seem that a copy of either the Balfour or the Milner draft declaration was sent with this. There is a certain air of casualness about the whole thing, even of diffidence on Cecil's part, as the addition of the word "unofficially" suggests.

Yet, whatever importance may or may not have been attached to a statement of views from Washington at this moment, His Majesty's Government had been committed by the War Cabinet to the receiving of one before proceeding further; and as the week went by, the Foreign Office grew impatient for the reply that had not yet come. On Saturday, September 8, Chaim Weizmann had an interview at the Foreign Office with Sir George Clerk, who seems to have told him in general terms what the situation was. The next day, Weizmann wrote Clerk a short note that the Jewish New Year was to be celebrated on Monday the seventeenth, and that "it would be simply splendid if we could publish the Declaration of the British Govmt. here and in America, S. Africa, Canada and also Russia by Friday or Saturday." By Tuesday, the Foreign Office had prepared this query for dispatch to the British military intelligence office in New York: "Has Colonel House been able to ascertain whether President favors declaration of sympathy with Zionist aspirations as asked in my telegram of September 3rd? We should be most grateful for early reply as September 17th is the Jewish New Year and announcement of sympathy by or on that date would have excellent effect."

This message was not sent, however; for a reply finally arrived from Washington that had been sent out on September 10, the day before. In it, House said the president's opinion was that "the time is not opportune for any definite statement further perhaps than one of sympathy provided it can be made without conveying any real commitment. Things are in such a state of flux at moment that he does not consider it advisable to go further." This message is, in itself, as perplexing as the original Cecil query was offhanded. What would the president have considered a reasonable statement of "sympathy" or an unreasonable "real commitment"? Were the two draft declarations statements of sympathy and no more, or were they real commitments? There are indications that the sort of commitment in Palestine Wilson feared most at this time was one regarding suzerainty—whether British, American, or a combination of the two—but this was precisely what all the drafts of a declaration had carefully eschewed. The problem, of course, was that neither Wilson nor House had apparently seen any text of a declaration at all. And if there had indeed been discussion of an American protectorate when House was in London in February 1916, then doubtless he and the president were apprehensive that something suggesting this idea might be taken up in a British declaration. Whatever the message meant, however, its effect in London certainly was to give support, at least for a moment, to those who sought a delay in the issuance of any kind of declaration. On September 18, Weizmann wrote to Harry Sacher that "to my great astonishment I hear that Wilson thinks the time not yet ripe for this Declaration."

But since this apparent stance on the president's part does not accord with one that Brandeis was to claim for him only two weeks after House's disappointing message, we are led back to the question of the true intention or even validity of that communication of September 10. There even is reason to wonder how much of it was Wilson and how much was Colonel House. On September 7, three days before it, House had written the president a memorandum asking him: "Have you made up your mind regarding what answer you will make to Cecil concerning Zionist Movement? It seems to me that there are many dangers lurking in it, and if I were the British I would be chary about going too definitely into that question." This is somewhat more negative than the message subsequently sent on the tenth; but since Wilson's attitude was to prove more positive than that message, we may infer that what House did in it was strike a balance between his own view and the president's—one, moreover, that they may have arrived at in a passing moment of conversation. Once again, the keynote of the whole business seems to be its odd casualness.

It was Weizmann who led the way in beginning to elicit a different sort of Wilsonian attitude. At a meeting of the London Zionist Political Committee on September 11—the storm of his threatened resignation now abating—Weizmann conveyed information he had received from the British Government about the decision to wire Wilson for his approval, and it was requested that he in turn wire Brandeis asking him to use his influence with the president. Weizmann sent this message through British military intelligence the next day:

> Following text declaration has been approved by Foreign Office and Prime Minister and submitted to War Cabinet.
> "(1) H.M. Government accept the principle that Palestine should be reconstituted as the national home of the Jewish people.
> "(2) H.M. Government will use its best endeavors to secure the achievement of the [sic] object and will discuss the necessary methods and means with the Zionist Organization."
> May expect opposition from assimilationist quarters.
> Would greatly help if President Wilson and yourself would support text. Matter most urgent. Please telegraph.
> Weizmann

With only one inadvertent error—"the" for "this" in the second clause—Weizmann had conveyed the text, not of Balfour's modified version, but of the draft prepared by Sokolow and sent to the foreign secretary by Lord Rothschild on July 18. Weizmann was certainly not correct in saying it had been approved by the Foreign Office as such, and it probably had not yet even gone to the prime minister. Yet even this relatively strong version was acceptable to Brandeis—who finally received it on September 19—and, it would seem, to Wilson as well. "From talks I have had with President," Brandeis wired back on the twenty-fourth, "and from expressions of opinion given [by him] to closest advisers I feel sure I can answer you that he is in entire sympathy with declaration quoted in yours of nineteenth as approved by Foreign Office and the Prime Minister. I of course heartily agree." This certainly conveyed a different Wilson from the one in House's telegram of two weeks before, although a close inspection of the message can lead one to wonder if Brandeis had actually seen Wilson on this particular occasion. The "talks I have had" is a vague formulation, and the "expressions of opinion" relayed by advisers would hardly seem necessary if Brandeis had specifically discussed the matter with the president. Yet it is reasonable to suppose that Brandeis had at least discussed the matter with Colonel House, who evidently had undergone a change of heart. This would not have been the first time House was ready, whatever his more private thoughts, to speak favorable words to a Zionist when actually confronted by one—in February, he had written to Rabbi Stephen S. Wise, "I hope the dream which we have may soon become a reality"—and he had a particular respect for Brandeis. Furthermore, this may have been the first time he was actually seeing a text, and it must have struck him as not so bad as he expected.

Brandeis sent Weizmann another message that same day. "It would be wise," he said, "for you to get French and Italians to inquire what attitude of President is on declaration referred to in yours of the nineteenth. Please let me know steps taken by them." This further suggests that Colonel House and the president were still more concerned about the attitude of the Allies than they were about the nature of their own commitment to Sokolow's draft declaration, and that their strange coolness of two weeks earlier followed by their present warm acceptance had to do with concern over the question of suzerainty, which the declaration proved itself not to be taking up. At any rate, nothing came of this suggestion of Brandeis's, since Sokolow had really settled the matter in his talks in Paris and Rome the previous spring.

The forces favoring delay having had their triumph at the September 3 War Cabinet, there was no way to get the machinery for a declaration moving again until Balfour and Lloyd George were back in Whitehall. Balfour returned from his holiday on September 14, and Weizmann saw him five days later. "I had the pleasure of seeing Mr. Balfour this afternoon," he wrote to Philip Kerr on September 19:

He told me of the fate which has befallen the "declaration." The matter came up for discussion before the War Cabinet at a meeting when neither the P.M. nor Mr. B. were present. It was dealt with in a rather casual way and as there were not many who knew much about the question or realized how far it has gone it was decided to postpone it until a later date. So far so good, but Edwin Montagu violently attacked Zionism and it was his interference that brought about the attitude of the Cabinet. Then apparently somebody suggested that one should wire to Wilson and ask his opinion. I don't know the text of the telegram which was sent, but I understand that Wilson although sympathetic is also for postponement.

Weizmann told Kerr that "Mr. Balfour promised to see the P.M. about that and my hearty request goes out to you to put the matter before the P.M." Kerr was one of Lloyd George's most influential advisers at this point and was wholly sympathetic to Zionism; but the matter could not be put before the prime minister until he was back to work from his sickbed. The fact that everyone was "sympathetic"—a point Balfour had stressed to him—made the whole thing only the more perplexing to Weizmann.

"Although fully appreciating the reasons which cause it," Sir Ronald Graham wrote in a Foreign Office memorandum on September 24,

> I cannot regard without some concern the delay that is taking place in giving the Zionists some assurance of sympathy for their aims and aspirations on the part of His Majesty's Government. The result of this delay is that the Zionist leaders are rendered uncertain, if not dissatisfied, and that their propaganda on behalf of the Allies has practically ceased.

Graham mentioned that the emissary who had finally been sent by Weizmann to Russia that summer, Boris Goldberg, had done useful work and that Sokolow was soon to go to Russia to do more—but that Sokolow would not leave until armed with a British assurance. He stressed that Zionist propaganda was also still desirable in the United States. "In the meantime," he went on, "the Germans have become seriously apprehensive that the Zionist forces will be mobilized on behalf of the Allies. An organized campaign . . . is now proceeding in the German Press in favor of Jewish claims to Palestine." As evidence for this point, Graham annexed an extract from an article in the *Jewish Chronicle* of September 21, which reviewed a number of recent articles in the German press calling for some kind of stance to counter the increasingly evident British tendency to favor Zionist aspirations in Palestine. Graham warned of the danger of worldwide Zionist feeling becoming divided as a result of this agitation, especially if the Germans were to persuade the Turks to make concessions to Zionism. "It should be remembered," he added for further incentive, "that the French Government has already given the Zionists a somewhat vague letter of sympathy which, however, appears to satisfy them. I do not see why we should not go as far as the French in the matter." He concluded that, despite the appearance of Jewish opinion being divided on the subject, the "recent struggle in the Jewish community in England has shown that the Zionists are in the majority." Graham insisted that, furthermore, in other countries, including the United States, "the anti-Zionist forces are recruited from the Jewry of international finance which, if not hostile to the Allies, has never been strongly in our favor and whose interests lie in an inconclusive peace." He was not aware that Jacob Schiff had recently expressed sympathy both with Zionism and with the Allied cause.

"Pace Mr. Montagu," minuted Lord Hardinge on Graham's memorandum, "I think we might and ought to go as far as the French." "Yes," Balfour agreed in his own minute. "But as the question was (in my absence) decided by the Cabinet against the Zionists I cannot do anything until the decision is reversed." There is a refreshing candor in Balfour's characterization of the September 3 War Cabinet decision as having been "against the Zionists."

The prime minister was the crucial factor, and he had finally returned to work on the 23rd. As had so often been the case in the past, the issue was thrust back to his attention by C.P. Scott, who saw him on Friday the twenty-eighth. After breakfast, Scott, Lloyd George, and Philip Kerr prepared to leave 10 Downing Street for a stroll in Saint James's Park. "I had asked Weizmann to come," Scott records in his diary, "in case George should like to see him, and they had a few words downstairs, and George, on Weizmann's representation of urgency, told [his secretary William] Sutherland to put down 'Palestine' for the next War Cabinet." It was scheduled for the following Thursday, October 4.

In the meantime, Montagu had not relented in his campaign. On September 4, he had written a letter to Lord Robert Cecil against an accusation that his views represented those of only a minority of Jews. He remained insistent that it was only among foreign-born Jews that Zionism was the belief of a majority. But he now was developing a different approach from that of his previous paper, which had essentially been an echo of the assimilationist arguments of the Conjoint Foreign Committee. His new position with the India Office gave him a different perspective. About to leave on a personal visit to India, he now viewed the Middle East from the vantage point of Delhi and Baghdad, and no longer saw Palestine merely the way insular assimilated Jewish Englishmen did. At the moment, in fact, he could see the matter with eyes no less authoritative than those of Miss Gertrude Bell, who had just prepared a series of papers on Ottoman Asia.

Montagu found particular ammunition in Chapter Four of her series, which was entitled "The Arab Provinces—Syria." After a lament upon the devastation that Syria had been suffering at the hands of the Turk during the war, Miss Bell went on to describe the "peculiarly varied, not to say incongruous" state of the Syrian population, tending toward compromise of the ideal of national unity for the country. "East of Jordan," she wrote,

> the disintegrating influence of tribal authority forbid [sic] the development of a true national sentiment. From Damascus northward a greater homogeneity prevails, but even here each separate religious sect . . . revolves around its own axis and regards as comparatively unimportant its connection with the system of which it forms a part.

But this was by no means all. "Not least among the denationalizing forces," she continued,

> is the fact that a part of Syria, though like the rest mainly inhabited by Arabs, is regarded by a non-Arab people as its prescriptive inheritance. At a liberal estimate the Jews of Palestine may form a quarter of the population of the province, the Christians a fifth, while the remainder are Mohammedan Arabs. Jewish immigration has been artificially fostered by doles and subventions from millionaire co-religionists in Europe; the new colonies have now taken root and are more or less self-supporting. The pious hope that an independent Jewish state may some day be established in Palestine no doubt exists, though it may be questioned whether among local Jews there is any acute desire to see it realized, except as a means of escape from Turkish oppression; it is perhaps more lively in the breasts of those who live far from the rocky Palestinian hills and have no intention of changing their domicile.

She then repeated an anecdote that the late Lord Cromer had been fond of telling, of a prominent English Jew who said, "If a Jewish Kingdom were to be established at Jerusalem I should lose no time in applying for the post of Ambassador in London." She concluded:

Apart from the prevalence of such sentiments two considerations rule out the conception of an independent Jewish Palestine from practical politics. The first is that the province as we know it is not Jewish, and that neither Mohammedan nor Arab would accept Jewish authority; the second that the capital, Jerusalem, is equally sacred to three faiths, Jewish, Christian and Moslem, and should never, if it can be avoided, be put under the exclusive control of any one local faction, no matter how carefully the rights of the other two may be safeguarded.

After a final passing reflection on whether or not "it could be turned into a fitting home for millionaires," she turned to a physical description of Palestine.

These do not seem always to have been Miss Bell's sentiments on the Palestine question. In January 1915 she had written to her beloved friend, Lieutenant Colonel C.H.M. Doughty-Wylie: "I told you how Herbert Samuel wrote and asked me if I thought we could turn Palestine into a Jewish state under British protection? ... I told him I had alway wanted to create a neutral belt, if Turkey broke up, between French Syria and the Egyptian frontier. ... Then I plotted out for him Palestine Prima, under the guarantees of the Powers." But much had changed since then: Doughty-Wylie had been killed in the first landing at Sedd-el-Bahr in Gallipoli, that campaign had failed, and Miss Bell had gone out to Cairo, Basra, and now, Baghdad. Having once again encompassed that Middle East which was the consistent and surviving great passion of her life, she seems to have grown intolerant at the prospect of any impositions from the outside, as she conceived them, upon its already ravaged purity. Visions of recasting the world according to Britain's will had perhaps died for her by now. But there is an irony in her testy vision of Jewish millionaires coming out to violate the rocky Palestinian hills: for some of the most ardent Christian supporters of Zionism back home were also not inclined to like the wealthy, assimilated Jews of the West—Chaim Weizmann had given some support to such a feeling—and were eager to see them cured by a revival of Jewish nationhood. If a Balfour or a Sykes did not want to see them overwhelm London, Miss Bell seems to have felt the same way about them in Judea: it was partly a question of which terrain one cherished most as one's inviolable preserve.

During that same summer, a dissenting voice perhaps as significant as her own, though far less celebrated, had also been heard from. One of Sir Mark Sykes's most trusted sources of information in Cairo was a Levantine Catholic merchant from Jerusalem named A.P. Albina. On August 10, Albina had sent a letter surveying some aspects of the general Middle Eastern situation as he had learned them through his contacts in Cairo. In it was a warning about Palestine and the Jews. "The rumor spreading about," he wrote,

> and the propaganda undertaken in the Press, that the Jews will be given possession of Palestine, or at least will be granted extensive privileges there, are causing a feeling of fear and great anxiety amongst the Christian and Moslem Arabs. You know my opinion in the matter. Besides racial considerations of the highest importance, the question of Palestine is closely connected with the whole Moslem and Christian world. Jerusalem, as I have pointed out in former reports, is the most sacred city in the world to Christians and the third holy place to Moslems. The Jews have nothing there but memories of the past. Would England and France allow them to dispossess the Mohammedans of the Mosque of Omar and convert it into a Jewish temple? Or are the Jews (who at present are not even allowed to pass by the church of the Holy Sepulcher) to keep order between the different Christian sects in the Basilica? Such prospects are too absurd to be entertained.
>
> With regard to the racial question, how can the Allies conciliate [sic] their engagement of freeing small nationalities, by imposing upon the Palestinian Arabs, who are the original settlers of the country, the rule of a foreign and hated race, a motley crowd of Poles, Russians, Roumanians, Spaniards, Yemenites, etc., who can claim absolutely no right over the country, except that of sentiment and the fact that their forefathers inhabited it over two thousand years ago? The introduction into Palestine of Jewish rule, or even Jewish predominance, will mean the spoliation of the Arab inhabitants of their hereditary rights and the upsetting of the principles of nationalities. Why should not the Palestinians share the same fate like the rest of their countrymen in Syria?
>
> Politically, a Jewish State in Palestine will mean a permanent danger to a lasting peace in the Near East.

This is one of the more vigorous among the earliest statements on record of the anti-Zionist case coming directly from the Middle East; and there are signs that Sykes, though he certainly had answers ready to many of its points, was seriously troubled by it. Up to this time, the empirical Sykes, whose own views were often subject to modification from one day to the next, had been inclined to play the whole set of Middle Eastern nationalities questions "by ear," so to speak—to orchestrate the dissonances and harmonies of Jewish, Arab, and Armenian aspirations as they emerged with the rapidly changing times. But lately, he had been somewhat under siege from various directions. No sooner had he returned from Cairo in mid-June, for example, than he found himself confronted by Sir Louis Mallet's drive for a separate peace with Turkey. "On my arrival," he had written back to Clayton on July 22,

> I found that the Foreign Office had been carefully destroying everything I had done in the past 2 years. Stimulating anti-Entente feeling, and pushing separate negotiations with Turkey ideas. Indeed I arrived in the nick of time. Luckily Zionism held good and the plots to bring Morgenthau over and negotiate a separate peace with Turkey in Switzerland were foiled. Morgenthau was met at Gibraltar by Weizmann on behalf of British Zionism and was obliged to admit that no useful negotiations could be undertaken with the Turks until another victory had been gained.

The matter had not quite ended there, however: Mallet subsequently presented a paper arguing the reasons for a separate peace with Turkey, and Sykes had been impelled to reply with a long memorandum on July 29.

Apart from practical considerations, Sykes was firmly convinced that the whole character of the war had changed over the past year or so: out of a clash of conflicting expansionist ambitions had come a moral crusade. "Colonialism is madness," he wrote in his July 22 letter to Clayton,

> and I believe Picot and I can prove it to [the French]. Lawrence's move is splendid and I want him knighted. Tell him that now he is a great man he must behave as such and be broad in his views. Ten years' tutelage under the Entente and the Arabs will be a nation. Complete [immediate] independence means Persia, poverty, and chaos. Let him consider this as he hopes for the people he is fighting for.

Such views were not to keep Lawrnece from considering the co-author of the agreement that was continually being called "Sykes-Picot" as one of the chief villains of Middle Eastern colonialism. "I submit," Sykes began one July memorandum in reply to a Foreign Office paper by Harold Nicolson summing up the various Middle

Eastern commitments to date, "that the Anglo-French Agreement should be called the Anglo-French-Arab agreement in such papers and not the Sykes-Picot Agreement." Furthermore, he went on in response to Nicolson,

> I am of opinion that this paper does not attribute sufficient importance to the moral side of the question and to the ideals for which the best elements in this war are fighting, viz: the liberation of oppressed peoples and the maintenance of world peace. If the problem of Turkey-in-Asia is approached from a narrow Imperialistic view we shall find ourselves completely at variance with the strong moral forces which will weigh down the scales at the end of the war, with the result that our enemies the Central Powers will by a little agility gain their ends.

These mounting attitudes reached their virtually inevitable conclusion on August 14, when Sykes submitted a "Memorandum on the Asia-Minor Agreement" that began: "I believe that the time has now come when, in the interests of both Great Britain and France, discussion and interchange of views would be desirable in regard to the Asia-Minor Agreement." Sykes had not yet quite come to the extreme of suggesting a revision of the geographical boundaries agreed upon with Picot more than a year and a half before, but he did think "the two powers should discuss frankly and freely the attitude they intend to adopt towards the populations inhabiting those regions.

"When the agreement was originally drawn up," he went on,

> I think it was then in consonance with the spirit of the time that certain concessions were made to the idea of nationality and autonomy, but an avenue was left open to annexation. The idea of annexation really must [now] be dismissed, it is contrary to the spirit of the time, and if at any moment the Russian extremists got hold of a copy they could make much capital against the whole entente;* this is especially so with the Italian claim which runs counter to nationality, geography and common sense, and is merely Baron Sonnino's concession to a chauvinist group who only think in bald terms of grab.

In then mentioning some of the considerations he thought should be dealt with between the two powers, Sykes spoke firmly once again of

---

* They were to do precisely that; in December 1917, the Bolshevik government published all the wartime secret agreements found in the tsarist archives.

Arab, Armenian, and Zionist aspirations as three parts of a single aim. He also made it clear that he thought Great Britain should be "appointed trustee of the Powers for the administration of Palestine"—a reiteration of the novel but highly significant "mandatory" idea he had, perhaps for the first time, aired at the beginning of March.

A few days after this memorandum, he received another warning from Cairo regarding the Zionist aspect of the question, this time from Clayton. "I am not sure," Clayton said in response to word of the pondered declaration, "that it is not as well to refrain from any public pronouncement just at present. It will not help matters if the Arabs . . . are given yet another bone of contention in the shape of Zionism in Palestine as against the interests of the Moslems resident there." This, along with Albina's letter of August 10, seems to have had some effect upon Sykes, who was now bent entirely on balancing the moral equations that had emerged out of the Middle Eastern calculations of previous years. Sometime in late September, he produced a "Note on Palestine and Zionism," evidently for cabinet use, which made a few emphases he had not been making in recent months and tended to hedge the Zionist demands. In the course of a long presentation of the Zionist case, the note says at one point that

it would be as well to rehearse precisely what the Zionists desire and what they do not desire. What the Zionists do not want is:
I. To have any special political hold on the city of Jerusalem itself or any control over the Christian or Moslem Holy places.
II. To set up a Jewish Republic or other form of state in Palestine or any part of Palestine.
III. To enjoy any special rights not enjoyed by other inhabitants of Palestine.
On the other hand the Zionists do want:
I. Recognition of the Jewish inhabitants of Palestine as a national unit, federated with national units in Palestine.
II. The recognition of [the] right of bona fide Jewish settlers to be included in the Jewish national unit in Palestine.

It is significant that, although Sykes had submitted an earlier draft of this paper to Weizmann for approval and corrections, this passage had not appeared in it. On the surface of it, everything here was within limits that Sykes and the Zionist leaders had more or less agreed upon, but the emphases certainly would have been disturbing to Weizmann. To be sure, a Jewish state was no more the *immediate* aim than was an Arab state or states in the adjacent regions; but was it true to the spirit of Zionist aspirations to say they "do not want" one? The firm exclusion of Jerusalem raised a similar question. As for the exclusion of "special rights," this was in principle beyond reproach; but, so stated, what did it do to the Zionist desire for a chartered company? And finally, the last thing the Zionists desired in the long run was to see the Jews of Palestine as part of a federation of national units there. This was not the first time that Sykes had for a moment sought to leap ahead of his usual empirical approach and try to formulate a vision for the near future of Palestine that was a bit too exact to be practicable.

Sykes may even have had some second thoughts about his "Note on Palestine and Zionism," for the record gives no indication that it had official circulation either at the cabinet or at the Foreign Office. Nevertheless, there are signs that at least Lord Curzon got to see it, and it is reasonable to infer that other cabinet members saw it as well. Similarly, although the Edwin Montagu memorandum containing the Gertrude Bell paper on Syria survives in the Foreign Office archives with the date October 9 on it, we may be virtually certain that at least some members of the cabinet got to see the paper before the meeting of October 4. For, about half an hour before that meeting, as Leopold Amery was to recall, he was asked by Lord Milner—still seeking a suitable revision of the earlier drafts—to try drawing up a version of the declaration on Palestine "which would go a reasonable distance to meeting the objections both Jewish and pro-Arab without impairing the substance of the proposed declaration." In effect, this was to mean provisos responding to the Jewish assimilationist objections that Montagu had revived and to the concern about the implications for the Arabs of Palestine that had recently been adumbrated through Sykes and by Gertrude Bell.

By the time the cabinet meeting began, Amery and Milner had produced this new version of a declaration text:

His Majesty's Government views with favor the establishment in Palestine of a national home for the Jewish race, and will use its best endeavors to facilitate the achievement of this object; it being clearly understood that nothing shall be done which may prejudice the civil and religious rights of existing non-Jewish communities in Palestine, or the rights and political status enjoyed in any other country by such Jews who are fully contented with their existing nationality [and citizenship].*

The major change was, of course, represented by the two provisos introduced by the phrase "it being clearly understood." As Amery was to explain years later: "The reference to Jews outside Palestine was, of course, to satisfy Montagu. The provision about non-Jewish communities in Palestine was, no doubt, Curzon's, but I cannot remember definitely." As a former viceroy of India, Curzon was beginning to show concern about the Muslim side of the question and was not yet to be placated even by this amendment.

After several other pieces of cabinet business, the matter of a Palestine declaration was opened by Balfour. Just the day before, Weizmann and Lord Rothschild had sent him a letter urging passage of the declaration—which they still knew only in the draft Lord Rothschild had sent to Balfour on July 18. Weizmann even, it would seem, was prepared to state his case in person, and at the cabinet there was a last-minute decision to send for him, but he could not be located in time. On the other hand, Montagu was present.

Balfour began his presentation by saying that "the German Government were making great efforts to capture the sympathy of the Zionist movement. This Movement," Balfour insisted, "though opposed by a number of wealthy Jews in this country, had behind it the support of a majority of Jews, at all events in Russia and America, and possibly in other countries." Balfour said he "saw nothing inconsistent between the establishment of a Jewish national focus in Palestine and the complete assimilation and absorption of Jews into the nationality of other countries. Just as English emigrants to the United States became, either in the first or subsequent generations, American nationals, so, in future, should a Jewish citizenship be established in Palestine, would Jews become either Englishmen, Americans, Germans, or Palestinians. What was at the back of the Zionist Movement was the intense national consciousness held by certain members of the Jewish race. They regarded themselves as one of the great historic races of the world, whose original home was Palestine, and these Jews had a passionate longing to regain once more this ancient national home. Other Jews had become absorbed into the nations among whom they and their forefathers had dwelt for many generations."

* The last two words, "and citizenship," were added at the meeting.

At that point, Balfour read "a very sympathetic declaration by the French Government which had been conveyed to the Zionists, and he stated that he knew that President Wilson was extremely favorable to the Movement." In response to this last remark, someone observed that there was a contradiction between the telegram that Colonel House had sent on September 10 and the one that Brandeis had sent to Weizmann on the twenty-fourth.

Montagu, far from placated by the draft Lord Milner was offering, then "urged strong objections to any declaration in which it was stated that Palestine was the 'national home' of the Jewish people." Stressing that he "regarded the Jews as a religious community and himself as a Jewish Englishman," he again spoke of "the prejudicial effect on the status" of any like himself that such a statement would have. "Whatever safeguarding words might be used in the formula," he said, with perhaps a glance at Milner, "the civil rights of Jews as nationals in the country in which they were born might be endangered."

Then he came up with a pointed argument that he may have discussed with Curzon. "How would he negotiate with the peoples of India on behalf of His Majesty's Government," Montagu asked regarding himself, "if the world had just been told that His Majesty's Government regarded his national home as being in Turkish territory?" Referring to the recent struggle between Zionists and anti-Zionists in the Conjoint Foreign Committee, Montagu pointed out that the former had won only by the very narrow majority of fifty-six to fifty-one. And what did that small majority consist of? "He also pointed out that most English-born Jews were opposed to Zionism, while it was supported by foreign-born Jews, such as Dr. Gaster and Dr. Hertz, the two Grand Rabbis, who had been born in Roumania and Austria respectively, and Dr. Weizmann, President of the English Zionist Federation, who was born in Russia." Montagu's conclusion was "that the Cabinet's first duty was to English Jews, and that Colonel House had declared that President Wilson is opposed to a declaration now."

Joining the negative perspective on Zionism that seemed now virtually to emanate from India, Lord Curzon spoke up, urging "strong objections upon practical grounds. He stated, from his recollection of Palestine, that the country was, for the most part, barren and desolate; there being but sparse cultivation on the terraced slopes, the valleys and streams being few, and large centers of population scarce, a less propitious seat for the future Jewish race could not be imagined. How was it proposed," he asked, "to get rid of the existing majority of Mussulman inhabitants and to introduce the Jews in their place? How many [Jews] would be willing to return and on what pursuits would they engage?" Curzon said that securing "for the Jews already in Palestine equal civil and religious rights seemed to him a better policy than to aim at repatriation on a large scale. He regarded the latter as sentimental idealism, which would never be realized, and that His Majesty's Government should have nothing to do with it."

Someone pointed out in reply to Curzon "that during recent years before the War, Jewish immigration into Palestine had been considerably on the increase, and that several flourishing Zionist colonies were already in existence." With that, the Milner-Amery draft was submitted, and the War Cabinet members came to the conclusion that:

> Before coming to a decision they should hear the views of some of the representative Zionists, as well as of those who held the opposite opinion, and that meanwhile the declaration, as read by Lord Milner, should be submitted confidentially to—
>
> (a.) President Wilson.
> (b.) Leaders of the Zionist movement.
> (c.) Representative persons in Anglo-Jewry opposed to Zionism. The Secretary [Sir Maurice Hankey] was instructed to take the necessary action.
>
> The War Cabinet further decided that the opinions received upon this draft declaration should be collated and submitted to them for decision.

With that, they moved on to other business.

·43·

THE THIRD SALLY:
THE DECLARATION AT LAST

Aaron Aaronsohn arrived in London on October 1, assigned there by military intelligence after a fruitful stint in Egypt of nearly ten months. There are signs that his advice and information were of value in the renewed Palestine campaign that was about to begin. He had been able to give General Allenby, in a long interview in July, a solid evaluation of the political attitudes of the Palestine population, Jewish and non-Jewish alike, and of the condition of the Turkish army and its leadership. And in addition to whatever practical help he had been able to provide, Aaronsohn had proved to be—despite or perhaps because of his unorthodoxy in relation to the Zionist establishment—a potent instrument of living propaganda for the Zionist cause. He deeply stirred those with whom he came into contact. "I have seen a great deal of Aaronsohn," Philip Graves had written to Sykes in March, before the latter's arrival in Egypt. "He is good stuff with lots of knowledge and grit and reconciles me much more to Zionism." Graves was to become a firm supporter of Zionism, as Ormsby-Gore had become through contact with Aaronsohn before moving on to London early in the year, and as Major Wyndham Deedes, successor to Ormsby-Gore as Aaronsohn's closest collaborator in Cairo intelligence, had now also become.

Aaronsohn was for the moment being replaced in Cairo by his brother Alexander, who had returned from his two years of propaganda work in the United States—passing through London at around the time of the British publication of his book, *With the Turks in Palestine*—and had obtained a commission with British military intelligence in Egypt. Aaron, who now went to see all the Zionist leaders in London whom he had avoided during his last, secretive sojourn there, wasted no time about asking Weizmann to send a message to

Cairo for relaying to the rest of his family in Zichron Ya'akov. For the Aaronsohn spy network was possibly in trouble on its home ground.

After the departure of Alexander and Aaron, the intelligence operation at Athlit had been taken over at first by Absalom Feinberg; but he was killed at the end of 1916 in a mission in the Negev. The leadership then had been taken over by Sarah Aaronsohn. Now twenty-seven, this woman who had left a husband in Constantinople and lived through the death of her beloved friend and co-worker in espionage, seems to have exercised upon those with whom she was closely associated—especially the men—a personal force as powerful as her will to carry out the dangerous work that had devolved upon her. "I see you sitting quiet and wonderful," wrote Liova Schneerson, her closest co-worker since Absalom's death, in his diary one evening, "with your wonderful white hands, and your slim fingers, of such loveliness and beauty as I have never seen." Fair-complexioned, blue-eyed, with flowing golden hair, she stands within the mist of legend surrounding her as the pillar of strength upon which rested the spy network that had, since Aaron's departure, taken for itself the code name of Nili. The word was an acronym of those spoken by the prophet Samuel (1 Samuel 15:29) in his anger at Saul for not having completely destroyed Amalek: *Netzach Yisroel lo yishaker*—"the Strength of Israel will not lie" ("nor repent," Samuel adds). Soon after that, Samuel anoints the young David. Did Sarah and her comrades now perhaps see her as the prophet in Israel who would reject all those who flinched at destroying the Turks and appoint the true succession?

Sarah had actually made her way to Cairo in April, to consult with Aaron and British intelligence, but despite pleas that she remain she returned to Zichron Ya'akov in June. The decision proved fatal. Early in September the Turks discovered the Nili operation—apparently through the capture of a carrier pigeon—and by the beginning of the following month had traced it to the Aaronsohn home in Zichron Ya'akov. Sarah and her sixty-eight-year-old father were beaten and tortured in an effort to extract information from them about their activities. "I've been given the most murderous beatings," she wrote in a final letter. "They have tortured me with terrible tortures. They chained me with iron chains." Returned home under house arrest on Friday, October 5, she found a pistol and shot herself; but even this was a prolongation of agony, for she did not die until four days later. It was two days after that that there arrived in Zichron Ya'akov the message relayed to her by Alexander in

Cairo from Weizmann in London. "We are doing our utmost," it said, "to secure a Jewish Palestine under British auspices. Your heroic sufferings are greatest incentive our difficult work. Our hopes are great. Be strong and of good courage until Land of Israel liberated." The news of Sarah's death was not to reach London for several weeks.*

On October 6, the day Weizmann sent his message in vain to Sarah Aaronsohn, two important letters were sent out from Whitehall in implementation of the War Cabinet decision of two days before. One was from Balfour to Colonel House in Washington. "In view of reports," it said,

> that the German Government are making great efforts to capture the Zionist Movement, the question of a message of sympathy with the Movement from H.M. Government has again been considered by the Cabinet. Following formula is suggested. [Here follows the Milner-Amery draft declaration.] Before taking any decision the Cabinet intend to hear the views of some representative Zionists and anti-Zionists, but meanwhile they would be most grateful if you found it possible to ascertain the opinion of the president with regard to the formula.

On the same day, the cabinet secretary, Sir Maurice Hankey, sent out copies of the draft declaration to eight prominent English Jews: four of them Zionists or favorable to Zionism, four of them either opposed or indifferent. The four on the Zionist side were Weizmann, Sokolow, Lord Rothschild, and Chief Rabbi Hertz; the opposing four were Claude Montefiore, Leonard Cohen (the chairman of the Jewish Board of Guardians), Sir Philip Magnus (a Liberal M.P. and prominent Hebrew educator), and Sir Stuart Samuel (Herbert Samuel's elder brother, who was the MP from Whitechapel and the newly elected president of the Jewish Board of Deputies). Hankey's covering letter to them read in part:

* Among the legends that have come to surround the memory of Sarah Aaronsohn, one of the most remarkable is the widespread belief that she is the mysterious "S.A." to whom T.E. Lawrence dedicated the *Seven Pillars of Wisdom*. This has generally not been accepted by Lawrence biographers. There is extremely little likelihood that Lawrence ever met her, though he surely had heard of her. Lawrence did know Aaron Aaronsohn; they had met for the first time on August 12, 1917, in Cairo, and Aaron had disliked him intensely. "Thinks very highly of himself," Aaronsohn wrote; and when Lawrence discussed the place of the Palestine Jewish settlements in the future scheme of things, it seemed to Aaronsohn that he "was attending a Prussian anti-Semitic lecture."

I am directed by the Prime Minister to inform you that at the instance of the Secretary of State for Foreign Affairs, the question of drawing up a formula setting forth the attitude of His Majesty's Government towards the Zionist Movement in general and to the future of Palestine in particular, has been under preliminary decision by the War Cabinet.

In view of the apparent divergence of opinion expressed on the subject by Jews themselves, the War Cabinet decided that they would like to receive in writing the views of representative Jewish leaders, both Zionist and non-Zionist, upon the form and wording of the proposed draft declaration that had been submitted to the War Cabinet for consideration.

The letter then gave the text of the draft declaration, and asked that a reply embodying the recipient's views might be made within a week. It concluded with a list of the names of the persons to whom copies of it were being sent.

This was not the end of solicitation in the eventful few days following the October 4 cabinet meeting. On the ninth, Weizmann sent a wire to Brandeis giving the text of the draft declaration and concluding:

Most likely [I] shall be asked to appear before Cabinet when final discussion takes place about a week. It is essential to have not only President's approval of text but his recommendation to grant this declaration without delay. Further your support and enthusiastic message to us from American Zionists and also prominent non-Zionists most desirable at once. Assimilants doing utmost to defeat us. Your support urgently needed.

Weizmann sent similar messages to Baron de Rothschild in Paris, and to Israel Rosov, president of the Russian Zionist Organization. Then the English Zionist Federation drafted a circular letter calling for mass meetings of Jewish groups throughout the country and living under the British flag abroad, and requesting that this basic outline resolution be passed:

(1) That this meeting being unanimously in favor of the reconstitution of Palestine as the National Home of the Jewish People, trusts that His Majesty's Government will use its best endeavors to facilitate the achievement of this object.

(2) That this mass meeting pledges itself to support the Zionist leaders in their efforts towards the realization of the Zionist aims.

This letter went to Cairo and as far away as Australia, as well as to many congregations and organizations at home. Weizmann wrote a letter restating his case to Philip Kerr, and to Herbert Samuel he sent a report on all that had transpired thus far.

The responses were vivid. Mass meetings endorsing the proposed resolution were held in various parts of London, in Manchester, Leeds, Liverpool, Birmingham, Cardiff, Glasgow, Dublin, and many other communities in the United Kingdom. In Cairo, some three thousand Jews were to convene to endorse it before the end of the month.

As for President Wilson, we finally hear his own voice for the first time among the documents that survive of the peculiar episode of British solicitation of his opinion on the declaration that had begun on September 3. "I find in my pocket," he wrote on October 13 to Colonel House, "the memorandum you gave me about the Zionist Movement. I am afraid I did not say to you that I concurred in the formula suggested by the other side. I do, and would be obliged if you would let them know it." In his pocket! It is tempting to believe, as some have done, that Wilson was here responding for the first time to the queries he had received early the previous month. But this clearly is his answer to the query sent out after the War Cabinet meeting of October 4. The story ends as casually as it had begun.

On October 16 the British intelligence chief in New York wired London: "Colonel House put formula before President, who approves of it but asks that no mention of his approval shall be made when his Majesty's Government makes formula public, as he has arranged that American Jews shall then ask him for his approval, which he will give publicly here." The American Zionist leaders, in sending their approval, seem either to have suggested two changes in the text of the draft resolution or to have endorsed two changes suggested by Sokolow: most likely it was the latter. The first change was to restore the term "Jewish people" in place of "Jewish race" which had unfortunately made its way into the Milner formula. The other change was to reformulate the whole final clause so as to read: "or the rights and political status enjoyed by Jews in any other country." Both these changes were to be found acceptable.

The Jewish notables were prompt in their replies to the letter Hankey had sent them. Claude Montefiore took issue with the term "national home" and thought it significant that, as he put it, "anti-Semites are always very sympathetic to Zionism." For him, true Jewish well-being still lay in "emancipation and liberty in the countries of the world"—and as for the words "who are fully contented with their existing nationality and citizenship." he thought this put the case quite inadequately. "When thousands of Jews," he wrote, "are fighting with passion and ardor for their respective countries, they are not merely *contented* with their nationality. It is bone of their bone and spirit of their spirit." Yet, he said, he and his friends had no desire to impede Jewish immigration and colonization in Palestine, and furthermore, if His Majesty's Government regards it as being in the British interest to publish this formula, "I would of course subordinate my Jewish feelings, wishes and interests to the interests of England and the Empire." He then proposed an alternative draft declaration of his own:

> His Majesty's Government is anxious that free and unimpeded Jewish immigration into Palestine should be established. It views with favor unrestricted Jewish colonization in that country. It will do its best to facilitate such immigration and colonization, and will also seek to secure such municipal and local autonomy for the Jews as may be found possible, it being clearly understood, etc.

This of course eschewed the statement of essential national principle that the Zionists wanted; though the day would come when they were to wish they had pressed as firmly as Montefiore does here for an explicit statement favoring unrestricted Jewish immigration.

Leonard Cohen and Sir Philip Magnus also sent in alternative draft declarations of their own. Cohen's text was in the spirit of Montefiore's:

> His Majesty's Government, viewing with favor the settlement of Jews in Palestine, will use its best endeavors to facilitate their immigration and colonization in that country, and to secure for them the enjoyment of civil and religious liberty, together with municipal privileges, in the towns and colonies inhabited by them; it being clearly understood, etc.

Magnus, with whom Weizmann had held a not unsympathetic interview back in December 1914, presented himself as a sort of non-Zionist Ahad Ha'am, an interested Hebraist without the nationalism:

> His Majesty's Government views with favor the establishment in Palestine of a center of Jewish culture, and will use its best endeavors to facilitate the achievement of this object; it being understood, etc.

As for Sir Stuart Samuel, he simply stated it as his view that the vast majority of the Jews living in Great Britain were in favor of the position represented by the War Cabinet's proposed declaration. Years later in his memoirs, Herbert Samuel was to describe his brother without qualification as having been in favor of the declaration.

On the positive side were Herbert Samuel—who was, in effect, a ninth participant—Weizmann, Sokolow, Lord Rothschild, and Chief Rabbi Hertz. "It is," wrote Dr. Hertz,

> with feelings of the profoundest gratification that I learn of the intention of His Majesty's Government to lend its powerful support to the re-establishment in Palestine of a National Home for the Jewish people. . . . I must, as Chief Rabbi, thank the Prime Minister, the Secretary of State for Foreign Affairs and the members of the War Cabinet for their striking sympathy with Jewish aspirations and assure them that the overwhelming majority of Anglo-Jewry, as well as of the Jewries of His Majesty's Overseas Dominions, will rejoice with me at this broad humanity and far-sighted statesmanship of the men who guide the destinies of the Empire.

This was no small assurance: the appointment of Rabbi Hertz just before the war had been an unexpected and sumptuous gift to British Zionism.

Chaim Weizmann, in his letter of assent, could not resist the opportunity to deliver a final few blows to his assimilationist opponents before returning to his corner. "Although it is unfortunately true," he wrote, "that a certain number of Jews, chiefly in Western countries, are opposed to the idea of a Jewish national home in Palestine, it is no less true that these opponents, who are comparatively few in number, are almost exclusively to be found amongst those Jews who by education and social connections have lost touch with the real spirit animating the Jewish people as a whole." This was particularly in response to Edwin Montagu, who had sailed for India by now, but had left behind him yet another memorandum summing up the anti-Zionist views of a wide array of prominent Jews in Britain, America, and Western Europe. Montagu had even added a draft declaration of his own to the list of those submitted. "His Majesty's Government," it ran,

> accepts the principle that every opportunity should be afforded for the establishment in Palestine of those Jews who cannot,

and will not, remain in the lands in which they live at present, will use its best endeavors to facilitate the achievement of this object, and will be ready to consider any suggestions on the subject which any Jewish or Zionist organizations may desire to lay before it.

This, along with all the other suggested alternative drafts, was printed up for cabinet circulation.

Originally it had been supposed that the War Cabinet would come around to a reconsideration of the draft declaration within about two weeks of the October 4 meeting, or virtually as soon as all the answers to queries were received; but this was not the case. By Sunday the twenty-first, Weizmann was under the impression that the matter would be on the agenda two days hence, but there still were delays. Then it was actually put on the agenda for Thursday the twenty-fifth; but it was again postponed. For Weizmann, fate seemed to be conspiring against him. "I shall never in my life forget this day," Weizmann wrote to Ahad Ha'am on the twenty-fifth: "I was awaiting the decision in the morning, and it ended with a postponement. I went wearily to the Laboratory and found that there had been a fire and that half of it was burnt out. For a few days until things get straightened out please do not phone me at the Laboratory (the telephone was destroyed by the fire)."

Weizmann was not the only person whose patience was being strained. Just the day before, Sir Ronald Graham had written another memorandum on the subject. "I beg respectfully to submit," he wrote,

that this further delay will have a deplorable result and may jeopardize the whole Jewish situation. At the present moment uncertainty as regards the attitude of His Majesty's Government on this question is growing into suspicion, and not only are we losing the very valuable cooperation of the Zionist forces in Russia and America, but we may bring them into antagonism with us and throw the Zionists into the arms of the Germans who would only be too ready to welcome this opportunity.

After reminding his colleagues once again that the French and Italian governments, the Vatican, and now President Wilson, had all given their assurances of sympathy to the Zionists, Graham returned to the Russian situation, where bolshevism and antiwar sentiment were making great advances—greater even than Graham realized. "Information from every quarter," he wrote,

> shows the very important role which the Jews are now playing in the Russian political situation. At the present moment the Jews [of Russia] are certainly against the Allies and for the Germans, but almost every Jew in Russia is a Zionist and if they can be made to realize that the success of Zionist aspirations depends on the support of the Allies and the expulsion of the Turks from Palestine we shall enlist a most powerful element in our favor.

Graham pointed out that Yehiel Tschlenow was on his way to England at that moment and that it was most desirable that a British assurance on Zionism could be given by the time of his arrival. Graham further stated that Weizmann was ready to proceed to Russia, once a declaration was given, to take charge of a pro-Ally propaganda campaign there. As a final fillip, Graham noted that, though some have contended "that the feeling of the British Jews is against Zionism," the fact was that "within the last week 300 representative Jewish bodies have forwarded unanimous resolutions in favor of the movement."

Wickham Steed at *The Times* also had noticed the delay. In an October 14 letter to his publisher, Lord Northcliffe, who was visiting the United States, he had written about the general Zionist situation at home. Describing Montagu's tactics, he said that Curzon and Bonar Law had been giving these tactics support and had succeeded in delaying an outcome. But Steed said he had been doing all he could to help the Zionists and had been given a rather free hand in this by the editor, Geoffrey Dawson. Steed proved this point on October 26, when *The Times* ran a leader called "The Jews and Palestine." "The direct appeal," it began,

> recently made by more than 250 Jewish institutions, communities, and organizations throughout the country to His Majesty's Government "in favor of the reconstitution of Palestine as the National Home of the Jewish people," is too significant not to merit earnest attention. It would scarcely have been made had there not been reason to believe the Government disposed to respond to it. It is, indeed, no secret that the question of re-establishing the Jews in Palestine has for months been under consideration by the British and Allied Governments, and

not by them alone. But with a British army actually in Palestine, it is naturally to Great Britain that the Jews look for a directly helping hand in the achievement of their age-long aspiration. Yet a public announcement of our policy in this matter has been unaccountably delayed.

The article went on to sum up the reasons for making this announcement as soon as possible.

Steed seems to have been correct in his estimate of who in the cabinet were the major sources of the delay. "Bonar Law the difficulty," C.P. Scott had written in his diary on the 19th after seeing Weizmann, who certainly had inside information. "Not hostile, but pleading for delay." Bonar Law, in his inclination never to move too swiftly to any conclusion, was Asquith's true successor in the methods of cabinet government. His apparent hesitation about a pro-Zionist declaration does not seem to have had roots in any deep-lying negative attitude, however. The same could not be said of Lord Curzon, who was the reason for the postponement of the October 25 date for discussion; for he was at that moment preparing a long memorandum on the question, which he did not have ready for submission until the next day.

With clearly intended reference to Herbert Samuel's now-classic paper of 1915, Curzon's memorandum also was called "The Future of Palestine." Curzon began by calling attention to what he saw as a number of contradictions in the views of the proponents of a Jewish Palestine—in particular, over the matter of whether or not a state was what they ultimately sought. This of course was a point regarding which vagueness for the time being had become a policy, so that Curzon did not stand on firm ground in criticizing it.

The larger part of his paper was devoted to the question he had raised at the last War Cabinet discussion of the draft declaration—that of Palestine's capacity to absorb a large immigrant Jewish population. Curzon had visited the country shortly before the war and was impressed both by its smallness and by its relative aridity. "Palestine," he wrote, "would appear to be incapacitated by physical and other conditions from ever becoming in any real sense the national home of the Jewish people." He pointed out significantly that it was "a country calling for prolonged and patient toil [even] from a people inured to agriculture," whereas the Jews were "to a large extent trained in other industries and professions." Evidently he had not met Aaron Aaronsohn.

"There arises the further question," he went on,

what is to become of the people of this country, assuming the Turk to be expelled, and the inhabitants not to have been exterminated by the War? There are over half a million of these, Syrian Arabs—a mixed community with Arab, Hebrew, Canaanite, Greek, Egyptian, and possibly Crusaders' blood. They and their forefathers have occupied the country for the best part of 1,500 years. They own the soil, which belongs either to individual landowners or to village communities. They profess the Mohammedan faith. They will not be content either to be expropriated for Jewish immigrants, or to act merely as hewers of wood and drawers of water to the latter.

Curzon also dwelt upon the problem of Jerusalem. He knew that some dreamed of it as the capital of a Jewish state, but, he said, "such a dream is rendered wholly incapable of realization by the conditions of Jerusalem itself." Too many peoples and religions had a "passionate and permanent interest" there. He appreciated that, as he saw it, "the wisest of the Zionists" were satisfied to have Jerusalem "remain as a sort of enclave in international, if not in British, hands."

He then spelled out what he thought would be the most effective policy in Palestine once the Turks were turned out:

(a) Set up some form of European administration (it cannot be Jewish administration) in that country.

(b) Devise a machinery for safeguarding and securing order both in the Christian and in the Jewish Holy Places.

(c) Similarly guarantee the integrity of the Mosque of Omar and vest it on some Moslem body.

(d) Secure to the Jews (but not to the Jews alone) equal civil and religious rights with the other elements in the population.

(e) Arrange as far as possible for land purchase and settlement of returning Jews.

None of this, to be sure, was incompatible with the declaration now under consideration, and Curzon seems to have been aware of that in the literal sense. "If this is Zionism," he went on, "there is no reason why we should not all be Zionists," and he would gladly support their policy. But he feared that the idea of a "national home" represented "romantic and idealistic aspirations" that could not be realized. In his judgment, he concluded, Palestine would not "provide either a national, or material, or even a spiritual home for any more than a very small section of the Jewish people."

This was serious enough to provoke a reply from Sykes, who on the 30th issued a long, unsigned paper that surely had been drawn up with Aaronsohn's help. Referring to his own personal acquaintance with Palestine dating back to 1886, Sykes addressed himself exclusively to the assertion that the land was too barren to support a large immigrant population. Its apparent barrenness, he said in a sudden display of his mordant wit of prewar years, was due to:

(1) Indiscriminate charity of missionary bodies of all denominations which has tended to make pauperism profitable. . . .

(2) The tourist traffic, which has produced an immense number of muleteers, cicerones, guides etc., who make an income in the 2 months season and [are] idle the rest of the year.

(3) Want of roads, want of security, oppressive military service, uneconomic taxation, want of accessible parts.

(4) The cumulative effects of all these factors on a naturally idle and indolent race.

He then proceeded to spell out what the country's agricultural resources actually were—and, in particular, had become under organized settlement—mentioning, among other things, the orange groves, olive production, and the wine industry, all of which were flourishing. "The Jordan Valley," he said, "is a gigantic natural hothouse, capable of producing tropic and sub-tropic vegetables." So also was the area beyond the Jordan capable of development, and as for the Galilee, it already had become an example of what could be done.

To defend his view that colonization would have an immense effect on the productivity of Palestine, Sykes pointed out that no form of it so far had failed to have some positive result. Among the examples he referred to were the monks on Mount Carmel, the German colony at Haifa, and the Zionists. The monks, he pointed out, "were not trained colonists and restricted to an apparently barren rock"; the German colony "was not supported by the German Government"; and the Zionists "were hampered by the [Turkish] Government." Nevertheless, he went on, "these colonies have all caused the so-called desert to flourish, and are self-supporting and prosperous. I should not speak so strongly had I not seen these colonies grow up under my own eyes. Since I first knew Palestine the area of sporadic cultivation has practically quadrupled in spite of every discouragement." He thought that with "the abolition of . . . unnatural restrictions" the Palestine population could be quadrupled and even quintupled within forty years. "If Zionists do not go there," he concluded, "I am confident that some one will; nature abhors [a] vacuum. It took the Turks and all their men to keep the country a desert before the war, and if it remains in their hands after the war they will be too exhausted to resist the spirit of the age."

Nor could the War Cabinet go on resisting the spirit of the moment. The draft declaration was to come up for final consideration at last the following day.

It was on the day of the War Cabinet meeting scheduled to deal for the third time with the draft declaration that the British army won its first major victory in Palestine. This was the culmination of the change in atmosphere that had been occurring since Allenby's arrival in Egypt four months before. The Sinai front had now been strengthened by the arrival of two additional divisions. As promised, Allenby had established his general headquarters near the front, just to the north of Rafah. As if to emphasize the move from Cairo, where his predecessor had maintained headquarters, Allenby had even taken with him General Murray's old chef, a Frenchman who in peacetime had been proprietor of a café in Alexandria. The name of the Sinai desert village at which Allenby established himself was Umm el Kelab ("the Mother of Dogs"). An atmosphere of desert legend seemed to surround him there. At around this time there came to light an Arab prophecy that the Turks would be driven from Jerusalem only "when a prophet of the Lord brought the waters of the Nile to Palestine." The waters indeed had been brought by pipeline; and as for a "prophet of the Lord," speakers of Arabic knew that the new commander's name could be spelled out in their alphabet to read "Allah en-nebi," which meant precisely that.

The British had their code letters concerning Allenby, too. For whenever the commander was suddenly off on another of his well-known trips to examine some minor installation with his own eyes, the wireless would buzz with the signal "B.L."—meaning "Bull loose." Allenby left no opportunity for study unexplored; as one biographer has put it, he went about "with the diligence of a student working for a doctorate, as much as of a General about to conquer the land." He studied the Bible carefully, perhaps with a special zeal on account of the personal tragedy that had struck shortly after his assumption of the Egyptian command—the death of his only child Michael on the western front. He also carefully read George Adam Smith's classic work of 1894, *The Historical Geography of the Holy Land*—which Lloyd George claimed to have recommended to him and which, in a subsequent edition, was to include accounts of Allenby among those of various historic conquerors of Palestine. He also read two other contemporaries—his colleague David G. Hogarth's *Ancient East* and J.L. Myres's *Dawn of History*—as well as Herodotus. He would send to London for relevant papers appearing in the *Geographical Journal*, and at one point he sent back to Cairo for some passages in Strabo, which he himself translated from the original Greek. Allenby also studied flora and fauna, and was in fact an ardent amateur ornithologist, as were some members of his staff. "Along the water's edge," he wrote to his wife after an examination of the enemy lines near the coast below Gaza, "are queer crabs, big and little, many sandpipers and stints and some lovely blue kingfishers. They are the Spanish kingfisher; very like the English, but bluer. They pick up the little fish in the pools, and are quite tame and friendly."

In their examinations of troop distributions and the lie of the land, Allenby and his advisers had come to a significant conclusion: that Gaza itself, having become a major Turkish position since the element of surprise had been lost by the British, was now no longer the viable objective. As Lloyd George was to put it, with characteristic scorn toward the British military establishment, "Allenby was not wedded to the fantastic obsession which dominated the War Office and Headquarters in France, that the best place to attack the enemy was at his strongest point." At the very moment when the British armies in the west were once again learning the deadly futility of this obsession, at the third battle of Ypres—or Passchendaele—Allenby was making the decision that the place to attack was on the enemy's weak left flank at Beersheba. "Nothing," writes George Adam Smith of Beersheba, "could more aptly illustrate the defencelessness of these southern slopes of Judah than that this site which marked the frontier of the land was neither fortress nor gateway, but a cluster of wells on the open desert." The principle remained that whoever had control of those wells—the town's name probably originated in the meaning "seven wells" or "well of the seven"—was master of the entire surrounding arid region.

Allenby and his advisers were correct both as to the fact that Beersheba was a weak position—it was garrisoned by about five thousand troops, most of them Arab—and in assuming that the enemy expected the third major British assault to be made directly upon Gaza once again. But a danger was looming that could have upset their calculations had they moved too slowly. For the Turks and their German advisers in Syria were at this very time preparing a major offensive, to be made up primarily of troops that, owing to the slowing of action on the Caucasus front against a Russia weakening under the impact of revolution, were gathering in Aleppo. The operation—given the code name "Yilderim," the Turkish word for "lightning"—was the creation of Field Marshal Erich von Falkenhayn, who, recently demoted from supreme command of the German general staff on account of the failure to break through at Verdun, was now trying out his talents in Ottoman Asia. The ultimate purpose of Falkenhayn's mission was the reconquest of Baghdad, a far more important point than southern Palestine in the scheme of German oriental hegemony; but the first element in its strategy was to eliminate the Egyptian Expeditionary Force as a threat upon the right flank of a Turkish offensive in Mesopotamia. The peculiar irony was that Falkenhayn was planning to attack Allenby's army at its right flank, precisely the sector in which the British were now preparing to make their own move.

Of the problems facing Allenby as he prepared his offensive, the first and perhaps most urgent was secrecy. Surprise had failed at Gaza, and Gaza had become impregnable; surprise had to prevail at Beersheba. On the other hand, Allenby knew that it was impossible for the Turks and their German advisers not to know of British preparations regarding Beersheba—of reconnaissance expeditions or even of the attack itself, which had to be made with supply lines across more than ten miles of desert. The task was to persuade the enemy that all moves in the direction of Beersheba were only a feint, and that Gaza was indeed to be the objective of the main British attack. To this end, it was planned to precede the offensive by a week-long bombardment of Gaza.

Even more brashly, the British undertook an adventure in counterintelligence that came to be known as the "haversack ruse." The idea was that a staff officer, pretending to be on reconnaissance among Turkish desert outposts, would get himself chased, appear to be wounded and make off in great haste, his haversack fallen to the ground. Inside it, the Turks would find all they needed to know about the planned attack on Gaza. Two attempts were made and failed: the first time, the Turks did not notice the fallen haversack; the second, they did not even pursue the wounded officer. The third try was undertaken by the director of intelligence at general headquarters in the field, Colonel Richard Meinertzhagen, another admirer of Aaronsohn's and a man by this time persuaded that the reconquest of Palestine for the Jews was a task of virtually biblical import.

"I was well mounted," Meinertzhagen later wrote in his diary, "and near Girheir I found a Turkish patrol who at once gave chase. I galloped away for a mile or so and then they pulled up, so I stopped, dismounted and had a shot at them at about 60 yards. That was too much for them, and they at once resumed the chase, blazing away harmlessly all the time. Now was my chance, and in my effort to mount I loosened my haversack, field-glasses, water-bottle, dropped my rifle—previously stained with some fresh blood from my horse—and, in fact, did everything to make them believe I was hit and that my flight was disorderly. They had now approached close enough, and I made off, dropping the haversack which contained the note-book and various maps, my lunch, etc. I saw one of them stop and pick up the haversack and rifle, so I now went like the wind for home and soon gave them the slip, well satisfied with what I had done and that my deception had been successful. If only they act on the con-tents of the notebook, we shall do great things."

They did. On the night of October 30-31, some forty thousand British troops of all arms were moved out into the desert to take their positions. There were no viable roads, so that the only forms of transport were foot, horse, and camel. In the desert heat, the total water requirement for the striking force—including animals—in a single day was some four hundred thousand gallons, of which fully one-quarter, the human requirement, had to be carried. With the help of thirty thousand camels, this enormous requirement was pro-vided for—but for one day, and no more. The next day's supply had to be obtained in Beersheba itself—or back on base, after a retreat. And Beersheba had to be taken with the wells intact, before a de-feated enemy saw fit to destroy them.

The attack, which began at dawn, was carried out by three in-fantry divisions and two mounted divisions, with a camel brigade attached to each grouping. There also was an independent raiding party of Hejaz Arabs, mounted on camels and commanded by Lieu-tenant Colonel S.F. Newcombe, who had worked with Lawrence and Woolley on their expedition mapping the Sinai desert back in Janu-ary 1914. The assault was begun by the three infantry divisions, with their camel brigade, from the south and the southwest of the village, where the land provided no natural barriers and the defenses were upheld chiefly by barbed wire. By 1:30 P.M. they had established themselves in a solid line along a southwestern perimeter about three miles outside the village. There, according to plan, they stopped, while the actual assault upon the village was carried out by the mounted troops.

During the night, the mounted divisions had ridden all the way round to the east of the village, where they established themselves on heights from which they could see Beersheba and their own infantry below. They had begun their own assault at about 9:00 A.M., but were unexpectedly held up by a particularly strong Turkish defensive position at Tel es Saba. It was not until 3:00 P.M. that they were able to take this flat-topped, steep-walled mound with a machine-gun emplacement on it. For a moment there was uncertainty whether the right thing to do was to reduce other outside positions as planned or to aim directly at the village itself. It was the same crucial moment of decision near the end of the day that had ended in success at Magdhaba and in failure at the first battle of Gaza.

Then, almost simultaneously, General Allenby issued an order to take the village immediately, and the Anzac commander, General H.G. Chauvel, decided to do so before the order even got to him. This time there was a British will to victory blowing in the hot desert air. A classic charge began, the riders of the Desert Mounted Corps galloping over two lines of trenches, some of them dismounting to finish off the holders of those positions with bayonets, others thundering straight into Beersheba, where they overran guns, vehicles, and a mass of soldiers suddenly broken into a wild disorder. It was a far cry from that western front where Allenby had spent three frustrating years and where his son had just been killed. It was more like the era of Kipling in which he had been young, and of South Africa, where he had gained his first experiences as a soldier. There was something about this war in Palestine and Arabia that quickened the spirit.

Other than the revised text of the Milner-Amery draft declaration, the principal document before the War Cabinet as they turned to consider that question on October 31 was the Curzon memorandum. Balfour, in his opening remarks on the declaration addressed himself primarily to Curzon, who was present, and secondarily to Edwin Montagu, who was not. He said he "gathered that everyone was now agreed that, from a purely diplomatic and political point of view, it was desirable that some declaration favorable to the aspirations of the Jewish nationalists should now be made. The vast majority of Jews in Russia and America, as, indeed, all over the world, now appeared to be favorable to Zionism. If we could make a declaration favorable to such an ideal," he said, "we should be able to carry on an extremely useful propaganda both in Russia and America."

He then summed up the two main arguments that he gathered were still being put forward against Zionism:

(a.) That Palestine was inadequate to form a home for either the Jewish or any other people.

(b.) The difficulty felt with regard to the future position of Jews in Western countries.

Addressing himself to the first argument, Balfour said he understood "that there were considerable differences of opinion among experts regarding the possibility of the settlement of any large population in Palestine, but he was informed that, if Palestine were scientifically developed, a very much larger population could be sustained than had existed during the period of Turkish misrule. As to the meaning of the words 'national home,' to which the Zionists attach so much importance, he understood it to mean some form of British, American, or other protectorate, under which full facilities would be given to the Jews to work out their own salvation and to build up, by means of education, agriculture, and industry, a real center of national culture and focus of national life. It did not necessarily involve the early establishment of an independent Jewish State, which was a matter for gradual development in accordance with the ordinary laws of political evolution." The key word here was "early"; otherwise, the statement makes it quite clear that Balfour envisaged the eventual emergence of an independent Jewish state. Doubtless he had in mind a period somewhat longer than a mere thirty years; but the same could also be said of Chaim Weizmann.

Balfour now turned to the second argument, saying he felt that, "so far from Zionism hindering the process of assimilation in Western countries, the truer parallel was to be found in the position of an Englishman who leaves his country to establish a permanent home in the United States. In the latter case there was no difficulty in the Englishman or his children becoming full nationals of the United States, whereas, in the present position of Jewry, the assimilation was often felt to be incomplete, and any danger of a double allegiance or non-national outlook would be eliminated." The argument was perhaps overly ingenious, but the point to which it was addressing itself was really no longer a problem. Assimilationist opposition had been disarmed by the response to the Conjoint Foreign Committee's letter in *The Times* of May 24 and by provisos in the declaration's text; furthermore, Montagu was no longer present to be contended with.

The principal opposition present at the table, Lord Curzon, spoke up. He said he "admitted the force of the diplomatic arguments in favor of expressing sympathy, and agreed that the bulk of the Jews held Zionist rather than anti-Zionist opinions. He added that he did not agree with the attitude taken up by Mr. Montagu. On the other hand, he could not share the optimistic views held regarding the future of Palestine. These views were not merely the result of his own personal experiences of travel in that country, but of careful investigations from persons who had lived for many years in the country. He feared that by the suggested declaration we should be raising false expectations which could never be realized. He attached great importance to the necessity of retaining the Christian and Moslem Holy Places in Jerusalem and Bethlehem, and, if this were to be effectively done, he did not see how the Jewish people could have a political capital in Palestine." Having made his arguments, he then conceded that "some expression of sympathy with Jewish aspirations would be a valuable adjunct to our propaganda, though he thought that we should be guarded in the language used in giving expression to such sympathy." Yet he did not now offer—nor had he ever done so—any revision in the language of the declaration. With that, the vote was taken, and the revised draft was passed. Balfour was instructed to make it public at a suitable opportunity.

Sykes, who was present, left the room with the approved final text and brought it to Weizmann, who this time was waiting right outside. "Dr. Weizmann," he said, "it's a boy."

Two days later, Balfour made his official reply to the letter Lord Rothschild had sent him on July 18, presenting a declaration rather different from the draft that had then been submitted. It read:

Foreign Office,
November 2nd, 1917.
Dear Lord Rothschild,
    I have much pleasure in conveying to you, on behalf of His Majesty's Government, the following declaration of sympathy with Jewish Zionist aspirations which has been submitted to, and approved by, the Cabinet:

    "His Majesty's Government view with favour the establishment in Palestine of a national home for the Jewish people, and will use their best endeavours to facilitate the achievement of this object, it being clearly understood that nothing shall be done which may prejudice the civil and religious rights of existing non-Jewish communities in Palestine, or the rights and political status enjoyed by Jews in any other country."

I should be grateful if you would bring this declaration to the knowledge of the Zionist Federation.

Yours,
Arthur James Balfour

·44·

THE HIGH WALLS
OF JERUSALEM

Although the leadership of the English Zionist Federation was duly informed of Balfour's letter to Lord Rothschild within two or three days of its issuance, its contents were not made public for a week. On November 2, the day of the letter, the news of the fall of Beersheba appeared in the headlines. In the meantime, General Allenby, exploiting the principle of continued pursuit after a victorious surprise attack, had continued his offensive against the Turkish left and successfully rolled back that flank. Braced for a moment against a major attack from the south, even after Beersheba, the Turks at Gaza found the British still coming mainly from the east. Instead of fighting any longer, they evacuated the town, and British troops entered on the morning of the 7th to find it abandoned. The third battle of Gaza had ended in a victory at last. This was published in Britain on the 8th.

The wait for news of the first substantial British victories in Palestine was apparently among the reasons for the delay in the publication of the declaration. On November 7 C.P. Scott wrote to Weizmann congratulating him on this success, and added: "We are at liberty, I gather, to publish the important news in tomorrow's paper." That would have been Thursday the eighth; but the news did not appear anywhere until Friday. The reason for this further delay appears to have been Leopold Greenberg and the *Jewish Chronicle*. That paper was a weekly, published on Fridays. Greenberg, having heard about the declaration on the day of its issuance, was most anxious that the news should not break before the ninth, when he could present it at the same time as everyone else. Weizmann and

Sokolow were not pleased at the idea, but Greenberg prevailed upon Lord Rothschild, who wrote to Balfour requesting the November 9 publication date.

The timing could hardly have been worse. On the sixth the long-expected Bolshevik uprising had occurred, and the All-Russian Congress of Soviets had convened the next day to elect Vladimir Ilyich Lenin as president of the First Council of People's Commissars. The news reached Britain in time for Friday's editions. "ANARCHY IN PETROGRAD," *The Times* headline read, "POWER SEIZED BY LENIN." Next to this was a small box headed "Palestine for the Jews—Official Sympathy," which began: "Mr. Balfour has sent the following letter to Lord Rothschild in regard to the establishment of a national home in Palestine for the Jewish people." The text of Balfour's letter followed—but nothing more. There was no leader on the subject, nor would there be for several weeks. *The Times*, which had urgently called for this declaration just two weeks before, now had nothing to say about it. On October 26 it had written: "Have our Government, for instance, considered the value of Jewish influence in counteracting the insidious German propaganda in Russia?" But now the argument that the Jews of Russia, swayed by a pro-Zionist declaration, might be able to prevent the radicalization of the revolution there was manifestly being swept into the dustbin of history at the very moment the declaration became a reality.

The argument for winning American-Jewish support of the Entente also had become irrelevant. Oddly, little excuse for the declaration was left outside of the idealism that above all had motivated its principal makers.

The idealism of it was certainly what was celebrated by the rest of the British press, which, unlike *The Times*, was prompt to respond vividly to the event. "Epoch-making is perhaps not too strong a term to apply to Mr. Balfour's letter to Lord Rothschild," wrote the *Daily Chronicle* on the day of its publication, noting that, in the moment of General Allenby's victories, "the declaration has a significance that cannot be mistaken." "Never since the days of the Dispersion," wrote the *Manchester Guardian*, "has the extraordinary people scattered over the earth in every country of modern European and of the old Arabic civilization surrendered the hope of an ultimate return to the historic seat of its national existence." Characteristically, C.P. Scott's newspaper did not hesitate to go beyond the text of the declaration and offer a vigorously Zionist view of the British endorsement of that return. "What it means," the leader went on, is that, assuming our military successes to be continued and the whole of Palestine to be brought securely under our control, then on the conclusion of peace our deliberate policy will be to encourage in every way in our power Jewish immigration, to give full security, and no doubt a large measure of local autonomy, to the Jewish immigrants, with a view to the ultimate establishment of a Jewish State.

For the *Jewish Chronicle* the occasion, headlined "A Jewish Triumph," was one for celebrating the confluence of two great national destinies. "In this joyous hour," it said,

we English Jews turn with feelings of deepest pride and reverence to great and glorious Britain, mother of free nations and protectress of the oppressed, who has thus taken the lead in the Jewish restoration. The friend of our people for generations, who has raised her voice times out of number for our suffering martyrs, never was she truer to her noble traditions than today—never more England than now!

This was not far from the mood of Chaim Weizmann himself, who, despite some disappointment at the compromises in the text, wrote to Lord Rothschild on November 2 describing the declaration as "the Magna Charta of Jewish liberties," and was soon to write to Balfour comparing it to the proclamation of Cyrus the Great calling upon the Jews to return to Jerusalem and rebuild the Temple—the comparison Lord Ashley had made when Palmerston proposed returning the Jews to Palestine more than three-quarters of a century earlier.

In the next few days there were similar responses in the influential weeklies, as well as in the provincial press. "There could not have been at this juncture a stroke of statesmanship more just or more wise," the *Observer* said. The *Nation* recognized the moral significance of this outcome in terms of the Russian problem in particular. "One of our solidest reasons for welcoming the Russian Revolution," it wrote, "was that it had freed the whole Alliance from complicity in the sins of one of its chief partners towards the Jews. To end this record by restoring the dispersed and downtrodden race to its own cradle is a war aim which lifts the struggle in this region above the sordid level of Imperial competition." The *New Statesman*, calling the declaration "one of the best pieces of statesmanship that we can show in these latter days," was reminded of its own contribution to the discussion that had helped bring it about. "Early in the war," it said, referring to its issue of November 21, 1914, "*The New Statesman* published an article giving the main reasons why such a step should be taken, and nothing has occurred to change them." The author of that article, Albert M. Hyamson, who had since published a book on Palestine and had been working closely with Weizmann on the London Zionist Political Committee, was in fact at this very time appointed to head a new Jewish section of the Foreign Office's Information Department. There had been a curious muffling of the declaration at first, but the British Government was now going to miss no opportunity to publicize it.

The first significant public response to the declaration came on Sunday, December 2, when a mass meeting to celebrate it was held at the London Opera House. Lord Rothschild presided over a roster of eminent Jewish and non-Jewish speakers. Herbert Samuel stood up and gave, for the first time in public, the arguments for a Jewish Palestine that he had been presenting to members of the cabinet since November 1914. He concluded his speech with the exhortation that ends the traditional Passover service: "*l'Shanah haba'ah b'Yerushalayim*" ("Next Year in Jerusalem"). Such an utterance in Hebrew from the lips of an eminent Anglo-Jewish statesman was bound to make a deep impression upon this audience—which was largely drawn from the East End—and carry implications of virtually messianic significance. This mood was enhanced by Chief Rabbi Hertz, who reminded his listeners of the Proclamation of Cyrus and repeated the 126th Psalm, which celebrates the ensuing return from Captivity. Then Moses Gaster—recalling an old legend to the effect that, when the Temple was destroyed, fragments of its stones had embedded themselves in the hearts of every Jew—said that "I feel the stone in my heart already loosening." Israel Zangwill signaled the new era by offering to Zionism the cooperation of his Jewish Territorial Organization. Messages of support were read from, among others, Lord Grey and Lord Crewe, those champions of the cause in a bygone era.

The most important speeches had been made by the two most prominent Gentiles on the platform, Lord Robert Cecil and Sir Mark Sykes. Cecil, who again was filling in as acting foreign secretary while Balfour recovered from a minor illness, spoke of the declaration as the first constructive effort that we have made in what I hope will be the new settlement of the world after the war. I do not say that that is the only thing involved. It is not only the recognition of a nationality, it is much more than that. It has great underlying ideals of which you will hear this afternoon, and of which it would be impertinent of me to speak. It is, indeed, not the birth of a nation, for the Jewish nation through centuries of oppression and captivity have preserved their sentiment of nationality as few peoples could; but if it is not the birth of a nation, I believe we may say it is the re-birth of a nation. I don't like to prophesy what ultimate results that great event may have, but for myself I believe it will have a far-reaching influence on the history of the world and consequences which none can foresee on the future history of the human race.

In terms of the newly emerging Middle East, Cecil had made it quite clear earlier in the speech what his vision was: "Our wish," he said, "is that Arabian countries shall be for the Arabs, Armenia for the Armenians, and Judea for the Jews." The man who was soon to be one of the world's foremost activists for a League of Nations, and eventually the winner of a Nobel Peace Prize, was here expressing his firm belief in the compatibility of these national revivals.

For Sykes, the achievement of such compatibility was his overriding concern now that the declaration on Zionism was a reality. This was the burden of his speech; but first, he began it with a significant personal tribute. "My Lords, ladies and gentlemen," he said,

I should like to say, before I say one other word, that the reason I am interested in this movement is that I met one some two years ago who is now upon this platform, and who opened my eyes as to what this movement meant. He is on the list of speakers; . . . his name is known to most in the records of Zionism: I mean Dr. Gaster.

This surely helped loosen the stone from Gaster's heart. Then Sykes broached his main subject in characteristically rambling syntax. "I see," he said,

speaking to you as a watcher—now you, in a sense, are perhaps watchers also—perhaps you see something, perhaps you see three nations stricken with plague, cumbered with ruin, and Europe a welter of blood. Perhaps you see these three nations, and you realize that it may be your destiny to be a bridge between Asia and Europe, to bring the spirituality of Asia to Europe, and the vitality of Europe to Asia. That I firmly believe is the mission of Zionism. I see here something which is greater than a dream or a League of Nations. It is a league of continents, a league of races, and finally a league of ideals.

Reverting to history, Sykes then observed:

It is said that the Jewish people have a long memory. I believe that you remember Cordova, where your influence on modern civilization was at its zenith, and I think you remember what you owed to the Arabs in Cordova. You remember in the days when the Jews were so oppressed in Russia what you owed to the Armenians, who were your companions in oppression These tragedies are very different in their nature, and three tragedies destined to unite in one triumph. If all three hold together, the realization of your ideal is certain.

And he concluded:

You want to see Armenia free because you want to know that all people are free. You want to know the Arab is free, because he is, and always will be, your neighbor. Lastly, I would also say this: I look forward through difficulty and through pain to see Armenia free, and to prove the inevitable triumph of right over the greatest might there may be. I look to see the Arab civilization restored once more in Bagdad and in Damascus, and I look to see the return of Israel, with his majesty and tolerance, hushing mockery and dispelling doubt; and all three nations giving out to the world the good that God has infused into them.

Even as he spoke these words, Sykes's ears may have been ringing with the dispatch that had arrived only three days before from Sir Reginald Wingate in Cairo. "Recent announcement of His Majesty's Government on Jewish question," it said, "has made profound impression on both Christians and Moslems who view with little short of dismay prospect of seeing Palestine and even eventually Syria in hands of Jews." But Sykes, who had even found two Arabs as well as an Armenian to speak on this occasion, was not alone among the creators of the Balfour Declaration in believing that God and British good government would bring about a reconciliation in the end.

Chaim Weizmann ended the meeting by asking everyone to rise and repeat the celebrated oath from the 137th Psalm: "If I forget thee, O Jerusalem, let my right hand forget her cunning." This was followed by the singing of the two relevant national anthems, "Hatikvah" and "God Save the King." In the circumstances, the convergence of these strains was an echo of the convergence of British armies upon Jerusalem that was taking place at that moment.

When Lloyd George had spoken to Allenby in June before sending him to his new command, he had suggested a most desirable gift for Government and country: "Jerusalem before Christmas." Could this wish be satisfied? After Gaza on November 7, Jaffa had fallen on the sixteenth—a climax to the campaign that had begun with the roll-up of the Turkish flank at Beersheba. With winter now coming on, there were good arguments for calling this the end of the campaigning season. Allenby was badly in need of reinforcements, but the War Office could not supply them. Just two years earlier to the month, in another of this war's rare campaigns of movement, General Townshend had overextended himself in Mesopotamia, and the result had been retreat to Kut-el-Amara and the disastrous siege there. Furthermore, if Jerusalem was the objective, what confronted Allenby's soldiers was no longer desert and plain, in which they had achieved such mastery, but the steep, jagged, and rocky hills of Judea.

"A long series of valleys running south from Aijalon to Beersheba," writes George Adam Smith in *The Historical Geography of the Holy Land*, "separate the low loose hills of the Shephelah [the lowlands adjacent to the Coastal Plain] from the lofty compact range to the east—*the hill-country of Judaea*. This barrier, which repelled the Philistines, even when they had conquered the Shephelah, is penetrated by defiles, none more broad than those of Beth-horon, of Wady 'Ali along which the high-road to Jerusalem travels and of Wady es-Surar up which the railway runs. Few are straight, most sharply curve. The sides are steep, and often precipitous, frequently with no path between save the torrent bed, in rapids of loose shingle or level steps of the strata, which at the mouth of the defile are often tilted almost perpendicularly into easily defended obstacles of passage. The sun beats down upon the limestone; springs are few, though sometimes generous; a thick bush fringes the brows, and caves abound and tumbled rocks."

Smith's text gave Allenby ample warning of what he would be up against. "Everything conspires," it went on, "to give the few inhabitants means of defence against large armies. It is a country of ambushes, entanglements, surprises, where armies have no room to fight, and the defenders can remain hidden; where the essentials for war are nimbleness and the sure foot, power of scramble and of rush." Apart from the railway that the French had built before the war, the only good access to Jerusalem from the west was the road up from Jaffa that pilgrims had followed through the ages. It was the one road from that direction suitable for wheeled transportation. But—steep, winding, and often surrounded by commanding heights—it was hard to travel in the best of circumstances and easily defensible in war.

"Yet with negligent defenders," Smith adds, "the western border of Judaea is quickly penetrated. Six hours will bring an army up any of the defiles, and they stand on the central plateau, within a few miles of Jerusalem or of Hebron." Well, the Turks had often enough shown themselves to be negligent defenders, and Falkenhayn's Yilderim army had still not come down to Jerusalem. Allenby, who established his new headquarters at Junction Station, a point south of Ramleh at which the railway tracks from Jerusalem branched northward and southward, was determined to give it a try. He gave his troops one day's needed rest and began his Jerusalem campaign on November 18.

At first he thought he would again use his fine mounted troops; but a day of fighting in the defiles caused him to realize that the task was now mainly one for infantry. Allenby's maps of the region dated back to the era of the Palestine Exploration Fund, and many of the routes marked on them really were suitable for no adequate beast of burden other than the donkey—and, in fact, some two thousand donkeys had been brought up from Egypt for the campaign. Accordingly, three infantry divisions were sent into the hills. One of them, the Seventy-fifth—which was made up largely of Gurkhas and other Indian troops—was to follow the main road up from Jaffa, stop a few miles short of Jerusalem, and turn off to the northeast. Another, the Yeomanry Division, was to follow the Beth-horon route mentioned by Smith, a few miles to the left of the Seventy-fifth. Between them, to maintain support and contact, the Fifty-second Division was to advance from the Vale of Ajalon. To their right, one Australian mounted brigade was to lend support by advancing along the Wadi es-Surar, the railway route.

Jerusalem itself, which was well fortified and to which Allenby did not want to cause physical damage—he had given an order that no fighting was to take place within six miles of the city—was not the immediate objective. Rather, the objective was Jerusalem's best road, which ran from the city directly north to Nablus and was the main Turkish supply route. Allenby's plan was that the three attacking infantry divisions should converge upon the road north of the city and choke off the Turkish garrison. On the nineteenth, the second day of the campaign, this goal seemed well on its way toward realization, despite the sudden onset of winter rain—of the stone-soaking wetness that can make the Judean hills in November and December seem like the chilliest place on earth, especially when, like Allenby's troops in their thin khakis, with few blankets and no overcoats, one is prepared only for blazing sun. On that day, the Seventy-fifth Division—seasoned by experience of similar terrain on the northwestern frontier of India—made the crucial ascent on the main road up the steep Bab el Wad defile. The other two divisions also fought their way successfully to their designated first objectives west and southwest of Ramallah: the Yeomanry to Beit Ur et Tahta; the Fifty-second to Beit Likia.

November 20, another cold and rainy day, started out similarly well. The Seventy-fifth continued its rugged progress up the main road, facing a machine-gun battery on a high eminence at Kuryet el Enab (Kiryat Anavim). A fog rolled in, and under cover of it three battalions charged up to the machine guns with fixed bayonets. They had won the position by sundown. The Fifty-second Division also made some progress; but the Yeomanry, making its crucial thrust for the Nablus road, had been stopped at Beitunia by a force of some three thousand Turkish soldiers. Despite a number of successes, then, the three-pronged assault had come to the end of its third day without achieving its main objective.

But this did not prevent the indefatigable men of the Seventy-fifth from scoring their greatest triumph the following day. Having secured Kiryat Anavim, they made that position their right flank, swinging off the main road and heading northeast toward the Nablus road. On the way, they found the historic village of Nebi Samwil ("Prophet Samuel," who is said by tradition to be buried there) standing high on a cone-shaped hill and dominated by a minaret visible for miles around. One brigade assaulted it and gained the summit by midnight. From it could be seen many of the Turkish defenses and even Jerusalem itself. Richard Coeur de Lion is said to have stood at this spot in the spring of 1191, weeping at the sight of the city he knew he could not recapture from Saladin, for the Third Crusade had disintegrated by then. The Turks knew that the village was a prize, for they were to make three vigorous counterattacks upon it within as many days. All were repulsed by the men of the Seventy-fifth, who considered themselves to have captured the "Key to Jerusalem." Eventually they were to adopt a symbolic key as their divisional badge.

The energies of assault were rapidly being depleted, however. For the next three days, the Seventy-fifth and the Fifty-second took turns attacking the strong Turkish position just to the north of Nebi Samwil at El Jib, the biblical Gibeon: "Then spake Joshua to the Lord in the day when the Lord delivered up the Amorites before the children of Israel, and he said in the sight of Israel, Sun, stand thou still upon Gibeon; and thou, Moon, in the valley of Ajalon." But the sun kept rounding the earth from the 22nd to the 24th of November 1917, and the position was not taken. In the meantime, the Yeomanry Division, similarly frustrated, had fallen back to the Beth-horon defile at the village of Beit Ur el Fauka. On the twenty-fourth, Allenby gave orders to discontinue all attacks and consolidate the line that had been gained. Was Judea to be another Gallipoli after all?

It was not. During the next two weeks, Allenby replaced the three divisions that had fought in the hills with relatively fresh ones—veterans of the recent campaigns that at least had enjoyed a few days' respite. During that time, several Turkish counterattacks at various positions were repulsed. A new line of attack was projected by General Philip Chetwode, now one of Allenby's corps commanders. Still aimed at the Nablus road, his plan was not to attack it from the rugged defiles to the north as before, but to move upon it straight from the Jaffa-Jerusalem road, sweeping past the western outskirts of the city itself. Yet this plan proved unnecessary when the major assault was begun on December 8 and 9. After only one day of fighting, during which the British took Ein Karem—believed to be the birthplace of John the Baptist—the Turkish will to fight suddenly collapsed. By the morning of the ninth, Jerusalem was empty of Turkish soldiers.

Some last-ditch fighting was still going on on the Mount of Olives above when members of the Sixtieth Division saw a man, who turned out to be the mayor of Jerusalem, emerging from the Jaffa Gate, white flag in his hands. Ready to offer the keys of the city and a letter of surrender to the first British soldiers he encountered, Mayor Husseini approached Sergeants Hurcombe and Sedgewick of the 2/29th London Regiment. They declined the honor. Then he tried two artillery majors, who in turn sought out two other officers for a solution to this problem of protocol. Finally, a brigadier general appeared, and he tried to deal with the by now excited mayor. The matter was then referred to the Sixtieth Division commander, Major General J.S.M. Shea, who consulted General Chetwode. Chetwode advised him that he could accept the surrender on General Allenby's behalf, and he did so from an undoubtedly grateful mayor at 11:00 A.M.

When the news of the fall of Jerusalem reached Allenby, he was in his tent at Junction Station, in the middle of an interview with Major T.E. Lawrence. Lawrence had been ordered to fly in from Aqaba to report on some of his recent activities, which had not been going entirely well. Less than three weeks before, he had spent perhaps the worst night of his life—one during which, as he was to write, "the citadel of my integrity had been irrevocably lost." Captured by the Turks while spying at Deraa in the Hauran, he had been beaten, whipped, tortured, and in some way sexually assaulted; but he managed somehow to escape. Another recent setback had been his failure to blow up a bridge across the Yarmuk River south of Deraa—a mission that, if accomplished, would have greatly hindered the provisioning of the Turkish forces at Jerusalem. But when he spoke to Allenby that December 9, Lawrence found the general "so full of victories that my short statement that we had failed to carry a Yarmuk bridge was sufficient, and the miserable details of failure could remain concealed."

Far from resenting Lawrence's failure, Allenby invited him to participate in the official entry into Jerusalem. This took place on December 11. "It was a brilliant day," Allenby later wrote to his wife; "hoar frost here, in the early a.m., and then iced sunshine; with no wind. We could see, from the top of the house where I met Chetwode, the mountains of Moab; deep blue and huge. The Dead Sea lay too low to be seen."

The ceremony had been the subject of planning by telegram between London and Cairo since November 8, the day after Gaza fell. Sykes had wired innumerable suggestions as they came to him, ranging in their concern from the proper ways to handle various religious groups and their Holy Places to questions of a decidedly political nature. Sir Reginald Wingate was not to attend the ceremony, for example, because Sykes thought his presence would make it seem as though the Egyptian administration were simply being extended across the border in a purely annexationist move. The French and the Italians were to be kept firmly if delicately in their place, though they were of course to take part in the ceremony. Picot, who had been in Cairo ready to enter Jerusalem since November 25, even had a new title: French high commissioner in Palestine and Syria. General Clayton, who had replaced Sykes as chief political officer on the staff of the British army in Palestine, had no such title. But Picot's troubling claim could be handled by a simple expedient: until further notice, Allenby was establishing a temporary *military* administration in Palestine, and that would be only British.

Allenby, who, as Lawrence was to put it, had "made ready to enter in the official manner which the catholic imagination of Mark Sykes had devised," rode on horseback at the head of a procession through the new part of Jerusalem. But he dismounted when he reached the Jaffa Gate, strode past the honor guard, and entered the Old City on foot. "There was no great pageantry of arms," according to the *Illustrated London News*, "no display of the pomp and circumstances of a victorious army." This was a far cry from the grand entry made by the kaiser in October 1898, when a part of the wall alongside the low Jaffa Gate had been demolished to enable him to enter on horseback. It was the entry of a liberal conqueror, who, though he was the first Christian to capture the city since the Crusaders, was eager to point out that his army contained Muslim contingents as well. One such unit, from India, was at that very moment guarding the Haram-esh-Sharif, the sacred enclosure of the Dome of the Rock. The all-Jewish units would be arriving in less than three months.

Entering through the Gate just behind Allenby were the commanders of the small French and Italian units that had been serving under him. Behind them was a group of British officers that included Chetwode, Clayton, and Lawrence, the latter wearing a uniform pieced together from among his colleagues to replace his customary disarray. In Lawrence's opinion, he was sharing in "the supreme moment of the war."

The procession made its way to the nearby Citadel, where Allenby read a proclamation:

> To the inhabitants of Jerusalem the Blessed and the people dwelling in its vicinity:
>
> The defeat inflicted upon the Turks by the troops under my command has resulted in the occupation of your City by my forces. I therefore here and now proclaim it to be under Martial Law, under which form of administration it will remain so long as military considerations make it necessary.
>
> However, lest any of you should be alarmed by reason of your experiences at the hands of the enemy who has retired, I hereby inform you that it is my desire that every person should pursue his lawful business without fear of interruption. Furthermore, since your City is regarded with affection by the adherents of three of the great religions of mankind, and its soil has been consecrated by the prayers and pilgrimages of devout people of those three religions for many centuries, therefore do I make known to you that every sacred building, monument, holy spot, shrine, traditional site, endowment, pious bequest, or customary place of prayer, of whatsoever form of the three religions, will be maintained and protected according to the existing customs and beliefs of those to whose faiths they are sacred.

Translations of this into several languages, including Hebrew and Arabic, then were read in turn. Afterward, the notables of the city were presented to Allenby. Then the procession returned to the Gate and the modest ceremony ended.

Lunch was served at General Shea's headquarters, and it was here that Picot spoke up. "And tomorrow, my dear general," he said, according to Lawrence, "I will take the necessary steps to set up civil government in this town."

Lawrence describes the astonishment of everyone present. "Salad, chicken mayonnaise and foie gras sandwiches hung in our wet mouths unmunched, while we turned to Allenby and gaped. Even he seemed for the moment at a loss." But the general had received his instructions.

"In the military zone," Allenby replied, "the only authority is that of the Commander-in-Chief—myself."

"But Sir Grey," Picot protested, "Sir Edward Grey . . ." His attempt to invoke a name from a bygone era was cut short.

"Sir Edward Grey," Allenby said, "referred to the civil government which will be established when I judge that the military situation permits."

Perhaps this was the moment in which the Sykes-Picot Agreement began its surrender to the biggest battalions. After aspiring for so long—even for centuries—to keep the French out of it, the British were to have Jerusalem after all.

EPILOGUE

·1918–1948·

·45·

FROM WAR TO PEACE

On February 2, 1918, the Thirty-eighth Royal Fusiliers, made up almost entirely of "Russian" aliens from the East End, marched in ceremony from the City of London into Whitechapel. In the lead was Lieutenant Colonel John Henry Patterson on horseback; on foot with the men was the newly commissioned Lieutenant Vladimir Jabotinsky. "There were tens of thousands of Jews," Jabotinsky was to recall, "in the streets, at the windows and on the roofs. Blue-white flags were over every shop-door; women crying with joy, old Jews with fluttering beards murmuring, '*Shehechey-anu*';* Patterson on his horse, laughing and bowing, and wearing a rose which a girl had thrown him from a balcony." Two days later the "tailors," as they were called, sailed from Southampton on their way to Palestine.

The war in Palestine was largely quiescent during the spring and summer of 1918. In those months the burden of Allied energies shifted even more heavily than before to the West, where the Germans—after concluding the Treaty of Brest-Litovsk, which removed Russia from the war—staged a succession of powerful and nearly overwhelming offensives. But these ultimately were frustrated, owing in part to the substantial presence of American troops, and the tide began to turn in September. General Allenby then launched a new offensive in Palestine.

Allenby once again relied upon his cavalry for the main assault: indeed, this was to be the last great cavalry battle in history. As before, the infantry opened the way: its attack began on the morning of September 18 along the coast north of Jaffa, aided by artillery and aircraft. By nightfall it had swung back the Turkish forces in a

---

* The traditional Jewish prayer thanking God for having made it possible to survive to see this day.

wheeling movement northeastward that was like the opening of a great gate. Through the opening rode the Desert Mounted Corps, sweeping in an arc whose left wing thundered into Nazareth in the early morning hours of the twentieth. General Liman von Sanders, commanding from that ancient city, was so taken by surprise that he had to retreat in his pajamas. Only Mustafa Kemal, commanding the Turkish Seventh Army, fought with any distinction on the enemy side; but he, too, was forced to retreat. At the center of the great swath made by the British cavalry were the ruins of the ancient city of Megiddo, the Armageddon of the Bible, and it was from this site that the battle was appropriately to take its name.

Taking advantage of the disarray into which the Turks had been thrown, the British right proceeded up the Jordan Valley from its original position just north of Jericho. Among the troops fighting in this sector were the three battalions constituting what was now generally referred to as the Jewish Regiment and would be remembered in history as the Jewish Legion—the Thirty-eighth Royal Fusiliers, or "tailors"; the Thirty-ninth, made up primarily of volunteers from the United States and Canada; and the Fortieth, composed almost entirely of Palestinian Jews from the Alexandria barracks and from the liberated areas in the south of the country. Enduring summer heat that ranged from 100 to 120 degrees Fahrenheit, surrounded by mosquitoes, centipedes, and stinging spiders, the Jewish battalions took part in the capture of Es Salt, a key position in the Hills of Moab on the way eastward to Amman, on September 23. "The dust on the hills was worse than the smoke in the valley had been," Jabotinsky was to recall. "It hung over the ground without a breath of wind to disturb it, and instead of air we breathed and swallowed dust." Amman was taken on the twenty-fifth, as was Samakh, on the southern shore of Lake Tiberias.

It was not until September 22 that Allenby made clear his intention to continue the pursuit all the way to Damascus. The success of this aim depended upon Lawrence, Feisal, and their Arab troops, who formed an irregular wing to the east of Allenby's conventional right in the Jordan Valley. Their zone of battle had been the Hejaz railway, which by now had been so battered by their raids that it was virtually under their control south of Deraa. The Turkish garrison at Medina, still holding out against the two-year-long Arab siege, had lost all hope of a successful outcome. The last important link between it and Damascus was Deraa, the junction between the Hejaz line and the branch that ran westward to Haifa and other points in Palestine. The Arabs began their assault on the twenty-sixth, with the capture by Auda abu Tayi of a train that yielded some two thousand prisoners, including Germans and Austrians. Deraa itself, hastily abandoned by the main body of Turks, was taken the next day. That same day, the twenty-seventh, Quneitra was taken by Allenby's cavalry. All the key positions on the way to Damascus were now in Arab and British hands.

Since Damascus—perhaps the most ancient continuously inhabited city in the world—stood at the center of trade routes and had never been built for self-defense, the entry into it was only a matter of time. Indeed, this now was a political problem more than a military one. Allenby's victories had already begun an effective revision of the Sykes-Picot Agreement: whatever hopes the French still cherished in the Middle East, they were no longer to be even partially in control of the destiny of Palestine. But Damascus was another matter. Though designated by the Agreement for Arab autonomy, it nevertheless, as part of Area A, was to be firmly under French hegemony. What would happen to this arrangement if Feisal's Arabs entered the city first, as Lawrence so ardently desired?

The question was made more complicated by a curiously ill-considered statement the Foreign Office had allowed to be issued on June 16. In Cairo, seven Arab nationalist leaders from various parts of Ottoman Asia, who asked to remain anonymous, had submitted a formal inquiry to Sir Reginald Wingate as to the nature of British war aims in the region. The reply had stated that the region under consideration fell into four categories:

> 1. Areas in Arabia which were free and independent before the outbreak of war;
> 2. Areas emancipated from Turkish control by the action of the Arabs themselves during the present war;
> 3. Areas formerly under Ottoman dominion, occupied by the Allied forces during the present war;
> 4. Areas still under Turkish control.

In the areas comprised in the first two categories, the statement went on, the British Government recognized "the complete and sovereign independence" of the Arabs living there. Regarding the third category, the statement called attention to the proclamations issued by General Maude in Baghdad and General Allenby in Jerusalem when they respectively occupied those cities, and added:

It is the wish and desire of His Majesty's Government that the future government of these regions should be based upon the principle of the consent of the governed and this policy has and will continue to have the support of His Majesty's Government.

As for the fourth category, Britain desired "that the oppressed peoples of these areas should obtain their freedom and independence and towards the achievement of this object His Majesty's Government continue to labor."

The Declaration to the Seven, as it came to be called, was in the spirit of the Fourteen Points proclaimed by President Wilson the preceding January; but it contained implications that, in the light of other commitments, were to be difficult or impossible to honor.* How could the "consent of the governed" be reconciled with either the Sykes-Picot Agreement or any revision of it that would still designate areas of French or British control whether the local populations wanted it or not? And if the principle applied to the population of Palestine as it then was constituted, it hardly was compatible with the Balfour Declaration, which would surely have been opposed by the Arab majority there. As for areas emancipated by the Arabs, this would have made Damascus a problem indeed had Lawrence and Feisal had their way.

In the race for Damascus, two Arab contingents arrived at its outskirts on the night of September 30; but its surrender did not take place until the following morning with the arrival of an Australian light horse brigade. Allenby made his formal entry on October 3 and then held a conference with Feisal, who had entered the same day. Allenby said he would recognize an Arab military administration in Damascus; but he reserved Palestine and northern coastal Syria for British and French military administrations, respectively. He also informed Feisal of the Sykes-Picot Agreement. When the young Hashimite objected strongly, Allenby turned to Lawrence, who was present, and asked:

"But did you not tell him that the French were to have the Protectorate over Syria?"

"No, Sir," Lawrence replied, "I know nothing about it."

---

* The essentials of this pledge were reaffirmed by an Anglo-French declaration issued on November 7, a week after the Turkish armistice, which stated that the object of the victors was "the establishment of national governments and administrations deriving their authority from the initiative and free choice of the indigenous populations."

"But you knew definitely that he, Feisal, was to have nothing to do with the Lebanon."

"No, Sir," Lawrence said, "I did not."

With that, Allenby explained the situation to Feisal and said the final outcome remained to be decided after the end of the war. When Feisal left, Lawrence—not at all eager at the prospect of working with a French liaison officer—announced that he was due for a leave and that he had better take it now and go to England.

"Yes," said Allenby. "I think you had!"

Lawrence left the next day, knowing at once, he was to recall, "how much I was sorry." His wartime struggle for Feisal and the Arab revolt was over, his peacetime one about to begin. Turkey surrendered on October 30, four days after the British capture of Aleppo and twelve days before the end of the war in the West.

If Foisal had indeed been ignorant of French claims in Syria until the capture of Damascus, he had at any rate not been so regarding the Jewish claims in Palestine. News of the Balfour Declaration had reached the ears of King Hussein and other Arab leaders by the end of 1917, and they had sought further elucidation about it. Clayton had sent a telegram about the matter to Sykes, who wired back on January 4 instructing him to tell Arab leaders:

> That so far as Palestine is concerned we are determined that no people shall be subjected to another, but . . . since the Jewish opinion of the world is in favor of a return of Jews to Palestine and inasmuch as this opinion must remain a constant factor, and further as His Majesty's Government view with favor the realization of this aspiration, His Majesty's Government are determined that in so far as is compatible with the freedom of the existing population both economic and political, no obstacle should be put in the way of the realization of this ideal.

Within a few days of the arrival of this message, Commander D.G. Hogarth was in Jeddah relaying its contents to the king in person. Hogarth added that the leaders of the Zionist movement were ready to offer friendship and cooperation with the Arabs and that this offer was "not one to be lightly thrown aside." Hussein had accepted this explanation—and so, apparently, had Feisal. For, in a succession of encounters with Chaim Weizmann from the middle of 1918 to early

1919, Feisal showed a willingness to cooperate with the Zionist movement and achieve a modus vivendi with its aspirations in Palestine.

The first meeting between Feisal and Weizmann took place during the first half of June 1918 at Feisal's camp in the Hills of Moab near Maan. Weizmann had arrived in Palestine at the beginning of April as leader of a nine-man Zionist Commission, appointed by the War Cabinet to begin coordinating Jewish affairs there, to act as a liaison between the military government and the Jewish population, and to try to establish links between the Jewish and Arab communities. It seems to have been General Clayton who suggested a meeting between the Zionist leader and the Hashimite prince. Weizmann gladly took up the idea and made the arduous roundabout voyage to Feisal's camp—by way of Suez, the sea, and Aqaba—necessitated by the fact that the Turks were then still in control of the Jordan Valley. Weizmann made the last part of the journey on foot, from the heat of the valley to the fresh breeze of the mountaintops. "It was a brilliant moonlit night—Palestinian moonlight," Weizmann later recalled, "—and I looked down from Moab on the Jordan Valley and the Dead Sea and the Judean hills beyond. I may have been a little lightheaded from the sudden change of climate, but as I stood there I suddenly had the feeling that three thousand years had vanished, had become as nothing."

It was an atmosphere in which Jew and Arab could readily fall back upon their ancient history as Semitic cousins. "He is the first real Arab nationalist I have met," Weizmann was to write admiringly to Vera: "He is a leader! He's quite intelligent and a very honest man, handsome as a picture! He is not interested in Palestine, but on the other hand he wants Damascus and the whole of northern Syria. He talked with great animosity against the French, who want to get their hands on Syria. He expects a great deal from collaboration with the Jews!" Clayton later expanded upon this in his own report of the conversation, which was held through an interpreter but with occasional direct exchanges in French. "Weizmann pointed out," Clayton wrote,

> that a Jewish Palestine would assist the development of an Arab Kingdom and that an Arab Kingdom would receive Jewish support. Weizmann explained the Zionists did not propose to set up a Jewish Government, but wished to work if possible under British guidance in order to colonize and develop the country without encroaching on other legitimate interests.

Colonel P.C. Joyce, like Lawrence a British officer attached to the Arab revolt, had escorted Weizmann in Lawrence's absence. He reported to Clayton that in his opinion

> Feisal really welcomed Jewish cooperation and considered it essential to future Arab ambitions though unable to express any very definite views in absence of authority from his father. It is Colonel Joyce's opinion that Feisal fully realizes the future possibility of a Jewish Palestine, and would probably accept it if it assisted Arab expansion further north.

At the end of their conversation, the two Semitic nationalist leaders posed for pictures together, Weizmann wearing an Arab *kefiyah*. Later that summer, after he had returned to Tel Aviv, Weizmann received word that King Hussein wanted to see him too, but the trip no longer seemed feasible at that point.

Weizmann was back in London by the beginning of November, as was T.E. Lawrence, whom he began seeing with some frequency after the German armistice was signed and preparations for the Peace Conference began. Lawrence and Weizmann got on well, despite the impression Aaron Aaronsohn had that Lawrence was anti-Semitic and despite the frequent allegations of anti-Zionism that were ever to be made against him—which Weizmann was to deny vigorously in his autobiography. As far back as his first journey to Palestine in 1909, Lawrence had described the Jewish colonies there as "bright spots in a desert," and by the end of 1918 he had become outspoken in the view that Jews and Arabs could get along in Palestine so long as Britain was in control there.

In December, prior to attending the Peace Conference due to open in Paris the following month, Feisal came to London, and Lawrence, who acted as his escort, arranged another meeting between him and Weizmann. This took place on December 11 at the Carlton Hotel, where Feisal was staying; Lawrence acted as interpreter for the occasion. Feisal began the conversation with a denunciation of the Sykes-Picot Agreement, which he said he hoped the Americans would be able to destroy at the Peace Conference. Weizmann replied that he had long been aware of the Agreement and had protested against it whenever he could. He told Feisal that a delegation of American Zionists was on its way to London and that it "would use its influence in favor of both Jews and Arabs."

The discussion then turned to the friction that was growing between Jews and Arabs in Palestine itself. Feisal thought this was being "fomented by Turkish and pro-Turkish propaganda. The Turks always ruled by trying to divide the races under their sway. The Arabs in Palestine are still used to the methods of Turkish propaganda, but he was quite sure that he and his followers would be able to explain to the Arabs that the advent of the Jews into Palestine was for the good of the country, and that the legitimate interests of the Arab peasants would in no way be interfered with." Later, Feisal remarked that "it was curious there should be friction between Jews and Arabs in Palestine. There was no friction in any other country where Jews lived together with Arabs." He seems to have forgotten for the moment that Jews were not claiming a national home in any other country. Perhaps the real truth of his attitude lay in something Weizmann had noticed at their meeting in June. "He is contemptuous of the Palestinian Arabs," Weizmann had written to his wife at the time, "whom he doesn't even regard as Arabs!" But whatever his underlying feelings were, Feisal, according to Weizmann's account, expressed the view in this London conversation that there was land enough in Palestine for both Jews and Arabs.

Feisal asked for some details of the Zionist program, and Weizmann replied with seven points: (1) the expectation that Feisal and the Peace Conference would "recognize the national and historical rights of Jews to Palestine"; (2) the desire for Great Britain to be "the Trustee Power, which would set up a Government in Palestine in which the Jews would expect to take an adequate share"; (3) land reform in Palestine, which would render the large, unused tracts "now in the hands of the Effendis and Usurers available for colonization"; (4) public works and improvements allowing the possible settlement even of "four or five million Jews, without encroaching on the ownership rights of Arab peasantry"; (5) that the Jews of Palestine be ready to assist Feisal with knowledge and money in his own national revival; (6) that the details of boundary and religious jurisdictions be left until after the settlement of the larger questions; (7) repudiation of all insinuations that the Jews intended to interfere with the Muslim Holy Places.

Feisal responded by assuring Weizmann "on his word of honor that he would do everything to support Jewish demands, and would declare at the Peace Conference that Zionism and the Arab movement were fellow movements, and that complete harmony prevailed between them. He would try his best to obtain the British Government as Trustee Power for Arabia and, if he did not succeed, he would try to get America to act." He expressed his wish that the Zionists would help him and said that if he failed to achieve an Arab state by peaceful means he would have to take up arms to do so. With that, the meeting ended.

After meeting again at a dinner party at the home of Lord Rothschild, Weizmann and Feisal convened with T.E. Lawrence on January 3, 1919, to sign a formal agreement. This nine-part document, with a preamble speaking of "racial kinship and ancient bonds" between Jews and Arabs and of "the consummation of their national aspirations," refers throughout to "the Arab State" and to Palestine as two distinct and separate entities. Largely reiterating the points agreed upon in the December 11 conversation, it rose to its greatest significance in the third and fourth articles:

ARTICLE III

In the establishment of the Constitution and Administration of Palestine all such measures shall be adopted as will afford the fullest guarantees for carrying into effect the British Government's Declaration of the 2nd of November, 1917.

ARTICLE IV

All necessary measures shall be taken to encourage and stimulate immigration of Jews into Palestine on a large scale, and as quickly as possible to settle Jewish immigrants upon the land through closer settlement and intensive cultivation of the soil. In taking such measures the Arab peasant and tenant farmers shall be protected in their rights, and shall be assisted in forwarding their economic development.

On the eve of the Paris Peace Conference, then, Feisal was accepting the Balfour Declaration as policy regarding Palestine, and acknowledging the principle of unrestricted Jewish immigration there. Feisal's only reservation—and it was a strong one—had to do with his own ambitions rather than the Jewish ones. Before signing the agreement, he placed a proviso at the bottom in Arabic, which was translated thus by Lawrence:

If the Arabs are established as I have asked in my manifesto [to be] addressed to the British Secretary of State for Foreign Affairs, I will carry out what is written in this agreement. If changes are made, I can not be answerable for failing to carry out this agreement.

Years later, Feisal's historian George Antonius was to describe Lawrence's rendering of the proviso as a "loose and misleading paraphrase" and to translate it thus:

> Provided the Arabs obtain their independence as demanded in my Memorandum ... to the Foreign Office of the Government of Great Britain, I shall concur in the above articles. But if the slightest modification or departure were to be made, I shall not then be bound by a single word of the present Agreement which shall be deemed void and of no account or validity, and I shall not be answerable in any way whatsoever.

It was, of course, the Lawrence version that Weizmann considered to be Feisal's statement. The two leaders then signed the document.

The Paris Peace Conference was convened on January 18, 1919. Feisal and Weizmann were to present their respective cases in person before its Supreme Council of Ten; but in the meantime, Lloyd George and Georges Clemenceau—the French prime minister since November 1917—had already agreed upon a major revision of the Sykes-Picot arrangements. "When Clemenceau came to London after the war," Lloyd George writes, "I drove with him to the French Embassy through cheering crowds who acclaimed him with enthusiasm. After we reached the Embassy he asked me what it was I especially wanted from the French. I instantly replied that I wanted Mosul attached to Irak, and Palestine from Dan to Beersheba under British control. Without any hesitation he agreed. Although that agreement was not reduced into writing, he adhered to it honorably in subsequent negotiations." That was not quite the end of Anglo-French discussions of the matter, but the final results indeed were to be what Lloyd George describes as the outcome of this seemingly impromptu exchange.

Feisal appeared before the Council of Ten on February 6, with Lawrence at his side. "These two remarkable men," according to Lloyd George, "were arrayed in the flowing robes of dazzling white in which they were appareled when they led their mounted warriors to battle against the Turks." Lawrence further impressed the gathering by translating Feisal's remarks from Arabic into both English and French. In presenting his case for Arab independence in the region specified by the correspondence between his father and Sir

Henry McMahon in 1915, Feisal explicitly set aside Palestine as a separate matter.

Before the turn of the Zionists came to present their case, a tragedy—both personal and historic—intervened and cast a shadow over the prospects of Arab-Jewish cooperation. Shortly after the conference began, Sir Mark Sykes—now a parliamentary under-secretary of state for foreign affairs—arrived in Paris after another round of diplomatic travels in the Middle East. Sokolow was startled at his appearance, for he had become "frightfully thin. He had lived the whole time on 'German sausages' and had suffered much from digestive troubles. It only transpired later, that he had spent sixteen hours a day in Aleppo working under almost impossible conditions on behalf of the Arabs and Armenians."

Sykes then settled down to working as hard as ever in Paris, except for a three-day interval, during which he went home and then returned with his wife. Shortly afterward, Edith Sykes came down with influenza—this was the time when an epidemic of "Spanish flu" was taking a toll in lives ultimately to rival that of the western front. Her case was not serious, however. On the morning of February 14, Sokolow was to recall, Sir Mark sent word that his wife was better, "but that he himself was taken ill. 'I have got it,' he said to Sergeant Wilson when he went to bed." The next day Lady Edith sent for Sokolow, saying her husband wanted to know how Zionist matters were going at the conference. She told him "that her husband would have to remain in bed for a few days," and afterward they "intended to go to England for a week or so to recuperate."

On the following day, February 16, Harold Nicolson, who was with the British delegation, saw Sergeant Wilson in the Champs-Elysées, "great tears pouring down his cheek." Wilson told him Sykes was dying. On February 17, Nicolson recorded in his diary:

> Mark Sykes died last night at Hotel Lotti. I mind dreadfully. . . . It was due to his endless push and perseverance, to his enthusiasm and faith, that Arab nationalism and Zionism became two of the most successful of our war causes. To secure recognition of these his beliefs he had to fight ignorance at the F.O., suspicion at the I.O., parsimony at the Treasury, obstruction at the W.O., and idiocy at the Admiralty. Yet he conquered all this by sheer dynamic force. He made mistakes, of course, such as the Sykes-Picot Treaty, but he kept to his ideas with the fervor of genius.

Sokolow wrote that "he fell as a hero at our side." Sykes was not yet forty when he died. Would the subsequent history of the Middle East have been different had he been granted a normal lifespan?

Bereft of their good friend and colleague, Sokolow and Weizmann made their appearance before the Council of Ten on February 27. Reading from a memorandum that the Zionists had already submitted, Sokolow called for recognition of "the historic title of the Jewish people to Palestine and the right of the Jews to reconstitute in Palestine their National Home." He placed this demand within the framework of the most important achievement at the Peace Conference so far, the League of Nations plan, and of its accompanying new concepts of "mandatory" and "mandate"—one of the originators of which may have been Sir Mark Sykes. "The sovereign possession of Palestine," Sokolow urged, "shall be vested in the League of Nations and the government entrusted to Great Britain as Mandatory of the League." Actually, the British delegation had arrived in Paris still determined to sound out the idea of American or Anglo-American control in Palestine, but the Americans had proved utterly disinclined to it. Their attitude, along with Allenby's troops and Clemenceau's acquiescence, was conspiring to give British Zionism exactly what it wanted in this respect.

Sokolow went on to call for this special condition under the mandate:

> Palestine shall be placed under such political, administrative and economic conditions as will secure the establishment there of the Jewish National Home, and ultimately render possible the creation of an autonomous Commonwealth, it being clearly understood that nothing shall be done which may prejudice the civil and religious rights of existing non-Jewish communities in Palestine, or the rights and political status enjoyed by Jews in any other country.

Weizmann, during the course of his own remarks, added to these demands that the mandatory power shall:

> (a) Promote Jewish immigration and close settlement on the land, the established rights of the present non-Jewish population being equitably safeguarded.
>
> (b) Accept the cooperation in such measures of a Council representative of the Jews of Palestine, and of the world, that may be established for the development of the Jewish National

Home in Palestine and entrust the organization of Jewish education to such Council.

(c) On being satisfied that the constitution of such Council precludes the making of private profit, offer to the Council in priority any concession for the development of natural resources which it may be found desirable to grant.

For the time being, such a council was the Zionist commission, which had remained in Palestine after Weizmann's departure in the fall.

After Sokolow and Weizmann there were three more speakers. The poet André Spire appeared on behalf of French Zionism, and the veteran Zionist Menahem Ussishkin spoke on behalf of his colleagues in Russia. The French orientalist and member of the Alliance Israélite Universelle, Sylvain Lévi, who had been with Weizmann on the Zionist Commission, also spoke, taking an anti-Zionist position. Weizmann and Sokolow were dismayed, but did not feel they could properly request time for a rebuttal. Suddenly, however, Weizmann was given the floor again when Robert Lansing, the American secretary of state, asked him to explain the term "Jewish National Home." Did it, he wanted to know, mean an autonomous Jewish government? Weizmann said no, explaining that the Zionist organization merely wanted to establish,

under a Mandatory Power, an administration, not necessarily Jewish, which would render it possible to send into Palestine 70,000 to 80,000 Jews annually. . . . Thus it would build up gradually a nationality, and so make Palestine as Jewish as America is American or England English. Later on, when the Jews formed the large majority, they would be ripe to establish such a Government as would answer to the state of the development of the country and to their ideals.

Weizmann then went on to deal with Lévi's remarks.

After that small mishap, things again seemed to be going well for the Zionists. Then, on March 1, the daily *Le Matin* carried an interview with Feisal, which quoted him as saying that the Jews were welcome to find a refuge in Palestine under a Muslim or Christian government responsible to the League of Nations, but that if they wanted "to establish a state and claim sovereign rights in the country, I foresee and fear very serious dangers and conflicts between them and other races." Startled at this, the Zionists promptly demanded clarification from Feisal's secretary, who replied that all

Feisal said was: "If the Zionists wished to found a Jewish state *at the present moment* [italics added], they would meet with difficulties from the local population." This correction was conveyed to *Le Matin*.

To clear the matter up further, a meeting was arranged between Feisal and Professor Felix Frankfurter, who was in Paris representing American Zionism. Lawrence was present at the meeting, and at the end of it he was delegated to write up Feisal's position in the form of a letter to Frankfurter. "We Arabs," the letter said in part,

> especially the educated among us, look with the deepest sympathy on the Zionist movement. Our deputation here in Paris is fully acquainted with the proposals submitted by the Zionist Organization to the Peace Conference, and we regard them as moderate and proper. We will do our best, in so far as we are concerned, to help them through; we will wish the Jews a most hearty welcome home.

This was signed by Feisal and published on March 5 in *The New York Times*.

Whatever the real prospects may have been for cooperation between a Jewish Palestine and an Arab Middle East ruled by Feisal and the Hashimites, they were not to be tested owing to the latter's subsequent decline in fortunes. Feisal could do nothing to stem the tide of French ambitions in northern Syria, which became all the stronger after the renunciation of Palestine and, later, of Cilicia, which was reclaimed by a Turkey turned nationalist under the rule of Mustafa Kemal. The upshot was that, in defiance of the old Arab demand for Damascus, Homs, Hama, and Aleppo, the French were granted all of the newly formed entity of Syria and Lebanon as a mandate. This proved to be entirely against the wishes of the Syrian National Congress, an assembly of tribal chieftains and religious and local notables that had first been convened in July 1919. On March 11, 1920, the congress reconvened and elected Feisal king of a United Syria—which was meant to include Lebanon and Palestine as well. Feisal's destiny was now on a direct collision course with French aspirations and British intentions. To make matters worse, when the mandate was officially assigned to France in April, the Syrian Congress refused to recognize it. In July the French presented Feisal with an ultimatum, and while he played for time their

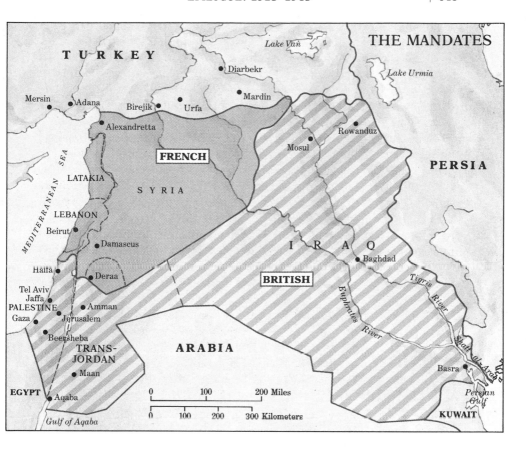

troops advanced upon Damascus. On the twenty-fifth they entered the city and he was deposed.

It was under the strain of this setback that Feisal lost his ability to see eye-to-eye with the Zionists. In an interview at the British Foreign Office on January 20, 1921, he suddenly insisted that Palestine had not been excluded from the area promised to the Arabs in the correspondence between his father and Sir Henry McMahon in 1915. "The Arabs," he said, "had always regarded both Palestine and the hinterland of Syria as being covered by the pledges" then given. This point was argued with him—perhaps he was reminded that he had already taken public positions entirely inconsistent with his present remarks—and he backed down. But he continued to maintain that "as the Arabic stood, it would clearly be interpreted by any

Arab, and had been so interpreted by King Hussein, to refer to the four towns and their immediate surroundings. . . . Palestine did not lie to the west of the four towns [and] was therefore . . . included in the area for which His Majesty's Government had given pledges to his father." That was all for now, but he had effectively seen to it that the British Government would not be allowed to forget the McMahon "pledge" for the entire era of the mandate.

The British soon found a way of dealing with the problem of Feisal and with another problem at the same time. For the last six months of 1920, there had been an Arab insurrection in Iraq, a protest against the British mandatory government that had been assigned there in April. Feisal was brought there in June 1921 by the high commissioner, Sir Percy Cox, and, with the help of his oriental secretary, Miss Gertrude Bell—who became Feisal's new Lawrence for the occasion, rarely leaving his side—organized a plebiscite that proclaimed him king of Iraq by a 96 percent majority. That Hashimite throne, at any rate, was to last until the Iraqi revolution of 1958.

King Hussein, Feisal's father and the man with whom it all had begun, did not fare so well. The war had not long been over when Abdul Aziz ibn Saud—the India Office's "horse," ridden by another colorful British orientalist, H. St. John Philby—began to prove that he had been the best bet after all. It was in May 1919 that his forces won their first victory over Hussein. Then Ibn Saud took Asir in August 1920, Hail in November 1921—thereby disposing at last of the ancient enemy of his family, the Ibn Rashids—and finally Taif in the Hejaz in September 1924. On October 3 of that year, Hussein abdicated in favor of his son Ali, who then had to evacuate Mecca when Ibn Saud took it ten days later. Ali abdicated in turn after the fall of Medina in December 1925, and Ibn Saud, after taking Jeddah, proclaimed himself king of the Hejaz in January 1926. From then on he and his descendants were the sole rulers of what is now called Saudi Arabia.

With the fall of Hussein came also the end of the Caliphate, which had been claimed by him after its abolition in Turkey early in 1924. Once a prize in Muslim politics, it has ceased since then to be an issue at all.

The only Hashimite regime to survive to the present time was created in the Transjordanian Emirate that the British carved out of their mandated territory in 1921. Hussein's son Abdullah was made ruler there, and he survived to become monarch of the independent Hashimite kingdom of Jordan in 1948. Three years later he was shot and killed by a Palestinian Arab youth, evidently out of revenge for his having sought—in the tradition briefly established by his late brother Feisal—to reach an accommodation with the new Jewish state. His grandson Hussein rules there today, the surviving royal descendant, and the namesake, of the short-lived "king of the Arab countries."

The Hashimite dream of a unified Arab world was not to be easily realized. As for the problem of Arab-Jewish relations with which Feisal had tried, however briefly and inadequately, to deal, it proved to be one outside his purview in any case. For it was a Palestine problem above all.

·46·

BRITISH PALESTINE
1918–1948

The makers and supporters of the Balfour Declaration tended to view Arab nationalism as a pan-Arab phenomenon or at any rate one whose smallest subdivisions in the former Ottoman Asia were Arabian, Iraqi, and Syrian. The separate Palestinian Arab nationalism that we know today did not exist at the time of the Balfour Declaration; indeed, it may be said to be one of the declaration's offspring. From the point of view of Zionism and its friends, a relatively small corner of Ottoman Asia was being set aside for Jewish national aspirations, while the rest of that vast region was given over to the development of the Arab political future. As for the Arabs of Palestine, the more concerned Zionists foresaw that their standard of living would be raised by Jewish economic growth and that their eventual status in the country would be as a minority—a *millet*, in the Ottoman tradition—enjoying full civil and religious rights. To the extent that they had political aspirations, these were seen as Arab or Syrian rather than specifically Palestinian, and such aspirations were expected to enjoy full realization in the neighboring countries. For political fulfillment, they could look to Mecca or Damascus; at home in Palestine, they would enjoy greater civic and economic well-being than they had known before. This vision was based upon the expectation of universal Arab-Jewish friendship in the region.

However reasonable this vision may have seemed to a Zionist or even to a pan-Arab leader, it was not likely to be acceptable to an Arab of Palestine if given his choice. Such was the view of, among other outside observers, Henry C. King and Charles R. Crane, two Americans sent to Syria in the spring of 1919 at the head of an investigating commission that was originally to have been inter-

Allied, but from which France and Britain both withdrew. The King-Crane Commission returned to Paris that summer recommending, among other things, "serious modification of the extreme Zionist Program for Palestine of unlimited immigration of Jews, looking finally to making Palestine distinctly a Jewish State." The erection of such a state, its report went on, cannot "be accomplished without the gravest trespass upon [in the words of the Balfour Declaration] the 'civil and religious rights of existing non-Jewish communities in Palestine.'" According to the King-Crane survey, "the non-Jewish population of Palestine—nearly nine-tenths of the whole—are emphatically against the entire Zionist program."

There were only two possible responses to such estimates of Palestinian Arab feeling as far as Zionism was concerned. One was that of Arthur James Balfour himself, made in a memorandum on Syria in general that he prepared in August 1919. "The four Great Powers are committed to Zionism," he wrote. "And Zionism, be it right or wrong, good or bad, is rooted in age-long traditions, in present needs, in future hopes, of far profounder import than the desires and prejudices of the 700,000 Arabs who now inhabit that ancient land." The other response was that represented by Chaim Weizmann, who came to be admired for his moderation by opponents of Zionism in both England and Palestine precisely because he eschewed discussions of a distant future on public platforms. In his heart, he envisioned as much as the most radical Zionist did a Palestine "as Jewish as America is American or England English," but to Arab and non-Zionist listeners he protested during the months following the Balfour Declaration that he and his colleagues were seeking the establishment, not of a Jewish government, but of a British one. And this was quite sincere with reference to the near future, which was all that Weizmann, a scientist after all, felt reasonably able to discuss in public. The far future was to be reached only through trial and error: too much haste might produce an explosion, whereas deliberateness and caution might enable Arabs to accept the Jewish entity growing quietly in their midst.

It was during his sojourn in Palestine with the Zionist Commission in the spring and summer of 1918, as he went about the country seeking to assuage Arab leaders with his immediate program, that Weizmann began to sense that all was not going well. "A striking illustration of this condition of affairs," he wrote on April 16 to Major Ormsby-Gore, who was political officer with the commission, "occurred in Jerusalem only last week. On the 11th of April the Military

Governor of Jerusalem was present at a performance in aid of a Moslem Orphanage. We [on the Zionist Commission] have seen extracts from two speeches delivered by Arabs on that occasion, one of them certainly in the presence of the Military Governor. Both speakers used the kind of language which would be appropriate if an attempt were on foot to enslave and to ruin the Arabs of Palestine. They called on the Arab nation to awake from its torpor, and to rise up in defense of its land, of its liberty, of its sacred places against those who were coming to rob it of everything. One speaker adjured his hearers not to sell a single inch of land. Nor is that all. Both speakers took it for granted that Palestine was and must remain a purely Arab country. In fact, a map of Palestine, bearing the inscription 'La Palestine Arabe,' was prominently displayed, and the speeches concluded with the expressions 'Vive la Nation Arabe, Vive la Palestine Arabe.' "

Weizmann was perturbed not only by this display of Arab anti-Zionist sentiment but also by the comportment for the occasion of the military governor of Jerusalem—who was Lieutenant Colonel Ronald Storrs, appointed to the position on December 28. "And while the speakers," Weizmann continued, "had no scruple about avowing these unmistakably anti-Jewish sentiments in the presence of the representative of the British Government, the Military Governor, so far as our information goes, uttered no word to suggest that there was any discrepancy between those sentiments and the Government's policy. It is true he avoided the expression 'La Palestine Arabe' and concluded his speech with 'Vive la Nation Arabe. Vivent les habitants de la Palestine.' But this rather subtle difference of phraseology cannot have suggested to the audience that he meant to correct or modify the sentiments expressed by the Arab speakers who preceded him."

Reflecting years later on his tenure of the governorship of Jerusalem, Storrs was to write: "Being neither Jew (British or foreign) nor Arab, but English, I am not wholly for either, but for both. Two hours of Arab grievances drive me into the Synagogue, while after an intensive course of Zionist propaganda I am prepared to embrace Islam." In the immediate circumstances, his elegantly orientalist sensibility might not always have impelled him to such evenhanded responses. "It will be seen," he wrote to the Foreign Office of a copy of a speech Weizmann had given on April 27, 1918, to some Arab notables in Jerusalem, "that the document is a frank, and, from the Arab point of view, somewhat drastic exposition of the theme of 'back to the land' with the subtle distinction that the land in question is not for the moment the national property of those who propose to go back to it. From an oratorical point of view the speech was not impressive, being neither rhetorically nor, as English, accurately pronounced." Speaking classical Arabic, Greek, and several modern languages besides, but no Hebrew, "Don Rinaldo Orientale"—as an Italian member of the Zionist Commission liked to refer to him—was not the ideal man to deal with the fervid Russian-Jewish polemicists and restless state builders who would come to him with their complaints. "He was everyone's friend," Weizmann later wrote; "but, try as he might, he failed to gain the confidence of his Jewish community." Other Zionist estimates of him were less generous.

One thing that had happened was that, in spite of Sykes's determination not to let it appear so, Cairo had to a large extent transferred itself to Palestine after all. This was perhaps inevitable, but it also inevitably meant an administration whose outlook was not well suited to the special case that was Palestine. "Whatever addition to the Administration has been made," Weizmann had written home to Sokolow on April 19, 1918, "is recruited out of the mass of Anglo-Egyptian Officials, people who are not favorable to us."

This applied even to Brigadier General Sir Gilbert Clayton, who at the beginning had been inclined to be sympathetic to Zionism, but who had growing reservations. Now military governor of Occupied Enemy Territory Administration (OETA) South,* as Palestine was designated for the time being, Clayton remained utterly cordial in his relations with Weizmann and eager, as in the case of the latter's first meeting with Feisal, to promote Arab-Jewish understanding. But, in his communications with London, he was frank in his view that the Balfour Declaration represented a policy not compatible with acceptance of a British mandate by the Arabs of Palestine. They "desire their country for themselves," he wrote, "and will resist any immigration of Jews . . . by any measure in their power including active hostilities." He insisted that the mandatory power would not be able to carry through the Zionist program except by force. And he added emphatically: "by Zionist program I do not mean the interpretation of extreme Zionists but the comparatively moderate program presented to the Peace Conference." Until August 4, 1918, Clayton and the OETA in Palestine did not even treat the Balfour Declaration as Government policy. On that date, they were officially informed that it was, but did not publicize the fact.

---

* The other OETA divisions were to be North and West (under the French and centered in Beirut) and East (under Feisal and centered in Damascus).

Even then, there simply were differing interpretations of what the Balfour Declaration meant. Was a "national home" policy necessarily anything more than cultural, applied to one group among others? The King-Crane Commission asserted flatly that it was "not equivalent to making Palestine into a Jewish State." Balfour knew better what he had intended. "My personal hope," he had told a luncheon gathering that included Asquith and Lord Rothschild on February 7, 1918, "is that the Jews will make good in Palestine and eventually found a Jewish State. It is up to them now; we have given them their great opportunity." But the military administrators in Palestine did not necessarily see it that way. On the contrary, by standing as they did upon the traditional principle of status quo for military administrations—whereby any changes are eschewed as having political import, proper only for a permanent civil government—they placed themselves in direct conflict with virtually all efforts on the part of Jewish groups to implement the Balfour Declaration as they understood it. This led to growing antagonism between the Jews and the administration in Palestine.

The result was an inevitable polarization of the opposing elements. On the one hand, there were Zionists in Palestine who by no means shared Weizmann's moderation or even his fondness for British ways. A conference held in Jaffa on December 18, 1918, produced an "Outline for the Provisional Government of Palestine," which called for, among other things, the immediate changing of the country's name to Eretz Israel (Hebrew for "the Land of Israel") and official adoption of the Jewish flag. This threatened some realization of the Arabs' fears that the Jews were going to take over right away. When the Zionist Commission was reorganized in 1919, its new vice-president—and hence the man who represented Jewish interests in Palestine to the British during Weizmann's absences abroad—was Menahem Ussishkin, who had nearly succeeded in splitting the Zionist movement in 1903, when he led the extreme opposition to Herzl and the East Africa proposal. Even the ardently pro-Zionist Colonel Richard Meinertzhagen, who was appointed chief political officer at Cairo headquarters in September 1919 as a gesture to Jewish opinion, had to describe Ussishkin's attitude as being "at the outset of overbearing intolerance with a contempt for compromise."

In time, the most formidable of the Zionist extremists in Palestine was to be Vladimir Jabotinsky, whose fury steadily mounted during the military administration toward the England he once had so ardently admired. His Jewish Legion had at last achieved realization in war; but at least equally important for him was that it also be realized in peace. His vision always had been of a Jewish unit helping to liberate Palestine from the Turks and then staying on there to become the nucleus of a Jewish national army. But the three Jewish battalions had been demobilized shortly after the war's end, and it was the explicit policy of the administration to let no one bear arms but British troops. Jabotinsky was soon to begin organizing a clandestine army; but in the meantime, as political officer of the Zionist Commission, he allowed his resentments to accumulate against the worst elements in the OETA. No stranger to British traditions of fair-mindedness, he nevertheless felt that the novel complexities of the situation in Palestine had caused among some of the military administrators "an unprecedented epidemic of anti-Semitism. I repeat: unprecedented. Not in Russia, nor in Poland had there been such an intense and widespread atmosphere of hatred as prevailed in the British army in Palestine in 1919 and 1920."

This may be exaggerated on the whole, but there were indeed some administrators who seem to have answered to Jabotinsky's description. There was, for example, General Sir Arthur Money, who became chief administrator in Palestine in 1919 after Allenby left to become high commissioner in Egypt, and who once remained seated at a Jewish gathering during the playing of "Hatikvah," the Zionist national anthem. Colonel Vivian Gabriel, financial adviser to the administration, and Lieutenant Colonel Hubbard, the military governor of Jaffa, were both notorious for taking openly anti-Zionist and even anti-Jewish positions. Colonel Hubbard was reputed to have said that if Arabs were to riot against the Jews he would not interfere.

Feelings of this sort soon had opportunity enough to be gratified. In February 1920, a party of Arab raiders suddenly attacked the Jewish settlements of Tel Hai and Metullah in the extreme north of the country. Among the defenders who fell at Tel Hai was Joseph Trumpeldor, who had returned to Palestine after going to revolutionary Russia in 1917 to organize young pioneer groups. This sent a shock through the Palestine Jewish community, but it was only a foreshadowing of things to come. On April 4, an Arab procession for the festival of Nebi Musa—the Prophet Moses—in Jerusalem deteriorated into an anti-Jewish riot that lasted three days. Synagogues were desecrated and burned, property destroyed, six persons killed, and two hundred wounded. Weizmann, who blamed the disaster on "poisonous agitation" and "inflammatory speeches" that had been permitted for too long by the authorities, did not hesitate to point out in a telegram to Lloyd George that Arab policemen had partici-pated in the excesses. "Unanimous Jewish public opinion," he said, was that the "outbreak could have been prevented [or at] any rate stopped immediately trouble began."

By this time Jabotinsky had organized secret Jewish defense groups. He had even tried to create a legal Jewish police force to balance the Arab one in Jerusalem, but Storrs had refused his re-quest. During the riots, Jabotinsky at first obtained permission to enter the Old City with a hundred armed men; but then the decision was reversed before he entered and he was arrested upon doing so. After a trial, he was sentenced to fifteen years' penal servitude. He was to serve a few months until he was amnestied. He was now more determined than ever that a real Jewish defense force—in Hebrew, a *haganah*—should become organized, even if clandestinely, to be ready to fight for the future of a Jewish Palestine.

After the rioting of April 1920, things seemed to take a decided turn for the better from the Zionist point of view. At the end of that month, the San Remo Conference finally drew up the terms of the peace with Turkey, and the mandate for Palestine was assigned to Great Britain by the Council of Ten. Although Balfour had retired by then and been replaced by the less friendly Lord Curzon as foreign secretary, Lloyd George was still prime minister and as strong a supporter of Zionism as ever. That spring he invited Herbert Sam-uel, just returned from a tour of Palestine, to become the first Brit-ish high commissioner there. Samuel accepted, was knighted, and took over the post with a small ceremony in Jerusalem on July 1, 1920. Later that month, Chaim Weizmann was formally elected pres-ident of the World Zionist Organization.

Samuel had expressed some reservations at first as to whether a Jew should be the British high commissioner for Palestine. When he did assume the post many Jews found it an occasion for rejoicing; but this feeling was to change rapidly. In May 1921, another serious outbreak of Arab rioting occurred against Jews, this time in Jaffa as well as in Jerusalem. Samuel's administration regarded this latest manifestation of Arab discontent as a direct result of the large influx of Jewish immigrants—some ten thousand in less than a year—that had followed upon an ordinance allowing virtually free immigration, which had been passed immediately after the start of the mandate. The Government therefore decided to place a tempo-rary ban on Jewish immigration, and this was first announced by the high commissioner at a gathering of Arab notables. Zionist leaders were as dismayed at the manner of the announcement as they were at its substance. Perhaps some of them recalled how, during the wartime controversy over Russian-Jewish aliens and military service, Samuel had proved more severe toward them than were many of his non-Jewish colleagues. The ban was lifted two months later, but immigration continued to be more restricted than before.

Samuel also amnestied the instigators of the new pogroms, as he had previously amnestied most of the principals in the April 1920 disturbances, including Jabotinsky. What was to bother Zionists increasingly about this decision was the fact that one of its beneficiaries was Haj Amin al-Husseini, a member of one of the two leading Arab families of Jerusalem, and before long, the principal opponent in Palestine of Jewish national aspirations there. Indeed, soon after his release, the administration was to help in the consolidation of his power by securing his election to the lifetime post of Grand Mufti, tho highoot Muolim rcligiouo officc in Jcruoalcm. From thio vantagc point, al-Husseini was able to achieve leadership of the Supreme Muslim Council, which, in the wake of consistent Arab refusals to participate in a civil administration that included Zionists, became in effect the chief Arab political body in the land.

Samuel further offended the Zionists at around this time by granting the somewhat obscure claims of a group of Bedouin tribes to a vast tract of land south of Lake Tiberias that had officially become state-owned under the Turks. As a result, thousands of acres of potentially cultivable land continued for decades to lie fallow. The official policy of the administration was "equality of obligation toward Arabs and Jews," but even moderate Zionists such as Weizmann thought the Jewish Sir Herbert Samuel was bending over backward to make the point.

Yet another action often held against Samuel by Zionists in later years was the creation of a separate Transjordan. At first the Palestine mandate extended eastward to the borders of Iraq and Arabia, far beyond what anyone could reasonably have called the historic boundaries of the country. On the other hand, most Zionists and many authoritative Englishmen—including the researchers for the Palestine Exploration Fund—regarded the historic frontier to extend somewhat eastward of the Jordan River, though not as far as the Hejaz railway. Others assumed that the Jordan was the boundary; and in fact, with only one exception on the southern shore of Lake Tiberias, there were no Jewish settlements east of that river in 1921.

It was in that year that the mandatory offered an arrangement to Abdullah, who had come up into Transjordan leading an army to defend his brother Feisal against the French. "To allow the British mandatory area to be used as a base for an attack on our French neighbors would never do," Sir Herbert Samuel later wrote; "on the other hand we had no force available to stop it; and in any case we did not want to be led into a clash with our Arab friends." Samuel's administration decided to propose to Abdullah that he "give up his campaign against the French and settle down in Transjordan; let him be recognized as ruler there and be given the help of a few British advisers, and the moderate subsidy essential for a proper government." Abdullah accepted, and the whole mandated territory east of the Jordan (with a border modification at Degania on Lake Tiberias) was removed from the purview of the Balfour Declaration and placed under his nominal rule.

Early in 1921 jurisdiction over the British mandates was at last transferred from the Foreign to the Colonial Office, and Winston Churchill, his star in the ascendant once again, was appointed colonial secretary. One of Churchill's first acts in office with regard to the Middle East was to convene a conference in Cairo in order to review the entire situation and reformulate policy. Held in March, the Cairo Conference was attended by such luminaries of British orientalism as T.E. Lawrence, Gertrude Bell, and Sir Percy Cox, as well as by Sir Herbert Samuel and by Churchill himself. It was at this gathering that the decision was made to give Feisal the kingship of Iraq and, as if to compensate his brother for this prize, to confirm the creation of a separate administrative entity that was soon to become the emirate of Transjordan under Abdullah. Decisions also were made regarding Palestine west of the Jordan, and these came to be summed up the following year in a statement of policy—subsequently known as the Churchill White Paper—that was issued in London by the colonial secretary on July 1, 1922.

The paper addressed itself to what it deemed the main apprehensions on both the Arab and the Jewish sides about British intentions in Palestine. As far as the Arabs were concerned, the paper said, these apprehensions were based in part on "exaggerated interpretations" of the meaning of the Balfour Declaration. "Unauthorized statements," it said,

> have been made to the effect that the purpose in view is to create a wholly Jewish Palestine. Phrases have been used such as that Palestine is to become "as Jewish as England is En-

glish." His Majesty's Government regard any such expectations as impracticable and have no such aim in view.

This was a direct rebuke to Weizmann, normally the British Government's favorite voice of Zionist moderation, who had spoken words to this effect before the Council of Ten in February 1919. In compensation, the Churchill paper now made a special point of the modified, Basel-inspired wording that Lord Milner had brought into the text of the Balfour Declaration. "His Majesty's Government," it said,

> would draw attention to the fact that the terms of the Declaration referred to do not contemplate that Palestine as a whole should be converted into a Jewish National Home, but that such a home should be founded *in Palestine*.

Then addressing itself to Jewish apprehensions, the paper stressed that although the national home policy did not mean "the imposition of a Jewish nationality upon the inhabitants of Palestine as a whole," it did mean "the further development of the existing Jewish community, with the assistance of Jews in other parts of the world, in order that it may become a center in which the Jewish people as a whole may take, on grounds of religion and race, an interest and a pride." And for the sake of its future favorable development, this community should know "that it is in Palestine as of right and not on sufferance." Here was, among other things, a firm repudiation of a movement then afoot in the House of Lords to repeal the Balfour Declaration.

The paper also made a point of dealing with the insistence now mounting in some quarters that McMahon had not excluded Palestine from the land he "pledged" to the Arabs. A delegation of Arab leaders in London at that very time were making this claim. "This representation," the paper says,

> mainly rests upon a letter dated the 24th October, 1915, from Sir Henry McMahon, then His Majesty's High Commissioner in Egypt, to the Sherif of Mecca, now King Hussein of the Kingdom of the Hejaz. That letter is quoted as conveying the promise to the Sherif of Mecca to recognize and support the independence of the Arabs within the territories proposed by him. But this promise was given subject to a reservation made in the same letter, which excluded from its scope, among other territories, the portions of Syria lying to the west of the district of Damascus. This reservation has always been regarded by His

Majesty's Government as covering the vilayet of Beirut and the independent Sanjak of Jerusalem. The whole of Palestine west of the Jordan was thus excluded from Sir H. McMahon's pledge.

Another convenience of this interpretation of McMahon's wording, of course, was that it, by implication, excluded the country east of the Jordan from the purview of the Balfour Declaration.

There were elements in this paper that Weizmann and the Zionists did not care for, despite its gratifying assertion that the Jews were in Palestine "as of right and not on sufferance." In speaking of future immigration into Palestine, it suggested limitation according to the country's "economic capacity" to absorb new arrivals—an ominously broad qualification. It recommended a legislative council that, being based on the current population of the country, would have more Arab than Jewish seats. It in effect excluded Transjordan from the national home policy. But despite reservations about these and other aspects of it, the Zionist organization accepted the white paper policy. The Palestinian Arab leadership did not, however. As a result, no legislative council was created, and the administration was forced to govern without an indigenous representative body.

Later that month, on July 24, 1922, the mandate for Palestine was at last officially approved by the League of Nations. The delay had been due to the ambiguous political situation in Turkey, where a nationalist revolt was being led by the great war leader, Mustafa Kemal. The San Remo Conference had culminated in the Treaty of Sèvres, signed on August 10, 1920, by the weak sultanate left in the wake of the collapse of the Committee of Union and Progress. But this had been repudiated by Kemal, and after his assumption of complete power, a new treaty had to be negotiated. This was to be signed at Lausanne in July 1923; but in the meantime, the League of Nations had gone ahead and officially assigned the mandates.

The text of the Palestine mandate gave firm support to the Balfour Declaration, which it cited in its preamble. Article 2 then said:

> The Mandatory shall be responsible for placing the country under such political, administrative and economic conditions as will secure the establishment of the Jewish national home, as laid down in the preamble, and the development of self-governing institutions, and also for safeguarding the civil and religious rights of all the inhabitants of Palestine, irrespective of race and religion.

Article 4 in effect acknowledged the Zionist demand for a chartered company by allowing for an "appropriate Jewish agency" to deal with the Palestine administration in matters relating to the development of the national home and by recognizing the Zionist organization in this capacity.* Article 6 called for the facilitating of Jewish immigration "under suitable conditions" and the encouragement of "close settlement by Jews on the land." Article 22 included Hebrew along with English and Arabic as the official languages of the country. Only article 25, which was inserted in August 1921 and provided for the possible exclusion of the lands east of the Jordan from the national home policy, represented any kind of compromise to what was otherwise a thorough endorsement of Zionist aims.

A period of peaceful growth ensued, during which many Zionists came to believe that their dream might be realized within the framework of good relations with the Arabs. Between 1924—when immigration to the United States was severely restricted for the first time—and 1926 some fifty thousand Jews entered Palestine; yet, far from causing serious friction, this influx coincided with a time in which Arabs and Jews seemed to be discovering friendship and mutual prosperity. At the Fourteenth Zionist Congress in Vienna in 1925, Weizmann proclaimed Palestine to be the quietest part of the Middle East. Sokolow foresaw the prospect of a Palestinian Arab-Jewish Congress one day, and the rising young Palestinian labor leader David Ben-Gurion urged Jews to sympathize with the national aspirations of other oriental peoples.

Even the mandatory administration now looked good to Zionist leaders. Sir Herbert Samuel had retired from the high commissionership in 1925 in an atmosphere of revived cordiality between himself and Weizmann, and his successor, Field Marshal Lord Plumer, soon came to appear the ideal that the Zionists had been seeking. One day, the popular story goes, the Grand Mufti went to Plumer and said that if a certain Jewish procession were held, he could not be responsible for law and order. "You need not worry about law and order," Plumer had replied. "That is my responsibility."

Jewish institutions flourished, primarily under the tutelage of the labor Zionist movement that now was the dominant force within the country itself. Each new land purchase by the Jewish National

---

* The Jewish Agency, made up of non-Zionists as well as Zionists throughout the world, was founded for this purpose in 1929.

Fund was followed by the erection of new settlements by groups of young pioneers. The *kibbutz*, or collective farm, was the basic form of such settlement in this period; but another prominent form was the *moshav*, or cooperative settlement, which bought and sold goods and owned equipment communally, but in which the individual farmer worked his own holding. In the towns, labor was organized under the Histadrut, a vast institution that in time became a welfare state within the state—providing medical and other social services—as well as the country's major entrepreneur. Hebrew flourished as the spoken language of the Jewish community and in a lively vernacular theater, press, and literature. But perhaps the crowning Jewish cultural achievement in Palestine—certainly for Weizmann, who had been the foremost worker on its behalf since his earliest days in the Zionist movement—was the Hebrew University. During his first sojourn with the Zionist Commission in 1918, his proudest act had been to lay the cornerstone of the university on Mount Scopus overlooking the Old City. Another of his life's happiest moments came on April 1, 1925, when he presided over the university's official inauguration ceremony. The principal speaker was Lord Balfour.

A sign that all was not really well, however, was provided after the ceremony when Balfour traveled on to Damascus. There the reception was so hostile to the man who had reportedly come to "hand over" Palestine to the Jews—some Arabs believed he was a Jew himself—that he had to leave hurriedly and surreptitiously. The fact was that, no matter how often Arab and Jewish intellectuals gathered together in the bookstores and cafés of Jerusalem, or even in one another's homes, and no matter how many political leaders, merchants, or laborers from the two groups dealt cordially with each other over common concerns, the basic problems remained unresolved. Apart from the overarching political problem, there were economic, social, and religious ones as well. Arab laborers in Palestine had indeed become more prosperous than their counterparts in other countries; but their wages still were far lower than those of their Jewish compatriots. They also found themselves excluded from the best jobs. There was an ideological reason for this: labor Zionism insisted that Jews had to create their own proletariat, scorning the reliance on cheap native labor that characterized the classic European *colon* and that would have compromised their becoming a fully rounded nation. But in practice, this could only have seemed a demonstration of racial prejudice in the eyes of the Palestinian Arabs.

Furthermore, as Arab-owned lands were bought by the Zionists, Arab tenant farmers often were dispossessed.

As for religious matters, there was inevitable tension surrounding the ancient Temple Mount in Jerusalem. At the top of it, on the site of the spiritual and geographical center of ancient Israel, stood the third holiest shrine in the Muslim world; and at the side of the temple mount stood the site most sacred to modern Judaism, the surviving Western (or "Wailing") Wall. Fronted by narrow streets and a Muslim religious endowment, or *waqf*, the Western Wall had been a scene of Arab-Jewish tension at every major Jewish holiday, when large numbers of worshipers gathered there.

It was after an incident at the wall in August 1929, when Jews had gathered to commemorate the fast of the Ninth of Ab, that groups of young Arabs suddenly appeared and attacked Jews, first in Jerusalem, then in Hebron, Safed, and other towns throughout the country. By the time these riots had ended, nearly one hundred and fifty Jews were dead, and hundreds more were wounded. The disaster was worse than Kishinev. And it proved to be a turning point: from then on, hopes for reconciliation between Jews and Arabs in Palestine rapidly diminished. Jewish hopes for the mandate—now under the high commissionership of Sir John Chancellor, whom Weizmann described as "a man of much smaller caliber" than his predecessor Lord Plumer—also waned.

A British investigating commission headed by Sir Walter Shaw came to the conclusion that the real cause of the riots was Arab apprehension about Jewish intentions in Palestine and pointed to Jewish immigration among other things as a source of the trouble—even though it had, in fact, declined sharply in the previous two years and many Jews had emigrated. A decree restricting Jewish immigration was issued in May 1930; but this led to widespread protests, and in August the League of Nations Mandates Commission concluded that the British administration had been at fault in the 1929 riots for not having provided adequate police protection. Meanwhile, another British investigating commission had gone out to Palestine under Sir John Hope Simpson, and it produced a report in October. Its findings were embodied in a white paper issued later that month by Lord Passfield (the former Sidney Webb), the colonial secretary in Ramsay Macdonald's Labour Government. The Passfield White Paper castigated the Histadrut for its virtually exclusive labor policy, called for restrictions in land purchase by the Zionists, suggested the tightening of Jewish immigration, and urged Jewish leaders to consider making concessions in their national home policy.

This was met by a storm of protest and was then quietly retracted.

These events brought to the surface deep-lying divisions in the Zionist movement. As the paragon of reconciliation with the British, Weizmann found himself subject to growing criticism. To demonstrate his vehement opposition to the Passfield White Paper, he had resigned the presidency of the World Zionist Organization when it was issued; but at the congress of July 1931 in Basel, he was not reelected. The move to overthrow him was led by Vladimir Jabotinsky, who had resigned from the Zionist executive in 1923 and was taking an increasingly independent and radical course. Still motivated above all by the ideal of Jewish self-defense, he had founded a quasi-military youth organization that he called, in honor of his fallen comrade, Brith Trumpeldor* (abbreviated *Betar*). As this organization spread through the Jewish communities of Europe and America, it formed the rank and file of a virtual new party, called the Revisionists, within the Zionist movement. At the 1931 Zionist Congress, Jabotinsky hoped to achieve the presidency in Weizmann's place. Instead, the election was won by Nahum Sokolow. This represented no significant change of policy, and Jabotinsky and his followers soon were to leave the Zionist organization and form one of their own, the New Zionists.

Hitler's accession to power in 1933 gave rise to a wave of Jewish immigration into Palestine greater than any that had preceded it. In the next three years more than 150,000 Jews entered the country. In 1936, the Jewish population of Palestine was 384,000; the Arab population 920,000.

That year saw a new outbreak of anti-Jewish riots, and the formation, under the leadership of the Grand Mufti, of the Arab Higher Committee, which assumed the leadership of a rapidly spreading general strike. The committee announced that the strike would continue until Jewish immigration was suspended. This was the beginning of a full-fledged rebellion against the mandate and the Balfour Declaration policy, and Arab volunteers began arriving from neighboring countries to take part in it. The British Government dealt with the situation by sending out a new investigating commission under Lord Peel, a former secretary of state for India. Among those from whom the Peel Commission heard testimony in Jerusalem was

---

* "Trumpeldor League." Its Hebrew initials, by which it was most commonly known, spell Betar, the town at which Bar-Cochba ended his revolt against Hadrian of the years 132–135.

Chaim Weizmann, who had regained the presidency of the World Zionist Organization the previous year.

The Peel Commission report, published on July 8, 1937, not only made the usual diagnosis of Palestine's ills, but this time offered a radical new cure. It recommended the partitioning of the country into three entities: a Jewish state, an Arab state, and a British mandated territory. The latter was mainly a whittled-down version of the old Jerusalem enclave, extending to Jaffa but not including it, the purpose of which was to keep the Holy Places under a regime responsible to the League of Nations; it also included Haifa. The Jewish state was to consist of the coastal plain from Tel Aviv to a point just south of Haifa, the Valley of Jezreel, most of the Galilee, and an area south of the Jerusalem enclave: it would contain about 300,000 Jews and a slightly smaller number of Arabs. The rest of the country, including Jaffa, was to be the Arab state, united with Transjordan.

The proposal aroused vehement protests among Jews and Arabs alike. But Chaim Weizmann, struck by its call for a sovereign Jewish state, felt that it "held out great possibilities and hopes," and tried to persuade his colleagues to accept it at the Twentieth Zionist Congress that August. After some stormy sessions, a resolution was passed calling the scheme "unacceptable," but nevertheless empowering the Zionist executive to enter into negotiations on the basis of it. But in Syria the following month, a pan-Arab congress voted overwhelmingly and unequivocally against the Peel recommendations. Arab intransigence grew, and despite the arrest and deportation of members of the Arab Higher Committee in October—the Grand Mufti taking refuge in Syria—the rebellion even at times reached the point of pitched fighting in Palestine.

Jewish self-defense grew under these circumstances in spite of the ban. The Haganah was now a virtual underground national army and even had found experienced leadership in a young British officer stationed in Palestine, Orde Wingate—a cousin of Sir Reginald Wingate of Egypt and the Sudan—who trained defense units that he called "special night squads." Some were to refer to him in time as "Lawrence of Judea." But whereas the Haganah remained true to an official Zionist policy of *havlagah* ("self-restraint"), fighting only in self-defense and not against the British, other newly forming Jewish organizations adopted a more aggressive policy. Foremost among these was the Irgun Zvai Leumi ("National Military Organization")—generally known abroad as the Irgun—which was made up largely of members of Betar, but whose resort to terrorist tactics aroused protests from Jabotinsky himself.

Eager to wash its hands of the Palestine mess, and in effect no longer committed to the Balfour Declaration, the Government of Neville Chamberlain—that master of destructive compromises—came up with a radical solution in May 1939. It issued another white paper, this one calling for the creation within ten years of an independent Arab-Jewish binational state. Over a five-year period, another 75,000 Jews would be allowed to enter Palestine. After five years Jewish immigration was to stop altogether, unless the Arabs of the country were to agree to let it continue. No worse moment could have been chosen for such a policy. The Arab Higher Committee rejected it as always; but now the Jews rejected it, too. Great Britain had become a virtual enemy to the Zionists; but beginning that September there was a far greater enemy to fight first. "We shall fight with Great Britain in this war as if there was no White Paper," said David Ben-Gurion, now the preeminent Jewish leader in Palestine, "and we shall fight the White Paper as if there was no war."

The next six years were a major disaster to mankind and the greatest disaster in all of Jewish history. At the end of them, nothing was as it had been. Emerging from her own heroic struggle, bleeding Britain had to confront the moral fact of a Jewish people that had lost six million of its sons and daughters, and of which there were now hundreds of thousands of displaced persons longing for a home. Even Winston Churchill, a warm friend of Zionism as always, had not felt able under the imperatives of war to make an overt challenge to the white paper policy, and an illegal immigration into Palestine had provided only the smallest outlet to a European Jewry fleeing slaughter. After Hitler's concentration camps, the sight of Jewish refugees detained in British camps on account of their lack of authorization to enter Palestine was not something the world could easily bear. The same was true of the sight of refugee ships being turned away from Haifa port.

When the new Labour Government of Clement Attlee took office in July 1945, there were hopes that a solution might still be found under the mandate. But its foreign minister, Ernest Bevin, soon grew weary and embittered at the task. Jewish opposition to British rule in Palestine became a virtual war of rebellion. The Haganah stood ambivalently between this new situation and the old policy of self-restraint; but the Irgun—now under the leadership of a young former soldier in the Polish army and ardent follower of Jabotinsky,

Menachem Begin—and its even more radical offshoot, the Stern group, moved on to a policy of terrorism. Jabotinsky, who died of a heart attack in 1940 while visiting a Betar camp in the United States, had not lived to see this development among his spiritual offspring.

The British Government finally referred the whole Palestine question to the United Nations in April 1947. On November 29, the General Assembly voted in favor of the partition of Palestine into a Jewish and an Arab state. This was accepted by the Zionist leadership, and rejected not only by the Arab Higher Committee but by the governments adjacent to Palestine, organized since 1945 into the Arab League. As the mandate neared its end, the new Jewish state in embryo found itself already at war with troops unofficially provided by the Arab League countries, fighting under the eyes of the British.

On May 14, 1948, the Union Jack was lowered over Palestine and the Jewish provisional government in Tel Aviv proclaimed the State of Israel: its prime minister was to be David Ben-Gurion and its president Chaim Weizmann. Troops of the Arab League countries now prepared a full-scale invasion from three sides in the first Arab-Israeli war. Before the day's end, President Harry S. Truman had announced de facto American recognition of the Jewish state.

Notes and Bibliographies

Because this book takes on a wide variety of subjects in the pursuit of its own main theme, there would be little value for the reader in a single bibliography giving a long and formidably varied list of relevant titles in alphabetical order. Instead, I propose to give, under each chapter heading—and often under each separate section of a chapter—a list of the books consulted specifically for that chapter or section. The reference notes for the chapter or section then will follow, many of them citing the books listed just above.

There are, however, a few books and other sources that should be mentioned at the outset as having been of general value through this entire work. Foremost among the books, as I have suggested in the Preface, is *The Letters and Papers of Chaim Weizmann*, Series A: *Letters* (London, then New Brunswick, N.J., and Jerusalem, 1968-). I used Volumes 1 through 9 of this monumental work, and especially Volume 7, edited by the late Leonard Stein. (All references to volumes in this series will be in this abbreviated form: *CW Letters*, followed by the volume number, the page number and by the footnote number if that is what is referred to.) The natural companion to this, and an indispensable source, is Weizmann's autobiography, *Trial and Error* (New York, 1949), though it must be used with caution: it is full of the inevitable distortions of recollection long after the fact. There is an almost musical relationship between the autobiography and the letters: the former provides atmosphere and the general outlines of the story; the latter correct its facts and abundantly fill out the detail.

Two previous studies on the making of the Balfour Declaration were of great value: Leonard Stein, *The Balfour Declaration* (New York, 1961), and Isaiah Friedman, *The Question of Palestine, 1914-1918* (London, 1973). Stein's book is in some respects virtually another original source: a friend and associate of Weizmann's and a lifelong activist in Zionist and Jewish affairs, Stein brought personal recollections and interviews with some participants to bear in his work. His deductions are remarkable, considering that he did not have the official government archives at the Public Record Office at his disposal—they were not released for this period until later in the 1960s—but these deductions also inevitably fall short of the mark at times for the same reason. As for Professor Friedman, although—less interested than I in the personal side of the story—he makes little use of the Weizmann letters, he has covered well that vast territory of Public Record Office documents. I find, however, after my own scrutiny of them, that he and I often differ in our sense of their import.

Another work that is both a history and a primary source in its own right is Nahum Sokolow, *History of Zionism, 1600-1918*, 2 vols. (London, 1919; one-volume reprint, New York, 1969). Sokolow was a main participant in the events described in my book, and this work by him includes not only personal recollections but compendious documentation as well. An indispensable source collection is J.C. Hurewitz, ed., *The Middle East and North Africa in World Politics: A Documentary Record*, 2 vols. (New Haven and London, 1975).

Other books on the subject in general that should be mentioned here are: N.M. Gelber, *Hatzharat Balfour v'Toldoteyha* (Jerusalem, 1939), and Esco Foundation for Palestine, *Palestine: A Study of Jewish, Arab and British Policies*, 2 vols. (New Haven, 1947).

Of the periodicals I used as original source materials, three in particular were consulted throughout: *The Times* and the *Jewish Chronicle*, both of London, and the *Manchester Guardian*.

Of the various archives I consulted, the principal one was the Public Record Office, London (PRO). Most of the PRO materials used in this book are Foreign Office (FO) documents, usually of the FO 371 series (followed by a slash and a volume number; also by a page number for those volumes that have been paginated): in these cases I shall not mention the archive. Other materials at that archive will be mentioned with the designation PRO preceding them.

Another important archive is the Private Papers Collection at the Middle East Centre, St. Antony's College, Oxford. Many of the collections in this archive are photocopies of collections housed elsewhere—for example, the papers of Sir Mark Sykes, which are now, in the originals, mainly in the University of Hull, as well as at Sledmere, the Sykes family estate in Yorkshire: because they all were at first located at the estate, they are still known as the Sledmere Papers, and will be so referred to in these notes. Also at St. Antony's Middle East Centre are photocopies of the relevant papers of Herbert (Viscount) Samuel, housed in their originals at the Israel State Archives, Jerusalem. Other collections I consulted at the Middle East Centre were the Allenby Papers and the "Balfour Declaration" file.

The diaries of C.P. Scott, a major source for this book, are on deposit at the British Library, London. A large selection from them has been published in Trevor Wilson, ed., *The Political Diaries of C.P. Scott* (Ithaca, N.Y., 1970). The diaries and other papers of Dr. Moses Gaster are on deposit at the Mocatta Library, University College, London. The papers of David Lloyd George are in the House of Lords Record Office. A substantial part of Chaim Weizmann's papers is at the Weizmann Archives, Rehovoth, Israel, as are Vera Weizmann's diaries; the latter also are amply quoted in Vera Weizmann, *The Impossible Takes Longer* (New York, 1967)—her memoirs, as told

to David Tutaev. The Sokolow papers are still partly in the private possession of the Sokolow family, but some are on deposit at the Central Zionist
Archives, Jerusalem.

I conclude these prefatory remarks with a note on the epigraph. It is
from Thomas Heywood's *The Foure Prentises of London, With the Conquest
of Ierusalem*, written in about 1600 and reproduced in *The Dramatic Works
of Thomas Heywood* (London, 1874); the passage quoted is on page 229 of
that edition. I am grateful to Barbara W. Tuchman, who in her book *Bible
and Sword* (New York, 1956) calls attention to this play and this remarkable
speech, all conveying a peculiarly Anglo-Judaic vision of the First Crusade.
At least in imagination, the English were aspiring to rebuild a Jewish Jerusalem even in Heywood's time.

Here, now, are the chapter-by-chapter bibliographies and page-by-page
notes.

1. LONDON AND JERUSALEM: A VICTORIAN ROMANCE

The principal work and compendium of sources on our subject for this period of
Palmerston, Shaftesbury, and Montefiore is Sokolow's *History of Zionism*. The other
crucial source collection for the period under discussion is Albert M. Hyamson, *The
British Consulate in Jerusalem in Relation to the Jews of Palestine, 1838-1914*, 2 vols.
(London, 1939). A good recent biography of Palmerston is Jasper Ridley, *Lord Palm-
erston* (London, 1970), and the standard biography of Montefiore is Paul Goodman,
Moses Montefiore (Philadelphia, 1925).

Page

4   "There exists at present . . .": Palmerston to Ponsonby, August 11, 1840;
      quoted in Hyamson, *Consulate*, 1:33-34.

4   "would tend greatly to increase . . .": Palmerston to Ponsonby, August 20,
      1840. Ibid., p. 38.

4   "to afford protection to the Jews generally": John Bidwell to W.T. Young,
      January 31, 1839. Ibid., p. 2.

5   "Palmerston had already been chosen . . .": Diary of the Earl of Shaftes-
      bury, August 1, 1838; quoted in Sokolow, *History*, 1:123.

5   "the growing interest . . . will immediately go thither": Quoted in Sokolow,
      History, 1:124.

5   "a prelude to the Antitype . . .": Shaftesbury Diaries; quoted in ibid., p. 126.

6   Figures on the Jewish population of Jerusalem and of Palestine in this
      period are to be found in Hyamson, *Consulate*, 1:5; and in another work by
      Hyamson, *Palestine: The Rebirth of an Ancient Nation* (New York, 1917),
      pp. 60-61.

6-7   "From all information I have been able to gather . . . to return to Pal-
      estine": L. Loewe, ed., *Diaries of Sir Moses and Lady Montefiore*, 2 vols.
      (London, 1890), 1:167.

7   For Montefiore-Palmerston exchange of April 30, 1840, see ibid., p. 214.

Of the many biographies of Disraeli, two are indispensable: the official one by
William Flavelle Monypenny and George Earle Buckle, *The Life of Benjamin Disraeli, Earl of Beaconsfield*, 6 vols. (London, 1910-1920; new revised ed., complete in 2
vols., New York, 1929); and the most ambitious of the one-volume works, Robert

Blake, *Disraeli* (New York, 1967). The edition I used of several of Disraeli's novels is that of 1904, reissued in London under the general heading "Young England."
Page

8	"the good Bishop . . .": Disraeli, *Tancred*, p. 225.
8	"All is race . . .": Ibid., p. 176.
8	"Christianity is completed Judaism": Disraeli, *Sybil*, p. 150.
8-9	"penetrate the great Asian mystery": Disraeli, *Tancred*, p. 147.
9	"for this English youth . . . by the laws of Sinai": Ibid., pp. 313-14.
9	"to free your country . . .": Ibid., p. 305.
9	"the Arabs are only Jews upon horseback": Ibid., p. 299.
9	"will ever remain . . . the throne of David": Ibid., p. 203.
9	"to disembarrass itself . . .": Ibid., p. 202.
9	"I am not, alas, a true Arab . . .": Ibid., p. 564.
9-10	"If the English . . . 'I hope not,' said Tancred": Ibid., p. 296.
10	"Let the Queen . . . Levantine coast": Ibid., p. 311.

The classic work on Disraeli and the Near Eastern crisis of 1876-1878 is R. W. Seton-Watson, *Disraeli, Gladstone, and the Eastern Question* (London, 1935; reprint, New York, 1972).
Page

11   For Gladstone's comments on the "Bulgarian horrors" and his response to *Tancred* and Judaic feeling, see Philip Magnus, *Gladstone: A Biography* (New York, 1964), pp. 242, 244.

A good survey of the work of the Palestine Exploration Fund is in Frederick Jones Bliss, *The Development of Palestine Exploration* (New York, 1906). The best sources are the books and articles published by the Fund itself, which are too numerous to mention here.
Page

12   Quotations from Charles Warren's *The Land of Promise* can be found in Sokolow, *History*, 2:274, 269 72.

The definitive biography of George Eliot is the one by Gordon S. Haight, *George Eliot: A Biography* (Oxford, 1968). Haight is also the editor of *The George Eliot Letters*, 6 vols. (New Haven, 1955). The edition I used of *Daniel Deronda* was that of Harper Torchbooks (New York, 1960). On Emanuel Deutsch, one should consult Emily Strangford, *Literary Remains of the Late Emanuel Deutsch, with a Brief Memoir* (New York, 1874).
Page

13	"the Industrial Plantation . . .": Sokolow, *History*, 1:161.
14	"must be a Jew . . .": Eliot, *Daniel Deronda*, p. 355.
14	"Revive the organic centre . . . transmission and understanding": Ibid., p. 400.
14	"the world will gain . . .": Ibid., p. 402.
14-15	"That is impossible . . .": Ibid., p. 497.
15	"identify myself, as far as possible . . .": Ibid.
15	"to make his life a sequence . . .": Ibid., p. 353.
15	"to become better acquainted . . . over the face of the globe": Ibid., p. 606.
15	"Doubtless . . . the wider public . . .": Haight, *George Eliot*, p. 483.
15	"When I want to read a novel . . .": Blake, *Disraeli*, p. 191.

Of the several biographies of Laurence Oliphant, the ones I used were: Philip Henderson, *The Life of Laurence Oliphant* (London, 1956); and the part memoir, part collection of letters published by his cousin, the popular novelist Margaret Oliphant,

Memoir of the Life of Laurence Oliphant, 2 vols. (New York, 1891). The edition I used of Oliphant's *The Land of Gilead* is the original one, published in London in 1880.

Page

15 17   Oliphant's letter to Lord Salisbury is excerpted at length in Henderson, *Life*, pp. 204-6.

15-16   "any amount of money . . . by their pilgrims": Margaret Oliphant, *Memoir*, 2:169.

17   "the kindest encouragements . . . cordial sympathy": Laurence Oliphant, *Gilead*, p. xxxv.

17   "the western section . . .": Ibid., pp. 300-301.

17   "would put the colony . . .": Ibid., p. 302.

17   "the true outlet for its produce": Ibid., p. 301.

17   "under the auspices of the Sultan . . .": Ibid., p. xxxii.

17-18   "The nation . . . that espoused . . .": Ibid., p. 503.

18   "for as we have special interests . . .": Ibid., p. 524.

18   "that the Liberal leaders . . .": *Jewish Chronicle*, April 9, 1880, as quoted in ibid., p. xxix.

2. HERZL IN ENGLAND

There are several biographies of Theodor Herzl, but the classic one is Alex Bein, *Theodor Herzl* (Philadelphia, 1941; reprint, New York, 1962). The definitive edition, in English translation, of Herzl's diaries is Raphael Patai, ed., *The Complete Diaries of Theodor Herzl*, trans. Harry Zohn, 5 vols. (New York, 1960). The most comprehensive history of Zionism is Walter Laqueur, *A History of Zionism* (New York, 1972; reprint, 1976); an important standard work is Israel Cohen, *The Zionist Movement* (London, 1945).

Page

19   "I am Daniel Deronda . . .": Patai, *Diaries of Theodor Herzl*, 1:282.

19   "There is an immense movement . . .": Margaret Oliphant, *Memoir of the Life of Laurence Oliphant*, 2 vols. (New York, 1891), 2:218.

20   "attended a meeting . . .": Ibid., p. 219.

20   The best book on the history of Jewish settlement in Palestine is Alex Bein, *The Return to the Soil* (Jerusalem, 1952). On Baron de Rothschild's colonizing work, see Simon Schama, *Two Rothschilds and the Land of Israel* (New York, 1978).

21   "the power to stir people": Patai, *Diaries of Theodor Herzl*, 1:228.

22   "we are an historical unit": Ibid., p. 276.

22   "this was the idea of *Daniel Deronda*": Ibid., p. 279.

22-23   Herzl's visit to Sir Samuel Montagu is from ibid., p. 280.

23-24   Herzl's visit to Colonel Goldsmid is from ibid., pp. 281-83.

25   Gladstone . . . had found its subject "highly interesting": Ibid., p. 360.

25   "from Constantinople the *presque-certitude* . . .": Ibid., p. 406.

25   "stirred . . . under everybody here": Ibid.

26   "Edmond Rothschild's sport. . .": Ibid., p. 420.

26   "People crowded into every corner . . .": Ibid., p. 418.

26   "As I sat on the platform . . .": Ibid., p. 421.

27   "Now it really depends . . .": Ibid., p. 419.

27   "downright dangerous": Ibid., p. 427.

27   "It is no longer the elegant . . .": Quoted in Bein, *Herzl*, p. 231.

27   "At Basel I founded the Jewish State . . .": Patai, *Diaries of Theodor Herzl*, 2:581.

27   For the Basel Program, see Sokolow, *History*, 1:xliv; and Israel Cohen, *Zionist Movement*, p. 73. In the official language of the Congress, German, the original of "a home in Palestine secured by public law" is "*öffentlich-rechtlich gesicherte Heimstätte.*"

28   England as the "Archimedean point": Bein, *Herzl*, p. 263.

On Jewish immigration to Britain and the Aliens Bill, see Elie Halévy, *A History of the English People in the Nineteenth Century*, vol. 5, *Imperialism and the Rise of Labor, 1895-1905* (New York, 1961), pp. 371-75; V.D. Lipman, *Social History of the Jews in England* (London, 1954), p. 143; and L.P. Gartner, *The Jewish Immigrant in England* (London, 1959).

Page

29   "It was their insatiable appetite . . .": Halévy, *History of the English People*, 5:372.

29-31   Herzl's testimony before the Aliens Commission is in the official *Report of the Royal Commission on Alien Immigration* (London, 1903), pp. 211-21. The report is in double columns, and the citations below indicate column a or b.

30   "the recognition of Jews . . .": Ibid., p. 212b.

30   "a diverting of the stream . . .": Ibid., p. 213a.

30   "The Jews of Eastern Europe . . .": Ibid.

30   "when you want a great settlement . . .": Ibid., p. 217b.

30   "whether you mean that . . .": Ibid., p. 219a.

30   "Now, it is certainly the goal . . .": Ibid.

30   "I will not say the dream . . .": Ibid., p. 219b.

31   "thought that I could carry out . . .": Patai, *Diaries of Theodor Herzl*, 4:1295.

31   "I believe Lord James . . .": Ibid., p. 1296.

31-32   For Herzl's meeting with Joseph Chamberlain on October 22, 1902, see ibid., pp. 1360-63.

32   "a great man": Ibid., p. 1370.

32   For Herzl's meeting with Lord Lansdowne on October 24, 1902, see ibid., pp. 1370-71.

32-33   For Herzl's memorandum for Lansdowne, see ibid., pp. 1364-67.

33   "Is it possible . . .": Ibid., p. 1372.

33   "that no sanguine hopes . . .": Bein, *Herzl*, p. 424.

33   "historic document": Ibid., p. 425.

33   "alternative proposal": Patai, *Diaries of Theodor Herzl*, 4:1419.

34   "only surplus Nile water . . .": Ibid., p. 1446.

34   "the most disagreeable Englishman . . .": Ibid.

On the "Uganda" or East Africa proposal, see Robert G. Weisbord, *African Zion* (Philadelphia, 1968).

Page

34-35   "I have seen a land . . . I have to": Patai, *Diaries of Theodor Herzl*, 4:1473.

35   "If Dr. Herzl were at all inclined . . .": Weisbord, *African Zion*, p. 30.

35   "an ingenious bit of fantasy . . .": Theodor Herzl, *The Jewish State*, trans. Harry Zohn (New York, 1970), pp. 27-28.

36   "I hope that Dr. Herzl . . .": Bein, *Herzl*, p. 440.

36   For Lloyd George's role in the East Africa project, see Lloyd George Papers 9/33/1/16.

36-37   Sir Clement Hill's letter on the East Africa offer is cited in Weisbord, *African Zion*, p. 79.

37   "amazement, admiration . . .": Bein, *Herzl*, p. 455.

38   "traitor": Ibid., p. 461.

38   For Herzl's remarks to his friends at the end of the sixth congress, see Patai, *Diaries of Theodor Herzl*, 4:1547.

3. TURKEY ENTERS THE WAR

One of the best introductions to Turkish history until the start of the twentieth century is Lord Kinross, *The Ottoman Centuries* (New York, 1977). Illuminating for the first four decades of the twentieth century is the same author's *Atatürk: A Biography of Mustafa Kemal, Father of Modern Turkey* (New York, 1978). Bernard Lewis, *The Emergence of Modern Turkey* (Oxford, 1961; 2nd ed., 1968), is a fine work of interpretation for the initiated; readers unfamiliar with the subject should begin with Kinross. The classic work on the diplomatic problem of the Ottoman Empire—mainly with regard to its European part—through the centuries is J.A.R. Marriott, *The Eastern Question: An Historical Study in European Diplomacy* (Oxford, 1917; later editions through 1947). Edward Meade Earle, *Turkey, the Great Powers, and the Baghdad Railway* (New York, 1923), is the classic study on that subject.

For the incidents of the Turkish battleships, and of the *Goeben* and the *Breslau*, the principal sources I used were: Winston S. Churchill, *The World Crisis* (abridged ed. in one volume, New York, 1931) and *The Aftermath* (New York, 1929); Djemal Pasha, *Memories of a Turkish Statesman, 1913-1919* (London, n.d.); Henry Morgenthau, *Ambassador Morgenthau's Story* (New York, 1926); and contemporary newspaper accounts. There is a very fine account of the whole set of incidents in Barbara W. Tuchman, *The Guns of August* (New York, 1962), Chapter 10.

Page

41   "There seemed to be . . .": Churchill, *World Crisis*, p. 113.

41   "Never, never . . .": Djemal, *Memories*, p. 116.

41-42   "Agents had gone . . .": Morgenthau, *Story*, p. 76.

42   "this incident justified . . .": Djemal, *Memories*, p. 117.

42   "far outstripped in speed . . .": Churchill, *World Crisis*, p. 121.

42   "Very good . . . Hold her . . .": Ibid., p. 124.

43   "against superior forces": Ibid., p. 122.

43   "sinister fatality . . . Admiralty clerk": Ibid., p. 144.

43   "consent to the two ships . . .": Djemal, *Memories*, p. 119.

44   "I asked the press . . .": Ibid., p. 120.

44   "As we shall insist . . .": Earl of Oxford and Asquith, *Memories and Reflections*, 2 vols. (Boston, 1928), 2:32.

44   "now pending with the Ottoman Government . . .": *The Times* (London), August 13, 1914.

44   *Jawuz Sultan Selim* and the *Midilli*: Ibid., August 15, 1914.

44   "One day . . . disappeared down stream": Morgenthau, *Story*, p. 79.

44-45   "I have terrible news . . . captured Turkey": Ibid., p. 81.

46-47   "It is a wonderful brew . . . other men's ideas": Sir Mark Sykes, *The Caliphs' Last Heritage: A Short History of the Turkish Empire* (London, 1915), pp. 494-95.

48   "almost more German than Turkish": Morgenthau, *Story*, p. 32.

48   "he had learned to speak German . . .": Ibid.

48   For Wangenheim's June 1913 telegram requesting a German general, see Otto Liman von Sanders, *Five Years in Turkey* (Annapolis, Md., 1927), p. 1.

49   "German training . . .": Sykes, *Last Heritage*, pp. 510-11.

49-50   "disgraceful career . . . petty chicanery": Ibid., pp. 548-49.

50   "It enabled the Turkish War Office . . .": Ibid., p. 522.

There are innumerable biographies of T.E. Lawrence, but the most ambitious of the recent ones, and particularly good on the Carchemish period, is John E. Mack, *A Prince of Our Disorder: The Life of T.E. Lawrence* (Boston, 1976). The origin of the spying charge against Hogarth, Lawrence, and their circle is Phillip Knightley and Colin Simpson, *The Secret Lives of Lawrence of Arabia* (London, 1969). There are many source works and collections on Lawrence, but the ones most relevant to this section are: David Garnett, ed., *The Letters of T.E. Lawrence* (New York, 1939); Sir Leonard Woolley, *Dead Towns and Living Men* (London, 1920, 1954); A.W. Lawrence, ed., *T.E. Lawrence, By His Friends* (New York, 1937); and Hubert Young, *The Independent Arab* (London, 1933).

Page

51   "always wore a blazer . . .": Woolley's account in A.W. Lawrence, *Lawrence, By His Friends*, p. 73.

51   "a marked ascendancy . . .": Woolley, *Dead Towns*, p. 72.

51   "Tonight one of these engineers . . .": Garnett, *Letters*, pp. 126-27.

52   "Now these earth mounds . . .": Woolley, *Dead Towns*, p. 85.

52   "The natives, of course . . .": Ibid., p. 88.

52   "because they did not know . . . despise them". Woolley's account in A.W. Lawrence, *Lawrence, By His Friends*, p. 75.

53   "Whenever Basrawi went in to Aleppo . . .": Young, *Independent Arab*, p. 17.

53   "a well-meaning man . . .": Woolley, *Dead Towns*, p. 92.

53-54   Lawrence's description of the incident between Kurds and Germans is from his letter to James Elroy Flecker, June 1914; reproduced in Garnett, *Letters*, pp. 172-75.

Descriptions of the Haifa Technical College controversy are in the following: Israel Cohen, *The Zionist Movement* (London, 1945), pp. 101-2; Alex Bein, *The Return to the Soil* (Jerusalem, 1952), pp. 138-45; and Albert M. Hyamson, *Palestine: The Rebirth of a Nation*, (New York, 1917), pp. 241-43. The controversy is mentioned *passim* in *CW Letters*, vol. 6.

Page

56   "the Hebraization or Germanization . . .": Weizmann to H. Infeld, January 26, 1914. *CW Letters*, 6:230.

56   "a *Stützpunkt* . . .": Weizmann to Judah L. Magnes, December 3, 1913. Ibid., p. 175.

57   "There is only a feeling . . .": *Manchester Guardian*, September 12, 1914.

57   "alarming rumors . . . net effect . . .": Ibid., October 2, 1914.

4. HERBERT SAMUEL RAISES THE PALESTINE QUESTION

Herbert Samuel wrote an autobiography, which in the United States is entitled *Grooves of Change* (Indianapolis, 1945); the standard biography is John Bowle, *Viscount Samuel, a Biography* (London, 1957).

Page

58   Asquith's Guildhall speech of November 9, 1914 appeared in *The Times* (London), November 10, 1914.

59   "I don't know whether you have read . . .": Weizmann to three Zionist colleagues in New York. *CW Letters*, 7:36.

59   "The Prime Minister, in his speech . . .": *Jewish Chronicle*, November 13, 1914.

60   "This war will inevitably . . .": Ibid.

60   ". . . restoring a real Judaea": H.G. Wells to Israel Zangwill, in *Daily Chronicle*, November 4, 1914.

61   "Your 'War in the Air' . . .": Ibid., November 9, 1914.

61   "the first member . . .": Samuel, *Grooves*, pp. 171–72.

63   "has traveled in East Africa . . .": *Jewish Chronicle*, January 12, 1906.

63   "With plenty to do elsewhere . . .": Samuel, *Grooves*, p. 171.

64   "the moment Turkey entered the war . . .": Ibid.

64   "who was to succeed the Turk . . .": Ibid.

64   "long conversation . . . favorably to Palestine": Gaster Diaries.

Sir Edward Grey has written his memoirs: Viscount Grey of Fallodon, *Twenty-Five Years, 1892–1916*, 2 vols. (New York, 1925). For many years the standard biography was G.M. Trevelyan, *Grey of Fallodon* (London, 1937, 1948), but now there also is Keith Robbins, *Sir Edward Grey* (London, 1971).

Page

65   For Lloyd George's scathing estimate of Grey and his class, see David Lloyd George, *War Memoirs of David Lloyd George*, 6 vols. (Boston, 1933–1937), 1:88.

65   "The lamps are going out . . .": Trevelyan, *Grey*, p. 266.

66   "to support Arabs against Turkey . . .": Grey to Mallet, August 29, 1914. FO 371/2138.

66–69   The Samuel-Grey conversation of November 9, 1914 is from a note of it made by Samuel, reproduced entirely in *Grooves*, pp. 172–74.

67   For Grey, Greenberg, and the El Arish plan in 1906, see Lloyd George Papers 9/33/1/16.

5. LLOYD GEORGE TAKES NOTE

On Lloyd George throughout this book, I have made use of Frank Owen, *Tempestuous Journey: Lloyd George, His Life and Times* (New York, 1955); there are several other biographies as well. Another major printed source is David Lloyd George, *War Memoirs of David Lloyd George*, 6 vols. (Boston, 1933–1937).

Page

70–73   "The Future of Palestine": *New Statesman*, November 21, 1914.

73   "I was brought up . . .": Lloyd George speech to the Jewish Historical Society of England, 1925 (reproduced as the Afterword in Philip Guedalla, *Napoleon and Palestine* [London, 1925], pp. 49–51).

73-74   "The spiritual wants . . .": Owen, *Tempestuous Journey*, p. 59. The story of Elisha and Gehazi is in 2 Kings 5.

74   " . . . Brummagem and Jerusalem": Owen, *Tempestuous Journey*, p. 139.

74   "a British subject born in Ontario . . .": Ibid., p. 141.

74   "only think talking": Earl of Oxford and Asquith, *Memories and Reflections*, 2 vols. (Boston, 1928), 2:76. Asquith says this of two members of his cabinet: the other is Winston Churchill.

75   "The present Chancellor of the Exchequer . . .": Lloyd George, *War Memoirs*, 1:14.

75   "among Philistines . . .": Frederic Morton, *The Rothschilds* (New York, 1962), p. 238.

75   "Lord Rothschild, we have had . . .": Lloyd George, *War Memoirs*, 1:104.

75-76   "The Turk . . . is the greatest enemy . . .": Lloyd George's speech apeared in *The Times* (London), November 11, 1914.

76   "thinks imperially": Lloyd George, *War Memoirs*, 1:15.

76   For Greenberg and Lloyd George in 1906, see Lloyd George Papers 9/33/1/16.

76   friendly message to a Zionist meeting in Cardiff: Stein, *Balfour Declaration*, p. 142.

On C.P. Scott, there are, in addition to the diaries cited in the introduction to these notes: a biography by J.L. Hammond, *C.P. Scott of the Manchester Guardian* (London, 1934); David Ayerst, *The Manchester Guardian: Biography of a Newspaper* (Ithaca, N.Y., 1971), with a good deal of material on Scott; and a memoir, "C.P. Scott," in Arnold J. Toynbee, *Acquaintances* (London, 1967), pp. 228-30.

Page

76-79   For the Scott-Lloyd George conversation, see Scott Diaries, November 27, 1914.

6. THE GENTLEMAN FROM PINSK

There are short biographies of Weizmann by Julian L. Meltzer, *Chaim Weizmann* (London, 1962), by Barnet Litvinoff, *Weizmann: Last of the Patriarchs* (New York, 1976), and by Harold M. Blumberg, *Weizmann, His Life and Times* (New York, 1975); and at least two collections of memoirs of Weizmann edited by Meyer W. Weisgal, *Chaim Weizmann, Statesman and Scientist* (New York, 1944), and *Chaim Weizmann: A Biography by Several Hands* (New York, 1963), coedited by Joel Carmichael. There has yet to be a definitive study. Indispensable for students of Weizmann are the *Letters* and *Trial and Error*, both cited in the introduction to these notes. Sir Charles Webster, in his collection of essays, *The Art and Practice of Diplomacy* (New York, 1962), discusses Weizmann in part of the title essay and in all of "The Founder of the National Home" (pp. 113-32), in which he gives his opinion that Weizmann's achievement was "the greatest act of diplomatic statesmanship of the First World War." See also Isaiah Berlin, *Chaim Weizmann* (New York, 1958).

Page

80   "Starting with nothing I . . .": *CW Letters*, 7:58.

80   "Who are the persons representing . . .": Wolf quoted in a letter from Leon Simon to Weizmann, November 27, 1914, Weizmann Archives; cited in *CW Letters*, 7:57, n.48/2.

80-81   "My success . . . the Jewish people": *CW Letters*, 7:58.

81   "The townlet of my birth . . .": Weizmann, *Trial and Error*, p. 3.

81   "In those days . . .": Mendele Moicher S'forim, *The Travels and Adventures of Benjamin the Third*, trans. Moshe Spiegel (New York, 1949, 1968), p. 19.

82   "At table grandpa . . .": Weizmann, *Trial and Error*, p. 7.

82   "A remarkable change . . .": Jacob Prelooker, *Under the Tsar and Queen Victoria* (London, n.d.), p. 9, quoted in Jacob S. Raisin, *The Haskalah Movement in Russia* (Philadelphia, 1913), pp. 241–42.

82   "And please, my dear teacher . . .": Weizmann to Shlomo Tsvi Sokolovsky, Summer, 1885. *CW Letters*, 1:35–36. This is the very first letter in the collection.

82-83   For Weizmann's education and early career, see Leonard Stein's introduction in ibid., p. 14.

83   Plekhanov "was debunked and routed . . .": Weizmann to Leo Motzkin, November 23, 1901, Ibid., p. 210.

84   "with a vehement gesture": Weizmann, *Trial and Error*, p. 85.

84   "*Monsieur le Président* . . .": Ibid., p. 87.

84   "Congress does not conceive . . .": *CW Letters*, 3:xxv.

84   "a positive attitude": Ibid., p. xxv.

84-86   The account of Weizmann's trip to London in the fall of 1903 is based on ibid., pp. 43–54.

85   "I have reached the inescapable conclusion . . .": Ibid., p. 48.

85   "unharnessed the horses . . .": Weizmann, *Trial and Error*, p. 7.

85   "We must also thank . . .": *CW Letters*, 1:37.

85   "this monstrous London": Ibid., 3:44.

85   "Lord, what horror! . . .": Ibid.

85   "This is the hub of the world . . .": Ibid., p. 48.

86   "about my wish to move . . .": Ibid.

86   "I have also enquired . . .": Ibid., p. 52.

86   "He is no longer . . .": Ibid., p. 270.

87   "There was a certain freedom . . .": Weisgal, *Weizmann: A Biography*, p. 91.

87   "in my time . . .": Agate quoted in David Ayerst, *The Manchester Guardian: Biography of a Newspaper* (Ithaca, N.Y., 1971), p. 339.

Material on the Jews of Manchester in this period was provided by a special supplement to the *Jewish Chronicle* of June 15, 1906, called "The Manchester Jewish Community." Material on the relationship between Weizmann and Charles Dreyfus comes from *CW Letters*, vols. 3 and 4, *passim*, and the biographical note on Dreyfus in *CW Letters*, vol. 3, p. 386. Dreyfus and his wife also are mentioned in the *Jewish Chronicle* special supplement just cited. The remarks about Dreyfus in *Trial and Error* are wholly unreliable, as is often the case in that book when Weizmann is dealing with someone for whom fondness has faded along with memory.

Page

88   "Greenberg and Cowen are wooing me": Weizmann to Vera Khatzman, January 23, 1905. *CW Letters*, 4:12.

88-89   "the introduction of politics into Zionism . . . in which Zionists should assist": From account of meeting in *Jewish Chronicle*, January 27, 1905.

89   "ultra-*Palestinian* . . .": *CW Letters*, 4:13.

89   "Yesterday I went . . .": Weizmann to Vera Khatzman, January 28, 1905. Ibid., pp. 18–19.

89-90   "The local Zionist leader . . . rendered completely paralyzed": Weizmann to Menahem Ussishkin, January 29, 1905. Ibid., p. 21.

On Balfour, the standard work is still the one by his niece, Blanche E.C. Dugdale, *Arthur James Balfour, First Earl of Balfour*, 2 vols. (New York, 1937). A more recent and more astringent study is Kenneth Young, *Arthur James Balfour* (London, 1963). For a general view of the Balfour government, one can do no better than the standard histories: Elie Halévy, *A History of the English People in the Nineteenth Century*, vol. 5, *Imperialism and the Rise of Labor, 1895-1905* (New York, 1961); and Sir Robert Ensor, *England: 1870-1914*, Oxford History of England, vol. 14 (Oxford, 1936; 1968), pp. 353-81.

Page

90   "So far as he knew . . .": *Parliamentary Debates* (Commons), July 10, 1905, O.R. col. 155.

90   "may be classed as 'blood money' . . .": *Jewish Chronicle*, April 28, 1905.

90   On the Aliens Act, see ibid., August 18, 1905, and subsequent issues; also, Halévy, *History of the English People*, 5:373-75.

My account of the January 1906 election is gleaned from contemporary newspaper accounts, primarily in *The Times*, the *Manchester Guardian*, the *Observer*, and the *Jewish Chronicle*.

Page

91   list of all the Jewish candidates: *Jewish Chronicle*, January 12, 1906.

91   "I should have thought it hardly necessary . . .": *The Times* (London), January 4, 1906.

91   "sympathy with Jews in Russia . . .": Ibid., January 6, 1906.

On Churchill in Manchester, see Randolph Churchill, *Winston S. Churchill, Young Statesman*, vol. 2 in the official biography of Churchill (Boston, 1967).

Page

91   "sham [that] contained absurdities . . .": *Jewish Chronicle*, October 13, 1905.

91-92   "Mr. Churchill, in addressing a Jewish audience . . .": *Manchester Guardian*, January 9, 1906.

92-93   "I have delayed to answer . . .": *The Times* (London), January 2, 1906; further information in *Jewish Chronicle*, January 5, 1906.

93   For Churchill and Weizmann in December 1905, see *CW Letters*, 4:207-8, 215-16.

93   "prepared to receive a Zionist delegation . . .": Ibid., p. 220.

94   Sir Francis Montefiore's open letter to the candidates is in *The Times* (London), January 12, 1906.

95   250 favorable replies: *Jewish Chronicle*, January 26, 1906.

95   the prime minister's brother Gerald: *The Times* (London), January 6, 1906: *Manchester Guardian*, January 6, 1906.

95   "I had a meeting with Balfour today . . .": *CW Letters*, 4:219.

95-96   "I saw Balfour . . .": Weizmann to David Wolfssohn, November 4, 1906. Ibid., p. 336.

96   "He delivered the best platform speeches . . .": Dugdale, *Balfour*, 1:323.

96-97   Weizmann's account of this meeting, including all quotations, is from Weizmann, *Trial and Error*, pp. 109-11.

97   For the election results, see *The Times* (London), January 15, 1906.

97-98   "Much excitement and enthusiasm . . .": *Jewish Chronicle*, January 19, 1906.

98   "I had a most interesting conversation . . .": Weizmann, *Trial and Error*, p. 111.

98   "Balfour has written to Dreyfus . . .": *CW Letters*, 4:262.

98   "the Russian gentleman who had the honor . . .": Dreyfus to Balfour, March 24, 1906. Quoted from Dugdale Papers in Stein, *Balfour Declaration*, p. 152, n. 21.

98   "a Jewish friend—an anti-Zionist": Stein, *Balfour Declaration*, p. 152. These are Stein's own words based on information he obtained privately.

98   "I enclose a letter from Dr. Dreyfus . . .": Letter of April 13, 1906. Quoted from Dugdale papers in ibid.

7. DR. WEIZMANN MISSES LLOYD GEORGE AND SEES HERBERT SAMUEL INSTEAD

Page

99   For developments in the EZF and Weizmann's prewar activities, see *CW Letters*, vols. 5 and 6, *passim*.

100   "Without me the Zionists . . .": Ibid., 6:304.

100   On Israel Zangwill, see Joseph Leftwich, *Israel Zangwill* (New York, 1957), and Maurice Wohlgelernter, *Israel Zangwill: A Study.* (New York, 1964).

100-101   "I regret deeply . . . the good of Jewry": Ibid., 7:18-19.

101-2   "your letter leaves me . . .": Ibid., p. 25, n. 22/1.

102-3   "My plans . . . than 17 inch guns": Ibid., pp. 25-28.

103   "six or seven million . . . patience of the authorities": Ibid., pp. 28-29, n. 22/10.

103   "any national view . . .": Ibid., p. 109.

There are four accounts, whole or partial, of Weizmann's first encounter with C.P. Scott: Weizmann, *Trial and Error*, pp. 148-49; Vera Weizmann, *The Impossible*, pp. 51-52; David Ayerst, *The Manchester Guardian: Biography of a Newspaper* (Ithaca, N.Y., 1971), p. 381; and Weizmann to Leopold Greenberg, September 16, 1914, *CW Letters*, 7:9-10. I have assembled my own account from these.

Page

104   "And what is your office?": Vera Weizmann, *The Impossible*, p. 52.

104   "I had a long talk . . .": *CW Letters*, 7:9-10.

105   "Things have moved quicker . . . glad to hear from you": Ibid., pp. 38-39.

105   Scott replied by inviting Weizmann: Ibid., p. 43, n. 38/1.

105-6   "so unaffected, so open . . .": Weizmann, *Trial and Error*, p. 149. Writing more than a quarter of a century later, Weizmann in this passage has confused this November visit to Scott with the first one in September. The letters show him to be mistaken, and I have taken the liberty to correct him.

106   "for the kindness you have shown . . .": *CW Letters*, 7:44-45.

106   I was immensely interested . . .": Ibid., p. 44, n. 39/2.

106   "I have just had a letter . . .": Ibid., p. 65.

107   "Unable arrange George away": Ibid., p. 66.

107   For Weizmann's activities from December 3 to December 12, 1914, see Ibid., pp. 66-83, 110-17.

107-10   For the Weizmann-Samuel conversation of December 10, 1914, see Ibid., pp. 110-12. This is part of a report on his activities sent by Weizmann on

January 7, 1915, to two members of the Zionist executive recently arrived in England, Nahum Sokolow and Yehiel Tschlenow.

8. MR. BALFOUR

In addition to the Balfour materials already cited under Chapter 6, I should add here Balfour's unfinished autobiography: Arthur James, First Earl of Balfour, *Retrospect, An Unfinished Autobiography, 1848-1886* (Boston, 1930). Balfour's three philosophical works are *A Defence of Philosophic Doubt* (1879), *The Foundations of Belief* (1895), and *Theism and Humanism* (1916). Large extracts from these books and other writings of Balfour's are in Wilfrid M. Short, *The Mind of Arthur James Balfour* (New York, 1918). Also relevant is *Opinions and Argument from Speeches and Addresses of the Earl of Balfour, 1910-1927* (New York, 1928).

Page

111　"a special Palestine association": *CW Letters*, 5:15, 16.

111　"I know Balfour . . . lines indicated above": Ibid., pp. 266-67.

111　"I am at present engaged . . .": Ibid., p. 269.

112　"It has not now been possible . . .": Ibid., p. 271.

There has yet to be an adequate biography of Nahum Sokolow. Simcha Kling, *Nachum Sokolow, Servant of His People* (New York, 1960) is slim, sketchy, and hagiographical; so also is the work, in Hebrew, of Sokolow's son, Florian Sokolow, *Avi, Nahum Sokolow* (Tel Aviv, 1970), though this has some valuable passages based on Sokolow's personal papers.

Page

112　"promised to write to you and Balfour . . .": *CW Letters*, 5:312.

112　Dreyfus replied that Balfour: Ibid., n. 203/3.

113　"By the way . . .": Ibid., p. 346.

113　"I have written to Balfour . . .": Ibid., 7:37.

113　"After I had written to Balfour . . .": Ibid., p. 45.

113　"I have the liveliest . . .": Ibid., n. 40; also, Stein, *Balfour Declaration*, p. 153.

An example of the widespread view of Balfour as a listless and unfeeling decadent is the profile of him in Piers Brendon, *Eminent Edwardians* (London, 1979), pp. 67-129. One of the classic correctives to this view is the profile of Balfour in Winston S. Churchill, *Great Contemporaries* (London, 1937; Chicago, 1973), pp. 237-57.

Page

114　"a lust for slaughter . . . his languid life": Blanche E.C. Dugdale, *Arthur James Balfour, First Earl of Balfour*, 2 vols. (New York, 1937), 1:110.

114　"Presently . . . from behind the speaker's chair . . .": Quoted in Kenneth Young, *Arthur James Balfour* (London, 1963), pp. 170-71.

115　"aghast at the halting nature . . .": Sir Ian Malcolm, *Lord Balfour, A Memory* (London, 1930), p. 23.

115　"No Minister in charge of a Bill . . .": Churchill, *Great Contemporaries*, p. 252.

115　"I say what occurs to me . . .": Ibid., p. 250.

115　"the curious thing . . .": Malcolm, *Lord Balfour*, p. 23.

115　"He saw a great deal of life from afar": Quoted in Churchill, *Great Contemporaries*, p. 237.

116　"Do it if you like . . .": Dugdale, *Balfour*, 1:5.

116   "Morality is more than a bare code of laws . . .": Short, *Mind of Arthur James Balfour*, p. 232.

116-17   "something more important . . .": Ibid., pp. 232-33.

117   On T. H. Huxley's response to Balfour's work, see William Irvine, *Apes, Angels and Victorians* (New York, 1955, 1959), pp. 354-57.

117-18   Balfour's essay on Handel is reproduced almost in its entirety in Short, *Mind of Arthur James Balfour*, pp. 218-29.

117   "on the whole it would, I suppose . . .": Ibid., p. 220.

117   "It seems at first sight strange . . .": Ibid.

117   "the rivalries and quarrels . . .": Ibid., p. 221.

117   "in the age of Voltaire and of Hume . . .": Ibid., p. 227.

117-18   few "have succeeded in touching . . .": Ibid., p. 225.

118   "the most splendid inspirations . . .": Ibid.

118   "it stands out . . .": Ibid., p. 223.

118   "a state of things . . .": *Parliamentary Debates* (Commons), July 10, 1905, O.R. col. 155.

118-19   "The letter you send me . . .": Quoted from the Dugdale Papers in Stein, *Balfour Declaration*, p. 165.

119   "peopled with endless Sassoon girls . . .": Young, *Arthur James Balfour*, p. 139.

119   Lady Battersea . . . was to remember: Lucy Cohen, *Lady Rothschild and Her Daughters* (London, 1935), p. 250.

The main source for the Balfour-Weizmann conversation of December 12, 1914, is Weizmann's report, already cited, of January 7, 1915, to Sokolow and Tschlenow (*CW Letters*, 7:114-15). But there is additional material in Weizmann's letters of December 13, 1914, to C.P. Scott (Ibid., p. 80) and of December 14-15, 1914, to Ahad Ha'am (Ibid., pp. 81-82). I have drawn upon all three sources to reconstruct the conversation.

Page

119   "I spoke to him practically in the same strain . . .": *CW Letters*, 7:114.

119   "You may get your things done . . .": Ibid., p. 81.

119-20   "would remain insoluble until . . .": Ibid.

120   Cosima Wagner: Ibid., pp. 81, 114.

120   Wotan a "tiresome old gossip": Malcolm, *Lord Balfour*, p. 9.

120   "and offered to tell him . . . at the hands of the Jews": *CW Letters*, 7:114.

120   "that Germans of the Mosaic faith . . .": Ibid., p. 81.

120   "The essential point . . .": Ibid., p. 114.

120   "absorption": Ibid., p. 82.

120   "Grandees": Ibid., p. 114.

120   "they must hide their Judaism . . .": Ibid., pp. 114-15.

120   Weizmann thought he saw tears: Ibid., p. 82.

120   Balfour . . . took his visitor by the hand: Ibid.

120-21   "Palestine and the building up . . .": Ibid., p. 115.

121   For Russian Jewry and Claude Montefiore, see ibid.

121   "What a great difference . . .": Ibid., p. 82.

121   "regretted that he had known . . .": Ibid., p. 115.

121   "that fatal error . . .": Ibid., p. 82.

121   "to explain to him how great and deep . . .": Ibid.

121   "the military situation became clearer": Ibid., p. 115.

121   Weizmann's reports give slightly differing versions of Balfour's parting words; I used the one in the letter to Ahad Ha'am, ibid., p. 82.

121   For Balfour's speech in Bristol, see *The Times* (London), December 14, 1914.

9. LLOYD GEORGE SEES DR. WEIZMANN, AND HERBERT SAMUEL PRESENTS HIS MEMORANDUM

Page

125   "I received today . . .": Earl of Oxford and Asquith, *Memories and Reflections*, 2 vols. (Boston, 1928), 2:64.

125   "All the wars of the world . . .": Winston S. Churchill, *The World Crisis* (New York, 1931), p. 298.

125-26   For Lloyd George's memorandum of January 1, 1915, see David Lloyd George, *War Memoirs of David Lloyd George*, 6 vols. (Boston, 1933-1937), 1:322-30. All the Lloyd George quotations in these pages are from this source.

On Kitchener, the two basic works are the official biography by Sir George Arthur, *Life of Lord Kitchener*, 3 vols. (London, 1920); and the more recent and more critical one by Philip Magnus, *Kitchener, Portrait of an Imperialist* (New York, 1959). On Churchill in this period, the basic work is Volume 3 of the official biography: Martin Gilbert, *Winston S. Churchill: The Challenge of War, 1914-1916* (Boston, 1971).

Page

127   a telegram sent by Sir George Buchanan: Gilbert, *Churchill*, 3:232.

127   "The feeling here is gaining ground . . .": Magnus, *Kitchener*, pp. 310 11.

127   Kitchener's other move . . . was to contact Winston Churchill: Churchill, *World Crisis*, pp. 325-26.

128   "I wanted Gallipoli attacked . . .": Gilbert, *Churchill*, 3:231; also Churchill, *World Crisis*, p. 325, without "Turkish."

128   "mere demonstration": Churchill, *World Crisis*, p. 326.

128   "I do not see . . . Constantinople was threatened": Ibid.

129   "might be forced . . .": Carden quoted in ibid., p. 330.

129   Carden's . . . fully wrought plan of attack: Ibid., pp. 331-32.

129   "produced a great impression . . .": Ibid., p. 332.

129   "the Fleet would proceed up . . .": Cabinet Papers. PRO: CAB 22/1.

129   "tremendous enthusiasm": Quoted from Sir Maurice Hankey by Gilbert in *Churchill*, 3:252.

129   For Lloyd George's and Kitchener's reactions, see PRO: CAB 22/1.

129-30   For Weizmann-Gaster-Samuel conversation of December 25, 1914, see part of Weizmann's report to Sokolow and Tschlenow, January 7, 1915. *CW Letters*, 7:116-17.

130-31   For Weizmann's conversation with Baron de Rothschild of December 28, 1914, see part of report of January 7, 1915. Ibid., pp. 117-18.

131-32   For Sokolow's arrival in London, see Florian Sokolow, *Avi, Nahum Sokolow* (Tel Aviv, 1970), p. 139.

132   "Mr. Lloyd George, whom I have seen . . .": Weizmann Archives, quoted in Stein, *Balfour Declaration*, pp. 139-40.

132   "You will probably find . . .": Ibid., p. 140.

133   "I was terribly shy . . .": Weizmann, *Trial and Error*, p. 150.

133   "When Dr. Weizmann was talking of Palestine . . .": Ibid., p. 152.

133-37   A copy of Herbert Samuel's draft memorandum of January 1915 on Pal-
         estine is in the Grey Papers, PRO: FO 800/100, pp. 482-506.
138   "I have just received . . .": Asquith, *Memories*, 2:70-71.

10. ISRAEL IN EGYPT

The principal sources used on the Palestine Jewish community during the First
World War are: Frank E. Manuel, *The Realities of American-Palestine Relations*
(Washington, D.C., 1949); Arthur Ruppin, *Memoirs, Diaries, Letters* (New York, 1971);
Rahel Yanait Ben-Zvi, *Coming Home* (New York, 1969); and—above all—contemporary
newspaper accounts, especially in the *Jewish Chronicle*.

Page
139   "The months of August and September . . .": *Jewish Chronicle*, October 2,
         1914.
139-40   For Morgenthau and the *North Carolina* relief mission, see ibid., October
         9, 1914.
140   "On the morning of the 24th September . . .": Ibid., October 23, 1914.
140-41   For the round-up in Jaffa of December 15, 1914, see ibid., January 1, 1915;
         Manuel, *Realities*, pp. 122-31; Ruppin, *Memoirs*, pp. 153-54.
141   "At the harbor that evening . . .": Ruppin, *Memoirs*, p. 153.
141   "Although these expulsions . . .": Ibid., pp. 153-54.
141   "nearly 4,000 . . .": Ibid., p. 154.
141-42   On Beha ad-Din, see ibid., p. 155; Manuel, *Realities*, p. 127.
142   "The Government . . .": Manuel, *Realities*, p. 129.
142   On Captain Decker and the *Tennessee*, see ibid., p. 127.
142-43   "Further statements . . .": *Jewish Chronicle*, February 5, 1915.

The standard biography of Jabotinsky is the two-volume work by Joseph Schecht-
man, *The Vladimir Jabotinsky Story*; the period covered by the present work is entirely within Volume 1, *Rebel and Statesman: The Early Years* (New York, 1956).
Jabotinsky wrote a brief *Autobiography* (Jerusalem, 1947) in Hebrew; but his book
The Story of the Jewish Legion (New York, 1945) is entirely autobiographical in approach and is the major source here for this aspect of the story.

Page
143   "A few days ago . . .": Jabotinsky, *Jewish Legion*, p. 29. Jabotinsky says
         "early in December," but his recollection is obviously incorrect.
144   "Jabotinsky, the passionate Zionist . . .": Weizmann, *Trial and Error*, p. 63.
144   "The Young Turks then ruled . . .": Jabotinsky, *Jewish Legion*, p. 30.
144   "I read in a poster . . .": Ibid., p. 29.
144-45   "had been a mere observer . . .": Ibid., p. 30.
145   "The appeal to a Holy War . . .": Ibid., p. 33.
145   "lively Zionist atmosphere": Ibid.
145   Hotel Metropole: *Jewish Chronicle*, January 22, 1915.
145   "stuffy unattractive building . . .": Ronald Storrs, *The Memoirs of Sir
         Ronald Storrs* (New York, 1937), p. 23.
145   For Emile Cattaui and other shelter operations, see *Jewish Chronicle*, Feb-
         ruary 5, 1915.
145-46   "A special department was created . . .": Jabotinsky, *Jewish Legion*, p. 33.
146   "two kitchens . . .": Ibid., pp. 33-34.
146   "organized a football club . . .": Ibid., p. 34.

146   a letter to a Zionist colleague in Russia: This letter, to Israel Rosov, is in
       Jabotinsky Institute, Tel Aviv; listed and summarized in *Ig'rot Ze'ev Jab-
       otinsky*, 2 vols. (Tel Aviv, 1972), 1:37, letter 115.
146   On Nordau's doubts, see Jabotinsky, *Jewish Legion*, p. 31.

The principal sources on the January–February 1915 attack on the Suez Canal
are: Djemal Pasha, *Memories of a Turkish Statesman, 1913–1919* (London, n.d.); Archibald P. Wavell, *The Palestine Campaigns* (London, 1931; New York, 1972); and Cyril
Falls and General Sir G. MacMunn, *Military Operations, Egypt and Palestine*, 2 vols.
(London, 1928). The last work, which is part of the British official history of the war, is
based entirely upon military reports and interviews with the participants. Wavell's
book, a more concise account, draws upon these sources and Falls and MacMunn, and
also upon his own experiences in that theater of the war. These two works, along with
contemporary newspaper accounts and other sources that will be cited in their place,
are the principal sources for the accounts of the Egypt and Palestine campaigns in
general in the present book.

Page
147   "an armed camp . . .": *Jewish Chronicle*, November 20, 1914.
147   "Up to December 18 . . .": *The Times* (London), January 1, 1915.
147   "On December 19 . . . the Holy Banner . . .": Ibid.
147   "the luckless population of Syria": Ibid., January 14, 1915.
147   "The Arab and Syrian troops . . .": Ibid.
148   "desert ration": Djemal, *Memories*, p. 149.
148   "I can have no greater duty . . .": Ibid., p. 153.
148   "the majority of the Arabs . . .": Ibid.
148   "Unfortunately . . . there was some slight delay . . .": Ibid., p. 155.
149   "Morning broke as the pontoons . . .": Ibid.
149   "Your Excellency . . .": Ibid., p. 157.
149   "Is the garrison of Egypt . . .": Wavell, *Palestine Campaigns*, p. 32.
149   "The position was an unpleasant one . . .": Jabotinsky, *Jewish Legion*, p. 36.
150   "And at that interview, I . . .": Ibid.
150   "Hush . . . your young fellows": Ibid., p. 37.

There is no biography of Joseph Trumpeldor, though a brief, somewhat hagio-
graphic account of his life has been published under official auspices: Pesah Lipovet-
zky, *Joseph Trumpeldor, Life and Works* (Jerusalem, 1953). An identical collection, one
in Hebrew and one in German, of Trumpeldor's letters and diaries (all originally in
Russian) was published in the 1920s, each with its own different biographical introduction. I used the German one for this book: Joseph Trumpeldor, *Tagebücher und Briefe*
(Berlin, 1925).

Page
151   "with his one arm . . .": Joseph Baratz, *A Village by the Jordan: The Story
       of Degania* (Tel Aviv, 1956), p. 76.
151   "We ran after them . . .": Ibid., pp. 76–77.
151   "I found him at home . . .": Jabotinsky, *Jewish Legion*, pp. 38–39.
152   "the English would not . . .": Ibid., p. 40.
152   "to form a Jewish Legion . . .": Ibid.
152   "How many men . . .": Ibid., p. 41.
152   For conversation with General Maxwell, see ibid.
153   "a most unflattering sound . . .": Ibid., p. 42.
153   For the debate in the hotel room, see ibid.
153   "Maxwell's offer accepted": Ibid., p. 43.

11. ENGLAND PREPARES TO SMASH THE TURKS

On the Dardanelles campaign and Gallipoli, the chief sources used in this book are: Winston S. Churchill, *The World Crisis* (New York, 1931); Martin Gilbert, *Winston S. Churchill*, vol. 3, *The New Challenge of War, 1914-1916* (Boston, 1971); Brigadier General C.F. Aspinall-Oglander, *Military Operations, Gallipoli*, 2 vols. (London, 1929)—part of the official history of the war; Alan Moorehead, *Gallipoli* (New York, 1956); and contemporary newspaper accounts. On the general background and history of the First World War, a most convenient and lucid work is that of Cyril Falls, *The Great War, 1914-1918* (London, 1959; New York, 1961). For the naval part of the Dardanelles campaign, the volumes in the official history to consult are: Sir Julian S. Corbett, *History of the Great War, Naval Operations*, 2 vols. (London, 1920).

Page

155-56   On the War Council of March 3, 1915, see PRO: CAB 22/1.

156-57   "The course of recent events . . .": The French original of Sazonov's message is reprinted in E.L. Woodward and R. Butler, eds., *Documents on British Foreign Policy, 1919-1939* (London, 1952), series 1, vol. 4, pp. 635-36. This translated version is in Hurewitz, *Middle East and North Africa* 2:17.

157   "Admiral Carden is asking . . .": Gilbert, *Churchill* 3:336.

157   "that both we and France . . .": PRO: CAB 22/1.

157   "the Russians were so keen . . .": Ibid.

157   "as soon as . . . in this country": Ibid.

157-58   "Subject to the war being carried on . . .": Hurewitz, *Middle East and North Africa*, 2:17-18; from Woodward and Butler, *Documents*, ser. 1, vol. 4, p. 636.

158   Grey attached a memorandum: Hurewitz, *Middle East and North Africa*, 2:18-19; from Woodward and Butler, *Documents*, ser. 1, vol. 4, pp. 636-38.

158   For Churchill's exchange with the Grand Duke Nicholas, see Gilbert, *Churchill*, 3:345.

159   War Council of March 10: PRO: CAB 22/1.

159   "it is a point of no ordinary importance . . .": *Jewish Chronicle*, February 12, 1915.

160   "La France du Levant . . . going to win their reward": Quoted by Bertie in a dispatch to the FO, December 30, 1914. FO 371/2480, p. 78. My translation from the French.

160   "Very French": Lancelot Oliphant's minute on Bertie's dispatch. Ibid.

160   "interfered with the population . . .": Weizmann was not to put it precisely this way until April 1917 (*CW Letters*, 7:376), but the opinion was already held at this time among British Zionists.

160   "has begun in deadly earnest . . .": *Jewish Chronicle*, March 12, 1915.

160-61   "I should be grateful to Your Excellency . . .": Hurewitz, *Middle East and North Africa*, 2:19; translated from the French text in J. Polonsky, trans., *Documents diplomatiques secrets russes 1914-1917 d'après les archives du ministère des affaires étrangères a Petrograd* (Paris, 1928), p. 288.

161   "The French ambassador . . .": Hurewitz, *Middle East and North Africa*, 2:19; from Polonsky, *Documents*, p. 290.

161   "Paléologue explains . . .": Ibid.

162   "Edmond de Rothschild sent . . .": Lady Algernon Gordon Lennox, ed., *The Diary of Lord Bertie of Thame*, 2 vols. (London, 1924), 1:105.

162 "It contemplates the formation . . .": Ibid.

162 Samuel-Grey conversation of February 5, 1915, is from a note by Samuel reproduced in his autobiography, *Grooves of Change* (Indianapolis, 1945), p. 176.

163 "A long line of statesmen . . .": *Manchester Guardian*, December 18, 1914.

163 "We both think that in the real interests . . .": Earl of Oxford and Asquith, *Memories and Reflections*, 2 vols. (Boston, 1928), 2:82.

163-64 "When I asked him what his solution was . . . a most formidable attack on Egypt": Samuel, *Grooves*, p. 176.

164 "I had a talk with L.G. . . .": Ibid., p. 175.

164 "it seems to me that something . . .": Stephen Graham, "Russia and the Jews," *English Review*, February 1915.

164 "I have read your Memorandum . . .": Samuel, *Grooves*, p. 176.

165 Samuel . . . was a guest at Tring: Note by Samuel, February 14, 1915. Samuel Papers.

165 ". . .the aspirations of most Nationalist Jews . . .": Claude G. Montefiore, *Outlines of Liberal Judaism, for the Use of Parents and Teachers* (London, 1912), p. 283.

165 "one with the nations . . .": Ibid., p. 292.

165 "on the ground that the Jews . . .": Note by Samuel, February 14, 1915. Samuel Papers.

165-66 "would be of use as bringing relief . . .": Ibid.

166 "H.S. told me about his visit . . .": *CW Letters*, 7:148-50.

166-68 "As far as Russia is concerned . . .": Ibid., pp. 153-55.

168 "I very much agree with your memorandum . . .": Samuel, *Grooves*, p. 176.

168 "I have had several conversations . . .": Quoted in Stein, *Balfour Declaration*, p. 132.

168-69 "I am very glad to state . . .": *CW Letters*, 7:181.

169 Samuel's conversations of January-February 1915 are from Samuel, *Grooves*, p. 177.

169 Samuel's final draft memorandum on Palestine is reproduced in full in John Bowle, *Viscount Samuel, a Biography* (London, 1957), pp. 172-77.

169-70 "H. Samuel had written . . .": These remarks of Asquith's have long been known in the abridged form in which they appear in *Memories*, 2:78. Their original appearance, in full, was as part of a letter Asquith wrote to Venetia Stanley on March 13, 1915. The full version given here is as quoted in Gilbert, *Churchill*, 3:342-44. *H. H. Asquith: Letters to Venetia Stanley*, edited by Michael and Eleanor Brock (Oxford, 1983), is a valuable recent collection.

12. ZION AT GALLIPOLI

In addition to the sources already cited under Chapter 11, the main source for this chapter is the enthusiastic account—published in 1916 in order to promote the idea of a Jewish legion—of his experiences with the Zion Mule Corps written by Lieutenant Colonel John Henry Patterson, *With the Zionists in Gallipoli* (New York, 1916).

Page

171 "It [is] not a question of 'crushing' Germany . . .": Scott Diaries, March 15, 1915.

172   "From the days of my youth . . .": Patterson, *With the Zionists*, p. 46.

173   "It certainly was curious . . .": Ibid., p. 47.

173   "I divided the Corps . . .": Ibid., p. 52.

173-74   "It was a most imposing ceremony . . . their modern leader": Ibid., pp. 49-50.

174   "Never since the days of Judas Maccabaeus . . .": Ibid., p. 53.

174   "was most complimentary on the workmanlike appearance . . .": Ibid., p. 56.

174-75   "We had a last big parade . . .": Ibid., p. 60.

177   "you have only to dig, dig, dig. . . .": Alan Moorehead, *Gallipoli* (New York, 1956), p. 155.

177-78   "The general attack on the Dardanelles . . .": *The Times* (London), April 27, 1915.

178   "As we plowed along . . . aid in its defense": Patterson, *With the Zionists*, p. 90.

178   "Soon battleships, cruisers and destroyers . . .": Ibid., p. 91.

178   "As we approached near . . .": Ibid., pp. 92-93.

178-79   "were slowly moving . . . by the landing parties": Ibid., p. 93.

179   "We watched the fight from our position . . .": Ibid., pp. 93-94.

179   "the guns from Asia . . . passed merrily along": Ibid., p. 105.

179-80   "On we squelched through the mud . . . linked up across the Peninsula": Ibid., p. 113.

180   "Gongs could plainly be heard . . .": Ibid., p. 114.

180   "We have a lot to do . . .": Trumpeldor to his fiancée, May 6, 1915; quoted in Joseph Trumpeldor, *Tagebücher und Briefe* (Berlin, 1925), pp. 109-10. My translation from the German.

180   "Sometimes while away . . . embrace him most tenderly": Patterson, *With the Zionists*, pp. 203-4.

180-81   "never once saw him give way . . .": Ibid., p. 204.

181   Hamilton's evaluation of the Zion Mule Corps is reproduced, among other places, in Vladimir Jabotinsky, *The Story of the Jewish Legion* (New York, 1945), p. 44.

181   Private M. Grushkovsky: *Jewish Chronicle*, June 4, 1915.

181   "The formation in Alexandria . . .": Ibid., April 30, 1915.

181   "one thing I admit . . .": Jabotinsky, *Jewish Legion*, p. 43.

13. DR. WEIZMANN IS ENLISTED IN THE WAR EFFORT

A basic source for Weizmann's wartime scientific work, and for the whole problem of solvents in munitions manufacture at the time, is in the official *History of the Ministry of Munitions*, 8 vols. (London, 1918-22), vol. 7, pt. 4, chapt. 4, sect. 1: "Acetone and the By-Products of Wood Distillation," pp. 65-73.

Page

182   "The news . . . that the fierce battle . . .": *The Times* (London), April 27, 1915.

183   "one campaign that brought him renown . . .": David Lloyd George, *War Memoirs of David Lloyd George*, 6 vols. (Boston 1933-1937), 1:170-71.

183   "Oh, it is terrible . . . shells that were wasted!": Ibid., p. 171.

183   "really distressed and preoccupied . . .": Earl of Oxford and Asquith, *Memories and Reflections*, 2 vols. (Boston, 1928), 2:79.

183-84   "There is no evidence in my possession . . .": Lloyd George, *War Memoirs*, 1:172.

184   "it is quite on the cards . . .": Asquith, *Memories*, 2:79.

184   "We are fighting Germany, Austria and Drink . . .": Quoted in Wilson, *Political Diaries of C.P. Scott*, p. 121.

185   "NEED FOR SHELLS . . .": *The Times* (London), May 14, 1915.

186   "THE SHELLS SCANDAL . . .": Quoted in Philip Magnus, *Kitchener, Portrait of an Imperialist* (New York, 1959), p. 336.

186   "extremely delicate": Lloyd George, *War Memoirs*, 2:47.

187-88   For Rintoul's visit to Weizmann, see *CW Letters*, 7:145; Weizmann, *Trial and Error*, pp. 171-72.

188   "The people from Nobel's spent . . .": *CW Letters*, 7:162.

188   down payment of £3,000: Ibid., p. 189.

188   "excellent": Weizmann, *Trial and Error*, p. 172.

188   "my solicitor's advice is *not* to budge": *CW Letters*, 7:189.

188   patent . . . granted on March 29: Ibid., p. 183, n. 146/1.

189   For Nathan's contacts and interview with Weizmann, see ibid., pp. 268, 193. On pp. 268-71 of *CW Letters*, vol. 7, there is a letter from Weizmann to Nathan of February 27, 1916, largely summarizing their history together to that point. On pp. 193-94 is Weizmann's initial report to Nathan of April 25, 1915.

189   "I am handing over the whole process . . .": *CW Letters*, 7:195.

190   "One curious detail . . .": Ibid., p. 198.

191   "I had an opportunity of talking . . .": Ibid., p. 181.

191-92   "As far as letters from B. and G. . . .": Ibid., p. 171.

192   "I read your excellent paper . . .": Quoted in John Bowle, *Viscount Samuel, a Biography* (London, 1957), p. 178.

There is a bit of a puzzle regarding one figure at the Admiralty—there until the middle of May 1915—who had shown considerable interest in Zionism before and would do so again: Winston Churchill himself, the first lord until Balfour replaced him in the cabinet upheaval. If he was giving any thought at this time to the future of Palestine, the record does not show it. Preoccupied day and night with the Dardanelles campaign, he seems to have thought of virtually nothing else; and, as we have seen, he even insisted at War Council meetings that the time was not ripe for discussing postwar political arrangements.

Yet he could not have been oblivious to the fact that, toward the end of April—some three weeks before his downfall—the Admiralty was taking on for scientific work one of England's leading Zionists, with whom he had even had personal dealings regarding Jewish matters during the Manchester elections nine years before. As a matter of fact, Weizmann claims in *Trial and Error* that he was taken to see Churchill personally when hired for the Admiralty job. "Mr. Churchill . . . ," he writes, "was brisk, fascinating, charming and energetic. Almost his first words were: 'Well, Dr. Weizmann, we need thirty thousand tons of acetone. Can you make it?' " Weizmann says that Churchill then went on to give him "carte blanche" for his experiments (p. 173).

Is this story reliable, or is it another of the tricks of memory that abound in the pages of *Trial and Error*? Weizmann dates the event a year later than it could possibly have happened. There is nothing about it in Weizmann's letters as we now have them—but there is a three-week hiatus in these between May 5 and May 26, 1915, which is precisely when the meeting with Churchill would have occurred, if it did occur. But the strangest aspect of the story as Weizmann tells it is that it shows no sign of acknowledgment between the two men that they had already met.

Page

192-93   "I told him of my problem . . .": Lloyd George, *War Memoirs*, 2:48.

194   "I am going up to London again today . . .": Weizmann to Roszika (Mrs. Charles) Rothschild, June 6, 1915. *CW Letters*, 7:204.

194   "If you are seeing Dr. Weizmann tomorrow . . .": Stein, *Balfour Declaration*, p. 141, n. 11.

194   "He was rather keen . . .": *CW Letters*, 7:205-6.

194   "only for a very few minutes . . . mentioned under point 1)": Ibid., p. 206.

195   Weizmann's letter to Lloyd George, June 9, 1915, is in ibid., pp. 206-7.

196   For Lloyd George's lunch with C.P. Scott, see Scott Diaries, June 16, 1915.

14. THE BEGINNINGS OF A MIDDLE EASTERN POLICY

Page

197   "Dardanelles . . . drive us into the sea": Scott Diaries, June 16, 1915.

On Italian diplomacy during the war, see René Albrecht-Carrié, *Italy at the Paris Peace Conference* (New York, 1938; Hamden, Conn., 1966).

Page

198   the secret London Agreement of April 26: Great Britain, *Parliamentary Papers*, 1920, misc. no. 7, cmd. 671. Reproduced in Hurewitz, *Middle East*, 2:22-24.

198   "We never stipulated . . .": G.M. Trevelyan, *Grey of Fallodon* (London 1937, 1948), p. 302.

199   March 19 War Council meeting: PRO: CAB 22/1.

199-200   "M. Cambon informed me today . . .": Grey to Bertie, March 23, 1915. FO 371/2486, p. 2.

200-208   For the de Bunsen Committee and its report, see PRO: "British Desiderata in Turkey and Asia: Report, Proceedings and Appendices of a Committee Appointed by the Prime Minister, 1915." CAB 27/1. The Report (without the Proceedings or Appendices) is reproduced in Hurewitz, *Middle East*, 2:26-46.

15. THE ARABIAN SWEEPSTAKES

A helpful handbook on the Arab Middle East, past and present, is *The Middle East: A Political and Economic Survey*; I have used the fourth edition, edited by Peter Mansfield (Oxford, 1973), but there are subsequent ones. An important work also is Elizabeth Monroe, *Britain's Moment in the Middle East, 1914-71* (Baltimore, 1981; new and rev. ed.); and most useful is Howard M. Sachar, *The Emergence of the Middle East, 1914-1924* (New York, 1969). For the history of what is now Saudi Arabia, one should consult: H. St. John Philby, *Arabian Jubilee* (New York, 1953), *Sa'udi Arabia* (London, 1955; Beirut, 1968), and other works by this man who became part of the history he wrote about. Two fine recent works are David Holden and Richard Johns, *The House of Saud* (New York, 1982), and Robert Lacey, *Kingdom* (New York, 1982). As for the Sherif Hussein, the Hejaz, and the Arab revolt, the standard work is George Antonius, *The Arab Awakening* (New York, 1946; Capricorn ed., 1965—my citations are from this). Much of Antonius's book is based upon his personal interviews with Hussein and his family, so that the book is somewhere between history and memoir. It must be read with caution, since history is reasonably scientific but memoir is not; and the line between them in this book is not always clear. But as memoirs above all, it is one of the major sources for its subject. Another basic work is David G. Hogarth, *Hejaz Before World War I* (Cairo, 1916, 1917; Cambridge, England, 1978)–this is a reprint of the official handbook on the subject prepared by the Arab Bureau in 1916.

Page

209   "You should inform Wingate . . .": Grey to McMahon, April 14, 1915. FO 371/2486, p. 7.

210   "Term 'independent sovereign State' . . .": McMahon to Grey, May 14, 1915. Ibid., p. 9.

210-11   For the "veiled protectorates," see, for example, Hurewitz, *Middle East and North Africa*, 1:432, 464-66, 475-77.

211-12   "the big race: the Arabian Stakes": Philby, *Arabian Jubilee*, p. 9.

212   "The theory . . . is that the English traveler . . .": Alexander Kinglake, *Eothen* (1844; Everyman ed., London, 1908; 1954), p. 147.

212-13   "to ascertain how much . . .": Sir Richard F. Burton, *Personal Narrative of a Pilgrimage to al-Madinah and Meccah*, 2 vols. (1855; New York, 1964), 1:141.

213   "to the solitary wayfarer . . .": Ibid., p. 149.

213   As for me who write . . .": Charles M. Doughty, *Travels in Arabia Deserta*, 2 vols. (New York, 1937), 1:95.

213   "So here we are . . .": Lady Bell, *The Letters of Gertrude Bell*, 2 vols. (London, 1927), 1:334-35.

213   "In practice the Englishman . . .": T.E. Lawrence's introduction to Doughty, *Arabia Deserta*, pp. 20-21.

213   "the test of nomadism . . .": Ibid., p. 21.

213   " 'Arabs' we call them . . .": Bell, *Letters*, 1:68.

213   "all in all, the worst type of humanity . . .": Charles Francis Tyrwhitt Drake, "The Fellahin," in Sir Charles Wilson et al., eds., *Survey of Western Palestine: Special Papers on Topography, Archaeology, Manners and Customs*, Palestine Exploration Fund (London, 1881), p. 311.

214   "the Syrian merchant is separated . . .": Gertrude Bell, *Syria: The Desert and the Sown* (London, 1907; 1928) p. 140.

214   "One point struck me at once . . .": Burton, *Personal Narrative*, 2:190.

214   "The Semites are like to a man . . .": Doughty, *Arabia Deserta*, 1:95.

214   "Like to this . . . nomad custom should hold": Ibid., p. 269.

215   For Gertrude Bell's report of September 5, 1914, see FO 371/2141.

216-17   On Shakespear, see H.V.F. Winstone, *Captain Shakespear* (London, 1976).

217   "I am in camp here with Bin Saud . . .": H.V.F. Winstone, *Gertrude Bell* (New York, 1978), pp. 151-52.

217-18   "Idrisi's approaching us . . .": Aden Resident (D.G.L. Shaw) to FO, March 15, 1915. FO 371/2478, p. 161.

218   For treaty with Idrisi (draft and correction), see ibid., pp. 275-77. Reproduced in Hurewitz, *Middle East and North Africa*, 2:24-26.

218   "Arabia for the Arabs . . .": Lord Hardinge, Viceroy of India, to IO (India Office). FO 371/2478, p. 176.

219   "Mahdi of Asir" . . . " . . .the winning horse": The reference to the "Mahdi of

Asir" is by G.S. Symes in a letter to Clayton in Cairo, June 15, 1915. Kitchener's remark is on the FO folder containing this letter and accompanying ones. FO 371/2479, pp. 30-36.

219-22   The sources on Abdullah's visits to Cairo in early 1914 are Antonius, *Arab Awakening*, pp. 126-29; Ronald Storrs, *The Memoirs of Sir Ronald Storrs* (New York, 1937), p. 135; and "Material on the Sherif of Mecca," report of December 13, 1914, from Sir Milne Cheetham in Cairo containing summaries of all dealings with the Sherif and his family to that date. FO 371/1973.

220   "who must anyhow be the eyes . . .": Storrs, *Memoirs*, p. 65.

220   "I visited him in the Abdin Palace . . .": Ibid., p. 135.

221   "Short and thick built . . .": Hogarth, *Hejaz*, p. 55.

221   "I think it's rather a triumph . . .": Bell, *Letters*, 1:70.

221   "Traveling by a series . . .": Storrs, *Memoirs*, p. 135.

221-22   "the extension of the railway . . . should the occasion arise": Report by Storrs on conversation with Abdullah, written on April 19, 1914; in "Material on the Sherif of Mecca." FO 371/1973.

223   "Tell Storrs to send . . .": Kitchener to Cheetham, September 24, 1914. FO 371/2139.

223-24   The narrative of Messenger *X* is reproduced verbatim in Storrs, *Memoirs*, pp. 164-66.

224   "Messenger has returned from Mecca . . .": Cheetham to FO, October 31, 1914. FO 371/2139.

225   ". . . Lord Kitchener's salaam . . .": Kitchener to Cairo, October 31, 1915. Ibid. Also reproduced in Storrs, *Memoirs*, p. 166, with slight variations from original.

225-28   The Storrs-Ruhi message to Abdullah, on the basis of Kitchener's October 31 letter is in "Materials on the Sherif of Mecca." FO 371/1973. Abdullah's reply to the Storrs-Ruhi message and his oral communication to the messenger are from the same source.

16. PROMISING LANDS

In addition to George Antonius, *The Arab Awakening* (New York, 1946; Capricorn ed., 1965), the principal books relating to this chapter are: Sylvia G. Haim, ed., *Arab Nationalism: An Anthology* (Berkeley, Calif., 1962, 1976); Elie Kedourie, *England and the Middle East* (London, 1956), *The Chatham House Version and Other Middle Eastern Studies* (New York, 1970), and *In the Anglo-Arab Labyrinth: The McMahon-Hussein Correspondence and Its Interpretations, 1914-1939* (Cambridge, England, 1976); and Zeine N. Zeine, *The Emergence of Arab Nationalism* (Beirut, 1958; 1966). Isaiah Friedman, *The Question of Palestine*, has a chapter thoroughly examining the McMahon-Hussein correspondence on the basis of the FO archives (pp. 65-96), and he comes to conclusions different from my own. This subject will ever give rise to as much disagreeement among historians as it did among its contemporary political interpreters.

Page

230   "are the best able to bear hardships . . .": Abd al-Rahman al-Kawakibi, "The Excellences of the Arabs," in Haim, *Arab Nationalism*, pp. 78-80.

230-31   "in a whisper . . .": Antonius, *Arab Awakening*, pp. 149-50.

231   Damascus Protocol: Ibid., pp. 157-58.

231-32   "A North African or near eastern vice-royalty . . .": Quoted by Kedourie in "Cairo and Khartoum on the Arab Question, 1915-1918," *Chatham House Version*, p. 17. This and other materials quoted by Kedourie in this study are in the Wingate Papers, School of Oriental Studies, University of Durham, England.

232   "is deputed by a central committee at Baghdad . . .": Cheetham to Grey, August 24, 1914. FO 371/2140.

234   "nearly all of us rallied": T.E. Lawrence, *Seven Pillars of Wisdom* (New York, 1938, de luxe ed.), p. 57.

234   On Sir Reginald Wingate, see Sir Ronald Wingate, *Wingate of the Sudan* (London, 1955).

234-35   "I—who so warmly supported the Turk . . .": Quoted in Kedourie, *Chatham House Version*, p. 15.

235   "the most suitable man . . . the most competent Power": Wingate to FO on al-Mirghani, May 15, 1915. FO 371/2486, p. 26.

235   "I am well aware . . .": Ibid., pp. 24-25.

236   "Mr. Chamberlain is inclined to think . . .": Ibid., pp. 39-41.

236   "The Government of His Majesty . . .": Ibid., p. 45. Hardinge's reaction is on p. 33.

237-54   The English texts of the McMahon-Hussein letters as given here are Antonius's translations, located in *Arab Awakening*, pp. 413-27.

237-38   Hussein letter of July 14, 1915 is from ibid., pp. 413-15.

238   "He knows . . . he is demanding . . .": Kedourie, *Chatham House Version*, p. 21.

238   "His pretensions are in every way exaggerated . . .": FO 371/2486, pp. 101-2.

238   "Mr. Chamberlain agrees . . .": Ibid., pp. 104-5.

239   "if the Sherif . . .": Grey to McMahon, August 25, 1915. Ibid., p. 109.

239   "The moment in my opinion has not yet arrived . . .": Ibid., p. 129.

239   McMahon's reply to Hussein, August 30, 1915, is from Antonius, *Arab Awakening*, pp. 415-16.

239-40   Hussein to McMahon, September 9, 1915, is from ibid., pp. 416-18.

241   "In the present confusion . . . its Patron and Protector": Wingate to FO, August 25, 1915. FO 371/2486, pp. 183-86.

242-44   Clayton's report on al-Faruqi is in ibid., pp. 222-38. Other material on al-Faruqi is in FO 371/2491—this is Sir Ian Hamilton's letter of August 25, 1915, describing al-Faruqi's surrender on the Gallipoli front.

243   inspired by a passage in Chapter 58 of . . . Gibbon: E. Marmorstein, "A Note on Damascus, Homs, Hama and Aleppo," in *St. Antony's Papers No. XI* (Oxford, 1961). Marmorstein thought the suggestion may have come from Sir Mark Sykes, but Sykes had not yet arrived in Cairo. Kedourie, *Anglo-Arab Labyrinth*, pp. 84-88, very persuasively argues for Storrs.

244   "the Palestine portion of British territory . . .": FO 371/2476.

244   "under the nominal suzerainty . . .": Ibid.

244   "Palestine might be the subject . . .": FO 371/2486, p. 186.

245   "A buffer State is most desirable . . .": Storrs to FitzGerald, December 28, 1914, in Kitchener Papers. PRO: 30/57/45, item 0073.

245   "It was the most unfortunate date in my life . . .": Quoted in Kedourie, *Chatham House Version*, p. 14.

246   "A powerful organization . . .": FO 371/2486, p. 191.

246   "The Government . . . are most desirous . . .": Ibid., p. 196.

246-47   "From further conversation with Faroki . . . in Basrah Vilayet": Ibid., pp. 205-6.

247   "You can give cordial assurances . . .": Ibid., p. 208.

247-48   McMahon to Hussein, October 24, 1915, is in Antonius, *Arab Awakening*, pp. 419-20.

249   "The problem of Palestine . . .": India Office Records PRO: L/P and S/10/523, p. 4082/1915. Quoted in Kedourie, *Anglo-Arab Labyrinth*, p. 106.

249-51   On *wilayah* and *wilayat*, see, for example, ibid., p. 101.

251   "that it was not intended by me . . .": Letter in *The Times* (London), July 23, 1937.

251   "My reasons . . . for restricting myself . . .": McMahon to Shuckburgh, March 12, 1922. FO 371/7797.

251-53   McMahon's explanatory letter to FO, October 26, 1915, is in FO 371/2486, p. 274.

253   "Luckily . . . we have been very careful . . .": Quoted in Kedourie, *Chatham House Version*, p. 22.

253-54   "in a very curious letter . . .": Quoted in Kedourie, *Anglo-Arab Labyrinth*, pp. 120-21.

254   "I cannot decide here what weight . . .": FO 371/2486, pp. 313-14.

254   "your advocacy of speedy action . . .": Hussein to McMahon, November 5, 1915. Antonius, *Arab Awakening*, p. 422.

17. M. PICOT PRESENTS TERMS

In addition to works cited under Chapters 15 and 16, a valuable book in connection with this chapter is Jukka Nevakivi, *Britain, France and the Arab Middle East* (London, 1969).

Page

256   "délégué chargé d'établir . . .": FO 371/2486, pp. 348-49.

256   Committee to Discuss Arab Question and Syria: Ibid., p. 350.

257   incoherent and unreal: Elie Kedourie, *The Chatham House Version and Other Middle Eastern Studies* (New York, 1970), p. 20.

257   "It was decided . . .": FO 371/2486, p. 350.

257   "Make it clear . . .": Ibid., p. 350 and verso.

257-58   "Our case for doing . . .": Ibid., p. 439.

258   "that no French Government . . . to throw Mosul into the Arab pool . . .": Ibid., p. 438 and verso.

258   "observed that when he was lately in Cairo . . .": Ibid., p. 438 verso.

258   "the Turks and Germans being able . . .": "Note on the Arab Movement" by Major General G.E. Calwell and Lieutenant Colonel A.C. Parker. Ibid., p. 434.

258   "though an Arab union . . .": Ibid., p. 438 verso.

259   "held out *no* hopes whatever": "Note on the Arab Movement," Ibid., p. 434.

259   "It was further urged on him . . . by the French public": Ibid., p. 439.

259   "M. Picot is to submit a report . . .": Ibid., p. 438 verso.
259   "intimated his readiness . . . as we had suggested": Ibid., p. 439 verso.
259   "The Arabs will not now be gained . . .": Ibid.
259-61 "Note on the Arab Movement": Ibid., p. 434-36.
261   "Selection of Picot . . .": Ibid., p. 480.
261-62 "fully understood your statement . . .": McMahon to Hussein, December 13, 1915. George Antonius, *The Arab Awakening* (New York, 1946; Capricorn ed., 1965), p. 423.
262   "M. Picot is now in Paris . . .": FO 371/2486, p. 479 and verso.
262   "We can await the return . . .": Ibid., p. 479.

18. THE TRAVELS OF SIR MARK SYKES

There are two biographies of Sir Mark Sykes: Shane Leslie, *Mark Sykes: His Life and Letters* (London, 1923), the rather informal tribute of a friend, part memoir, part miscellaneous collection of quotes from Sykes's papers; and a recent scholarly biography by Roger Adelson, *Mark Sykes: Portrait of an Amateur* (London, 1975). In addition, there are two important shorter studies: a portrait of his father is sketched by Christopher Sykes in the essay on Zionism, "The Prosperity of the Servant," in his book, *Two Studies in Virtue* (London, 1953), pp. 107-249; and Nahum Sokolow provides an impassioned memoir, written immediately after Sykes's death, in the introduction to volume 2 of his *History of Zionism*.

Page
263   "I am waiting here . . .": FO 371/2486, p. 374.
265   Sykes to Churchill, August 24, 1914, and Churchill's reply are quoted in Adelson, *Mark Sykes: Portrait*, p. 175.
266   Sykes to Churchill, February 26, 1915, is quoted in Martin Gilbert, *Winston S. Churchill*, vol. 3, *The Challenge of War, 1914-1916* (Boston, 1971), p. 317.
267   "that it is important that Great Britain and France . . .": FO 371/2490.
267   "that the French will give up the coast . . .": Ibid.
267   "could then be under the government . . .": Ibid.
267-68 "He was one of those few . . .": Ronald Storrs, *The Memoirs of Sir Ronald Storrs* (New York, 1937), p. 211.
268   "He would take an aspect of the truth . . .": T.E. Lawrence, *Seven Pillars of Wisdom* (New York, 1938, de luxe ed.), p. 58.
268   For Sykes's impressions of India, see Leslie, *Mark Sykes: His Life*, p. 246.
268-69 "As the result of my tour . . .": FO 371/2491.
269   "I believe that the moment has now come . . .": Ibid.
269-70 Sykes's six-point formula for British policy in the Middle East is in FO 371/2486, p. 474.
270   "inoffensive to French susceptibility": Ibid., p. 374.
271-72 For Sykes's interview with al-Faruqi, see ibid., pp. 379-80.
272   "that Arabs, Christians and Moslems alike . . .": Sykes to FO from Petrograd, March 14, 1916. FO 371/2767.
273   "Jews will be governed by a special law": FO 371/2486, p. 238.
273   "With regard to France and Arabs . . . as certain winners": Ibid., pp. 383-84.
273-74 "on the Armenian scale . . . French prospects in Syria": Ibid., p. 431.

19. SYKES AND PICOT ARE BROUGHT TOGETHER

Page
276-78   Sykes's appearance before the War Committee, December 16, 1915, see PRO: CAB 42/6/9 and 10.
278-81   For Crewe-Bertie exchange of letters, December 17 and December 21, 1915, see PRO: CAB 42/6.
281   For Picot's new proposal to the Nicolson Committee, December 21, 1915, see FO 371/2486, p. 500.
281   "give up the coast to the South of Akka": FO 371/2490.
282   For Paris meeting of December 5, 1915, see Earl of Oxford and Asquith, *Memories and Reflections*, 2 vols. (Boston, 1928), 2:132-33.
282-83   "After the Committee . . .": Sykes's prefatory note to his memorandum with Picot of January 5, 1916. FO 371/2767.

20. TRIALS AND ERRORS OF A CHEMIST AT WAR

Page
284   "The Admiralty decided not to concern themselves . . .": Weizmann to Ahad Ha'am, August 27, 1915. *CW Letters*, 7:235.
286   "He was one of the subtlest brains . . .": David Lloyd George, *War Memoirs of David Lloyd George*, 6 vols. (Boston, 1933-37), 1:221.
286   "he agreed both with my criticism . . .": Weizmann to C.P. Scott, July 15, 1915. *CW Letters*, 7:224.
286-87   Weizmann received a telegram from Bern: Ibid., p. 225.
287   "I think that I'll leave for France . . .": Ibid., p. 236.
287   "I think . . . from the extremely candid way . . .": Scott Diaries, October 4, 1915.
287-88   "the question of chemical munitions . . .": Ibid., October 14, 1915.
288   "will be set into motion next week": Weizmann to Dorothy de Rothschild, *CW Letters*, 7:242.
288   "I saw the French Naval Attaché . . .": Ibid., p. 243.
288   "would enable me to get into touch . . .": Ibid., p. 244.
288   "My object in seeing him . . .": Scott Diaries, November 15, 1915.
289   "Jews and the War": *Manchester Guardian*, June 25, 1915.
290-91   "The Defense of Egypt": Ibid., November 22, 1915.
291   "Saw Lloyd George's Secretary . . .": Scott Diaries, November 26, 1915.
291-94   For the luncheon on November 26, 1915, see ibid.
294-97   For Lloyd George, Scott, Weizmann, and Nathan at the Ministry of Munitions, see ibid.
298-99   "Please don't be surprised . . . and appeal to you": Weizmann to Scott, December 1, 1915. *CW Letters*, 7:253-54.
299   "I am afraid . . .": Ibid., p. 254, n. 224/6.
299   "an amusing account of his encounter . . .": Scott Diaries, December 14, 1915.
299-300   "battled hard against it . . . acetone will be needed": *CW Letters*, 7:257.
300   "a distinguished *homme de lettres* . . . is in this country": Ibid., p. 256.

21. SYKES COMES TO TERMS WITH PICOT,
AND THE BROWN AREA EMERGES

Page

303-7   Sykes's and Picot's memorandum on Ottoman Asia of January 5, 1916, is in FO 371/2767.

308   "I must confess . . .": Ibid.

308   "We are only waiting for an opportunity . . .": Hussein to McMahon, January 1, 1916. Quoted in George Antonius, *The Arab Awakening* (New York, 1946; Capricorn ed., 1965), p. 426.

308-9   "We cannot aford to waste any time . . .": FO 371/2767.

309   Captain W.R. Hall's response to the January 5 memorandum is in ibid.

310   Admiral Fisher was . . . chairman of an "Inventions Board": *The Times* (London), July 5, 1915.

22. ZIONISM AT THE FOREIGN OFFICE, I:
A YEAR OF INDIFFERENCE

Page

311-12   Norman Bentwich's memorandum on Palestine, January 22, 1915, and FO comments upon it are in FO 371/2482.

312   For U.S.S. *Vulcan*, and "only render less harmonious . . .": See FO 371/2140, *passim* and p. 321.

313   For Grey's assurance to Leopold de Rothschild, see *Jewish Chronicle*, February 26, 1915.

The main source on the life and career of Lucien Wolf is the biographical introduction by Cecil Roth to the posthumous publication of Lucien Wolf, *Essays in Jewish History* (London, 1934).

Page

314   "for dealing with the Jewish questions . . . arising out of the War": From the "Report of the Delegation of the Jews of the British Empire" to the Paris Peace Conference, 1919; quoted in Stein, *Balfour Declaration*, p. 173.

315   "that it might be possible under certain conditions . . .": Weizmann's report on January 7, 1915, to Sokolow and Tschlenow. *CW Letters*, 7:115.

315-17   The Conjoint Foreign Committee-Zionist meeting of April 14, 1915, is in FO 371/2488.

318   "I am in agreement . . .": *Jewish Chronicle*, January 26, 1906.

318-19   There are two sources for the August 18, 1915, meeting between Weizmann and Lord Robert Cecil, since each participant wrote a description of the meeting immediately afterward. Cecil's is in the Grey papers at the PRO: FO 800/95. Weizmann's is in his letter to Harry Sacher, August 21, 1915 (*CW Letters*, 7:232) and his letter to Ahad Ha'am, August 23, 1915 (ibid., p. 234).

319-20   "There are signs . . . that the Germans . . .": *The Times* (London), November 23, 1914.

321   "Berlin and Vienna . . .": Ibid., November 28, 1914.

321   "syndicate of Jews . . .": FO 371/2480, pp. 4-10.

321   a book called *Die Juden der Türkei*: Quoted in Stein, *Balfour Declaration*, p. 212.

On the whole subject of the German Zionists and the Ottoman Empire in this period, see Isaiah Friedman, *Germany, Turkey and Zionism, 1897-1918* (Oxford, 1977).

Page
322   "Jewish activities designed to promote . . .": Quoted in Stein, *Balfour Declaration*, p. 213.

322   "This Committee maintains . . .": *Jewish Chronicle*, November 19, 1915.

On American Zionism, see Melvin I. Urofsky, *American Zionism from Herzl to the Holocaust* (New York, 1975); and Yonathan Shapiro, *Leadership of the American Zionist Organization, 1897-1930* (Urbana, Ill., 1971). On Brandeis, there is the classic biography by Alpheus T. Mason, *Brandeis: A Free Man's Life* (New York, 1946); this can be supplemented by Melvin I. Urofsky, *A Mind of One Piece: Brandeis and American Reform* (New York, 1971). Urofsky also is the coeditor, with David W. Levy, of the ongoing *Letters of Louis D. Brandeis*, (Albany, N.Y., 1971-   ); vols. 3 and 4 cover the period of the present book.

Page
324-25   Horace Kallen's memorandum on American-Jewish opinion regarding the war is in FO 371/2579.

325-30   Lucien Wolf's letter to the FO, December 16, 1915, with memorandum and enclosures is in ibid.

326   "The specific object . . .": Bigart to Wolf, December 10, 1915, ibid. My translation from the French.

326   "Rachmones Zionism": Weizmann to Zionist Executive, Berlin, May 5, 1912. *CW Letters*, 5:294.

331   "All the enemies of England . . .": Stephen Gwynn, ed., *Letters and Friendships of Sir Cecil Spring-Rice* (London, 1919), p. 309.

23. ZIONISM AT THE FOREIGN OFFICE, II: THE AWAKENING

Page
332   Report of the February 1916 conversation with Edgar Suarès is in FO 371/2671.

333-36   All FO remarks on the Suarès conversation are minuted on the folder containing the report of it; see Ibid.

334-35   For Colonel House at Lord Reading's dinner, February 14, 1916, see Charles Seymour, ed., *The Intimate Papers of Colonel House*, 4 vols. (New Haven, 1928), 2:179-81.

336-37   For Wolf-Oliphant conversation of March 2, 1916, see FO 371/2817, p. 5.

337   "Suggested Palestine Formula": Ibid., p. 12. The various FO comments that follow are on the folder containing this.

338   "On the chance of the F.O. doing anything . . .": Ibid., p. 18.

338   "There is, of course, a residuum . . .": *The Times* (London), December 15, 1915.

339   "the intangible nature . . . and so inform Mr. Wolf": FO 371/2817, p. 13 and verso.

339   "We should inform Mr. Wolf . . .": Ibid., p. 13 verso.

339-40   "The one ruling consideration . . . from them in return": Ibid., p. 16 and verso.

340-41   "not the general assurance . . . in the O'Beirne minute": Ibid., pp. 16 verso and 17.

341   "I am quite clear . . . of the whole community": Ibid., p. 17.

341   "May I add . . .": Ibid.

341   "I quite approve . . . Russia to realize this": Ibid.

341-42   Crewe's letter on Palestine to Bertie and Buchanan is in ibid., pp. 20-23.

343   "We are all 'Weizmannites' . . .": Vera Weizmann Diaries, March 20, 1916; quoted in Vera Weizmann, *The Impossible*, p. 57.

344   "we do not desire . . .": FO 371/2817, p. 23.

344   Buchanan's replies of March 14 and 15, 1916, are in ibid., pp. 34, 36.

24. SYKES DISCOVERS A NEW ENTHUSIASM

Page

345-47   Sykes's letter to Herbert Samuel, February 26, 1916, is in Samuel Papers.

347-49   Sykes's response of March 14, 1916, to Crewe note on Palestine and the FO minutes regarding it are in FO 371/2767.

349-51   Sykes's message of March 16, 1916, and O'Beirne's response to it are in ibid.

350   "As regards Palestine, Russian Government . . .": Ibid.

350-51   "My informal discussion . . .": Ibid.

351   "to those Members of the Cabinet . . .": Samuel Papers.

351   "British colonists are liars or Jews . . .": Shane Leslie, *Mark Sykes: His Life and Letters* (London, 1923), p. 70.

351   "O dear no! . . .": Ibid., p. 72.

352   "and as for the speech of women . . .": Ibid., p. 148.

352   "The Diaspora": This cartoon faces p. 85 in ibid.

352   "The Jews at Nisibin . . . adopt my suggestion": Mark Sykes, *Dar ul-Islam* (London, 1904), pp. 140-41.

353   The most significant defense by a Zionist of this aspect of Sykes's personality is offered by Nahum Sokolow in his biographical sketch of Sykes at the beginning of volume 2 of his *History of Zionism*.

353   "that mighty genius . . .": Leslie, *Mark Sykes: His Life*, p. 209.

353   "It is very wonderful . . .": Ibid., p. 152.

353   "Zionism was backed . . .": Sir Mark Sykes, *The Caliphs' Last Heritage: A Short History of the Turkish Empire* (London, 1915), p. 509.

353   "dis man is more vile . . .": Mark Sykes, *Through Five Turkish Provinces* (London, 1900), p. 5.

353-54   "I feel such an intense prejudice . . .": Ibid., p. 79.

355-56   Bertie's March 22 reply to Crewe's letter on Palestine is in FO 371/2817, p. 38.

355   "nettement pro-German . . .": Basch's report is enclosed with a letter from Lucien Wolf to the FO, March 9, 1916. Ibid., p. 26.

356-57   Oliphant's and O'Beirne's minutes on Bertie's reply are in ibid., p. 37 and verso.

25. SYKES AND GASTER: AN INTERLUDE

Page
358   "H. Samuel rang up . . .": Gaster Diaries, April 11, 1916.
359   settled in . . . the "Regent Palestine": Florian Sokolow, *Avi, Nahum Sokolow* (Tel Aviv, 1970), p. 139.
359-62   For Sokolow, Cumberbatch, and the two memoranda of April 13, 1916, see FO 371/2817, pp. 46-54.
362   "Sokolow, Waizman and Herbert Samuel . . . in Palestine": Gaster Diaries, April 16, 1916.
363   "I shall be seeing Samuel on Sunday . . .": *CW Letters*, 7:277.
363   "Sokolow for dinner . . .": Gaster Diaries, April 24, 1916.
364   "the opportunity of stating . . .": *The Times* (London), April 20, 1916.
364   "The suggestion about which . . .": Gaster Papers.
364-65   "I thank you very much . . .": Ibid.
365   "I write at the suggestion . . .": Ibid.
365   "If it would be equally convenient . . .": Ibid.
366   "Lt.-Col. Sir Mark Sykes . . . by *English* soldiers": Gaster Diaries, May 2, 1916.
366-67   For Gaster-Sokolow telephone conversation, see ibid.
367   "I write now . . . to ask you . . .": Gaster Papers.
367   "Told him about French maneuvers . . .": Gaster Diaries, May 3, 1916.
367   "Sir Mark and Picot . . . favorable to France": Ibid., May 10, 1916.
368   "disclosed the fact . . .": *The Times* (London), May 23, 1916.
368   "I was very grieved . . .": Gaster Papers.
368   "Never mind. Things may have taken . . .": Ibid.

26. DR. WEIZMANN'S TRIALS CONTINUE

Page
370   "On my arrival in London . . .": Vera Weizmann, *The Impossible*, p. 54.
370-71   "Besides . . . I don't think that the meeting . . .": *CW Letters*, 7:261.
371   "Sir Frederick is already installed . . .": Weizmann to Scott, December 30, 1915. Ibid., p. 258.
372   "you will be interested to know . . .": Ibid., p. 260.
372   "He told me that lots of people . . .": Ibid., p. 264.
372   "To London by night train . . .": Scott Diaries, January 24-29, 1916.
373   "took him to Munitions Office . . .": Ibid., February 22-23, 1916.
373   "entirely under the auspices . . .": Weizmann to Arthur Desborough, February 23, 1916. *CW Letters*, 7:267.
373-75   Weizmann to Sir Frederick Nathan, February 27, 1916, is in ibid., pp. 268-71.
375   "Another by-work . . .": Scott Diaries, February 29-March 3, 1916.
376   The lunch at the Astors' on March 15, 1916, is reported in Vera Weizmann Diaries and quoted in *The Impossible*, pp. 55-56.
376-77   The lunch at Dorothy de Rothschild's on March 16, 1916, is reported in Vera Weizmann Diaries and quoted in *The Impossible*, pp. 56-57.
377   "very discreet and careful . . .": Vera Weizmann, *The Impossible*, p. 61.

377-78   The dinner at the Astors' on March 25, 1916, is reported in Vera Weizmann Diaries and quoted in *The Impossible*, p. 62.

378-80   Weizmann's letter to Scott of April 5, 1916, is in *CW Letters*, 7:274-76.

380   "quite prepared to make an arrangement . . . raise this point there": Weizmann to Arthur Desborough, April 11, 1916. Ibid., p. 276.

380   "Mr. Scott was most confident . . .": Ibid., p. 277.

381   "he had seen Balfour twice . . .": Scott Diaries, May 8-11, 1916.

381   "that he would then and there . . . which indicated hesitation": Ibid., May 22-26, 1916.

381   "latest remarkable developments . . .": Ibid.

382   "It can easily be seen . . .": *CW Letters* 7:278.

382   "Prof. Fernbach and the Synthetic Products Co. . . .": Ibid., p. 280.

382-83   "He further informed me . . . with the Prime Minister": Weizmann to M. Atkinson Adam, June 4, 1916. Ibid., p. 282.

383-84   "as I have heard within the last few days . . .": Ibid., p. 283.

384   "I don't care whose process it is . . .": Scott Diaries, June 12-17, 1916.

27. THE REVOLT IN THE HEJAZ

Page

385   "news of a great Naval battle . . .": Vera Weizmann Diaries, June 2, 1916; quoted in *The Impossible*, pp. 62-63.

386   "could not have done better . . .": Vera Weizmann Diaries, July 13, 1916; quoted in *The Impossible*, p. 63.

386   "proclaimed the independence of the Arabs . . .": George Antonius, *The Arab Awakening* (New York, 1946; Capricorn ed., 1965), pp. 194-95.

386n   "This escape, at least . . .": David Lloyd George, *War Memoirs of David Lloyd George*, 6 vols. (Boston, 1933-37), 2:149.

387   "We had informed your Excellency . . .": Hussein to McMahon, February 18, 1916. Reproduced in Hurewitz, *Middle East and North Africa*, 2:54.

387   "It should be observed . . .": McMahon to Grey, April 19, 1916. FO 371/2768, pp. 159-60.

387   "We have gone far enough . . .": Ibid., p. 157 verso.

388   "which should receive copies of all telegrams . . .": Sykes to FO, October 9, 1915. FO 371/2491.

388   creation of the Arab bureau . . . "it should have agency in London . . .": FO 371/2670, pp. 543-46.

388-89   "I agree in general . . .": Ibid., p. 546.

For Lawrence at this time, one should consult, in addition to works already cited, his own *Seven Pillars of Wisdom* (New York, 1938, de luxe ed.)—there are various editions—and *Revolt in the Desert* (New York, 1927), an abridgement of the former. Among the numerous biographies, particularly useful for the details of the desert campaigns is B.H. Liddell Hart, *'T.E. Lawrence': In Arabia and After* (London, 1934).

Page

390   "nailed within that office at Cairo . . .": Lawrence to his mother, May 18, 1916. David Garnett, ed., *The Letters of T.E. Lawrence* (New York, 1939), p. 208.

391   "to watch the Turkish governor . . .": Antonius, *Arab Awakening*, p. 185.

391   "with the settled purpose . . .": Ibid., p. 188.
391   "moved heaven and earth . . .": Djemal Pasha, *Memories of a Turkish Statesman, 1913-1919* (London, n. d.), p. 217.
391   "pleaded with Jemal in person": Antonius, *Arab Awakening*, p. 189.
391   "it took the intercessions of his Constantinople friends . . .": T.E. Lawrence, *Seven Pillars*, p. 52.
392   "how shameless . . . God's curse be upon them!": Djemal, *Memories*, p. 220.
392   "Tab al-maut . . .": Antonius, *Arab Awakening*, pp. 190-91.
392   "gone beyond the bounds . . . battle cry of the Arab Revolt": Ibid., p. 190.
392   "your father is beginning to show . . .": Djemal *Memories*, p. 221.
392   "At that time I had no documentary evidence . . .": Ibid., p. 222.
392   "played his cards with consummate skill": Antonius, *Arab Awakening*, p. 193.
393   "to raise his father's crimson banner . . .": T.E. Lawrence, *Seven Pillars*, pp. 52-53.
393   "though the irony of the review . . . they are our guests": Ibid., p. 53.
393   "plead for the lives . . .": Ibid.
394   "but telegrams came from Medina . . .": Ibid.
394   "When he raised the Arab flag . . .": Ibid., pp. 53-54.
394   "Sharif's son Abdallah . . .": Ronald Storrs, *The Memoirs of Sir Ronald Storrs* (New York, 1937), p. 169.
394-97   For Storrs's journey to the Hejaz of May through July 1916, see ibid., pp. 169-77.
397   "Storrs returned yesterday . . .": McMahon to Grey, June 11, 1916. FO 371/2773.
398   "The Turks had fortified . . .": Philip Graves, ed., *Memoirs of King Abdullah of Transjordan* (London, 1950), p. 147.
399   "GREAT ARAB REVOLT . . . will now be removed": *The Times* (London), June 22, 1916.
400   "However it was . . .": T.E. Lawrence, *Seven Pillars*, p. 62.
400   "was permitted to carry on . . .": Ibid.
400   "The Arab Revolt became discredited . . .": Ibid.
401   "I'm going to have flavored gum . . .": M. Robert Lawrence, ed., *The Home Letters of T. E. Lawrence* (Oxford, 1954), p. 328. Letter of July 22, 1916.
401   "they were both younger . . .": Quoted in John E. Mack, *A Prince of Our Disorder: The Life of T.E. Lawrence* (Boston, 1976), p. 137.
401   "I had hardly returned to Alexandria . . .": Storrs, *Memoirs*, p. 185.
401   "third descent to the Hejaz . . .": Ibid., p. 186.
401   "took this strategic opportunity . . .": T.E. Lawrence, *Seven Pillars*, p. 63.
401   "I am going off tomorrow . . .": Quoted in Mack, *A Prince*, p. 147.
401   "the train from Cairo . . .": Storrs, *Memoirs*, p. 186.
402   "Abdullah, on a white mare . . . succeeded in revolutions": T.E. Lawrence, *Seven Pillars*, p. 67.
402   "Is this man God . . .": Storrs, *Memoirs*, p. 204.
402-3   "To Ali himself . . . with Ali for its head": T.E. Lawrence, *Seven Pillars*, pp. 76-77.
403   "My camel was a delight to me . . .": Ibid., p. 80.
403   "tired my unaccustomed muscles . . .": Ibid., p. 84.
403-4   "inner court . . . There was a quiver": Ibid., p. 91.

28. THE ADVENTURES OF AARON AARONSOHN

The principal source for this chapter is the diary of Aaron Aaronsohn. The original of this, written by Aaronsohn in French, is on deposit at the Aaronsohn Archive, Zichron Ya'akov, Israel. The complete diary was published in Hebrew translation: Aaron Aaronsohn, *Yoman, 1916-1919* (Tel Aviv, 1970); my quotations are my own translations from this edition. Only one, rather sketchy volume—apart from several fictional accounts—has been written in English on the Aaronsohn circle: Anita Engle, *The Nili Spies* (London, 1959). There is also a compilation in Hebrew, Eliezer Livneh, ed., *Nili* (Tel Aviv, 1961), but a fuller, more detailed and more critical book on this curious and exciting episode is very much needed.

Page

405   Aaronsohn's itinerary in the summer and fall of 1916 is given with exacting detail in the FO report on the "Inhabitant of Athlit," which is all of file no. 221220 in FO 371/2783.

407   "It was a marvelous tree nursery . . .": Rahel Yanait Ben-Zvi, *Coming Home* (New York, 1964), pp. 274-75.

407   "could read the fossils . . .": Ibid., p. 276.

408   Aaronsohn imported Palestine's first motor car: Arthur Ruppin, *Memoirs, Diaries, Letters* (New York, 1971), p. 92.

408   the only really good stretch of macadamized road: Norman Bentwich, *My 77 Years* (Philadelphia, 1961), p. 27.

408   "As a talker . . .": Brandeis to Norman Hapgood, June 16, 1913. Melvin I. Urofsky and David W. Levy, eds., *Letters of Louis D. Brandeis* (Albany, 1971-), 3:117.

408   "Airborne swarms of locusts . . .": Ruppin, *Memoirs*, p. 156.

408-9   "Not only was every green leaf devoured . . .": Alexander Aaronsohn, *With the Turks in Palestine* (Boston, 1916), pp. 51-52.

409-10   "We were disarmed . . .": Ibid., pp. 23-24.

410   "If a soldier of the Sultan . . .": Ibid., p. 28.

410   "military requisitions . . . more desolating": Ibid., p. 53.

411   "were very suspicious of Alex . . .": Quoted in Engle, *Nili Spies*, p. 55, from a personal communication from Sir Leonard Woolley.

412-13   "The English examining officers . . . passengers are astonished": Entry of October 22, 1916. Aaron Aaronsohn, *Yoman*, pp. 116-17.

413   "closer to Gaster's outlook . . .": Entry of October 27, 1916. Ibid., p. 119.

413-14   "The informant is a partisan . . .": "Inhabitant of Athlit" material. FO 371/2783.

414   "From the diplomatic point of view . . .": Entry of November 24, 1916. Aaron Aaronsohn, *Yoman*, p. 135.

414-15   Gribbon's thirty-four page typewritten report: FO 371/2783.

416   "that idiot named Sokolow": Entry of November 19, 1916. Aaron Aaronsohn, *Yoman*, p. 132.

416   "on Palestinian matters are not altogether the right ones": Weizmann to Magnes, April 14, 1914. *CW Letters*, 6:326.

416   "I told Sir M. . . .": Gaster Diaries, November 14, 1916.

29. A GATHERING OF FORCES

Page
417-19 Sacher finally published the volume of Zionist essays: Harry Sacher, ed., *Zionism and the Jewish Future* (London, 1916).

417-18 The Sokolow essay, "The New Jew: A Sketch," is in ibid., pp. 214-34.

418 The Gaster essay, "Judaism as a National Religion," is in ibid., pp. 87-98.

418 "the conception of a mere religious confraternity . . .": Ibid., pp. 92-93.

418-19 The Weizmann essay, "Zionism and the Jewish Problem," is in ibid., pp. 1-11.

418 "the position of the emancipated Jew . . .": Ibid., pp. 6-7.

418 "It is therefore no exaggeration to say . . .": Ibid., p. 3.

418-19 "When the aim of Zionism is accomplished . . .": Ibid., p. 8.

419 "Of all the constructive ideas . . . genuinely national state": *Manchester Guardian*, July 31, 1916.

419-20 review . . . by Lord Cromer: *Spectator*, August 12, 1916.

420-21 article called simply "Zionism": *Fortnightly Review*, November 1916, pp. 819-26.

421 "What evil genius . . . perilous article": *Jewish Chronicle*, November 3, 1916.

421 "the foulness of the blow . . .": Ibid., November 17, 1916.

421-22 Harry Sacher's letter is in the *Manchester Guardian*, November 6, 1916.

422-23 For the formation of the British Palestine Committee, see Herbert Sidebotham, *Great Britain and Palestine* (London, 1937), pp. 33-42.

424 "slackers" and "shirkers": See, for example, the *Jewish Chronicle* leader of August 4, 1916, "Mr. Samuel and Russian-Born Aliens."

424 "Mr. Samuel . . . towards the Jewish immigrant": *Manchester Guardian*, August 8, 1916.

425 "What a doctrine . . .": Reported in the *Manchester Guardian*, August 23, 1916.

425 "I saw S[amuel] . . .": *CW Letters*, 7:285-86.

425-26 "I have been approached . . . presented themselves for enlistment": Reported in the *Manchester Guardian*, August 23, 1916.

426 "odious" and "Our Committee . . .": *CW Letters*, 7:288.

426 Weizmann's letter to the local military authorities of August 31, 1916, is in ibid., pp. 289-90.

The material in the following section comes not only from Vladimir Jabotinsky, *The Story of the Jewish Legion* (New York, 1945), but also from FO 371/2835, in which file no. 18095 is largely devoted to the campaign of Jabotinsky and his friends for a Jewish legion.

Page
427 "my friend Mr. Jabotinsky": Scott to Cecil, December 11, 1915. FO 371/2835/18095.

428 "a Jewish legion . . .": Jabotinsky to C.F.G. Masterman, January 26, 1916. Ibid.

428 "Healthy, replete . . .": Jabotinsky, *Jewish Legion*, p. 60.

428 "vast difference between your boys and . . .": Ibid., pp. 66-67. The Liberal MP was Joseph King.

429-31 For the Weizmann-Wolf meeting on August 17, 1916, see FO 371/2817, pp.

164-222, and Weizmann's letter to Wolf of September 3, 1916, in *CW Letters*, 7:291-92.

431-32 One version of the "Programmatic Statement" is given in *CW Letters*, 7:543; another in Frank E. Manuel, *The Realities of American-Palestine Relations* (Washington, D.C., 1949), pp. 165-66. The latter is used here.

30. THE NEW GOVERNMENT

In addition to works already cited on the politics of this period, an indispensable source is Lord Beaverbrook, *Politicians and the War, 1914-1916* (London, 1928-1932; reprinted 1960), part memoir, part journalistic report, part history, by a great press lord who was one of the participants. One must also consult A.J.P. Taylor, *English History 1914-1945* (Oxford, 1965), which is volume 15 in *The Oxford History of England*. On Asquith, the two basic biographies are: J.A. Spender and Cyril Asquith, *The Life of Lord Oxford and Asquith*, 2 vols. (London, 1932); and Roy Jenkins, *Asquith* (New York, 1964).

Page

434 "'The Prime Minister . . .'": *The Times* (London), December 4, 1916.

435 "It was . . . a revolution, British-style": Taylor, *English History*, p. 73.

435 "there had never before been a 'ranker' . . .": David Lloyd George, *War Memoirs of David Lloyd George*, 6 vols. (Boston, 1933-37), 3:5.

436 "I intend as soon as possible . . .": Message of November 13, 1916, from GOC in C (General Officer Commanding in Chief), Egypt, to CIGS (Chief of Imperial General Staff), London, at the War Office. PRO: WO 33/905/6278-79.

436 "like that in Mesopotamia . . .": Lloyd George, *War Memoirs*, 4:82.

437 For the War Cabinet meeting of December 9, 1916, and Robertson's subsequent telegram to Murray, see PRO: CAB 23/1/1.

437 "My action subsequent . . . out of the question": Quoted in Cyril Falls and General Sir G. MacMunn, *Military Operations: Egypt and Palestine*, 2 vols. (London, 1928), 1:259.

437 "been seen by Prime Minister . . .": Ibid., p. 260.

438 "In my first appreciation . . .": Ibid.

438 "In order that any possibility . . .": Ibid., pp. 260-61.

439 "Operations will shortly be begun . . .": FO 371/2783.

439 "if the forthcoming operations . . .": PRO: CAB 23/1/8.

439 "with the utmost secrecy . . . rise against the Turks": Ibid.

440 "As they rode in the darkness . . .": Falls and MacMunn, *Military Operations*, 1:252.

440 "As our troops were not strong enough . . .": Quoted in ibid., from Kress von Kressenstein, *Mit den Türken zum Suezcanal* (Berlin, 1938).

31. PALESTINE: MAKING A BEGINNING

Page

446 For Bentwich and Aaronsohn, see Norman Bentwich, *My 77 Years* (Philadelphia, 1961), pp. 42-43.

446   Aaronsohn's report on Palestine is in FO 371/3049.

446-47 The sources for Jabotinsky and the Jewish Legion are Vladimir Jabotin-
        sky, *The Story of the Jewish Legion* (New York, 1945), pp. 77-82; Leopold
        Amery, *My Political Life*, 2 vols. (London, 1935), 2:117-18; *CW Letters*,
        7:328-29; the Jabotinsky-Trumpeldor Memorandum in CAB 24/9 and in
        Sledmere Papers, February 11, 1917; and the relevant parts of file no. 18095
        in FO 371/2835.

447-49 The first issue of *Palestine*: Palestine, the organ of the British Palestine
        Committee, vol. 1: January 26-July 1, 1917. All quotes but the last in this
        section are from vol. 1, no. 1, January 26, 1917. "Our Military Interest in
        Palestine" is from vol. 1, no. 2, February 1, 1917.

449-50 For the Lloyd George breakfast of January 26, 1917, see Scott Diaries,
        January 26-30, 1917.

449   For Scott's report on Walter Lippman's account of "pro-Germanism," see
        Scott to Lloyd George, December 24, 1916, reproduced in Wilson, *Political
        Diaries of C.P. Scott*, pp. 253-54.

32. SYKES MEETS THE ZIONIST LEADERSHIP

Page

451   "Saw Weizmann in morning . . .": Scott Diaries, January 26-30, 1917.

451   For the new Palestine-related appointments of Sykes and Picot, see FO
       371/3050.

451   The probable Gaster-Sykes meeting, January 8, 1917, is inferred from the
       Gaster-Sykes letters of January 5 and January 9, the first asking for an
       appointment on the eighth, the second implying that it had occurred. Gas-
       ter Papers.

452   For Samuel's renewed promotion of his Palestine memorandum, there
       is, for example, a letter to Samuel from Milner, January 17, 1917, thank-
       ing him for sending the memorandum, and offering comments. Samuel
       Papers.

452   For James de Rothschild, Sykes and racehorses, see Gaster Diaries, Janu-
       ary 30. 1917. On that day, Sykes gave Gaster some kind of account of the
       past few days' events.

452   "France was competing hard for Palestine . . .": Scott Diaries, January 26-
       30, 1917.

The somewhat puzzling role of James Malcolm in the first contacts between Sykes
and Weizmann is painstakingly pieced together by Leonard Stein in his *Balfour Declaration*, pp. 362-68. I quite disagree with Stein's reconstruction of what went on, but
I could not have arrived at my own without his pioneering attempt. The problem
stems largely from the fact that Malcolm, in later retrospective accounts, was eager to
inflate his own contribution to this historic moment.

Page

452-53 The Greenberg-Malcolm relationship is well formulated by Stein, largely
        from personal recollections obtained from Greenberg's daughter and an
        old colleague of the *Jewish Chronicle*.

453   "a curious story . . .": Scott Diaries, January 26-30, 1917.

453   *brasseur d'affaires*: Sokolow to Weizmann, April 20, 1917. Quoted in Stein, *Balfour Declaration*, p. 395.

454   For Weizmann's and Greenberg's call on Sykes, see Gaster Diaries, January 28 and 30, 1917.

454   "the honor of bringing . . .": Greenberg letter to the Zionist Executive of August 24, 1921. Quoted in Stein, *Balfour Declaration*, p. 363, n. 10.

454   "Message from Weizmann . . .": Gaster Diaries, January 28, 1917.

454   "One of my co-workers . . .": Gaster to Sykes, January 29, 1917. Gaster Papers.

455   "*Went to Sykes* . . . appointment with him that evening": Gaster Diaries, January 30, 1917.

455   "I hope to see Dr. W. this afternoon . . .": Gaster to Sykes, January 31, 1917. Gaster Papers.

455   "Had been introduced, as he alleged . . . other representatives": Gaster Diaries, January 31, 1917.

456   "Gaster thinks that he has got . . .": Weizmann to Sieff, February 3, 1917. *CW Letters*, 7:326.

456   Gaster had reported the results: Gaster to Sykes, February 1, 1917. Gaster Papers.

456   "very important": *CW Letters*, 7:327.

456   For the Gaster-Picot meeting of July 7, 1916, see Gaster Diaries.

456   Picot . . . asked Sykes to find a Zionist with a more realistic grasp: *La Terre Retrouvée* [Paris], April 1, 1939.

456-57   "that he was capable of setting . . .": Aaronsohn diary, April 27, 1917. Quoted in Stein, *Balfour Declaration*, p. 362, n. 4, in the original French. My translation is from that.

457   "hotly resented . . .": Gaster to James de Rothschild, February 9, 1917. Gaster Papers.

457   "forced upon . . .": Gaster Diaries, February 7, 1917.

457-62   Minutes to the meeting of February 7, 1917, probably composed by Sokolow, are on deposit at several archives, including Gaster Papers, Samuel Papers, Central Zionist Archives, Weizmann Archives.

462   Gaster was to write to James de Rothschild: Gaster to Rothschild, February 9, 1917. Gaster Papers.

462   "The most important meeting . . .": Gaster Diaries, February 7, 1917.

33. THE POLITICAL EMERGENCE OF SOKOLOW AND WEIZMANN

Page

463   "In our Palestinian affairs . . .": *CW Letters*, 7:328-29.

463-71   Sokolow's minutes of the three meetings of February 8, 9, and 10, 1917, are on deposit in Gaster Papers, Samuel papers, Central Zionist Archives, and Weizmann Archives.

468   "The world will not go under . . .": Weizmann, *Trial and Error*, p. 79.

471-73   For Weizmann's election as President of the EZF and his speech at the February 11, 1917, conference, see *Jewish Chronicle*, February 16, 1917.

473   For the evening meeting in Aldgate, see ibid.

473-74 "At a time when Palestine . . .": *Manchester Guardian*, February 1, 1917.

474-75 *Nation* leader of February 17, 1917, and Sidebotham's response are reprinted in *Palestine*, vol. 1, no., 6, March 1, 1917.

475   "The Boundaries of Palestine": Ibid., no. 4, February 15, 1917.

475   "Sir M. invited me today . . .": *CW Letters*, 7:330-31.

475   For Sieff's letter to Weizmann of February 19, 1917, see ibid., p. 332, n. 311/1.

475   "Letter received . . .": Ibid., p. 332.

475   "you can do what you please . . .": Ibid., p. 333.

476   "discipline and unity . . . contain a Jewish article . . .": Sieff to Weizmann, February 20, 1917. Ibid., p. 333, n. 311/3.

476   "Jewish Self-Government in Palestine": *Palestine*, vol. 1, no. 5, February 22, 1917.

476   For Weizmann's meeting with the British Palestine Committee on February 22, 1917, see *CW Letters*, 7:332, n. 311/2.

476   "I read Sidebotham's letter . . .": Ibid., p. 335.

34. SYKES PONDERS THE QUESTION OF CONTROL

Page

478   Sokolow's minutes of the Sykes-Sokolow conversation of February 22, 1917, are on deposit in Gaster Papers, Central Zionist Archives, and Weizmann Archives.

479-81 Sykes's letter to Picot of February 28, 1917, is in Sledmere Papers.

481-82 For the Sykes-Scott conversation of March 1, 1917, see Scott Diaries, February 26-March 1, 1917.

35. WALLS TUMBLING DOWN

Page

483   "REVOLUTION IN RUSSIA . . .": *The Times* (London), March 16, 1917.

483   "The new Government . . .": *Manchester Guardian*, March 17, 1917.

483   "At tea he did most of the talking . . .": Scott Diaries, March 17, 1917.

483-84 "That which has long been awaited . . . a dream?": *Jewish Daily Forward*, March 16, 1917. My translation from the Yiddish.

484   "JEWISH TROUBLES ARE AT AN END": Ibid., March 20, 1917.

484   "Yes, the events in Russia . . .": *CW Letters*, 7:345.

484   "rather lose Bagdad than Jerusalem . . .": *Manchester Guardian*, March 13, 1917.

484-85 "than he asked Chaim . . . inflict himself upon him": Vera Weizmann Diaries, March 13, 1917; quoted in Vera Weizmann, *The Impossible*, pp. 67-68.

485   "You must take me by storm . . . company and get ahead": Scott Diaries, March 15-17, 1917.

485   "merely academically": Vera Weizmann Diaries, March 13, 1917; quoted in Vera Weizmann, *The Impossible*, p. 68.

485   "the destruction of the barbarous . . . not to be thought of": Scott Diaries, March 15-17, 1917.

486   For the Baghdad Proclamation, see, for example, *Manchester Guardian*, March 19, 1917.

486   "Proclamation is addressed . . .": From General Officer Commanding Force "D" to IO, March 16, 1917. FO 371/3042.

487   "The Arabs are, with the Jews . . .": *Manchester Guardian*, March 20, 1917.

487–89   Weizmann's letter to Scott of March 20, 1917, is in *CW Letters*, 7:343-45.

490   Mr. Balfour . . . did not at first . . .": Weizmann to Scott, March 23, 1917. Ibid., p. 346.

490   "freely in favor of Zionism": Leopold Amery to Balfour, March 29, 1917. PRO: FO 800/204.

490–91   "I think I succeeded . . . interested to hear about that": Weizmann to Scott, March 23, 1917. *CW Letters*, 7:346-47.

491   "I have no hesitation in saying . . .": Weizmann to Brandeis, April 8, 1917. Ibid., p. 358.

491–92   For the first battle of Gaza, see Archibald P. Wavell, *The Palestine Campaigns* (London, 1931; New York, 1972); Cyril Falls and General Sir G. MacMunn, *Military Operations, Egypt and Palestine*, 2 vols. (London, 1928); and contemporary newspaper accounts.

492   For Murray's official report of March 28, 1917, see *The Times* (London), March 30, 1917.

492   "Victory in Palestine" and "Sir Archibald Murray . . .": Ibid.

493   "The dispatch about the Battle of Gaza . . .": *Manchester Guardian*, March 30, 1917.

493–95   For the Lloyd George breakfast of April 3, 1917, see Scott Diaries, April 2-5, 1917.

493   "was very emphatic . . .": Weizmann to Sokolow, April 4, 1917. *CW Letters*, 7:351.

494   "if the bearers of the idea are lost in France?": Jabotinsky to Weizmann, March 25, 1917. Ibid., p. 349, n. 326/2.

36. SYKES AND SOKOLOW IN PARIS AND ROME

Page

496   "In accordance with an understanding . . .": Sokolow to Samuel, March 30, 1917. Sokolow Papers; quoted in *CW Letters*, 7:349, n. 327/1.

497   "This work is very difficult . . .": Ibid., p. 354, n. 333/2.

497   "the importance of not prejudicing . . . to the British area": "Note of a Conference Held at 10 Downing Street, at 3.30 P.M. on April 3, 1917, to Consider Instructions to Lt. Col. Sir Mark Sykes, The Head of the Political Mission to the General Officer Commanding-in-Chief, Egyptian Expeditionary Force." Sledmere Papers.

497   "we could take care of the Holy Places . . .": Scott Diaries, April 2-4, 1917.

497–99   "After five days negotiations . . . in Blue Area or Area A": FO 371/3045.

499   "things here are not so bad . . . fairly well equipped": Sykes to Hankey, April 7, 1917. Sledmere Papers.

499–500   "In dealing with the question . . .": Bertie to Graham, April 12, 1917. FO 371/3052.

500   "Syrian party . . . but Haifa, never": Sykes to Graham, April 15, 1917. Sledmere Papers.

500   "The Parisian Jews . . .": Ibid.

501   "But . . . as I was crossing the Quai d'Orsay . . .": Sokolow, *History of Zionism*, 2:xxix-xxx.

501   For Sokolow's April 9, 1917, meeting at the Quai d'Orsay and "After favorable results . . .": see FO 371/3045.

501-2   For Sykes and Monsignor Pacelli, see Sykes to Graham, April 15, 1917. FO 371/3052.

502-3   Sykes's audience with Pope Benedict XV is in ibid.

503   "I visited Monsignor Pacelli . . .": Sykes to Sokolow, April 14, 1917. Ibid.

504-5   On the Italian role in Middle Eastern affairs, see Frank E. Manuel, "The Palestine Question in Italian Diplomacy, 1917-1920," *Journal of Modern History*, September 1955, pp. 263-80.

504   Saint Jean de Maurienne: See Ibid.

505-7   Graham's memorandum to Lord Hardinge, April 21, 1917, and Hardinge's and Cecil's minutes to it are in FO 371/3052.

507-8   "I must say . . . center of our activities": Sokolow to Weizmann, April 20, 1917. Sokolow Papers; quoted in Stein, *Balfour Declaration*, p. 395.

508   "for the definite purpose . . .": Sokolow to Weizmann, May 12, 1917. Weizmann Archives; quoted in Stein, *Balfour Declaration*, p. 405.

508   For "in spite of the extraordinary courtesy . . ." and the Gasparri interview, see Sokolow Papers; quoted in Stein, *Balfour Declaration*, p. 406.

508-9   For Sokolow's audience with Pope Benedict XV, see Florian Sokolow, *Avi, Nahum Sokolow* (Tel Aviv, 1970), pp. 148-51. My translation from the Hebrew.

509   "Have been received by Pope . . . most favorable attitude": Sokolow to Weizmann, May 7, 1917. FO 371/3053, p. 206.

509-10   "did not wish to treat . . .": Rodd to FO, May 10, 1917. Ibid., p. 221.

510   Sokolow went to see Prime Minister Paolo Boselli: Stein, *Balfour Declaration*, p. 415.

37. WEIZMANN CARRIES ON AT HOME

Page

511   "Here last week . . . friends on the other side": *CW Letters*, 7:350-51.

511   "For the Jews and the Arabs . . .": *The Times* (London) March 30, 1917.

512   "our position . . . a British protectorate": *CW Letters*, 7:357-60.

512   "I was very anxious . . .": Ibid., p. 350.

513   "Important progress . . .": Ibid., p. 360. My translation from the French.

513   "Result official interview . . .": Ibid., p. 362, n. 340/1.

513   "Heartfelt thanks . . .": Ibid., p. 362.

513   "Expect urgently . . .": Ibid., p. 365.

513   "Anxious absence news Nahum . . .": Ibid.

513-14   "Continuation work all right . . .": Ibid., n. 344/2.

514   "Very anxious absence all news . . .": Ibid., p. 366.

514   "Myself and friends . . .": Ibid., n. 347/3.

514-15   "Only yesterday Malcolm arrived . . . journey to Rome": Ibid., pp. 368-69.

515   "This was startling information indeed": Weizmann, *Trial and Error*, p. 191.

515   "Chaim and all those . . .": Vera Weizmann, *The Impossible*, p. 70.

516   For Scott's conversation with Milner on April 20, 1917, see Scott Diaries, April 19-21, 1917.

516   "certainly appears to me the most attractive . . .": Milner to Samuel, January 17, 1917. Samuel Papers.

516-17   For Weizmann's conversations with Samuel and with Graham on April 24, 1917, see Weizmann to Scott, April 26, 1917. *CW Letters*, 7:378-82.

517   "he couldn't go to Egypt . . .": Vera Weizmann Diaries, April 24, 1917; quoted in *The Impossible*, p. 70.

517   "nothing is clear . . .": *CW Letters*, 7:380.

517-20   There are two sources for the Weizmann-Cecil conversation of April 25, 1917—Weizmann's note of the conversation, in *CW Letters*, 7:375-78; and Cecil's memorandum on it, in FO 371/3053, p. 204.

520   "All unanimously agree . . .": Vera Weizmann Diaries, no date given; quoted in *The Impossible*, p. 70.

520   "Your work in France . . .": *CW Letters*, 7:384-85.

521   "After favorable results . . .": FO 371/3053, p. 180.

521   "In other words . . . if possible at once": *CW Letters*, 7:390-93.

522   "Astonished fallacious commentaries . . .": FO 371/3053, p. 204.

523   "had finally decided to postpone his departure": Scott Diaries, April 30–May 14, 1917.

523   "Dr. Weizmann inquires whether . . .": FO 371/3053, p. 202.

523   "I do not know what military situation is . . .": Ibid., p. 208.

524   "all your letters from Rome . . .": *CW Letters*, 7:401-3.

524   "Your telegram received . . .": Ibid., p. 405.

524   "It is only right . . .": Gaster to Weizmann, May 10, 1917. Gaster papers.

525   "I beg to thank you . . .": *CW Letters*, 7:408.

38. SOME DECLARATIONS

Page

526   "The Russian Revolution and Zionism": *Zionist Review*, May 1917.

526-28   Weizmann's speech at the May 20, 1917, conference of the EZF is quoted in full in Sokolow, *History*, 2:54-58.

529-31   The Conjoint Foreign Committee's open letter on Zionism is in *The Times* (London), May 24, 1917.

531   "A Grave Betrayal": *Jewish Chronicle*, May 25, 1917.

531   "I do not propose . . .": *The Times* (London), May 28, 1917.

531-32   "I consider it most unfortunate . . .": Ibid., May 28, 1917.

532   "It may possibly be inconvenient . . .": Ibid.

533   "The important controversy . . . Jewry everywhere": *The Times* (London), May 29, 1917.

533   eighteen prominent Jews: Ibid., June 1, 1917.

534   "You were good enough . . .": FO 371/3058, p. 153. The translation here is Sokolow's own, given in his *History*, 2:53; but I have edited it slightly in the light of the original.

535   Greenberg had sent a memorandum: FO 371/3052.

535   Cecil's telegram to Buchanan and Buchanan's response are in FO 371/3053, pp. 177-78, 182.

535   Sykes . . . opposing Buchanan's evaluation: Ibid., pp. 188-89.

535   "Tschlenow wires . . .": *CW Letters*, 7:408–9.

535–36   "Shall go to Petrograd . . .": FO 371/3053, p. 223.

536   "It is certain that Jewish influence . . .": Quoted in Stein, *Balfour Declaration*, p. 418.

536–37   Extracts from Tschlenow's address at the All-Russian Zionist Congress are in Sokolow, *History*, 2:39–40.

537   For Sokolow's message from Paris of June 6, 1917, see *CW Letters*, 7:430, n. 418/2.

537   For Sokolow's message from Paris of June 11, 1917, see ibid., p. 436.

537   "You are one of the Americans . . .": Blanche E.C. Dugdale, *Arthur James Balfour, First Earl of Balfour*, 2 vols. (New York, 1937), 2:168.

537–38   For the Drummond-Brandeis conversation of April 24, 1917, see FO 371/3053, pp. 300–301.

538–39   For the Wilson-Brandeis conversation of May 6, 1917, see note by Brandeis in de Haas Papers, Zionist Archives, New York.

539   "We approve your program . . .": *CW Letters*, 7:405, n. 380/6.

539   "I am a Zionist": Felix Frankfurter to Mrs. Dugdale, ca. 1934; quoted in Stein, *Balfour Declaration*, p. 428.

539   "Balfour was powerfully struck . . . won by Balfour": Ibid.

539   "so qualified as . . .": From de Haas Papers.

539–40   "A Jewish Republic in Palestine": FO 371/3053, pp. 289–92.

540–41   "a distinguished American Zionist . . . in this view": Graham memorandum, June 13, 1917. FO 371/3058, pp. 144–50.

541   "It would appear . . . results it would secure": Graham memorandum, June 13, 1917. Ibid.

542   "How can HMG . . .": Minuted by Balfour on Graham's memorandum of June 13, 1917. Ibid.

542   Graham's June 18, 1917, memorandum on Sokolow is in ibid., pp. 151–52.

542   "I never meant to suggest . . .": Ibid., p. 150 verso.

542   For Cecil's and Balfour's minutes, see ibid.

543   "Lord Rothschild and myself saw Mr. Balfour yesterday . . .": *CW Letters*, 7:445.

39. NEW BEGINNINGS IN EGYPT AND ARABIA

Page

544   "Further it was agreed by delegates . . .": Sykes to FO, April 30, 1917. FO 371/3053, p. 192.

544–45   "Sir Mark believes . . .": Entry of April 28, 1917. Aaron Aaronsohn, *Yoman, 1916–1919* (Tel Aviv, 1970), p. 253. My translation from the Hebrew.

545   "The sooner the French military mission . . .": Sykes to Wingate, May 5, 1917. Sledmere Papers.

545   "grateful to France . . .": Edouard Brémond, *Le Hedjaz dans la guerre mondiale* (Paris, 1931), p. 147. My translation from the French.

546   "Out of every thousand square miles . . .": T.E. Lawrence, *Seven Pillars of Wisdom* (New York, 1938, de luxe ed.), p. 189.

546   "tall, strong figure . . .": Ibid., pp. 221–22.

546–47   Foremost among Arab historians denying this and other claims of Lawrence's is Souleiman Mousa, *T.E. Lawrence: An Arab View* (London, 1966).

547   "most happy to surrender . . .": *Arab Bulletin*, no. 59. Reprinted in David Garnett, ed., *The Letters of T.E. Lawrence* (New York, 1939), p. 235.

547-48   "engineer in grey uniform . . .": Lawrence, *Seven Pillars*, p. 312.

The two foremost biographies of Allenby for this period are: General Sir Archibald Wavell, *Allenby: A Study in Greatness* (New York, 1941); and Brian Gardner, *Allenby of Arabia* (New York, 1965).

Page

548-49   "My word, he is a different man . . .": Quoted in Gardner, *Allenby of Arabia*, p. 117.

549-50   "It was a comic interview . . . his very greediest servant": Lawrence, *Seven Pillars*, pp. 321-22.

40. AFTER AN INTERMEZZO, A DRAFT DECLARATION

In addition to the Weizmann letters and autobiography, two important sources on the Morgenthau mission are: FO 371/3057, File no. 103481, *passim*; and Frank E. Manuel, *The Realities of American-Palestine Relations* (Washington, D.C., 1949), in which the account is from State Department papers.

Page

551   "opera bouffe intermezzo": Weizmann, *Trial and Error*, p. 195.

551   "certain concessions should be made to them": Charles Seymour, ed., *The Intimate Papers of Colonel House*, 4 vols. (New Haven, 1928), 3:58.

552   "under the leadership of Brandeis . . .": Manuel, *Realities*, p. 55.

552   "an effort to ameliorate . . .": *The New York Times*, June 20, 1917.

552-53   "to keep an eye on things": Weizmann, *Trial and Error*, p. 198.

553   "an American commission": Ibid., p. 195.

553   "if any Jew is to be sent . . .": Ormsby-Gore's report on the conversation with Weizmann and Malcolm, June 10, 1917. "Aubrey Herbert's Mission to the Turk." Sledmere papers.

553   "axiomatic that no arrangements . . .": Weizmann to Sacher, June 11, 1917. *CW Letters*, 7:437.

554   "One would feel absolutely safe . . .": Ibid., p. 453.

554   "a delightful companion . . . hastily withdrew": Weizmann, *Trial and Error*, p. 196.

555   "It was midsummer . . .": Ibid., p. 198.

555-56   Weizmann summarizes the Gibraltar meeting in two documents: a letter to Sir Ronald Graham of July 6, 1917, and a formal report of the same date. *CW Letters*, 7:461-65.

557   Sacher's first draft of a declaration is in Central Zionist Archives.

557   "the principle of recognizing Palestine . . .": Ibid.

557   "It is not here . . .": Sokolow to Cowen, July 9, 1917. Ibid.

557   "I am persuaded . . .": Sacher to Sokolow, July 9, 1917. Ibid.

557-58   "in a private way . . . get more and more": Sokolow to Sacher, July 10, 1917. Ibid.

558   "The definite form of such reconstitution . . .": Ibid.

558   "A Jewish State . . .": Ibid.

558-59   Sokolow's draft declaration of July 12, 1917, is in Weizmann Archives.

559　"It was feared . . .": Central Zionist Archives.
559　Draft version of July 18, 1917, is in FO 371/3083, pp. 43-53.
559-60　"At last I am able to send you . . .": Ibid.
560　"Many thanks for your letter . . .": Ibid.

41. THE DRAFT DECLARATION AT THE WAR CABINET:
THE FIRST SALLY

One should also consult Jon Kimche, *The Unromantics: The Great Powers and the Balfour Declaration* (London, 1968).

The sources on Edwin Montagu are: S.D. Waley, *Edwin Montagu* (London, 1964); Lord Beaverbrook, *Politicians and the War, 1914-1916* (London 1928-1932; reprinted 1960), which, in its close account of Asquith's last days in office, has a good deal on Montagu's role in the crisis; and Roy Jenkins, *Asquith* (New York, 1964), *passim*. There is a lively account of Montagu in Chaim Bermant, *The Cousinhood* (New York, 1971), pp. 249-67.

Page
561　Balfour's undated mid-August reply to Lord Rothschild, containing a draft declaration is in FO 371/3083, pp. 43-53.
563　"between deserting a sinking ship . . .": Beaverbrook, *Politicians and the War*, p. 498.
563　Montagu's poem to Lloyd George and the subsequent exchange of letters with Asquith are quoted in Frank Owen, *Tempestuous Journey: Lloyd George, His Life and Times* (New York, 1955), pp. 416-17.
564　"the Assyrian . . . Silken Tent": Jenkins, *Asquith*, p. 267.
564　"Is it race or religion . . .": Waley, *Montagu*, pp. 66-67.
564　"with all my love . . .": Jenkins, *Asquith*, p. 365.
564　"a disastrous policy": Quoted in Friedman, *The Question of Palestine*, pp. 22-23.
564-65　Montagu's comments on Jewish nationalism are quoted in Christopher Sykes, *Two Studies in Virtue* (London, 1953), pp. 212-14.
565-67　"The Anti-Semitism of the Present Government": FO 371/3083, pp. 64-65.
567-68　"Arrangements are now nearing completion . . .": *The Times* (London), July 28, 1917.
569　"I am waiting to learn . . .": Montagu, "Anti-Semitism." FO 371/3083, pp. 64-65.
569-70　For Scott's conversations with Nabokov and Derby, see Scott Diaries, August 29, 1917.
570　"country squire . . .": Vladimir Jabotinsky, *The Story of the Jewish Legion* (New York, 1945), p. 83.
571-72　"I wish to inform you . . .": *CW Letters*, 7:490.
571n　"a token reward . . .": Weizmann, *Trial and Error*, p. 174.
572　"believe me, my dear friend . . .": *CW Letters*, 7:491.
572　For Weizmann's attempted resignation on September 5, 1917, see ibid., p. 499.
572-73　"an act of treason . . .": Quoted in Stein, *Balfour Declaration*, p. 495.
573　"you were resigning your position . . .": Scott to Weizmann, September 12, 1917. Quoted in Stein, *Balfour Declaration*, p. 496.

573   "I am afraid . . .": Weizmann to Scott, September 13, 1917. *CW Letters*, 7:509.

573   "I'm glad that you are only . . .": Scott to Weizmann September 14, 1917. Weizmann Archives. Quoted in Stein, *Balfour Declaration*, p. 496.

573-77   For the War Cabinet of September 3, 1917, dealing both with Jewish regiment and with declaration on Palestine, see PRO: CAB 23/4, no. 227. Also enclosed in FO 371/3083, pp. 66-67.

574   "between our formula and the full Zionist scheme": Quoted in Friedman, *Question of Palestine*, p. 257.

575   For Milner's draft version, see PRO: CAB 21/58.

575   Ormsby-Gore's suggestion is in ibid.

42. THE DRAFT DECLARATION AT THE WAR CABINET: THE SECOND SALLY

Page

578   "We are being pressed here . . .": Relayed by House to Wilson, September 4, 1917. Quoted in Frank E. Manuel, *The Realities of American-Palestine Relations* (Washington, D.C., 1949), p. 167.

578   "it would be simply splendid . . .": *CW Letters*, 7:504.

578-79   "Has Colonel House been able . . .": Quoted in Stein, *Balfour Declaration*, pp. 504-5.

579   "the time is not opportune . . .": FO 371/3083.

579   "to my great astonishment . . .": *CW Letters*, 7:514.

579   "Have you made up your mind . . .": Manuel, *Realities*, p. 168.

580   "Following text declaration . . .": *CW Letters*, 7:505-6.

580   "From talks I have had with President . . .": Ibid., p. 506, n. 496/5.

581   "I hope the dream . . .": Manuel, *Realities*, p. 168.

581   "It would be wise . . .": *CW Letters*, 7:506, n. 496/5.

581-82   "I had the pleasure of seeing . . .": Ibid., p. 516.

582-83   Graham's memorandum of September 24, 1917, and the minutes on it by Hardinge and Balfour are in FO 371/3083, pp. 102-4.

583   "I had asked Weizmann to come . . .": Scott Diaries, September 26-28, 1917.

584-85   "The Arab Provinces—Syria": FO 371/3059.

585   "I told you how Herbert Samuel wrote . . .": H.V.F. Winstone, *Gertrude Bell* (New York, 1978), pp. 201-2.

586   "The rumor spreading about . . .": Albina to Sykes, August 10, 1917: Sledmere Papers.

587   "On my arrival . . . people he is fighting for": Sykes to Clayton, July 22, 1917. Sledmere Papers.

587-88   "I submit . . . gain their ends": "Memorandum by Sir Mark Sykes on Mr. Nicolson's Note Regarding our Commitments." FO 371/3044, pp. 294-95.

588   "I believe that the time . . . in bald terms of grab": "Memorandum on the Asia-Minor Agreement" by Sir Mark Sykes. FO 371/3059.

589   "I am not sure . . .": Clayton to Sykes, August 20, 1917. Quoted in Friedman, *Question of Palestine*, p. 225.

589   The earlier draft of Sykes's "Note on Palestine and Zionism" (just entitled "Note on Palestine") and the later one are both in the Sledmere Papers.

590   "which would go a reasonable distance . . .": Leopold S. Amery, *My Political Life*, 3 vols. (London, 1953), 2:116.

590-91   "His Majesty's Government views with favor . . .": PRO: CAB 23/4, p. 80 verso.

591   "The reference to Jews outside Palestine . . .": Amery to Leonard Stein, July 1, 1952. Quoted in Stein, *Balfour Declaration*, p. 522, n. 7.

In *Trial and Error*, Weizmann presents a rather more dramatic version of the effort to summon him to the cabinet than seems to have actually been the case, which is described in a vague and general way in a letter he wrote three days later to Brandeis (*CW Letters* 7:524).

Page

591-93   For the War Cabinet of October 4, 1917, see PRO: CAB 23/4.

43. THE THIRD SALLY: THE DECLARATION AT LAST

Page

594   For the Aaronsohn-Allenby interview of July 17, 1917, see Aaron Aaronsohn, *Yoman, 1916-1919* (Tel Aviv, 1970) p. 315.

594   "I have seen a great deal . . .": Graves to Sykes, March 18, 1917. Sledmere Papers.

595   "I see you sitting . . .": Anita Engle, *The Nili Spies* (London, 1959), p. 81.

595   "I've been given the most murderous beatings . . .": Ibid., p. 200.

596   "We are doing our utmost . . .": *CW Letters*, 7:523.

596   "In view of reports . . .": FO 371/4083.

596n   The "Lawrence-Sarah Myth": Engle, *Nili Spies*, pp. 229-38, has an appendix summarizing this phenomenon. The August 12, 1917, meeting between Lawrence and Aaron Aaronsohn is described in Aaronsohn, *Yoman*, pp. 328-29.

597   For Hankey's letter to the Jewish notables of October 6, 1917, see British Library, Add ms. 41,178A, "The Balfour Declaration."

597   "Most likely [I] shall be asked . . .": *CW Letters*, 7:530-31.

597   "(1)That this meeting . . .": The text of the basic resolution varies in different sources, including contemporary ones. This is essentially as given in Sokolow, *History*, 2:69.

598   "I find in my pocket . . .": Frank E. Manuel, *Realities of American-Palestine Relations* (Washington, D.C., 1949), p. 169.

598   "Colonel House put formula before President . . .": *Documents on British Foreign Policy, 1919-1939* (London,1952), series 1, vol. 4, no. 196, p. 281, n. 4.

598   two changes suggested by Sokolow: FO 371/3083, p. 73.

598-99   Claude Montefiore's covering letter is in Stein, *Balfour Declaration*, pp. 525-26; for his draft resolution, see FO 371/3083, p. 73 verso.

599   The draft resolutions of Leonard Cohen and Sir Philip Magnus are in FO 371/3083, p. 73 verso.

600   For Herbert Samuel on his brother's response, see Viscount Samuel, *Grooves of Change* (Indianapolis, 1945), p. 78.

600   Rabbi Hertz's response is quoted in Paul Goodman, ed., *The Jewish National Home, 1917-1942* (London, 1943), pp. xx-xxi.

600   "Although it is unfortunately true . . .": Weizmann to Hankey, October 15, 1917. *CW Letters*, 7:533.

600-601   Montagu's draft resolution is in FO 371/3083, p. 73 verso.

601   "I shall never in my life forget this day . . .": *CW Letters*, 7:540.

601-2   "I beg respectfully to submit . . . in favor of the movement": FO 371/3054, pp. 31-32.

602   Wickham Steed's letter to Northcliffe of October 14, 1917, is in "Balfour Declaration" file, Middle East Centre, St. Antony's College, Oxford.

602-3   "The Jews and Palestine": *The Times* (London), October 26, 1917.

603   "Bonar Law the difficulty . . .": Scott Diaries, October 19-21, 1917.

603-4   Curzon's memorandum, "The Future of Palestine," is printed in its entirety in David Lloyd George, *Memoirs of the Peace Conference*, 2 vols. (New Haven, 1939), 2:727-32.

605-6   Sykes's reply to the Curzon memorandum is in FO 371/3083, pp. 114-17.

606   "Allah en-nebi": Archibald Wavell, *Allenby: A Study in Greatness* (New York, 1941), pp. 203-4.

606   "with the diligence of a student . . .": Brian Gardner, *Allenby of Arabia* (New York, 1965), p. 127.

607   "Along the water's edge . . .": Wavell, *Allenby*, p. 200.

607   "Allenby was not wedded   ": David Lloyd George, *War Memoirs of David Lloyd George*, 6 vols. (Boston, 1933-1937), 4:96.

607   "Nothing . . . could more aptly illustrate . . .": George Adam Smith, *The Historical Geography of the Holy Land* (New York, 1966, Harper Torchbook ed.) p. 193.

608-9   "I was well mounted . . .": Quoted in Gardner, *Allenby of Arabia*, pp. 129-30.

610-12   For the War Cabinet of October 31, 1917, see PRO: CAB 23/4.

612   "Dr. Weizmann . . . it's a boy": Weizmann, *Trial and Error*, p. 208.

612-13   Balfour's letter to Lord Rothschild, November 2, 1917, is in British Library, Add ms. 41,178A, "The Balfour Declaration."

44. THE HIGH WALLS OF JERUSALEM

Page

614   "We are at liberty, I gather . . .": Stein, *Balfour Declaration*, p. 559.

614-15   reason for this further delay: Ibid., p. 560, based on information obtained by Stein personally.

615   "ANARCHY IN PETROGRAD . . .": *The Times* (London), November 9, 1917.

615   "Palestine for the Jews . . .": Ibid.

615-17   Responses in the British press are all quoted *in extenso* in Sokolow, *History*, 2:84-99.

616   "the Magna Charta of Jewish liberties": *CW Letters*, 7:542.

617-20   The speeches from the mass meeting at the London Opera House are printed in Sokolow, *History*, 2:99-113.

619   "Recent announcement of His Majesty's Government . . .": Wingate to Sykes, November 28, 1917. Sledmere Papers.

620   "Jerusalem before Christmas": David Lloyd George, *War Memoirs of David Lloyd George*, 6 vols. (Boston, 1933-1937), 4:94.

620-21   "A long series of valleys . . . of Jerusalem or of Hebron": George Adam Smith, *The Historical Geography of the Holy Land* (New York, 1966, Harper Torchbook ed.), p. 195.

624   "the citadel of my integrity . . .": T.E. Lawrence, *Seven Pillars of Wisdom* (New York, 1938, de luxe ed.), p. 447.

624   "so full of victories . . .": Ibid., p. 453.

624   "It was a brilliant day . . .": Archibald Wavell, *Allenby: A Study in Greatness* (New York, 1941), p. 231.

624-25   For the planning of the entry into Jerusalem, see FO 371/3061, file no. 214354 *passim*.

625   "made ready to enter . . .": Lawrence, *Seven Pillars*, p. 453.

625   "There was no great pageantry . . .": *Illustrated London News*, January 19, 1918.

625   "the supreme moment of the war": Lawrence, *Seven Pillars*, p. 453.

626   Allenby's proclamation is in Allenby Papers.

626-27   The Picot-Allenby exchange over lunch is in Lawrence, *Seven Pillars*, p. 455.

45. FROM WAR TO PEACE

Page

631   "There were tens of thousands . . .": Vladimir Jabotinsky, *The Story of the Jewish Legion* (New York, 1945), p. 104. See also John Henry Patterson, *With the Judeans in the Palestine Campaign* (New York, 1922).

632   "The dust on the hills . . .": Jabotinsky, *Jewish Legion*, p. 139.

633-34   For the Declaration to the Seven of June 16, 1918, and the Anglo-French Declaration of November 7, 1918, see Great Britain, *Parliamentary Papers*, 1939, Cmd. 5974, pp. 48-51; reprinted in Hurewitz, *Middle East and North Africa*, 2:111-12.

634-35   "But did you not tell him . . . I think you had!": John E. Mack, *A Prince of Our Disorder: The Life of T.E. Lawrence* (Boston, 1976), p. 173.

635   "how much I was sorry": T.E. Lawrence, *Seven Pillars of Wisdom* (New York, 1938, de luxe ed.), p. 660.

635   "That so far as Palestine is concerned . . .": FO 371/3054, pp. 418-19.

635   "not one to be lightly thrown aside": From text of Hogarth message; as reproduced in Hurewitz, *Middle East and North Africa*, 2:111.

636   "It was a brilliant moonlit night . . .": Weizmann, *Trial and Error*, p. 234.

636   "He is the first real Arab nationalist": *CW Letters*, 8:210.

636-37   "Weizmann pointed out . . . Arab expansion further north": FO 371/3398.

637   "bright spots in a desert": David Garnett, ed., *The Letters of T. E. Lawrence* (New York, 1939), p. 74.

637-39   The Feisal-Weizmann conversation of December 11, 1918, is described by Weizmann in a memorandum for the FO, December 16, 1918. See *CW Letters*, 9:70-71.

638   "He is contemptuous . . .": *CW Letters*, 8:210.

639   The Feisal-Weizmann agreement of January 3, 1919, is reproduced in facsimile in *CW Letters*, vol. 9, between pp. 86 and 87.

640   Antonius's translation of Feisal's proviso is in his *The Arab Awakening* (New York, 1946; Capricorn ed., 1965), p. 439.

The basic work on the Peace Conference is: H.W.V. Temperley, ed., *A History of the Peace Conference of Paris*, 6 vols. (London, 1920-1924). A fine one-volume work, part history, part memoir, is Harold Nicolson, *Peacemaking 1919* (New York, 1965).

Another important work is Lloyd George's *Memoirs of the Peace Conference*, 2 vols. (New Haven, 1939).

Page

640   "When Clemenceau came to London . . .": Lloyd George, *Peace Conference*, 2:673.

640   "These two remarkable men . . .": Ibid.

641-42   For the death of Sykes, see Sokolow, *History*, 2:xxxv-xxxvi; and Nicolson, *Peacemaking*, pp. 262-63.

642-43   Sokolow's and Weizmann's statements before the Council of Ten are in Lloyd George, *Peace Conference*, 2:747-48.

643   Sylvain Lévi: Weizmann, *Trial and Error*, p. 244; *CW Letters*, 9:118.

643   Feisal's *Le Matin* interview is in Esco Foundation, *Palestine*, 1:142-43.

644   Feisal's letter of retraction to Frankfurter is reprinted in Weizmann, *Trial and Error*, pp. 245-46.

645-46   "The Arabs . . . pledges to his father": FO 371/6237. Extracts in Friedman, *Question of Palestine*, p. 94.

46. BRITISH PALESTINE: 1918-1948

Among various histories of the Palestine Mandate, see especially: John Marlowe, *The Seat of Pilate* (London, 1959); Christopher Sykes, *Crossroads to Israel* (New York, 1965); and J.C. Hurewitz, *The Struggle for Palestine* (New York, 1950, and subsequent editions).

Page

648-49   For the King-Crane Commission and Report, see *Foreign Relations of the United States: Paris Peace Conference, 1919*, vol. 12, pp. 787-99. A large extract is in Hurewitz, *Middle East and North Africa*, 2:192-99; the passages quoted are on pp. 195-96.

649   "The four Great Powers are committed . . .": Hurewitz, *Middle East and North Africa*, 2:189. Balfour's reflections on Syria, Palestine, and Mesopotamia are reprinted in ibid., pp. 185-91, from *Documents on British Foreign Policy, 1919-1939*, ser. 1, vol. 4, pp. 340-49.

649-50   "A striking illustration . . . Arab speakers who preceded him": *CW Letters*, 8:128-29.

650   "Being neither Jew . . .": Ronald Storrs, *The Memoirs of Sir Ronald Storrs* (New York, 1937), p. 358.

650-51   "It will be seen . . .": FO 371/3395, p. 59.

651   "Don Rinaldo Orientale": Vladimir Jabotinsky, *The Story of the Jewish Legion* (New York, 1945), p. 168.

651   "He was everyone's friend . . .": Weizmann, *Trial and Error*, p. 220.

651   "Whatever addition to the Administration . . .": *CW Letters*, 8:149.

651   "desire their country . . . presented to the Peace Conference": Marlowe, *Seat of Pilate*, p. 70.

652   "not equivalent to making Palestine . . .": Hurewitz, *Middle East and North Africa*, 2:195.

652   "My personal hope . . .": Quoted in Richard Meinertzhagen, *Middle East Diary, 1917-1956* (New York, 1960), pp. 8-9.

652   "Outline for the Provisional Government of Palestine": Esco Foundation, *Palestine*, 1:152-53.

652   "at the outset of overbearing intolerance . . .": Quoted in Marlowe, *Seat of Pilate*, p. 77.

653   "an unprecedented epidemic of anti-Semitism": Jabotinsky, *Jewish Legion*, p. 171.

653   For General Money and Vivian Gabriel, see ibid., pp. 172-73. For Colonel Hubbard, see Weizmann, *Trial and Error*, p. 220.

653-54   "poisonous agitation . . . immediately trouble began": *CW Letters*, 9:334.

654-56   For Samuel's own view of his administration, see Viscount Samuel, *Grooves of Change* (Indianapolis, 1945), pp. 184-216.

656   "To allow the British mandatory area . . . essential for a proper government": Ibid., pp. 195-96.

On the Cairo Conference, see Aaron S. Klieman, *Foundations of British Policy in the Arab World: The Cairo Conference of 1921* (Baltimore, 1970).

Page

656-58   For the Churchill White Paper of July 1, 1922, see Great Britain, *Parliamentary Papers*, 1922, Cmd. 1700, pp. 17-21; reproduced in Hurewitz, *Middle East and North Africa*, 2:302-5.

658-59   For the text of the Palestine Mandate, see Great Britain, *Parliamentary Papers*, 1922, Cmd. 1785; reproduced in Hurewitz, *Middle East and North Africa*, 2:305-9.

659   On the Fourteenth Zionist Congress, see Walter Laqueur, *A History of Zionism* (New York, 1972; reprinted 1976), p. 243.

659   "You need not worry . . .": Marlowe, *Seat of Pilate*, p. 4.

660   For Balfour at the Hebrew University and in Damascus, see Weizmann, *Trial and Error*, pp. 318-23.

661   "a man of much smaller caliber": Ibid., p. 329.

663   "held out great possibilities and hopes": Ibid., p. 385.

663   "unacceptable": Ibid., p. 387.

664   "We shall fight with Great Britain . . .": Quoted, for example, in Christopher Sykes, *Crossroads to Israel, 1917-1948* (New York, 1965), p. 204.

Index